Evaluating Competencies

Forensic Assessments and Instruments

Second Edition

Perspectives in
Law & Psychology

Sponsored by the American Psychology-Law Society / Division 41 of the American Psychological Association

Series Editor: Ronald Roesch, *Simon Fraser University, Burnaby, British Columbia, Canada*

Editorial Board: Jane Goodman-Delahunty, Thomas Grisso, Stephen D. Hart, Marsha Liss, Edward P. Mulvey, James R. P. Ogloff, Norman G. Poythress, Jr., Don Read, Regina Schuller, and Patricia Zapf

Evaluating Competencies

Forensic Assessments and Instruments

Second Edition

Thomas Grisso

University of Massachusetts Medical Center
Worcester, Massachusetts

with

**Randy Borum, John F. Edens,
Jennifer Moye, Randy K. Otto**

KLUWER ACADEMIC / PLENUM PUBLISHERS
NEW YORK/BOSTON/DORDRECHT/LONDON/MOSCOW

Library of Congress Cataloging-in-Publication Data

Grisso, Thomas.
   Evaluating competencies: forensic assessments and instruments/by Thomas Grisso
with Randy Borum ... et al.].—2nd ed.
     p.   cm.—(Perspectives in law & psychology; v. 16)
   Includes bibliographical references and indexes.
   ISBN 0-306-47343-7 (HB) — ISBN 0-306-47344-5 (PB)
     1. Competency to stand trial—United States. 2. Insanity—Jurisprudence—United States.
3. Forensic psychiatry—United States. I. Borum, Randy. II. Title. III. Series.

KF9242 .G7 2003
345.73'04—dc21

                                            2002028691

ISBN HB: 0-306-47343-7
PB: 0-306-47344-5

©2003 Kluwer Academic / Plenum Publishers, New York
233 Spring Street, New York, New York 10013

http://www.wkap.nl/

10 9 8 7 6 5 4 3 2 1

A C.I.P. record for this book is available from the Library of Congress

Printed in the United States of America

To Saleem Shah
1931–1992

Whose misson of integrity and quality
nurtured and inspired this project, and many others,
for the benefit of public forensic mental health services

About the Chapter Authors

RANDY BORUM, PH.D. • Associate Professor in the Department of Mental Health Law and Policy, Louis de la Parte Florida Mental Health Institute, University of South Florida, where he also holds faculty appointments in the Department of Criminology and the College of Public Health.

JOHN F. EDENS, PH.D. • Assistant Professor in the Department of Psychology at Sam Houston State University, where he is a core faculty member in the Forensic Clinical Psychology Doctoral Program.

JENNIFER MOYE, PH.D. • Assistant Professor of Psychology, Department of Psychiatry, Harvard Medical School, and Director of the Geriatric Mental Health Clinic in the Boston VA Healthcare System at the Brockton campus.

RANDY OTTO, PH.D. • Associate Professor in the Department of Mental Health Law and Policy, Louis de le Parte Florida Mental Health Institute, University of South Florida. He also serves as adjunct faculty in the Department of Psychology at the University of South Florida and the Stetson University College of Law.

Preface to the Second Edition

The second edition of *Evaluating Competencies* (hereinafter, EC) retains the outline of the first edition, but it has a somewhat different purpose. When the first edition was published in 1986, it introduced an untested conceptual framework for organizing an empirical approach to competence assessments. It introduced the term "forensic assessment instruments" to the field. It borrowed on others' works and ideas, combining them for the purpose of proposing a systematic, cohesive foundation for the development of legally-relevant assessment tools.

Much of that purpose has been accomplished. The principles for conceptualizing what legally-relevant competence evaluations are about, and the values of an empirical foundation for competence assessments, are accepted by most forensic researchers and practitioners who entered the field in the 1990s.

Therefore, while the first edition of EC was an unveiling of principles for consideration, the second edition of EC is an affirmation of their continued value, evidenced by their survival and reflected in their absorption into the mainstream of forensic assessment. In addition, the book chronicles the significant progress that has been made in this field since the first edition.

Changes in the second edition will be described in more detail below, but first it is worthwhile to revisit briefly the function of the first edition of EC and the intellectual process that it reported.

ix

WHAT WAS EVALUATING COMPETENCIES?

One of the central and best-known features of the first edition of EC was its review of "forensic assessment instruments" (FAIs), tools that could provide an empirical foundation for clinicians' evaluations in a variety of areas of legal competence. But from the author's perspective, the value of those reviews to clinicians was almost secondary to a more fundamental purpose—the testing of an hypothesis that predicted the utility of a set of concepts. In other words, the process of writing EC was itself a research project, designed to test whether the author's theory would fit when applied to a wide range of legal competencies.

The "theory" proposed that all legal competencies—whether criminal or civil, and despite their very different histories of development in the law—had certain underlying features in common. Moreover, those features could be used to structure a legal or a clinical psychological inquiry about any legal competence. Structured in this way, both legal and clinical inquiries would be mutually consistent in form, terminology, and clarity of translation across legal and clinical domains. For the clinician, this would increase the potential for a legally-relevant assessment of characteristics of individuals about whom questions of legal competence are raised.

Six characteristics of all legal competencies were proposed (see Chapter 2, although they have been reduced to five in the second edition), based on an initial examination of the law's application of legal definitions for a variety of competencies. In addition, EC introduced a model for developing psychological tools structured to provide information related to those six characteristics (see Chapter 3). Then six chapters tested the application of these characteristics for six legal competencies. Each of those chapters first analyzed the legal competence in question to examine the fit of the model to the contours and details of legal definitions in that area. Then the chapter applied the same model to evaluate the potential utility of a variety of assessment tools for providing information to the courts relevant to the six-part model.

The hypothesis that the model would be applicable across legal competencies, and that it would have utility in analyzing potential assessment tools, was largely confirmed as a matter of conceptual feasibility. The process also revealed a number of ways in which existing instruments fell short of the demands placed on them by the model, leading to specific recommendations for the use of the model to drive future development of forensic assessment instruments.

Returning to my earlier note about the purpose of the current volume, the second edition is not a "replication" of the "experiment" that the first edition represented. It is best seen as a restatement of the theory, a review of what has happened to the field since the theory was first introduced 15 years ago, and its application to a new generation of forensic assessment instruments that has evolved in that time.

CONTENT OF THE SECOND EDITION

THE CONCEPTUAL CHAPTERS (1–3)

Chapter 1 of the first edition classified and described the many deficiencies in forensic mental health evaluations for legal competencies, identifying the need for a systematic and empirically-based foundation for legally-relevant competence assessments. The new Chapter 1 revisits these deficiencies and reviews empirical evidence regarding the degree to which the field has improved in subsequent years. There is evidence that it has, although the job is not done.

Chapters 2 and 3 of the second edition are almost identical to those in the first edition. These are the chapters that introduced the conceptual model of legal competencies, designed to improve the legal relevance and empirical quality of forensic clinical assessments for competencies. The only fundamental change is a reduction of the six-part model to five components of legal competencies. Experience indicated that one of them (the Contextual component) could be folded into another (the Functional component), reducing complexity with no appreciable loss for the model's utility.

THE REVIEW CHAPTERS (4–9)

The six review chapters in the second edition cover the same six legal competencies as in the first. Moreover, the chapter outline used in the first edition has been retained. But the content of these chapters has been greatly revised.

The first half of each chapter provides legal and psychological analyses of the competence in question. For most of the legal competencies, these analyses required substantial revisions in the second edition, related to the evolution of law and clinical practice in most of the competence areas during the past 15 years.

The second half of each chapter reviews tools and instruments for assessing abilities associated with the specific legal competence in question. It is here that the greatest revisions have been made. The first edition reviewed 26 instruments, while there are 37 in the second edition. But this is not merely the addition of 11 instruments. Only nine of the instruments reviewed in the first edition were retained for the present review (in addition to four instruments that were significantly revised versions of prototypes that were reviewed in the original EC). Thus 28 of the 37 instruments reviewed here—about three-fourths of the second edition's total—were not in the first edition.

In deciding what instruments to include, we focused primarily on tools that have been developed specifically for use in forensic evaluations of legal competencies. Moreover, instruments were required to have an available manual and at least a few studies examining their conceptual validity and psychometric properties.

Exclusion of instruments that had been reviewed in the first edition occurred for three reasons. First, most of the instruments reviewed in the areas of Parenting Capacity and Guardianship/Conservatorship in the first edition were not developed as "forensic assessment instruments." They had evolved in developmental or geriatric psychology and psychiatry for general (non-forensic) clinical and research applications. They were reviewed in the first EC, however, to stimulate the field's interest in the potential for some existing clinical instruments to meet our needs for assessments of functional abilities related to legal decisions about the need for guardianship/conservatorship. While the review of those instruments served a conceptual purpose, subsequently most of them did not acquire extensive use in forensic evaluations for legal competencies. Therefore, up-dated reviews would have been of questionable value.

Second, those same two areas of legal competence enjoyed a considerable growth in instruments designed specifically for use in assessing parents in custody cases or elderly persons with disabilities that might require guardianship. Thus the need to rely on *general* (*non*-forensic) clinical tools focusing on functional abilities—as well as review of those instruments—was reduced.

Finally, a few forensic assessment instruments reviewed in the first edition simply languished. Subsequently they received no discernable clinical use and produced no further research reports, thus warranting no further review.

THE CONCLUDING CHAPTER (10)

Although modified substantially, the final chapter has the same purposes as in the first edition. It summarizes the "lessons learned" for future research and development of forensic assessment instruments for legal competencies, and it applies the book's model as a guide for clinical forensic practice in assessments for legal competencies. It concludes with new observations about the questionable future of forensic assessment instruments, in light of practical and legal obstacles to clinicians' adoption of empirically-based assessment methods as "routine practice."

THE FUTURE: NO THIRD EDITION

It is not at all clear where the field of empirical forensic assessment is headed. Two directions for future evolution of the field seem to have equal potential, and neither leads to a need for a third edition of EC.

In the first scenario, forensic assessment instruments become a significant part of almost all competence evaluations. Examiners understand that scores should never define whether a person is legally incompetent, so that the instruments take their proper place as part of a broader assessment. Existing or new forensic instruments are adapted to computerized administration where feasible. Courts and attorneys learn the language of the instruments and come to understand their values and limitations. New forensic assessment instruments focus on specialized tools for particular populations and for use in various clinical–legal systemic contexts. This development is so substantial that instruments across six areas of legal competence can no longer be reviewed in a single volume. So a third volume of EC is not feasible. Instead, it becomes the prototype for similar volumes (by a variety of authors), each devoted to separate legal competencies.

In the second scenario, managed care continues to shrink the provision of mental health services to persons with mental illnesses and disabilities associated with old age. The needs of the mentally and physically disabled do not go away, requiring continued and increasing responsibility for the courts to identify and respond to them. The demands for competence evaluations grow to a proportion that places an inordinate emphasis on efficiency in obtaining clinical opinions in competence cases. Standardized empirical approaches to clinicians' evaluations are deemed unessential—indeed, extravagant—under these circumstances. Moreover, courts liberally allow testimony based on clinical interviews and theoretical impressions alone. In contrast, expert opinions based in part on the use of new forensic assessment instruments encounter increasingly difficult and time-consuming challenges to meet *Daubert* and *Frye* tests of admissibility of scientific evidence, threatening exclusion of the examiner's opinions altogether. Clinicians who can no longer support themselves under the squeeze of managed care turn in droves to forensic assessment as a source of income. Paid by the case, they learn to provide the courts with the minimally acceptable amount of information that can be obtained in the least possible time. Forensic assessment instruments languish under these withering demands, and a third edition of EC is deemed irrelevant.

May the eventual demise of *Evaluating Competencies* be for the former reason rather than the latter.

Acknowledgements

First, I acknowledge and apologize for my tardiness. *Evaluating Competencies* went into its second printing several years ago, has been a "best seller" in the *Perspectives in Law and Psychology Book Series*, and has been out of print for the past four years. There should have been a second edition well before now.

The maturing of the field of forensic psychological assessment had much to do with my negligence. During the 1990s I found it far more exciting to participate in this field's fast-paced development than to rework existing ideas. New territory kept opening up, and the task of retreading old ground could not compete with the lure of discovery. In addition, the rapid expansion of this field rendered the prospect of cataloguing its recent developments quite intimidating. Fifteen years ago it was possible to be a generalist, knowing most of what was happening in the many assessment areas that *Evaluating Competencies* described in the first edition. As I approached the second edition, however, I realized that I was no longer an "expert" in all of those areas. I finally solved this problem by inviting chapter authors—Randy Borum, John Edens, Jennifer Moye, and Randy Otto—and I am greatly in debt to them for the strength of their contributions and their willingness to help me finish this job.

While the first edition had no dedication page, this one does. The name of Saleem Shah is not well known to many of our second-generation colleagues in Psychology and Law. He performed little research, published few papers, and was not a clinical or forensic practitioner. Yet many who were there in Psychology and Law's early years of the 1970s and 1980s would argue that Saleem was one of the chief architects of the field, doing more than almost anyone else—in his role as administrator of the NIMH Center for Studies of Crime and Delinquency—to provide an opportunity for others to establish the foundations of mental health law research and forensic assessment. How he did this has been detailed in a series of articles (in *Law and Human Behavior*, 1993, Vol. 19, No. 1) that Hank Steadman and I edited soon after Saleem died when his car was struck by a drunk driver. The original *Evaluating Competencies* might never have evolved had I not been stimulated and encouraged by Saleem and then provided funding (RO1-MH-37231) for the project from his NIMH center.

Thanks many times over to Bruce Sales for serving as editor of the first edition of this book, to Alan Goldstein who browbeat me into finishing the second edition, and to Ron Roesch, current editor of the *Perspectives in Law and Psychology Book Series*, for tolerating my tardiness. The effort will have been worthwhile if *Evaluating Competencies* plays a part in stimulating a new generation of researchers and clinicians to use psychology with integrity, in service to the justice system and persons whose incapacities require special legal protections.

Finally, thanks to Paul Appelbaum with whom I have "talked legal competencies" for so many years, and to my other colleagues and friends in the Law and Psychiatry Program at the University of Massachusetts Medical School, a wonderful group with whom I've spent most of the years subsequent to the first edition. They have made every day an intellectual adventure that has had a cumulative effect in maturing my thoughts about the topics in this book.

Contents

CHAPTER 6. NOT GUILTY BY REASON OF INSANITY 193

Randy Borum

CHAPTER 7. PARENTING CAPACITY................................. 229

Randy K. Otto and John F. Edens

—————————— 1 ——————————

Advances in Assessments for Legal Competencies

In the 1986 first edition of *Evaluating Competencies* (hereinafter, EC), Chapter 1 was entitled "Problems in Assessments for Legal Competencies." During the past 15 years, researchers and clinicians in this field have devoted considerable energy to improving assessment practices in legal contexts. As the present edition will show, the field of forensic assessment for legal competencies has matured considerably. It is fitting, therefore, that the first chapter in this second edition focuses on the field's "advances" in dealing with the "problems" represented in the chapter's 1986 title.

Before turning to that review, the first section of this chapter repeats a series of brief sketches of the legal competencies nearly as they appeared in the first edition. This establishes the domain of the book for new readers. Then we describe the historical problems in forensic assessments for legal competencies that were of concern in the first edition of EC, and we review how far the field has advanced in dealing with these issues. The chapter concludes with a restatement of the need for a conceptual model to guide the development and implementation of methods for assessing legal competencies.

LEGAL COMPETENCIES

Criminal and civil courts frequently make legal decisions about individuals based in part on their physical, mental, and social capacities. Some of these legal decisions involve judgments about *legal competence*. For example, a court may have to consider an elderly person's prospect for managing day-to-day tasks of living, in order to determine whether to appoint a legal guardian to provide assistance to the elderly individual. A criminal court may need to determine whether a defendant with mental illness is able to participate in an upcoming trial.

There are many types of legal competencies in various areas of law. Yet all legal competencies have certain fundamental notions in common as legal concepts:

- All legal competencies recognize the rights of individuals to make decisions and have control of their own lives.
- Legal competencies recognize that some individuals may not have the capacities to make important decisions in their lives. This is of concern because their incapacities may jeopardize their welfare or that of others who will be influenced by their decisions.
- All legal concepts of competence provide a legal mechanism for identifying individuals for whom the relevant incapacities may exist.
- When legal incompetence is determined, it allows, obligates, or justifies the state's intervention in certain ways in order to protect the welfare of the individual, typically curtailing the individual's rights in the best interests of the individual and society.

A key point in concepts of legal competence is the need to weigh whether the individual's capacities are sufficiently impaired to require a finding of legal incompetence. Society authorizes courts to make these critical judgments, and courts often turn to mental health professionals to assist them in identifying individuals' capacities relevant for the decision that the court must make. Society and the law have long recognized psychiatrists and psychologists as experts in assessment and understanding of human abilities, emotions, and potentials. Further, many individuals whom the law declares legally incompetent manifest the same mental deficits that give rise to the need for clinical care. Therefore, legal codes and legal practice rely on mental health professionals to assist courts in their review of mental capacities related to the difficult issues posed by competence laws.

Beyond these common features, legal competencies in various areas of law have somewhat different criteria. Further, each type of legal competence may be defined somewhat differently across the statutes or case law of the nation's 51 legal jurisdictions. Subsequent chapters provide discussions of the major variations in legal definitions of each of six legal competencies reviewed in this volume. The present discussion provides a more general and very basic introduction to each of the legal competencies addressed in this book, and notes several other legal competencies that will not receive attention in later chapters. Complete citation of references supporting the descriptions of the six legal competencies are reserved for the more detailed discussions in subsequent chapters.

LEGAL COMPETENCIES IN THE CRIMINAL PROCESS

Several points in the criminal trial process may require legal decisions based wholly or in part on a consideration of a defendant's psychological capacities. These include the defendant's capacities: (a) to waive rights to silence and counsel "knowingly, intelligently, and voluntarily," prior to questioning by law enforcement officers; (b) to plead guilty or to dismiss counsel; (c) to stand trial (i.e., to function in the role of defendant in the trial process); (d) to possess the requisite cognition, affect, and volition for criminal responsibility (i.e., the insanity defense); (e) to serve a sentence; and (f) to be executed (i.e., to undergo capital punishment).

Three of these areas produce the most frequent requests for the assistance of mental health professionals: capacities related to standing trial, waiver of rights during police investigations, and criminal responsibility.

Competence to Stand Trial (Chapter 4)

Our legal doctrine of competence to stand trial evolved from English common law. Its earliest form focused simply on the capacity of the accused to plead, a ritualistic requirement without which the trial could not proceed. British common law distinguished allowable causes for remaining "mute" when asked to plead, recognizing that some defendants actually lacked the capacity to respond while others merely chose not to exercise their probable capacity to do so (sometimes motivated by a desire to delay the trial). A plea was not required for "idiots" and "lunatics," who were then excused from prosecution. Others were forced, by various means, to make a plea.

From this notion evolved a more complete doctrine of criminal competence based on a broader concern for fairness in the trial of persons accused of crimes. It was recognized that certain defendants with serious mental deficiencies might not be capable of defending themselves, putting them at risk of suffering the consequences of a miscarriage of justice.

Moreover, their inability to contribute meaningfully to the trial process could weaken the integrity of the justice system itself. In modern law, the definition of competence to stand trial was provided by the United States Supreme Court in *Dusky v. United States* (1960): "whether he [the defendant] has sufficient present ability to consult with his lawyer with a reasonable degree of rational understanding" and "whether he has a rational as well as factual understanding of the proceedings against him" (p. 402).

The question of a defendant's competence to stand trial is raised frequently, in comparison to other competencies in criminal law, although it arises only in a minority of a jurisdiction's total criminal cases. If the question is raised, this will usually occur prior to a hearing on the criminal allegations. The question can be raised, however, at any stage in the adjudication process, from arraignment through sentencing.

Determining whether a defendant is incompetent to stand trial requires an inquiry into the defendant's capacities as defined by the *Dusky* standard. Typically the question of incompetence is raised because of present or past evidence suggesting a serious mental illness or other psychological disabilities. An examination of the defendant's abilities by a mental health professional, therefore, is a standard part of the competence inquiry in most jurisdictions. The forensic examiner's findings are reported to the court in writing, and sometimes in oral testimony, for use during a competence hearing at which a judge weighs all relevant evidence and makes a finding of competence or incompetence. A finding of incompetence to stand trial usually will result in a delay of the trial process while the state employs involuntary treatment to bring the defendant to competence. The trial process resumes if and when the state's therapeutic intervention results in conditions suggesting that the defendant is capable of meeting the competence standard.

Capacity to Waive "Miranda Rights" (Chapter 5)

Law enforcement officers sometimes seek a statement from persons suspected of crimes. The statements that suspects make (e.g., offense-related information or confessions) may be entered into evidence in criminal proceedings against the defendant only if the defendant was afforded adequate opportunity to choose to withhold the information or to have the benefit of legal counsel at the time the statement was made. This protection arises from constitutional requirements designed to curtail the potential abuse of power by the state in seeking convictions and criminal sanctions against individuals.

A defendant's opportunity to claim the right to silence and to legal counsel requires not only freedom from coercive police actions, but also the defendant's knowledge that the rights are available and an understanding of the nature and significance of the rights. Police are required to inform the individual of the rights (*Miranda v. Arizona*, 1966) in what are called "*Miranda* warnings," usually consisting of four or five sentences describing the rights. The individual's subsequent choice to waive the rights and make a statement must be made "knowingly, intelligently, and voluntarily." If the waiver does not meet this test, then it was not made "competently," the waiver was invalid, and the information obtained by law enforcement officers would be inadmissible as evidence.

When a waiver's validity is questioned, the court must examine relevant facts to rule on the issue. Generally this will require consideration of circumstances of the police inquiry, as well as the psychological characteristics of the individual who was involved. Mental health professionals may be asked to examine the individual's abilities or mental status in order to provide information about the person's capacities to have understood and appreciated the rights of which the person was informed.

The court may determine that the individual had insufficient capacity to waive the rights knowingly, intelligently, and voluntarily. "Incompetence to waive *Miranda* rights," however, is neither a legal finding nor a formal legal concept. The individual's incapacity to waive *Miranda* rights is more like an intermediate conclusion that may be reached on the way to a legal finding of invalidity of the waiver. Thus, in contrast to incompetence to stand trial, an individual does not acquire a legal status of "incompetent to waive *Miranda* rights." Nevertheless, the concept of a person's capacities to waive the rights may be conceptualized, for purposes of forensic evaluation, as though it were a legal competence.

Criminal Responsibility (Chapter 6)

The law has long recognized two concepts on which responsibility for criminal actions depends: *actus reus*, requiring evidence that the accused person engaged in the alleged act; and *mens rea*, requiring a determination that the accused person manifested the requisite mental state to have intended committing the act or to have foreseen its consequences. The insanity defense doctrine acknowledges that individuals whose mental capacities did not allow them to appreciate the wrongfulness of their acts or to control their behavior should not be held responsible for acts that otherwise would be criminal. Thus a finding of insanity constitutes acquittal.

At issue when testing legal insanity is the individual's state of mind at the time of the offense. Somewhat different legal tests for insanity are used in different jurisdictions. All of them, however, refer in one way or another to cognitive, affective, and/or volitional capacities of the defendant, and to the impairment of those capacities as a consequence of mental disorder.

The insanity plea is asserted in a very small minority of criminal cases, and in most jurisdictions it results in acquittal in only a small fraction of the cases in which it is raised. Mental health professionals typically are asked to evaluate defendants about whom the question of criminal responsibility is raised. This provides the court with information about characteristics of the defendant relevant to the cognitive, affective, and/or volitional capacities at issue.

The concept of competence to stand trial must not be confused with the concept of insanity. In addition to referring to somewhat different mental states or capacities, they refer to abilities at different times. Competence to stand trial pertains to a person's abilities at the time of the trial process, while insanity refers to the person's mental condition at the time of the offense. One may be competent to stand trial yet insane, or incompetent to stand trial yet sane. Moreover, the defendant who meets criteria for the insanity defense is not declared "incompetent to have committed the crime." Nevertheless, this is the effect of a legal declaration of insanity, in that the defendant is seen as not having the requisite capacities to warrant a guilty verdict. Further, the court and the mental health professional are faced with much the same kind of task in insanity cases as in questions of other legal competencies: that is, assessment and consideration of the person's psychological capacities. Therefore, in this book, legal insanity is examined conceptually as a legal competence, despite recognition that the law formally does not apply the terms competence or incompetence to the concept of insanity.

Other Competencies in Criminal Law

Competence to plead guilty and competence to dismiss counsel refer primarily to capacities to make informed and rational decisions that may have serious consequences for the criminal defendant. A United States Supreme Court case, *Godinez v. Moran* (1993), decided that defendants who are competent to stand trial are competent to make the above decisions as well. Some courts may still consider these as competencies separate from competence to stand trial. Nevertheless, in Chapter 4 we will follow the precedent in *Godinez* that includes within the concept of competence to stand trial the abilities that would be necessary to make decisions about pleas and about dismissing counsel.

LEGAL COMPETENCIES IN CIVIL CASES

Many questions of civil law require legal decisions based substantially on a consideration of an individual's physical and psychological capacities. Some of the more common questions refer to a person's capacities: (a) to be responsible for meeting a child's needs, as a parent or caretaker; (b) to consent to medical or mental health interventions (e.g., treatment, counseling); (c) to consent to participation in research; (d) to care for oneself and one's property; (e) to make a contract; and (f) to make a will (testamentary competence).

Three of these competence questions will receive relatively greater attention in this book, because they more frequently involve the assistance of mental health professionals in determining related psychological capacities. These are the areas of parental competence, competence to care for self and property, and competence to consent to treatment.

Parental Competence (Chapter 7)

The *parens patriae* function of the state has long allowed legal intervention to terminate parental rights in relation to a child when the child's health and welfare are endangered by the parent's care. The decision to terminate a parent's rights requires a determination that the individual is not a "fit parent," as defined by statute. The state then may remove the child from the parent's custody for placement with a more suitable caretaker.

Parental fitness or competence frequently involves an examination of evidence concerning the parent's past abuse or neglect of the child. In addition, a mental health professional may be asked to evaluate the parents and children involved, in order to provide the court with information of a psychiatric, psychological, or social nature that might bear on the question of the parent's legal competence to meet the child's needs and to ensure the child's safety.

The question of parental competence may also be raised in divorce cases in which two parents are in contest concerning legal custody of their children. Such cases usually involve no formal finding of incompetence status to determine custody, and in many cases neither parent would meet the legal criteria for parental unfitness. The court's task in divorce-related cases is to determine which parental situation represents the best prospects for the child's general welfare. Yet when mental health professionals are asked to evaluate one or both parents and the child in such cases, frequently the capacities that are evaluated are much the same as in cases involving competence determinations for termination of parental rights.

Finally, parental competence is raised in legal decisions concerning a child's adoption, placement of a child with a family for foster care, or evaluation of families for their eligibility as a resource for foster care programs.

Competence to Care for Self or Property (Chapter 8)

The state is empowered to intervene in the lives of individuals who are incompetent to care for themselves or to manage their property, so as to ensure their protection and care in accordance with the best interests of the incompetent individual and society. A legal finding of incompetence to care for self or property allows the state to appoint a suitable guardian, who will be responsible for decisions affecting the incompetent person's care and protection. Medical doctors and mental health professionals may be consulted to provide courts with information about the individual's capacities related to this legal determination.

Guardianship is most commonly sought for children, persons with developmental disabilities and mental illnesses, and elderly individuals whose diminished capacities for self-care or property management raise concern for their safety. The guardian may be authorized to make whatever decisions seem necessary for the person's care, including decisions about medical care and institutionalization in mental hospital facilities, residential arrangements, and the conservation and expenditure of the incompetent person's financial resources.

Competence to Consent to Treatment (Chapter 9)

Law provides for the protection of individuals from medical or psychological interventions against their desires (except in certain emergency or court-ordered circumstances). Thus most situations involving proposed interventions by medical or mental health professionals require the consent of either the individual to whom treatment is being offered or a relative or guardian who is authorized to provide proxy consent.

The question of an individual's competence to consent to or refuse proposed treatment interventions arises from the doctrine of *informed consent*, which requires that the individual must (a) be provided information relevant for the decision, (b) make the choice voluntarily, and (c) be competent to decide. The question is most often raised when treatment decisions are being made by persons with developmental disabilities or mental illnesses, certain elderly persons, minors, or any individuals whose immediate medical conditions render them incapable of managing a request for consent. In these instances, mental health professionals may be asked to provide evidence concerning the individual's capacities to make decisions to accept/refuse the treatment in question.

The circumstances that raise the question of competence to consent reflect some of the more difficult issues currently facing mental health law. For example, they include the right and capacities of patients with mental illness to refuse highly intrusive treatments (such as medication, electroconvulsive treatment, and psychosurgery) and patients' rights to refuse life-sustaining treatment for terminal medical conditions.

Other Civil Law Competencies

Competence to consent to participation as a subject in research is less often raised for reasons of professional ethics and sometimes as a legal question. Special concerns about consent to participation in research arise with regard to minors, prisoners, or persons with mental disorders who are asked to be research participants. The evaluation of individuals for competence to consent to research has not been common in the past. It is becoming more frequent, however, as a consequence of recent inquiries into the participation of psychiatric patients in field trials of psychoactive medications (e.g., Appelbaum, 1998). Similarly, the competence of patients to consent to voluntary psychiatric hospitalization has begun to receive greater scrutiny in recent years (see *Zinermon v. Burch*, 1990; Appelbaum, Appelbaum, & Grisso, 1998; Poythress et al., 1996).

Competence to contract and competence to execute a will (testamentary competence) are concerned with an individual's capacities to make decisions about the management and disposition of financial assets. Thus they are special instances of the capacity to care for one's property, and they may require specialized assessment methods. Mental health professionals may be asked to form opinions about an individual's testamentary competence on the basis of past records, documents written by the deceased, and the recollections of friends or associates.

SUMMARY

No single legal criterion or test applies across all legal competencies. Each legal competence refers to somewhat different abilities related to various ordinary or extraordinary situations in the lives of defendants, patients, children and the elderly, or persons with no particular legal, developmental, or psychiatric status. The law, therefore, does not presume that legal incompetence in any of these areas renders an individual incompetent in any other area of legal competence.

All of the legal competencies, nevertheless, have in common a reference to human capacities that must be assessed in the process of applying legal criteria for decisions about competence. Courts have recognized the difficulties in assessing adequately the relevant capacities in individual cases, as well as the gravity of the assessment task in light of the consequences of legal competence decisions for the individuals involved.

These concerns have allowed mental health professionals to gain wide access to the legal process as examiners and advisors to courts. Later chapters will document that some courts have relied heavily on the judgments of mental health examiners, at times producing a record of legal decisions that nearly mirrored the clinical opinions offered by expert witnesses. Thus the quality of examiners' evaluations is of great concern for fairness in the legal system and to protect the welfare of individuals about whom the courts make competence decisions.

In this light, heavy criticism of clinicians' evaluations for legal competencies in past decades raised serious concerns about the value of mental health professionals' participation in the legal competence process. Although many of the field's shortcomings have been mitigated in recent years, it is important that we recognize their history. Some of the criticisms of earlier days are still valid in some jurisdictions, and they are prone to recur if we are not vigilant. Moreover, we need to know our progress in dealing with past weaknesses, in order to inform courts of our improved methods and to be forthright about things that still are in need of change.

Therefore, in the next discussion we review criticisms that have been made regarding forensic mental health evaluations for legal competencies, as well as advances in recent years in the field's attempts to mitigate its earlier shortcomings.

IMPROVING EVALUATIONS FOR LEGAL COMPETENCIES: HOW FAR HAVE WE COME?

In the first edition of EC, we reviewed a large body of literature prior to the mid-1980s that documented extreme discontent with the practices of mental health professionals in their assessments in legal cases (e.g., Bazelon, 1982; Bonnie & Slobogin, 1980; Brakel & Rock, 1971; Ennis & Litwack, 1974; Gutheil & Appelbaum, 1982; Halleck, 1980; Halpern, 1975; Meehl, 1971; Melton, Petrila, Poythress, & Slobogin, 1987; Melton, Weithorn, & Slobogin, 1995; Monahan, 1981; Morse, 1978a, b, 1982, 1983; Roesch & Golding, 1980; Shah, 1981; Stone, 1975, 1984). Criticisms raised in these works were summarized in three categories:

- *ignorance and irrelevance* in courtroom testimony;
- psychiatric or psychological *intrusion* into essentially legal matters; and
- *insufficiency and incredibility* of information provided to the courts.

Subsequent reviews have frequently referred to EC's characterization of these criticisms, which came to be known as the five "I's." We will return to those criticisms in a moment to assess their current relevance, but first it is worthwhile to set a context for their reconsideration.

When the first edition of EC was published in 1986, forensic psychologists and psychiatrists had only recently begun to build a theoretical and empirical foundation for their evaluations related to legal competencies. For example, the first substantial research study on evaluations for competence to stand trial was published only about 10 years earlier by forensic psychiatrist A. Louis McGarry (Laboratory of Community Psychiatry, 1973), and only 5 years had passed since the publication of the first book entirely devoted to the matter of competence to stand trial (Roesch & Golding, 1980). Nevertheless, during the 1970s and 1980s, mental health professionals were providing competence evaluations of various kinds with increasing frequency. Moreover, often they were practicing without adequate forensic training and without sound models, theories, or empirical work to guide them.

It is not surprising, therefore, that courts were increasingly registering their ambivalence, disenchantment, or outright frustration with clinicians' contributions in competence cases. Mental health professionals, it was said, often were not able to deliver what was expected, or they insisted on delivering much that the law did not desire. As a consequence, the future of mental health professionals in the courtroom was at stake. According to Alan Stone (1984), mental health professionals had not yet lost their place in the courtroom, but the battle to maintain the necessary credibility to continue in their role had left them "wounded and bloody" (p. 57).

The subsequent 15 years since the first edition of EC has witnessed a concerted effort by the field to improve the quality of forensic psychological assessments for the courts, including evaluations for legal competencies. These efforts emerged in the mid-1980s and early 1990s, represented by the publication of *Psychological Evaluations for the Courts* (Melton et al., 1987), the first edition of EC (Grisso, 1986), and the publication of the American Psychology-Law Society's *Specialty Guidelines for Forensic Psychologists* (Committee on Ethical Guidelines in Forensic Psychology, 1991). Up to that time there were almost no textbooks on forensic clinical assessment. Now there are enough of them to fill several shelves in a forensic examiner's office, and many provide conceptual and empirical foundations for forensic assessments that did not formerly exist. For example, only about 30 research articles on competence to stand trial evaluations had appeared in the literature prior to 1985. Rather suddenly, 51 empirical research articles in this area appeared during 1986–1990 (Grisso, 1992), with 69 articles added in 1991–1995 (Cooper & Grisso, 1997) and about 80 more in 1996–2000 (Mumley, Tillbrook, & Grisso, in press).

Recent years have also seen rapid growth of efforts to improve forensic assessment practices through educational opportunities for forensic specialization. The American Psychological Association took affirmative steps to promote the development of undergraduate, graduate, and postdoctoral education in Psychology and Law and forensic psychological practice (Bersoff et al., 1997). The American Academy of Forensic Psychology developed a substantial continuing education program that has been attended by thousands of forensic-specialty psychologists in the1990s, augmenting the equally ambitious educational efforts of the American Academy of Psychiatry and the Law.

Thus there has been ample opportunity for the field to achieve a higher level of quality in evaluations for legal competencies. But has the field actually attained that goal? Let us return to the criticisms of the 1980s, repeating them for those who are unfamiliar with that era, then examine the degree to which we have addressed them.

IGNORANCE AND IRRELEVANCE

One of the most pressing problems in the history of the courts' use of mental health experts was *examiners' failure to provide testimony that was relevant for the law's concerns* in legal competence cases. Complaints pointed to the fact that *many examiners seemed to be ignorant of the nature of the legal inquiry.*

"Diagnostic testimony" was the most frequently cited example of this failing. This occurs when the examiner provides a psychiatric diagnosis—for example, schizophrenia—and describes its symptoms, then testifies on that basis alone that the individual lacks the requisite capacities for competence to stand trial, to have been responsible for criminal actions, to manage the custody of a child, or whatever the legal competence in question. In contrast, the law does not presume that any psychiatric diagnostic condition is synonymous with any legal incompetence. Some individuals with psychoses or developmental disabilities are able nonetheless to function in a trial or to manage a child's custody, whereas others may not have those capacities.

Something more is needed, therefore, than a mere diagnosis of mental disorder, a reference to an individual's inadequate contact with reality, or a statement about general mental retardation. For clinical information to be relevant in addressing legal questions of competence, *examiners must present the logic that links these observations to the specific abilities and capacities with which the law is concerned.*

This first requires a clear recognition of the need to observe and describe specific abilities—not just diagnostic clinical conditions—associated with the legal competence in question (Grisso, 1986; Heilbrun, 2001; Melton et al., 1987, 1997). If the examiner believes that the person is deficient in these abilities associated with legal competence, and if a mental disorder exists, then the examiner must explain specifically how the symptoms of that disorder are relevant for that opinion (for example, how the mental disorder accounts for the deficits in relevant abilities). Failure to provide this information reduces the relevance of observations for the legal fact finder.

Some judges identified clinicians' failures to do this several decades ago and began admonishing them to correct their practice (e.g., see Bazelon, 1974, 1982). What progress have we made toward increasing clinicians' awareness of the need to explain how a person's mental illness addresses the questions before the courts in legal competence cases, rather than merely diagnosing mental disorder and declaring incompetence?

Much effort has been directed toward that end in the past 15 years. The mid-1980s saw the publication of the first comprehensive handbooks on forensic psychology and forensic psychiatry, all of which attempted to improve clinicians' awareness of the importance of translating clinical information so that it is legally relevant (e.g., Curran, McGarry, & Shah, 1986; Grisso, 1986; Gutheil & Appelbaum, 1982; Melton et al., 1987; Rogers, 1984; Weiner & Hess, 1987). Many other texts (which we will cite in later chapters) have joined them in the 1990s, describing to clinicians ways to accomplish this objective and the importance of doing so. The American Psychology-Law Society formulated and published specialty guidelines for forensic psychologists, including explicit recognition of the obligation to know the legal standards one is addressing and to explain the relation of one's clinical information to those legal standards (Committee on Ethical Guidelines for Forensic Psychologists, 1991).

Has practice improved in this regard? Currently there are no data to answer this question for evaluations of legal competencies in general. But several studies have examined forensic examiners' practices specifically in evaluations for competence to stand trial, and the following evidence indicates that, at least in that area of competence to stand trial, our evaluations have become more legally relevant.

Borum and Grisso (1995, 1996) surveyed diplomates in forensic psychology and forensic psychiatry regarding their perceptions of recommended practice for competence to stand trial evaluations and reports. They found an almost unanimous consensus that examiners should assess and describe examinees' specific functional abilities associated with the legal competence. Moreover, recent studies that have examined actual reports on competence to stand trial by forensic clinicians have found that they typically do observe and describe many of the abilities that are relevant for the specific legal competence in question (Robbins, Waters, & Herbert, 1997; Skeem, Golding, Cohn, & Berge, 1998). In addition, rarely does one encounter evaluations in recent years in which the examiner seems ignorant of the difference between competence to stand trial and criminal responsibility (Nicholson & Norwood, 2000).

These results are encouraging when compared to earlier studies from the 1970s showing that clinicians almost never included a description of defendants' legally-relevant abilities in their reports (e.g., Roesch & Golding, 1980). Yet current practice is not wholly satisfactory. For example, Skeem et al. (1998) found that the reports they reviewed rarely addressed certain types of abilities—especially defendants' decision making abilities—that have become increasingly important to evaluate as a consequence of modern legal decisions on competence to stand trial (see Chapter 4).

Having observed deficits in the person's abilities associated with the legal competence, clinicians must offer an explanation concerning how mental illness or disability is responsible for those deficits, thus linking the diagnostic condition to the legal question of competence. In their survey of forensic diplomates, Borum and Grisso (1996) found that 90% of the respondents agreed that this function of forensic reports on competence—the relation between the defendant's mental illness (if it existed) and the abilities with which the courts are concerned—was either essential or recommended. In contrast, in a study of actual competence to stand trial reports in two states, only 27% of the reports in which mental illness was present contained explanations of how defendants' symptoms influenced defendants' abilities related to legal competence to stand trial (Robbins, Waters, & Herbert, 1997). In another study in one state, only 10% of reports explained how a defendant's psychopathology compromised competence to stand trial abilities (Skeem et al., 1998).

In summary, recent research suggests some progress in everyday practice in improving the relevance of data in forensic evaluations for competence to stand trial. But the progress is only incremental, not complete, and we have no data on current evaluation practices for most other areas of legal competence.

INTRUSION

The history of mental health evaluations for the courts reveals that they have been criticized on another count, that of the *intrusion of psychiatry and psychology into the domain and authority of the legal factfinder*. When mental health professionals are asked to provide clinical information in a case related to legal competence, it is not uncommon for them to begin or end their testimony by offering their opinion concerning whether the individual in question is "competent" or "incompetent."

In the mid-1980s, authors writing about the development of standards for forensic evaluations were admonishing clinicians that this type of testimony—offering opinions about the "ultimate legal question"—was inappropriate, if not unethical (e.g., Grisso, 1986; Melton et al., 1987; Morse, 1978). Their viewpoint rested on the conviction that the final answer is not clinical in nature. A finding about legal competence is a statement about how the state should balance an individual's claim to legal rights of self-determination against the individual's or society's need for protection. It rests on a judgment that the defendant's incapacities are of sufficient magnitude to relieve the defendant of the autonomy to make important decisions that are otherwise protected by law.

This question—*how much of a deficit in abilities is enough to justify the restriction of individual liberties*—requires a moral and social judgment, not a scientific or clinical one. It cannot be answered without applying personal values or one's sense of what is just and right. When mental health professionals testify in court as experts, the area of expertise for which they are qualified is scientific and clinical, not as an arbiter of moral and social values. Therefore, these earlier texts argued, a clinician's offer of an opinion about an examinee's competence or incompetence is an inappropriate intrusion into the role of the legal fact finder.

What has happened to this issue in the ensuing 15 years? Although the second edition of *Psychological Evaluations for the Courts* (Melton et al., 1997) continues to take the above position, that view has been challenged from a consequentialist perspective (e.g., Rogers & Ewing, 1989; Slobogin, 1989), raising several arguments in support of ultimate opinion testimony. For example, stating an opinion about competence or incompetence might allow judges to better follow clinicians' testimony about individuals' deficits, having been provided a notion of the direction that the explanation will take. Moreover, judges are always free to reject clinicians' opinions about the ultimate legal question. And efforts to avoid stating an opinion about it are often artificial, inasmuch as a conclusory opinion is usually discernable anyway from one's clinical testimony about the defendant's specific capacities and deficits.

Evidence suggests that this issue has not been resolved. Borum and Grisso's (1996) survey of forensic psychiatry and forensic psychology diplomates found that about one-quarter of mental health professionals with specialization in forensic assessment believed that they should *avoid offering opinions* on ultimate legal questions of competence to stand trial. The remaining three-quarters of the respondents were equally divided between those who believe it is *important to offer* such opinions and those who were *neutral* about stating ultimate opinions, believing that they should be neither condemned nor required. Skeem et al. (1998) found that three-quarters of competence to stand trial reports reviewed in their study did include an ultimate opinion about defendants' competence, and only 4 out of the 66 reports examined by Robbins et al. (1997) did not offer ultimate opinions on competence.

Currently, therefore, it appears that authorities are divided on the question of the propriety of clinicians' statements of opinion on the ultimate legal question of competence. Moreover, at least for competence to stand trial, most experts in forensic psychiatry and psychology do not support the argument that such statements must be avoided, and most clinicians who perform evaluations in this area apparently do offer opinions on the ultimate legal question in their reports in everyday practice. Such testimony continues to be discouraged but allowed in formulations of ethical standards of forensic psychiatrists or psychologists, and typically it has been allowed by law (for an exception, see Chapter 6 on expert testimony in federal insanity cases).

One could concede that ultimate opinion testimony might do little harm when clinicians are careful not only to offer their opinion but also to explain their logic. Courts are capable of weighing the value of clinicians' opinions if clinicians clearly point out to the court the specific ways in which the defendant's mental condition influences the defendant's abilities to a degree that warrants the clinician's conclusion. Yet the results of studies cited earlier (see "Ignorance and Irrelevance" above) suggest that *most clinicians today do not offer such explanations in their competence to stand trial reports*. Without them, the court is given a clinician's observations and conclusion, but it is not provided the examiner's logic for arriving at the ultimate opinion. These are precisely the conditions that encourage judges simply to rely on the clinician's unexamined judgment, in effect placing the competence decision—a moral rather than a clinical matter—in the hands of the clinician rather than the law.

Until clinicians accept the responsibility to fully explain their logic for their competence opinions, there is no reason to alter the recommendation about "ultimate legal question" testimony expressed in the first edition of EC. Offering an opinion as to whether the examinee is "competent" or "incompetent," in the absence of an adequate explanation of the logic for one's opinion, should be considered unacceptable practice, even if the law does not object.

INSUFFICIENCY AND INCREDIBILITY

Mental health professionals have been criticized for *testimony based on assessments with insufficient evidence to support their conclusions, resulting in opinions that lack credibility*. This complaint is based not only on the empirical and scientific standards of examiners' disciplines, but also on the demands of legal evidence. Developments in the law during the 1990s regarding the admissibility of expert testimony (e.g., *Daubert v. Merrell Dow Pharmaceuticals, Inc.*, 1993) have increased the demands on mental health professionals to be able to support the reliability and validity of the evaluation methods on which their testimony is based.

One focus of this criticism is on the quality of the examiner's empirical foundation. Examiners sometimes may not obtain sufficient information about the examinee, in terms of quantity, type, or reliability of the observations, in order to reach certain conclusions credibly. In other instances, adequate data regarding the examinee may be available, but the interpretive meanings of the data in relation to the information needs of the court cannot be supported credibly by past research in psychiatry and psychology. The relevant research with which to interpret the data sometimes simply is not available. When research is available, its nomothetic and probabilistic findings often do not allow the definitive statements about individual cases that attorneys would prefer (Loftus & Monahan, 1980; Melton et al., 1998).

Concerning the first of these complaints, the use of specialized data collection methods developed for evaluations of various legal competencies holds the promise of improving the quality of information in competence evaluations. A major purpose of the first edition of EC was to review those specialized data-collection methods—"forensic assessment instruments"—that were available by the mid-1980s. As seen in later chapters, considerable progress has been made in the past 15 years in developing and refining clinicians' options for collecting more reliable data related specifically to legal competencies. Some companies that publish psychological tests now devote several pages to "forensic tests," whereas they listed virtually none 15 years ago. An increase in specialized assessment tools, however, does not necessarily mean improved quality; later chapters will review whether we have made progress not only in available options for systematic data collection, but also in the quality of the data that our instruments provide.

It is difficult to determine the degree to which clinicians have come to employ these specialized data collection methods in their evaluations for various legal competencies. Evidence offered in later chapters suggests that they have not become the norm with regard to practice in any area of legal competence, although they have been used more widely in some areas (e.g., parents' capacities in child custody evaluations) than in others (e.g., competence to stand trial).

A second form of criticism regarding credibility focuses on examiners' use of theory or "informed speculation" in courtroom testimony. Theories about human nature are an indispensable part of professional practice in the laboratory or clinic. A good theory uses existing information about a person to provide tentative explanations for the person's behavior or to guide speculation about future behavior. The value of these speculations, however, is not known until more data are collected in order to test the theoretical proposition. These tests would follow in the normal course of scientific endeavor (e.g., a new research study), clinical assessment (e.g., selecting an additional method for obtaining information needed to test the speculation), or therapeutic practice (e.g., beginning a treatment intervention on a speculative, trial basis).

Theoretical speculations in the courtroom, however, often have been spoken or heard as though they were facts, even when they might have had little or no empirical support. Further, testimony based on informed speculation frequently has not acknowledged equally plausible but alternative speculations based on different theories of human behavior. Critics, then, claim that examiners' conclusions too often are based on theory rather than empirically-verified logic, and that the tentative nature of theory-based speculation often is not acknowledged by either the expert or the court when dealing with expert opinions related to legal competencies.

One remedy for this state of affairs is to promote research that will provide the empirical base for interpreting the meaning of clinicians' data for the legal competence in question, and to promote clinicians' use of those research results in their own case-by-case interpretations. For example, what are the actual relations between various mental disorders and deficits in defendants' abilities associated with competence to stand trial? And how do defendants with those deficits actually perform when they are observed as participants in their trials? What deficits in parenting abilities actually make a negative difference in the upbringing of children? And when those deficits are measured in forensic evaluations, do they correspond to parents' performance in everyday life when they are acting as caretakers of their children?

When *EC* was first published, these were questions for which there were few empirical answers, thus requiring clinicians to rely almost entirely on theory in explaining the meaning of their data for the forensic questions that they were asked to address. Chapters in this book on each of the legal competencies will show that considerable research progress has been made toward providing empirical guidance for interpreting the data that clinicians collect in their evaluations for most of the competencies. Literature reporting research to improve interpretations in competence to stand trial evaluations, for example, has followed an ascending trajectory (as noted earlier in this chapter), increasing by about 25% in each of the past five-year periods (Grisso, 1992; Cooper & Grisso, 1997; Mumley, Tillbrook, & Grisso, in press). This increase in the availability of empirical information related to legal competencies is encouraging. Currently we have no evidence regarding clinicians' use of this information. But its availability, as well as work in progress, suggests that the field has developed far more resources than in earlier years to establish an empirical foundation for its evaluations related to legal competencies.

In summary, it is clear that the field has made significant strides to mitigate the problems in forensic competence evaluations associated with the "5 I's" of discontent regarding forensic practice. Yet evidence also indicates that this progress has been uneven and incomplete. The lessons of EC's first edition, therefore, are still needed.

THE VALUE OF A CONCEPTUAL MODEL

A primary contribution of the first edition of EC was the description of a conceptual model for structuring our thinking about legal competencies. The purpose of the model was to assist the field in overcoming the limitations and criticisms that we have just reviewed. The model was intended to frame and clarify our thinking about:

- what the law wants to know when it asks legal competence questions;
- what should be required of clinicians' evaluations for legal competencies; and
- what research is needed in order to assist clinicians in obtaining reliable data and making relevant interpretations pertaining to legal competencies.

EC's conceptual model appears to have had a significant impact on developments in the field of assessments for legal competencies in subsequent years, both in terms of research and the way that the assessment process has come to be described in texts that guide the field of forensic assessment. It is again offered in Chapters 2 and 3 of this book, with some modifications suggested by experience in using it during the past 15 years. Two premises originally influenced the development of the model.

- A conceptual model for assessments related to legal competencies must be based at the outset on *an analysis of the law's view of competencies.*
- The model must be consistent with, and must promote, the *scientific, empirical and ethical standards of mental health professionals' disciplines.*

The intention to develop assessments based on an analysis of the law's view of legal competencies does not concede that the law "knows more" about human capacities than do mental health professionals. To the contrary, assessments should make use of the special expertise of mental health professionals that qualifies them to enlighten legal decision makers. Their disciplines have developed many concepts, theories, and methods that can assist the courts. Yet these must be selected and used in accordance with the structures of the law and its standards for decision making. Therefore, an assessment model for legal competencies should reflect, not reform, the law's model for addressing legal competencies.

The intention to develop a conceptual model that is consistent with the scientific, empirical, and ethical standards of mental health professionals' disciplines is essential, because these are the standards that define mental health professionals' expertise in the courtroom. Theory, too, is essential; yet the use of theory alone does not distinguish the expertise of the scientist from that of the philosopher, theologian, or astrologer. The distinguishing characteristic is the essential requirement for empirical evidence to support the utility of the psychological theories that the scientist uses. A conceptual model for assessments must promote this empirical requirement in three ways: it must guide the collection of reliable case data, the use of empirical research results to interpret the data, and the development of new research to improve both methods and interpretations.

Chapters 2 and 3 describe the conceptual model for legal competence assessments that can meet these demands. The final section of Chapter 3 introduces Chapters 4 through 9, each of which describes the development and use of special assessment instruments that can assist in implementation of the conceptual approach. Chapter 10 summarizes the directions that should be taken in the future development and application of these instruments.

2

Legally Relevant Assessments for Legal Competencies

One of the primary contributions of the first edition of EC was the introduction of a model for conceptualizing all legal competencies. The model was first developed as an intellectual challenge. Could a set of concepts be constructed that would identify a common structure among legal competencies that are encountered throughout criminal and civil law? The model was published as a test of the hypothesis. Like a good theory, if the model had utility, it would survive and serve a heuristic function for the field across time.

The hypothesis seems to have been confirmed. The model has been cited widely and appears to have been useful for both researchers and practitioners across the past 15 years. Experience has identified a few features of the model that were unnecessarily complex. But the basic form of the model has encountered no serious challenges and continues to be of value as a structuring tool.

Therefore, in preparation for the instrument review chapters, the present chapter describes the model almost in the same form and with the same arguments that appeared in the first edition of EC. Where there have been minor changes, they are noted and explained.

INTRODUCTION

Legal competencies are constructs, in the same sense that this term is used in psychology and psychiatry. *Constructs* are hypothetical conditions or states that cannot be observed directly; only their behavioral signs can be observed. We use constructs to summarize our observations about individuals, and we presume that the inferred condition has some consequence for how individuals will behave or how we may want to respond to them. We may agree on certain observable phenomena to guide our use of the construct. Yet a construct is "open-textured" (Meehl, 1970); it can never be captured by an invarying set of facts. Its use may vary somewhat across cases, and it is open to various operational definitions. In summary, a construct is an abstraction; despite its inferred relation to observations, it retains the elusive quality of an idea.

Legal competencies have these same qualities (Roesch & Golding, 1980; Melton et al., 1997). Each competence (e.g., competence to stand trial, competence to care for self or property) is defined by broad statutory phrases and by case law interpretations of the statutory definition. For example, most states define an individual's competence to stand trial as a "sufficient present ability to consult with his lawyer" and a "rational as well as factual understanding of proceedings against him" (*Dusky v. United States*, 1960, p. 402). These conditions are said to be absent or present in individual cases on the basis of the court's consideration of relevant facts and circumstances in each case. Yet no particular set of facts ever defines the condition for all cases. The legal competence construct is an abstraction, unable to be defined by verbal precision or specific observations.

Gordley's (1984) essay on legal reasoning aptly describes why the law does not reduce its decision criteria to a set of specific facts or circumstances that would promote mechanical interpretations (or what behavioral scientists would call "operational definitions"). Legal authorities that frame the law's definitions recognize that the purpose of a definition is to contribute to just, right, or useful decisions. To enumerate the exact circumstances that must be present in order to arrive at these decisions would require the presumption that no other circumstances could arise that would achieve the legal purpose. Legal authorities recognize that the world is not that predictable: "No set of invariable rules," Gordley observed, "could even tell one the best way to make a trip downtown" (1984, p. 142), unless one presumes that there will never be changes in the weather, one's health, public transportation schedules, and so forth. Therefore, the law's definitions for legal competencies provide broad discretion in determining whether a set of case facts satisfies the criteria for competence or incompetence.

This quality of legal competencies as constructs tells us that we should not expect any clinical assessment to define operationally a legal competence. The results of an assessment may be more or less useful in providing information that assists courts to make legal competence decisions. Yet the decision will not depend on any particular set of assessment observations across cases.

Despite the elusive quality of legal competence constructs, one can discern a common structure in legal competencies as diverse as competence to stand trial, competence as caretaker of a child, and competence to manage one's property. The analysis in this chapter describes this structure, offering five components that define all legal competencies. As will be shown in the following discussion, this structure provides a model to guide assessments toward objectives that are consistent with the legal criteria and process in competence cases. The discussion at this point will not attempt to demonstrate how each of the five components applies to each legal competence. That evidence appears in subsequent chapters (4 through 9), wherein the utility of the five-component model is tested by its ability to structure and organize our thinking about legal competencies and related assessments.

The conceptual model offered here is essentially the same as the one that was first described in the 1986 edition of this book, but with one significant structural change. The original model consisted of six components that the legal competencies have in common. Experience has suggested, however, that the important aspects of one of these components (the *contextual* component) could be folded into one of the others (the *functional* component) without loss of meaning and with gains associated with simplification. In addition, the present version uses the term "components" of legal competencies rather than the term "characteristics" used in the original version. According to this model, the primary components of all legal competencies are: (1) Functional, (2) Causal, (3) Interactive, (4) Judgmental, and (5) Dispositional.

FIVE COMPONENTS OF LEGAL COMPETENCIES

FUNCTIONAL COMPONENT

Definition

Legal competence constructs focus on an individual's *functional abilities, behaviors, or capacities.* As used here, the term *functional abilities* refers to that which an individual can do or accomplish, as well as to the knowledge, understanding, or beliefs that may be necessary for the accomplishment. Examples of functional abilities include the capacity to engage in disciplinary responses to a child's misbehavior (relevant for parenting competence), and being able to keep track of one's financial expenditures (for questions of competence to manage one's property).

Functioning is related to, but distinct from, psychiatric diagnoses or conclusions about general intellectual abilities and personality traits. Psychiatric and psychological conditions (e.g., psychosis, abstract reasoning ability, introversion) are hypothetical constructs that are presumed to influence functioning. The functional component of legal competence constructs, however, refers to functioning itself and to specific knowledge or understanding for relevant functioning, not only to the hypothetical traits or psychodiagnostic conditions that might influence it.

The specific functional abilities that are relevant will vary depending on the legal competence construct in question. Each legal competence construct refers to a general environmental context that establishes the parameters for defining the relevance of particular functional abilities for the legal competence construct. The relevant environmental context is some class of external situations to which a person must respond. Various legal competencies examined in this book specify widely differing contexts: for example, criminal proceedings (trials), police interrogations, home life, and treatment services. Each context is presumed to require certain types of functional abilities in order to manage one's role within that context. Roles consistent with the contexts noted above would include, respectively, the role of defendant, suspect, manager of one's everyday affairs, and patient.

Different general contexts and roles are presumed to require somewhat different functional abilities. For example, a person's ability to discipline a misbehaving child may be quite relevant for the context and role with which legal definitions of parent competence are concerned, when applied in questions of child custody. Yet this functional ability would not be relevant for the legal construct of competence to stand trial, which refers specifically to the context of trials and defendants' roles in these proceedings. Conversely, a person's ability to understand the gravity of potential consequences of a criminal conviction may be relevant for competence to stand trial, but not for competence to care for a child. Clearly, there is no single construct of legal competence. There are several legal competencies distinguished by their different contexts, which in turn refer to different functional abilities.

The law, however, usually does not identify in great detail specifically which abilities are demanded of people in these general contexts. For example, guardianship cases generally apply the legal construct "ability to care for oneself and one's property," and competence to stand trial refers to "a defendant's ability to assist a lawyer in his defense." These guidelines and subsequent case law, however, do not provide a finite listing of functional abilities that are necessary in order to perform the role of manager of oneself or one's property, or the role of client/defendant in trial preparations with a lawyer. Both contexts merely define the parameters of a hypothetical domain of functional abilities. Identification of specific functional abilities that may be relevant for a legal competence requires some form of exploration and interpretation of this domain.

Assessment Implications

The most fundamental objective of a related assessment is to obtain information about a person's functional abilities—*what the person understands, knows, believes, or can do that is directly related to the competence construct.*

This objective contrasts with most clinical assessments designed to determine psychiatric diagnoses, to provide trait-based descriptions of examinees, and to recommend interventions. As explained in Chapter 1, mental health professionals often have assumed that a diagnosis of some major mental disorder is sufficient basis for determining legal incompetence. The functional characteristic of legal competencies, however, requires a good deal more, because neither the law nor theories of psychopathology assume that any mental disorder always renders individuals incapable of all intellectual, behavioral, and social functions. The assessment should be designed so that the examiner will not be caught unprepared when the judge asks: "We understand that the defendant is schizophrenic and has severe delusions, Doctor. But that is not entirely the point. What can he do and what is he not able to do that is relevant for the question before this court?"

In the past, mental health professionals often attempted to respond to questions of this type by inferring from a diagnostic or trait-based description the specific functional abilities with which the law is concerned. For example, an examiner might infer that an individual with a diagnosis of Major Depressive Episode will be unable to manage financial matters, such as buying necessities, paying bills, and keeping accounts. The logic is based on the symptomatic behaviors that the examiner observed in forming the diagnosis: the patient's prominent and persistent dysphoric mood, loss of energy, poor appetite, insomnia, decrease in sexual drive, slowed thinking, and perhaps even recurrent thoughts of death. Given these observations, the expert infers that the patient will be incapable of, or disinterested in, managing the tasks associated with daily financial transactions or maintenance of property.

In another case, an examiner may infer that a juvenile could not have understood the words and phrases that police used when they informed him of his *Miranda* rights, prior to his waiver of the rights and making a confession. This inference might be based on the juvenile's low intelligence test score, poor school achievement records, and the results of an interview.

The examiner's status as expert clearly allows opinions and inferences of this type in expert testimony (Federal Rules of Evidence, Article 7). Morse (1978a,b), though, produced the classic and still convincing argument that inferences of this type frequently are not "expert" at all. The mental health professional may be especially qualified to observe, summarize, and describe the behaviors that constitute the depressive disorder or the juvenile's intellectual development. Yet the expert's inferences about functional abilities specific to the legal competencies (paying bills, understanding police warnings), when based on these more general observations, are often no more than speculation. *The expert has not demonstrated special knowledge of the relation between the observed symptoms and the actual behaviors that are related to the law's concerns.*

Based on this argument, Morse concluded that mental health professionals should be limited to symptom descriptions, because their subsequent inferences about specific functional abilities are not based on any special knowledge about the relation of the symptoms or diagnoses to the functional abilities in question. This limitation is not necessary, however, if mental health professionals acquire special knowledge of the functional abilities and behaviors that are relevant for the legal competence question. In that case, neither the expert nor other participants in the legal process would need to rely on speculative inference about those abilities. *Whenever possible, therefore, forensic examiners should observe directly the functional abilities associated with a legal competence.*

The assessment of functional behaviors and abilities has a long tradition in psychology outside the specific area of forensic assessment. In the realm of clinical assessment, the measurement of competencies, aptitudes and abilities that are important for real-life functions has long been seen as having the potential to serve many of psychology's descriptive and predictive needs better than the measurement of intelligence (e.g., McClelland, 1973). Similarly, the assessment of specific, functional abilities relevant for legal competencies serve the needs of courts and forensic examiners better than the determination of diagnoses or the measurement of general personality traits alone.

The present model places the measurement of functional abilities at the core of an assessment for legal competence. Significant portions of later chapters in this book are devoted to methods for assessing legally relevant functional abilities. A later discussion in this chapter, however, will show that we should not discard the more traditional, trait-based assessment methods of psychiatry and clinical psychology, because they have an important supplemental function in legal competence assessments.

Having decided that functional abilities must be assessed, the next step in fulfilling that objective is to identify which functional abilities are especially relevant for a given legal competence. What criterion should we use to decide that a particular functional ability is or is not relevant for a particular legal competence construct?

One criterion, of course, is *theory*. We may decide, for example, that one's ability to display affection for a child is an important functional ability to assess in relation to legal questions of parental competence and child custody, because psychological theories of child development or parenting emphasize the importance of affection for a child's development. Alternatively, we may arrive at the same conclusion *empirically*, having observed in controlled research that children who have not received displays of affection have not thrived as well as children who have received affectionate caretaking. Finally, we may decide to assess the ability to display affection because it has been defined *legally* as a relevant variable for evaluating parental competence in child custody cases, or at least has received considerable attention in judicial deliberations in these cases.

The examiner's decision about which abilities to assess is relatively easy when there is basic agreement between theory, empirical observation, and legal requirements. Conflict or uncertainty arises, though, when particular functions may be considered relevant on the basis of one criterion but are not raised, or are actively rejected as irrelevant, by another criterion. For example, in relation to child custody questions, judicial thinking has given considerable weight to a parent's conventional lifestyle or moral virtues; yet these qualities have played a lesser role in psychology's theoretical and empirical perspectives on the essential dimensions of parenting (see Chapter 7). The theoretical concept of "psychological parent" (Goldstein, Freud, & Solnit, 1973) has been adopted in some jurisdictions as an important dimension from a legal perspective; yet several empirical studies have obtained results that question its usefulness as a concept applied to decisions about the best interests of children (see Chapter 7; also Reppucci, 1984). Both theoretical and empirical considerations suggest the importance of a parent's knowledge or capacity for manifesting consistent, contingency-based reinforcement for a child's behaviors; yet this parenting skill receives little or no reference in the body of laws and legal writings that guide or control judicial child custody decisions (Chapter 7).

   Given such conflicting criteria, which criterion should an examiner employ when deciding what functional abilities to assess in relation to the context of a legal competence? One could argue that legal criteria must take precedent: that the competence is defined by law, and that other criteria, therefore, do not have authority to define the nature of the legal competence. On the other hand, one could argue that psychological theory and empirical research should take precedent in deciding which functional abilities are relevant for legal competencies. After all, if the law is concerned with functioning in specific social contexts, one might assume that legal decision makers would not wish to assign weight to abilities that have no empirical relation to performance in those contexts.

   The present conceptual model suggests that assessments for legal competencies should be guided by all three legal criteria, because each provides a somewhat different perspective on the abilities of greatest relevance to legal questions within the defined context. Were we to require a mental health professional to assess only the abilities recognized in law and judicial perspectives, this might have several undesirable consequences.

   First, unquestioning adherence to legal preferences assumes the infallibility of legislative and judicial assumptions concerning which abilities are related to performance in the relevant contexts. This infallibility is not presumed even by the law itself (Gordley, 1984). Subsequent chapters will show that the law usually does not define the specific abilities related to a competence context, and judicial opinions often manifest uncertainty, openness, or lack of consensus concerning which abilities to consider.

   Second, if assessments are confined only to the abilities defined as relevant by law or judicial opinion, we are not stimulated to develop information and assessment methods that might inform lawmakers concerning the practical importance of other abilities outside the law's current perspective. Through our own empirical research or development of theory, we may discover the importance (or relative unimportance) of various abilities for performance in various contexts. These abilities might be among those already endorsed by lawmakers, or they might not have been apparent to them intuitively. By confining ourselves only to the law's perspective, however, we are less likely to discover these kinds of abilities. Further, we would be relinquishing our opportunity to contribute to the growth of law, and to rationality in judicial decisions, through our empirical perspective. In the last analysis, of course, the law and judicial opinion will determine whether one's selection of abilities yields probative or admissible evidence.

   In Chapters 4 through 9, we will examine all three criteria for determining the relevance of functional abilities in contexts specified by legal competencies. Judicial interpretations will be summarized, psychological theories will be examined as guides for selecting which abilities to assess, and empirical guidance will be sought wherever research has provided it.

CAUSAL COMPONENT

Definition

Legal competence constructs require *causal inferences to explain an individual's functional abilities or deficits related to a legal competence.* That is, when a person's deficient abilities related to the legal competence are known, the legal competence construct requires ascription of the likely reasons for those deficits.

Later chapters will show that statutory phrases defining competence constructs frequently contain references to causes of functional inabilities. For example, legal definitions applied in guardianship proceedings often require that "inability to care for oneself or one's property" must be "because of" or "as a result of" mental, developmental or physical disability, in order to meet the standard for legal incompetence and assignment of a guardian.

Why is the law concerned about the "cause" of one's functional deficits? If the individual does or does not manifest the ability to know, understand, believe or do those things that are relevant for a legal competence construct, why does the cause matter? There are two major reasons, both derived from the consequences of a finding of incompetence.

First, for some legal competencies, a legal finding of incompetence can lead to a positive consequence that offers an incentive for feigning diminished functional abilities. For competence to stand trial, for example, one of the consequences of a finding of incompetence is a delay of trial while defendants are provided some intervention that is intended to remediate their functional deficits that stand in the way of their participation in their trial. Some defendants may manifest poor functional abilities for reasons that are directly related to their mental disorder, and the delay of trial is intended to provide time for interventions that will reduce their symptoms and improve their functioning. Other defendants, however, will manifest similar deficits in their performance of functional tasks because they wish to appear incompetent, thereby gaining a delay of their trial. Courts obviously have an interest in avoiding this misuse of the legal process.

Second, findings of legal incompetence typically result in a temporary or permanent deprivation of rights that the individual otherwise would enjoy. This is done in order to protect the individual (or others) from the potential damages that might otherwise accrue (e.g., loss of finances as a consequence of poor judgment) as a consequence of the individual's functional deficits. Although the purpose is beneficent, our society and legal system do not take lightly the deprivation of individual liberties and personal self-determination, but require a sound reason for doing so.

In this context, it is important to recognize that some individuals may manifest deficits in functional abilities at a particular time for reasons other than mental illness or mental disability (even in cases in which the individual in question does have a mental illness or disability). For example, imagine that at the time the person's functional deficit was observed, the person had had no sleep the previous night. In another case, a defendant might demonstrate little knowledge of the importance of a judge in a trial, but otherwise seems capable of learning new information. In cases like these, the possible causes of the apparent functional deficits may seem easily remediable, thus changing their meaning and significance in deliberations about a person's legal competence.

In summary, the causal component of legal competence constructs focuses on explanations for an individual's apparent deficits in relevant functional abilities, in order to assure that the consequences of a finding of incompetence are not misapplied.

Assessment Implications

Assessments for legal competencies should provide information that will assist courts in judging the probable reasons for deficits in the functional abilities that have been assessed, as well as the potential for their stability, change, or remediation. Observation and measurement of the functional abilities alone, of course, usually will not provide sufficient information for this objective.

Psychiatry and psychology possess many resources for explaining functional behaviors and for estimating their future course. Various functional deficits may be seen as consequences of neurological or biochemical conditions, intellectual and cognitive capacities, motivations, emotions, learning histories, and social relations. When the law refers to "mental disorder" as a cause, the mental health professional turns to these biological and psychological constructs as potential sources for explanations of disorder in mental and behavioral activities. Existing tools and guides for working with these constructs are numerous.

First, mental health professionals have a wide range of methods and instruments for collecting reliable data on the variables just noted. Many of these tools, including biological and psychological tests and interview methods, can be used to describe examinees reliably in terms of their emotional or motivational characteristics, their intellectual or cognitive conditions, neurological abnormalities, social histories, and everyday behaviors.

Second, mental health professionals possess empirical research results that describe relations between the above types of information and other past, present, or future behaviors and outcomes. For example, research results frequently establish empirical links between individuals' past histories and current behavioral and psychological characteristics. They also may establish relations between two or more current conditions, as when a particular behavior is shown almost always to occur concurrently with a particular event or a certain emotional state. Other research demonstrates potentials for anticipating a future behavior or event based on current characteristics of an individual. Therefore, when assessment methods and instruments can identify certain biological or psychological characteristics of a given examinee, existing research on these characteristics sometimes can guide the examiner's inference to suggest or reject various causal explanations and predictions concerning a specific case.

Third, the disciplines of mental health professionals have theories of normal and abnormal behavior. A psychological theory is a system of interrelated constructs and assumptions about human behavior and its causes. A theory by itself is a convenient fiction that is useful for generating hypotheses about how various events, behaviors, and human characteristics interrelate. When these hypotheses have been tested in empirical research, the theory serves as a logical system for organizing and describing what is known empirically. In this role, it provides causal explanations for what is known. Such causes are never proven true or false by either research or the elegance of a theory. Theoretical causal explanations merely seem more or less plausible or useful, given the strength or weakness of the empirical research results that the theory has generated.

Each of these three tools has an important role in collecting and communicating information that will assist courts in addressing causal questions in legal competence constructs. Given that one has assessed an examinee's legally relevant functional abilities and deficits (in accordance with the Functional component noted earlier), theory and existing research results can be used to develop one or more hypotheses concerning causes of the functional deficits. The hypotheses then dictate one's selection of certain assessment methods or instruments that employ the theoretical constructs (e.g., intelligence tests, measures of personality or psychopathology, structured interview methods), and these methods would be used to test the hypotheses. The actual assessment process might not always follow this precise sequence, but testimony generally would unfold the assessment results in this logical manner. Thus the value of any theoretical explanations in testimony would be tested in court by the quality of the examiner's empirical evidence for the hypotheses, not merely by the elegance or intuitive plausibility of the theory that generated the causal hypotheses.

This view of the assessment process finds a role for theory in assessments, but considerable controversy has surrounded the use of psychiatry's and psychology's theoretical explanations for behavior in expert testimony. Morse (1978a, b; 1982, 1983), for example, contended that the results of forensic assessments should be reported only as descriptions of behavior or, when available, as relationships and predictions based on sound empirical research. He believes that theoretical explanations should not be offered, because: (a) too often they have little or no empirical support, and therefore are mere speculation; (b) theories of psychiatry and psychology nevertheless may seem "scientific" and thus may have an undo influence on the fact finder; and (c) legal fact finders—for example, judges and juries—probably are capable of drawing their own causal conclusions, given whatever descriptive and empirical research information the expert witness can provide. Other commentators (e.g., Bonnie & Slobogin, 1980; Melton et al., 1997) have not taken this position, but instead have pointed out potential values of testimony that informs the fact finder of theoretical explanations underlying the examiner's assessment results. The court can then take these theories into account in weighing the relevance of the person's deficits for the legal question.

In summary, to satisfy the causal requirements of a legal competence construct, the assessment should be designed to obtain data and to use empirical research results in a manner that will provide the court a theoretical explanation concerning any deficits in functional abilities that are relevant to the legal competence.

INTERACTIVE COMPONENT

Definition

Legal competence constructs focus on *person-context interactions*. A legal competence question does not merely ask the degree of functional ability or deficit that a person manifests. It asks further, "Does this person's level of ability meet the demands of the specific situation with which the person will be (was) faced?" Defined more formally, a decision about legal competence is in part a statement about *congruency or incongruency between (a) the extent of a person's functional ability and (b) the degree of performance demand that is made by the specific instance of the context in that case.* Thus an interaction between individual ability and situational demand, not an absolute level of ability, is of special significance for legal competence decisions.

The law provides ample evidence with which to identify the interactive component of legal competence constructs. This evidence is reviewed in later chapters, but a few examples will facilitate the following discussion:

- The court in *U.S. v. Wilson* (1966) ruled on the procedure for determining whether an amnesiac defendant is incompetent to stand trial. The court decided that this depends in part on the degree to which there is enough evidence without the defendant's recall to allow the defense to reconstruct the critical events associated with the alleged crime. The more deficient the case in sources of information critical to a defense, the greater the importance of the defendant's ability to recall the events.
- Repeatedly in cases from *In re Gault* (1967) to *Fare v. Michael C.* (1979), appellate courts have concluded that the competence of a juvenile's waiver of *Miranda* rights at the time of arrest depends not only on the capacities of the juvenile, but also on the manner and circumstances in which the police obtained the juvenile's waiver.
- Legal analysts (e.g., Anderer, 1990; Sales, Powell, Van Duizend, & Associates, 1982) have noted that abilities related to competence to care for one's property (as the concept applies to guardianship for the elderly or developmentally disabled) will depend in part on the size, type, and complexity of the individual's property and resources.

These examples clearly indicate that no absolute level of functional ability or inability signifies competence or incompetence. The individual's level of ability will be important to consider, yet the fact finder can assess its significance only when it is weighed against the demands of the individual's specific situation.

For example, two defendants may manifest equal deficiencies in their ability to manage the role of defendant in trials. Yet one of them, facing a trial that is expected to be relatively brief or simple, may be deemed competent, while the other, facing a more complex and lengthy trial, may be considered incompetent. The law labels the *person* incompetent, yet it is more accurate to say that *the law arrives at a conclusion about a condition of incompetence posed by person-context incongruency or mismatch.*

The term *context* has now been employed in two ways in this model, and it is worthwhile to make the distinction between its two uses.

In describing the Functional component, we noted that the functional abilities that are relevant for a particular legal competence depend on the context of the legal competence—e.g., for competence to stand trial, the abilities that are important for defendants to exercise in the role of defendant. Thus the context of the legal competence defines the *types* of abilities that are relevant. In contrast, context is used in the Interactive component to determine the *level or degree* of those abilities that are needed in the specific case in question.

In some cases, the specific instance of the context may even reduce to negligible levels the relevance of some ability that generally would be within the domain of a competence's context. An example outside of the law might be helpful. When evaluating the "competence" of automobiles, we would consider their ability to ascend hills as within the domain of relevant abilities to consider. Yet for the driver whose route includes no hills (the specific instance of the context), the automobile's "functional ability to ascend" may be of little importance in evaluating its competence for the journey at hand. By the same token, a knowledge of the automobile's ability to ascend will not be sufficient information with which to determine its competence to manage a hilly route. The driver will have to know also the probable degree of incline of the hills. Similarly, a consideration of the specific instance of the context is inextricable from the definition of a legal competence construct.

Specific instances of contexts for legal competencies almost always exist in the future or the past. The law wishes to know about a person's abilities in relation to situations that have already happened, such as the circumstances surrounding a crime or an arrest, or concerning situations that are anticipated, such as a trial. Therefore, consideration of the degree of person-context congruency necessarily directs one to address the probable demands of the past or future situation together with an estimate of the person's past or future functioning.

Assessment Implications

Psychology offers mental health professionals a number of theoretical models and concepts related to the interactive perspective of the law on competencies. Consistent with many of these contributions, behavior often is best understood as an interaction between personal consistencies in behavioral or cognitive functioning (e.g., traits, cognitive styles) and characteristics of the settings in which a person functions. (e.g., Bem & Allen, 1974; Magnusson & Endler, 1977; Mischel, 1983, 1984).

The interactive nature of legal competencies suggests that forensic examiners should consider collecting information about the specific environmental or social context in which the examinee will be expected to function. Doing this for various legal competencies might require discovering the demands of an upcoming trial (for competence, to stand trial), the special needs and characteristics of a specific child (for parental competence related to child custody), or the degree of certain skills and knowledge that will be required by the financial and residential circumstances of a specific elderly person (for competence to care for self/property as related to guardianship).

Assessment of the performance demands of the specific context has several objectives and benefits. One objective, of course, is to describe the degree to which the examinee's abilities (as described in the sections on the Functional component) exceed or fall short of these demands. Second, this approach clarifies for both the examiner and the court that legal competence is not a matter of the examinee's absolute level of ability alone, but rather the congruency between ability and demand. Third, considering the situation's demands in relation to the examinee's abilities has certain conceptual implications for reducing the incongruency between the two. That is, congruency (an approximation toward legal competence) may be increased not only by remediation of a person's deficits, but also by changing the performance demands of the relevant situation. For example, if an elderly person's abilities are incongruent with the demands of an anticipated living arrangement or financial situation, the interactive perspective offers three hypothetical responses to the incongruency: (a) declare the person incompetent and assign a guardian, (b) augment the elderly person's skills, or (c) find a living arrangement and financial situation with fewer demands, therefore producing greater congruency between the person's current abilities and the person's life situation.

Certain challenges are presented by the objective to assess dimensions of specific environmental or social contexts in a manner that will meet the objectives outlined above. Direct comparison of personal abilities and situational demands might be greatly facilitated if the dimensions for assessing situations were to parallel the dimensions used for describing personal abilities. Common examples of this approach may be found in educational and industrial psychology, in which performance levels among people in a particular work setting are measured and then used as the criterion measure for selecting future employees for that work setting. Psychology also has long had models for describing individuals and environments on parallel dimensions, an approach pioneered by Murray (1938) in his constructs of human "needs" and environmental "press."

Later chapters will note that very few assessment methods for addressing legal competencies have been developed with this conceptual perspective. The creative examiner, however, could find ways to employ this strategy in some cases. For example, an examinee in a child custody assessment might be evaluated for the ability to provide structure and consistency in child rearing, and the child might be evaluated concerning the degree of structure and consistency in parenting that the child requires. The use of the same dimension for both assessments facilitates the process of judging the person-situation congruency or incongruency on which competence decisions are based. Later chapters will consider further the value of this notion of parallel, person-context dimensions in assessments for various legal competencies.

<h2 style="text-align:center">JUDGMENTAL AND DISPOSITIONAL COMPONENTS</h2>

Definition

Legal competence constructs require a *judgment* that person-context incongruency is of a sufficient magnitude to warrant a finding of legal incompetence. Part of that judgment is based on the fact that when the judgment is made, law prescribes certain *dispositional* consequences. The competence decision sets a disposition in motion, and in that sense, the disposition is part of the legal competence construct.

The interactive component, as described above, addresses questions of the degree to which a functional ability exists, how much is demanded by the situation, and how much of a discrepancy exists between the two. The judgmental component then addresses the ultimate question: *How much incongruency is enough to warrant a finding of incompetence?*

Legal competence statutes are replete with phrases referring to this component of competence constructs. They use words such as "sufficient," "grave," "significant," "requisite," "unlikely to be able," and "reasonable degree" to refer to the extent of deficit or incongruency that will satisfy the legal standard. These terms have no static or absolute meaning. In theory, no particular degree of person-context incongruency is dispositive of the legal competence decision. The words and phrases noted above are interpreted with great discretion.

Legal competence constructs, nevertheless, are defined by law, no matter how vaguely. Therefore, the legal fact finder who employs discretion to answer the judgmental question of legal competencies must make a judgment based on the law. This requires a consideration of legal precedent and an interpretation of the standards of justice set forth by society, which formulates the law. When a legal fact finder states that a degree of functional deficit or person-context incongruency in a particular case is "enough" to warrant a finding of legal incompetence, that person interprets the meaning of justice in that instance.

Justice is required because a finding of competence or incompetence often designates a legal status and a related legal *disposition* for the person to whom it is applied. An individual's legal status of incompetence gives the state the authority to act in some way toward the individual. In some instances, the state's dispositional act may be automatic—that is, without further decision—once the person's legal incompetence status has been assigned. In these cases, the incompetence finding is at one and the same time a conclusion about person-context incongruency and a decision to apply the state's authority for subsequent action. In most instances, this action includes deprivation of fundamental rights, many of which are of grave natural consequence for the individual and for other persons in the community who may be affected by the decision.

Therefore, the judgmental and dispositional components identify the question, "how much incongruency is enough," as an interpretation of justice, in light of the instant circumstances and the dispositional consequences that will accrue for both the individual and society. This interpretation invariably constitutes a legal, moral, or social judgment, no matter how it is made. In the last analysis, interpretations of the sufficient conditions for depriving individuals of constitutional freedoms, even for their own good, are moral judgments requiring legal authority.

Assessment Implications

It follows logically from this description of the judgmental and dispositional components that forensic assessments for legal competencies should *address* but not *answer* the question of a person's legal competence or incompetence. Legal interpretations of justice are beyond the special expertise of mental health professionals, in that nothing in their training, experience, and education sets them apart from other laymen with regard to the ability to judge what is morally right or wrong. Many commentators, therefore, have recommended that mental health professionals should not offer an opinion on ultimate legal questions of competence ("Is the person legally competent or incompetent?") (Appelbaum & Gutheil, 1992; Grisso, 1986, 1988; Group for the Advancement of Psychiatry, 1974; Halleck, 1980; Heilbrun, 2001; Melton et al., 1997; Morse, 1983; Stone, 1975), urgings to the contrary notwithstanding (Federal Rules of Evidence, Article 7, Rule 704).

This general principle has several implications for assessments related to legal competencies. First, when assessing an examinee's degree of functional abilities relevant for the context of a legal competence, the examiner can be relatively unconcerned about translating the level of ability into some notion of legal sufficiency for a finding of competence or incompetence. The examiner's task is to describe as clearly and accurately as possible that which the defendant knows, understands, believes, or can do. If this is described on a measurement continuum, one need not try to establish a cutoff score representing legal acceptability or unacceptability of performance. Indeed, the mental health professional has no legal authority to do so. Further, the law itself recognizes no absolute level of any ability as dispositive of the legal question. The use of so-called "cutoff" scores on psychological tests, forensic or otherwise, to represent legal competence or incompetence is wholly illogical.

Second, when assessing incongruency between an examinee's abilities and the demands of a particular context (the Interactive component), the examiner should not attempt to establish criteria that define a particular amount of incongruency as suggestive of legal incompetence. The extent of the discrepancy itself should simply be described. Further, the examiner might be able to provide descriptive and empirical evidence concerning the probable consequences of the interaction (for example, that an elderly examinee with a particular degree of understanding of basic medical/nutritional needs, placed in a particular independent living situations, is not likely to maintain a medication schedule or an adequate diet unassisted). These results and predictions do not answer the ultimate legal question (Is the person legally competent or incompetent?). They are not judgments that an examinee should or should not be declared legally incompetent. In fact, the elderly person in the example above might *not* be found legally incompetent, if the fact finder determines that there is a realistic way to meet the person's needs without the appointment of a guardian.

Examiners may sometimes feel that the difference between answering the ultimate legal question and stating the degree of incongruency between ability and context demand is almost indistinguishable. For example, after assessing a defendant who cannot understand the English language, who appears to distort reality severely, and who behaves fearfully in any conversations with professionals, many examiners would feel quite justified in believing that the defendant "cannot communicate effectively with a lawyer in his own defense."

To state this conclusion in a forensic report, however, is to answer the ultimate legal question of competence to stand trial. In instances like this, it may be well to remember that it is literally not true that the defendant "cannot communicate," and whether or not he can "communicate effectively" (sufficient to render a *just* trial) is a moral or social judgment. If the examiner means that the lawyer will not learn from the defendant certain information that is needed in trials of the type anticipated, or that the lawyer will have extreme difficulty understanding the defendant, or that the consequences of this particular trial are too complex for the lawyer to convey in a manner the defendant can grasp, then the examiner should describe these incongruencies in this way. Whether or not these interactive conditions amount to client-lawyer communications that are so ineffective as to preclude a just trial ("cannot communicate effectively with one's attorney") can be left for the court to decide.

SUMMARY

Legal competence constructs focus on *functional* abilities: that which a person knows, understands, believes, or can do. The principal objective of an assessment related to legal competence should be the description of an examinee's functional abilities that are relevant conceptually for the legal competence in question. The abilities themselves should be observed, measured, or otherwise documented by reliable means, rather than relying solely on diagnoses of psychopathology, psychiatric symptoms, or assessment of personality traits and general intelligence to infer the examinee's functional abilities.

The functional abilities that are relevant for a legal competence depend on an analysis of the environmental context of the legal competence construct, focusing on the role to be filled by the person in that context. Legal, theoretical, and empirical criteria may be employed in this analysis and selection.

Deliberations about legal competencies require *causal* inferences regarding the hypothetical origins of current functional deficits, their relation to past or future events, and their stability, change, or remediation. Therefore, assessments should be designed to obtain supplemental data with which to assist courts in addressing causal, predictive, and remediation questions about the examinee's functional abilities. Data collection should be guided by theories and empirical research findings (within the examiner's areas of expertise) that provide the empirical relations and theoretical assumptions from which causal explanations and predictions generally are made in psychiatry and psychology. The data thus obtained may be offered to the court, along with relevant empirical research findings, allowing the court to make informed judgments about possible causal relationships. Theoretical speculation without empirical support should be avoided.

The *interactive* component of legal competencies requires consideration of the congruency or incongruency between a person's functional abilities and the degree of performance demand that is made by the specific instance of the context in that case. Thus a finding of legal incompetence speaks to a condition of person-context incongruency, not merely to a condition of the person alone. Therefore, assessments should strive to evaluate and describe the relevant environmental and social situations (e.g., the trial faced by the defendant, or the child for whom custody arrangements are to be made) to which to compare the examinee's abilities. Assessment of both the person and the situation on parallel dimensions will assist the examiner in describing the degree of congruency or incongruency between them.

Legal competence constructs are *judgmental*, in that they require a legal or moral evaluation that a person-context incongruency is sufficiently great to warrant a finding of incompetence. They are *dispositional* in that the finding authorizes particular legal response to the individual, often including deprivation of fundamental rights. These anticipated consequences are weighed when arriving at judgmental conclusions, making the conclusion about legal competence primarily a moral judgment. Therefore, the examiner should describe personal abilities, situational demands, and their degree of congruency in a way that avoids stating the ultimate judgment or conclusion about legal competence. That is, the examiner should offer no opinion concerning whether functional deficits or person-situation incongruencies are of sufficient magnitude to warrant a finding of legal incompetence.

The purpose of this model for describing and analyzing legal competencies is to increase both the relevance and credibility of assessments for legal competencies, by structuring them according to the logic of legal standards for competence. Forensic assessments, however, must do more than meet the demands of legal standards. They must also satisfy the scientific standards of the examiner's profession. These requirements are the subject of the next chapter.

3

Empirical Assessments for Legal Competencies

The conceptual approach to legal competence assessments outlined in Chapter 2 requires the assessment of functional abilities and behaviors related to the legal competence in question. Most assessment methods traditionally used in psychiatry and clinical psychology, however, were designed to assess psychopathological states, personality traits, and general intelligence. These assessment methods will continue to play an important role in many legal competence assessments (see Causal component, Chapter 2). Yet the previous analysis has shown that the use of these methods alone will not satisfy courts' needs for relevant and credible information about examinees' functional abilities related to legal competencies.

For this reason, a specialized set of assessment tools has evolved as a response to the special demands of assessments for legal competencies. The first part of this chapter defines this special class of instruments and provides a model that clarifies their objectives and value. The second section describes special issues in the evaluation of these instruments and establishes criteria for reviews that appear in later chapters. The third section briefly describes the criteria that were employed in selecting the instruments that are reviewed in Chapters 4–9, as well as the standardized outline for each of those review chapters.

FORENSIC ASSESSMENT INSTRUMENTS

The earliest, comprehensive effort to develop a specialized instrument for use in evaluating a legal competence—competence to stand trial—appeared in the early 1970s in the work of an interdisciplinary research team headed by a psychiatrist, A. Louis McGarry (Laboratory for Community Psychiatry, 1973). They proposed that legal criteria for competence to stand trial could be "accurately translated into psychological and clinical terms and retranslated into relevant legally oriented data" (Laboratory of Community Psychiatry, 1973, p. 4). Reviewing the law, they arrived at three broad classes of abilities and capacities of defendants that were relevant for determining competence to stand trial. They translated these legal concepts into 13 psychological "functions," or cognitive, attitudinal, and ability constructs that were believed to be important factors for describing the defendant role in trial settings (e.g., "Quality of Relating to Attorney," "Understanding of Court Procedure"; see Chapter 4 for a listing of the 13 functions). These functions were then used to create the content for two assessment instruments (reviewed in Chapter 4): the *Competency Assessment Instrument* and the *Competency Screening Test*.

The instruments were not intended to predict defendants' later functioning in trials, but rather to describe trial-relevant abilities at the time of the assessment itself. Further, the research team did not intend for the instruments to replace other clinical methods for assessment that might clarify pathological states or cognitive characteristics. These new instruments were to be used in conjunction with other clinical methods of assessment, especially in order to define and clarify the relation between "psychological and clinical terms" and "legal criteria for competence" (Laboratory for Community Psychiatry, 1973).

The efforts of that research group provided the earliest example of a systematic approach to assessment of abilities specifically relevant for a legal competence construct. During the 1980s, other researchers employed a similar logic to develop instruments for use in assessments related not only to competence to stand trial, but also to other legal competencies. For example, Grisso (1981) developed several instruments to assess juveniles' and adults' capacities to waive rights in police interrogations, and Weithorn (1980) and Roth et al. (1982) researched methods for evaluating competence to consent to treatment.

Each of these test developers employed a somewhat different approach to the task than did the pioneering Harvard group. Yet all of them had a similar purpose—to develop standardized, quantitative methods with which to observe and describe behaviors of direct relevance to the law's questions about human competencies and capacities. Recognizing that the law's questions about competencies usually cannot be answered by psychiatric diagnoses or personality descriptions alone, researchers and practitioners alike have sought instruments that assess functional abilities—what people know, understand, believe, or can do—related to specific environmental contexts to which legal competencies refer.

These instruments, whether developed specifically for legal purposes or adapted from other fields of psychology, were first grouped conceptually as a class of instruments in the first edition of EC, wherein they were referred to as "Forensic Assessment Instruments" (FAIs).

OBJECTIVES OF FORENSIC ASSESSMENT INSTRUMENTS

Test developers and forensic examiners seem to have perceived a need for FAIs in order to meet *conceptual objectives* and *procedural objectives*.

Conceptual Objectives

FAIs may improve our ability to conceptualize the relations between legal definitions of abilities and psychological constructs associated with human capacities. This objective is clarified in Figures 1 and 2, to which the following discussion refers.

In Figure 1, *A* represents any legal competence construct. In Figure 2, which applies the model to Competence to Stand Trial, *A* is stated as the *Dusky v. U.S.* (1960) standard for competence to stand trial (i.e., "rational as well as factual understanding of proceedings ... and sufficient present ability to consult with his lawyer with a reasonable degree of rational understanding"). *A* also would include interpretations and refinements of the *Dusky* construct, as applied and explained in subsequent legal cases.

Traditionally, mental health professionals employed general psychological theories and constructs (such as intelligence, reality testing, defense mechanisms, or psychiatric symptoms) as the conceptual basis for their assessments related to legal competencies. These clinical constructs, represented as *B* in Figure 1, often are defined operationally by clinical assessment instruments or methods, designated *B'*, that are designed to assess the clinical and personality attributes. Yet mental health professionals frequently were able to establish only a vague conceptual link between psychological theories (*B*) or data (*B'*) on the one hand, and legal competence constructs (*A*) on the other. Thus clinical data about psychological traits and states, no matter how reliable and valid, were difficult to employ when relating findings to the questions of legal competencies.

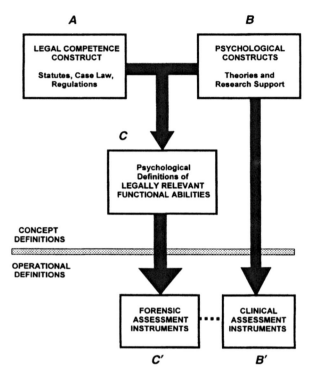

Figure 1. Conceptual and Operational Definitions for Forensic Assessments.

In Figure 1, C represents psychological definitions of functional abilities that have been derived logically from an analysis of a legal competence construct. For example (see Figure 2), the construct representing competence to stand trial (A) may be considered to include a number of functional ability concepts (C), one of them being "Capacity to Disclose to Attorney" (one of the 13 functions by Laboratory of Community Psychiatry, 1973). This legally relevant ability in turn is conceptualized as related to basic psychological constructs (B) such as "intelligence," "memory," and "interpersonal honesty and trust." The functional ability concept (C), therefore, acts as a conceptual link between the legal standard (A) and basic clinical or psychological constructs (B).

A forensic assessment instrument (C') is an operational definition of a legally relevant functional ability concept (C). Therefore, FAIs are intended to provide data that can manage the conceptual gap between legal constructs and psychological constructs. In addition, the dotted line in Figure 1 represents potential relations between FAI data (C') and information from

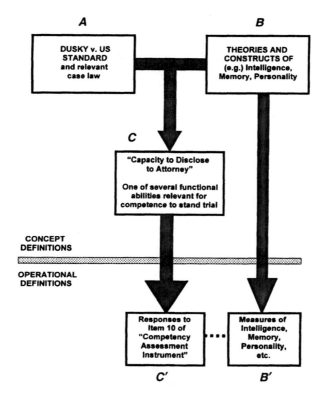

Figure 2. Conceptual Model Applied to Competence to Stand Trial.

traditional psychological tests and psychiatric methods (B') that operationally define psychological constructs. These relations provide a data base for making causal inferences relating psychological constructs (B) to legally relevant functional abilities (C). Figure 2 demonstrates these conceptual relations for one of the functional abilities in competence to stand trial.

These conceptual purposes of FAIs and functional ability concepts have an important limit. They are not intended to define the legal competence construct as a whole. They define only the human abilities and capacities to which the legal construct is believed to refer. Nevertheless, FAIs offer several logical benefits for forensic assessments.

First, *they provide structure for the examiner.* From the outset, FAIs make it clear to the examiner what it is that the law wants to know about human capacities, because these capacities are part of the structure of the FAI itself. Thus they can assist the examiner in arriving logically at data and inferences consistent with the purposes of forensic assessments outlined in Chapter 2.

Second, *FAIs may improve communication in legal settings.* FAI data in expert testimony clarifies for the judge and jury the relation between functional abilities and the legal competence construct. Data that are "face valid" in relation to the competence construct require less complex inferential processes than when one attempts to relate psychiatric symptoms or general personality traits to the legal competence construct. Therefore, expert testimony may be more understandable and useful. Judge and jury might find it possible to participate in the process of inference, rather than relying solely on the expert to manage esoteric and speculative relations between general psychological constructs (*B*) and legal competence criteria (*A*).

Finally, *FAIs facilitate empirical research on the associations between legally relevant functional abilities (operationally defined by FAIs) and the constructs of psychiatry and psychology (operationally defined by more traditional, clinical instruments).* These research findings produce an empirical basis for mental health professionals to employ when interpreting individual cases, thereby decreasing the necessity to rely on theory and speculation alone.

Procedural Objectives

FAIs can improve the quality of forensic assessments by providing relatively standardized and quantitative procedures for acquiring legally relevant assessment data. Unlike unstructured interviews or professionals' individualized approaches to assessing functional abilities, FAIs can offer procedures that are more replicable. That is, they can be repeated in approximately the same manner from one examiner to another and for various examinees. Further, examinees' abilities can be expressed in a uniform manner, using the instrument's methods for classifying or quantifying examinees' responses.

These procedural features of FAIs may have several possible benefits. First, uniform definitions and procedures for assessing legally relevant functional abilities *serve to reduce error and bias.* Some degree of error is inherent in any professional assessment, but generally it is decreased by standardization of procedure.

Second, uniform procedures for assessment *promote meaningful comparisons across time.* FAIs offer the potential to compare an examinee's functional abilities at two different times: for example, to assess the degree of gain in a defendant's abilities relevant for competence to stand trial after a period of treatment. Pre- and post assessments of this type are meaningful only to the extent that procedures for assessing functions are similar at the two times, which is possible with standardized methods using relatively objective ratings or scores.

Third, standardized, quantitative assessment methods *allow collection of data on normative samples*, which promotes the interpretation of examinees' performances by comparison to norms. Comparisons of this type are less meaningful when data have been collected with unstandardized interview or social history methods. Comparisons to norms offer considerable benefits in the inferential logic employed in interpreting individual cases.

Fourth, FAIs can *facilitate comparisons between examiners*. In forensic assessments, it is common for two examiners (testifying on opposing sides) to arrive at different conclusions or opinions about an examinee. Often this may be due to differences in their interpretation of data, but it can also be due to differences between the data bases about which they are making interpretations. If both examiners, however, have used the same standardized methods for obtaining data, it is often possible to determine whether differences in their opinions are due to differences in functional ability data manifested by the examinee, or whether instead the examiners arrived at different conclusions based on essentially the same data. Such comparisons may be difficult when the two examiners have obtained data in very different (unstandardized) ways.

Finally, FAIs *make possible programs of research on the empirical reliability of forensic examiners' methods* for assessing legally relevant functional abilities, as well as *research on the validity (empirical meanings) of their assessment data*. Without standardized methods for assessing legally relevant abilities, there is no way to demonstrate the consistency or dependability (reliability) of the expert's observations. Further, less standardized approaches severely limit our ability to engage in research to demonstrate that the examiner's methods "measure what they claim to measure," that is, that they are empirically valid indicators of the relevant ability concepts.

In summary, FAIs provide operational definitions for functional abilities that are related conceptually to legal competence constructs as well as our psychological and psychiatric constructs. Therefore, they offer two main potential benefits. One is to assist examiners in constructing assessments with conceptual relevance to legal criteria. The other is to contribute data to forensic assessments in a manner consistent with scientific standards for the reliability and validity of assessments.

THE NEED FOR EVALUATION OF FORENSIC ASSESSMENT INSTRUMENTS

The qualities of FAIs that offer potential benefits for competence assessments also constitute a potential for their misuse and misinterpretation. Thus we must approach FAIs with caution and careful scrutiny.

The conceptual relation of FAIs to legal standards could promote inappropriate attribution of meaning or legal relevance to FAI data solely on face value. The mere fact that an instrument possesses scale labels and content based on an analysis of legally relevant functional abilities does not allow us to assert that the instrument provides the law with a more objective, accurate, or meaningful definition of those abilities. This conceptual logic is an appropriate start, of course, and it greatly increases the potential for more useful forensic assessment data. Yet one must have evidence that the instrument can fulfill that potential, rather than reifying the results of FAIs merely on the basis of their appearance of conceptual relevance.

The standardized and quantitative nature of FAIs likewise may lead to premature optimism or misinterpretation. Merely standardizing our *procedures* does not necessarily mean that we have standardized our *assessments*. The latter depends on whether or not we employ procedures and instruments in the manner intended. Merely assigning scores to responses does not guarantee that they are more accurate or objective than nonquantified observations. Their accuracy depends in part on demonstrating with empirical research that quantification produces these qualities.

One must not assume that FAIs' psychometric properties replace the need for less standardized or nonquantitative methods in forensic assessments. No interpretations should be based on any single measure or index alone, no matter what level of reliability or validity may have been demonstrated for it. At best, FAIs must join other measures and methods in a multimethod approach to assessment.

Therefore, if the conceptual and procedural objectives of this new type of instrument suggest certain benefits, they also contribute to the possibility that FAIs will be misconstrued and misused. Their potential benefits can be maximized, and their misuses possibly avoided, if we carefully scrutinize the nature of these specialized instruments. That is one of the major objectives of the reviews of FAIs in subsequent chapters.

The review of this class of instruments is guided by three more specific purposes, associated with their development, their forensic application, and their use in legal settings.

One purpose for examining existing FAIs is *to provide test developers with information that can assist them to improve existing FAIs, and with principles that can guide the development of new instruments in the future.* Subsequent discussions will show that the development of FAIs offers challenges and potential pitfalls, many of which are related to their intended use in legal settings. The special demands of law, legal process and legal systems raises certain test construction issues that may be unique to this area of test development. This does not mean that general principles of test construction will not apply to the development of FAIs. Yet the application of these principles to FAIs offers new challenges.

A second purpose for evaluating FAIs is *to provide guidelines for examiners who wish to use and interpret them.* Examiners are responsible for understanding the limits of the methods that they employ. Further, they must stay abreast of new methods that might improve the quality of forensic assessments.

A third purpose is *to clarify for members of the legal profession the nature of the assessment methods used by mental health professionals in forensic assessments.* Judges and lawyers are responsible for both using and challenging the methods of forensic examiners. They should be sufficiently familiar with the mental health examiner's assessment methods to be able to scrutinize the examiner's choice of certain methods, the logic of the examiner's interpretation of data, and the soundness of the data base for the examiner's inferences. Their understanding of the values and limits of FAIs should improve their ability to meet these responsibilities and to make effective use of assessments for legal competencies.

Chapters 4 through 9 will evaluate FAIs for the three purposes just noted. The following section examines more closely some of the practical and scientific standards that must be met in the development and use of FAIs.

STANDARDS FOR FORENSIC ASSESSMENT INSTRUMENTS

Mental health professionals will be aware of many sources that provide and explain standards for psychological tests and measurements. Those standards should apply to the development and evaluation of FAIs (see Heilbrun, 2001), just as they do to other instruments for assessing human attributes. The relation of FAIs to legal constructs and legal uses, however, suggests a number of special issues concerning the application of scientific standards to the development and evaluation of FAIs. Some of these issues will be raised in this section, in preparation for later reviews of FAIs, whereas possible solutions will be considered in later chapters.

The outline used in this section will be applied in the chapters in which each FAI is reviewed. Standards are discussed in the following order: (1) conceptual basis, (2) psychometric development, (3) construct validation, (4) predictive or classificatory utility, and (5) potential for expressing person-situation congruency.

CONCEPTUAL BASIS: DEFINING LEGALLY RELEVANT
FUNCTIONAL ABILITIES

The Functional component of a legal competence construct (see Chapter 2) requires that a FAI should be an index of functional abilities. The functional abilities to be assessed should relate to the performance of a role in an environmental context specified by the legal competence construct. The Causal component suggests that the functional abilities assessed should be related to cognitive and behavioral constructs found in the basic theories and empirical findings of psychology and psychiatry. This is necessary if one expects to use existing theory and research to guide interpretations of deficits in legally relevant abilities.

These demands have important implications for the first steps in the development or evaluation of a FAI: concept definition and operational definition.

Concept Definition

This activity requires the determination of a set of functional ability concepts or dimensions (*C*, Figure 1) that is related logically to two, more general sets of constructs: the legal competence standard (*A*, Figure 1) and psychology's or psychiatry's basic theories and empirical knowledge about human attributes (*B*, Figure 1). When developing a FAI, these functional ability concepts must be carefully determined, then thoughtfully and completely defined by verbal description. An instrument is not likely to manifest construct validity in later evaluations if the instrument is not based at the outset on careful identification of the attribute dimensions to be measured (Guion, 1983).

When seeking to formulate a set of well-defined dimensions of functional ability for a specific purpose, it is convenient to think in terms of a hypothetical domain of abilities. The parameters or boundaries of this domain are specified generally by the legal competence construct, often in two ways. First, the competence construct will refer to an environmental context, as explained in Chapter 2, which generally identifies a performance role for the individual within that context. Second, legislative wording of legal competence standards, as well as appellate court opinions and other legal writings, may provide phrases referring to global functions with which the law is concerned. These verbal formulations of the legal competence construct, found in the law itself, sketch the boundaries of functioning within which are located an as yet undefined set of legally relevant functional abilities.

One then strives for a solution to the question of the functional ability dimensions that lie within that domain. The content validity of an instrument begins here. *Content validity* refers to the adequacy with which a test has sampled the behaviors or concepts associated with a particular domain. If an instrument begins with certain concept dimensions that are not relevant for the identified domain, or a set of dimensions that does not represent adequate coverage of the domain, then test items that later are devised to represent these dimensions cannot have adequate content validity for the domain.

Content validity does not rest with the mere appearance of relevance. The dimensions derive their relevance also from the method or process used for attaining the set of dimensions to represent the domain in question. Later chapters will review the methods employed by developers of FAIs for identifying functional ability concepts within legal competence domains. Generally, the methods and the task bear some resemblance to the efforts of industrial and organizational psychologists when doing a job analysis in preparation for the construction of job-related assessment instruments. Some jobs may be analyzed for their requisite tasks and functional abilities by systematically observing people performing the job or role. More complex jobs require the use of a theory about the job and its task requirements. Similarly, concept definition for FAIs may use empirical methods, a consideration of psychological or psychiatric theories about human behavior, and the less formal theories of experts who have been in a position to form impressions of the requirements of a particular environmental context. When the environmental context is one with which legal professionals have special knowledge (e.g., the performance of defendants in trial processes), the opinions of judges and lawyers may be sought concerning the relevant functional dimensions associated with the domain. Whatever the methods, the content validity of the resulting set of ability dimensions is judged by the quality of this process.

The related but distinct question of face validity takes on special significance in the selection of ability dimensions for use in legally relevant assessment instruments. In contrast to content validity, *face validity* refers to the appearance of relevance: that is, judgments concerning whether the final set of ability dimensions looks relevant to the purposes intended for the instrument.

With reference to FAIs, there can be no more important criterion for face validity than the opinions of judges and lawyers as prospective consumers of the results of one's anticipated assessment instrument. One should not progress beyond this point in test construction or selection without obtaining their judgments concerning the relevance of the ability dimensions for addressing the legal competence. This may save the test developer from the frustration of proceeding through the tasks of item construction and validation, only to learn that the conceptual dimensions at the foundation of the instrument simply do not comport with judges' legal sense of the competence construct in question. It is possible that no amount of empirical validity will be able to overcome a judicial belief in the face invalidity of an instrument's dimensions in relation to the legal construct.

One must realize, however, that the set of functional ability concepts that one eventually selects will not constitute a conceptual definition of the legal competence construct itself. The FAIs' ability concepts are only a conceptual definition of the functional abilities that appear to be relevant for the legal competence construct. As explained in Chapter 2 (Interactive and Judgmental components), a legal competence construct may refer to far more than a person's functional abilities alone. It may require, for example, considerations of situational variables, economic circumstances, and moral values of society. FAIs can never define legal competence, either conceptually or empirically. Therefore, their construction does not begin with this goal, but rather with conceptual definition of those aspects of the legal competence construct that refer to human functioning—those things that people know, understand, believe, or can do.

Finally, when one is forming a set of functional ability concepts related to the legal competence, it is equally important to be able to describe the assumed or hypothetical relations between these concepts and psychology's basic theories, constructs, and data for understanding human attributes. (This is the relation between *B* and *C* in Figure 1.) Various types of legal competencies may require reference to constructs in theories of psychopathology, theories of personality, developmental theories, or theories of emotion, motivation and cognition. These conceptual links between one's legally relevant ability concepts and basic theories of human behavior will be very important at a later point, when dealing with issues of construct validation and the interpretation of the meaning of functional deficits (see Causal component, Chapter 2).

Operational Definition

Once the legally relevant functional abilities are defined as concepts, they must be translated into content items for the instrument. The format of the items might be questionnaire statements with true-false or Likert-type response formats, or some other format that is more appropriate for various purposes: for example, checklists, structured and semistructured interview items, or categories of behavior to observe and record as manifested by examinees in naturalistic or assigned-task situations. In addition, some method for categorizing, rating, or scoring responses must be devised. The sum total of the content of the items, the method of administration, the response format, and the criteria for scoring or rating responses constitutes the operational definition of the legally relevant functional abilities (C' in Figure 1). These are the procedures with which the attributes of functional ability will be defined and measured.

Several issues require special comment at this phase of construction of a FAI. First, the same issues of content validity that were discussed in relation to concept definition are raised again in operational definition. Now, however, one is concerned with the process for arriving at a set of tasks or test items that will assure adequacy of sampling (in terms of content relevance and content coverage) of the domain of behavior within each functional ability to be assessed. This process is the second step by which content validity will be determined.

When we arrive at a set of tasks or items, we are faced again with the question of face validity as well. We may know by now that the functional ability concepts appear to be relevant to the legal competence construct, according to our assessment of the opinion of legal professionals. Yet is the specific content of the items that now operationally define the dimensions also perceived as legally relevant? Some procedure may be required to determine this before one proceeds further.

Second, the involvement of legal professionals during test construction becomes increasingly important if one intends to develop a system to score responses according to some absolute standard of correctness. For example, a test may instruct examiners to score examinees' responses as "adequate," "marginal," or "inadequate," and examinees' scores are then interpreted accordingly. When a FAI is constructed to incorporate judgments about adequacy of response into the scoring criteria, the assistance of legal authorities in the formation of those criteria is especially important. Chapter 2 identified questions of sufficiency of ability as being legal judgments—not empirical facts or psychological judgments—when data about the ability are applied to a legal definition of competence. Scoring criteria that define as "adequate" or "inadequate" an examinee's answer to a question or performance on a task at least imply a legal judgment when the test itself was developed to address aspects of a legal competence construct. The scoring criteria, therefore, should not be based on the opinions of the test developer alone.

A third issue is the similarity or dissimilarity between the test format and the environmental context to which the legal competence refers. For example, three tests assessing a defendant's ability to communicate with an attorney all might include an item with content that examines defendants' willingness to disclose information to their lawyer. Yet one instrument may pose the question in a true-false item on a paper-and-pencil task, the second in a hypothetical situation posed by a forensic examiner in a structured interview, and the third in a procedure in which the examiner observes the examinee interacting with the examinee's lawyer. The latter of the three tests clearly has the appearance of sampling behavior that most closely approximates the environmental context (communicating with an attorney) to which the construct of competence to stand trial refers.

It is often difficult, however, to approximate closely the environmental context in an examination procedure. In the area of job-related employment testing, for example, often it is not possible to reconstruct in standardized test formats the specific conditions that will confront an examinee on the job. This has produced considerable difficulty in legal determinations of the validity or fairness of employment tests (Haney, 1982). Similarly, certain legally relevant environmental contexts cannot (and often should not) be closely approximated in formats for FAIs. For example, one investigation (Ferguson & Douglas, 1970) confronted school children with an unexpected, quasi-investigative interview intended to produce an ecologically valid examination of children's abilities to understand Miranda warnings prior to waiver of rights. Ethical considerations for psychological harm to the examinee, however, may far outweigh the anticipated value of such research or testing procedures. Thus there is no simple answer to the question of the desirable or acceptable degree of similarity between test format and the legally relevant environmental context. One merely must be aware that this may be of concern, when examiners eventually are required to interpret the degree to which the results of FAIs can be generalized to real-life environmental contexts.

Finally, when constructing ability, attitude, and personality-trait instruments, psychometricians are accustomed to employing various statistical methods for producing homogeneity of items within a scale. The objective is to attain unidimensionality, or some assurance that the items refer or contribute to a single dimension or concept (the one that guided the process of content selection for the scale).

Psychometricians who attempt to develop instruments related to legal constructs might face conflict between this general practice and the demands for content relevance and coverage in relation to legal questions. For example, certain items may correlate poorly with other items in an ability scale of which they are a part, rendering them as suspect in one's search for a homogeneous set of items. Automatic exclusion of these items, however, may have the effect of decreasing both content and face validity, given that the items originally were included as a result of a careful job of content selection.

PSYCHOMETRIC DEVELOPMENT

Within the category of psychometric development are standards related to instrument standardization, reliability, and norms.

Standardization

The materials, administration, and scoring or rating procedures should be established and carefully described for examiners. The issue here, of course, is replicability. Attempts to establish the reliability or validity of a poorly standardized instrument are likely to be fruitless, due to error in measurement allowed by the vagueness of the test procedures themselves. Careful standardization, in turn, maximizes later gains in documenting reliability and validity. In addition, an examiner who can clearly describe to a court the standard procedure with which assessment data were obtained is likely to engender greater understanding on the part of judge and jury and a more firm base for credibility.

Standardization is not synonymous with the elimination of discretion in administration or scoring. Some abilities and attributes are assessed better with methods that are more flexible than questionnaire items and dichotomous response choices. Some behaviors cannot be scored by summing Likert-type responses; instead, examiners sometimes must be asked to rate the behaviors they observe. The objective of standardization is not to reduce all assessment to mechanical procedures, but rather to minimize bias and situational or examiner error to the degree that this is possible with the instrument's administration and quantitative format. Note, however, that this goal requires greater care and effort when defining procedures for subjective rating than when an instrument can be mechanically scored.

Reliability

There are many ways to examine the reliability of instruments, each offering an estimate of the error in measurement that derives from some source. Some forms of reliability estimate examiner error (due to variations in administration, rating, or scoring), whereas others estimate error in terms of changes in responses over time. Still others examine the relationship of items within a scale to each other, providing an index of internal consistency of the scale.

Not all FAIs will require high coefficients (demonstrations of low error variance) for all possible types of reliability. This is because low reliability coefficients need not be interpreted as error in all circumstances.

For example, low test-retest reliability need not be interpreted as a sign of error, if the instrument claims to measure attributes that are presumed in theory to be unstable for any given person across time (e.g., transient emotional states).

Error due to changes in examinees' responses over time takes on special significance in forensic assessments. Most legally relevant functional abilities probably will be conceptualized as relatively stable attributes (though modifiable with therapeutic or educational intervention). Typically, then, one might want FAIs to demonstrate acceptable coefficients of stability. Yet forensic assessments often occur at times and in places that subject examinees to unusual stress or affective arousal. In addition, the anticipated consequences of legal decisions may motivate some examinees to perform worse (malingering), or to exhibit more socially desirable responding (dissimulation), than is representative of their typical performance or attitudes.

All of these sources of error produce special challenges for evaluating the reliability of FAIs. Further, the above examples point up the importance of examining the reliability of a FAI by obtaining test samples in the types of settings, and with the types of populations, for which the instrument eventually will be employed. Reliability coefficients based on administration of a FAI to college sophomores cannot be trusted to provide estimates of measurement error that are meaningful for use of the instrument in pretrial examinations of criminal defendants or parents seeking custody of a child.

All FAIs should demonstrate acceptably low levels of error variance associated with examiner administration and scoring. Later chapters will refer to "inter-examiner reliability" when evidence addresses error due to different *administrators,* and "inter-scorer or inter-rater reliability" when error is assessed as a function of different *scorers* or raters of test samples. These are two distinctly different sources of examiner error, although test developers often do not separate the two in their calculations of examiner-related reliability.

Norms

The special purposes of FAIs do not call for any single standard concerning the development of normative data. Different purposes will call for different standards, and some of these require explanation.

First, some FAIs might be constructed to describe examinees' abilities in an absolute sense. That is, the purpose may be merely to describe that which the examinee can and cannot do, rather than to express the level of performance in relation to other persons. Instruments of this type, of course, are referred to as "content-referenced" or "criterion-referenced," rather than "norm-referenced" instruments. They do not require the development of sample distributions of scores with which to compare the performance of an examinee. We will return in a moment to discuss certain values of normative data in forensic situations. The matter of content- and criterion-referenced instruments for forensic assessments, however, requires special comment.

When an instrument is used in a *content-referenced* manner, an examinee's score is expressed merely as some proportion of the continuum of possible scores on the instrument. For example, on an instrument assessing a defendant's knowledge of trial proceedings, one might report that the defendant correctly answered 75% of the items related to functions of trial participants and 45% of the items dealing with trial procedures. One could also, of course, report the specific things that the defendant seemed not to know, that is, the content of items incorrectly answered. This type of evaluation does not rely on comparison to any other external criteria. A court receiving this information would be left to consider the overall adequacy of the defendant's understanding according to any discretionary standard that it wished to apply. This type of data might be quite appropriate for many legal situations. Indeed, it is consistent with the perspective discussed in Chapter 2 (see Judgmental component): that is, description, rather than evaluative statements about the sufficiency of examinees' abilities, may represent the most appropriate or important function for examiners in legal proceedings.

In contrast, instruments that are called *criterion-referenced* employ an external criterion with which to evaluate the quality of an examinee's score. Often this external criterion is some index of the degree of performance necessary to satisfy requirements in a situation external to the test. For example, examinees taking an exam for state licensing as a psychologist may have to obtain a particular threshold score in order to qualify, or an employer may require that applicants for a clerical position must type or take shorthand notes at a specified rate of words per minute. The cutoff score generally is set by a standard-setting group that makes a discretionary judgment that will apply across examinees. This approach is basically non-normative; the criterion score, not examinees' performances in relation to each other, determines the evaluation.

In one sense, criterion-referenced interpretations of FAIs are in conflict with requirements for forensic assessments outlined in Chapter 2. The Interactive component of legal competence constructs suggests that degrees of examinees' functional abilities are not to be viewed as sufficient or insufficient in and of themselves. Instead, sufficiency depends on a comparison of the person's degree of ability to the performance demands of their specific environmental situation (e.g., the demands of their upcoming trial, the needs of a particular child). Law does not instruct judges to consider any particular level of ability as indicative of competence or incompetence across cases. From this perspective, neither the mental health professional nor the judiciary is authorized to set cutoff scores as determinants of examinees' legal competencies.

On the other hand, one can argue that both mental health professionals and judges are free to determine cutoff scores for other purposes. For example, they might set a cutoff score on an instrument intended merely to screen defendants for those who are in need of more extensive evaluation for competence to stand trial. The cutoff score might be set conservatively, so that it screens out only defendants who are most clearly competent.

The danger in cutoff scores for FAIs, therefore, lies in their use. A test developer is not violating professional standards by publishing a cutoff score, if the developer satisfies the requirements to make explicit the acceptable and unacceptable uses of such criteria. On the other hand, test developers cannot control the use of their instruments, and the publication of cutoff scores inevitably will lead some examiners and legal professionals to apply them as definitions of a competence decision, rather than as one type of data among many for making a decision. For purposes of evaluating FAIs, therefore, one must consider whether the test developer may be endorsing or encouraging (without intent) the misuse of a FAI by adopting the criterion-referenced approach described above.

Turning now to *norm-referenced* considerations, we note that various legal questions may be addressed with a comparison of the examinee's abilities to those of normative groups. One major question will be the choice of a sample on which to develop test norms. Test developers and users typically are aware of the hazards of comparing examinees' performances to norms based on samples that differ markedly in their sociodemographic or other characteristics from those of the examinee.

This matter is not settled, however, by a simple admonition to avoid such a comparison, because the legal decision process sometimes might require it. For example, a court might wish to know the degree to which a juvenile's understanding of certain rights (for purposes of evaluating validity of waiver of rights) is different from that of adults. Thus an adult sample may provide the appropriate normative data for evaluating a juvenile's ability. In another instance, a court might recognize that practically no defendant will know everything about the roles and functions of participants in a trial. It may be helpful to obtain a perspective on a particular defendant's knowledge of these matters in relation to that of the "average person." Sometimes this "average person" will be represented better by random samples of the general population than by sampling from within populations with defendants' typical sociodemographic characteristics.

The general standard, then, is to select samples for development of FAI norms with careful attention to the intended use of the norms in legal settings. These might vary considerably from one area of legal competence to another.

CONSTRUCT VALIDATION

Historically, psychometricians attempted to identify several types of validity or validation procedures, making distinctions between content validity, concurrent validity, predictive validity, and construct validity. Each of these validities is somewhat different in its meaning and implication for the purposes for which tests may be used. Among them, however, the notion of *construct validity* is primary. As noted by Messick, "Construct validity is ... the unifying concept of validity that integrates criterion and content considerations into a common framework for testing rational hypotheses about theoretically relevant relationships" (Messick, 1980, p. 1015). Thus the validity of FAIs will be reviewed in this book without making fine, categorical discriminations between the traditional types of validity, including them generally under the heading of construct validation.

One argument against this choice might be the importance generally attached to predictive validity. This term refers to the degree to which an instrument is successful in predicting some criterion event, examinee behavior, or examinee standing on some other variable, given a time interval between examination and the future criterion index. A special interest in the predictive validity of FAIs is understandable, because legal competence constructs often refer to future consequences (e.g., subsequent trials, the future rearing of a child).

Therefore, the outline for evaluating FAIs in later chapters includes a special category entitled "Predictive or Classificatory Utility," which reviews studies that demonstrate what is generally referred to as predictive validity. Those studies, of course, will contribute also to our overall assessment of the construct validity of an instrument. The term *utility* was chosen, however, purposely to draw attention away from the tendency to perceive predictive validity as the *sine qua non* for instrument validity. The reasons that predictive data should not play such a strong role in overall evaluation of FAIs will be made clear in the discussion of utility, to which we will turn in a moment.

Construct validation refers to an accumulation of evidence concerning the degree of confidence with which a FAI can be interpreted as an index of the functional ability concepts that it claims to define operationally. Construct validity is not an absolute condition. Contrary to some test authors' claims, no instrument is ever simply "valid." At any given time, the evidence accumulated merely increases or decreases our confidence in the FAI as an operational definition of its functional ability concepts.

Many types of evidence can contribute to a FAIs construct validity (e.g., factor or item content analysis, and various methods for examining concurrent and predictive validity). One of the most important types of evidence, however, is the relation between the FAI as a measure of an ability construct and indexes of other psychological constructs that are expected on theoretical grounds to be related to the ability construct.

Let us refer back to Figure 1 to clarify this point. We noted that functional ability concepts for a FAI (C) are selected with close attention to the domain of a legal competence construct (A). In addition, though, the ability concepts should be defined with some conceptualization of their assumed relation to theories, constructs, and empirical findings in psychology and psychiatry (B) that are used to describe and understand human behavior generally. If this process has been carried out conscientiously, then we are prepared for the construct validation process noted earlier. That is, we can examine whether our FAI index of the functional ability (C') relates (dotted line) to indexes of the theoretical constructs in psychology (B') in the hypothesized manner.

To provide an example, imagine a FAI that operationally defines "comprehension of *Miranda* rights" by obtaining and scoring examinees' explanations of the meaning of the *Miranda* warnings (Grisso, 1981). We might expect that general intelligence or cognitive developmental maturity contributes to *Miranda* comprehension, but that the ability to understand these specific message contents may be influenced by other variables as well: for example, amount of past exposure to the warnings. Thus *Miranda* comprehension as an ability concept is perceived as related to the general cognitive constructs, but not necessarily overlapping them completely. All of these assumptions may be tested by comparing FAI scores to scores on measures of general intelligence, cognitive developmental maturity, some definition of "amount of prior exposure" (e.g., number of prior arrests), and so forth. The results contribute to construct validity—a sense of the meaning of *Miranda* comprehension as measured by the FAI—if the pattern of results emerges as expected.

In addition to providing general support for the instrument, results of this type become especially useful in relation to the causal characteristic of a legal competence construct (see Chapter 2). Construct validation research provides the logic with which an examiner may support an explanation for an examinee's functional deficits as measured by a FAI, or for considering the plausibility of various possible explanations. Thus when causal information and reasoning are requested by the court, the examiner may be able to use theory in an empirically informed, less speculative manner.

PREDICTIVE OR CLASSIFICATORY UTILITY

The category of predictive or classificatory utility considers the utility of a FAI for identifying persons who, at a later time, engage in a particular behavior or are classified by other means as having a particular psychiatric or legal status. For example, a FAI may be examined for its ability to predict a later manifestation of the functional ability, behavior, or attitude that it claims to assess, as when an examinee who manifests certain deficiencies in child-rearing abilities on a FAI later manifests deficiencies in actual child-rearing practice. Other examples would include the relation between a FAI for abilities related to competence to stand trial, and later performance of the defendant in the courtroom, or later judicial decisions about legal competence or incompetence of defendants. Special types of analyses (e.g., Receiver Operating Characteristics, or ROC, analysis) are available to demonstrate the degree to which a FAI performs better than chance in classifying examinees according to the criterion behaviors that one intends to predict.

When a FAI can be related empirically to future events, this contributes to its construct validity and to its possible utility for assisting the legal system in anticipating future consequences. Further, from both a scientific and public point of view, there is probably no other empirical evidence of an instrument's integrity that is more impressive than its demonstrated ability to predict the future accurately.

Nevertheless, FAIs should not be required to stand or fall on the basis of their predictive utility. In fact, the following discussion will argue that in the case of FAIs, predictive utility:

- may not be possible to test
- when it can be tested, is not sufficient by itself to justify predictive uses
- is not essential in relation to legal definitions or scientific standards
- is not a rational expectancy in light of current knowledge concerning the determinants of behavior; and
- is not appropriate, when the objective is the prediction of a legal (judicial) decision.

First, various circumstances pertaining to legal procedures and criteria suggest that *we may not be able to test the predictive utility of some FAIs*. A few examples will be offered, and others will arise in subsequent chapters.

For example, one would hope that functional deficits on a FAI that assesses abilities for competence to stand trial would be related to defendants' actual performances in subsequent trials. Yet if defendants manifest serious deficits in the course of a forensic examination, they are not likely even to reach trial until the court has evidence that the deficits have been remediated. As a consequence, researchers may never have the opportunity to test the relation between deficits measured by a FAI and behaviors observed in actual trial situations.

For some FAIs, no future criterion can be used in validity studies because the appropriate criterion event is in the past. For example, a FAI that measures capacities to understand *Miranda* warnings is intended to assist courts in judging whether suspects were able to understand their rights as described to them when they were arrested by police and prepared for interrogation. In order to test the utility of the FAI as a postdictive indicator of understanding, the researcher would need to compare FAI performance to measures of understanding manifested by suspects earlier, at the time of arrest. This would be very difficult in light of the uncontrollable circumstances and variations in the arrest and interrogation process. In summary, the real world might not allow one to test the predictive or postdictive validity of FAIs.

Second, *the predictive power of a FAI is not sufficient by itself to justify or support its use as a predictive tool for legal or scientific purposes.* Measurement theorists generally are in agreement that an empirical relationship between a measure and a future event does not justify the instrument's relevance or use if there is no underlying rationale for the relationship (e.g., Messick, 1975). This may be true especially in legal circumstances, where evidence must pass a legal test of probative value with regard to the question at hand. For example, imagine that one found that defendants' competence to stand trial could be predicted with high accuracy by adding their height to the number of state capitals they could name. No matter how powerful the prediction, it would not pass legal scrutiny concerning a rational or reasonable relationship between the scores and the issue at hand. In scientific terms, the measure would lack the support of underlying constructs that provide a cogent rationale for the relation of the index to the criterion.

Third, *FAIs do not necessarily need evidence of predictive utility in order to be used to assist legal decision making.* Construct validity itself can justify the use of an index for contributing to decisions when it is not possible to do critical predictive validity studies. One must simply avoid using or referring to the instrument as though it is known to account for some substantial proportion of variance in future performance, or as though it can provide actual probability estimates of future behaviors.

Fourth, *current theories of the determinants of specific behaviors would not lead one to expect that any measure of personal attributes alone will produce accurate behavioral predictions.* Considerable research has shown that a given individual does not behave consistently across all environmental and interpersonal situations. Instead, situations themselves elicit, modify, or inhibit the influences of personal attributes on behavior (Mischel, 1984; Monahan, 1981). Thus we should not require a FAI that measures personal abilities alone to have a high degree of predictive power; at best it might make some contribution to prediction when used with situational variables.

Similarly, a FAI might be unable to predict specific outcomes accurately, yet it might identify people who are at greater risk for certain future outcomes. For example, if a FAI is correct in predicting future child abuse in only 20 out of every 100 cases having a high score on the instrument, this may still be useful information for certain purposes if the base rate of child abuse in the catchment population is much lower than 20%. The FAI would be a very poor predictor of child abuse; yet it could serve an alerting function for certain purposes.

Finally, *it is inappropriate to judge the predictive utility of a FAI on the basis of its ability or inability to predict judicial decisions about legal competence or incompetence.* FAIs are not (or should not) be constructed for the purpose of making such predictions. Chapter 2 discussed legal competence decisions as depending on a consideration of person-environment interactions and incongruencies (interactive characteristic), and moral senses of justice (judgmental characteristic). In contrast, FAIs seek only to define and measure functional abilities that are relevant for these legal decisions. Judicial decisions to which the FAI is compared may have taken into account far more variables than the FAI was intended to measure. It is even possible that legal decision makers who form the predictive criteria in a validation study might have failed to take into account the very abilities that the legal standard requires and that the FAI claims to assess. Thus FAIs should not necessarily be evaluated negatively when they cannot mimic judicial decisions.

POTENTIAL FOR EXPRESSING PERSON-SITUATION CONGRUENCY

The person-situation congruency standard for evaluating FAIs is the only one that does not generally appear in standards applied to most psychological instruments. It is offered here not as an essential standard, but as a quality that may enhance the value of a FAI. The standard is related to the Interactive component of legal competence constructs. As described in Chapter 2, legal decisions about competencies depend in part on incongruency between an examinee's functional ability and the degree of demand for that ability in a specific environmental context faced by the examinee. For example, courts may consider not only a defendant's degree of ability to inform a lawyer about matters related to a defense, but also the degree to which the anticipated trial may require this ability. Similarly, a court may weigh the importance of a parent's pattern of child-rearing abilities or deficiencies against the caretaking needs of a specific child.

These comparisons of ability to situational demand suggest the need for assessment methods to describe both sets of information. Further, as noted in Chapter 2, especially desirable would be instruments that assess both an examinee and a specific situation using parallel sets of concepts or dimensions: for example, assessing a parent's ability to provide structure and a child's degree of need for structure.

Subsequent chapters will provide examples of parallel, person-environment assessment instruments that can address certain legal questions, although very few instruments currently offer this opportunity. When evaluating most FAIs, therefore, we will consider their potential to be translated into parallel dimensions for describing environmental contexts. A FAI that offers this potential has a better chance, given further development, to assist examiners in addressing the interactive questions in legal competence constructs.

ORIENTATION TO THE INSTRUMENT REVIEWS

The five categories of standards that we have just discussed will be used in the subsequent reviews of FAIs (Chapters 4 through 9) pertaining to six legal competencies. Before proceeding to those reviews, it may be helpful to describe the manner in which instruments were selected for review, as well as the standardized outline that is used across reviews.

DISCOVERY AND SELECTION OF THE INSTRUMENTS

For the first edition, a national mailed survey of forensic mental health professionals had been used to discover instruments for review, because in the 1980s, there were few published sources of information about forensic assessment instruments. In contrast, current books, journal articles, and internet search options provided ample resources for identifying instruments related to the six legal competencies of interest. Thus the national survey was not replicated in preparation for the second edition.

Certain general criteria were employed to select instruments for review:

- The instrument was developed specifically to address a forensic question of legal competence in one of the six areas.

- The instrument offered a method for expressing results in quantitative form.
- A published manual was available for the instrument, and its development was described in at least one journal article, book, or monograph.

In general, the choice of instruments to be included in the second edition was more selective than in the first edition. Far fewer instruments were available in the 1980s, and often instruments were included in the review even when they had not been developed for forensic purposes (and their use in forensic cases was unknown). In the second edition, the greater number of instruments available made it necessary to focus primarily on instruments that were developed with the intention for forensic use.

The selection of instruments also required somewhat different considerations in each of the assessment areas addressed in the book, resulting in the exclusion of certain instruments. These special selection criteria, and some of the instruments excluded from review, are noted in each of the review chapters.

Selection of instruments for this review should not be considered an endorsement of their value in forensic assessments. The purpose was to review how FAIs are developed, and to review current evidence for their utility and directions for further refinement. In most instances, the reviews provide no summary judgment concerning the overall quality of the various instruments. Judgment frequently cannot be passed on the basis of the characteristics of an instrument alone. Its acceptability will depend also on the specific situation and purpose for which its use is being considered. An instrument may be acceptable for some purposes and not for others. Clinicians and legal professionals themselves must make those judgments, weighing the qualities of the instruments as described here against the demands of specific circumstances that arise in their practice.

PURPOSES AND OUTLINE OF THE REVIEW CHAPTERS

The objective of each of the next six chapters (Chapters 4–9) is to review forensic assessment instruments:

- to test the value of the conceptual model of legal competence constructs (Chapter 2) as a tool for structuring forensic assessments and examining FAIs
- to review existing FAIs as case studies of test development and application, in order to identify issues and potential solutions to problems in the development of specialized FAIs, and

- to evaluate the utility and limitations of FAIs in their current state, for application by mental health professionals in forensic examinations.

Each of the six chapters achieves these purposes according to an identical outline with three major sections: The Competence Question; Evaluation of the Forensic Assessment Instruments; and Current Status of the Field.

The Competence Question

The first section of each chapter provides a description of legal and assessment issues associated with the legal competence with which that chapter is concerned. It has two subsections:

- *Law and Current Practice*: This subsection identifies the history, intent, and statutory definition of the legal competence ("Legal Standard"); legal and empirical information on the process for arriving at competence decisions ("Legal Process"); and current assessment practices by mental health professionals, as well as commentary and recommendations for assessment practice that exist in the literature ("Competence Assessment: Current Practice").
- *From Legal Standard to Forensic Assessment*: This subsection applies the five components of legal competencies (as defined in Chapter 2) in an analysis of the legal competence in question. This analysis is used to describe that which is required of forensic assessments to increase their legal relevance in future practice.

Review of Forensic Assessment Instruments

A major section on forensic assessment instruments reviews each of the selected FAIs separately. The review of each FAI follows the outline for evaluating FAIs described earlier in this chapter:

- Basic Description and Objectives
- Conceptual Basis (conceptual and operational definition of the legally relevant functional abilities)
- Psychometric Development (standardization, reliability, norms)
- Construct Validation
- Predictive or Classificatory Utility, and
- Potential for Expressing Person-Situation Congruency.

Current Status of the Field

A final section in each chapter provides a synthesis and discussion that uses the FAIs in the previous review to identify critical issues for FAI development and use in the legal competence area in question. It is divided into two subsections:

- *Research Directions*: Focus is on issues in the research and development of FAIs. The subsection is organized according to the five characteristics of a legal competency construct (Chapter 2).
- *Clinical Application*: This subsection summarizes the uses and limitations of the FAIs, in their current state, when employed by forensic examiners. Emphasis is on guidelines for the FAIs collectively within the legal competence area in question, although special suggestions for certain individual instruments are noted as well. The subsection is organized according to four general objectives of assessments: *Description* of an examinee; *Explanation* for abilities and deficits; *Prediction* of an examinee's behavior; and *Examiner Conclusions* concerning the implications for the assessment results for the questions facing the legal decision maker.

Finally, Chapter 10 represents a synthesis across the *Current Status* sections of the six review chapters. It uses the material in the *Research Directions* and *Clinical Applications* subsections in each of the previous chapters to achieve the broadest level of generalization concerning recommendations for the future development and use of FAIs.

───────4───────

Competence to Stand Trial

THE COMPETENCE QUESTION

The concept of competence to stand trial in criminal courts recognizes that a defendant's mental or emotional disabilities might interfere with the right to a fair trial. When it appears that these disabilities might render the defendant incapable of conducting an adequate defense, the law requires that the court must determine the defendant's competence to stand trial before proceeding further with the trial process. The inquiry involves a forensic evaluation by a mental health professional, with a court finding of incompetence subsequent to the evaluation often leading to involuntary hospitalization for treatment to bring the defendant to competence. Reevaluation by mental health professionals will be required periodically during the treatment process, in order to determine whether the defendant has improved sufficiently to warrant a return to court.

There are no national statistics on the number of defendants who are evaluated for competence in a given year. An estimate in the 1980s (Steadman et al., 1982) placed this figure at about 25,000 defendants nationally per year. There is no reason to believe that the number has decreased in recent years. Attorneys have concerns about their clients' competence in about 10% to 15% of their criminal cases, but they raise the question in fewer than one-half of those cases (Hoge et al., 1992; Poythress et al., 1994). Estimates of the proportion of cases found incompetent among those for which the question is raised have ranged from 10% (Melton et al., 1997) to 30% (Roesch & Golding, 1980). Psychosis is the most common diagnosis for persons found incompetent to stand trial (Nicholson & Kugler, 1991), and previous psychiatric hospitalization is common (Steadman et al., 1982). Several studies have reported that incompetence to stand trial is found more often among defendants with nonviolent or misdemeanor charges than for defendants with violent or more serious charges (Roesch & Golding, 1980; Bittman & Convit, 1993; Warren et al., 1991).

A series of articles since the publication of the first edition of *Evaluating Competencies* provides five-year updates of all psychological and psychiatric journal articles pertaining to evaluations for competence to stand trial, for the periods 1986–1990 (Grisso, 1992), 1991–1995 (Cooper & Grisso, 1997), and 1996–2000 (Mumley, Tillbrook, & Grisso, in press).

Careful scrutiny of competence evaluation procedures and related forensic evaluations is important because of the potentially serious consequences of competence proceedings for defendants and society. Fundamental fairness requires that defendants who truly are disabled in their ability to mount a defense should not be placed in jeopardy. On the other hand, both defendants and society have an interest in avoiding unnecessary delays in trial procedures, as well as any unnecessary hospitalization of defendants for evaluations or treatment as a result of an incompetence finding. These consequences justify considerable attention to the legal procedure, as well as the quality of evaluations, for competence to stand trial.

LAW AND CURRENT PRACTICE

Legal Standard

The standard for raising the question of competence to stand trial is very liberal. Cases (and many states' statutes) direct courts and attorneys to raise the question when there is a *"bona fide* doubt" about defendant's competence (*Drope v. Missouri*, 1975; *Pate v. Robinson*, 1966; *People v. Pennington*, 1967). This is typically interpreted to mean any possible doubt based on the behavior or history of the defendant, such as a record of mental disorder or a defendant's behavior while interacting with counsel suggesting any relevant mental disability that might interfere with trial competence.

DUSKY V. U.S.   The prevailing standard for determining competence to stand trial was stated in *Dusky v. United States* (1960): whether the defendant has "sufficient present ability to consult with his lawyer with a reasonable degree of rational understanding" and whether the defendant has a "rational as well as factual understanding of proceedings against him" (p. 402). Most states have adopted the *Dusky* standard intact or with minor modifications in wording.

Legal doctrine clearly distinguishes the standard for competence to stand trial from standards by which criminal responsibility ("insanity") is decided (e.g., *Lyles v. United States*, 1975). Questions of criminal responsibility (see Chapter 6) refer to mental state at the time of the offense, whereas competence to stand trial refers to a defendant's current mental state and functional capacities as they relate to a pending trial process. A defendant may be competent to stand trial yet have good grounds for an insanity defense. Incompetence and insanity questions are often raised within the same case, but they are distinctly separate questions controlled by different legal standards.

Some states' statutes manifest a set of legal guidelines for competence to stand trial determinations that specify factors to be weighed in competence assessments and judicial determinations. Florida (FL. R. Crim. Pro. § 3.211(a)), for example, identifies six factors, referring to the defendant's capacity to:

- Appreciate the charges or allegations against him
- Appreciate the range and nature of possible penalties, if applicable, which maybe imposed in the proceedings against him
- Understand the adversary nature of the legal process
- Disclose to his attorney facts pertinent to the proceedings at issue
- Manifest appropriate courtroom behavior
- Testify relevantly

Factors such as these typically have been derived from analysis of relevant functional abilities such as those recommended by McGarry and associates (Laboratory of Community Psychiatry, 1973) in a major research study to be reviewed later in this chapter. Legal instructions about factors to be weighed require only that the various elements must be considered. The law specifies no particular level of deficiency within any of these areas of functioning as dispositive of the legal competence question.

Some states have added the requirement that the defendant's deficiencies (as noted previously) must be attributable to "mental disease or defect." Case law, however, clearly indicates that the mere presence of a mental disorder or developmental disability, whatever its severity, is not a sufficient basis by itself for a finding of incompetence to stand trial (e.g., *Feuger v. United States*, 1962; *Swisher v. United States*, 1965; *United States v. Adams, 1969; Wieter v. Settle*, 1961). Mental disorder and mental retardation are related to the question of pretrial competence only insofar as they affect the defendant's understanding of the nature and process of the trial and the ability to assist counsel in a defense. Some defendants with psychotic or other serious diagnoses may pass this legal test, whereas others with similar diagnoses will not. (As described later, a few states also have made statutory provisions for "developmental immaturity" as a predicate condition for findings of incompetence to stand trial.)

In addition to a defendant's actual capacities and psychiatric or psychological conditions, certain trial circumstances must sometimes be considered when deciding how to apply the *Dusky* standard. For example, the court in *United States v. Wilson* (1968) affirmed that amnesia may or may not be a basis for an incompetence finding, depending (among other things) on the degree to which the defendant's recollection of the circumstances surrounding the alleged offense is necessary in order to assure a fair trial. Thus the anticipated nature of the trial, not merely the defendant's capacities, may play a role in deciding the question of pretrial competence.

GODINEZ V. MORAN.   The specific meaning of the legal standard for competence to stand trial underwent intense scrutiny in the courts and in scholarly treatises in the 1990s. Cases during earlier years had suggested disagreement in appellate courts regarding the meaning of the *Dusky* standard. For example, while some courts held to a uniform criterion across cases, others perceived the need for more demanding criteria for some purposes than for others, especially when cases required that defendants make decisions about the waiver of rights that might place them in special jeopardy. For example, *Westbrook v. Arizona* (1965) acknowledged a more demanding criterion than the *Dusky* standard when deciding competence to waive one's constitutional right to legal counsel.

Similarly, in *Sieling v. Eyman* (1973), a federal circuit court of appeals identified a "higher" standard for competence in order to make a "reasoned choice" about plea bargains, entering a plea of guilty, or waiving other important rights.

Identifying this issue, Bonnie (1992, 1993) proposed a reconceptualization of the standard for competence to stand trial, which he called "adjudicative competence," creating a two-part standard: general "competence to proceed" and specific "decisional competence." The first pertained to understanding and appreciating one's situation and the trial process sufficiently to assist counsel, allowing for a case to proceed. The second, "decisional competence," referred to the defendant's capacity to make important decisions about the waiver of constitutional rights in the trial process. Thus some defendants who might be capable of proceeding to trial competently might nevertheless be considered incompetent for certain purposes as the trial proceeded (e.g., if they decided to waive representation by counsel), if those purposes became relevant. But it would allow many defendants to proceed to trial without having to meet a more demanding standard regarding decisional abilities that might never arise in their cases.

This view seemed to have been rejected subsequently by the U.S. Supreme Court's decision in *Godinez v. Moran* (1993). The Court in *Godinez* found that there was only one standard for competence to stand trial—as defined by the *Dusky* standard—related to all aspects of a defendant's participation in the trial. Some analysts interpreted this to mean that defendants' decision making abilities need not be considered when making judgments about their competence, because the *Dusky* standard makes no specific reference to "decision making." Others recognized, however, that the *Godinez* decision explicitly identified the need for defendants to be able to make decisions about waiving important constitutional rights, and the point was affirmed in a subsequent U.S. Supreme Court decision in *Cooper v. Oklahoma* (1996).

By this analysis, the *Godinez* court included decision making abilities within the *Dusky* standard. In so doing, it may have "elevated" the standard for competence to stand trial by requiring that all defendants, to be considered competent, must be capable not only of basic understanding of the trial process, but also of making far-reaching decisions (which many of them will never have to make—for example, regarding dismissing counsel and representing oneself). Whether or not this interpretation resulted in changes in the proportion of defendants found incompetent (which is unknown), it drew new attention to the need to consider defendants' decision making abilities when applying Dusky to cases in which the question of competence to stand trial has been raised.

LEGAL STANDARD IN JUVENILE COURT.   Competence to stand trial did not apply to delinquency cases in the first half of the twentieth century because of the civil nature of delinquency cases in juvenile court. The concept arose in juvenile court only after *In re Gault* (1967), which extended to youths in delinquency hearings many of the rights and procedures that pertained to defendants in criminal court. By the late 1980s, about one-third of the states recognized by statute or case law the right of youths to be competent to stand trial in juvenile court (Grisso, Miller, & Sales, 1987). The issue was almost never raised, however, until reforms in juvenile law in the 1990s increased punitive sanctions for youthful offenders. As a consequence, more than two-thirds of the states recognized the concept of competence to stand trial in juvenile court by the late 1990s (Bonnie & Grisso, 2000), and the definition of the concept when applied in delinquency proceedings received increased attention (Grisso & Schwartz, 2000).

Almost all appellate courts that have addressed the issue have concluded that competence to stand trial applies in delinquency proceedings in juvenile court (Bonnie & Grisso, 2000). Their logic typically has referred to rights provided in *Gault* (e.g., the right to representation by legal counsel), concluding that those rights are meaningless without a competent juvenile defendant to assist counsel (see, e.g., a Georgia appellate court decision in *In re the Interest of S.H., a Child*, 1996).

Most states have also decided that the definition to be applied is the same as for criminal court proceedings (that is, the state's definition that parallels the *Dusky* standard). How this standard should be applied, however, is still evolving in the juvenile courts. For example, it is unclear in most states whether *juvenile* court adjudication requires the same level or degree of abilities to which *Dusky* refers as would be necessary for *criminal* court adjudication. Moreover, the historical development of the legal concept of competence to stand trial focused on mental illness and mental retardation as predicate conditions for incompetence, in some states explicitly requiring that deficits in relevant abilities must be due to these conditions. Some juveniles, however, may possess similar deficits not because of these clinical conditions, but merely as a consequence of cognitive or emotional immaturity (Grisso, 1997, 2000; generally, Grisso & Schwartz, 2000). While a few states now recognize this explicitly, the potential relevance of immaturity as a predicate legal condition for incompetence is still evolving or has not yet been raised in the majority of states.

Legal Process

There are five main stages in the procedure for determining and disposing of competence cases:

- Requesting a competence determination (often called "raising the question");
- The competence evaluation stage;
- The judicial determination of competence or incompetence; and in some cases;

- Disposition and provision of treatment; and
- Rehearings on competence.

REQUESTING A COMPETENCE DETERMINATION. In most jurisdictions, the question of a defendant's competence to stand trial may be raised by the defense, the prosecution, or the judge at any stage in the criminal court proceeding. Judges are allowed considerable discretion in determining whether there is a *"bona fide* doubt" of competence.

Forensic examiners should be aware that courts and attorneys sometimes have raised the question of pretrial competence for purposes other than those for which the competence doctrine exists. These inappropriate referrals for competence evaluation have been said to occur for several reasons. Some courts or defense attorneys apparently have sought competence evaluations primarily in order to obtain immediate treatment of a defendant's behavioral disorder, especially when other methods for obtaining treatment are either more difficult or unavailable (Bonovitz & Bonovitz, 1981; Gudeman, 1981; Warren et al., 1991). In addition, Roesch and Golding (1980) observed that the competence question is raised in some cases merely as a legal maneuver. Prosecutors might seek extra time to prepare the state's case, and defense attorneys sometimes call for competence evaluations in order to obtain information not about competence, but about the potential for a later insanity plea.

THE COMPETENCE EVALUATION STAGE. The present section focuses only on where, when, and by whom competence evaluations are performed; the actual substance of competence evaluations will be reviewed later.

Some states have developed a system for providing competence screening evaluations (Grisso, Steadman, Cocozza, Fisher, & Greer, 1994). Screening typically involves a brief evaluation, often at the time of arraignment, designed simply to determine if there is reason to believe that further evaluation is necessary. In this way a large number of the "easy" cases for which the competence question is raised (persons who are very clearly competent or very obviously incompetent) can be returned to court without requiring relatively lengthy, full competence evaluations.

Courts obtain their full competence evaluations in various ways across the 50 states (Grisso et al., 1994; Melton et al., 1997; Poythress, Otto, & Heilbrun, 1991). During the past two decades, courts have greatly reduced their reliance on inpatient evaluations for competence to stand trial, most states having moved to much greater use of evaluations performed while defendants are outpatients (that is, are awaiting trial in jail or in the community). Often these evaluations are performed by forensic examiners in community mental health clinics or by special arrangements between the courts and examiners in private practice in the community. Grisso et al. (1994) found that state systems for providing competence evaluations tend more often to employ clinical psychologists than psychiatrists, although the latter are still substantially involved.

Many statutes limit the length of evaluation commitments and the time within which an evaluation report must be made. Often they specify 30 days with possible extensions to 60 days. The CJMH standards (Standard 7-4.4, ABA, 1984) recommended 7 days when a defendant is in custody, 14 days when the defendant is at liberty (e.g., has been placed on pretrial release), and possible extension to 30 days for "good cause." These time limits underscore the fact that pretrial competence evaluation commitments are not intended to be a means for obtaining prolonged treatment of disordered defendants. The trend in recent years in state statutes controlling competence evaluations has been to shorten considerably the evaluation time allowed, requiring clinicians to become more efficient if they are to continue to provide evaluations of quality to the courts in competence cases.

The legal purpose of an assessment for competence to stand trial often requires attention to procedures that are not typical for other clinical assessments. For example, laws in many states, as well as general ethical guidelines for forensic evaluations (Committee on Ethical Guidelines for Forensic Psychologists, 1991; Heilbrun, 2001), require that defendants be informed about (a) the purpose of the evaluation, (b) potential uses of disclosures made during evaluation, (c) conditions under which the prosecutor will have access to information from the evaluation, and (d) consequences of defendant's refusal to cooperate in the evaluation. Defense counsel usually has the option to observe the evaluation. Audiotaped or videotaped recording of the evaluation is not legally required but is often recommended (e.g., Committee on Ethical Guidelines for Forensic Psychologists, 1991) in order to produce an evidentiary record.

JUDICIAL DETERMINATION OF THE COMPETENCE QUESTION. Judicial practice does not always require a formal hearing on the question of a defendant's pretrial competence after the evaluation. In fact, the CJMH standards (Standard 7-4.7, ABA, 1984) recommended that a court hearing on the issue may not be necessary if all parties have stipulated that they are in agreement on the defendant's competence or incompetence, and if the court concurs after considering the forensic evaluation results. Otherwise, a formal hearing generally will be required, offering opportunity for examinations of the forensic assessment results and challenges by either party during the hearing.

DISPOSITION AND PROVISION OF TREATMENT. Trial proceedings resume if the defendant is found competent to stand trial. If the defendant is found incompetent, however, the competence hearing turns to inquiry concerning the likelihood that treatment can render the defendant competent to stand trial.

This stage of the proceeding has been greatly influenced by the U.S. Supreme Court ruling in *Jackson v. Indiana* (1972). Prior to *Jackson*, many incompetent defendants who were involuntarily hospitalized for treatment did not improve, resulting in indefinite hospitalization. Their lack of improvement with treatment sometimes was a consequence of disabilities that were not likely ever to respond to treatment (e.g., severe mental retardation or brain damage). Thus they might spend years in involuntary confinement (often longer than if they had been tried, convicted, and served the usual sentence for their crime), with little likelihood of ever being brought to trial. Prior to the *Jackson* decision, researchers at one hospital (McGarry, Curran, & Kenefick, 1968) reported that the number of patients being treated for pretrial incompetence who were discharged as restored and returned to court was exceeded by the number whose hospitalization was terminated due to their natural death!

The court in *Jackson* ruled that incompetent defendants could not be held for treatment longer than the nature of their disorders warranted. Therefore, courts must determine whether the potential treatment of an incompetent defendant's disorder offers a reasonable prospect for bringing the defendant to competence. When the disorder cannot be treated, the incompetent defendant can neither be committed nor tried on the criminal charges. The state must either drop the charges and release the defendant or initiate commitment proceedings under the state's civil commitment criteria. Therefore, a forensic examiner's testimony about the defendant's mental disability and potential for treatment plays an important role in this stage of the legal inquiry.

If it appears that the defendant's incompetence can be treated, commitment to a state mental hospital or forensic treatment facility for that purpose is the most common disposition. Some statutes require that the defendant must be treated in the least restrictive setting that provides a reasonable opportunity for gaining pretrial competence. In general, courts have ruled that defendants have no right to refuse treatment (e.g., psychoactive medication) to restore their competence (Melton et al., 1997). The U.S. Supreme Court in *Riggins v. Nevada* (1992) required that courts consider whether medication, even if it reduced patients' symptoms, might also interfere with their ability to perform certain functions such as interaction with counsel or the provision of testimony at their trials.

REHEARINGS ON COMPETENCE. The need for forensic evaluations of competence to stand trial will occur periodically in the course of a defendant's treatment. Most states require reevaluation and court review of incompetent defendants at least once every six months during their treatment. At the review, typically a court must: (a) make a ruling on the question of competence if the forensic examiner and treating professional believe that competence has been restored; or (b) extend the commitment (e.g., another six months) if it appears that competence can be restored "in the foreseeable future"; or (c) terminate commitment if at any point pretrial competence appears not to be attainable (see also CJMH Standard 7-4.11, ABA, 1984). The cumulative results of several reports suggest that most defendants found incompetent to stand trial and provided treatment are found competent within 4 to 6 months (for reviews of these studies, see Cooper & Grisso, 1997; Grisso, 1992; Melton et al., 1997).

Competence Assessment: Current Practice

Assessments in competence to stand trial cases have received considerable scrutiny regarding the *settings and methods* that are employed, as well as the *content* of reports and testimony.

EVALUATION SYSTEMS AND METHODS. For many years competence to stand trial evaluations were performed in inpatient psychiatric hospitals, within either general units or specialized forensic units (Keilitz, 1982; Melton, Weithorn, & Slobogin, 1985; Roesch & Golding, 1980). This almost exclusive use of inpatient services for competence evaluations was eventually seen as unnecessarily costly and had important implications for the principle of *least restrictive alternative* in mental health services (e.g., Shah, 1981). By the 1980s there were several calls for the development of alternative systemic models for performing pretrial competence assessments (Fitzgerald, Peszke, & Goodwin, 1978; Holmstrup, Fitch, & Keilitz, 1981; Melton et al., 1985; Mental Disability Law Reporter, 1978; Schreiber, 1978: Schutte, Malouff, Lucore, & Shern, 1988).

By the 1990s, many states had reformed their systems for obtaining pretrial competence evaluations (Grisso et al., 1994; Poythress, Otto, & Heilbrun, 1991). The majority of states had developed outpatient mechanisms, typically private practitioners or forensically-specialized clinicians at community mental health centers, who evaluated defendants while in jail awaiting trial. Most of these states retained an inpatient option for cases requiring immediate psychiatric attention or more complex evaluations.

The time required for performing evaluations typically has been shorter in outpatient arrangements, while receiving generally favorable ratings from judges (Melton et al., 1985; Warren & Fitch, 1988). About one-fifth of the states, however, still rely primarily on inpatient evaluations for competence to stand trial, especially in western states with low population density and less comprehensive community mental health services (Grisso et al., 1994). Outpatient arrangements typically require greater quality control efforts on the part of state agencies than do inpatient arrangements, because the former involve a greater number of clinicians only some of whom will have extensive forensic evaluation experience. One study found similar scores on a competence assessment measure (the *MacArthur Competence Assessment Tool—Criminal Adjudication*) when comparing an outpatient to an inpatient evaluation system (Edens, Poythress, Nicholson, & Otto, 1999). Warren, Rosenfeld, Fitch and Hawk (1997), however, found that incompetence was found more often as a result of outpatient than inpatient evaluations, possibly because defendants are afforded more opportunity to regain competence while in inpatient settings where they receive psychiatric care during the period of the evaluation itself.

Another approach to reducing the number of inpatient pretrial competence evaluations has been the development of screening procedures (e.g., Fein et al., 1991). As many as 80% of defendants referred for pretrial competence evaluations in some jurisdictions are found competent after assessment (Melton et al., 1997; Roesch & Golding, 1980). Brief screening systems seek to reduce this proportion by diverting some defendants from the more costly forms of competence assessment. Screening evaluations may consist of a brief interview by a psychiatrist or a psychologist, and/or administration of a pretrial competence assessment instrument (e.g., see examples reviewed later in this chapter), often in the same setting in which the defendant is being detained for trial. Defendants for whom pretrial competence is still questionable or doubtful after screening are then referred for more extensive inpatient or outpatient assessment, whereas defendants who are judged as clearly competent by screening professionals are likely to proceed to trial.

Little is known empirically about the methods that clinicians actually use in collecting data for competence to stand trial evaluations. Textbooks generally emphasize the importance of obtaining hospital and offense records, information from third parties (e.g., attorneys' perceptions of their clients' deficits in assisting counsel), interviews to obtain clinical information as well as a direct assessment of defendants' functional abilities that are associated with the legal definition of pretrial competence, and psychological testing when it is necessary to identify important psychological deficits (Grisso, 1988; Heilbrun, 2001; Melton et al., 1997).

As documented in the first edition of *Evaluating Competencies*, the 1970s and 1980s saw the emergence of assessment instruments designed specifically to evaluate abilities related to pretrial competence. McGarry and coworkers (Laboratory of Community Psychiatry, 1973) analyzed the *Dusky* standard and its application by courts, and thereby arrived at a conceptualization of defendant capacities and specific abilities related to the legal standard. These concepts became the structure for a number of assessment tools designed to assist forensic examiners in maintaining a proper focus on essential criteria for competence to stand trial. By the mid-1980s, some of these forensic assessment instruments were being recommended for clinical use (Grisso, 1986, 1988; Gutheil & Appelbaum, 1982; Melton et al., 1987; Shah, 1981).

The development of instruments for pretrial competence evaluations proliferated through the 1990s, as evidenced in the reviews later in this chapter. There are little reliable data, however, on the extent of their use in current practice. Some evidence (Terhune, 1990) suggests that judges have more favorable perceptions of reports that include data from specialized pretrial competence assessment instruments. A recent survey (Borum & Grisso, 1995) suggested that the use of such instruments has become more frequent in subsequent years, at least among experienced (board-certified) forensic clinicians. Yet only about 40% of those respondents said that they used competence assessment instruments "frequently," while approximately 40% said that they never used them. This suggests that use of structured forensic assessment instruments for competence to stand trial evaluations has not yet become standard practice.

CONTENT ISSUES.   The first edition of *Evaluating Competencies* summarized a litany of complaints found in the literature regarding evaluations and reports for competence to stand trial. For example, examiners were accused of failing to address the legal standard for pretrial competence, neglecting to describe relevant functional abilities, and failing to provide reasoning to support their judgments about defendants' competence. This led to significant efforts, especially in the 1990s, to establish standards for forensic eval-uations in general (including competence to stand trial evaluations) (e.g., Committee on Ethical Guidelines for Forensic Psychologists, 1991; Heilbrun, 2001) and to promote these standards through increased training activities (Otto, Heilbrun, & Grisso, 1990). Perhaps stimulated by these developments, several researchers recently provided our first reliable view of the state of practice regarding pretrial competence evaluations (for a more comprehensive review, see Nicholson & Norwood, 2000).

There is some evidence that forensic clinicians' pretrial competence evaluations have improved in their appropriate focus on functional abilities associated with the legal question. For example, Robbins, Waters, and Herbert (1997) examined a sample of competence to stand trial reports in New Jersey and Nebraska. They developed a structured method to determine the degree to which reports provided information related to Grisso's (1986) six elements of legal competencies. In general, reporting of relevant functional abilities was relatively adequate (although far from complete).

However, LaFortune and Nicholson (1995) reported that while functional abilities were described in most reports in a sample in Oklahoma, some important abilities were only rarely included. Similarly, in an analysis of another state's pretrial competence reports, Skeem, Golding, Cohn, and Berge (1998; see also Skeem & Golding, 1998) concluded that attention to functional abilities associated with understanding of information related to trials was relatively good, but that little attention was paid to defendants' capacities to make decisions in the trial process. For example, only 12% of the reports addressed defendants' comprehension of the implications of a guilty plea, despite the fact that most defendants must decide how to plead (and frequently do plead guilty in the context of plea agreements).

Borum and Grisso (1996) surveyed experienced forensic psychologists and psychiatrists nationally (most of them forensic board-certified) regarding their opinions about the degree of importance for including each of 57 types of content in pretrial competence (and criminal responsibility) reports. They found substantial consensus among forensic clinicians (and across disciplines) regarding the degree of importance of the majority of items. Yet the respondents did not express a consensus that it was essential for reports to explain clinicians' reasons for their opinions.

Similarly, Skeem et al. (1998) found that in reports indicating deficits in competence-relevant abilities, only 10% provided reasoning that spelled out the relation between psychopathology and the compromised abilities. This has been perhaps the most frequently documented deficiency of competence evaluation reports in recent years (Otto et al., 1996; Nicholson et al., 1995; Robbins et al., 1997). These findings are in contrast to practice guidelines that urge clinicians in the strongest terms to provide such explanations for relevant functional deficits (Committee on Ethical Guidelines for Forensic Psychologists, 1991; Grisso, 1988; Heilbrun, 2001; Melton et al., 1997).

As a consequence of these findings, the long-running debate about testifying to the ultimate legal question (stating an opinion as to whether the defendant is or is not competent to stand trial) continues to be a relevant point of concern. Texts have long argued that a conclusion about legal competence or incompetence is not a matter of clinical expertise and therefore is inappropriate in expert testimony (Grisso, 1986, 1988; Melton et al., 1987, 1997). Arguments have been made to the contrary, however (e.g., Rogers & Ewing, 1989; Slobogin, 1989), and a majority of experienced forensic clinicians claim that reports of pretrial competence evaluations *should* answer the ultimate legal question, or that to do so is of no great consequence (Borum & Grisso, 1996). One of the strongest arguments for this position is that judges are free to accept or reject the clinician's opinion, after clinicians have explained the logic and reasons for arriving at the decision. Yet most of the foregoing studies of examiners' pretrial competence reports have found that most clinicians do *not* explain, for example, how symptoms of disorder are related to defendants' functional deficits. If they do not, they fail to provide an important part of the evidence that judges must have in order to weigh the value of clinicians' opinions on the ultimate legal question.

Almost all texts describing pretrial competence evaluations have agreed that examiners need structure and a clear conceptualization of their objectives, as well as appropriate methods, in order to perform evaluations that will have clinical quality, legal relevance, and practical utility to the courts. The remainder of the chapter addresses this need.

FROM LEGAL STANDARD TO FORENSIC ASSESSMENT

This section reviews the legal construct of competence to stand trial, using the five components of legal competencies described in Chapter 2. The discussion of each component provides guidelines for conceptualizing and performing assessments in this area.

Functional Component

Statutes, case law, and comments by legal analysts make it clear that competence to stand trial determinations require a consideration of the defendant's functional abilities (e.g., Grisso, 1988; Heilbrun, 2001; Melton et al., 1997; Laboratory for Community Psychiatry, 1973; Roesch & Golding, 1980. For legal citations see *Legal Standard* earlier in this chapter.) The central question is whether the defendant knows, understands, believes or can do certain things generally required by a particular context: the role of defendants in trials.

The standard in *Dusky v. United States* (1960) describes at the most general level the parameters for the domain of functional abilities with which the law is concerned: "sufficient present ability to consult with [one's] lawyer with a reasonable degree of rational understanding" and "rational as well as factual understanding of proceedings against [the defendant]" (p. 402). What are the more specific functional ability concepts that might be relevant for this functional domain?

The court in *Wieter v. Settle* (1961) listed eight "elements" of knowledge and ability related to the *Dusky* standard. These elements, however, were so minimal in their demands (e.g., an appreciation that "there is a judge on the Bench") that they did not describe adequately the type or range of abilities about which the law is concerned in pretrial competence cases.

Legal analysts and researchers have produced a number of lists of functional ability concepts related to the *Dusky* standard, the earliest being those of Robey (1965), Bukatman, Foy, and DeGrazia (1971), McGarry and associates (Laboratory of Community Psychiatry, 1973), the Group for the Advancement of Psychiatry (1974), and Ausness (1978). (See Grisso, 1988, for these lists of abilities.) There is much consensus among these lists, and they served a valuable purpose in orienting clinicians to pay attention to functional abilities rather than simply to infer competence or incompetence on the basis of psychiatric symptoms alone.

These lists of abilities relevant for pretrial competence, however, were developed more than 20 years ago, and they do not reflect modern changes in the conceptualization of pretrial competence. For example, they focus especially on defendants' performance during formal trials, despite the fact that competence to stand trial applies to pretrial participation as well. Moreover, at least 90% of criminal defendants' cases are resolved without a formal trial on the facts, typically as a consequence of guilty pleas that require the ability to understand, consider, and decide regarding "plea bargains." This has been increasingly recognized in recent years in scholarly analyses (e.g., Bonnie, 1992) and legal cases (e.g., *Godinez v. Moran*, 1993; *Cooper v. Oklahoma*, 1996).

Table 1 offers a list of functional abilities formed as a composite of these past lists, but supplemented by abilities associated with Bonnie's "decisional competence." They include a number of abilities associated with assisting counsel in a defense, understanding the basic purpose and process of criminal trials (factual understanding), and applying information to one's own trial circumstances (rational understanding in the decision making process).

TABLE 1. FUNCTIONAL ABILITY CONCEPTS ASSOCIATED WITH COMPETENCE TO
STAND TRIAL

Consulting and Assisting Counsel
- Understanding that counsel works for defendant
- Understanding counsel's inquiries
- Capable of responding to counsel's inquiries in a manner that provides relevant information for defense
- Can provide consistent account of events relevant to charges and a defense
- Can manage the demands of trial process (stress, maintaining demeanor)
- Capable of testifying if necessary

Factual Understanding
- That the defendant is accused of a crime
- That the court will decide on guilt or innocence
- That he trial could result in punishment
- Of the various ways that defendants may plead
- That certain sentences are possible (their nature and seriousness)
- Of the roles of various participants in the trial process
- Of the general process of trials

Rational Understanding (Decisional Abilities)
- Beliefs about one's own trial process are not distorted by delusional beliefs
- Appropriately motivated to further one's defense
- Reasoning ability sufficient to process relevant information during decision making

The distinction between *factual understanding* (basic knowledge) and *rational understanding* (the ability to apply knowledge to one's own situation) bears comment. Some defendants manifest a discrepancy between what they know about trials and what they believe will happen in their own situation. For example, a defendant might know that judges are supposed to uphold the law, and in this sense may have a factual understanding of the role of the judge in a trial. The same defendant, however, might nevertheless harbor a delusional belief that the judge in the court in which the defendant will appear is part of global conspiracy to do the defendant harm. Other defendants may have difficulty applying information to their own situation because of lack of motivation (e.g., depression so severe that they have no desire to defend themselves) or because of cognitive limitations that do not allow them to process and use various pieces of information to meaningfully engage in decision making. In cases like these, "factual understanding" does not tell the whole story, because deficits in "rational understanding" may preclude defendants' capacities to apply the information rationally to their own situations.

In Figure 1 of Chapter 3, these ability concepts would appear in "C: *Psychological Definitions of Legally Relevant Functional Abilities.*" Methods

for assessing these functional abilities relevant to the role of defendant (C')
are reviewed later in this chapter.

Causal Component

The legal construct of competence to stand trial suggests that courts
should be informed not only about deficits in a defendant's functional
abilities to perform the defendant role, but also: (a) the nature of a defendant's psychological disorder, if any; and (b) the relation of the disorder
to deficits in the legally relevant functional abilities (see *Legal Standard*
earlier in this chapter). This information assists the court in formulating
causal explanations for the observed functional deficits.

There are several reasons why courts are concerned with explanations for functional deficits related to a defendant's trial participation.
One reason is to assure that the functional deficits are beyond the control
of the defendant. For example, functional deficits in understanding of
trial processes or attorney-client relations will not suggest a finding of
incompetence if the defendant appears to be malingering. Attention to the
possibility of malingering and other "response biases" in pretrial competence examinations has been discussed and strongly recommended by
commentators on forensic examinations (e.g., Gothard, Rogers, & Sewell,
1995; Grisso, 1988; Heilbrun, 2001; Heilbrun, Bennett, White, & Kelly,
1990; Miller & Germain, 1987).

A second reason is to assure that observed deficits in trial-related
functioning are not merely a consequence of conditions that could be
remediated easily without the need for psychiatric treatment. For example,
mere ignorance of the nature of trial procedures (without evidence of
underlying disorder) is not consistent with a finding of incompetence,
because the defendant might easily be prepared for trial (assuming adequate intellectual capacities) by simply engaging in efforts to educate
the defendant concerning the nature of trials. Similarly, if a defendant's
ability deficits may be related merely to fatigue or other transient, non-
pathological conditions at the time of examination for functional abilities,
these conditions might be easily remedied without the need to declare
incompetence and to pursue treatment.

A third reason arises in decisions about treatment to restore competence in defendants who are found incompetent. The nature of the psychological disorder, and its relation to legally relevant functional deficits,
will have implications for deciding the type of treatment necessary. In
some cases the condition apparently responsible for the deficits might
be essentially untreatable, requiring a declaration of incompetence and

dismissal of charges (with or without involuntary civil commitment proceedings).

When addressing any of these questions, the identification of a mental disorder is not the only task in a causal analysis. The mere coexistence of a mental disorder and a functional deficit does not provide sufficient information with which to form an explanation for the deficit. For example, when a defendant diagnosed with mental retardation manifests important deficits in understanding of trial procedures and charges, these deficits might be related to the defendant's limited intellectual capacities. On the other hand, some individuals with mental retardation may nevertheless be able to understand the general nature and purpose of a trial. Further, such an individual's trial-related deficits might be for reasons other than mental retardation. For example, some patients with diagnoses of mental retardation also have psychotic conditions, and diagnosis of any disorder does not automatically rule out malingering or other response biases.

Establishing possible relations between mental disabilities and functional deficits generally will require observation and description of symptoms or psychological characteristics that are more specific than broad diagnostic classifications. For example, establishing the relation between a defendant's schizophrenia and functional deficits in relating to an attorney might require detailed examination of the content or focus of the defendant's paranoid delusion, as well as how that delusion plays a specific role in the defendant's perception of defense counsel.

Other disorders might require assessment of psychological functions such as memory, motivational states, or cognitive complexity in order to establish the relation between mental disorder and functional deficiency. Psychological characteristics that may be relevant for developing such causal connections include general intelligence, memory, contact with reality, motivation, reasoning or problem solving, and emotional control. Cases involving adolescent defendants may also require assessment of cognitive, emotional and social immaturity as a potential factor accounting for deficits in functional abilities for the defendant role (Barnum, 2000; Grisso, 1998a, 2000).

Forensic examiners have a wide range of methods for assessing diagnostic conditions and psychological characteristics that might address causal questions about deficits in functional abilities. Among these are mental-status exams, instruments for the assessment of intellectual and memory abilities, and tests that assist in determining personality traits, psychopathological conditions, and behavioral predispositions. Only a few studies, however, have focused on establishing relations between these indexes of psychological constructs and the functional abilities of primary concern in competence to stand trial cases. (See Nicholson & Kugler, 1991, for a review of relations between incompetence and characteristics of psychopathology and personality; see also research results with instruments reviewed later in this chapter.)

Interactive Component

No particular degree of deficits in trial-related capacities signifies competence or incompetence to stand trial. Instead, legal determinations of incompetence require a consideration of the degree of incongruency between a defendant's functional abilities and the anticipated demands of the defendant's trial. This interactive characteristic of the legal construct suggests that forensic assessments should be conducted with a consideration of the attorney-client circumstances and probable trial demands in the instant case.

The best example of courts' interactive reasoning in pretrial competence cases is provided by court opinions involving defendants' claims of amnesia for events surrounding the alleged offense (e.g., *Hansford v. United States*, 1966; *United States v. Sermon*, 1964; *Wilson v. United States*, 1968). Defendants in these circumstances have argued that their inability to provide their attorneys with an account of facts surrounding the alleged offense precludes their ability to adequately assist in their defense. In turn, courts generally have reasoned that amnesia *per se* is not adequate to establish incompetence to stand trial. Amnesia suggests incompetence only if circumstances in that particular case disallow acquisition of evidence by defense counsel in any way other than by the defendant's report, and if the evidence is important to an adequate defense (see *Wilson v. United States*, 1968, for more specific enumeration of guidelines). In other words, one amnesiac defendant might be found competent to stand trial and another might be found incompetent, because of different evidentiary needs of the two defendants' trial circumstances.

The assessment of trial demands in relation to a defendant's functional deficits will require some sense of the dimensions with which trial circumstances can be described, as related to questions of pretrial competence. A perusal of references cited throughout the foregoing discussions of competence to stand trial suggests that the following variables might be relevant:

- Complexity and multiplicity of charges
- Particular events associated with the alleged offense
- Range of possible penalties for this alleged offense, and probabilities of their occurrence

- Range and types of evidence available to counsel without defendant's report
- Simplicity or complexity of the legal defenses available
- Necessity for defendant's own testimony at trial
- Probable length of trial
- Probable complexity of trial (e.g., types and numbers of witnesses)
- Potential of trial to arouse emotion (e.g., due to the nature of offense, relation of parties in the trial process)
- Sources of social support for defendant during trial process.

This list is neither exhaustive nor the product of definitive research. It represents merely a compendium of variables mentioned by commentators in past literature. Currently no researchers have reported systematically studying or assessing trial demands for purposes of comparing them to trial-related functional abilities of defendants. We have no systematic methods for assessing and describing future trials and no methods designed to compare defendants' abilities to trial demands.

Nevertheless, it is possible for forensic examiners to employ this component in their evaluations and reports (e.g., "My conclusions about the defendant's potential for decompensation under stress may be important in light of counsel's statement that defendant's testimony may be needed"). In doing so, however, forensic examiners who attempt to describe incongruencies between defendant abilities and trial demands must rely on logic and speculation, rather than standardized method and empirical support for interpretations. Sources of data that might be relevant for addressing this interactive aspect of pretrial competence would include police reports of the alleged offense and subsequent events; information about defense counsel's past behavior and relations to clients; and the opinions of legal professionals concerning such variables as the probable demands of the upcoming trial or the nature of available defenses.

Judgmental and Dispositional Components

No particular degree of incongruency between defendant ability and trial demand is determinative of the pretrial competence question. Whether the extent of incongruency in a case reaches criteria for incompetence will require an interpretation of society's sense of justice. The basic concern underlying the legal construct of competence to stand trial is the fairness of the future trial. This concern requires that one balance protections for defendants against society's interests in criminal cases, taking into account the dispositional consequences of a competence or incompetence finding. Would proceeding to trial be a just or fair outcome for this defendant, and does the consequence of probable involuntary hospitalization for treatment represent a fair outcome for the defendant and society?

Clearly these are moral questions that go beyond the limits of expertise claimed by mental health professionals. Forensic assessment might provide a comparative description of a defendant's abilities and probable trial demands. Yet one makes a moral judgment when one concludes that the degree of incongruency between these two sets of observations is too great to warrant a finding of competence.

Therefore, an opinion on the ultimate legal question ought not to be an objective of forensic assessments related to competence to stand trial. If examiners offer such opinions, they should explain why they believe that the individual's deficits do or do not meet a legal standard for competence to stand trial, so that the court can weigh the logic of their opinions.

REVIEW OF FORENSIC ASSESSMENT INSTRUMENTS

Mental health examiners may improve their assessments related to competence to stand trial by evaluating functional abilities that are especially relevant for the legal definition of the competence. This section reviews 6 assessment instruments that were designed for this purpose. The first 3 instruments reviewed here were developed anew since the time of the first edition: the *MacArthur Competence Assessment Tool-Criminal Adjudication*, the *Fitness Interview Test-Revised*, and the *Competence Assessment for Standing Trial-Mental Retardation*. The original *Fitness Interview Test* was published soon after the first edition of EC, and the revised version has taken its place; thus the original FIT is described but not reviewed in detail in the section on the FIT-R. The *Georgia Court Competence Test*, reviewed in the first edition of this book, has been revised as the *Georgia Court Competence Test-Mississippi State Hospital*; only this newer version is reviewed in this edition. Finally, the review includes 2 instruments that were described in the first edition and have not been revised by their authors: the *Competence to Stand Trial Assessment Instrument* and the *Competence Screening Test*.

Several instruments that have been developed for use in competence to stand trial assessments were not selected for review. Three are from an earlier era, providing "checklists" of information to be obtained in competence evaluations but no quantitative scores or ratings (Bukatman, Foy, & De Grazia, 1971; Lawrence, 1981; Robey, 1965). Another (the *Computer-Assisted Competence Assessment Tool*) was not included because no manual was available (for a review of this instrument, see Melton et al., 1997, pp. 143–144). The *Interdisciplinary Fitness Interview* (IFI), which was reviewed in the first edition of EC, was not re-reviewed because no further work on the IFI has been published since the review in the first edition.

Finally, at the time this chapter was written, a manual for the *Evaluation for Competency to Stand Trial-Revised* (ECST-R) by Rogers, Tillbrook, and Sewell (undated) was in preparation but not yet in final form. The instrument's constructs and semi-structured interview items include the full range of abilities typically associated with competence to stand trial, a format for identifying the relation of psychiatric symptoms to defendants' deficits on those abilities, a system of rating the items, and an index for detecting feigning of symptoms. Initial promising information on the instrument has been published (Rogers, 2001; Rogers, Grandjean, Tilbrook, Vitacco, & Sewell, 2001; Rogers, Sewell, Grandjean, & Vitacco, in press; Tillbrook, 2001).

In each of the following reviews, citations are made to lettered references (for example, a, b, c) that appear at the end of the instrument's review.

MacArthur Competence Assessment Tool-Criminal Adjudication (MacCAT-CA)

Authors

Poythress, N., Nicholson, R., Otto, R., Edens, J., Bonnie, R., Monahan, J., & Hoge, S.

Primary Author Affiliation

Florida Mental Health Institute, University of South Florida, Tampa FL

Primary Reference

Poythress et al. (1999). *The MacArthur Competence Assessment Tool-Criminal Adjudication: Professional manual.* Odessa, FL: Psychological Assessment Resources.

Description

The *MacArthur Competence Assessment Tool-Criminal Adjudication* (MacCAT-CA) was developed to assess abilities associated with "adjudicative competence." As discussed later in this review, adjudicative competence is a concept that recognizes the broad range of factors that may be involved in legal determinations of defendants' "competence to proceed (assist counsel)" and their "decisional competence." (b) The adjudicative competence concept was one of the guiding structures for an effort during the 1990s by the MacArthur Research Network on Mental Health and Law to develop improved measures of capacities associated with competence to stand trial. The Network project resulted in a research tool, the *MacArthur Structured Assessment of Competencies of Criminal Defendants* (MacSAC-CD), that manifested substantial psychometric values and evidence of construct validity. (g) The MacSAC-CD, however, exceeded reasonable lengths of administration time for the typical demands of clinical evaluations for competence to stand trial. Therefore, the MacArthur Network researchers then developed the MacCAT-CA as "a clinically portable measure for actual use in clinical practice" (j) while retaining essential features of the MacSAC-CD.

The MacCAT-CA is a structured and highly standardized interview that consists of 22 items organized in three parts called Understanding, Reasoning and Appreciation. (k) The eight Understanding items and eight Reasoning items are based on a brief vignette, introduced at the beginning of the interview, regarding two men who get in a fight in a bar while playing pool. One of the men is arrested and faces charges and a trial process.

In this hypothetical context, the *Understanding* items ask questions of the examinee to determine the examinee's comprehension of eight things:

- roles of defense and prosecution attorneys
- the elements of an offense with which the defendant could be charged
- elements of a lesser included offense
- role of the judge
- role of the jury
- the consequences of conviction
- consequences of pleading guilty
- rights waived when one pleads guilty.

For 6 of these items, an examinee's failure to give an adequate response results in the examiner employing a brief, standardized "teaching" process regarding the element that is being tested, with a subsequent repeat of the question to determine whether the defendant can now provide an adequate response. For the 2 items about nature of the offense, the items begin with a "teaching" disclosure without a "pre-test" of the defendant's knowledge.

The examinee's responses are examined with objective scoring criteria in the manual, classifying them as 2, 1, or 0 (adequate, questionable, inadequate). The item score for each of the six items that have a "pre-test" and a potential "teaching" section is the examinee's score on the pre-test if it was adequate (2 pt.) or, if teaching was needed, the score obtained after the teaching process.

The eight *Reasoning* items are of two types. Five of the items offer two "facts" about the incident and ask the examinee which of the two would be more important for the defendant to tell his lawyer. The other three items are based on a description of two pleading choices: pleading guilty under the conditions of a plea agreement with the prosecutor, and pleading not guilty and going to trial. The items focus on the decision process, not the choice: whether the examinee seeks more information before deciding, offers both an advantage and a disadvantage for the chosen option, and manifests evidence of having compared the chosen option to the rejected option. Responses are scored (2, 1, 0) according to objective criteria provided in the manual.

The six *Appreciation* items are not based on the hypothetical case used in Understanding and Reasoning, but on the examinee's own legal situation. The examinee is asked whether, "compared to other people who are in trouble with the law," the examinee thinks that he or she is "more likely, less likely, or just as likely" to:

- be treated fairly in the legal process
- be assisted by defense counsel
- fully disclose case information to his or her defense attorney
- be found guilty
- get the same punishment as others if found guilty
- plead guilty

Examinees are then asked for an explanation for their choice, and queries are made to determine whether the examinee's explanation contains evidence of "unrealistic or idiosyncratic beliefs that defendants have about themselves or their situations" such that they are "clearly implausible and colored by symptoms of mental illness (e.g., delusions)" (k, p. 13). Items are scored not on the basis of the choice, but according to the explanation that is provided. Items are scored 2, 1, or 0 based on objective criteria for "implausibility" of response described in the manual.

The process yields Understanding, Reasoning, and Appreciation scores, but the manual does not provide or encourage a "total MacCAT-CA score" such as a sum of the three scale scores. The examinee's scores can be compared to norms, provided in the manual, for three groups of adult defendants involved in research during the instrument's development: non-selected jail detainees, defendants with mental illness but presumed competent, and defendants who had recently been found incompetent to stand trial. Tables offer percentages of persons in each of these groups who obtained each of the possible scores on the three scales. The tables also offer recommended cut-off points for levels of performance designated "minimal or no impairment," "mild impairment," and "clinically significant impairment." The authors explain that these are not meant to define competence or incompetence, but to assist in describing the degree of deficits or strengths that the defendant manifests.

Conceptual Basis

CONCEPT DEFINITION. Two sets of concepts played central roles in the development of the MacCAT-CA: adjudicative competence as conceptualized by Bonnie (b), and the three elements of Understanding, Reasoning, and Appreciation.

Bonnie's theory of adjudicative competence employs two components: *competence to assist counsel* and *decisional competence*. Competence to assist counsel includes a basic understanding of matters pertaining to the trial process, as well as the ability to work with one's attorney and to assist the attorney by relating pertinent factors that may assist the defense. Decisional competence refers to abilities needed for "autonomous decision making with respect to strategic issues that arise in the course of prosecution" (k, p. 2). This includes abilities associated with the cognitive processing of information in order to arrive at decisions. The concept recognizes also that decisions might be reached on illogical bases if the individual has delusional beliefs that could interfere with the individual's interpretation of his or her own legal situation.

The elements of Understanding, Reasoning, and Appreciation were derived from earlier work in the structuring of decision making abilities associated with competence to consent to or refuse treatment, as identified through case law reviews (a, n) and employed in other studies of assessment of abilities associated with competence to consent (d). According to Grisso and Appelbaum (d), Understanding refers to basic comprehension of relevant facts. Reasoning refers to the ability to process information (e.g., seek information, weigh advantages and disadvantages of options) in the course of decisionmaking. Describing the MacCAT-CA concepts, Otto et al. also include in Reasoning the "ability to discern the potential legal relevance of information" (j, p. 436). Appreciation refers to "rational awareness of the meaning and consequences of the proceedings in one's own case" (j, p. 436). This element focuses specifically on distorted application of information to one's own situation due to delusional beliefs associated with mental disorder.

As conceptualized by Grisso and Appelbaum (d), these elements are inter-related but sufficiently discrete to warrant separate concepts.

For example, one might fully understand the facts of trials, yet have difficulties manipulating the information in a decision process. Or one might have the cognitive capacities to process information quite well in arriving at a decision using simple logic, while also being at risk of making a decision based on a delusional belief (e.g., regarding one's immortality or invulnerability) that does not allow one to realistically appreciate the significance of the trial for oneself.

The specific content to be employed in each of these three sections of the MacCAT-CA derived from various sources. The content of the Understanding section borrowed from an evolving consensus in law and clinical practice (as manifested in many other psycholegal instruments) regarding the specific things that defendants are expected to know about charges and trials when questions of their competence are raised. The content domains of the Reasoning and Appreciation sections are more novel and were determined by the researchers in consultation with members of the MacArthur research network that sponsored the development of the instrument.

OPERATIONAL DEFINITION. The various item strategies employed in the MacCAT-CA (such as the use of a hypothetical case, the teaching process of the Understanding items, the Reasoning section's method for assessing ability to perceive relevant facts and to process information, and the Appreciation section's format) had been used in the MacSAC-CD, which had demonstrated the viability and value of these strategies in earlier studies with criminal defendants (g). They were refined in the course of a group process of discussion and revision that involved a broader community of researchers and law scholars (the MacArthur Research Network on Mental Health and Law). Example responses for use in the scoring criteria were also derived from the earlier MacSAC-CD and from piloting of the prototype MacCAT-CA.

CRITIQUE. The use of two sets of concepts to guide the development of the MacCAT-CA anchors it in both law and existing psycholegal concepts for structuring the assessment of relevant abilities for legal competence. It is unique, for example, in focusing part of the assessment on decision making abilities associated with competence to stand trial, which have achieved greater attention in practice as a result of their recognition in the U.S. Supreme Court decision in *Godinez v. Moran*. The decision to use the three elements that have been derived in other areas of legal competence also increases its potential to contribute to a more unified conceptualization of legal competencies.

The absence of separate *competence to assist counsel* and *decisional competence* sections of the MacCAT-CA seems logical. The authors explain that the Understanding items and some of the Reasoning items are especially associated with the competence to assist counsel component, and the Appreciation items and some of the Reasoning items are especially associated with decisional competence. But these two concepts, while capturing somewhat different aspects of competence to stand trial, are not completely discrete. Understanding of essential facts is necessarily required for meaningful decision making, and delusional beliefs can impair one's ability to assist counsel. Thus, the choice not to try to structure the instrument too rigidly along the lines of these two concepts seems wise.

As acknowledged by the MacCAT-CA authors (k), the MacCAT-CA does not collect information on all of the abilities and deficits that might be relevant for competence to stand trial evaluations. Among those that are not included, for example, are the defendant's ability to engage in logical communications with a defense attorney, the ability to testify, and the ability to manage the stress of trial. This is not a weakness unless a measure's items insufficiently represent the primary psycholegal constructs that have guided the development of the instrument. In this sense, the MacCAT-CA items seem to have been chosen meaningfully.

The high degree of structure employed in the MacCAT-CA offers excellent potential for the instrument to be used not only in clinical assessments but also in research, and it provides the opportunity for constructing meaningful norms and demonstration of its psychometric properties. The use of a hypothetical case, as well as the rigid standardization of questions and inquiries, reduces the examiner's ability to explore issues that may arise specific to individual defendants (e.g., probing the nature of their misunderstanding of concepts, determining whether they understand their own charges and their consequences). Rogers (l) criticized the MacCAT-CA's reliance on defendants' responses to hypothetical offenses and offenders, pointing out that such data were insufficient to address case-specific issues in actual forensic assessment practice. The MacCAT-CA authors were clearly aware of this. They acknowledged (j, k) that the instrument was not intended to provide all of the information that a clinician will need when assessing defendants' abilities; it should be supplemented with mental status examination and inquiries designed to assess the defendant's grasp of information specific to his or her own circumstances. Use of those more individualized methods alone, of course, would provide no way to compare defendants to norms regarding degrees of ability related to competence to stand trial. This is the value of using multiple methods, some highly structured like the MacCAT-CA and others with greater capacity to capture nuanced information specific to the individual.

The use of a teaching mechanism in the Understanding items is unique. It incorporates the notion, suggested in various texts on psycholegal assessment (c, h), that it is the capacity to understand, not merely the amount one currently understands, that is most relevant for competence to stand trial. When defendants at first appear not to understand certain aspects of trials, examiners typically are encouraged to attempt to "teach" them and to assess their capacity to grasp the matters with instruction. The MacCAT-CA makes this a standard part of the competence assessment process. It is not clear why the authors did not construct a subscale of Understanding that expresses the defendant's original level of understanding, in contrast to the final Understanding score based on their performance after having been taught. This could be done by examiners, but the MacCAT-CA manual and current research provide neither a procedure with which to do this nor normative data to which to compare the defendant's initial understanding.

Similarly, one should be aware that the Reasoning scale contains two relatively distinct sets of items. Five items pertain to the defendant's ability to make inferences about the relevance or irrelevance of facts in the case for purposes of building a defense. Three other items focus on the individual's processing of a decision (e.g., whether they attend to both advantages and disadvantages of options). While all of those items can be conceptualized as related to a concept called Reasoning, the fact that they are of two different types raises the possibility that they might create a scale with less internal consistency than one might wish.

A review of the scoring criteria reveals scoring distinctions, explanations, and examples that generally will not be difficult for clinicians to comprehend or to explain to courts that inquire about the basis for their scores. One exception is the scoring for the Appreciation items. The concept of Appreciation refers specifically to evidence of the presence or absence of "implausible" explanations based on delusional beliefs. The Appreciation scoring system, however, gives "0" credit for two types of responses. One is for "reasons that are clearly implausible ... based on a delusional premise or a serious distortion of reality." The other is for cases in which the defendant "offers no reason or fails to answer the question." Due to the second of these criteria, a low summary Appreciation score cannot be interpreted as signifying the concept that Appreciation represents—that is, "implausibility due to delusional content"—because in some cases it will represent mere failure to respond. In clinical practice, one can easily interpret what a defendant's Appreciation score means by examining the specific responses of the defendant. But this creates greater problems for researchers, who will not be able to make meaningful comparisons of Appreciation scores across studies (unless they examine every research subject's "0" responses on Appreciation to discover and report the proportion that are delusional responses and the proportion that are "I don't know" responses).

Psychometric Development

STANDARDIZATION. Instructions for administering the MacCAT-CA are clear, highly structured, and aided by a standardized form for administration, response recording, and scoring. Scoring criteria are explicitly defined and supplemented with example responses.

RELIABILITY. Interrater reliability was established by examining responses on 48 protocols in the sample on which the MacCAT-CA norms were developed, with eight of the study's research assistants scoring all protocols (other than the six that a given research assistant had originally scored) (j, k). Intraclass correlations for scale scores were .90 for Understanding, .85 for Reasoning, and .75 for Appreciation. All items but two in Reasoning and three in Appreciation manifested intraclass correlations above .60. Test-retest reliability has not been examined.

NORMS. Currently the original validation study for the MacCAT-CA is the source for normative data on the MacCAT-CA (j, k). The study involved administration of the MacCAT-CA and other clinical measures to:

- 283 defendants admitted to forensic psychiatric units after being adjudicated incompetent to proceed (HI: hospitalized incompetent),
- 249 defendants in jail who were receiving treatment for mental health problems but who were presumed competent (JT: jail treated), and
- 197 randomly selected jail inmates who were presumed competent (JU: jail unscreened).

The sample was obtained from data collection in six states in a study that managed consistency across sites in test administration and the data collection process. Defendants were between the ages of 18 and 65. Males made up about 90% of the sample, with about one-half being non-Hispanic white defendants. Gender, race, age, and educational level were not markedly different across the three comparison groups. The MacCAT-CA manual provides the percentile rank for scores on each of the three MacCAT-CA scales separately, for the HI group and for the combined JU/JT groups. Certain scores are designated "mild impairment" and "clinically significant impairment" based on their departure below the mean of the JU/JT group by 1.0 and 1.5 standard deviations, respectively.

CRITIQUE. The degree of standardization of administration provided by the MacCAT-CA, as well as evidence for interscorer reliability, inspires confidence in the norms and their application in clinical cases. These psychometric features also provide excellent potential for the instrument's use in research. This psycholegal assessment instrument is the first in its area to offer meaningful norms to which to compare scores in individual cases involving defendants whose competence to stand trial is questioned and evaluated. Moreover, data were obtained from a number of sites nationally, which increases confidence in the generalizability of the norms.

One unanswered question is whether the norms can be applied to women. Only small proportions of the validation samples were women, and reports of the instrument's development did not indicate whether any differences were found (or whether the small female sample could have provided such information with confidence).

Although the authors devised cut-off scores, they have been very careful (k) to discourage users from employing these criteria as indicators of "competence" or "incompetence." As long as they are not misused in that way, the cut-off scores offer a useful tool for making comparative statements about the performance of defendants in individual assessment cases.

Construct Validation

In the original study (i, j), Cronbach's alpha was .85 for Understanding, .81 for Reasoning, and .88 for Appreciation. The mean inter-item correlations within each of these scales was .42 for Understanding, .36 for Reasoning, and .54 for Appreciation. Overall these results suggest that items within each scale are assessing something in common associated with the scale's construct.

Reports of the original study did not describe the degree to which the three scales of the MacCAT-CA are measuring distinctly different domains of ability (e.g., interscale correlations or factor analytic structure). Rogers et al. (m) performed a factor analysis on a new sample of 149 defendants, achieving both two-factor and three-factor solutions with factor eigenvalues over 1.0. The three-factor solution, which accounted for more of the variance, manifested a distinct Appreciation factor and two other factors that corresponded roughly to the Understanding and Reasoning constructs. However, the Reasoning factor contained the five items (out of eight) that focused on defendants' capacities to infer relevance and irrelevance of information for a defense. Concerning the other three Reasoning items that focus on the reasoning process, two loaded on a factor with the majority of the Understanding items and did not load significantly on any of the factors.

The study producing the norms for the MacCAT-CA (j, k) found significant correlations between the MacCAT-CA scales and a number of clinical variables, the most significant being Full Scale IQ (with Understanding, .41; Reasoning, .34; Appreciation, .14), the Psychoticism scale of the Brief Psychiatric Rating Scale ($r = -.40$ to $-.52$), and Psychoticism on the Minnesota Multiphasic Personality Inventory-2 ($r = -.21$ to $-.33$).

CRITIQUE.   Available evidence suggests good internal consistency for the MacCAT-CA scales. More evidence is needed to examine empirically the degree to which the three scales are sufficiently distinct to warrant the basic three-scale structure of the MacCAT-CA. Preliminary factor-analytic evidence from Rogers et al. (m), however, suggest a rough correspondence with the intentions of the instrument's authors.

Note that Understanding and Reasoning were related more substantially to Full Scale IQ than was Appreciation. This is consistent with findings of Grisso et al. (f) for another psycholegal measure (the *MacArthur Competence Assessment Tool—Treatment*) that used the same three constructs for that instrument's structure. The Understanding and Reasoning constructs would be expected to be related more closely to measures of general cognitive ability, while the Appreciation concept focuses on individual's beliefs and affective reactions to their own circumstances.

The finding that the MacCAT-CA scales are most consistently related to psychoticism is in agreement with findings in many other studies (e.g., i) that psychotic disorders constitute the most frequent clinical condition found in persons who are considered incompetent to stand trial in actual practice.

Predictive or Classificatory Utility

The original MacCAT-CA norming study (j, k) compared the jail unscreened, jail treated, and hospitalized incompetent samples on the MacCAT-CA scales. Moreover, because many of the hospitalized incompetent defendants were residing in hospital programs for the restoration of incompetence, clinicians were asked to make independent evaluations and decisions (without exposure to MacCAT-CA data) for each of the defendants hospitalized for incompetence, indicating whether they appeared to be competent or incompetent to stand trial at the time of the MacCAT-CA evaluation. Significant differences were found on all three MacCAT-CA scales between the HI defendants who were judged competent and those judged incompetent by clinicians. Scale scores were correlated with these competence judgments for all three scales (Understanding, .36; Reasoning, .42; Appreciation, .49). Moreover, both of the HI groups were significantly lower than the jail unscreened and jail treated groups (presumed competent) on all three of the MacCAT-CA scales.

The MacCAT-CA manual includes tables that provide "hit rates" and various indicators of predictive utility (e.g., sensitivity, specificity, false negative rate, positive and negative predictive value) for each score on all three of the MacCAT-CA subscales.

CRITIQUE.   The evidence regarding the relation between MacCAT-CA scores and independent criteria for competence to stand trial is very encouraging. The findings need to be supported in other studies, but the likelihood that these results will be replicated is increased by the fact that the original sample was obtained from a number of sites nationally.

Potential for Expressing Person-Situation Congruency

The MacCAT-CA is based largely on stimuli that use a hypothetical case. It does not seek to assess the individual's understanding and reasoning abilities in relation to the individual's own circumstances. Therefore, it does not provide a means for comparing individuals' abilities to actual demands of their situations.

References

(a) Appelbaum, P., & Grisso, T. (1988). Assessing patients' capacities to consent to treatment. *New England Journal of Medicine, 319*, 1635–1638.

(b) Bonnie, R. (1992). The competence of criminal defendants: A theoretical reformulation. *Behavioral Sciences and the Law, 10*, 291–316.

(c) Grisso, T. (1988). Competence to stand trial evaluations: A manual for practice. Sarasota, FL: Professional Resource Press.

(d) Grisso, T., & Appelbaum, P. (1998). *Assessing competence to consent to treatment: A guide for physicians and other health care professionals.* New York: Oxford University Press.

(e) Grisso, T., & Appelbaum, P.S. (1995). The MacArthur Treatment Competence Study, III: Abilities of patients to consent to psychiatric and medical treatment. *Law and Human Behavior, 19*, 149–174.

(f) Grisso, T., Appelbaum, P.S., Mulvey, E., & Fletcher, K. (1995). The MacArthur Treatment Competence Study, II: Measures of abilities related to competence to consent to treatment. *Law and Human Behavior, 19*, 127–148.

(g) Hoge, S., Bonnie, R., Poythress, N., Monahan, J., Feucht-Haviar, T., & Eisenberg, M. (1997). The MacArthur adjudicative competence study: Development and validation of a research instrument. *Law and Human Behavior, 21*, 141–179.

(h) Melton, G., Petrila, J., Poythress, N., & Slobogin, C. (1997). *Psychological evaluations for the courts.* New York: Guilford.

(i) Nicholson, R., & Kugler, K. (1991). Competent and incompetent criminal defendants: A quantitative review of comparative research. *Psychological Bulletin, 109*, 355–370.

(j) Otto, R., Poythress, N., Edens, N., Nicholson, R., Monahan, J., Bonnie, R., Hoge, S., & Eisenberg, M. (1998). Psychometric properties of the MacArthur Competence Assessment Tool-Criminal Adjudication. *Psychological Assessment, 10*, 435–443.

(k) Poythress, N., Nicholson, R., Otto, R., Edens, J., Bonnie, R., Monahan, J., & Hoge, S. (1999). *The MacArthur Competence Assessment Tool—Criminal Adjudication: Professional manual.* Odessa, FL: Psychological Assessment Resources.

(l) Rogers, R. (2001). Focused forensic interviews. In R. Rogers (Ed.), *Handbook of diagnostic and structured interviewing* (pp. 296–357). New York: Guilford.

(m) Rogers, R., Grandjean, N., Tillbrook, C., Vitacco, M., & Sewell, K. (2001). Recent interview-based measures of competence to stand trial: A critical review augmented with research data. *Behavioral Sciences and the Law, 19,* 503–518.
(n) Roth, L., Meisel, A., & Lidz, C. (1977). Tests of competence to consent to treatment. *American Journal of Psychiatry, 134,* 279–284.

FITNESS INTERVIEW TEST—REVISED (FIT-R)

Authors

Roesch, R., Zapf, P., Eaves, D., & Webster, C.

Primary Author Affiliation

Mental Health, Law, and Policy Institute, Simon Fraser University

Primary Reference

Roesch, R., Zapf, P., Eaves, D., & Webster, C. (1998). *Fitness Interview Test (Revised Edition).* Burnaby, British Columbia, Canada: Mental Health, Law and Policy Institute, Simon Fraser University.

Description

The original 1984 version of the *Fitness Interview Test* (FIT) (d) was based on the *Competence Assessment Interview* (CAI) (see review later in this chapter). It included all of the functional ability items of the CAI as well as additional items related to understanding of trial procedures. Further, a separate section of 12 items guided examiners' evaluations of defendants' relevant clinical mental status. Research in the 1980s reported the structure, reliability, validity, and utility of the FIT (a, b, c). The revision of the instrument, resulting in the *Fitness Interview Test-Revised Edition* (FIT-R) (e), was begun soon after Canada's 1992 revision of its Criminal Code (called Bill C-30) that offered a statutory definition of "unfit to stand trial" replacing earlier Canadian reliance on case law definitions (as described later).

The revisions in the FIT were extensive. Although some of the items were retained in the FIT-R, some were eliminated and other new ones added and regrouped, the FIT's clinical mental status items were deleted, and the scoring system was completely revised. Thus research evidence on the original FIT cannot be extrapolated to address the properties of the FIT-R.

The FIT-R is a structured interview that was designed to assist clinicians in obtaining information on "all important aspects of fitness to stand trial" (e, p. 17), while recognizing that clinical opinions about fitness would require combining this information with clinical information obtained from an additional process for determining the presence and symptoms of mental disorder. The interview begins with four "background" questions (e.g., Do you have a lawyer at this point?"). This is followed by 70 questions, grouped according to 16 items that are clustered in 3 sections. The 3 sections, their items and number of questions are:

- Section I: Understanding the Nature or Object of the Proceedings: Factual Knowledge of Criminal Procedure
    1. Understanding of Arrest Process (5 questions)
    2. Understanding of the Nature and Severity of Current Charges (5 questions)
    3. Understanding of the Role of Key Participants (9 questions)
    4. Understanding of the Legal Process (4 questions)
    5. Understanding of Pleas (8 questions)
    6. Understanding of Court Procedure (5 questions)
- Section II: Understanding the Possible Consequences of the Proceedings: Appreciation of Personal Involvement in and Importance of the Proceedings
    7. Appreciation of the Range and Nature of Possible Penalties (4 questions)
    8. Appraisal of Available Legal Defenses (3 questions)
    9. Appraisal of Likely Outcome (3 questions)
- Section III: Communicate with Counsel: Ability to Participant in Defense
    10. Capacity to Communicate Facts to Lawyer (3 questions)
    11. Capacity to Relate to Lawyer (5 questions)
    12. Capacity to Plan Legal Strategy (6 questions)
    13. Capacity to Engage in Own Defense (3 questions)
    14. Capacity to Challenge Prosecution Witnesses (2 questions)
    15. Capacity to Testify Relevantly (2 questions)
    16. Capacity to Manage Courtroom Behavior (3 questions)

Although the questions should be posed in the sequence and wording provided in the manual, it is appropriate for examiners to probe regarding examinees' initial answers if they need clarification. When the interview is completed, examiners rate each item (2, 1, 0) based on a consideration of the examinee's responses to all of the questions associated with that item. The manual urges examiners to rate according to their opinions about the examinee's abilities, not simply with regard to the specific words used in the examinee's answers. General paragraph explanations are provided concerning the meaning of each item, but specific examples or scoring criteria are not provided. A 2 rating indicates "severe impairment of ability," 1 indicates "moderate impairment of ability," and 0 indicates "little or no impairment of ability" to meet the legal criterion.

The manual offers a coding sheet for recording these ratings, as well as assigning a single summary rating (2, 1, 0) for each of the three Sections. The examiner then indicates on the coding sheet an "overall judgement of fitness" (Fit, Questionable, Unfit). The FIT-R system does not provide any "formulas" for combining the item ratings to arrive at this final judgment, because not only the functional ability ratings, but also other evidence related to the presence and nature of mental disorder, must be taken into account to reach a final opinion about fitness. In addition, no specific level of ability is necessarily required for all types of defendant trials and circumstances.

Conceptual Basis

CONCEPTUAL DEFINITION. As noted earlier, the FIT-R was constructed to be compatible with 1992 changes in the Criminal Code of Canada (known as Bill C-30). The three sections of the FIT-R, therefore, followed the new definition of unfitness:

> Unable on account of mental disorder to conduct a defence at any stage of the proceedings before a verdict is rendered or to instruct counsel to do so, and, in particular, unable on account of mental disorder to (a) understand the nature or object of the proceedings, (b) understand the possible consequences of the proceedings, or (c) communicate with counsel (Criminal Code of Canada, Section 2, 1992).

OPERATIONAL DEFINITION. The items for each section were partly drawn from the FIT (which had been influenced by the content of the CAI, reviewed later in this chapter) with a few additions and modifications of content. The specific questions, however, are largely original (not borrowed from other instruments) and were developed by the authors as tools for probing the examinee's knowledge and inferential processes associated with the items in question. For example, Item 6, "Understanding of Court Procedure," is assessed with the following questions:

- Who is the only one at your trial who can call on you to testify?
- After your lawyer finishes asking you questions on the stand, who can ask you questions next?
- Why does the Crown counsel (prosecutor) ask you questions?
- What will the judge do if you plead guilty?
- What questions would you ask your lawyer before you decide whether or not to plead guilty?

CRITIQUE.   The logic for structuring the FIT-R according to Canadian law is quite clear. Moreover, it does not limit the FIT-R to application in Canada. Most of the concepts assessed in the interview are relevant for U.S. definitions of competence to stand trial. As noted in the third item above, the wording of questions in the FIT-R manual recognizes the potential application of the instrument in other countries.

It is instructive to compare the content of the FIT-R to that of the *MacArthur Competence Assessment Tool-Criminal Adjudication* (MacCAT-CA), reviewed earlier in this chapter. The first sections of both instruments focus on "understanding" of information about charges, penalties, and legal process, and they have considerable content overlap. The second section of the MacCAT-CA, called "Reasoning," focuses on the defendant's abilities to make inferences about the importance of facts that might be relevant to communicate to counsel. This is most similar to Section III of the FIT-R, although the inquiry for this section in the FIT-R is much broader, including a wider range of "ability to participate in defence" items and questions than is found in the MacCAT-CA (e.g., questions about ability to testify at one's own trial, capacity to manage behavior in the courtroom).

The title of the FIT-R's Section II (Understand the Possible Consequences of the Proceedings) uses the term *understanding*. But the criterion phrases describing the three items in this section clearly indicate that their purpose is similar to that of the "Appreciation" section of the MacCAT-CA. That is, Section II is intended to identify whether the defendant has a "realistic" perception of the penalties, possibilities for defense, and outcome. The focus, therefore, is not merely on understanding of facts, but whether or not defendants have beliefs about how those matters apply to their own circumstances that are distorted by delusional or idiosyncratic beliefs. As such, the content of this section of the FIT-R seems to depart from the plain wording of Canada's Criminal Code definition, which says nothing specifically about distorted beliefs ("appreciation," or in *Dusky v. U.S.*, "rational understanding" as contrasted with "factual understanding"). Thus whether (and, if so, how) Section II is relevant for application to Canadian fitness hearings requires further explanation, although inclusion of this "appreciation" factor clearly increases the instrument's potential application to U.S. definitions of competence to stand trial.

Other significant differences in format between the FIT-R and the MacCAT-CA include the FIT-R's focus on the defendant's own circumstances (compared to the MacCAT-CA's reliance on questions about a hypothetical criminal case), as well as the FIT-R's far more diverse set of questions to explore the nature of defendants' abilities. In contrast, the

MacCAT-CA's more narrow and more highly standardized format allowed for the development of highly objective scoring criteria. These are sacrificed in the FIT-R, which uses more general opinion rating criteria, in favor of allowing the influence of clinical judgment that the MacCAT-CA's strict "correct" or "incorrect" scoring criteria do not allow. Neither of these approaches is necessarily better than the other, but each has its own advantages and limitations. For example, in principle, the MacCAT-CA's more highly standardized format offers greater potential for inter-examiner reliability, while the FIT-R provides greater opportunities for individualized deficits (and their explanations) to arise in the fitness interview.

Psychometric Development

STANDARDIZATION. Questions are asked in a standardized sequence, although probing of examinees' answers are at the examiner's discretion. Rating criteria for the various items are in the form of a paragraph description of the concept covered by each item, but without specific guides for 2, 1, or 0 ratings.

RELIABILITY. In the only study of interrater reliability of the FIT-R (f), 49 professionals (psychiatrists, psychologists, graduate students, and nurses) were provided training in the FIT-R, then asked to perform FIT-R ratings for defendants observed in two FIT-R videotaped interviews. Intraclass correlation coefficients were calculated separately for each profession and showed only occasional differences between professions. Averaged across professions, correlations for most items were in the .80 to .95 range, with a few in the .70s. Only one item fell below this average ("Appraisal of Likely Outcome," .67). Average correlations for the three Section ratings were not as good (I = .70, II = .54, III = .59), but the average correlation for the overall judgment of fitness was .98.

NORMS. The FIT-R manual provides no norms, and none have been published to date in other sources.

CRITIQUE. The lack of specific scoring criteria apparently decreases the degree of interrater reliability found on the MacCAT-CA for some items. Most are satisfactory, however. More troublesome are the relatively low agreements on the Section II and III summary ratings. It is also difficult to understand why the overall judgments of fitness with the FIT-R manifests such high agreement, when there is only modest agreement between raters on the sections that represent the major components examiners are supposed to take into account when making a final fitness rating. Further research might profitably seek an explanation for this anomaly.

Construct Validity

In a study in British Columbia involving 76 male forensic inpatients remanded for fitness evaluations, FIT-R scores were moderately (but significantly) related to scores on two other measures of "Competence to Confess" and "Competence to Plead Guilty" (g). Fitness/Unfitness on the FIT-R corresponded with competence/incompetence conclusions based on the competence to confess measure 85% of the time, and with competence/incompetence conclusions based on the competence to plead guilty measure 81% of the time.

Both the MacCAT-CA and the FIT-R were administered to 100 male forensic inpatients remanded for fitness evaluations (i). There was considerable overlap in results, in that 28% were found to be "impaired" on both instruments and 48% were found "unimpaired" on both instruments (76% agreement). But more patients were found impaired on the MacCAT-CA (48%) than on the FIT-R (32%). The report did not specifically describe how a conclusion of impairment on either instrument was defined. But by extrapolation from tables in the report, it appears that patients were considered impaired on the FIT-R if they were rated as impaired on any one of the three Sections of the FIT-R, and impaired on the MacCAT-CA if they fell below the impairment cut-off scores (as defined in the MacCAT-CA: see previous MacCAT-CA review) on any one of the three main sections of the MacCAT-CA. This same report indicated that almost all of the patients were either unimpaired on all three sections of the FIT-R or impaired on all three sections; only 9% were impaired "selectively" on some section(s) and not others. In contrast, on the MacCAT-CA, 35% of the patients were "selectively impaired" on some section(s) but not others.

CRITIQUE.   Theoretically, there should be some degree of consistency in findings across various measures of fitness or competence in the criminal process. The results of these studies suggest that the FIT-R produces findings that are consistent with this theoretical notion. However, the differences between the FIT-R and the MacCAT-CA in the comparative study could have been found for either of two reasons. First, the FIT-R uses examiners' judgments to make ratings of abilities, while the MacCAT-CA uses more highly structured scoring criteria. A tendency for greater similarity in a defendant's ratings across the three sections of the FIT-R might arise if raters form general impressions of a defendant's fitness that then influence their judgments in their ratings for the three sections. Second, it is possible that the three sections of the FIT-R simply measure abilities that are less distinct from each other than are the sections of the MacCAT-CA. Factor analysis of the FIT-R might help to address the likelihood of this second interpretation.

Predictive of Classificatory Utility

Although two reports have compared the FIT-R to clinicians' independent judgments about patients' fitness, the earlier of these reports (h) used a sample that appears to have been incorporated later into a larger sample in the second report (j). Therefore, only the results of the second report are described here.

Two samples were included, obtained from the same Canadian forensic inpatient facility where men were remanded for fitness evaluations (during two different years). The first included 250 inpatients, and the second included 100 who were diagnosed with psychotic disorders. The FIT-R and the Structured Clinical Interview for DSM-III-R—Patient Edition (SCID-P) were administered to the first sample, while the FIT-R and the BPRS were administered to the second. Fitness evaluations and opinions on these patients were also obtained from forensic examiners at the facilities who had no knowledge of the results of the above measures. The independent examiners reached unfitness conclusions for only 4% of the first sample and 10% of the second sample, while the FIT-R produced unfitness conclusions for 13% of the first sample and 32% of the second sample. For both samples, only 2% of patients were identified as fit by the FIT-R and unfit by the institution's examiners.

CRITIQUE. The authors of the FIT-R have pointed out that while the instrument can serve as part of a broader fitness evaluation, it may also be used as a screening tool. As with all screening instruments, it would be expected to identify more patients as impaired—as it did in this study— than might be found unfit in comprehensive evaluations. This same result could be found, however, if the FIT-R is more sensitive to the full range of abilities associated with the legal construct of fitness than are forensic clinicians. In other words, there is no guarantee regarding the integrity or superiority of the standard to which the FIT-R was being compared.

Potential for Expressing Person-Situation Congruency

The FIT-R manual does not offer specific instructions to consider the degree of the defendant's abilities in relation to the demands of the defendant's specific legal situation. However, the flexibility of the rating system would allow for such judgments to be made, given that the examiner has some knowledge of the defendant's trial circumstances.

References

(a) Bagby, R., Nicholson, R., Rogers, R., & Nussbaum, D. (1992). Domains of competence to stand trial: A factor analytic study. *Law and Human Behavior, 16*, 491–506.

(b) McDonald, D., Nussbaum, D., & Bagby, R. (1991). Reliability, validity and utility of the Fitness Interview Test. *Canadian Journal of Psychiatry, 36*, 480–484.

(c) Roesch, R., Jackson, M., Sollner, R., Eaves, D., Glackman, W., & Webster, C. (1984). The Fitness to Stand Trial Interview Test: How four professions rate videotaped fitness interviews. *International Journal of Law and Psychiatry, 7*, 115–131.

(d) Roesch, R., Webster, C., & Eaves, D. (1984). *The Fitness Interview Test: A method for examining fitness to stand trial.* Toronto, Ontario, Canada: Research Report of the Centre of Criminology, University of Toronto.

(e) Roesch, R., Zapf, P., Eaves, D., & Webster, C. (1998). *Fitness Interview Test (Revised Edition).* Burnaby, British Columbia, Canada: Mental Health, Law and Policy Institute, Simon Fraser University.

(f) Viljoen, J., Roesch, R., & Zapf, P. (in preparation). *Interrater reliability of the Fitness Interview Test across four professional groups.* Burnaby, British Columbia, Canada: Simon Fraser University.

(g) Whittemore, K., Ogloff, J., & Roesch, R. (1997). An investigation of competence to participate in legal proceedings in Canada. *Canadian Journal of Psychiatry, 42*, 869–875.

(h) Zapf, P., & Roesch, R. (1997). Assessing fitness to stand trial: A comparison of institution-based evaluations and a brief screening interview. *Canadian Journal of Community Mental Health, 16*, 53–66.

(i) Zapf, P., & Roesch, R. (2001). A comparison of the MacCAT-CA and the FIT for making determinations of competence to stand trial. *International Journal of Law and Psychiatry, 24*, 81–92.

(j) Zapf, P., Roesch, R., & Viljoen, J. (2001). Assessing fitness to stand trial: The utility of the Fitness Interview Test (Revised Version). *Canadian Journal of Psychiatry, 46*, 426–432.

COMPETENCE ASSESSMENT FOR STANDING TRIAL FOR DEFENDANTS WITH MENTAL RETARDATION (CAST-MR)

Authors

Everington, C., & Luckasson, R.

Primary Author Affiliation

Department of Psychology, Miami University (Ohio).

Primary Reference

Everington, C., & Luckasson, R. (1992). *Competence Assessment for Standing Trial for Defendants with Mental Retardation: Test manual.* Worthington, OH: IDS Publishing Corp.

Description

The *Competence Assessment for Standing Trial for Defendants with Mental Retardation* (the CAST-MR) (c) was developed to respond to needs that were considered unique for defendants with mental retardation. The instrument forms the basis of a structured interview. It consists of 50 questions organized in three sections:

- I: Basic Legal Concepts
- II: Skills to Assist Defense
- III: Understanding Case Events

Section I includes 25 questions that focus on assessing defendants' "knowledge of the criminal justice process" (c, p. 3). In general these questions use the words "What is ____" or "What does _____ mean" or "What does it mean to _____," and they focus on the following:

- The roles of several of the persons in trials
- The meanings of words and concepts (hearing, sentence, maximum/ minimum sentence, crime, guilty, innocent, acquitted, felony, misdemeanor, plead guilty, penitentiary, time served, probation, plea bargain, fine)
- The meanings of certain functions (What happens when you go to court, in a trial, when a prosecutor asks you questions, when you go to a penitentiary)

Section II consists of 15 questions addressing defendants' "understanding of the client-attorney relationship" (c, p. 3). The items are questions that pose circumstances ("What if ___" or "Let's pretend ___") to which the defendant is asked to respond with an appropriate answer: for example, "What if your lawyer asks you to do something you don't want to do like getting a haircut? What would you do?" "Let's pretend that you took something from the store and you got arrested for it. You didn't mean to do it, and you felt really bad about it. When your lawyer asks you if you did it, what would you do?" Some of the questions focus on attorney-client interactions, some on events outside the courtroom (e.g., talking to other detainees about one's situation), and many focus on potential responses to events in the courtroom (including witnessing events or testifying at one's own trial).

Each of the questions in Sections I and II has three multiple choice response options. For each question, the defendant is asked to listen to all three optional answers, then select "the one that is right." In contrast, Section III consists of 10 open-ended, very brief questions focusing on defendants' ability to "discuss the facts concerning the incident in a coherent manner and to understand the relationship between the alleged facts in the case and the subsequent arrest and charges" (c, p. 3). The questions are more or less chronological in orientation, beginning with "What were you doing that caused you to be arrested," continuing through questions focusing on where and when the events occurred, what happened when the police arrived, and the charges that were filed.

Administration instructions include practice questions to give examinees prior to each section, in order to orient examinees to the task and to determine whether they can manage the response format. The manual provides instructions for how to manage cases in which examinees have difficulty grasping the nature of the task. The materials include an Examiner Form that has the questions, response options, and indicators for the correct answers, as well as a Subject Form that is given to the examinee during the evaluation. The Subject Form provides the questions and the multiple choice options visually (without correct answers indicated) while the examiner reads the same material aloud to the examinee, to which the examinee responds verbally. Questions may be read to examinees up to three times for Sections I and II, and up to two times in Section III, and certain allowable non-leading prompts are described in the manual.

Scoring of responses in Sections I and II simply requires assigning 1 point for each correct answer. Thus subscores range from 0 to 25 on Section I and 0 to 15 on Section II. Responses to Section III questions are scored according to a more detailed set of scoring criteria provided in the manual. Each Section III item may receive 0, .5, or 1 credit, allowing for a subscale III range of 0 to 10. Total scores may be calculated (the sum of points on all 50 items), ranging from 0 to 50.

Conceptual Basis

CONCEPT DEFINITION. The manual indicates that the areas of knowledge and ability related to the three sections were chosen in light of case law and psychological literature on competence to stand trial (c), but further detail is not provided.

OPERATIONAL DEFINITION. Decisions about operationalizing the three concepts were based substantially on the authors' intentions to construct a competence to stand trial instrument that would be especially suitable for administration to persons with mental retardation. A multiple-choice format, for example, was considered superior to an open-ended format because it was expected to place less of a demand on the respondent to answer independently. In addition, vocabulary and syntax were kept to the simplest possible level so that persons with mental retardation would not be unfairly penalized because of their lower level of linguistic ability.

To refine the format and content of the instrument, the authors asked 10 experts on criminal disability law to rate various parts of the CAST-MR for legal appropriateness of content, format with reference to the abilities of persons with mental retardation, and usability (e.g., clarity) (a). In general, ratings on the various features of the instrument were primarily "good" or "excellent," although some respondents felt that the format might be too difficult for persons with mental retardation. Readability analyses placed the reading level of the text at about grade 2 to grade 6.

CRITIQUE.   The types of abilities that directed the content development of the CAST-MR are much like those of other instruments for use in competence to stand trial evaluations. Like most such instruments, it was not developed to assess all relevant abilities. But the variety of the questions, especially in Section II (how defendants would respond to hypothetical situations from arrest to sentencing), is somewhat greater than in other instruments of its type.

The notion to develop an instrument specifically for defendants with mental retardation is novel and raises two general points. First, the logic for using a multiple choice format seems clear. Persons with mental retardation often have language deficits, making it difficult for them to express answers in open-ended response formats despite the fact that they might actually comprehend the information or concept for which they are being tested. A multiple choice format removes the necessity for constructing one's answers. This is not to say that the multiple choice format, however, makes for an easier response format. Choosing from among three answers, after they are presented to the individual verbally, requires auditory reception and retention, as well as a subsequent review and comparison of the three options, in the process of selecting the correct answer. This process itself is relatively more difficult for persons with mental retardation than for persons of average cognitive and functional capacity.

Second, given that the multiple choice format is successful in removing the effect of expressive deficits when assessing defendants' knowledge and functional responses to trial circumstances, one must recognize that this response format is a bit further removed from the types of functioning that are actually needed during trial participation. During the pretrial and trial process, defendants frequently will not be offered alternative interpretations of what is happening to them. In addition, they may sometimes be required to employ those same receptive and expressive abilities that the format of the CAST-MR was designed to avoid.

This being said, the logic of the multiple choice format is sound in theory, in that it is likely to help avoid penalizing persons with mental retardation who may grasp the nature of the trial and its participants yet have difficulty expressing what they know. Moreover, Section III does provide the examiner the opportunity to test whether the defendant has the expressive capacities necessary to communicate essential facts and defendant opinions to counsel in construction of a defense.

Psychometric Development

STANDARDIZATION. Administration of the CAST-MR is described very clearly, including the invariant sequence of the items and the allowable probes (c). Scoring is absolute on Sections I and II, requiring no examiner judgment. The scoring criteria for Section III (involving open-ended responses that require scoring judgments on the part of the examiner) are clearly defined in the manual, which, for each Section III item, offers general and specific criteria as well as scoring examples for 0, .5, and 1 point responses.

RELIABILITY. Interscorer agreement for Section III items (Section I and II provide scores requiring no examiner judgment) was examined in two studies. In one (a), observations between pairs of scorers on 10 cases manifested 80% agreement on individual items and 88% agreement on total Section III score. Another study (b) compared 11 scorers (who had obtained half-day training) to the CAST-MR authors' scores on at least three cases per scorer. Mean level of agreement was reported as 87%. Concerning test-retest reliability, a Pearson correlation of .90 was found between two administrations of the CAST-MR (two week interval) for 23 persons in group homes for persons with mental retardation (a).

NORMS. The manual (c) provides means and standard deviations for groups of individuals with and without mental retardation, as described later in "Construct Validation."

CRITIQUE. Standardization of the CAST-MR is quite good, allowing for adequate interscorer reliability and reasonable confidence in the ability of different examiners to produce similar results with a given examinee. Normative data currently are based on relatively small samples (see "Construct Validation").

Construct Validation

Concerning internal consistency, two studies involving persons with and without mental retardation reported Cronbach's alpha (a) and Kuder-Richardson coefficients (b) for the various sections of the CAST-MR. These were reported as follows: .93 and .92 for Section I; .76 and .73 for Section II; and .83 and .84 for Section III.

In one study (b), IQ was correlated substantially with scores on CAST-MR Sections I (.64), II (.54) and III (.59), and with total CAST-MR scores (.66). Correlations with other defendant characteristics have not been reported.

The first validation study (a) for the CAST-MR compared four groups of defendants who were expected to manifest progressively lower CAST-MR scores:

- A: defendants with no mental retardation ($n = 46$),
- B: defendants with mental retardation but not referred for competence evaluations ($n = 24$),
- C: defendants with mental retardation who were referred and found competent ($n = 12$), and
- D: defendants with mental retardation who were referred and found incompetent ($n = 11$).

A significant group effect was found for all 3 Section subscores and the total CAST-MR scored. The mean for Group D (mental retardation and found incompetent) was significantly different from those of all other groups on all four of the comparisons, and Group A's means (no mental retardation) were significantly different from those of Groups B and C except for Section III scores (A was not significantly different from B).

The second CAST-MR validation study (b) compared CAST-MR means for defendants with mental retardation whom clinicians recommended as competent ($n = 15$) and incompetent ($n = 20$). Clinicians making the competence judgments were specialized forensic examiners who did not have knowledge of the CAST-MR scores. Statistically significant differences were found between the two groups, with the "incompetent" group having lower mean scores for each of the sections of the CAST-MR and for total CAST-MR score. Seven items (3 from Section I and 3 from Section III) manifested significant differences between the two groups at or above $p < .01$.

CRITIQUE. The sample sizes of the validation studies are somewhat small. But within those limits, internal consistency appears to be satisfactory, and CAST-MR scores appear to be related to intellectual functioning (and mental retardation status) in a manner that would be expected based on theoretical inference. An examination of the absolute differences in mean scores, however, indicates that mean differences between competent and incompetent groups were not substantial, and it is interesting that only 7 of the 50 items appeared to contribute to the mean differences on the subscales. The stability of those findings is worth determining in future research.

Predictive or Classificatory Utility

In the first validation study (a), a discriminant function analysis correctly classified 9 of the 16 defendants judged competent by independent examiners and 7 of the 11 defendants judged incompetent. In the second validation study (b), better agreement between cut-off scores and independent examiner judgments were produced by Section I and Section II scores than by Section II or total CAST-MR scores. On Sections I and II, scores above 13 on Section I, and scores above 9 on Section II, produced 71% agreement. The pattern for both of these sections indicated that the CAST-MR was able to correctly classify about two-thirds of defendants judged competent and two-thirds of the defendants judged incompetent.

CRITIQUE. These results may not appear encouraging. On the other hand, they are similar to results found with other competence to stand trial screening instruments (reported elsewhere in this chapter). Moreover, the authors (b) correctly note that clinicians' judgments about competence among persons with mental retardation are probably less reliable than for defendants with mental illnesses. Thus one does not know whether the less-than-satisfying results of the CAST-MR's classification validity is due to error in the instrument or error in the criterion to which it was being compared.

Future research might examine the relation of the CAST-MR to competent and incompetent groups of persons with mental retardation in interaction with other variables. For example, persons with mental retardation might differ in capacities relevant for defendant participation as a function of age and legal experience. Perhaps the CAST-MR might play a more effective role in discriminating between competent and incompetent defendants when variance related to these other variables is controlled.

Potential for Expressing Person-Situation Congruency

The CAST-MR offers no quantitative method for comparing specific types of deficits of defendants in relation to the specific demands posed by their own trial circumstances. However, one of the interesting features of the CAST-MR is its range of content and its potential for qualitative interpretation. For example, Section II uses items that focus on a number of specific circumstances that are more or less likely to arise depending on the nature of the defendant's case, such as being questioned by the prosecutor or having to testify in a manner consistent with previous counsel between attorney and client. Defendants' responses to those items may be of greater importance in cases where defendant testimony is especially likely to be needed, offering information for interactive interpretation apart from CAST-MR scores.

References

(a) Everington, C. (1990). The Competence Assessment for Standing Trial for Defendants with Mental Retardation (CAST-MR): A validation study. *Criminal Justice and Behavior, 17*, 147–168.
(b) Everington, C., & Dunn, C. (1995). A second validation study of the Competence Assessment for Standing Trial for Defendants with Mental Retardation (CAST-MR). *Criminal Justice and Behavior, 22,* 44–59.
(c) Everington, C., & Luckasson, R. (1992). *Competence Assessment for Standing Trial for Defendants with Mental Retardation (CAST*MR): Test manual.* Worthington, OH: IDS Publishing Corporation.

GEORGIA COURT COMPETENCE TEST—MISSISSIPPI STATE HOSPITAL (GCCT-MSH)

Authors

Wildman, R., Batchelor, E., Thompson, L., Nelson, F., Moore, J., Patterson, M., & deLaosa, M.

Primary Author Affiliation

Central State Hospital, Milledgeville, GA

Primary Reference

For the original GCCT: Wildman et al. (1978). *The Georgia Court Competence Test: An attempt to develop a rapid, quantitative measure of fitness for trial.* Unpublished manuscript: Forensic Services Division, Central State Hospital, Milledgeville, GA.

For the GCCT-MSH: Nicholson, R., Briggs, S., & Robertson, H. (1988). Instruments for assessing competence to stand trial: How do they work? *Professional Psychology: Research and Practice, 19*, 383–394. (GCCT-MSH published as an Appendix to the article.)

Description

The *Georgia Court Competence Test-Mississippi State Hospital* (GCCT-MSH) (b) is a revision of the original *Georgia Court Competence Test* (GCCT) by Wildman et al. (h). The original GCCT was intended to provide "a rapid, quantitative measure of the knowledge and skills necessary for competence for trial" (h, p. 2). It was developed at the Forensic Services Division of Central State Hospital in Millidgeville, Georgia and first described in 1978 (h). According to Wildman (personal communication), the GCCT was not developed with the intention of widespread dissemination and use; it evolved from experience and local need, rather than from a research project. Nevertheless, it came into use by other mental health professionals, primarily in southern states. At least two revisions of the GCCT evolved in the 1980s, one of them by psychologists at Mississippi State Hospital. That revision, the GCCT-MSH, has been most often cited in subsequent research and practice. This review examines only studies performed with the GCCT-MSH, not the GCCT.

The original GCCT consists of 17 questions that are asked of the examinee in the context of a pretrial competence assessment by the examiner, usually requiring about 10 minutes for its administration. The questions are grouped in the following six categories and sequence:

1. *Picture of Court*: Seven questions focus on the examinee's description of the location of participants in a courtroom (e.g., "Where does the Judge sit?" "Where will the witness sit to testify?"). The questions are accompanied by a drawing of a courtroom that does not contain depictions of participants themselves. The examinee points to the area of the drawing to signify answers to the questions.
2. *Functions*: Five questions inquire about the functions of the Judge, jury, defendant's lawyer, prosecutor, and witnesses (e.g., "What does the jury do?").
3. *Charge*: Two questions, 'What are you charged with?" and "What does that mean?"
4. *Helping* the *lawyer*: One question asks how the examinee plans to help the examinee's lawyer in a defense.
5. *Alleged crime*: One question asks the examinee to describe "what actually happened about the charge you are here on?"
6. *Consequences*: One question asks what the examinee expects will be done to him/her if a guilty verdict is returned.

The GCCT-MSH differs from the GCCT in only two ways. First, 4 new questions were added in order to provide additional information about defendants' knowledge of courtroom procedures and ability to assist counsel. Specifically, 2 questions were added to #2 above, asking what is done by people watching the trial, and what "you will do during the trial." Two other questions were added to #4 above ("What is your attorney's name?" and "How can you contact him/her?"). Second, some of the maximum possible scores for each item were changed, and scoring criteria for questions about charges and possible penalties were redefined for improved clarity.

The maximum points possible vary from item to item, with the total possible being 50. Brief scoring criteria are provided for each question that does not have an obvious correct or incorrect answer. Points are multiplied by 2 to obtain a total score between 0 to 100. The original GCCT used 69 or below to suggest possible incompetence, and the GCCT-MSH has retained this cut-off (b).

Conceptual Basis

CONCEPT DEFINITION. The authors' examination of competence to stand trial standards, and the opinions of forensic experts in several states, led them to the following conceptual definitions for abilities related to legal competence to stand trial: knowledge of the charge; knowledge of the possible penalties; some understanding of courtroom procedure; and the ability to communicate rationally with an attorney in the preparation of a defense.

OPERATIONAL DEFINITION. Test items were developed logically to relate to the four conceptual definitions. Scoring decisions allowed some items to contribute a greater proportion to the total score than others, based on the authors' perceptions of the relative importance of each ability when one assumes the presence of a competent and helpful attorney (h).

CRITIQUE. The logical derivation of the concepts to be measured has not been described fully by the authors. The concepts themselves, however, seem to grasp some minimum of abilities relevant to pretrial competence.

Differences of opinion might arise concerning the criteria for adequacy or inadequacy of certain examinee responses. On the item, "What do witnesses do?" for example, some test users might disagree that the response, "Answers questions about the case," demonstrates adequate understanding of the witness function, although this receives full credit by the test's scoring criteria.

The choice of a picture stimulus (courtroom) for one set of items is unique among competence to stand trial instruments. The authors did not explain the reasoning for this choice; one possible rationale for a picture stimulus is the structure it provides early on in the test process, as well as establishing a concrete visual image that can facilitate exploration of the examinee's overall knowledge of the trial process.

Psychometric Development

STANDARDIZATION.   Specific questions are asked in a given sequence. Scoring criteria (right and wrong answers) are briefly characterized, with example responses offered for some items.

RELIABILITY.   Two studies have examined inter-rater reliability. One reported an intraclass correlation of .95 between two trained raters (c) and the other .82 (e). No test–retest reliability figures have been published for the MSH version. Test–retest reliability for the original GCCT was reported as .79 when the instrument was first developed (h). But it is uncertain whether this can be generalized to the GCCT-MSH, due to some changes in its scoring criteria.

NORMS.   No norms as such have been published. But mean GCCT-MSH scores for a group of defendants in a competence restoration program were 81.8 ($SD = 8.8$) for defendants considered restored and 43.2 ($SD = 18.4$) for defendants continuing to be seen as incompetent (g). Another study involving defendants referred for CST evaluations reported mean scores of 81.2 ($SD = 18.3$) for defendants considered competent and 51.3 ($SD = 24.8$) for those considered incompetent (d).

CRITIQUE.   Overall the GCCT-MSH appears to have adequate inter-rater reliability and internal consistency. It should be noted that the study (e) reporting lower alpha coefficients also reported lower inter-rater reliability, and the latter would typically result in lower alpha coefficients. Alternatively, the lower alpha for that study might be due to sample differences, over half of the subjects having not been drawn from the CST evaluation or restoration processes that characterized samples in the comparison studies.

Construct Validity

Internal consistency was demonstrated by alpha coefficients of .88 and .89 in two studies involving defendants in the CST evaluation or restoration process (b, g). But a marginal alpha of .70 was found in a study for which half of the subjects were mentally ill offenders not involved in the CST process (e). An average item-to-total score correlation has been reported as ranging from .47 to .67 (b), and inter-item correlations have averaged .28 (g) and .36 (b).

Two factor analyses of the GCCT-MSH, with defendants referred for CST evaluations, independently arrived at three-factor solutions with factors representing (I) most of the courtroom location items, (II) items involving the functions of participants, and (III) items involving the circumstances of one's own trial, charges and penalties (a, b). Two other factor analyses with different types of samples, however, claimed that a two-factor solution better fit the data (f, g). One of these studies found that the two-factor solution outperformed the aforementioned three-factor solution in a confirmatory factor analysis applied to a sample of defendants in a CST restoration program (f).

The GCCT-MSH was identified in one study (of defendants referred for CST evaluations) as correlating significantly (negatively) with mental retardation and with race (being non-white) but not with psychosis, and positively with years of education (b). In a sample of persons involved in CST restoration, multiple analysis of variance found no relation between GCCT-MSH competent and incompetent patients on any of the diagnoses provided by the SCL-90-R (g). In the same study, however, low IQ, psychotic disorder, and non-psychotic affective disorder did account for significant portions of the variance in GCCT-MSH competent and incompetent classifications.

Finally, the relation of the GCCT-MSH to the Competence Screening Test (CST) (see review in this chapter) was examined in two studies. One found a correlation of .76 between continuous scores on the two measures (b), while the other found a correlation of .47. In the latter study, the two instruments agreed on competence and incompetence classification (using their recommended cut-off scores) in only 63% of 85 cases.

CRITIQUE.   The results of the factor analyses of the GCCT-MSH are very difficult to interpret. This is in part due to reporting problems; for example, one study (g) attempted to compare its factor analysis to that of Nicholson et al. (b), but the factor loadings from Nicholson et al. that were "reproduced" in the report were not the same as those shown in the Nicholson et al. article itself. Difficulty in interpreting the results is also due to differences in samples. The two studies involving defendants referred for CST evaluations are in agreement on a three-factor structure, while the two studies using other types of samples (Ustad et al.'s restoration patients, and Rogers et al.'s mentally ill offenders with no referral for CST) claim the superiority of a different solution. For examiners concerned about the use of the GCCT-MSH with defendants referred for CST evaluations, it is reasonable to give greater weight to the results of the two studies that employed samples drawn from that population.

Similarly, the GCCT-MSH correlated substantially with another competence instrument (the CST) in a study involving defendants referred for competence evaluations, but not in a study involving patients who had all been found incompetent at one time and were now in various stages of restoration. These conflicting results either render the issue equivocal, or one accepts the results as population-specific. At any rate, if GCCT-MSH scores correspond only very imperfectly to classifications provided by the CST instrument, this does not argue against the concurrent validity of the GCCT-MSH, since the validity and utility of the CST itself has been questioned independent of these results (see review of the CST instrument in this chapter).

Predictive or Classificatory Utility

In one study (resulting in two journal reports), the GCCT-MSH cut-off score produced classifications of 140 defendants that correlated .44 with independent forensic professional staff decisions about competence and incompetence (b), identifying as incompetent 10 out of 14 persons (71%) who were classified incompetent by staff (b). The GCCT-MSH over-identified incompetence, however, so that the instrument was "right" only 3 in 10 times when it classified defendants as incompetent.

In a meta-analytic study, Nicholson and Kugler (c) reported that GCCT scores correlated on average .42 with independent clinical judgments of competence, based on results of four reports: the two identified above (which actually reported a single study), as well as the original Wildman et al. study of the GCCT and an unpublished study.

CRITIQUE. The correspondence of the GCCT-MSH to clinical judgments about competence is relatively uncertain, in that there has been only one study examining the present MSH version of the GCCT. That result suggests that the GCCT-MSH over-predicts incompetence, a result that is not of particularly great consequence in that the instrument is intended as a screening tool, resulting simply in further evaluation for examinees scoring below the cut-off score. One can tolerate a significant number of false positives under those circumstances.

Potentially more troubling is the fact that the study suggested a sensitivity rate of only 71%. This would mean that if the instrument were used to determine who would receive more comprehensive evaluations, it would fail to "screen in" more than one-quarter of the incompetent defendants in the population (who, hypothetically, would proceed to trial because their potential for incompetence had failed to be identified). Concern about this figure is mitigated, however, by two things. First, the baserate of incompetence was very low in this study sample, thus making the predictive task very difficult for any instrument. Second, there is no reason to believe that the professional judgments about incompetence, the criterion to which the GCCT-MSH was being compared, were themselves reliably made or were valid as indicators of defendants' actual capacities.

Potential for Expressing Person-Situation Congruency

The GCCT-MSH includes no assessment of the trial situation facing the examinee, and the primary reference does not mention examination of responses in light of the specific demands and circumstances of the examinee's future legal situation.

References

(a) Bagby, R., Nicholson, R., Rogers, R., & Nussbaum, D. (1992). Domains of competence to stand trial: A factor analytic study. *Law and Human Behavior, 16*, 491–507.

(b) Nicholson, R., Briggs, S., & Robertson, H. (1988). Instruments for assessing competence to stand trial: How do they work? *Professional Psychology: Research and Practice, 19*, 383–394.

(c) Nicholson, R., & Kugler, K. (1991). Competent and incompetent criminal defendants: A quantitative review of comparative research. *Psychological Bulletin, 109*, 355–370.

(d) Nicholson, R., Robertson, H., Johnson, & Jensen, G. (1988). A comparison of instruments for assessing competence to stand trial. *Law and Human Behavior, 12*, 313–321.

(e) Rogers, R., Grandjean, N., Tillbrook, C., Vitacco, M., & Sewell, K. (2001). Recent interview-based measures of competence to stand trial: A critical review augmented with research data. *Behavioral Sciences and the Law, 19*, 503–518.

(f) Rogers, R., Ustad, K., Sewell, K., & Reinhardt, V. (1996). Dimensions of incompetence: A factor analytic study of the Georgia Court Competence Test. *Behavioral Sciences and the Law, 14*, 323–330.

(g) Ustad, I., Rogers, R., Sewell, K., & Guarnaccia, C. (1996). Restoration of competence to stand trial: Assessment with the Georgia Court Competence Test and the Competence Screening Test. *Law and Human Behavior, 20*, 131–146.

(h) Wildman, R., Batchelor, E., Thompson, L., Nelson, F., Moore, J., Patterson, M., & deLaosa, M. (1980). *The Georgia Court Competence Test: An attempt to develop a rapid, quantitative measure for fitness for trial.* Unpublished manuscript, Forensic Services Division, Central State Hospital, Milledgeville, GA.

COMPETENCE TO STAND TRIAL ASSESSMENT INSTRUMENT (CAI)

Authors

McGarry, A.L. and Associates, Laboratory of Community Psychiatry, Harvard Medical School

Primary Author Affiliation

Harvard Medical School

Primary Reference

Laboratory of Community Psychiatry, Harvard Medical School (1973). *Competence to stand trial and mental illness.* Rockville, MD: NIMH, Department of Health, Education, and Welfare. DHEW Publication No. (ADM) 77-103.

NOTE ON SECOND EDITION REVIEW.   Since 1986, only one research article
has published results using the CAI. Thus the present review offers little
more than did the first edition with regard to empirical support for the
instrument. The review is included here primarily for its historical value,
because the CAI influenced the development of almost all other instruments for competence to stand trial evaluations. The DHEW monograph
that constituted the CAI manual is no longer available from NIMH,
although it is still found in some university libraries.

Description

The *Competence to Stand Trial Assessment Instrument* (CAI) was developed to deliver clinical opinion to the court in language, form, and substance sufficiently common to the disciplines involved to provide a basis
for adequate and relevant communication. The purpose of the instrument
was to standardize, objectify, and quantify, the relevant criteria for competence to stand trial (d, p. 99). An interdisciplinary team of psychiatrists,
psychologists, and lawyers developed the instrument at Harvard's
Laboratory of Community Psychiatry during a project funded by a
research grant from the Center for Studies of Crime and Delinquency,
NIMH. It was intended as a companion instrument for the *Competence
Screening Test* (described later in this chapter).

The CAI describes 13 functions related to a defendant's "ability to
cope with the trial process in an adequately self-protective fashion" (d,
p. 99). These functions are examined in an interview procedure that
employs the 13 functions as items, with two or three recommended interview questions for each item. The following are brief descriptions of the
functions and their content, as well as a sample question for each of them
(worded as in d, pp. 101–114):

1. *Appraisal of available legal defenses*: the accused's awareness of his
   possible legal defenses and how consistent these are with the reality of his particular circumstances ("How do you think you can be
   defended against these charges?").
2. *Unmanageable behavior*: the appropriateness of the current motor
   and verbal behavior of the defendant and the degree to which this
   behavior would disrupt the conduct of a trial ("What do you think
   would happen if you spoke out or moved around in the courtroom
   without permission?").
3. *Quality of relating to attorney*: interpersonal capacity of the accused
   to relate to the average attorney ("Do you have confidence in your
   lawyer?").

4. *Planning of legal strategy including guilty pleas to lesser charges where pertinent*: degree to which the accused can understand, participate, and cooperate with his counsel in planning a strategy for the defense that is consistent with the reality of his circumstances ("Is there anything that you disagree with in the way your lawyer is going to handle your case, and if so, what do you plan to do about it?").

5. *Appraisal of role of*: (a) defense counsel, (b) prosecuting attorney, (c) judge, (d) jury, (e) defendant, (f) witnesses ("In the courtroom, during a trial, what is the job of ...").

6. *Understanding of court procedure*: degree to which the defendant understands the basic sequence of events in a trial and their import for him ("After your lawyer is finished asking you questions on the stand, who then can ask you questions?").

7. *Appreciation of charges*: the accused's understanding of the charges against him and, to a lesser extent, the seriousness of the charges ("Do you think people in general would regard you with some fear on the basis of such a charge?").

8. *Appreciation of range and nature of possible penalties*: the accused's concrete understanding and appreciation of the conditions and restrictions which could be imposed on him and their possible duration ("If you're found guilty as charged what are the possible sentences the judge could give you?").

9. *Appraisal of likely outcome*: how realistically the accused perceives the likely outcome and the degree to which impaired understanding contributes to a less adequate or inadequate participation in his defense ("How strong a case do they have against you?").

10. *Capacity to disclose to attorney available pertinent facts surrounding the offense*: the accused's capacity to give a basically consistent, rational, and relevant account of the motivational and external facts ("Tell us what actually happened, what you saw and did and heard and thought before, during, and after you are supposed to have committed this offense").

11. *Capacity to realistically challenge prosecution witnesses*: the accused's capacity to recognize distortions in prosecution testimony ("Suppose a witness against you told a lie in the courtroom. What would you do?").

12. *Capacity to testify relevantly*: the accused's ability to testify with coherence, relevance, and independence of judgment (no example questions are provided in the primary reference).

13. *Self-defeating versus self-serving motivation (legal sense)*: the accused's motivation to adequately protect himself and appropriately

utilize legal safeguards to this end ("Suppose the District Attorney made some legal errors and your lawyer wants to appeal a guilty finding in your case-would you accept that?").

The interview is structured by the 13 functions and recommended questions. Instructions, however, urge clinicians to conduct the interview with appropriate clinical flexibility rather than as a recitation of questions. The authors suggest that examination and scoring with a defendant who is in relatively good contact with reality will require no more than one hour.

Each item is given a rating by the examiner, ranging from 1 (total lack of capacity to function) to 5 (no impairment, no question that defendant can function adequately), or 6 if the available data permit no rating within reasonable clinical certainty. Each rating pertains to the degree of impairment or functioning on that item (function) only; a rating of 1 on any single item does not necessarily constitute a clinical decision about overall incapacity to function in a trial setting. Rating proceeds on the assumption that the defendant will be adequately assisted by counsel, and that the professional who has administered the assessment interview has a basic understanding of realities of the criminal justice system. No specific rating criteria are provided, but clinical case examples are given for certain ratings on each of the 13 functions/items.

The 13 scores are neither summed nor weighted. They are left to stand individually for use in forming testimony when combined with information from other sources. The authors note that the CAI is not intended to predict a defendant's performance in a future trial, because "with the passage of time and variations in clinical status, even from day to day, a given defendant will vary in the scores attained" (d, p. 100).

Conceptual Basis

CONCEPT DEFINITION.   During the first year of a four-year project, the interdisciplinary team (including lawyers, psychiatrists, and psychologists) performed reviews of appellate cases and legal literature, observed pretrial competence hearings, and interviewed attorneys and judges. This allowed them to arrive at a three-part definition of the competence to stand trial standard: an ability to cooperate with one's attorney in one's own defense; an awareness and understanding of the nature and object of the proceedings; and an understanding of the consequences of the proceedings.

The functions (items) and their definitions were derived logically from the same review and observation process. Early versions of the CAI used 15 functions, but 2 were eliminated because they seemed duplicative of other functions.

OPERATIONAL DEFINITION. The recommended interview questions for eliciting defendant information relevant for the 13 functions were devised and refined in a process involving administration of early drafts of the instrument to nonhospitalized defendants preparing for trial and committed patients at Bridgewater State Hospital (Massachusetts). Further refinement occurred with administration of the CAI, at a later stage of its development, to Bridgewater examinees who had been committed to determine their competence to stand trial. Case examples to assist interviewers in assigning ratings on each function were drawn from experiences with the latter group of defendants.

CRITIQUE. The method for arriving at the 13 functions of the CAI offers no empirical assurance that the instrument covers the range of potentially relevant functions associated with pretrial competence. Nevertheless, the listing seems relatively complete in its coverage on a rational basis, and each of the functions focuses the examiner on elements that seem to have considerable content relevance for the issues in competence to stand trial determinations.

Controversy arose very soon after the publication of the CAI regarding the definitions of certain functions and their case examples. Brakel (a) argued that the rating criteria for certain functions contained presumptions and prejudices that would penalize some defendants unfairly. For example, Brakel noted that one of the case examples under "Quality of Relating to Attorney" was of a black defendant who was rated a 4 ("mild degree of incapacity") because he said that he did not yet know whether he had confidence in his public defender, but that he did not think the attorney was very interested in his case. Other functions (e.g., "Appraisal of Available Legal Defenses") require examiners to use their own presumptions concerning when legal strategies such as plea bargaining generally are realistic or desirable. Brakel's argument, then, charged the CAI with bias of two types: bias against persons who, for political or personal reasons, simply do not have confidence in the criminal trial process; or bias due to examiner assumptions about the general nature of trial circumstances and attorney performances, to which a defendant's response about specific attorneys or trial circumstances may be compared unfairly.

In defense of the CAI against these charges, its authors clearly specified their intention to evaluate defendants' perceptions of attorneys, judges, and trial processes under the assumption that the defendant will be represented by competent counsel and tried by a legal standard of fairness. As long as this is made clear to the court during testimony, there would seem to be no need for concern about the presumptiveness of the examiner because the court may weigh the matter based on its better knowledge of the quality of counsel in the immediate case. In addition, in evaluating the defendant's perceptions of legal defenses, the examples provided in the CAI manual indicate that the examiner should pay special attention to the logical process employed by the defendant, more than the defendant's final choice of defense strategy.

It is unfortunate that the CAI was not developed with more specific guidelines concerning what questions to ask and which aspects of examinees' responses are critical for ratings. For example, the function "Planning for Legal Strategy" focuses the examiner on the degree to which the accused can understand and cooperate with counsel in planning a realistic strategy of defense. The related text focuses the examiner on the content area of plea bargaining, and the questions to be asked direct one toward discovering which defenses the examinee would prefer or accept. Only by extrapolation from the case examples does it become apparent that it is the defendant's reasoning, not simply the choice of defense, that contributes to the rating.

Psychometric Development

STANDARDIZATION.   Few instructions are provided for administration of the CAI. For example, the authors provided no instructions in the primary reference (d) for introducing the CAI interview to defendants, for the sequence with which the various functions should be assessed, or for the extent of additional inquiry that may be necessary beyond the basic questions to be asked. The standard questions themselves are described as "sample questions," and many of them require only a "yes" or "no" answer by the examinee. Undoubtedly, examiners were expected to probe beyond the responses to these questions. Consequently, it is likely that different examinees receive somewhat different stimulus questions from different examiners.

No specific criteria are provided for each of the 1 to 5 ratings on each function. Standardization of rating depends on paragraph definitions of the function and three case vignettes per function, for which the authors' ratings are provided.

RELIABILITY.   Interrater reliability was established by examining intraclass correlations for a group of three experienced raters and a group of three inexperienced raters (d). In all cases, raters apparently observed (but did not themselves conduct) the interviews to be rated. Across CAI functions, correlations between the experienced raters ranged from $r = .84$ to .97 (average .92), compared to $r = .43$ to .96 (average .87) between inexperienced raters. Correlations may have been attenuated by the fact that raters discussed the ratings they had given after viewing each interview. Currently there are no data on temporal consistency of CAI ratings or on reliability as a function of different interviewers administering the CAI.

NORMS.   Neither norms nor mean scores for relevant samples is available.

CRITIQUE.   The CAI offers consistency and reliability for pretrial competence evaluations in the sense that it assures that each CAI-assisted evaluation will provide data on 13 functions. Beyond this, however, very little is known about the consistency or stability of CAI ratings. The rating system produced adequate interrater agreement for very experienced raters in the setting in which the CAI was developed. Yet without a description of standard instructions for CAI administration, one does not know whether one's own way of administering the CAI in everyday practice is similar to the interview procedure on which reliability ratings were performed. Published details of standard administration would be necessary before meaningful studies of interrater reliability could be performed.

Construct Validation

Schreiber (f) compared CAI-based recommendations for competence/incompetence to those based on two other instruments designed to be relevant for the construct of competence to stand trial. The study employed actual defendants to whom the CAI was administered in conjunction with the *Competence Screening Test* and/or the *Interdisciplinary Fitness Interview*. Statistically significant agreement was found between the CAI and both of the other instruments, although the CAI tended to find a somewhat greater number of defendants incompetent than did the *Interdisciplinary Fitness Interview*.

Schreiber, Roesch, and Golding (c, g) reported that competence judgments based on the CAI corresponded to the consensus of expert panels in about 78% of cases. Schreiber (e) found that CAI-based evaluations recommended findings of competence in all cases in which defendants had not received a psychotic diagnosis, and for incompetence in one-half of the psychotic cases. Finally, in one study, CAI scores were significantly related to behavioral observation ratings of defendants while they performed in the role of defendant in a mock trial setting (b).

CRITIQUE.   The existing research lends only meager evidence for the construct validity of the CAI. Nevertheless, it does appear to correlate with other instruments designed to assess the same construct underlying the development of the CAI. Further, it does not automatically produce incompetence findings for individuals diagnosed psychotic, although it does produce competence findings for defendants without significant psychosis. These results generally are consistent with legal presumptions about pretrial competence as a construct. The finding that CAI scores were related to observations of defendants' behaviors during mock trials is intriguing and may offer a method that can be used in future research on other measures of abilities related to competence to stand trial.

Predictive or Classificatory Utility

McGarry (d) reported that in a series of 15 cases in which the CAI formed the basis for expert testimony in Massachusetts Superior Court, judicial determinations of pretrial competence/incompetence matched the CAI-based recommendations in all but one case. The judicial decisions, however, were made with judicial knowledge of the CAI data. In another study in which CAI-based recommendations were not available to the court, those recommendations matched with the competence or incompetence decisions of the courts in 82% of the cases (c, f, g).

CRITIQUE. The existing evidence suggests that the CAI produces results similar to independent court opinions about competence or incompetence to stand trial. This is based on only one study, however, and it is not known whether CAI-based evaluations are any more effective in this regard than are traditional assessments for competence to stand trial. Courts' acceptance of CAI results in expert testimony, and legislative or administrative encouragement of its use, clearly has not been based on demonstrated empirical validity of the instrument.

There is some evidence, in fact, that it is the conceptual structure of the CAI rather than its operational or metric features that contributed to its acceptance in many legal and mental health systems. Schreiber (e) examined usage of the CAI and its companion instrument (the *Competence Screening Test*) in four states. He found that the CAI's 13 functions were being used to structure evaluators' observations and reports, but that the CAI's rating system itself either was actively opposed or simply was not being used. Further, in the survey inquiry that was performed for the first edition review of instruments in this book, many respondents reported using their own "modified McGarry interview," involving slightly altered versions of the CAI's 13-function outline without employment of the rating system.

The lack of research on the empirical validity of CAI ratings, therefore, was probably a consequence of users' lack of interest in, or their judgments about the questionable value of, its quantification. The CAI continues to be used as a conceptual tool—a way to think about functional abilities—with apparently very little use of the instrument as a scorable tool. Indeed, the CAI does not really have the status of an "instrument." Without the use of the quantified rating system, and with no standardized description of the interview process, the CAI's sole remaining contribution is a list of 13 legally relevant concepts and definitions. Valuable as this may be, it neither calls for nor can receive empirical support without greater attention to the quantitative aspect of the original CAI.

Potential for Expressing Person-Situation Congruency

The CAI includes no systematic evaluation of the trial circumstances or attorney relations facing the examinee. Three of the functions/items, however, instruct the examiner to compare the examinee's knowledge, perceptions or capacities to the "reality of his particular circumstances" (Function 1, Appraisal of Available Legal Defenses; Function 4, Planning of Legal Strategy; Function 9, Appraisal of Likely Outcome). Thus for some functions, the CAI asks the examiner to evaluate the congruency or incongruency between the examinee's ability and these aspects of the demands or reality of the situation. Yet the CAI provides no dimensions or guidelines for characterizing the environmental situation itself. Examiners might be greatly assisted by the development of such guidelines.

References

(a) Brakel, S. (1974). Presumption, bias, and incompetence in the criminal process. *Wisconsin Law Review*, pp. 1105–1130.
(b) Gannon, J. (1990). Validation of the Competence Assessment Instrument and elements of competence to stand trial. *Dissertation Abstracts International, 50-B*, 3875.
(c) Golding, S., Roesch, R., & Schreiber, J. (1984). Assessment and conceptualization of competence to stand trial: Preliminary data on the Interdisciplinary Fitness Interview. *Law and Human Behavior, 8*, 321–334.
(d) Laboratory of Community Psychiatry, Harvard Medical School. (1973). *Competence to stand trial and mental illness* (DHEW Pub. No. ADM-77-103). Rockville, MD: Department of Health, Education and Welfare.
(e) Schreiber, J. (1978). Assessing competence to stand trial: A case study of technology diffusion in four states. *Bulletin of the American Academy of Psychiatry and the Law, 6*, 439–457.
(f) Schreiber, J. (1983). *Evaluation of procedures for assessing competence to stand trial.* (Final Report of NIMH Research Grant No. ROI-MH33669.) Rockville, MD: Center for Studies of Antisocial and Violent Behavior, National Institute of Mental Health.
(g) Schreiber, J., Roesch, R., & Golding, S. (1987). An evaluation of procedures for assessing competence to stand trial. *Bulletin of the American Academy of Psychiatry and the Law, 15*, 143–150.

COMPETENCE SCREENING TEST (CST)

Authors

Lipsitt, P., & Lelos, D., with McGarry, A. L. and Associates, Laboratory of
Community Psychiatry, Harvard Medical School

Primary Author Affiliation

Massachusetts General Hospital, Harvard Medical School (Community
Mental Health-Law Program)

Primary Reference

Laboratory of Community Psychiatry, Harvard Medical School (1973). *Competence to stand trial
    and mental Illness* (DHEW Publication No. ADM 77-103). Rockville, MD: NIMH,
    Department of Health, Education, and Welfare.

NOTE ON SECOND EDITION REVIEW.   This review has changed little since
the first edition, because only a few studies have been performed with the
instrument since that time. The DHEW monograph that constituted
the CAI manual is no longer available from NIMH, although it is still
found in some university libraries.

Description

The *Competence Screening Test* (CST) was intended as a brief, psychometric instrument that would help to decide whether more extensive assessment for competence to stand trial was needed. The authors hoped that the
CST, in conjunction with a brief psychiatric interview, might serve a screening function to divert clearly competent defendants from the lengthy hospitalization that was typically required (in past decades) for full competence
assessments. Thus the CST sought to identify persons who clearly were
competent to stand trial. The identification of incompetent defendants
apparently was not a formal goal in the development of the CST; defendants' low scores "raise the issue of (in)competence" (c, p. 74), but do not
provide evidence for incompetence itself. The CST, therefore, can be
viewed as a psychometric definition of a threshold for recommending or
ruling out further evaluation related to legal decisions about pretrial
incompetence.

The CST was developed by an interdisciplinary team of psychiatrists,
psychologists, and lawyers, funded by a research grant from the Center
for Studies of Crime and Delinquency, NIMH. The instrument was
intended as a companion to the *Competence To Stand Trial Assessment
Instrument* (CAI) reviewed earlier in this chapter.

The CST consists of 22 items, each of which is the beginning of an incomplete sentence. The sentence stems are

1. The lawyer told Bill that
2. When I go to court the lawyer will
3. Jack felt that the judge
4. When Phil was accused of the crime, he
5. When I prepare to go to court with my lawyer
6. If the jury finds me guilty, I
7. The way a court trial is decided
8. When the evidence in George's case was presented to the jury
9. When the lawyer questioned his client in court, the client said
10. If Jack has to try his own case, he
11. Each time the D.A. asked me a question, I
12. While listening to the witnesses testify against me, I
13. When the witness testifying against Harry gave incorrect evidence, he
14. When Bob disagreed with his lawyer on his defense, he
15. When I was formally accused of the crime, I thought to myself
16. If Ed's lawyer suggests that he plead guilty, he
17. What concerns Fred most about his lawyer
18. When they say a man is innocent until proven guilty
19. When I think of being sent to prison, I
20. When Phil thinks of what he is accused of, he
21. When the jury hears my case, they will
22. If I had a chance to speak to the judge, I

The examinee's sentence completions are scored according to the 22 sets of definitions and examples provided in the CST manual. For example, the scoring criteria for Item 1 are as follows:

1. The lawyer told Bill that
   (a) Legal criteria: ability to cooperate in own defense, communicate, relate
   (b) Psychological criteria: ability to relate or trust
   Score 2: includes obtaining and/or accepting advice or guidance

   Examples: "he should plead not guilty," "he was free," "he should plead nolo," "he should plead guilty," "he would take his case," "he would need to know all the facts concerning the case," "he should turn himself in," "the outlook was good," "he will try to help him."

   Score 1:

   Examples: "he is innocent," "everything is all right," "be truthful," "he will be going to court soon," "he is competent to stand trial," "it will be filled."

Score 0: includes regarding lawyer as accusing or judgmental

Examples: "he was wrong in doing what he did," "he is guilty," "he is going to be put away," "no comment."

Each response is scored 2, 1, or 0, and scores are summed to arrive at a total CST score (range, 0–44). In the manual, a total score below 20 was used as a signal to raise the question of incompetence (c, p. 74). Another reference by the authors (d, p. 138), however, designates "low scorers" as those obtaining CST scores of 20 or below, and this rule has been used most often in subsequent research with the CST.

Conceptual Basis

CONCEPT DEFINITION.   During the first year of the 4-year project in which the CST was developed, the interdisciplinary team performed reviews of appellate cases and legal literature, and made observations in many pretrial competence hearings and in interviews with attorneys and judges. This allowed the team to arrive at a three-part definition of the competence to stand trial standard: an ability to cooperate with one's attorney in one's own defense; an awareness and understanding of the nature and object of the proceedings; and an understanding of the consequences of the proceedings.

These legal concepts were modified to provide a structure for developing the CST items. The three measurement constructs used in writing items were:

- the potential for a constructive relationship between the client and his lawyer,
- the client's understanding of the court process, and
- ability to deal emotionally with the criminal process (c, p. 27).

OPERATIONAL DEFINITION.   The three measurement constructs were used to structure the writing of 50 sentence stems. Pilot work reduced these to 22 items, refined the "legal criteria" and "psychological criteria" statements for each item, and developed definitions and examples for 2, 1, and 0 scores for each item. Each of the three measurement constructs is represented by about one-third of the CST items (although scores are summed only for total CST, not for construct dimensions).

CRITIQUE.   Questions about the content relevance of the CST can be addressed at three points in the translation process: the derivation of measurement constructs, the development of test items, and the formulation of scoring criteria.

Concerning the first, Brakel (b) severely criticized the CST authors for what he believes were unwarranted and dangerous presumptions when measurement constructs were developed to represent the *Dusky* standards. For example, where *Dusky* calls for an examination of a defendant's "ability to assist in one's defense," the CST construct inquires about "constructive relationship with one's lawyer." Brakel claims that these are not the same constructs, because a good relationship with a good lawyer would promote an adequate defense, but a good relationship with a poor lawyer would not. The issue of assisting in one's defense, he claims, is broader than the nature of one's ability to relate to a lawyer. Similarly, where legal standards call for "an understanding of the consequences of the proceedings," the CST counterpart focuses on "an ability to deal emotionally with the criminal process." Thus the legal construct is cognitive, whereas the measurement construct refers to an affective component.

Whether or not Brakel's criticism is fair depends on the CST authors' purposes in translating competence standards into measurement constructs. If they intended to produce three psychiatric constructs each of which would parallel the three *Dusky* (legal) components, then Brakel's criticisms are sound. At face value, the three measurement constructs seem essentially different from the three legal components derived more directly from *Dusky*.

On the other hand, it would seem likely that the three measurement constructs were intended to capture three psychological factors, each of which may contribute to *any* of the *Dusky* components: a social or interpersonal construct ("relationship"), a cognitive construct ("understanding"), and an affective or coping construct ("deal emotionally"). From this perspective, the CST attempts to measure three psychological functions, but using content specific to trial contexts (lawyers, trial events, criminal court outcomes) rather than assessing them in the abstract as in more general psychological tests of relating to others, intellectual abilities, and affective coping mechanisms. If that is the case, however, it is still true that the concepts themselves are considerably different than those that are used in modern interpretations of the constructs associated with competence to stand trial.

The second question of content relevance concerns translation of the measurement constructs into test items. The decision to develop approximately an equal number of items for each of the three constructs seems benign. Yet this means that CST total scores give equal weight to all three measurement constructs in all cases. It should be recognized when interpreting CST scores that low scores may be achieved because of marked deficits in only some areas of the CST, or because of moderate deficit across all areas.

At face value, several of the items (sentence stems) seem to have been worded in a manner that might result in interpretive error, in relation to the constructs that were to be assessed. For example, the first two items are intended to assess one's relationship capacities in interaction with one's lawyer. Yet the items do not specify a defense lawyer or one's own lawyer, but rather a lawyer of undefined role ("The lawyer told Bill that …," "When I go to court the lawyer will …"). This leaves open the possibility that the examinee may complete the sentence to express perceptions of prosecutors rather than defense attorneys.

The third question concerns the development of scoring criteria. Apparently the CST authors made no concerted attempt to determine whether professionals in law or in mental health outside of the project's research team would perceive the 2, 1, and 0 credit criteria or examples as relevant and appropriate to the legal purposes of the instrument. This is of concern because, at face value, it is often difficult to trace the logical connection between many of the scoring examples and the criteria that were written for the corresponding items. For example, for "The lawyer told Bill that …," it is not clear why the completion "… he should plead guilty" should receive 2 points, indicating fulfillment of the item criterion "Ability to relate or trust."

In other instances it is difficult to distinguish conceptually between 2 points and 1 or 0 points credit. For example, on item 6 ("If the jury finds me guilty, I …"), the response "… will serve my sentence" receives 2 points, whereas "… will take the punishment" receives 1 point. (The item intends to assess the defendant's realistic assessment of consequences.) A 0-point credit on the same item is assigned if the defendant responds, "… will be sentenced to the maximum penalty"; yet this may be a very realistic assessment of consequences in certain circumstances and for certain defendants.

Psychometric Development

STANDARDIZATION. The CST was designed as a paper and pencil test, although researchers (k, n) have administered it orally (with oral responding) when examinees lacked sufficient reading abilities. A standard set of instructions (c, p. 74) informs the examinee that the items deal with courtrooms and the law, that there are no right or wrong answers, and that one is to complete the sentences with first impressions. Scoring is standardized by way of brief general criteria for each item and numerous specific item responses for each scoring category on each item.

RELIABILITY. There are five published reports of interscorer reliability for total CST scores, using scorers with various degrees of training in the method (c, e, j, k, n). Different statistical tests of reliability were used in the various studies, and coefficients of correlation have been uniformly high, generally .93 or higher. There have been no reports of temporal consistency (test-retest reliability) of CST scores.

NORMS. No norms are provided as such, but Lipsitt, Lelos, and McGarry (d) described mean CST scores for several hospitalized and non-hospitalized samples employed in initial studies with the CST: competence examinees, 18.4; college students, 25.9; mental hospital control group, 24.6; men's club, 24.3; state hospital civil commitments, 23.8. Ustad et al. (p) provided means for competent (25.4) and incompetent (11.92) defendants in a competence restoration program.

CRITIQUE. Interscorer agreement for the total CST scores generally has been quite good, despite observations that several of the examples provided in the manual for 2-point and 1-point responses appear to be quite similar to each other. No studies have examined interscorer agreement on individual items, however; it may be that CST total scores are highly comparable between scorers despite scoring disagreements on some of the individual items. Thus criticisms of CST scoring criteria may be important when making inferences about individual item responses, but relatively unimportant when employing total CST scores to make clinical decisions.

Construct Validation

The internal consistency (Cronbach's alpha) of the CST was identified as .85 in one study (e) and .79 in another (p). Inter-item correlation in those two studies was .28 (e) and .14 (p). Differences between the two studies might be related to sample differences, the second study having been performed with defendants who were in a competence restoration program.

In the original study of the CST (c), factor analyses were performed with two samples of CST data: 91 patients representing a mix of the general hospital population and competence assessment defendants at Bridgewater State Hospital, and 83 persons who were not patients. The first analysis (hospitalized examinees) used an orthogonal rotation that produced six rotated factors accounting for 56.3% of the total variance on the test. The authors described these six factors (b, p. 28) as reflecting: (I) relationship of defendant to attorney, (II) understanding of court process, (III) responsiveness and reaction to accusation and guilt, (IV) a second factor for understanding of court process, (V) trust and confidence in lawyer, and (VI) future orientation. The factor analysis with the second ("normal") sample produced markedly different factors; in the authors' opinion, these factors did not seem to represent any concepts related to pretrial competence definitions.

A factor analysis performed by Nicholson et al. (e) produced three factors that were quite different from those in the original study and were essentially uninterpretable when examined for the content of items loading strongly on the various factors. A re-analysis of the Nicholson et al. data by Bagby et al. (a) using a six-factor solution (like the original validation study) produced results only slightly more like those found in the original study. Ustad et al. (p) also reported efforts to factor analyze the CST, having failed because a large number of subjects (in a competence restoration program) simply could not complete the instrument, either being unable to respond to some sentence stems or simply choosing to discontinue.

Schreiber (m) found that the CST produced competence/incompetence findings in proportions significantly similar to those based on interviews with the *Competence Assessment Instrument* (CAI: see previous review). Disagreements between the two instruments were all in the direction of CST incompetence findings in cases considered competent by CAI interviewers. Ustad et al. (p) found that scores on the CST correlated only .45 with those on the *Georgia Court Competence Test-Mississippi State Hospital* (GCCT-MSH: see accompanying review), and the measure agreed with competence/incompetence classification on the GCCT-MSH in only 61% of the cases.

One would expect pretrial competence to be related at least moderately to general intellectual ability. More specifically, individuals with very low levels of intellectual ability might be expected to perform poorly on the CST. Among patients with adequate intellectual functioning, however, variance due to psychopathology might obscure any effects related to intellectual capacity. Correlations between CST scores and IQ measures in three studies have been very low ($r = .10$) (p), low ($r = .24$) (o), and moderate ($r = .42$) (l). A fourth study (h) reported a moderately greater proportion of mental retardation diagnoses among low CST scorers (30.7%) than among high CST scorers (13.5%), and a fifth (g) reported a correlation of $-.33$ between mental retardation and CST scores.

Within mental hospital samples, one would expect type or severity of diagnoses to be related to CST scores. Several studies have reported that a diagnosis of schizophrenia accounts for a greater proportion of low CST scorers than of high CST scorers. In three studies, the proportions of schizophrenic diagnoses in low and high CST groups, respectively, were 37.5% and 4.5% (h), 81.8% and 60.0% (p), and 73.9% and 50.0% (d). One study (g) reported a correlation of $-.12$ between psychosis and CST scores.

Studies examining the criterion validity of the CST, of course, provide further empirical information concerning construct validity. These will be examined in the next section.

CRITIQUE. The factor analysis of CST scores indicates that the CST's content is somewhat more complex conceptually than would be suggested by the three measurement concepts with which the authors began. Moreover, factor analyses subsequent to the original report cast considerable doubt on the stability of conceptual meaning for the CST across different samples.

Predictive or Classificatory Utility

Eleven studies have compared total CST scores to either judicial decisions about competence or concurrent findings of forensic clinicians who had performed comprehensive competence assessments and made recommendations (d-2 studies, e, g, h, i, j, k, l, n, o).

All studies employed a CST score of 20 or lower as the cutoff score. Most of the studies used consecutive or randomly selected admissions of competence examinees to forensic assessment units of hospitals. In all cases, criterion decisions (judicial decisions or conclusions of forensic evaluations) were made without knowledge of the defendants' CST scores.

Nicholson and Kugler (f) reviewed all of these studies and calculated effect sizes to summarize the relation of independent competence judgments to scores above and below the cut-off on the CST (and those of several other competence assessment tools). The meta-analytic finding of $r = -.37$ was poorer than for the other instruments reviewed ($-.42$ to $-.52$).

Typically, studies have found that the CST identifies far more defendants as potentially incompetent than are found incompetent by independent clinical judgments. For example, in their meta-analysis, Nicholson et al. (g) found that about 78% of criterion incompetent defendants made scores below the cut-off on the CST (sensitivity), while about 70% of criterion competent defendants scored above the cut-off (specificity). Had the CST been used as a screening tool in that sample, it would have identified about 34% of the sample as in need of further evaluation, and about 23% of those who were further evaluated would have been found incompetent. Only 3% of those above the cut-off on the CST were criterion incompetent. However, those defendants accounted for nearly one-quarter of the incompetent defendants in the study. Some other studies have found somewhat better results with the CST, especially with samples that have baserates of criterion competence above 20% (the baserate in the Nicholson et al. meta-analysis was about 10%). Overall, however, the Nicholson et al. results are representative of other studies with baserates of competence that approximate the 10–15% baserate reported in many forensic services in the U.S.

CRITIQUE. The available data suggest two answers to the question of the CST's utility in identifying "clearly competent" defendants, as judged against criteria such as final court decisions and the outcome of more extensive psychiatric evaluations.

In jurisdictions with competence examinee populations that have a greater than 20% base rate of incompetence, about 9 out of 10 high CST scorers would meet judicial or comprehensive evaluation standards for pretrial competence. Stated another way, if the CST were the primary factor for decisions to proceed to trial, 1 out of every 10 defendants who met the CST criterion (above 20 cutoff score) would be tried unfairly, that is, would be falsely identified as competent. If low CST scores were the deciding factor in commitment for extensive competence evaluation because of "questionable competence," about one-third of those defendants would eventually be found competent. In contrast, in jurisdictions with very low base rates of pretrial incompetence (e.g., less than 15%), it is likely that the use of the CST as a screening device would produce a hit rate poorer than would be attained if one simply concluded that all defendants are competent.

Potential for Expressing Person-Situation Congruency

The CST makes no attempt to examine the defendant's knowledge or ability in relation to the idiosyncratic demands of the defendant's own specific trial circumstances. The conceptual development of the CST suggests three dimensions of the environment corresponding to the three measurement construct originally associated with the CST: interpersonal qualities and skills of the defense attorney; the complexity of the anticipated trial; and anticipated characteristics of the trial and its probable outcomes, especially its potential for affect arousal and induction of stress reactions.

References

(a) Bagby, R., Nicholson, R., Rogers, R., & Nussbaum, D. (1992). Domains of competence to stand trial: A factor analytic study. *Law and Human Behavior, 16*, 491–507
(b) Brakel, S. (1974). Presumption, bias, and incompetence in the criminal process. *Wisconsin Law Review*, pp. 1105–1130.
(c) Laboratory of Community Psychiatry, Harvard Medical School (1973). *Competence to stand trial and mental illness* (DHEW publication No. ADM 77-103). Rockville, MD: NIMH, Department of Health, Education, and Welfare.
(d) Lipsitt, P., Lelos, D., & McGarry, A. L. (1971). Competence for trial: A screening instrument. *American Journal of Psychiatry, 128*, 105–109.

(e) Nicholson, R., Briggs, S., & Robertson, H. (1988). Instruments for assessing competence to stand trial: How do they work? *Professional Psychology, 19*, 383–394.

(f) Nicholson, R., & Kugler, K. (1991). Competent and incompetent criminal defendants: A quantitative review of comparative research. *Psychological Bulletin, 109*, 355–370.

(g) Nicholson, R., Robertson, H., Johnson, W., & Jensen, G. (1988). A comparison of instruments for assessing competence to stand trial. *Law and Human Behavior, 12*, 313–321.

(h) Nottingham, E., & Mattson, R. (1981). A validation study of the Competence Screening Test. *Law and Human Behavior, 5*, 329–335.

(i) Pope, B., & Scott, W. (1967). *Psychological diagnosis in clinical practice.* New York: Oxford University Press.

(j) Randolph, J., Hicks, T., & Mason, D. (1981). The Competence Screening Test: A replication and extension. *Criminal Justice and Behavior, 8*, 471–481.

(k) Randolph, J., Hicks, T., Mason, D., & Cuneo, D. (1982). The Competence Screening Test: A validation in Cook County, Illinois. *Criminal Justice and Behavior, 9*, 495–500.

(l) Roesch, R., & Golding, S. (1980). *Competence to stand trial.* Champaign, IL: University of Illinois Press.

(m) Schreiber, J. (1983). *Evaluation of procedures for assessing competence to stand trial* (Final Report for Grant No. R0I-MH33669). Rockville, MD: Center for Antisocial and Violent Behavior, National Institute of Mental Health.

(n) Shatin, L. (1979). Brief form of the Competence Screening Test for mental competence to stand trial. *Journal of Clinical Psychology, 34*, 464–467.

(o) Shatin, L., & Brodsky, S. (1979). Competence for trial: The Competence Screening Test in an urban hospital forensic unit. *Mt. Sinai Journal of Medicine, 46*, 131–134.

(p) Ustad, I., Rogers, R., Sewell, K., & Guarnaccia, C. (1996). Restoration of competence to stand trial: Assessment with the Georgia Court Competence Test and the Competence Screening Test. *Law and Human Behavior, 20*, 131–146.

CURRENT STATUS OF THE FIELD

The first part of this section reviews collectively the methods and approaches that have been used to develop the competence to stand trial FAIs described in this chapter. These discussions lead to specific suggestions for further research and development of FAIs in this area. The second part of this section suggests the uses to which the instruments may be put in evaluations, given what is known currently about their reliability and validity.

RESEARCH DIRECTIONS

Functional Component

In the first edition of *Evaluating Competencies*, four suggestions were made for improving the process of selecting and defining the specific abilities that should be assessed by future FAIs related to competence to stand trial. Four of the six instruments reviewed in the present chapter have been developed since the first edition, and there is some evidence that their development was consistent with some of the suggestions offered 15 years ago, while in some cases it was not.

EMPIRICAL ANALYSIS OF THE ABILITY DOMAIN. The 22 items of the MacCAT-CA, the 13 CAI functions, and the items of the other instruments reviewed here represent these instruments' operational definitions of a domain of abilities—things that a defendant must know, understand, appreciate or be able to do—to which the components of the legal competence standard are presumed to refer. How did the test developers discover and define these specific abilities within the domain?

Collectively, they used three methods: review of statutes and appellate case opinions; the researchers' own experiences with courtrooms, defendants, and trial lawyers; and consensual agreement among the researchers themselves, often working as an interdisciplinary team. While these methods are appropriate, they have not made significant use of a different strategy: systematically sampling the types and range of abilities that are manifested when one enacts the role of defendant. We have no systematic job description for defendants based on controlled observation of samples of defendants participating in trial processes. For example, only anecdote informs us about how defendants and their attorneys arrive at mutual agreements on pleas and defense strategies, or in what ways defendants typically assist their attorneys in trial processes.

Therefore, we need empirical information on the typical roles and functions of defendants in trial and pretrial activities. This information would provide an empirical basis for defining the specific abilities that may be important for participation in a trial. This, in turn, would assist us in deciding which functional abilities to include in construction of instruments related to pretrial competence.

There are two views concerning the propriety of this approach to the development of FAIs for competence to stand trial. One view would consider this approach inappropriate, arguing that it is law, not empirical research, that defines abilities relevant for legal competence. Thus it is the responsibility of developers of FAIs in this area to do just what they have done—review and analyze the law, and arrive at a domain of abilities that is consistent with centuries of judicial interpretation of legal requirements.

The second view approaches the task with a more dynamic perspective, arguing that legal definitions are evolving concepts that can be informed and changed by empirical research findings about human behavior. If empirical analyses of defendants' tasks were to find functions that are not now included in legal constructions of competence, these findings might eventually improve the law's ability to construct definitions of competence that more closely represent the real demands of the defendant's role. Instruments based on such empirical findings need not ignore the law's current definitions. New abilities discovered empirically could be represented in adjunct sections of instruments that assess the traditional abilities associated with legal competence to stand trial.

LEGAL CONSENSUS FOR TEST CONTENT.   To the extent that FAIs should be guided by legal definitions, it is encouraging to see that at least some instruments reviewed here (e.g., CAST-MR) have included an assessment of judicial and/or attorney opinion among their methods for deciding on their relevant content. After test developers have determined the specific abilities that they believe may be important for test contents, they should submit these ability concepts to samples of judges or lawyers in order to obtain opinion consensus regarding the legal relevance of each of the abilities for pretrial competence determinations. This is encouraged for all future development of instruments in this area.

STIMULUS AND RESPONSE FORMAT.   Tests of functional abilities generally should attempt to use stimulus and response modes that are as similar as possible to those that are required in the criterion context: in this instance, in trials or in client-attorney consultations.

With the exception of the CST's sentence completion format, instruments for pretrial competence assessment have used interview questions requiring examinees' oral responses. Some of these questions are consistent with the aforementioned principle. For example, asking examinees to recount their version of the alleged offense approximates a request that might be made in client-attorney consultations or in courtroom testimony. On the other hand, asking examinees how they might interact with an attorney ("Would you feel free to confide in him?") does not approximate the behaviors about which the examiner is concerned. Observing a defendant in interaction with an attorney might provide a more ecologically valid indicator of that which the examiner wishes to know.

Newer FAIs in this area have tended simply to follow the lead of earlier instruments' focus on verbal response. Other stimulus approaches would be possible. For example, only one instrument currently uses a visual stimulus (a drawing). One might display videotaped trial events and ask examinees to answer a standard set of questions about the events and participants that are portrayed, rather than asking the examinee to deal with the material in a more abstract sense (e.g., "What is the role of a judge?"). Future developers of pretrial competence instruments might consider a range of optional response formats (as pioneered in the CAST-MR) rather than assuming that interview procedures are the preferred or necessary format in this area of competence.

VALIDATION OF THE INSTRUMENTS.   After 20 years of development of FAIs for assessing abilities related to competence to stand trial, no study has described an attempt to validate the instruments' scores against observations of the abilities they are said to measure. Instead, validation continues to focus on the correspondence of instrument scores or instrument-based conclusions to decisions reached by other instruments, traditional forensic examinations, or judicial hearings.

The use of judicial decisions or expert clinical judgments as a "gold standard" to which to compare instruments in this area will probably continue. But the limitations of this approach to validation must be kept in mind. Instruments for assessing abilities related to competence to stand trial cannot—and should not be expected to—define competence judgments. Judicial competence decisions (see Chapter 2, on the judgmental aspect of legal competence) are based on considerations that go beyond questions of defendant ability alone. In addition, we have no evidence regarding the reliability or validity of competence conclusions reached by forensic examiners or judges who form the criterion.

Causal Component

In the forensic assessment process, a defendant's poor performance on the instruments reviewed in this chapter will raise the question of reasons for the performance. Courts will wish to know whether the poor performance is in part a consequence of interference by psychopathological symptoms, mental retardation, or developmental disability, or whether it may be related to alternative explanations such as poor motivation during the examination or simulation of incompetence. Some advances have been made in this regard and are worth noting for their value in guiding future research and development of CST instruments.

SIMULATION DETECTION. None of the newer instruments reviewed here have chosen to include an index of potential feigning of symptoms, despite the legal relevance of this information for explaining deficits in the behaviors that the instruments claim to measure. An instrument currently under development called the *Evaluation of Competency to Stand Trial-Revised* (ECST-R) (Rogers, Tillbrook, & Sewell, undated) will offer this feature. Researchers wishing to follow this lead in developing future instruments may wish to review other examples of this strategy. For example, Nussbaum, Mamak, Tremblay, Wright, and Callaghan (1998) recently developed a prototype CST instrument called the *METFORS Fitness Questionnaire* (MFQ). Several of the items are 6-option multiple-choice questions, with only one choice correct, three incorrect but not unreasonably so, and the remaining two "absurd." Probability tables were used to identify the possibility of malingering when a defendant endorses a greater than chance number of "absurd" choices. Frederick, Carter, and Powell (1995) modified the *Symptom Validity Test* in order to assess feigned short-term memory deficits, and they published illustrations of its use in the detection of possible malingering in CST assessment cases.

ABILITY TO BENEFIT BY INSTRUCTION. The introduction to this chapter explained that a legal determination of incompetence to stand trial is not justified in cases where the defendant is merely ignorant of the nature of a trial. If the defendant has the capacity, with relatively brief effort, to learn the necessary aspects of trials and attorney consultations, education rather than treatment would be appropriate.

Although this notion of capacity to learn has long been recognized in clinical practice, the MacCAT-CA is the first CST instrument to employ a method to assist in identifying it. Several of the Understanding items in the MacCAT-CA assess unaided understanding (e.g., of the roles of trial participants), then provide information for examinees with incomplete knowledge and re-test for the examinee's grasp of the information that was provided. This strategy could profitably be used in new instruments that are developed in the future or revisions of existing instruments. Improvements on the MacCAT-CA procedure are possible, in that the MacCAT-CA scoring system does not include a standard procedure for calculating an "unaided understanding" score to compare to the final (post-teaching) Understanding score.

DEVELOPMENTAL CAUSES OF DEFICITS IN ABILITIES. As noted in the introduction to this chapter, youths' capacities as trial defendants has become an important focus of attention in recent years due to changes in laws that give new relevance the concept of pretrial competence in juvenile cases. Mental illness and developmental disability (mental retardation) have been the primary focus of incompetence to stand trial throughout the legal history of the concept. Empirically, it would seem likely that some youths will manifest relatively intractable deficits in the abilities measured in pretrial competence instruments (Grisso, 1997, 2000; see generally, Grisso & Schwartz, 2000), not for these reasons, but simply due to developmental immaturity. This is especially likely with regard to reasoning and decision making capacities. Yet currently there are few studies of the performance of youths on these measures (Cooper's [1997] use of the GCCT-MSH with adolescents is an exception). Research could profitably be directed toward the examination of youths' performance on instruments reviewed in this chapter, as well as methods to determine possible relations between their deficits and their cognitive or emotional immaturity.

Interactive Component

By definition (see Chapter 2), the interactive nature of legal competence constructs requires knowledge not only of the person's capacities but also the demands of the specific, legally relevant situation that the person faces. Further, decision makers must weigh the congruency or incongruency of these two realities.

None of the FAIs for pretrial competence have attempted to devise methods that would systematically provide comparisons of defendants' degrees of ability to the actual demands of their own trial circumstances. Such efforts would require the development of methods to assess and characterize trial environments, providing descriptions of individual trial contexts on certain standardized dimensions.

Research would need to proceed first to determine the relevant dimensions of trials that describe demands placed on defendants. Either of two approaches to this step might be used. One approach would involve systematic observation of a sample of trials to arrive at empirical dimensions. A second approach would develop dimensions conceptually, creating environmental counterparts of ability dimensions employed in existing pretrial competence instruments. For example, many of the CAI's 13 functional concepts suggest complementary environmental dimensions:

- Function 2 (Unmanageable Behavior): Anticipated length and arousal potential of trial
- Function 3 (Quality of Relating to Attorney): Quality of the attorney's relations with clients
- Function 7 (Appreciation of Charges): Nature and seriousness of charges as perceived by the public
- Function 8 (Appreciation of Range and Nature of Possible Penalties): Empirical range and nature of possible penalties, based on similar cases in the past.

The next research step, of course, would be to arrive at operational definitions for the dimension concepts, then to collect data on each dimension for a number of trials in order to arrive at normative descriptions to which individual trials could be compared. Finally, one would need standard methods for collecting information on each dimension for a given trial in conjunction with a defendant's assessment. With the resulting instrument, an examiner could summarize for the court the degree of anticipated demands of the trial on each dimension, as well as the examinee's degree of functional ability (according to existing competence instruments) on dimensions complementary to those used to characterize the trial environment. Whether assessment schemata of this type would be feasible, or would be acceptable to courts as data for pretrial competence examinations, is beyond the scope of this discussion. The potential is offered here merely as a conceptualization that is at least logically consistent with the model of legal competence constructs.

Judgmental and Dispositional Components

Chapter 2 described reasons why judgments about legal competence are beyond the expertise of mental health professionals. Nevertheless, all of the current pretrial competence instruments except the MacCAT-CA encourage a clinical recommendation of competence or incompetence in courtroom testimony. The FIT-R, for example, directs examiners to make a final competence judgment. This feature of the instruments encourages the mental health professional to answer the ultimate legal question (even though the test authors may not endorse that position).

Many courts allow and/or require the mental health professional to offer a conclusive opinion on the ultimate legal question. From this perspective, the competence instruments are designed to assist examiners to do what they must do. The instruments' provisions for conclusory statements about legal competence, however, are not consistent with the view that these judgments require weighing not only descriptive and theoretical evidence about defendants' capacities, but also social and moral concerns regarding the consequences of a finding of competence or incompetence. Concluding that a defendant is incompetent is not the same as concluding that a defendant is sorely deficient in capacities to participate in a trial. Yet the competence instruments, designed to assess the latter question, might inadvertently lead the examiner to state conclusions about the former question.

Future developers of pretrial competence instruments should decide whether they wish to encourage ultimate competence and incompetence recommendations by mental health professionals, or whether they wish to restrict the product of the assessment instrument to a description of functional abilities, causal information, and person-situation congruency. The latter approach, of course, would be consistent with the legal analysis of the competence construct offered in Chapter 2.

CLINICAL APPLICATION

Description

One of the purposes of pretrial competence assessments is to collect data with which to provide a legally relevant description of the defendant. Data collection and description in this assessment area were entirely unstandardized prior to development of the FAIs. Two examiners of the same defendant, therefore, might collect different types of information, thereby confounding later attempts to compare their opinions. Further, the information with which they described defendants often bore little relation to the law's concern for certain functional abilities of the defendant related to the specific context of trial participation. In contrast, all of the instruments reviewed here standardize the collection of information across defendants and across examiners. They provide some assurance that the data obtained will have legal relevance to the court in making a competence decision.

Further, there is evidence that trained interviewers/raters can quantify their data reliably with these interview methods. In contrast, the legal relevance or empirical grounding for unstandardized (traditional) forensic interview methods is essentially unknown. The advantages of standardization, therefore, strongly recommend the use of one of the instruments within the context of any assessment related to the question of competence to stand trial.

Historically, the content of FAIs in this area focused heavily on cognitive understanding of basic features of trials. In contrast, events of the 1990s (Bonnie, 1992; *Godinez v. Moran*, 1993) have placed increasing attention on defendants' decision making capacities associated with the waiver of important constitutional rights in the trial process. The MacCAT-CA and the FIT-R come closer than earlier instruments to providing information that goes beyond "factual understanding" to begin to address questions of defendants' decision making capacities. This is an important advance, and instruments that do not provide such information are not in step with the evolution of the legal construct of competence in recent years.

Explanation

Examiners are expected to provide possible explanations for the deficits in functioning that they describe for a defendant. Currently it must be assumed that poor scores or responses on the pretrial competence instruments may be obtained for any of a number of reasons. Among various possible conditions are psychopathological states and developmental disabilities. Other explanations that generally would not be consistent with a judicial finding of legal incompetence are malingering, adverse motivational conditions, or easily remediable lack of knowledge on the part of the defendant.

Potential explanations for functional deficits in trial abilities will require data beyond the item and summary scores of the instruments. Among these data may be content analyses of responses on the instrument; comprehensive mental status interview results; data from psychological tests of general intelligence, personality, and psychopathology; and reports and observations of the examinee's past and present behaviors in settings other than the examination session. Thus FAIs related to competence to stand trial must be used in the context of a broader assessment strategy and data collection plan. Currently, however, there are few empirical guidelines for relating FAI results to these other constructs or clinical measures.

Prediction or Classification

Published hit rates of the pretrial competence instruments are applicable to one's own setting only if the proportion of incompetent defendants (based on judicial criteria, for example) in the local population of examinees is similar to the proportions in past research samples. Further, pretrial competence instruments are likely to be of no value as predictors of judicial conclusions, or traditional forensic assessment conclusions, in jurisdictions in which the base rate of incompetence to stand trial is less than 15% of the defendants referred for competence evaluations.

The previous review identified variability in the degree to which the instruments reviewed here correspond to judicial competence decisions or more extensive forensic examinations. It can be argued, however, that the question of their correspondence is moot. For example, there is no assurance that judicial competence decisions are valid indicators of trial participation abilities. Further, these instruments need not mimic judicial decisions in order to be of considerable value in conveying legally relevant information to the decision makers.

Correspondence with judicial decisions is, perhaps, more relevant when evaluating the effectiveness of screening instruments like the CST and GCCT-MSH. They need not agree with judicial decisions, but they should at least not screen out too many cases that are eventually judged by courts to be incompetent. In this regard, the data in the previous reviews raise some doubts as to their utility. This is especially true given that they do not provide any information on defendants' decision making capacities. Thus some defendants might receive "passing" scores based on their ability to manage the "factual understanding" criteria that constitute the primary focus of the instruments. This would normally result in a recommendation for "no further evaluation," which would allow those defendants with distorted views of the application of information to their own situation, or deficits in decision making capacities, to proceed to trial with their deficits undetected.

The pretrial competence assessment instruments do not attempt to address three important questions that examiners generally must consider in pretrial competence assessments: the likelihood that the defendant, even if currently found competent to stand trial, might decompensate during a trial; the likelihood that a defendant, if currently found incompetent, can benefit by treatment or remediation directed toward augmenting the functions associated with competent participation in trials; and, if incompetence is remediable, the proper place and length of time required for the remediation or treatment.

Conclusions and Opinions

Thus the instruments alone currently do not provide empirical grounds for an examiner's conclusion that "the defendant cannot meet the demands of his future trial." FAIs in this area may contribute to this type of conclusion in some cases, as standardized and reliable methods for describing defendants' legally relevant abilities. But the conclusion itself would require other sources of data, especially about the nature of the pending trial, that would allow one to compare the defendant's degree of ability or disability to the anticipated trial demands and to comment on the implications of the incongruencies in this comparison.

Even when conclusions about incongruencies can be reached, nothing about FAIs justifies an examiner's testimony that the discrepancy between the defendant's abilities and the anticipated trial demands renders the defendant competent or incompetent to stand trial. As explained earlier in the chapter, that is a moral and legal judgment. The instruments provide no basis for going any further than the descriptive, explanatory, and comparative testimony previously described.

5

Waiver of Rights to Silence and Legal Counsel

THE COMPETENCE QUESTION

Adult criminal and juvenile delinquency suspects are provided the right to avoid self-incrimination and to have legal counsel when they are arrested and questioned by law enforcement officers (*Miranda v. Arizona*, 1966; *In re Gault*, 1967; *Fare v. Michael C.*, 1979; *Dickerson v. U.S.*, 2000). If they waive the rights to silence and counsel, their confessions can be admitted as evidence against them in later court proceedings only if their waiver was valid—that is, has been made by the suspect "voluntarily, knowingly, and intelligently" (*Miranda v. Arizona*, 1966).

When defendants have sought to exclude the use of their confession as evidence on the grounds that waiver was invalid, courts have found it necessary to consider the capacities or competence of defendants to have understood their rights and to have waived them voluntarily prior to making the confession to police officers. A defendant's capacities or abilities, however, are not the only consideration. Courts must also review the procedures used by the law enforcement officers to inform the person of the rights, as well as other circumstances of the arrest and questioning

149

event that might have contributed to, or detracted from, a "voluntary, knowing, and intelligent" waiver.

A judicial decision about the validity or invalidity of a defendant's waiver confers no legal status of incompetence on the defendant, even though the defendant's deficient capacities might have played a significant role in the decision. Therefore, competence or incompetence to waive rights is not in itself a legal disposition (as in "competency to stand trial"). Instead, it refers merely to the capacity of the defendant as one major factor to consider when reaching legal conclusions about the validity of the rights waiver.

Mental health professionals frequently have been asked to assess the capacities of defendants to understand and appreciate the rights that they waived at the time of their arrest and interrogation. The possible invalidity of an adult defendant's waiver of rights has been raised most commonly for individuals with significant intellectual deficits or psychological disorders, or when it has been alleged that police employed waiver procedures that might fall short of legal requirements and due process. In addition, many courts have dealt with questions of the capacities of juveniles to validly waive rights to silence and counsel, noting that their relative immaturity suggests greater vulnerability and potentially diminished cognitive capacities to understand their rights (e.g., *Fare v. Michael C.*, 1979; *In re Gault*, 1966; *People v. Lara*, 1967).

The question of capacity to waive *Miranda* rights needs to be distinguished from the matter of "false" or "unreliable" statements by suspects. One may be able to make a valid waiver of rights yet be susceptible to offering a statement to police officers that is untrue, partly true, or greatly distorted. Some suspects have been known to confess to offenses primarily on the basis of reconstructions of the offense provided by police officers, despite their own inability to clearly recall any participation in the offense in question (see Barthel, 1977 for a case example). Moreover, social psychological studies suggest that individuals differ in their capacities to resist suggestions supported by social consensus or by authority figures (Gudjonsson, 1992; Kassin, 1997; Kassin & McNall, 1991). Information about a defendant's susceptibility to making false confessions may be important for purposes of the weight that judges or juries should place on a defendant's confession. But the issue of false confessions requires separate inquiry from the legal question of capacity to waive *Miranda* rights voluntarily, knowingly and intelligently. Thus it is not reviewed in this chapter.

LAW AND CURRENT PRACTICE

Legal Standard

U.S. Supreme Court decisions (*Miranda v. Arizona*, 1966; *In re Gault*, 1967; *Fare v. Michael C.*, 1979; *Dickerson v. U.S.*, 2000) affirm that the validity of waiver of rights at the time of police questioning requires a weighing of the *totality of circumstances*. Application of this "test" of valid waiver raises two general considerations: the suspect's capacities, and the procedures and circumstances surrounding the waiver. The ultimate question of the validity of the waiver, and the subordinate questions of competency of the individual and the adequacy of police procedures for obtaining the waiver, are all judged according to the *voluntary, knowing, and intelligent* standard acknowledged in the decisions noted previously. The following discussion uses the three components in this standard to analyze legal requirements for capacity of the individual to make a competent waiver, and to comment on judgments about capacity in relation to procedural circumstances.

"*KNOWING*" *WAIVER*.   *Miranda v. Arizona* (1966, pp. 444–445, 478–479) specified the now-famous "*Miranda* warnings" that must be given to suspects: that the suspect has a right to remain silent, that any statements made can be used as evidence against the suspect, that the suspect can have an attorney present before and during interrogation, and that an attorney can be appointed if the suspect cannot afford one. Some confessions may be valid even if not preceded by *Miranda* warnings—for example, confessions made spontaneously, without inquiry by police officers. When officers are inquiring, however, waivers are invalid if police officers fail to provide the warnings to the suspect (recently reaffirmed by the U.S. Supreme Court in *Dickerson v. U.S.*, 2000).

No particular degree of capacity to understand these rights and entitlements necessarily satisfies the "knowing" component (Grisso, 1981). Consistent with the "totality of circumstances" approach, courts usually have decided whether a suspect's capacity to understand was sufficient in each specific case in light of circumstances of the waiver (e.g., the manner in which police informed the suspect, and whether the suspect was given assistance by counsel, parents, or friends in understanding the rights: *West v. United States*, 1968).

On the other hand, courts sometimes have addressed the "knowing" component on the basis of the suspect's presumed capacities alone. For example, one court (*United States ex rel. Simon v. Maroney*, 1964) believed that a retarded, 18-year-old suspect was incapable of understanding Miranda warnings, even though police had offered them clearly and properly. Another court (*State v. Prater*, 1970) decided that a suspect had such a great capacity to understand his rights (due to frequent previous exposure to police arrest procedures) that the hasty and incomplete reading of the rights by police officers did not invalidate the waiver. In general, though, legal standards usually construe "knowing" as a sum of suspects' abilities to understand plus the manner in which they are informed.

"INTELLIGENT" WAIVER. The distinction between the "intelligent" and "knowing" elements of capacity to waive rights is seen in a California Supreme Court case (*In re Patrick W.*, 1978, p. 738), in which the court noted that the suspect "showed understanding of the *Miranda* admonitions" ("knowing") but was not likely to "fully comprehend the meaning and effect" of his decision to waive the rights and make incriminating statements to police officers." (See also *People v. Lara*, 1967.) For example, a suspect might *understand* that she has a right to speak with an attorney, as the *Miranda* warnings indicate; but she might not *grasp the significance* of being able to speak with an attorney (for example, might not know what an attorney is or does) and therefore be unable to "intelligently" decide about whether to claim or waive the right. Some courts have even questioned suspects in the courtroom to assure that they understood not only what the *Miranda* warnings said, but also to determine whether they comprehended what manner of legal assistance they refused when they waived the right to legal counsel, or whether they understood the concept of a "right" (e.g., *People v. Baker*, 1973; *Coyote v. U.S.*, 1967).

Some courts, however, have disagreed with this interpretation of the *Miranda* standard, holding that only a "basic understanding" is necessary. For example, in *People v. Bernasco* (1990), the Supreme Court of Illinois defined the requisite knowledge as "understand[ing] the very words used in the warnings. It need not mean the ability to understand far-reaching legal and strategic effects of waiving one's rights ... [or] ... how widely or deeply an interrogation may probe" (p. 964). By this type of ruling, a "knowing" waiver might be made if one knows that one can get a lawyer (which is all the *Miranda* warnings say), without the need for an inquiry into whether the suspect also understands the roles a lawyer might play in legal proceedings. In this context, it is unclear what the law intends when it refers to an "intelligent" waiver of rights, or whether the term has any meaning separate from "understanding."

Equally unclear is the role of mental illness when courts apply the "intelligent waiver" standard. A suspect, for example, might understand what he is being told when issued the *Miranda* warnings, yet may have a delusional belief that renders the information inapplicable (in the suspect's mind) to his circumstances. This might seem to negate the value of the suspect's adequate understanding, since it nullifies the relevance of the warnings for oneself. Few courts, however, have verified this interpretation, and at least one court has found that it is not relevant for judging "intelligent" waiver. In a case in which the suspect appeared to understand the *Miranda* warnings but had a delusional belief that God would protect him if he confessed, the Supreme Court of Michigan decided that all that mattered was "whether the defendant understood ... that the state could use what he said in a later trial against him," saying that the lower court had erred when it "focused on *why* defendant was confessing rather than considering whether defendant could in fact understand" (*Michigan v. Daoud*, 2000).

Therefore, in states like Michigan that construe the issue narrowly, it is not at all clear what is meant by the term "intelligent" in the "knowing, intelligent, and voluntary" standard, since the inquiry regarding "knowing and intelligent" appears to be satisfied if defendants simply "know" what they were told when given the *Miranda* warnings. In states like California, however, what defendants believed when they applied the warnings to their own situation ("fully comprehend the meaning and effect" of warnings: *People v. Lara*, 1967; *In re Patrick W.*, 1978) is part of the inquiry regarding the validity of waiver of rights during police interrogation.

"VOLUNTARY" WAIVER.   This component requires that the waiver decision must be a consequence of the suspect's will, rather than a product of coercion. How this has been interpreted has varied considerably across courts and circumstances.

Especially with reference to juveniles, some courts have used terms such as *dependency, immaturity, compliance*, and *deference* to refer to characteristics of suspects that may be relevant when considering the coercive effects of police interrogation (Grisso, 1981). Similarly, in *In re Gault* (1967), the U.S. Supreme Court remarked on the likelihood that youths' waivers of rights might be influenced by "fantasy, fright and despair" associated with their immaturity.

At least in cases involving adult suspects, however, appellate court decisions have tended to focus on the actions of police when examining the voluntariness of a confession, excluding a consideration of the degree to which the suspect "felt" coerced. In *Colorado v. Connelly* (1986), the U.S. Supreme Court considered whether a suspect made a voluntary waiver of rights when he believed that God was commanding him to confess a murder to police officers. The Court decided that the purpose of the voluntariness inquiry was to assure that the actions of police officers were not of a coercive nature. Because police actions were considered to be proper in *Connelly*, the waiver was deemed voluntary despite Connelly's claim that his delusion was "coercive."

Therefore, the "voluntariness" component of the "knowing, intelligent and voluntary" standard need not involve inquiry into the state of mind of the suspect as a matter of U.S. Constitutional protections. This does not mean, however, that the characteristics of the suspect are irrelevant when judging voluntariness. Courts must still weigh whether police actions were coercive in light of the "totality of circumstances" (as discussed in more detail below). For example, in other cases, the U.S. Supreme Court has made it clear that juveniles require special care regarding potential coercion because of their relatively immature status; circumstances of police interrogation that are not necessarily coercive with adult suspects might be coercive with juveniles (*In re Gault*, 1967; *Fare v. Michael C.*, 1979; see also *Haley v. Ohio*, 1948; *Gallagos v. Colorado*, 1962).

Judicial reasoning when applying the "voluntary, knowing, and intelligent" standard is structured by two additional types of legal provisions, which may be called *decision rules* and *decision variables*.

DECISION RULES.   The law provides two approaches to deciding the question of the validity of waiver of rights to silence and legal counsel. They are called the *per se* approach and *the totality of circumstances* approach. A *per se* law codifies the automatic invalidation of a waiver in every case in which a certain fact or circumstance is shown to have been present. In contrast, the totality of circumstances approach requires a discretionary determination based on the individual circumstances of each case.

Currently, no states have *per se* rules based on capacities or characteristics of suspects alone. For example, no statute considers all mentally retarded defendants or all children automatically incompetent to waive *Miranda* rights. Some states, however, consider juveniles incompetent to waive their rights *unassisted*. In those states, juveniles' waivers are automatically (*per se*) invalid if they have not been advised by parents or other "friendly adults" (that is, if one of these persons was not present at the waiver) (Feld, 2000; Grisso, 1981, 1998a). *Per se* rules of this type specify conditions for determining invalidity of waiver, but not validity. In such states, for example, the presence of a parent at a juvenile's waiver does not automatically validate the waiver, because the juvenile in question might have been incapable of understanding the warnings even with assistance.

The *totality of circumstances* approach has predominated in this area of law (*Fare v. Michael C.*, 1979). This approach simply disallows the presumption that any particular fact, characteristic of suspects, or circumstance is sufficient to decide the validity or invalidity of waivers across all cases (Frumkin, 2000). Given two individuals with similar capacities, the waiver of one might be valid and the other invalid, depending on differences in circumstances between the two cases.

DECISION VARIABLES.   Leading cases have provided courts with lists of characteristics to consider when determining the capacities of suspects to waive *Miranda* rights (e.g., *Coyote v. United States*, 1967; *Fare v. Michael C.*, 1979; *Johnson v. Zerbst*, 1938; *State v. White*, 1973; *West v. United States*, 1967). A composite of these lists includes the following factors: age, intelligence, education, amount of prior experience with police, physical condition, background, and conduct. Other cases have cited additionally a suspect's psychotic condition. Courts providing these lists, however, have not confined judicial considerations to these characteristics alone.

Courts also have provided lists of procedural factors to be considered when judges determine whether suspects, given their degree of capacity, could have made a valid waiver in the instant circumstances. For example, the Court in *West v. United States* (1968) underscored a consideration of the manner in which police informed the suspect, whether the suspect was held incommunicado for a long period of time prior to questioning, and several other procedural variables. (See Grisso, 1998a, for an extended description of relevant circumstances of actions of police officers.) How these factors are applied, however, is a matter of considerable judicial discretion, as well as appellate uncertainty. It is somewhat more typical, however, for courts to have accepted suspects' waiver of rights even when police provide misleading information to suspects about available evidence against them (e.g., in *State v. Jackson*, 1983, in which suspect was told, falsely, that he was seen by an eyewitness and his fingerprints were found on the gun).

In general, however, when courts apply the totality of circumstances approach, police procedures are taken into consideration along with the capacities of the suspect in determining whether a waiver of rights was "knowing, intelligent, and voluntary."

Legal Process

Modern police practice strongly discourages the "third-degree tactics" of an earlier era. Current manuals for police investigation emphasize a friendly and concerned type of questioning, noting that this is both more humane and often more effective than aggressive intimidation in obtaining a suspect's cooperation (Inbau, Reid, & Buckley, 1986). The importance of obtaining confessions that will stand up to legal challenges has stimulated some law enforcement departments to urge officers to employ care in abiding by the letter of the law. On the other hand, interrogation manuals (e.g., Inbau et al., 1986) encourage relatively sophisticated methods for inducing waivers and confessions, employing psychological tactics for persuasion such as minimization, maximization, implied but unstated threats and promises, and suggested negative and positive incentives (see Kassin, 1997; Kassin & McNall, 1991; Oberlander & Goldstein, 2001). As coercive as these tactics may seem, they are generally allowable from a legal perspective.

Actual practices with mentally or developmentally disabled criminal suspects have not been documented or studied. Interrogation practices with juveniles apparently almost always result in a waiver of rights.

Grisso and Pomicter (1977) found that the rate of refusal to waive rights was only about 9% of juvenile cases in which waiver of rights was requested by police (compared to about 42% for adult suspects, according to Seeburger & Wettick, 1967). Juveniles most often were questioned at police stations or juvenile detention centers, and parents were present in the majority of cases. Other evidence, however, indicated that few parents explained the *Miranda* warnings to their children or provided advice concerning how the child should respond at the time of the waiver decision (Grisso, 1981), and that parents often believe they should encourage their children to cooperate with police officers in interrogation circumstances (Grisso & Ring, 1979).

Questions of invalidity of waiver are most likely to be raised by defense attorneys during the weeks or months following a defendant's questioning and confession to police. An assessment may be sought to evaluate the defendant's capacities to have understood the *Miranda* warnings or to have waived the rights voluntarily. Not all cases will involve evaluations, however, as sometimes the question of a waiver's validity may be raised primarily on the grounds that police procedures were inadequate to meet legal, threshold requirements of *per se* rules for procedures in dealing with suspects.

Little is known about the actual manner in which courts weigh the procedural circumstances and characteristics of suspects to arrive at decisions about the validity of rights waiver. In one review of appellate cases involving juveniles (Grisso, 1981), suspects 12 years of age or younger usually were perceived by courts as lacking in understanding of *Miranda* warnings; decisions in cases of 13- to 15-year-olds were more variable, whereas waivers in cases of juveniles 16 years and above were perceived as valid more frequently than in cases involving younger juveniles. Courts frequently associated very low IQ scores (e.g., below 75) with insufficient understanding of the warnings. Intelligence test scores often were cited in conjunction with poor academic records or reading abilities. Finally, suspects' number of prior contacts with police often were cited as relevant to courts' opinions about requisite understanding, with more prior contacts suggesting better understanding.

Many courts have recognized that a defendant's current level of comprehension of the *Miranda* rights (i.e., at the time of an evaluation or a court hearing) might not represent a suspect's capacities at the time that waiver of the rights actually was obtained (that is, at an earlier time of arrest, rights waiver, and questioning by police) (Grisso, 1981). For example, a court may decide that even though a defendant currently manifests only mild intellectual deficiencies, certain circumstances surrounding the arrest and waiver process were likely to have impaired the defendant's ability to use his or her modest intellectual potential. Therefore, judicial deliberations frequently involve a difficult process, taking into consideration the defendant's current capacities, information about the procedure and atmosphere of the past arrest and police questioning, and how these two sets of factors might have interacted to affect the defendant's comprehension and decision-making process at the past time in question.

Competency Assessment: Current Practice

Appellate case opinions provide ample evidence that courts have long relied on mental health professionals' assessments of defendants' capacities when the question of valid waiver is raised, especially in cases involving juveniles or persons with mental illness or developmental disabilities (Frumkin, 2000; Grisso, 1981). Yet, at the time of the first edition of EC, mental health professionals had little guidance in performing evaluations related to waiver of *Miranda* rights, other than the results of one substantial study of juveniles' capacities to waive *Miranda* rights (Grisso, 1981). Subsequently, literature offering such guidance has increased (Frumkin, 2000; Fulero & Everington, 1995; Grisso, 1998a; Melton, Petrila, Poythress, & Slobogin, 1997; Oberlander & Goldstein, 2001), and at this writing, two major studies were underway to replicate, update, and extend the earlier research by Grisso (1981) on juveniles' capacities to waive *Miranda* rights.

In general, these references describe a process involving the collection of detailed data on the circumstances of the arrest and interrogation, and relevant psychological characteristics of the suspect. Typically this includes clinical information (e.g., level of intelligence, mental disorder) and direct questioning about what the defendant currently can comprehend regarding the *Miranda* warnings. The inferential process described in these sources is complex, requiring retrospective interpretations of the defendant's capacities based on evidence of current capacities, reports of the defendant's behavior and state of mind at the time of the interrogation, and knowledge of a wide range of circumstances of the interrogation. There has been no research, however, describing the degree to which clinicians employ these models and guidelines for evaluations of defendants' capacities related to waiver of *Miranda* rights.

FROM LEGAL STANDARD TO FORENSIC ASSESSMENT

Functional Component

Grisso (1980, 1981) has described several broad abilities, or areas of functioning, associated with the concept of capacity to waive rights to silence and legal counsel. These abilities were derived from comprehensive reviews of appellate cases by a research panel of lawyers and psychologists. They provide conceptual definitions of what a person should be able to know, understand, believe or do (functional abilities) in order to make an informed decision about waiver of rights at the time of police investigations. A review of more recent case law in the area suggests only minor cautions, as noted later, regarding that earlier analysis.

The first area of functioning is the person's *understanding of the rights warnings*. Thus the suspect's understanding of the words and phrases usually used by police to inform suspects, as provided in *Miranda v. Arizona* (1966), would seem to be the proper focus for obtaining data associated with this part of the legal inquiry.

The second area of functioning is the suspect's *perceptions of the intended functions of the* Miranda *rights*. For example, suspects might understand that they have a right to an attorney; but their ability to consider the rights intelligently might be impaired if they do not understand the function of an attorney in legal proceedings, or if they have delusional or seriously distorted beliefs about the implications of waiving the right to avail themselves of an attorney's counsel. As noted above in "Legal Standards," this function will be more relevant in some states than in others, depending on whether or not they restrict the inquiry about "knowing and intelligent" waiver to a simple matter of understanding the words and phrases that the *Miranda* warnings provide. Grisso outlined three content areas within this function that seemed to be important to assess:

- the suspect's accurate perception of the nature of interrogation (e.g., its adversarial quality)
- the suspect's accurate perception of the attorney–client relationship (e.g., its advocacy quality), and
- the suspect's accurate perception of the irrevocable protection from self-incrimination (e.g., that the right is more "powerful" than police or judicial discretionary powers).

A third function is the suspect's *capacities to reason about the probable consequences of waiver or nonwaiver decisions*. For example, some suspects' capacities to reason, or in the case of juveniles, their immature perspective, might impair the process by which they decide about their waiver and confession. Cases in which this might be of greatest importance would involve persons whose mental retardation seriously limits their abilities to process information (Ellis & Luckasson, 1985; Everington & Fulero, 1999; Fulero & Everington, 1995), and youths whose developmental capacities might limit their ability to weigh the consequences of their decisions (e.g., limited time perspective required to anticipate short-range and long-range events, limited capacities to generate optional responses: see generally: Scott, 1992; Scott, Reppucci, & Woolard, 1995; Steinberg & Cauffman, 1996).

Grisso (1981) did not include a "voluntariness" component in his analysis of capacities to waive rights, because it was not clear that the law conceptualizes voluntariness as a capacity to be evaluated apart from the procedures with which a waiver was obtained. Some courts have expressed concerns that some suspects might choose to waive rights because they are especially acquiescent—for example, some children and adolescents who are vulnerable to "fantasy, fright and despair" (*In re Gault*, 1967). The voluntariness of statements, however, typically has not been judged on the basis of defendants' specific capacities. As noted earlier, courts have looked to the behavior of police officers when judging voluntariness (*Colorado v. Connelly*, 1986), or occasionally at the simple fact of youthfulness as increasing the risk of involuntary (simply acquiescent) agreements to waive rights in cases involving children. Thus it is difficult to postulate a concept of "capacity for voluntariness" that could offer meaningful guidance for psychological inquiry to assist the courts.

The components reviewed above suggest that forensic assessments for competence to waive *Miranda* rights should examine several functional capacities of examinees:

- understanding of the *Miranda* warnings (i.e., the words and phrases used to convey to them the rights to silence and legal counsel)
- perceptions of the intended functions of the rights
- expectancies and reasoning concerning probable outcomes of waiver or nonwaiver of the rights.

For conceptual convenience (but not necessarily for purposes of legal definition), the first function seems to parallel the "knowing" element of the legal standard (understanding), and the second and third components parallel the "intelligent" element (awareness of functions of rights, expectancies, reasoning). The forensic assessment instruments reviewed later in this chapter were intended to provide direct indexes of these specific abilities associated with defendants' capacities to waive rights to silence and counsel.

Causal Component

Laws controlling legal decisions about the validity of waiver do not specifically require the establishment of a causal connection between deficits in the above areas of functioning and psychological disorders or disabilities (e.g., mental illness or mental retardation). Nevertheless, appellate cases demonstrate courts' close scrutiny of these relationships (Grisso, 1981). When testimony suggests that a defendant may have had poor understanding of the *Miranda* warnings, courts will attend closely to information about general intellectual ability, age and developmental status, mental disorder, or prior experiences (such as numerous contacts with police) that might bear on the defendant's general knowledge of the rights.

One of the reasons for inquiry into this relationship is a concern that a defendant may manage the appearance of deficiency in understanding of rights, in order to suppress a confession and weaken the state's case against him. For example, in *State ex rel. Holifield* (1975), the appellate court noted that the juvenile defendant had incorrectly answered several questions posed to him at the lower court hearing concerning the meaning of the *Miranda* warnings. The court acknowledged that the juvenile's testimony might have been "self-serving." Nevertheless, the court believed that substantial questions about the juvenile's competency were raised by his answers, when considered in light of his age and testimony about his poor academic and intellectual capacities. As demonstrated in this court's reasoning, many courts look to relationships, or causal connections, between functional deficits (specific to the legal context in question) and psychological characteristics, in order to judge whether the deficits appear to be real—that is, beyond the person's control—or whether they may be feigned.

Therefore, an important task in a forensic assessment will be to collect and describe information about a defendant's psychological characteristics that bear some logical relation to the functional abilities associated with competence to waive rights. Which psychological characteristics will be important to assess?

In an empirical study involving 359 juveniles, Grisso (1981) found that understanding of *Miranda* warnings was related significantly to both age and IQ scores, with these two variables independently accounting for significant variance in scores on measures of *Miranda* comprehension. Juveniles' amounts of prior exposure to the warnings (i.e., number of prior felony arrests) were related to *Miranda* comprehension only for white juveniles. These results provide one source of information for forensic examiners who must consider the relationships between *Miranda* comprehension and other psychological characteristics in individual cases. For example, if a juvenile responds incorrectly to inquiries about the *Miranda* warnings read to him in an examination session (see instruments reviewed later in this chapter), the examiner might be led to question the accuracy of this assessment if the juvenile falls into the higher IQ range (average range) or upper age levels (16 or 17) of juveniles in the Grisso studies. Additional information regarding relevant characteristics for the causal question is provided for adults with mental retardation (Everington & Fulero, 1995; Fulero & Everington, 1999).

Beyond these empirical guides, however, examiners must look to psychology's general theories of intelligence, cognition, development, memory, and information processing. Theory and research in these areas might assist the examiner in forming expectancies concerning the relation between a measure of general cognitive ability and degree of manifest understanding of *Miranda* warnings. Causal interpretations might then be checked by comparing results on the measure of general cognitive ability to the examinee's answers to questions about the meanings of the *Miranda* warnings, in order to determine whether they are consistent or inconsistent with theoretical expectancy. Grisso (1988) provided a review of this inferential process and examples of its application to cases, especially in dealing with questions of malingering of deficits in capacities to comprehend information relevant for criminal competencies.

Interactive Component

As explained earlier, a court's decision about the validity of a suspect's past waiver of the rights to silence and counsel generally requires an examination of the "totality of circumstances." This concept clearly identifies the validity of a waiver of *Miranda* rights as neither a function of the suspect's capacities alone nor the circumstances of the situation, but as a question of the degree of capacity of the suspect weighed in relation to the demands of the situation. There may be exceptions, such as cases in which police fail to provide the *Miranda* warnings. But most cases will manifest this interactive perspective in arriving at a conclusion about the validity of *Miranda* waiver.

In this sense, a suspect's capacities to waive *Miranda* rights (or the validity of waiver) requires an examination of the congruency or incongruency of the suspect's functional abilities and the demands of the specific situation that the suspect encountered when arrested and questioned by law enforcement officers. This interactive characteristic of the legal competency suggests that forensic assessments should include, whenever possible, a comparison between the functional capacities of the examinee and various circumstances of the instant waiver situation.

A general review of appellate cases in this area (described earlier in this chapter) suggests several circumstances of waiver situations that are perceived as bearing on the comparison of a suspect's capacities and situational demands. One set of circumstances focuses largely on the opportunity for the suspect to be informed of the rights and to consider them carefully. These circumstances include:

- the words and phrases actually used to inform the suspect (e.g., the wording of the *Miranda* form used by police, variations in words, or message sequence, used by police when informing the suspect)
- manner of presentation ("boilerplate" or hasty reading of the rights; careful, slow presentation; attempts to explain or interpret the warnings for the suspect; attempts to elicit suspect's understanding of the warnings), and
- presence or absence of a consultative person (e.g., whether parents or attorney were present, whether or not they actually gave advice or were passive).

Several other circumstances noted in appellate opinions seem to relate primarily to questions of voluntariness of waiver:

- time of day or night
- length of time suspect was held incommunicado
- where the suspect was held prior to waiver and questioning
- conditions under which suspect was held (e.g., was or was not provided necessary food or water)
- opportunities for suspect to contact attorney or other supportive persons, and
- police demeanor (e.g., urgings, suggestions, persuasive tactics, forceful or coercive behaviors).

Finally, courts have considered situational states of the suspect at the time of the waiver: for example, states of intoxication or drug influence, fatigue, or physical illness.

Thus, suspects who are intoxicated, or who are offered only a formal, "boilerplate" reading of the *Miranda* warnings, or who are held incommunicado for several hours prior to a reading of rights and questioning, have greater demands placed on their capacities to understand the rights or to make a voluntary choice regarding waiver. When a suspect's capacities themselves are deficient, the interaction may be construed as constituting a degree of incongruency between ability and demand.

Assessing the demand, however, may be quite difficult for the forensic examiner. Many of the potential demand characteristics require a fact-finding process for which the examiner may be ill-equipped or unqualified. Indeed, the examiner might be in conflict with the function of the court in attempting to establish the facts of the waiver situation, inasmuch as these are likely to be contested by the parties in the case.

Judgmental and Dispositional Components

A decision as to whether the degree of incongruency between a suspect's capacities and situational demands constitutes an invalid waiver requires a judgment about justice. In some cases, suspects' capacities may be so extremely deficient that almost anyone's sense of justice would lead to a conclusion of invalidity of waiver. Yet in most cases, courts must wrestle with the question of "how much incongruency is enough" when weighing whether the decision should favor the suspect's protection or the claims of the state.

The latter consideration must take into account the dispositional gravity of the decision that a waiver is or is not valid. At stake for the defendant is possible conviction of a crime, partly or largely on the basis of the confession obtained after waiver. Convictions on the basis of a waiver made involuntarily or without understanding threaten constitutional safeguards protecting citizens against the state's abuse of its powers. On the other hand, leaning too heavily toward protection of criminal suspects threatens the ability of the state to prosecute offenders.

When forensic examiners merely report data on suspects' capacities for understanding of *Miranda* warnings, as well as possible relations between these characteristics and the demands of waiver circumstances, they are not stating conclusions about justice or the balance of individual liberties and state interests. They step very close to this conclusion, however, when they attempt to answer the question, "Did this suspect understand the *Miranda* warnings, at the time of waiver, sufficiently to make a knowing, intelligent, and voluntary waiver of rights?" This question posed by the legal standard cannot be answered by any set of observations made by the examiner. Deciding the degree of understanding or reasoning that is required in order to satisfy the legal standard is a moral or legal judgment beyond the proper role of the mental health expert witness.

REVIEW OF FORENSIC ASSESSMENT INSTRUMENTS

Assessments related to defendants' capacities to waive rights to silence and legal counsel will benefit by the evaluation of functional abilities or capacities that are recognized by legal standards as relevant for competent waiver of rights. This section reviews four assessment instruments related to this objective, which are the only instruments specifically designed for this purpose: *Comprehension of Miranda Rights, Comprehension of Miranda Rights-Recognition, Comprehension of Miranda Vocabulary,* and *Function of Rights in Interrogation.* These instruments have been published as a set (Grisso, 1998b), although they are reviewed separately.

Readers may also be interested in examining the *Gudjonsson Suggestibility Scale* (Gudjonsson, 1992). The instrument was developed to examine suspects' individual differences in the degree to which they may yield to suggestions by police officers, thus providing a distorted or false confession. The instrument is not reviewed here because the reliability of suspects' statements, and factors that may cause them to be distorted, is a separate issue from the validity of their waiver of *Miranda* rights. The instrument is described in a book by Gudjonsson (1992) and has been the focus of much research (for reviews, see Gudjonsson, Rutter, & Clare, 1995; Gudjonsson & Sigurdsson, 1995, 1996).

COMPREHENSION OF MIRANDA RIGHTS (CMR)

Author

Grisso, T.

Author Affiliation

Department of Psychiatry, University of Massachusetts Medical School

Primary Reference

Grisso, T. (1998b). *Instruments for Assessing Understanding and Appreciation of Miranda Rights.* Sarasota, FL: Professional Resource Press

Description

The *Comprehension of Miranda Rights* (CMR) measure was developed to assess adolescents' and adults' understanding of the rights to silence and to legal counsel, as these rights are conveyed by a standard form used in law enforcement procedures. The CMR is one of four instruments developed in an NIMH-funded research project (c), completed in 1980, to address the capacities of juveniles (and adults) to provide a meaningful waiver of the rights to silence and counsel. The instrument was intended as a research tool and as a method for evaluating defendants' capacities in actual cases in which their ability to understand their *Miranda* rights has been raised as a legal question. Subsequently it has been used clinically in cases in which examiners are asked to evaluate the capacities of defendants in cases in which valid waiver of *Miranda* rights are being questioned.

The CMR is administered with the aid of a "flip-chart," desk-top easel that shows examinee stimuli on the side facing the examinee and administration instructions on the side facing the examiner (d). The stimuli consist of the four *Miranda* warnings, shown individually, as follows:

1. You do not have to make a statement and have the right to remain silent.
2. Anything you say can and will be used against you in a court of law.
3. You are entitled to consult an attorney before interrogation and to have an attorney present at the time of the interrogation.
4. If you cannot afford an attorney, one will be appointed for you.

Each stimulus sentence is shown to the examinee and read aloud by the examiner in the testing session. After each stimulus the examiner asks: "Tell me in your own words what is said in that sentence." Standardized inquiry questions are printed on the examiner side of the easel pages, requesting information when the examinee's response uses certain phrases verbatim rather than paraphrased, and when the initial response is vague or confusing.

The manual (d) provides scoring criteria and examples for assigning each of the four responses 2-point (adequate), 1-point (questionable), or 0-point (inadequate) credit, so that total points range from 0–8. If an examinee's first response to an item is less adequate than a later response following one of the standardized inquiry questions, generally the examinee is credited with the best response. Scores may be compared to norms for juveniles or for adults (provided in the manual), and/or they may be used as absolute indicators of the defendant's understanding of each *Miranda* warning statement.

Conceptual Basis

CONCEPT DEFINITION.   The project within which the CMR was developed analyzed the valid waiver of *Miranda* rights as depending on two broad classes of circumstances: procedural circumstances (e.g., time and place of the waiver), and nonprocedural circumstances involving primarily the characteristics of the defendant. The latter set of circumstances was conceptualized as addressing "competence to waive rights."

A review of legal cases (c) suggested three components defining the concept of competence to waive rights:

- comprehension of rights (understanding the rights and entitlements)
- beliefs about the legal context (understanding and belief concerning the significance of the rights in the context of interactions with law enforcement officers, legal counsel, and the court), and

- problem solving (capacities to weigh and consider the rights and to form meaningful expectancies in the process of deciding whether to waive rights).

Therefore, "comprehension of rights" (the focus of the CMR) was seen as only one of three components for considering a defendant's capacities to waive *Miranda* rights, pertaining only to the defendant's ability to understand what rights were said to be available, as informed by *Miranda* warnings. Further, although the three components together might serve to represent a defendant's waiver competence, the validity of waiver was recognized to be a broader, legal construct encompassing not only waiver competence but also procedural and circumstantial characteristics of the waiver event itself.

OPERATIONAL DEFINITION. The CMR was developed as one of three operational definitions of the comprehension of *Miranda* rights component of waiver competency (see also CMR-R and CMV, in this chapter). The items for the CMR were the four *Miranda* warning statements used in actual waiver situations by law enforcement officers in St. Louis County at the time of the original study. Scoring criteria were developed (c) in a process involving:

- collection of a large number of responses in a pilot procedure within a juvenile court detention center population,
- study and recommendations by several panels of legal consultants (local and national) to categorize and define these responses as adequate, questionable, and inadequate,
- development of formal scoring criteria and sets of examples for each item on the basis of the panel recommendations, and
- development and empirical study of the use and reliability of a scoring manual with additional sets of juveniles and adults in legal settings.

Consultation involving legal professionals was an integral part of this process. For example, an interdisciplinary team of psychologists and attorneys (in juvenile courts and in an advocacy juvenile law center) worked together to produce the system for categorizing responses incorporated into the scoring manual. The tentative scoring criteria were submitted for review and comment to a national panel of juvenile court attorneys, juvenile law advocates, and judges.

CRITIQUE. The definition of the construct underlying the CMR (comprehension *of Miranda* rights) clearly indicates that it does not define competence to waive rights, but rather defines one cognitive component that contributes to that broader construct as defined by legal interpretations of competence to waive *Miranda* rights. The primary reference indicates that comprehension of *Miranda* rights is presumed to relate to psychological constructs of a developmental, cognitive nature (e.g., general intelligence, formal cognitive development), as well as learning and exposure to information concerning rights in legal contexts.

The development of the CMR manifests considerable attention to content relevance and face validity. For example, the instrument uses the same *Miranda* warning items used in police procedures, and the scoring system represents a legal consensus (based on panels of lawyers with considerable experience in juvenile and criminal law) about the adequacy or inadequacy of understanding manifested in various paraphrased responses.

A chief concern, however, is the wording of the warnings used in the instrument, which were the wordings used by the St. Louis Police Department at the time of the study. Grisso (c) claimed that the wordings used in the CMR were similar to those used in other jurisdictions. However, while most jurisdictions use the same four general warnings, a wide range of variations in wording have developed across the past two decades. Some police departments, for example, use the word "questioning" instead of the word "interrogation" that appears in the standardized CMR administration. Some use "lawyer" instead of "attorney." Some add a fifth warning, to the effect that if the suspect waives the rights and agrees to talk to police officers, the suspect still has the right to stop at any time (in other words, may re-invoke the rights after having waived them).

In actual practice, it is possible to substitute local wordings of the warnings for those in the CMR, because the scoring system is such that it can be applied to suspects' responses regardless of the wording of the warnings. However, if these warnings are worded very differently from the standardized statements in the CMR, the scores obtained cannot be compared meaningfully to the norms provided in the manual (which were obtained with the standardized wording of the warnings).

The CMR was not conceptualized as an index of the examinee's understanding of *Miranda* rights at the time of police interrogation, but rather at the time of the assessment itself. Inferences about the relation of current understanding to understanding in situations in the past would require additional evidence and reasoning beyond CMR performance in an evaluation session.

The choice of a paraphrase response format is well grounded in past research on the evaluation of knowledge and understanding. Paraphrase formats, however, may be subject to interpretation error due to verbal expressive difficulties of many delinquent youths (and some adults). That is, some examinees might not be able to express verbally what they understand. This problem is mitigated by the availability of parallel instruments using other response formats (see CMR-R and CMV), but it suggests caution if the CMR is administered as the sole measure of comprehension of *Miranda* rights in a clinical assessment.

Psychometric Development

STANDARDIZATION.   Administration and scoring criteria are described in detail in the primary reference and are highly standardized. For example, only certain inquiry questions may be asked and only under particular, narrowly defined response circumstances. Scoring criteria are provided by general statements of principle for each level of scores, by numerous specific examples, and by a description of the scoring process itself.

RELIABILITY.   The manual (d) provides interrater reliability coefficients between pairs of three experienced raters and an inexperienced rater, at different levels of experience during a research project, for individual CMR items and for CMR total scores. Generally, interrater coefficients are reported in the range of .80 to .97, with 90% perfect scoring agreements in one sample of 912 scoring events (c, p. 243). Better than 90% agreement was also reported by two other studies involving independent scoring of protocols by multiple raters, using samples of adult defendants with and without mental retardation (a, b). Test-retest within 48 hours for a sample of 24 juveniles (IQ = 69–117, M = 97.2) yielded a Pearson correlation coefficient of .84 (c).

NORMS.   Juveniles' and adults' CMR scores may be compared to normative data on juveniles and adults collected in the research project for which the CMR was developed (c). The juvenile sample consisted of 431 juvenile court detainees and residents of juvenile delinquency rehabilitation centers in St. Louis, Missouri. Ages ranged from 10 to 16, about two-thirds were male, and about three-fourths were white. Intelligence test scores ranged from 70 and below (11%) to 101 and above (22%) (M = 88), and most youths had one or more court referrals prior to their current referral. The adult sample included 203 offenders residing in halfway houses in St. Louis that took referrals from state and federal correctional agencies for offenders reentering the community. The mean age was 25 (lowest age is 17), about 80% were male and 40% were white. In the normative tables, CMR means are provided separately for juveniles and for adults for age-by-IQ classifications.

CRITIQUE.   Standardization appears to be adequate. Scoring manifests the capacity for good rater reliability with adequate training or practice.

The normative data are based on population samples with particular relevance for individual legal cases in which the instrument may be employed clinically. Some care should be taken in employing the juvenile norms in jurisdictions where juvenile court populations manifest a higher proportion of racial minorities than in the normative samples.

One concern with the norms and their current utility is the fact that they were collected over 20 years ago. It may be that youths and adults today have no greater familiarity with *Miranda* rights than in the late 1970s, but it is possible that such matters are better understood by some youths in the 21st century. No research other than the original study that produced the CMR has produced norms for general juvenile justice or criminal justice populations. At this writing, two large studies are underway to replicate, update, and extend the original studies with the CMR and its companion instruments. These studies will help to address whether the current norms should continue to be applied.

Construct Validation

In the original study (c), correlations between scores on the four CMR items were relatively low ($r = .20-.30$), while item scores correlated substantially ($r = .55-.73$) with total CMR scores. Thus each item may be assessing considerably different content from other items, yet with sufficient commonality to suggest their interpretive relation to a single construct.

In the juvenile sample of the original study ($n = 431$), CMR scores correlated adequately with scores on two companion tests, all three instruments having been developed in relation to the same construct and using similar content but different stimulus and response formats (correlation with CMV, .67; with CMR-R, .55). (See CMV and CMR-R reviews in this chapter.) No correlations between these tests were reported for the adult sample.

CMR scores correlated .47 with short-form Wechsler intelligence test scores for juveniles. In analyses of variance, CMR scores were significantly related to IQ scores for juveniles and adults, independent of variance related to race and socioeconomic status (c). In a separate study, significantly lower CMR scores were found for persons with mental retardation than for persons without mental retardation (a).

CMR scores manifested a small, significant correlation with age within the original juvenile sample ($r = .19$), but not in the adult sample (c). Very significant differences in CMR scores were found between the juvenile and adult samples (which did not differ significantly in mean IQ or socioeconomic status). For the juveniles with IQ scores above 80, CMR performance appeared to reach a plateau (similar to average adult performance) at about age 16; among juveniles with IQ scores of 80 and below, however, CMR performance generally was poorer than that of adults with similarly low IQ scores. Juveniles below 14 years performed significantly more poorly than did juveniles 14 to 16 and adults (c).

Above IQ scores of 80, CMR was not related to race in the juvenile sample; below this IQ, African-American juveniles in general performed significantly more poorly on the CMR than did white juveniles with similarly low IQ scores.

In the original CMR study, adult defendants with greater experience with the justice system (e.g., number of prior court felony referrals) had a significantly greater mean CMR score than those with less experience. Similarly, another study found that CMR mean scores for persons with mental retardation were greater for those currently involved in the criminal justice system (on probation) than for those who were contacted through sheltered workshops (b).

In the original juvenile sample, however, amount of prior experience was not related to CMR scores; instead, it was related positively (and significantly) to CMR scores for white juveniles, and negatively for African-American juveniles (c). That is, African-American juveniles with more court experience manifested poorer CMR scores than did African-American juveniles with less court experience.

CRITIQUE.   The relations between CMR scores and performance on its companion measures suggests that the instruments focus on a common construct. The significant but relatively lower correlation between these instruments and IQ scores suggests that the construct assessed is not merely general intelligence, but rather a construct that is more specific to the content of the instruments.

Several of the results are consistent with what would be predicted on the basis of age and developmental perspectives concerning cognitive capacities of juveniles and adults. For example, the poor performance of juveniles under 14, relative to older juveniles and adults, is consistent with the theoretical view that the age range of 11 to 14 is a critical period for the development of formal operational thinking typical of adults' cognitive processes. Tables in the original reference and the manual (c, d) show several expected mental-age effects when age and intelligence test scores are employed together in analyses of CMR scores.

Some results related to race suggest caution in interpretation of the CMR with African-American juveniles. Specifically, African-American juveniles with low IQ scores performed more poorly than white juveniles with similar ages and low IQ scores. This may be due to the paraphrase format of the CMR, which requires decoding of a message in standard (and somewhat legalistic) English and encoding to produce a response expressing one's understanding intelligibly to another person. Both the encoding and decoding processes might be more difficult for some subset of African-American juveniles with cultural exposure to a linguistic background other than standard English. Thus they may be at a particular disadvantage in understanding the message of *Miranda* warnings in their usual form. In addition, however, the CMR format might place them at a special disadvantage to manifest what they do understand about the rights to silence and counsel.

The CMR offers no safeguards against attempts by examinees to appear less knowledgeable about the *Miranda* rights than they might actually be. At least some examinees might understand the potential benefits of exclusion of their confession from trial evidence, as well as the role of the examiner's test results in a court's deliberations about the validity of the waiver and the confession. Knowing this, they might attempt to dissimulate by providing inadequate CMR responses. Detection of dissimulation might be enhanced by comparing CMR responses to other data about the examinee's general intelligence, or by an examination of patterns of errors across the CMR and its companion tests (CMR-R, CMV).

Predictive or Classificatory Utility

There have been no studies of the relation of CMR scores to juveniles' or adults' *Miranda* understanding or their waiver choices at the time of actual police interrogation procedures. Further, no studies have examined CMR scores in relation to independent judgments (e.g., by judges or attorneys) concerning individuals' competence to waive *Miranda* rights or to understand *Miranda* warnings.

CRITIQUE.   CMR scores obtained in an assessment at some time after police interrogation and rights waiver cannot be used as an empirical definition of the examinee's degree of understanding of the *Miranda* warnings at the time of the waiver event. Inferences of this type would require additional information, as discussed in the last section of this chapter.

Potential for Expressing Person-Situation Congruency

The CMR procedure and its use of a standardized wording of the *Miranda* rights sometimes will not parallel the actual manner in which a juvenile or adult was informed of the rights by police officers in an earlier arrest situation. Officers may have given only a cursory, "boilerplate" reading of the warnings, or they might have taken great pains to give the warnings in a simplified fashion. The question may arise, then, whether the comprehension demands of the police procedure were greater or less than that of the CMR procedure in an examination session, and whether an examinee's CMR performance therefore offers a reasonable basis for making inferences about understanding of the rights at the time of the arrest.

One approach to this problem would be to modify the CMR procedure to approximate more nearly the wording used by police officers in a particular case. This, of course, would require a transcript of the wording used by police, and transcripts or audiotapes of these events usually are not available. Even if this strategy were possible, however, other demand variables (e.g., time of day, suspect's fatigue, pressures and anxieties engendered by questioning at a police station) that might impair understanding of the warnings generally cannot be studied in the CMR procedure.

Some jurisdictions have prepared standard warnings to suspects that employ somewhat different wording than that used in the CMR. The relation of an examinee's CMR performance to the demands of these other wordings might be compared by subjecting the jurisdiction's standard form to a readability formula, which analyzes verbal material for its reading or comprehension difficulty using sentence lengths and syllables per 100 words (e). The CMR wording of the warnings used in the original study was identified in this way as being at an eighth grade level of reading difficulty, corresponding to the reading ability of the average 14-year-old (c). The demand of other *Miranda* warning forms could be examined in like manner.

References

(a) Everington, C., & Fulero, S. (1999). Competence to confess: Measuring understanding and suggestibility of defendants with mental retardation. *Mental Retardation, 37*, 212–220.
(b) Fulero, S., & Everington, C. (1995). Assessing competency to waive *Miranda* rights in defendants with mental retardation. *Law and Human Behavior, 19*, 533–543.
(c) Grisso, T. (1981). *Juveniles' waiver of rights: Legal and psychological competence*. New York: Plenum Press.
(d) Grisso, T. (1998b). *Instruments for assessing understanding and appreciation of Miranda rights*. Sarasota, FL: Resource Press.
(e) Grunder, T. (1978). Two formulas for determining the readability of subject consent forms. *American Psychologist, 33*, 773–775.

COMPREHENSION OF *MIRANDA* RIGHTS—RECOGNITION (CMR-R)

Author

Grisso, T.

Author Affiliation

Department of Psychiatry, University of Massachusetts Medical School

Primary Reference

Grisso, T. (1998b). *Instruments for Assessing Understanding and Appreciation of Miranda Rights.* Sarasota, FL: Professional Resource Press

Description

The *Comprehension of Miranda Rights—Recognition* (CMR-R) was originally entitled the *Comprehension of Miranda Rights—True/False* (b), but was retitled when the instrument was published commercially (c). It was developed as a companion measure to the CMR and CMV (see reviews preceding and following this review), in order to assess understanding of standard *Miranda* warnings concerning the rights to silence and legal counsel at the time of questioning and arrest by law enforcement officers. It was intended to complement the other two measures in that it demands less of examinees by way of verbal expressive capacities (b).

The CMR-R is administered with the aid of a "flip-chart," desk-top easel that shows examinee stimuli on the side facing the examinee and administration instructions on the side facing the examiner (c). The stimuli consist of the four *Miranda* warnings, each shown individually, and worded according to the four standard *Miranda* warning statements used in the CMR (see preceding review). The examinee is shown and read the first warning statement and is told:

> I will read three more statements. Each statement means either the same thing or not the same thing as the [sentence on the card]. I want you to tell me whether each statement is the same or different from the sentence on the card. (b, p. 234)

On the stimulus page facing the examinee, three sentences are printed beneath the warning statement. The examiner then reads the first of these sentences and asks whether it means the same thing or is different from the *Miranda* warning at the top of the page. The same is done for the second and third alternatives. For example, the three stimulus sentences for the first *Miranda* warning ("You do not have to make a statement and have the right to remain silent") are:

1. It is not right to tell lies.
2. You should not say anything until the police ask you questions.
3. You do not have to say anything about what you did.

The administration then proceeds to the second *Miranda* warning and its three corresponding same-or-different items. In each triad there are either one "same" and two "different" alternatives, or one "different" and two "same" alternatives (6 "same" and 6 "different" alternatives in all), and the arrangement of "same" and "different" items varies across the four *Miranda* statements. One point is received for each correct response, so that scores on the CMR-R range from 0 to 3 for each of the four *Miranda* warnings and 0 to 12 for the total CMR-R.

Conceptual Basis

CONCEPT DEFINITION.   The instrument was intended to assess "comprehension *of Miranda* warnings," the same construct defined in the preceding review of the CMR.

OPERATIONAL DEFINITION.   The CMR-R was intended to offer a method for assessing *Miranda* comprehension by recognition of similar meanings, rather than by ability to construct a paraphrase response as in the CMR. This dictated its format and content. The sentences providing similar and dissimilar meanings were selected from among a larger number by eliminating sentences that did not manifest heterogeneity of scores.

CRITIQUE.   The method used in the CMR-R would seem to have the potential to reduce measurement error due to examinees' difficulties in encoding a message to express that which they understand, since it requires virtually no verbal expressive ability. Thus it could reduce the instances in which examinees may be perceived as lacking essential understanding merely because they cannot verbalize what they know. The use of the CMR-R in conjunction with the CMR and CMV offers a multimethod approach to the assessment of comprehension of *Miranda* rights, with the potential to reduce interpretative error that may result from assessment by a single method.

The CMR-R format does not provide sufficient evidence that examinees have usable knowledge of the *Miranda* warnings, because they might not have grasped the meaning of the warnings until they were supplied with various interpretive sentences with which to evaluate the warning. This is not necessarily a weakness in the CMR-R, given its objectives. It was not intended to be the sole index of *Miranda* comprehension in an assessment. The logic of its format merely underscores the importance of administering it in conjunction with its companion measures.

Psychometric Development

STANDARDIZATION.   Administration is highly standardized, and scoring requires no discretionary judgment.

RELIABILITY.   Test-retest stability of the CMR-R has not been examined. No examination of interscorer reliability is required, due to the completely objective scoring criteria.

NORMS.   CMR-R scores may be compared to norms in the original research samples (b, c), including 105 juveniles and 203 adults. These samples were similar to those described in the previous review of the CMR in terms of age, race, gender, and prior justice system experiences.

CRITIQUE.   Psychometric development appears to be adequate except for the lack of empirical information on the stability of CMR-R scores. Use of the norms should take into consideration the racial or socioeconomic composition of the normative sample, in relation to these characteristics of the examinee in an individual case.

Construct Validation

The original research study (b) demonstrated a correlation of $r = .55$ between the CMR-R and the CMR, administered to a sample of 105 juveniles in a court detention center. CMR-R scores were significantly related to IQ scores ($r = .43$) and to age of juveniles ($r = .21$). Similar analyses for adults were not performed, but another study (a) found that adults with mental retardation scored substantially poorer than the adult sample in the original study.

Most of the more detailed analyses of relations between comprehension measures and juveniles' characteristics in the original research study (b) did not employ the CMR-R, due to the smaller size of the CMR-R sample as well as its secondary research importance in relation to the other two measures. It was used to test one hypothesis concerning the significant relation between race and CMR scores (African-Americans obtained significantly lower CMR scores than whites, even when variance due to differences in IQ scores was statistically controlled). It was suspected that African-Americans might have obtained a lower mean CMR score because of a greater number of African-American subjects having greater difficulty in encoding (paraphrasing) what they understood in standard English. The same race/comprehension effect was obtained, however, when comprehension was defined as CMR-R scores (requiring no verbal expression). Therefore, racial differences in performance might lie in the decoding portion of the process, and in differences in linguistic background between at least some African-American juveniles and the white juvenile sample.

CRITIQUE.   Little is known empirically about the relation of the CMR-R to indexes of psychological development and experience of juveniles and adults, compared to information available on the CMR. Its stronger relation to the CMR than to IQ scores, however, does provide evidence that it assesses an ability concept specific to the understanding of *Miranda* warning content, not merely general intellectual capacity. Further, the relation between the CMR and CMR-R supports the use of these two instruments together in order to examine similarities and differences in an examinee's performance errors on the two measures. This type of comparison may be useful in providing multimethod evidence for an examinee's misunderstanding of particular elements in the *Miranda* warnings, and may be useful in detecting inconsistencies in errors. Inconsistencies might be evidence of examinee confusion and anxiety or might suggest attempts to feign ignorance (but without ability to maintain dissimulation across different response modes).

Predictive or Classificatory Utility

There have been no studies of the relation of CMR-R scores to actual responses of juveniles or adults at the time of a police request for waiver of rights to silence and legal counsel, or to indexes of understanding obtained at the time of rights waiver in actual police interrogation situations. Further, no studies have examined the relation of these scores to independent judgments (e.g., by judges or attorneys) concerning individuals competency to waive *Miranda* rights or to understand *Miranda* warnings.

CRITIQUE.   CMR-R scores obtained at some time after police interrogation and rights waiver cannot be used as an empirical definition of understanding at the time of the interrogation event. Inferences of this type would require additional information, discussed in the last section of this chapter.

Potential for Expressing Person-Situation Congruency

Potentials here are the same as those discussed under this heading for the CMR (see preceding review).

References

(a) Fulero, S., & Everington, C. (1995). Assessing competency to waive *Miranda* rights in defendants with mental retardation. *Law and Human Behavior, 19,* 533–543.
(b) Grisso, T. (1981). *Juveniles' waiver of rights: Legal and psychological competence.* New York: Plenum Press.
(c) Grisso, T. (1998b). *Instruments for assessing understanding and appreciation of Miranda rights.* Sarasota, FL: Resource Press.

COMPREHENSION OF *MIRANDA* VOCABULARY (CMV)

Author

Grisso, T.

Author Affiliation

Department of Psychiatry, University of Massachusetts Medical School

Primary Reference

Grisso, T. (1998). *Instruments for Assessing Understanding and Appreciation of Miranda Rights.* Sarasota, FL: Professional Resource Press

Description

The *Comprehension of Miranda Vocabulary* (CMV) was developed as a companion instrument for the CMR and CMR-R (previous reviews) to assist in the assessment of juveniles' and adults' understanding of *Miranda* warnings concerning the rights to silence and legal counsel. Whereas the CMR and CMR-R assess understanding of the overall message conveyed by the standard *Miranda* warnings, the CMV was intended to assess examinees' understanding of specific words within the warnings. Thus it might provide information with which to interpret errors in an individual's responses on the other two measures (b).

The CMV is administered with the aid of a "flip-chart," desk-top easel that shows examinee stimuli on the side facing the examinee and administration instructions on the side facing the examiner (c). The CMV requires that examinees be presented with six specific words taken from the standard wording of the four *Miranda* warnings (see *Description* in the CMR review): consult, attorney, interrogation, appoint, entitled, and right. A word appears on the easel page facing the examinee, along with a sentence in which the word is used (e.g., "Entitled: He is entitled to the money."). The examiner reads the word and the sentence aloud to the examinee, who is then asked to give the meaning of the word. The manual specifies certain conditions in which further inquiry may be made to allow the examinee to elaborate or clarify the response.

Each response is scored 2 (adequate), 1 (questionable), or 0 (inadequate) according to scoring criteria and examples provided for each CMV stimulus word (c) (very similar to the criterion format for the Vocabulary subtest of the Wechsler intelligence tests). Total CMV scores can range from 0 to 12. Results may be examined for the nature of specific errors, and scores may be compared to the performance of juvenile and adult samples in the research study for which the instrument was developed.

Conceptual Basis

CONCEPT DEFINITION.   Unlike the CMR and CMR-R, the CMV was not intended to assess understanding of the *Miranda* warnings, but understanding of specific words within the warnings. It is possible that a person may understand the individual words within a message yet misunderstand a message that employs those words. Conversely, one can sometimes understand a message without understanding the meaning of each of its words outside the context of the message. Therefore, although the CMV was expected to have some relation to the "comprehension of *Miranda* rights" concept, it was conceptualized primarily as an adjunct instrument with which to explain or account for CMR errors, not as a measure to be used alone.

OPERATIONAL DEFINITION.   The six words of the CMV were chosen from among a larger number appearing in the standard *Miranda* warnings, primarily by eliminating words that were defined adequately by almost all juveniles in pilot studies. The general format for administration and scoring (except for use of the words in a sentence) was borrowed from the Vocabulary subtest of the Wechsler intelligence scales. Specific scoring criteria were the product of decisions made by a team of psychologists and legal professionals in juvenile law, with a second review process by a national panel of lawyers experienced in juvenile law and juvenile court work (b).

CRITIQUE.   The ability to define vocabulary words is a conceptual component of many measures of general intelligence. For this reason, the CMV might be perceived as a conceptual link between the three comprehension of *Miranda* rights measures (CMR, CMR-R, CMV), which share a similar content, and the more general psychological construct of intellectual capacity. If this assumption is supported in construct validation research (see following), then the CMV may play an important role in interpreting overall *Miranda* comprehension results in assessments with this purpose.

Development of the scoring procedure manifests adequate attention to legal consensus regarding adequacy or inadequacy of responses. Unlike the CMR scoring system, which may be employed with somewhat different wordings of *Miranda* warnings that might be found in various jurisdictions, the CMV scoring system can be employed only with the words that were chosen for the measure. This will restrict its use in some jurisdictions.

Psychometric Development

STANDARDIZATION.   The administration procedure is highly standardized and clearly described in the manual, including specific limits on
inquiry concerning vague responses.

RELIABILITY.   Test-retest stability of CMV scores is not known.
Interrater reliability is reported as $r = .97$ to .98 for total CMV scores, with
correlations in the .90s for individual items, using pairs of trained (experienced and inexperienced) scorers (b). In another study with mentally
retarded adults, interrater agreement was reported as "above 90%" (a).

NORMS.   Normative data are available in the form of CMV results
with the large samples of juveniles and adults described in "Psychometric
Development" in the previous review of the CMR. Individuals' CMV
scores may be compared to those of normative groups of similar age-by-
IQ classification (b, c).

CRITIQUE.   Interpretation of CMV scores must take into account the
lack of information concerning test-retest stability of scores. Interrater
agreement, on the other hand, is exceptionally good, suggesting the
potential for highly objective scoring despite the need or some degree of
discretionary judgment in application of the scoring criteria. The availability of normative tables are helpful in clinical application of the CMV.

Construct Validation

CMV items were intercorrelated to a relatively low degree ($r = .14–.47$) in a juvenile sample, but correlated substantially with total CMV
scores ($r = .51–.72$) (b). CMV scores correlated substantially with CMR
scores ($r = .67$) among juveniles.

In the research study for which the CMV was developed (b), CMV
scores of juveniles were significantly related to IQ scores ($r = .59$) and to
age ($r = .34$), both of which contributed significant sources of variance
independently in analyses of variance. CMV scores were not related to
amount of prior experience with the justice system. Among adults, CMV
scores were related significantly to IQ, but not to age.

CMV performance was significantly poorer for juveniles overall than
for adults, but with the 16-year-old group generally achieving a mean
CMV score closely approximating that of adult age groups of similar IQ.
Adults with mental retardation performed on average substantially more
poorly on the CMV than did adults in the original sample (a).

CRITIQUE.   The substantial relation ($r = .67$) between CMV and CMR
scores probably reflects in part the similarity in their content and suggests
that they tap a particular knowledge construct in common. On the other

hand, the CMV was related more closely to IQ ($r = .59$) than to the CMR ($r = .47$), suggesting that CMV performance may bear a greater relation to general intelligence (as a construct defined by IQ tests) than does CMR performance. The CMV, therefore, may have interpretive value as a conceptual link between the general psychological construct of intelligence and the specific ability construct of comprehension of *Miranda* rights.

In general, CMV performances at various ages and IQ levels appear to be consistent with what would be predicted based on psychological notions of cognitive development in early adolescence and beyond. In fact, it may be more sensitive to cognitive development than to experience variables; for example, the CMV did not manifest a relation between amount of prior experience with police (prior arrests) and comprehension of *Miranda* content, which was found with the CMR.

As in the other *Miranda* comprehension measures, the CMV provides no particular safeguard for detecting dissimulation. On the other hand, it may be useful in detecting dissimulation by employing it with its companion measures to examine consistencies and inconsistencies across tests in the kinds of errors made by an examinee.

Predictive and Classificatory Utility

As with the other *Miranda* comprehension measures, no studies have been developed to examine the relation of CMV scores to understanding at the time of actual arrest and rights waiver or to judicial opinions concerning juveniles' competence to waive rights knowingly, intelligently, and voluntarily.

CRITIQUE.   Currently the CMV does not provide empirical evidence with which to make inferences about examinees' abilities at the time of prior encounters between the examinee and police officers. Inferences of this type must use additional information, to be discussed in the last section of this chapter.

Potential for Expressing Person-Situation Congruency

The format of the CMV would not seem to make it amenable to modification in jurisdictions in which police officers use warnings containing different words than those in the standardized CMV. Current scoring criteria might not be suited to accurate scoring of responses to different words.

References

(a) Fulero, S., & Everington, C. (1995). Assessing competency to waive *Miranda* rights in defendants with mental retardation. *Law and Human Behavior, 19,* 533–543.

(b) Grisso, T. (1981). *Juveniles' waiver of rights: Legal and psychological competence*. New York: Plenum Press.
(c) Grisso, T. (1998b). *Instruments for assessing understanding and appreciation of Miranda rights*. Sarasota, FL: Resource Press.

FUNCTION OF RIGHTS IN INTERROGATION (FRI)

Author

Grisso, T.

Author Affiliation

Department of Psychiatry, University of Massachusetts Medical School

Primary Reference

Grisso, T. (1998b). *Instruments for Assessing Understanding and Appreciation of Miranda Rights*. Sarasota, FL: Professional Resource Press

Description

Function of Rights in Interrogation (FRI) was developed as a research and clinical instrument to assess one's perceptions of the function and significance of rights to silence and legal counsel in the arrest and adjudication process. Three other measures developed in the same research project (a) examined one's understanding of the rights in the *Miranda* warnings (see CMR, CMR-R, and CMV reviewed previously in this chapter). In contrast, the FRI was intended to assess one's beliefs about how the rights function and what their importance might be to the juvenile or criminal court defendant.

The FRI is organized according to three content areas, each of which focuses on the relationship between a criminal or juvenile defendant and various persons or events that defendants typically encounter in the justice system. The three areas comprise three subscales of the FRI:

1. *Nature of Interrogation*: one's perceptions concerning the roles of police and suspects in interrogations
2. *Right to Counsel*: one's perceptions of the roles of attorneys and suspects in attorney/client relationships
3. *Right to Silence*: one's perceptions of the power of the right to silence, especially the degree to which it limits the discretionary power of legal authorities (e.g., police, judges)

The FRI is administered with the aid of a "flip-chart," desk-top easel that shows examinee stimuli on the side facing the examinee and administration instructions on the side facing the examiner (b). The FRI stimuli consist of four pictures, corresponding hypothetical vignettes (hereafter, "stories"), and 15 questions (5 for each of the 3 subscales).

Picture 1 depicts a suspect and two police officers at a table in a bare room. The accompanying story, read aloud by the examiner, explains:

> This is a picture about a boy/man named Joe. The policemen in the picture have brought Joe into the detention/police station. There has been a crime. The policemen want to talk to Joe. Remember that Joe is in detention/police station and the policemen want to talk to him/her. (b)

The examinee then is asked five questions relating to the "Nature of Interrogation" subscale (e.g., "What is it that the policemen will want Joe to do?" "How is Joe probably feeling?").

Picture 2 shows a suspect seated with a lawyer, and the story identifies this as a meeting between the suspect and the suspect's lawyer prior to questioning by police. Four questions related to the "Right to Counsel" subscale are asked (e.g., "What is the main job of the lawyer?" "While he is talking with his lawyer, what is Tim supposed to do?"). Picture 3 is another interrogation scene with three questions related to the "Right to Silence" subscale (e.g., "Finish this sentence: If Greg decides to tell the police about what he did, then the things he says …"). Picture 4 shows a court hearing in process. The story identifies the participants and leads to three questions, one of them relating to "Right to Counsel" and the other two related to "Right to Silence" (e.g., "Greg did not tell the police anything about what he did. Here in court, if he were told to talk about what he did that was wrong, will he have to talk about it?").

Scoring criteria for each of the 15 questions provide abstract definitions and specific examples of answers that receive 2-, 1-, or 0-point credit. In general, 2-point answers on the "Nature of Interrogation" subscale are those that indicate an appreciation of the suspect's jeopardy; on the "Right to Counsel" subscale, a recognition of the advocacy nature of the attorney/client relationship; and on the "Right to Silence" subscale, a recognition of the irrevocable or absolute power of the right to silence. For example, in the first story, responses to the question "How is Joe feeling" receive 2 points credit if the answer indicates that the examinee recognizes the unpleasantness or danger of the interrogation for the hypothetical suspect.

Examinees receive three subscale scores (each ranging from 0–10) and a total FRI score (range = 0–30). Scores may be compared to those of juvenile and adult samples in the research project for which the FRI was developed (a). In general, FRI scores are interpreted as an index of examinees' awareness of various aspects of the legal process, without which the perceived importance or significance of the rights to silence and legal counsel might be reduced. Poorer scores, then, suggest that the examinee might not be prepared to weigh the matter of waiver of the rights, even if the examinee appears (on other instruments) to understand the *Miranda* warnings themselves.

Conceptual Basis

CONCEPT DEFINITION.   Grisso's (a) review of case law for the validity of confessions indicated that some courts examined not only suspects' knowledge of the *Miranda* rights (which the FRI's companion instruments were intended to assess), but also suspects' awareness of why the rights might be important in the legal process and how they might function in a protective manner in the course of police investigations and prosecution. The FRI was intended to assess this latter awareness. Grisso (a) conceptualized this awareness as comprising knowledge of certain aspects of the legal process as well as beliefs about the process. For example, in order to consider meaningfully the waiver of right to counsel, one would need to know that an attorney is supposed to be an advocate, and one would have to believe that an attorney in fact would play that role if one requested an attorney.

The three content areas chosen for the FRI were awareness of the adversarial nature of the suspect–police relationship, the advocacy and cooperative nature of the suspect–attorney relationship, and the irrevocable nature of the right to silence (that is, that the right could not be abridged by legal authorities in the interrogation and adjudication process). These were not construed as comprising a single construct, but merely as representing the content of a domain of knowledge and belief relevant to the law's concern that suspects are aware of the significance of the rights when considering waiver.

OPERATIONAL DEFINITION.   The use of picture stimuli was intended to augment the examinee's attention to the task, to establish a contextual set for responding, and to avoid the need for more lengthy verbal descriptions of the situation in hypothetical vignettes (a). Items for each of the three content areas were developed by a research team of psychologists and lawyers, guided by concerns expressed in past case opinions by courts. Extensive pilot work led to the final selections. Scoring criteria also were developed by the interdisciplinary group and were reviewed by a national panel of six juvenile court judges and juvenile law attorneys, whose suggested revisions were incorporated into the final criteria.

CRITIQUE.   The selection of the three content areas seems logical. The proper attitude within which to consider jeopardy associated with waiver of rights to silence and counsel would seem to include a perception of police as adversary, counsel as friend and confidante, and rights as guarantees that cannot be rescinded by legal authorities.

On the other hand, these content areas might not cover the range of considerations that would be relevant in individual cases, especially in juvenile cases. For example, do juveniles understand that their probation officer, heretofore perhaps a friendly counselor in whom they could confide, might have to adopt a law enforcement officer's adversarial role when they are suspected of reoffending? That is, do they understand that the trust they may have placed in their probation officer could act to their disadvantage if they now made incriminating statements in that relationship? Another aspect of jeopardy not covered by the FRI is the suspect's understanding of the potential long-range consequences of waiving rights and making a statement to police. For example, does the individual have a grasp of the possible penalties associated with conviction or adjudication as a consequence of confession?

Despite these questions of content coverage, content relevance seems adequate in light of the procedures used in selecting the content areas and devising test items (e.g., literature and legal review, interdisciplinary research team, legal panel consultation). Further, the use of picture stimuli might be of special help to clinicians when assessing juvenile defendants who may benefit from a more concrete anchor for the response process.

Psychometric Development

STANDARDIZATION.   Instructions to examinees, stories, questions, and scoring are described clearly in the manual (b), and they allow little discretion or flexibility by the examiner.

RELIABILITY.   Interscorer reliability for several pairs of scorers has been reported (a) as $r = .71$ to 1.00 for the various items, $r = .80$ to .94 for the various subscales, and $r = .94$ to .96 for total FRI scores. Test-retest stability of FRI scores has not been examined.

NORMS.   The primary reference and manual provide FRI means and standard deviations for large samples of delinquent adolescents and adult offenders in the original research study (a, b). These samples were drawn from a juvenile detention center and adult halfway houses for offenders in St. Louis County. Means are provided for various age groups, levels of IQ, race, and socioeconomic status.

CRITIQUE.   Research is needed to determine the stability of FRI scores, because their use in making inferences about an examinee's abilities at the time of rights waiver requires empirical evidence that FRI scores do not fluctuate greatly across periods of days or a few weeks (the usual time between waiver and clinical assessments to examine waiver competency).

Construct Validation

In the original research study (a), the three FRI subscales did not correlate substantially with each other for either juveniles or adults (the highest intercorrelation being $r = .24$ between the second and third subscales, for juveniles). Correlations between total FRI scores and the three subscale scores for juveniles were .48, .63, and .83, respectively, and for adults were .36, .59, and .83. The first subscale's lower relationship to total FRI scores apparently was due to extreme homogeneity of scores on the first subscale (Nature of Interrogation), most research participants having obtained very high scores on this subscale.

Total FRI scores and subscale scores correlated minimally with CMR, CMR-R and CMV scores (see earlier reviews), the correlations ranging from .05 to .27. Age was significantly related to FRI scores among adolescents, but not among adults; further, all adolescent age groups performed significantly more poorly on the FRI than did the adult group (a). An age-by-IQ interaction, however, indicated that differences between juveniles and adults were most pronounced at lower IQ levels, with juveniles of higher IQ differing little in FRI scores from adults with similar IQ scores. FRI scores were significantly and positively related to juveniles' amount of prior experience with courts (as indicated by number of prior felony referrals) when statistical analyses controlled for IQ.

CRITIQUE.   The lack of substantial correlations between subscales of the FRI suggests that the three subscales are relatively independent of each other in terms of their content; therefore, the FRI does not appear to assess any single construct. Further, the FRI does not relate substantially to the *Miranda* comprehension measures (CMR, CMR-R, CMV), which themselves have substantial intercorrelations (see earlier reviews). This finding is consistent with the author's expectations that individuals who understand *Miranda* warnings may or may not be aware of the function and significance of *Miranda* rights.

In general, research results with the FRI are consistent with expectations based on theory and empirical information about cognitive development and knowledge acquisition at adolescent ages. More research is needed, however, to examine the relation of FRI scores to developmental indexes in samples other than those employed in the research project for which the instrument was developed.

Predictive or Classificatory Utility

There have been no studies of the relation of FRI scores to actual responses of juveniles or adults to police requests for waiver of silence and legal counsel. Further, no studies have examined the relation of these scores to independent judgments (e.g., by judges or lawyers) concerning individuals' competency to waive *Miranda* rights.

CRITIQUE. Currently there is no empirical evidence with which to make inferences based on FRI data concerning examinees' understanding of the function of rights at the time of prior encounters between the examinee and police officers.

Potential for Expressing Person-Situation Congruency

Several situational circumstances might be relevant when comparing an individual's degree of appreciation of the function of *Miranda* rights to the degree of appreciation required by a specific waiver case. For example, a case in which police officers played an especially benign and friendly role (e.g., as a strategy to obtain cooperation from the suspect) would seem to demand a more firm awareness by the suspect of the adversarial nature of the suspect–police relationship, in order to be adequately prepared to consider the consequences of rights waiver and a confession. In contrast, the presence of a truly supportive and knowledgeable friend or adult to advise the suspect during the rights waiver process would seem to decrease the demand for personal knowledge or belief represented by the FRI. The FRI itself, of course, does not assess these situational demand variables, nor are there other systematic methods for doing so.

References

(a) Grisso, T. (1981). *Juveniles' waiver of rights: Legal and psychological competence.* New York: Plenum Press.
(b) Grisso, T. (1998). *Instruments for assessing understanding and appreciation of Miranda rights.* Sarasota, FL: Resource Press.

CURRENT STATUS OF THE FIELD

The first part of this section reviews the need for further research with FAIs that evaluate functioning relevant for waiver of rights to silence and legal counsel. The second part discusses uses of the instruments in forensic evaluations.

RESEARCH DIRECTIONS

Functional Component

COVERAGE OF FUNCTIONAL COMPONENTS. The first section of this chapter contained a review of three functional components related to the law's perspective on competent waiver of rights to silence and counsel:

- understanding of the *Miranda* warnings (i.e., of the words and phrases used to convey to suspects the rights to silence and legal counsel)
- perceptions of the intended functions of the rights
- expectancies and reasoning concerning probable outcomes of waiver or nonwaiver of the rights, and possibly

Collectively, the instruments reviewed in this chapter address the first and second of these components, but not the third. It would be helpful for future research to develop a method that would complete an assessment's coverage of the ability components: that is, a method to assess functional abilities associated with reasoning (the third capacity) about waiver of the rights.

An instrument designed to address this third component might focus on the process and outcome of a suspect's reasoning concerning the choice to waive or not to waive rights in certain arrest and interrogation circumstances. Grisso (1981) developed a research procedure, the *Waiver Expectancy Interview*, for examining juveniles' reasoning about the waiver decision in hypothetical arrest and interrogation events. The procedure was modeled on research methods developed by Spivack and Shure (1974) for examining children's problem-solving abilities. It was successful in producing information about juveniles' reasoning and expectancies concerning the consequences of rights waiver, classifying their responses in order to express frequencies of types of consequences that they anticipated for various decisions, and producing quantitative indexes of certain formal problem-solving elements (e.g., time perspective, ability to generate a variety of potential options and consequences). In general, however, the instrument is in need of further refinement in order to maximize its utility in clinical cases, because it is probably too lengthy and complex for use in most forensic cases.

CRITERION VALIDITY STUDIES. Currently there is no empirical evidence for relations between scores on any of the instruments reviewed in this area and judicial decisions concerning the validity of rights waiver (or suspects' competency to waive *Miranda* rights) in actual cases. Research to fill this gap is not likely to be forthcoming. The question of validity of waiver is raised for judicial review only occasionally in most jurisdictions, for which reason researchers will find it difficult to achieve adequate sample sizes with which to test the relationships in question. Even if the relation were tested, a lack of correspondence between instrument scores and judicial decisions about validity of waiver would not necessarily reflect poorly on the forensic assessment instruments (see the discussion of standards for empirical validity in Chapter 3). This is because each instrument claims to measure only one functional ability of the examinee (e.g., understanding of the Miranda warnings), whereas judges must consider many other variables in addition to these in arriving at decisions about the validity of a waiver (e.g., see the first section of this chapter).

NORMATIVE REPLICATION. The four instruments for assessing understanding and appreciation of *Miranda* warnings were the result of research in a single jurisdiction (the St. Louis metropolitan area) over 20 years ago. If these instruments are to continue to be of use to examiners, researchers must perform studies that provide norms for youths and adults today. Arguments can be made that youths of the present decade are more "sophisticated" (knowledgeable of the world) than youths several decades ago, rendering inapplicable norms developed in the 1970s. One can also argue, of course, that youths have not changed—that their apparent sophistication is only superficial and that as a group they manifest characteristics of "teenagers" of any era within the past 50 years. Arguing these positions, of course, is fruitless without new data that will update the norms for the measures. Fortunately, at least two major studies to do this were underway at this writing, both by researchers who were not involved in the original development of the *Miranda* instruments.

The wording of the *Miranda* warnings in the *Miranda* comprehension instruments has created significant difficulties for forensic examiners, because wordings in various jurisdictions are somewhat different from those in the instruments. Revising the wording of the *Miranda* warnings in the instruments (for example, for a re-norming study) will be of no value unless some version of the warnings enjoys some degree of consensual use across some majority of U.S. jurisdictions. It is not known whether such a version exists. If there is none, any wording that is chosen for research purposes will be unequivocally applicable only in certain limited jurisdictions; any wording will be open to the same criticism that is raised about the one used currently in the instruments. Thus, research that examines the degree of difference in performance associated with a few different forms of the *Miranda* warnings would be helpful in determining the importance of this issue.

Causal Component

It would be helpful to know more about the relation between performance on the instruments in this competence area and developmental, personality, or psychopathological characteristics of criminal/juvenile suspects. Interpretations in individual cases could be made more confidently to the extent that performance on the tests (in research studies) were known to follow predictions made on the basis of broader theoretical expectations. For example, do scores on the *Miranda* measures of comprehension of rights vary in relation to indexes of legal socialization or the development of the concept of a right (Grisso & Schwartz, 2000)? Results of studies focusing on such questions would assist examiners in interpreting the validity and potential meaning of measurement data when using the instruments in individual cases.

Interactive Component

There is probably little that research can do to assist clinicians or courts to examine the interaction of person and arrest/interrogation circumstances in *Miranda* waiver cases. The process would seem to require classification of interrogation events using standardized, operational definitions of variables that would characterize the salient features of the events. Research to describe interrogation events, however, would be quite difficult because of legal, political, or logistic barriers to observing them. Further, examiners might find little use for the research results in individual cases; even if reliable methods were available for categorizing various circumstances of interrogation events, examiners in actual cases generally will not have the opportunity to observe the events in question.

Judgmental and Dispositional Components

The measures reviewed in this area of legal competence were not developed to assess "competence to waive rights knowingly, intelligently, and voluntarily." The various instruments do not provide cutoff scores or statements of competence. Some of the measures do describe the relative adequacy of responses to individual items, but they do not classify the examinee's overall performance on the instruments as "adequate" or "inadequate." They provide conceptual and operational definitions with which examiners may describe to courts what an examinee seems to know, understand, or be able to do, and with which to compare an examinee's performance to empirical norms (e.g., the average performance of various age groups).

These limited purposes of the current instruments are entirely consistent with the viewpoint that the degree of ability required to satisfy legal standards for competence or incompetence is a moral judgment, not an empirical question. Further, the answer to the moral question will vary from case to case depending on circumstances that go beyond the question of a defendant's degree of ability. It would be inconsistent with this view for researchers to develop psychometric criteria concerning how much of an understanding of *Miranda* warnings is sufficient to warrant a finding of competence or incompetence to waive rights to silence and legal counsel.

CLINICAL APPLICATION

Description

All of the instruments reviewed in this chapter offer conceptual and empirical advantages over previous methods for describing abilities related to the competent waiver of rights to silence and legal counsel. Prior to development of the *Miranda* comprehension instruments, an examinee's ability to understand the *Miranda* warnings could be inferred only indirectly from measures of general intelligence or from unstandardized interview procedures. In contrast, the *Miranda* comprehension instruments offer indexes of knowledge and awareness for the specific content with which the law is concerned when considering an individual's capacity to waive rights in interrogations. Data are obtained in a standardized fashion. They can be used to summarize what an examinee appears to understand, then can be summarized objectively and reliably in quantitative fashion that is amenable to normative comparisons.

Published norms for the instruments in this chapter generally have derived from research meeting necessary scientific standards. Nevertheless, the use of these norms to describe the performance of examinees must consider the possible implications of background differences (e.g., economic, racial, cultural) between the examinee and the samples from which normative data were obtained. Moreover, as noted earlier, differences in wording of *Miranda* warnings across jurisdictions place limits on the way that results can be applied in individual cases.

Explanation

Poor scores or responses on the instruments in this chapter may be obtained for any of a number of reasons, some of which would not be consistent with legal notions of incapacity to waive rights knowingly, intelligently, and voluntarily (e.g., malingering, transient motivational states at time of testing). Therefore, testimony based on results of the instruments should make the court aware of the various explanations for the examinee's poor performance that cannot be ruled out by other assessment data.

The various Miranda comprehension measures are best employed together in assessments rather than administering only one of them. Research evidence suggests that whereas there is considerable correspondence between the instruments in the results produced (presumably because of their shared content), their different stimulus formats and response modes constitute three different methods for assessing the knowledge or understanding in question. Errors in interpretation may result from the use of any one index alone, due to individual differences among examinees in abilities to decode or encode information in the stimulus format and response mode of any one instrument. Thus the use of all three indexes guards against misinterpretation based on test-specific responding. In addition, examination of consistencies and inconsistencies in the content of inadequate responses across tests might assist the examiner in detecting various examinee conditions that could account for inadequate performance (e.g., malingering, or inconsistency resulting from cognitive and emotional confusion of the examinee).

Interpretation of results of the instruments in this chapter will require data beyond the item and summary scores of the instruments. Several types of data might be useful in explaining the meaning of adequate or inadequate responses on these instruments: for example, content analyses of responses on the instruments, comprehensive mental status interview results; observation and summary of the examinee's past and present behaviors in settings other than the examination session; and data from psychological tests of general intelligence, academic abilities, personality, and psychopathology. Therefore, FAIs assessing waiver-related abilities should be employed in the context of a broader assessment, designed to provide confirming and disconfirming evidence for various explanations for the degree of ability manifested on the forensic instruments.

Postdiction

The Miranda comprehension instruments provide indexes of current functioning. There is little empirical evidence to assist examiners in making inferences, based on these performance indexes, about functioning at an earlier time, such as a past arrest and interrogation event. Further, the instruments provide no special method for examining the relation of the examinee's abilities to the demands of the specific waiver situation with which the examinee was faced. Thus comparisons between an individual's abilities and the demands of the waiver situation must be inferred with great caution. Examples and further guidance for this process have been provided by Grisso (1998a).

Conclusions and Opinions

When circumstances allow the examiner to conclude that the individual probably understood very little about the rights at the time that they were waived, this still does not justify expert testimony concerning the validity of waiver (i.e., testimony that the waiver was or was not made "knowingly, intelligently, and voluntarily"). Nothing about the empirical nature of the forensic assessment instruments justifies testimony by expert witnesses on questions that require moral and social judgments in the application of the legal standard.

---------6---------

Not Guilty by Reason of Insanity

RANDY BORUM

THE COMPETENCE QUESTION

To establish that one is guilty of a crime, the law typically requires proof that an individual engaged in proscribed (unlawful) conduct (*actus reus*) and did so with unlawful intent (*mens rea*). The necessary degree of intent is usually specified as a statutory element of the offense. While the law presumes that persons act according to "free will" and should be held responsible for their own behavior, it also recognizes that there are individuals who have some form of severe mental illness or disability that impairs either their *cognitive abilities* (e.g., the ability to accurately perceive reality and to make rational and reasonable inferences based upon them) or their *volitional abilities* (e.g., the ability to control their own behavior) in such a way, and to such an extent, that their free will is compromised.

If one's capacity to exercise rational will in forming an intent to act is impaired by illness, disease, or defect (as opposed, for example, to voluntary intoxication), then the law stipulates that the individual's moral and legal culpability (blameworthiness) is diminished. This is the basis for the

193

legal doctrine of the insanity defense, and for the designation of *not guilty by reason of insanity* (NGRI).

To establish an insanity defense, it must be proven that at the time of the offense, the defendant had a severe mental illness or disability and that the condition impaired his or her cognitive and/or volitional capacities in certain ways. If these conditions are met, and the defendant is found to be NGRI, that individual is deemed "not guilty" in the legal sense and therefore is not subject to criminal sanctions for the behavior; however, he or she is likely to be civilly committed to a psychiatric hospital. This disposition is rooted, in part, in a belief that punishment would not serve as a deterrent and that treatment (usually with confinement) is a more appropriate disposition than imprisonment. Accordingly, when the defense is asserted, mental health professionals are almost always called upon to examine the defendant in order to provide relevant evidence about the presence or absence of illness and/or impairment at the time that the defendant committed the act.

Although there is a legitimate role for mental health professionals in these proceedings, it is important to understand two clinical-legal distinctions in criminal responsibility assessments. First, the assessment of insanity or mental state at the time of the offense (MSO) does involve an appraisal of capacity, but it is not customary to refer to this ability as a legal "competency." One would not refer to a defendant who meets criteria for legal insanity as being legally incompetent. As explained in Chapter 1, assessments of criminal responsibility/insanity are covered in this book (which otherwise focuses only on legal competencies) because they are among the more common questions posed in criminal forensic assessment, because they focus on human capacities and mental states, and because there is potential heuristic value in submitting the insanity question to analysis based on the assessment model for legal competencies.

Second, although clinical and mental health expertise may be relevant for an appraisal of insanity, the concept and definition of insanity in the law is legal, not clinical. The term "insanity" in criminal proceedings has a very specific legal meaning, and is not equivalent to simply having a mental illness. People can be mentally ill—even actively psychotic—at the time they commit a crime, but not be legally insane. Indeed, most offenders with mental illness do not meet the legal criteria for insanity. Mental illness or disability is a necessary but not a sufficient condition for legal insanity. Moreover, the law even determines what constitutes a mental illness, disease or defect for purposes of the defense, and legal definitions often are not synonymous with clinical convention, official diagnostic nomenclature, or other clinical criteria such as those found in DSM-IV (American Psychiatric Association, 1994). An officially recognized diagnosis in DSM-IV sometimes will not be considered sufficient to meet the legal threshold for a predicate mental impairment. Likewise, a particular condition, syndrome or set of symptoms may be qualified as a mental disease under legal definitions, even if the specific clinical diagnosis is unclear.

Mental health professionals who conduct MSO evaluations or insanity assessments should know not only the doctrine of insanity and the relevant legal standard, but also how the defense operates in actual practice.

The insanity defense is rarely used and, when used, is usually not successful. In fact, on average the insanity defense is raised in less than 1% of all felony cases, and is only successful about 25% of the time (Perlin, 1994; Melton, Petrila, Poythress, & Slobogin, 1997). The publicity of these cases makes them seem much more common (Silver, Cirincione, & Steadman, 1994). In a survey of seven states, the rate of insanity pleas ranged from .29 to 1.73 with an average of .85 (less than 1%) per 100 felony indictments. The aggregated success rate for insanity pleas in that survey was 28.1% (Cirincione, Steadman, & McGreevy, 1995). Similar findings have emerged from at least two other multi-state studies (Pasewark & McGinley, 1986; Steadman et al., 1993).

The insanity defense is raised in cases ranging for misdemeanors to serious violent felonies. Cases in which a defendant accused of a homicide raises an insanity defense often receive the greatest public attention. Murder cases, however, account for only about one-third or less of insanity defenses (Rodriguez, LeWinn, & Perlin, 1983), and the rate of success (NGRI acquittal) for these defendants is no better than for those accused of other offenses (Steadman, Keitner, Braff, & Aravanites, 1983). In addition, research suggests that, on average, insanity acquittees do not tend to be more dangerous or to be at greater risk of recidivism than other defendants convicted of felony offenses (Pasewark, Pantle, & Steadman, 1979; Steadman & Braff; 1983). For example, Steadman and Braff (1983) reported that 39% of convicted felons in their sample were re-arrested compared to 35% of NGRI acquittees.

These concerns underscore the need for mental health professionals to develop a clear understanding of how the defense operates in practice so that they have an appropriate context for their assessments in insanity cases.

LAW AND CURRENT PRACTICE

Legal Standards

The insanity defense doctrine has been a well-established part of Anglo-American criminal law since at least the 17th century. Through the years, the substantive standards and criteria have changed (e.g., wild beast test, "good and evil", "right and wrong"), but most states currently use one of two insanity defense standards: the *McNaughtan* standard, or the standard provided in American Law Institute (1962) Model Penal Code (called the "ALI standard"). About one-half of the states use *McNaughtan* and one-half the ALI standard. (Only New Hampshire employs a distinctly different standard, based on *Durham v. U.S.* [1954], which requires showing only that the unlawful act was the "product" of mental disease or defect.)

The *McNaughtan* standard requires proof that, at the time of the offense, as a result of a mental disease or defect, the defendant did not know the nature or quality of his act or did not know that the act was wrong. This standard arose out of England's case of Daniel McNaughtan (*McNaughtan's Case*, 1843), who mistakenly shot the secretary of Prime Minister Robert Peel (his intended target) and was acquitted as not guilty by reason of insanity. There was a tremendous public outcry about this verdict. Queen Victoria was outraged and demanded clarification from the House of Lords concerning the rules governing insanity. The Supreme Court of Judicature responded to the Lords' request and answered in part with the following statement: "(T)o establish a defense on the ground of insanity, it must be clearly proved that at the time of the committing of the act, the party accused was labouring under such a defect of reason, from disease of the mind, as not to know the nature and quality of the act he was doing; or if he did know it, that he did not know he was doing what was wrong" (*McNaughtan's Case*, 1843, p. 722.).

Some states adopted the *McNaughtan* standard strictly, while others supplemented it with an "irresistible impulse" test. The rationale for this expansion was that the strict *McNaughtan* standard considered only knowledge and cognitive considerations, not permitting courts to consider mental impairments that may have affected the defendant's ability to *control* his or her own actions, also known as volitional impairments (Morris, 1975).

The American Law Institute (1962) formally included a volitional component in the test of insanity when it drafted its Model Penal Code (Sect. 4.01). The ALI standard provides that: "a person is not responsible for criminal conduct if at the time of such conduct as a result of mental disease or defect he lacks substantial capacity either to appreciate the criminality [wrongfulness] of his conduct or to conform his conduct to the requirements of the law." Because this ALI standard is broader, allowing either cognitive or volitional impairment to qualify, the *McNaughtan* standard is generally considered to be the more conservative of the two.

In the *ABA Criminal Justice Mental Health Standards* project, the American Bar Association (1989) attempted to achieve equipoise between the narrow "knowledge" standard in *McNaughtan* and the broad "conform" element of ALI. It proposed using language from the cognitive prong of the ALI test, without the language from the volitional prong. Thus, the project proposed that the test of insanity should be: "A person is not responsible for criminal conduct if, at the time of such conduct, and as a result of mental disease or defect, that person was unable to appreciate the wrongfulness of such conduct" (American Bar Association, 1989, Standard 7-6.1, p. 330). This was intended to focus the test on issues more typically within the purview of mental health expertise (cognitive and affective functioning) rather than on the perceived strength of one's desire or impulse and the capacity to control it.

A few states have chosen, however, to abolish the insanity defense altogether. Montana and Idaho eliminated their insanity defense provisions before John Hinckley was found not guilty by reason of insanity for his assassination attempt on President Ronald Reagan, and Utah abolished its insanity defense shortly thereafter (Steadman et al., 1993). Nevada and Kansas followed suit in the mid-1990s.

While the insanity defense is intended to designate individuals who are not guilty or not criminally responsible due to impairment from a mental disability, some states also have a designation for offenders who have a mental illness, but who *are* held criminally responsible for their acts. This provision is known as *guilty but mentally ill* (GBMI). Since the first GBMI provision was enacted in Michigan in 1975, approximately 12 other states have created similar laws. The GBMI verdict was initially created as an alternative verdict to NGRI for use when it was proven that a defendant had a mental illness, but otherwise did not meet the insanity defense criteria. The statutory provisions for GBMI vary across the states, but they generally recognize either (a) that the defendant *is currently mentally ill* or (b) that the defendant *was mentally ill at the time of the offense.* However, unlike the insanity defense, this recognition does not affect the defendant's culpability or criminal disposition.

The original intent of GBMI was twofold: (a) to reduce the number of insanity acquittals by allowing jurors an explicit mechanism to convict mentally ill persons who did not meet the insanity defense criteria, and (b) to assure treatment for such individuals within a correctional setting (Robey, 1978). Recent research suggests, however, that in many instances these objectives have not been achieved (Borum & Fulero, 1999). In addition, the American Bar Association's Criminal Justice Mental Health Standards, the American Psychiatric Association's Statement on the Insanity Defense, the National Mental Health Association's Commission on the Insanity Defense, the American Psychological Association, and the National Alliance for the Mentally Ill all have opposed or recommended against adoption of GBMI.

It is important for evaluators to understand the distinction between NGRI and GBMI. The insanity defense is an affirmative *defense* to a crime. If defendants meet all criteria in the standard, they may be deemed "not guilty" (not criminally culpable) in the eyes of the law. Accordingly, they may be subject to *civil* proceedings for their confinement, but not to *criminal* incarceration or punishment. In contrast, GBMI is a verdict that implies that one is "guilty" (criminally culpable) and is subject to criminal sanctions including incarceration and possibly death (*Harris v. State*, 1986; *People v. Crews*, 1988). The addition of "but mentally ill" only denotes a finding that the defendant had a mental disorder at the time of the offense (or sentencing), but it does not lessen his or her guilt or culpability. As noted above, all states (except Utah and Nevada) with GBMI have *added* it to their existing insanity defense. The GBMI verdict is not considered in detail in the remainder of this chapter because it seems to raise no special assessment questions concerning a defendant's capacities in relation to the alleged criminal act.

Legal Process

Because the insanity defense is an affirmative defense, it is an issue raised most often by defense counsel. When the question is raised, mental health professionals often conduct assessments in inpatient psychiatric settings, although since the mid-1980s there has been a significant shift toward greater use of community-based forensic assessments (Grisso et al., 1994). Some states conduct full assessments in the community, while others use community-based evaluations for screening and then refer a defendant to an inpatient unit for a full evaluation if necessary. As noted in Chapter 4 ("Legal Process"), some judges routinely request simultaneous evaluations of criminal responsibility and competency to stand trial. This obscures the differences in purpose and definition between the two legal concepts, and creates some evidentiary challenges concerning disclosure of, and access to, potentially incriminating information (Keilitz, Farthing-Capowich, McGraw, & Adams, 1984).

Although numerous issues of legal procedure affect the operation of the insanity defense in U.S. courts (e.g., instructions to jury, burden of persuasion on prosecution or defense, forms of verdict), most do not directly affect the way that the examiner conducts the evaluation or how the expert offers opinions and evidence. There are, however, two notable exceptions.

First, jurisdictions differ with regard to the nature and scope of opinions on the issue of insanity that an expert is permitted to offer. In general, the Federal Rules of Evidence offer broad latitude to experts in providing any opinion that may assist a judge or jury in determining a fact at issue. In fact, in most cases, Rule 704 even permits an expert to offer an opinion on the "ultimate issue" of whether the elements of a particular legal standard are met in a given case. This is not true, however, for opinions on the issue of insanity. Mental health professionals are explicitly prohibited from offering opinions on the ultimate issue of a defendant's mental state or condition in federal proceedings involving the insanity defense (Rule 704b). Similarly, some state courts, such as California, expressly prohibit mental health professionals from testifying as to whether the mental state of the defendant meets the requirements of the legal standard. The rationale for excluding such testimony is that the ultimate judgment of insanity (excusing one from criminal responsibility) is a moral or normative decision, not a clinical one. To allow a mental health professional to offer an opinion on this issue would arguably invade the province of the judge or jury as fact finder. Examiners, therefore, should be familiar with the relevant evidentiary rules in the jurisdictions in which they practice.

A second procedural issue concerns the introduction of potentially incriminating information gained directly from the defendant about the act with which he or she is charged. Evaluators routinely inquire into the defendant's actions, thoughts, and emotions at the time of the alleged offense as part of gathering relevant information about the defendant's mental state. The evaluator often must disclose or refer to that information in testimony when describing the bases for his or her opinion, yet that information may incriminate the defendant. Possible remedies, including instructing the jury to disregard self-incriminating testimony (American Bar Association, 1989) and creating separate fact finding processes for the act and the mental state, have met with limited success.

Insanity Assessment: Current Practice

Little empirical evidence is available on the nature or quality of mental health professionals' assessments related to the question of insanity. Some surveys, however, have suggested that judges often use the testimony of mental health professionals in insanity cases and typically find it helpful and important (Melton, Weithorn, & Slobogin, 1987; Petrella & Poythress, 1983).

RELIABILITY AND VALIDITY. Because evaluations for mental state at the time of the offense (MSO) are conducted in the context of an adversarial process, an important fundamental question is whether different examiners reach the same conclusions regarding a defendant's mental state.

Psychometrically, this is the issue of reliability (inter-examiner reliability). Fukunaga, Pasewark, Hawkins, and Gudeman (1981) examined the reliability of MSO assessments in a naturalistic, archival sample of 355 cases in Hawaii. Courts in that state often appoint at least two independent examiners when the issue of a defendant's sanity is raised, but those examiners are not barred from communicating with one another before submitting their own reports. The frequency with which such communication occurs, however, is not known. Nevertheless, it is encouraging that pairs of independent evaluators agreed on the ultimate conclusion of sanity/insanity in 92% of the cases.

That study does not account, however, for the biases that may occur when the experts are in a more typical and explicitly adversarial relationship. Otto (1989) examined a phenomenon known as "forensic identification" in MSO assessments. The notion of forensic identification posits that when examiners are retained by a given party (as opposed to being court appointed) during an adversarial proceeding, they are likely to experience a subtle influence that causes them to interpret information or to form conclusions in a light most favorable to that side. Indeed, using written scenarios in an analogue study where the designation of the retaining party was randomly assigned, Otto found that participants given an identical set of facts were more likely to assign an ultimate conclusion that favored the side by which they were retained.

If the judgments are reliable, one may inquire as to whether they are valid. Determining the validity of judgments about MSO is challenging because there is no "gold standard" criterion that is unaffected by the opinion rendered in the evaluation itself. The conventional approach has been to examine the concordance between examiners' opinions and ultimate legal judgment/determinations. The obvious limitation with this strategy is "criterion contamination;" the legal determination typically is informed or affected by the results of the mental health evaluation. Studies that have assessed validity in this way, however, have consistently found very high rates of agreement—on average, 95%—between expert opinions and legal determinations (Albers & Pasewark, 1976; Fukunaga et al., 1981).

THE ASSESSMENT PROCESS.   There is a dearth of professional or scientific literature describing normative practice in MSO evaluations. What little empirical information is available can only be inferred from mental health professionals' reports in insanity cases. At the broadest level, all forensic reports, including MSO reports, should include (a) data, (b) clinical and forensic opinions, and (c) some indication of how the opinions arise from, or are supported by, the data (Melton et al., 1997).

Accordingly, the first question about the assessment process is what sources of data an evaluator should seek, use, and consider when arriving at an opinion on a defendant's MSO. Based on an analysis of recent sources of authority on forensic assessment practice, information from multiple sources appears critical. The following data sources are frequently recommended (Heilbrun, 2001; Melton et al., 1997; Rogers & Shuman, 2000; Shapiro, 1999):

- Extensive interviews with the defendant, focusing on the events surrounding the offense, the defendant's mental state before and during the offense, and their relation to each other.
- Comprehensive review of police reports and other legal documents related to the alleged offense.
- Review of criminal justice and mental health system records of the defendant's life prior to the event.
- Review of jail and/or hospital ward notes and records concerning the defendant's incarceration between the time of arrest and the assessment, and during the period of time over which the assessment process occurs.
- Collateral interviews with any individuals who were in contact with the defendant in the period of time leading up to, during, and after the alleged offense, or reviewing written statements by these individuals.
- Collateral interviews with the defendant's family members and friends.
- Interview with the defendant's attorney (if appropriate with regard to the expert's role in the case) to obtain information of which the expert might not be aware from other sources, as well as the attorney's direct observations of the defendant.
- Conducting or ordering neurological, psychological, and/or neuropsychological testing when such information may address specific questions raised by data from other sources.

The second, related question is what specific information (data) should be collected or analyzed from these sources. This selection should be informed and guided by the three key objectives: (a) to assess the nature and severity of any mental illness or disability that the defendant may have had at the time of the alleged offense; (b) to assess the defendant's thought processes and emotional states before and during the act; and (c) to assess the relationship between them.

Borum and Grisso (1996) surveyed experienced forensic psychologists and psychiatrists regarding the importance of specific elements in insanity/criminal responsibility reports. Although these opinions were asked with respect to report writing, they also have implications for understanding recommended practice, since gathering and analyzing particular information would be necessary to include in the report. The consensus of these expert forensic examiners was that the following data elements were essential for the MSO report. "Essential" means that participants felt that these elements must be included in a competent forensic report, and excluding the information would suggest that the report was below acceptable standards.

- *Psychiatric History*: Information that addresses whether or not defendant has a history of mental illness (or mental retardation).
- *Current Mental Status*: Information (data) about defendant's current mental status, derived at least in part from direct observation of defendant by examiner (must be a description of mental state at the time of the evaluation). (For example, describing delusions or other symptoms, describing thoughts or thought processes, describing level of intelligence at present time).
- *Formal Mental Status Exam*: Description of mental status that comments on the following: Orientation; Memory; Emotion; Behavior; Thought.
- *Psychotropic Medication*: Statement identifying defendant's current use of psychotropic medication (since time of arrest and at time of evaluation) or absence of it.
- *Psychological Testing*: Among *Forensic Psychiatrists*, 61% rated testing as either essential or recommended, with only about a third (37%) rating it as optional. Among *Forensic Psychologists*, 68% rated testing as either essential or recommended, with 32% rating it as optional.
- *Mental Health Records*: Includes a statement indicating that some document(s) from previous mental health evaluation/treatment was reviewed by examiner, or that such records were not available when an attempt was made to obtain them.
- *Information from Police*: Description of information (data) from police concerning defendant's behavior at time of arrest OR statement indicating that the examiner made an effort to obtain information from police, but such information was not made available to the examiner.
- *Prior Diagnosis*: Statement indicating a diagnosis from earlier medical or psychiatric treatment, or indicating the absence of earlier diagnosis or treatment history.

- *Alcohol/Substance Abuse*: Statement identifying presence and degree, or absence, of alcohol or other substance abuse in the past (prior to current charges).
- *Defendant's Disclosure*: Information (data) about defendant's behavior at time of the alleged offense based on the defendant's own report; or a statement indicating that the examiner made an effort to obtain the information, but defendant was not willing or able to provide a description of behavior and events at time of alleged offense.
- *Collateral Description*: Information (data) from interview with witness(es) concerning defendant's behavior at time of the alleged offense, or from others who encountered the defendant soon before or after the alleged offense; or a statement that no persons are known to have had contact with the defendant immediately before, during or after the alleged offense, or that potential informants were contacted by the examiner but were either unwilling or unable to provide relevant information.

It is the process prior to the reporting of data, however, that requires far more attention than it has been given. Remarkably little is documented concerning the process with which examiners collect and interpret data to describe a defendant's past mental state, to rule out alternative states, and to relate the defendant's pathological thoughts or feelings to the behaviors in question. Our frequent inability or disinclination to specify the evidence and logic with which we "postdict" diagnoses and mental processes in insanity cases has been one of the courts' greatest concerns (e.g., Bazelon, 1982). The following discussion continues the search for ways to better articulate the logic involved in clinical inferences related to the legal question of insanity.

FROM LEGAL STANDARD TO FORENSIC ASSESSMENT

Functional Component

As noted above, insanity is not designated a legal competence. The general assessment model used in this book (Chapter 2), however, may still have heuristic or conceptual value to structure or organize an evaluator's thinking about the requirements of legal standards for insanity. Thus, we begin by examining the functional capacities and contexts of existing tests of insanity.

Between the two major standards currently used in the U.S.—*McNaughtan* and ALI—there are two significant domains of functional capacity: cognitive and volitional. In the *McNaughtan* test, the cognitive component refers to "knowing," whereas in the ALI standard the cognitive element refers to "appreciation." Many legal scholars have noted that these two concepts are distinct and distinguishable. From a psychological perspective "knowing" is a relatively narrow process, typically referring to an individual's storage of information and capacity to retrieve it. In subsequent legal analysis in the United States, the word *know* in the *McNaughtan* test was interpreted to refer to the capacity to be aware of or to comprehend the character of the act and its probable or possible consequences (Goldstein, 1967).

Legal scholars have suggested that the shift from "know" to "appreciate" in subsequent tests of insanity was deliberate, intending to broaden relevance beyond rote knowledge or memory or the existence of a law or social proscription, thus including "an ability to recognize and understand the significance of [one's] personal actions" (American Bar Association, 1989, p. 343). Knowledge is a predicate condition. Appreciation extends further to one's capacity to understand how that knowledge may apply— and its implications—in relation to one's own situation or a given set of facts. For example, one may "know" that an automobile engine requires oil; yet one does not "appreciate" the engine's need for oil unless one comprehends and can rationally evaluate the potential risks and consequences of failure to put oil in the engine. Thus, the functional capacities that may be the object of assessment are broader in relation to the ALI and ABA standards than for the *McNaughtan* standard.

That which one must be capable of knowing (*McNaughtan*) or appreciating (ALI, ABA) is specified as the "criminality" or as the "wrongfulness" of the act. Courts in the U.S. have interpreted these terms in somewhat different ways. Some have interpreted this element strictly to refer to a defendant's recognition that the conduct was illegal or against the law, while others have focused on the defendant's apprehension of moral wrongfulness or transgression.

The term *criminality*, on its face, implies a focus on the illegality of the act. "Knowledge of criminality" of one's act seems to require only that one has stored in memory, and can retrieve, the fact that the act is prohibited by law. Appreciation of criminality would seem to require more. Knowledge is necessary, but one must also have the ability to comprehend his or her own situation in regard to a potential breach of that law. One might need to comprehend and believe that if the law is transgressed, that he or she may be subject to certain consequences. For example, one may know that it is unlawful to kill another person, but believe that the "laws of man" do not apply to or affect him because he is acting as an agent of God. The individual may believe that God will not allow any punishment to come to him and therefore not appreciate the likely consequences of his act.

Although the term *wrong* may be more readily associated with moral transgression, wrong in the *McNaughtan* standard has generally been regarded as referring to legal rather than moral proscription. Wrongfulness in the ALI and ABA standards, however, was intended to focus inquiry more broadly on "prevailing social morality" and views of "moral justification" (American Bar Association, 1989, p. 343) with regard to one's conduct, not merely on whether the act was illegal. Therefore, *knowledge of wrongfulness* of one's act would require that one has stored in memory and can retrieve the fact that prevailing moral standards (not merely laws) hold the act unjustifiable. Beyond that knowledge, an appreciation of wrongfulness would require one to have the capacity to comprehend and incorporate the prevailing moral standards that may undergird the formal laws.

If assessing one's functional capacity to know or appreciate the wrongfulness of the act seems challenging and complex, the appraisal of *volitional* capacity required by the ALI standard (the ability to "conform one's conduct to the requirements of law") is, in many ways, even more thorny and ambiguous. The general psychological capacities associated with this legal component might be construed as abilities to inhibit affective or behavioral reactions, to modulate impulses or desires to act, to delay one's responses, or to redirect one's responses toward options that might have less harmful consequences. Specifically, the issue for the legal standard is the defendant's capacity to have behaved in some other (nonoffending) manner at the time of the offense. Historically, some have suggested using the "policeman at the elbow" test; that is, would the defendant have committed the act even if there had been a police officer standing next to him?

Fundamentally, the ultimate distinction regarding the volitional element of the insanity standard is between an irresistible impulse and an unresisted (although resistible) impulse, which the American Psychiatric Association (1982) and others have rightly characterized as an often subtle differentiation. Moreover, the ALI standard requires that the impairment in volitional capacity be substantial, so that deficits or impairments that are less serious might have little or no relevance concerning the defendant's claim of incapacity at the time of the offense. This is made even more challenging by the fact that the appraisal must focus on the defendant's capacity at some prior point in time (not currently) and under the particular set of conditions (including perceptions and emotions) that existed when the defendant committed the act.

In summary, translating concepts in insanity standards into functional ability constructs amenable for assessment is a different task than for other legal standards that are designated as legal competencies. This is partly because the focus in an insanity assessment is on the individual's mental state at a particular moment in time in the past. Concepts and terms in other legal competencies relate primarily to an individual's current abilities. Depending on the circumstances, one's current capacity may have limited relevance to the postdictive question. Nevertheless, the deconstruction of these concepts into their psychological components may help to guide one's questioning and analysis of data and help to structure one's reasoning and communication of opinions in these cases.

Causal Component

Both of the major insanity standards (*McNaughtan* and ALI) require a causal connection between a "mental disease or defect" and the functional cognitive and/or volitional impairment. Because the analysis in these cases is postdictive, establishing the relation of the two elements poses some unique challenges. In assessing most legal competencies, the examiner first assesses a current functional deficit, then hypothesizes and tests potential causes. The law is concerned specifically with the defendant's mental state *at the time of the offense*, rendering this approach less practical. Unlike functional abilities in other legal competencies, the deficits neither stand alone nor are assessed alone. The deficits also do not typically provide evidence of the disorder; rather, the predicate mental condition provides evidence for the deficits.

The matter of what constitutes a "mental disease or defect" has been the subject of some debate. Typically, courts have determined that the condition must be characterized by a severe disorder of thought or mood and, typically, must interfere with one's capacity accurately to perceive reality. What is most important for the examiner to consider is that the standard of "mental disease or defect" is established by the fact finder, not by clinical opinion or convention. The inclusion of a syndrome in the DSM-IV (American Psychiatric Association, 1994) is neither necessary nor sufficient to satisfy the legal standard.

The definition of "mental disease or defect" in the ALI standard specifically excludes abnormalities "manifested only by repeated criminal or otherwise antisocial conduct." Arguably, this would exclude a diagnosis like Antisocial Personality Disorder, as it is currently defined in the DSM-IV. Similarly, the Criminal Justice Mental Health Standards project (American Bar Association, 1989) noted that, generally, "defects of character or strong passion" should not satisfy the "mental disease" requirements of the insanity defense. If they were included, the report said, "the defense would have no threshold at all; every abnormal defendant—and every normal defendant who became abnormally impassioned—could be said to have a 'mental disease'" (American Bar Association, 1989, p. 346).

Traditionally, voluntary intoxication (influence of alcohol or drugs) at the time of the offense has not been accepted as a condition fulfilling the "mental disease or defect" element of the insanity defense (American Bar Association, 1989). Circumstances in which alcohol or drug use might be relevant to the predicate mental condition, however, include potentially the alcohol-induced precipitation of a psychotic episode in a person already predisposed, or chronic alcoholism that has produced organic brain pathology (which itself is the mental disease resulting in incapacities relevant for the insanity defense).

The question of the presence or absence of a mental disease or defect is often the focal point of disagreement between different examiners in insanity cases. Data concerning the defendant's actual behavior typically do not produce much disagreement. No objective data, however, can be available on the defendant's actual perception of wrongfulness or ability not to act in a certain way. Evidence for impairment in cognitive or volitional capacity can be inferred only from history and behavior around the time of the offense. Present abilities are less relevant here.

Differences occur in the inferences, explanations, or causal attributions for the defendant's behavior. For example, if a defendant burned a victim's body, one expert might infer that this behavior was consistent with the subject's delusional belief that the victim was possessed by demons that needed to be "purged," while another might infer that this was done to destroy evidence of the crime. The same behavior could be used by different experts to argue for cognitive or volitional impairment (arising from a mental disease), and for the existence of a rational process indicating that the defendant was not disorganized or mentally ill. Thus, the causal element (mental disease or defect) is almost always inferred from the behavior. In contrast to the inferences required for most legal competencies, the judgments and interpretations required for insanity evaluations rely more heavily on theoretical speculation.

Interactive Component

Application of the insanity doctrine does not seem to require a consideration of the degree of a defendant's abilities in contrast to the demands of the defendant's particular external circumstances. Environmental circumstances certainly are considered in a number of ways in insanity cases, especially as explanations for the mental disorder, as triggering events for the offensive act, or as precipitants of heightened affective arousal. Nevertheless, insanity decisions seem to focus primarily on the defendant's presumed perceptions or interpretations of events rather than on the events themselves. Thus if two psychotic defendants both had commands from God to kill, but external conditions subjected one but not the other to extreme stress before the command or during the act, logically the degree of external stressors would make no difference in the application of the insanity standard as long as evidence for the disease and arguments for the delusions themselves were convincing.

Therefore, insanity cases seem not to require the same types of interactive information as the legal competencies. That is, the fact finder is not expected to consider the degree of congruency between the individual's capacities and the demands placed on the individual by external conditions. The insanity decision depends on assumptions about the characteristics of the defendant alone.

Judgmental and Dispositional Components

The "ultimate issue" issue is perhaps most debated in insanity cases (Rogers & Ewing, 1989). The dispute is about whether it is appropriate for mental health professionals to offer a clinical opinion that the defendant was or was not insane at the time of the offense, was or was not criminally responsible, or is recommended as NGRI.

As noted in Chapter 1 and in discussions of other specific legal competencies, there is arguably a line between clinical and legal issues that should be drawn at the dispositive issue of sanity or insanity. A finding that one is insane in a criminal proceeding implies, by definition, that one should not be held criminally responsible or blameworthy for an act that she or he committed. Some professionals and scholars have argued that this threshold decision is a moral or normative judgment and not a clinical one. The argument is that mental health professionals may have expertise and offer evidence regarding a defendant's mental condition, and potential impairments in functional cognitive and volitional capacities, but that addressing the threshold (whether the defendant was "crazy *enough*" or whether the nature and severity of the impairments were *sufficient* that he/she should not be held morally or criminally blameworthy) is rightfully a question only for the factfinder (judge or jury), not the expert. Accordingly, critics, including the American Psychiatric Association (1982) and the American Bar Association (1989), assert that mental health professionals should not testify as experts to the ultimate issue of sanity or insanity. As noted earlier, Federal Rules of Evidence (704b), as well as some states, do not allow such testimony by experts in insanity cases.

Other scholars and many forensic practitioners, however, believe that offering ultimate issue testimony on the issue of a defendant's sanity is entirely appropriate and, in fact, may help to reduce confusion or lack of clarity about the substance of one's opinions (Rogers & Ewing, 1989). In support of their argument, they point to empirical studies showing that the form of an expert's testimony—ultimate vs. non-ultimate issue—does not significantly affect verdicts or decisions (Fulero & Finkel, 1991; Rogers, Bagby, Crouch, & Cutler, 1990). They support the permissibility of "reliable and well-substantiated testimony that speaks to the ultimate issue" (Rogers & Shuman, 2000, p. 46). Moreover, among a national sample of experienced forensic psychologists and psychiatrists, only 17–19% held the position that offering such an opinion in a report would be inappropriate (Borum & Grisso, 1996).

All mental health professionals conducting insanity assessments must determine for themselves the propriety of offering an opinion on the ultimate legal issue. That decision, however, should be informed by a careful analysis of the ethical, professional and empirical arguments on both sides of the debate.

REVIEW OF FORENSIC ASSESSMENT INSTRUMENTS

There are only two known forensic assessment instruments designed specifically for use in evaluations for the question of insanity. Neither of these is a test in the strict sense; they are better seen as guides to help structure the assessment process. For consistency, the reviews are outlined in the same manner as the instrument reviews for the various legal competence areas in other chapters, except for the deletion of the category entitled "Potential for Expressing Person-Situation Incongruency" (which the previous discussion concluded to be of no apparent conceptual relevance for legal definitions of insanity).

MENTAL STATE AT THE TIME OF THE OFFENSE SCREENING EVALUATION (MSE)

Authors

Slobogin, C., Melton, G., & Showalter, C.

Primary Author Affiliation

College of Law, University of Florida

Primary Reference

Slobogin, C., Melton, G., & Showalter, C. (1984). The feasibility of a brief evaluation of mental state at the time of the offense. *Law and Human Behavior, 8*, 305–320

Description

The *Mental State at the Time of the Offense Screening Evaluation* (MSE) is a semi-structured interview guide to assist in assessments of a defendant's mental/psychological condition at the time of the alleged offense. It was intended for use in screening out cases where an insanity defense would clearly not be applicable and for identifying the "obviously insane individual for whom a more comprehensive evaluation is unnecessary" (b, p. 235). When MSE results indicate that a significant mental abnormality may have existed, there would typically be a recommendation for a more extensive evaluation.

The MSE has three sections that occur in the following sequence: I, Historical Information; II, Offense Information; and III, Present Mental Status Examination. Each section of the MSE outlines the interviewer's goals but does not specify the actual interview questions that the examiner should ask. Information from the interview may be supplemented by examination of available records of criminal or psychiatric history.

Section I (Historical Information) consists of five' subsections (A–E) and focuses on ruling out various "significant mental abnormalities" in the examinee's past. Subsection A is typical of the format of these subsections (f, p. 319):

A. Does the defendant have a history of prolonged bizarre behavior [i.e., delusions, hallucinations, looseness of association of ideas (thought processes incoherent and illogical), disturbance of affect (behavior disorganized, aggressive, intensely negativistic or withdrawal)]? If not, exclude:
1. Organic brain syndromes of progressive or chronic nature
    a. Dementia
    b. Organic personality syndrome
2. Psychoses
    a. Schizophrenia
    b. Paranoid disorders
    c. Schizophreniform disorders
    d. Affective disorders

Subsections B–E use a similar format to deal with convulsive disorders (B), bizarre behaviors suggestive of psychotic or various neuropsychological conditions (C), episodic bizarre behavior (D), and mental retardation (E). One always proceeds to Section II even if the above disorders are ruled out in the historical evaluation.

Section II (Offense Information) has two subsections for information from the defendant (A) and external sources (B). This section focuses on the examinee's mental state at the time of the offense. Categories of information to be obtained in each section are:

A. From the Defendant
   1. Defendant's present general response to offense
   2. Detailed account of offense
   3. Events leading up to offense
   4. Postoffense response
B. From extrinsic sources
   1. Indictment, information or complaint
   2. Confessions, preliminary transcripts, statement of the police
   3. Attorney's notes
   4. Autopsy reports
   5. Witness accounts

Section III (Present Mental Status Examination) is completed by employing any typical mental status examination, such as the Folstein Mini-Mental Status Examination (Folstein, Folstein, & McHugh, 1975), focusing on the person's mental state at the time of the interview.

After data collection, the examiner judges whether, on the basis of the data, "significant mental abnormality may have affected the defendant's actions at the time of the offense" (f, p. 311) or that there is "probably no evidence of 'significant mental abnormality' approaching legal relevance" (f, p. 319). No formulas are provided for arriving at these decisions from MSE data. The authors note, however, that the use of diagnoses in the MSE only serves as a tool for decision making; diagnoses are not dispositive of the evaluation question. For example, the mere presence of a significant mental abnormality at the time of the offense, without evidence that it impaired the examinee's functioning at that time, should lead to the recommendation that there is little likelihood of any insanity defense on the basis of mental state. Further, evidence of severe cognitive, affective, or volitional impairment at the time of the offense may warrant further evaluation, even when no signs of significant mental abnormality can be found.

Conceptual Basis

CONCEPT DEFINITION.   The authors developed the concept of "significant mental abnormality." This refers to any mental disorder that could serve as a predicate for a legal insanity defense, based on a review of statutes defining legal insanity and diminished capacity.

OPERATIONAL DEFINITION.   The authors extracted all diagnoses that they felt would constitute "significant mental abnormality" as defined above from DSM-III (a) (the version of the American Psychiatric Association's diagnostic manual that was being used at the time the instrument was developed). They prepared a logical argument for the choices, based on probable or possible effects of the diagnostic disorders on one's functioning in an aggressive, antisocial, or violent manner. The diagnoses chosen were:

- Dementia
- Organic personality syndrome
- Schizophrenias
- Paranoid disorders
- Schizophreniform disorders
- Affective disorders
- Epileptic disorders
- Brief reactive psychosis
- Intermittent and isolated explosive disorder
- Automatism (Post-concussion syndrome, Temporal lobe epilepsy, Cerebral anoxia)
- Dissociative disorders (Psychogenic future, Sleepwalking)
- Withdrawal, delirium, or hallucinations associated with psychoactive substance use
- Moderate to severe retardation

The format of the instrument operationalizes several concepts that frequently arise in courts' examination of evidence in insanity cases. For example, inclusion of a section concerning the defendant's mental state in an historical (preoffense) perspective, as well as current mental state, allows one to address the continuity or persistence of significant mental abnormality for a defendant. This is relevant for weighing questions of malingering and current treatment needs if the defendant is found legally insane. The section on mental state at the time of the offense inquires not only about mental state, but also how it affected the examinee's actions at the time of the offense, because functional ability (not merely diagnosis) is at the heart of the legal question of insanity.

CRITIQUE.   To screen for "significant mental abnormality," the authors began with a review of relevant diagnoses in the DSM-III. Subsequently, there have been two new versions of that diagnostic manual (DSM-III-R and DSM-IV). More important, however, the current scheme does not include consideration of some diagnoses and clinical syndromes that have permissively served as the basis for successful insanity pleas, such as severe personality disorders and certain dissociative disorders (c, d, e). As a practical matter, the exclusion of these diagnoses would not necessarily negate the merit of the screening system. Diagnoses are merely a tool, they note, not a deciding factor.

Potentially more problematic from a conceptual view, the grouping of symptoms in some cases is inconsistent with DSM and standard diagnostic nosology. Rogers and Shuman (g, p. 225) provide a detailed listing of these inconsistencies, which include:

- Hallucinations and delusions are listed as "bizarre behavior"
- Disorganized behavior is included as a "disturbance of affect"
- Disturbances of affect for assessment of mood disorders do not include depressed or elevated moods
- Mood disorders are limited arbitrarily to "prolonged' periods"
- Looseness of association is linked with incoherence
- Mood disorders are subsumed under psychotic disorders
- Sudden alterations of consciousness are subsumed under "bizarre behavior"
- Delirium can be excluded diagnostically without an assessment of consciousness.

Psychometric Development

STANDARDIZATION.   As noted above, the MSE is not a test or psychometric measure. Because it is a semi-structured guide, even the administration and classification/interpretation of responses is not formalized or standardized.

RELIABILITY.   Inter-rater reliability has not been established (or investigated) either for the classification of symptoms and impairment or for ultimate opinions and conclusions regarding the defendant's MSO.

NORMS.   (Not applicable)

CRITIQUE.   The absence of any empirical evidence relating to observations or conclusions from the MSE does limit the confidence that one can place in the opinion derived from it. If the MSE is to remain viable as one of the two existing guides for assessment of insanity, studies demonstrating both aspects of reliability should be a primary consideration.

Construct Validation

The single study of the MSE is best discussed under the following heading.

Predictive or Classificatory Utility

The authors of the MSE trained 24 psychiatrists and doctoral level clinical psychologists to use the instrument (f). Pairs of trainees each evaluated three cases (36 cases), which were selected randomly from admissions to a hospital forensic unit. Trainees were provided little information on defendants' past histories. Because the MSE was intended for use as a screening device, examiners were instructed to use a low threshold for the possible presence of a significant mental abnormality (in other words, if necessary, to err on the side of overidentification). In addition, all defendants were also evaluated independently by hospital forensic teams (consisting of a psychiatrist, a psychologist, and a social worker) who typically perform the required insanity assessments for the court. Cases were then followed through the court dispositions process.

In 72% of the 36 cases, the MSE-informed conclusion agreed with the conclusion of the forensic team based on their comprehensive evaluation. The MSE and hospital team agreed about all 16 "screen out" cases (those where a condition of legal insanity was clearly not present). There was substantially less agreement, however, about the 20 cases identified by the MSE pair as having sufficient merit to warrant further consideration. Of these cases, the hospital team agreed in 10 and disagreed in 9 cases. (One remaining case produced unresolvable disagreement between the two trainees in a pair.)

Of the 20 cases determined by the MSE pair to pass a screening threshold, the court found 2 cases insane, 6 cases had charges *nol-prossed*, 4 were convicted of a lesser charge, and 6 were convicted as charged. (The research report does not account for the remaining 2 cases.) Of the 10 cases identified by the hospital team as having potential merit for an insanity defense, 2 cases were found insane, 7 were *nol-prossed* and 1 was convicted as charged. For all 16 "screen out" cases, the court either convicted as charged or gave mitigated dispositions (unrelated to mental abnormality). No validity data are reported with regard to MSE conclusions about specific symptoms, disorders, or the severity of impairment.

CRITIQUE. The authors of the study discussed the results in terms of classification error rates. It is interesting to translate these rates into hypothetical consequences if the trainees were to have constituted an actual screening process in the mental health criminal justice system. Sixteen of the 36 defendants would have been screened out instead of being committed to a hospital for further evaluation. The results indicate that none of them would have been wrongly denied an insanity verdict. (That is, as defendants in this study, all of them were seen as ineligible by the hospital forensic team, *and* none of them received an insanity verdict in court.)

The number of cases sent to the hospital for a costly inpatient evaluation, however, would have been reduced by about 45%, and the court would have avoided delays in these cases.

Of course, based on MSE screenings, several defendants who the inpatient team would deem ineligible for an insanity defense would still be sent to them for evaluation. Yet this type of error is of less concern than screening out defendants who might otherwise be eligible for an insanity defense, from the point of view of fairness and defendants' fundamental rights.

While the agreement rate of 72% with no false negatives is promising, the limited sample size suggests that further research and replication is necessary. Furthermore, Rogers and Shuman (g) point out that although the MSE is intended to be used as a screening device, neither this nor any subsequent investigation has tested its effectiveness in a screening context or with a population that truly represents an outpatient forensic sample. Moreover, paired evaluation teams are not typical for screening or outpatient assessments.

A screening system of any type, though, might meet with opposition from some defense attorneys. One could argue that regardless of the empirical validity of the screening instrument, the principles of due process or equal protection are violated when the defendant is not provided the benefit of a full or comprehensive evaluation, especially when it is provided for some defendants and not others.

On the other hand, the empiricist will ask whether comprehensive evaluations are any more valid than briefer methods such as the MSE, especially because the more comprehensive evaluation methods rarely have been examined for their validity. Indeed, there may be no way to examine any insanity evaluations for their true validity (see Chapter 3).

References

(a) American Psychiatric Association (1980). *Diagnostic and Statistical Manual of Mental Disorders, Third Edition*. Washington, DC: APA.

(b) Melton, G., Petrila, J., Poythress, N., & Slobogin, C. (1997). *Psychological evaluations for the courts*. New York: Guilford.

(c) Pasewark, R. (1981). Insanity plea: A review of the research literature. *Journal of Psychiatry and Law, 9,* 357–401.

(d) Pasewark, R., Pantle, M., & Steadman, H. (1979). Characteristics and dispositions of persons found not guilty by reason of insanity in New York State, 1971–1976. *American Journal of Psychiatry, 136,* 655–660.

(e) Phillips, B. & Pasewark, R. (1980). Insanity plea in Connecticut. *Bulletin of the American Academy of Psychiatry and Law, 8,* 335–344.

(f) Slobogin, C., Melton, C., & Showalter, C. (1984). The feasibility of a brief evaluation of mental state at the time of the offense. *Law and Human Behavior, 8,* 305–320.

(g) Rogers, R. & Shuman, D. (2000). *Conducting insanity evaluations (2d ed.)*. New York: Guilford.

ROGERS CRIMINAL RESPONSIBILITY ASSESSMENT SCALES (R-CRAS)

Author

Rogers, R.

Author Affiliation

Department of Psychology, University of North Texas

Primary Reference

Rogers, R. (1984). *Rogers Criminal Responsibility Assessment Scales*. Odessa, FL: Psychological Assessment Resources

Description

The *Rogers Criminal Responsibility Assessment Scales* (R-CRAS) is designed to structure and quantify the decision making process in assessments of legal insanity. After the examiner conducts a thorough evaluation including relevant interviews and reviews of pertinent records, the R-CRAS presents 30 items called "Psychological and Situational Variables," which must be assigned a numerical rating. The examiner uses these ratings and the assessment information in a decision tree analysis, which leads to a conclusion that the defendant is either "sane" or "insane" according to the relevant legal standard.

Rogers (a) emphasizes that the R-CRAS can only be used by trained forensic examiners and does not substitute for clinical judgment. It does not provide a simple recipe for decision making or relegate the ultimate conclusion to a cutting score.

The examiner provides a numerical rating for each of the 30 items called "Psychological and Situational Variables" (hereafter, the "PSV items"), then uses ratings and other data to proceed through a decision tree to arrive at an opinion regarding legal insanity.

PSYCHOLOGICAL AND SITUATIONAL VARIABLES. There are 5 groups of PSV items in the instrument. These groupings have been used by Rogers as scales, especially for purposes of research with the R-CRAS:

A. *Patient's Reliability (2 items)*
   1. Reliability of patient's self-report which is under voluntary control
   2. Involuntary interference with patient's report

  B. *Organicity (5 items)*
      3. Level of intoxication at time of crime
      4. Evidence of brain damage or disease
      5. Relation of brain damage to commission of alleged crime
      6. Mental retardation
      7. Relation of mental retardation to commission of alleged crime
  C. *Psychopathology (10 items)*
      8. Observable bizarre behavior
      9. General level of anxiety
     10. Amnesia about the alleged crime
     11. Delusions
     12. Hallucinations
     13. Depressed mood
     14. Elevated or expansive mood
     15. Level of verbal incoherence
     16. Intensity and appropriateness of affect
     17. Evidence of formal thought disorder
  D. *Cognitive Control (4 items)*
     18. Planning and preparation
     19. Awareness of the criminality of behavior
     20. Focus of the crime (e.g., selective vs. random focus)
     21. Level of activity in commission of alleged crime
  E. *Behavioral Control (7 items)*
     22. Responsible social behavior during week prior to alleged crime
     23. Patient's reported self-control
     24. Examiner estimate of patient's self-control
     25. Relation of loss of control to psychosis
     26. Impaired judgment
     27. Impaired behavior
     28. Impaired reality testing

Two additional PSV items do not contribute to any conceptual scale (29, Capacity for self-care; 30, Awareness of wrongfulness).

The manual describes each PSV item to help provide conceptual anchors for the rating. Each item is rated on a 5- or 6-point scale, with a 0 indicating that no information is available, a 1 that there is "no symptomatology or disorganization," and a 2 that the factor is clinically insignificant. Ratings from 2 to 5 or 6 designate increasing degrees of severity or symptom impairment as specified in the item description. The ratings may be summed to produce subscores for the five summary scales, or they may stand simply as 30 item ratings with which to approach the following process.

R-CRAS DECISION MODELS. The R-CRAS was designed primarily to focus on insanity assessments using the American Law Institute (ALI) standard, but it may also be used with the *McNaughtan* standard and a Guilty but Mentally Ill (GBMI) standard. The analytic logic to apply the ratings is guided by separate decision trees. For example, the ALI model has six decision points (a, p. 33), each of which corresponds to a major interpretive issue (e.g., malingering; presence or absence of organic disorder) or to a component of the ALI standard (e.g., loss of cognitive control). "Yes" and "no" answers by the examiner at each of these decision points provide branching routes for arriving, ultimately, at a clinical opinion concerning whether or not the defendant meets the psychological criteria for insanity according to the ALI standard.

The examiner considers the numerically summarized data from the PSV items when making each of the judgments in the decision model. Further, the manual provides paragraph supplements defining each of the decision points in the decision models, as well as several case studies demonstrating the PSV item scoring and use of the decision models with individual defendants.

Conceptual Basis

CONCEPT DEFINITION. By conducting a review of existing statutes, case law, and legal analyses, Rogers identified the specific cognitive and/or volitional elements for each of the major insanity standards. He then attempted to identify known psychological constructs that would correspond to the functional legal element. For example, the following constructs are proposed for the ALI standard: (a, pp. 34–35):

- *Organicity*: an organic mental disorder.
- *Major Psychiatric Disorder*: functional disorders as defined by DSM-III, excluding disorders that "by definition would not have significant impact on a legal standard" (a, p. 34). [Organicity and Major Psychiatric Disorder together define the ALI's "mental disease or defect."]
- *Loss of Cognitive Control*: loss of ability to recognize, at the time of the crime, that the conduct was criminal.
- *Loss of Behavioral Control*: loss of ability to choose and to withhold important behaviors (e.g., "delusional ideation may leave no recourse and 'demand' a particular behavior response") (a, p. 35).

OPERATIONAL DEFINITION. The above four psychological definitions, together with the question of malingering and the legally required causal element (mental disease or defect), form the basis of the six decision nodes on the R-CRAS for the ALI standard. (Other constructs and decision models were developed for *McNaughtan* and for Guilty but Mentally Ill.) The logic of the legal standards also was translated into the "yes-no" pathways between the decision nodes in the decision models.

The selection and development of the 30 PSV items were derived from consensus ratings of five experienced forensic psychologists and psychiatrists for the ALI standard, and from another panel of three experts for the *McNaughtan* standard and the Guilty But Mentally Ill standard (GBMI criteria) (a). Rogers states that the structure of the R-CRAS rating system and derivation of decision models was heavily influenced by the *Schedule of Affective Disorders and Schizophrenia* (h, i).

CRITIQUE.   The general process of arriving at concepts to be assessed was systematically logical. The legal standard was analyzed as a construct with abstract elements, and Rogers translated these elements into psychiatric or psychological concepts. These, in turn, were defined operationally as several subclasses of symptoms, behaviors, and (despite the manual's reference to "Loss of Cognitive Control" rather than the broader "cognitive-affective" concept of "appreciation") both cognitive and affective states that might be inferred regarding the defendant's state at the time of the crime.

The strength of the model is that it provides a structured and standardized way to think about symptoms and levels of impairment. The limitation is that, while it creates constructs by relating legal elements to psychological functions, it does not—and arguably cannot—structure the application of those constructs to the ultimate threshold questions. For example, several items are related to the construct "Loss of Behavioral Control"; yet there is no specific guidance about how to conclude from these items whether the defendant had "no recourse" but to act in accord with his delusions. Some would argue that this is because those thresholds mark the division between psychological and moral/normative judgments. Regardless, Rogers notes that some examiners might wish not to employ these aspects of the decision tree model (a, pp. 32–33).

Psychometric Development

STANDARDIZATION.   Administration of the R-CRAS is not standardized in the formal sense. The relevant factors are specified and defined, but the R-CRAS does not require the examiner to ask any particular set of questions. Thus, the instrument specifies what type of information should be gathered, but does not require that it be gathered in any particular way. Similarly, PSV item scores are related to the decision nodes in a very structured way, but the ultimate conclusion is not standardized or driven by cutoff scores.

RELIABILITY. Rogers (a) simultaneously examined inter-examiner and test-retest reliability in a sample of 76 defendants in a forensic hospital for insanity evaluations. Each case was interviewed twice, on the average of 2.7 weeks between interviews, by different psychiatrists or psychologists trained in using the R-CRAS. Pairs of examiners demonstrated high agreement on the diagnostic variables, insanity variables, and ultimate conclusions in the ALI decision model. Rates of agreement ranged from 85% to 100%, with kappas between .48 and .94. Examiners agreed on the ultimate conclusion in 97% of cases (kappa .94). Interrater agreements on individual PSV items averaged $r = .58$, with lower correlations (below $r = .40$) on three items (7: Retardation and the crime; 16: Intensity of affect during crime; 21: Level of activity in committing the crime). Eighteen item correlations achieved very high statistical significance ($p = .0001$).

Rogers (a) reported alpha coefficients for internal consistency of the five summary scales of the R-CRAS: Patient's Reliability, .28; Organicity, .52; Psychopathology, .80; Cognitive Control, .64; and Behavioral Control, .77.

NORMS. The R-CRAS manual (a) provides summary scale means and 95% confidence levels for three sample sets ($n = 73$, $n = 111$, $n = 76$) of persons judged by forensic examiners (using the R-CRAS ALI decision model) to be legally insane or sane.

CRITIQUE. The R-CRAS seems to provide considerably greater standardization of the insanity assessment process than would be expected for assessments by examiners not employing the system. Yet it also provides sufficient flexibility in data collection to meet the requirements of specific cases.

Although interrater agreement on individual PSV items was less than one would hope, measures of interrater reliability for the components of insanity are strong (.75 for cognitive control and .80 for behavioral control) and those for the ultimate conclusions (sane/insane) are impressive (.94). It is possible that greater specification of item rating criteria and the inclusion of additional rating examples for each item could improve scoring standardization and inter-examiner reliability of item ratings.

The normative samples were drawn from forensic assessment centers in Chicago and Toledo, with secondary (smaller) samples drawn from several centers in other geographic areas. Therefore, the information on norms may be generalizable to various settings where insanity assessments are performed.

The low internal consistency of the Patient's Reliability summary scale probably is due to the presence of only two PSV items in this scale. Further, one would not expect these two items to be related. The first item refers to the veracity or unreliability of the patient's report as a function of voluntary

truthfulness or distortion, whereas the second refers to involuntary interference with the patient's report (e.g., because of delusional thought).

Construct Validation

Factor analysis of a set of R-CRAS protocols produced three factors (c):

- *Bizarre behavior*: lack of awareness; self-reported low control over crime; delusions; and final R-CRAS insanity decision.
- *High activity*: inappropriate, intense affect; self-reported low control over crime; absence of intoxication; and final R-CRAS insanity opinion.
- *High anxiety*: malingering; depressed feelings; lack of reliability of self-report; and self-reported low control over crime.

Rogers (a) reported a discriminant analysis using the five summary scales as predictors, and final R-CRAS opinions of the examiners (does or does not meet the ALI standard using the R-CRAS model) to define criterion groups. In the original and cross-validation attempts respectively, false positive rates were 5.7% and 16.7%, and false negative rates were 1.3% and 3.6%.

Rogers and Sewell (e) conducted a further examination of the construct/structural validity of the R-CRAS using discriminant analysis on each component (e.g., loss of cognitive control, loss of volitional control). As predicted, they found patterns of items that distinguished the constructs (average hit rates of 94%), and the results indicated that the items helped to "explain" the constructs (explaining, on average, 64% of the variance).

No significant relations have been found between final R-CRAS insanity opinions and age, race, gender, education, work history, competency to stand trial, prior felony arrests, and several other legal variables (a).

CRITIQUE.   Factor analysis of the R-CRAS items did not produce factors similar to the five summary scales, but rather factors that might describe three prototypic insanity assessment cases. One wonders, therefore, whether the summary scales should be conceptualized as scales as such, rather than simply as groups of PSV items. More research on the structure of the R-CRAS is needed to address this question.

One should note that the discriminant analysis described previously does not demonstrate the R-CRAS' external validity, but rather the degree of consistency between its summary scale ratings and the final opinions of insanity made by examiners using the *same* ratings along with the ALI decision model. Interestingly, the results suggest that use of the statistical analysis of summary scale ratings to make the final insanity classification usually will produce the same result (in 93–97% of the cases) as if the examiners had made the final decisions. This result speaks well for the internal validity of the R-CRAS system. Examiners, however, should not take these results to suggest that the R-CRAS is a valid indicator of insanity in the sense of external validity.

Finally, the study's use of examiners' final insanity decisions as a dependent variable or criterion should not be taken as a justification for testifying to these decisions in actual practice; arguably these opinions about the ultimate legal question are beyond the proper scope of expert testimony.

Predictive or Classificatory Utility

To examine the external validity of the R-CRAS, Rogers (a) examined the rate of agreement between R-CRAS-based opinions about sanity or insanity and court dispositions for a sample of 93 defendants. To avoid criterion contamination, courts were not advised of R-CRAS results for these defendants. The overall hit rate of the R-CRAS-based opinions was 88.3%, with 4.8% false negatives and 26.7% false positives. (Base rate of insanity verdicts was 32%). The chance-corrected kappa coefficient averaged .72. The rate of agreement for cases the evaluators assessed as sane was higher (95%) than for those assessed as insane (73%). Further analysis revealed that cases in which there was a disagreement between the R-CRAS opinion and the verdict were primarily cases in which the severity of psychopathology was moderate. Greater agreement was reached when the severity rating was either extremely high or extremely low.

CRITIQUE. The false positive rate in this study seems higher than would be desirable. On the other hand, Rogers (a) correctly notes that comparison of R-CRAS results to court determinations is an equivocal test of the instrument. One does not know (nor can one test) the validity or accuracy of judicial decisions, because there is no appropriate external criterion. At a minimum, at least the R-CRAS provides some evidence for *known* error rates in relation to *some* criterion, and this is more than currently exists for unaided or unstructured insanity assessments.

References

(a) Rogers, R. (1984). *Rogers Criminal Responsibility Assessment Scales.* Odessa, FL: Psychological Assessment Resources.
(b) Rogers, R. & Cavanaugh, J. (1981). The Rogers Criminal Responsibility Assessment Scales. *Illinois Medical Journal, 160,* 164–169.
(c) Rogers, R., Dolmetsch, R., & Cavanaugh, J. (1981). An empirical approach to insanity evaluations. *Journal of Clinical Psychology, 37,* 683–687.
(d) Rogers, R., Seman, W., & Wasyliw, O. (1983). The R-CRAS and insanity: A cross-validation study. *Journal of Clinical Psychology, 39,* 554–559.
(e) Rogers, R. & Sewell, K. (1999). The R-CRAS and insanity evaluations: A reexamination of construct validity. *Behavioral Sciences and the Law, 17,* 181–194.

(f) Rogers, R. & Shuman, D. (2000). *Conducting insanity evaluations (2d Ed.)*. New York: Guilford.
(g) Rogers, R., Wasyliw, O., & Cavanaugh, J. (1984). Evaluating insanity: A study of construct validity. *Law and Human Behavior, 8,* 293–303.
(h) Spitzer, R. & Endicott, J. (1978). *Schedule of affective disorders and schizophrenia.* New York: Biometrics Research.
(i) Spitzer, R., Endicott, J., & Rollins, E. (1975). Clinical criteria and DSM-III. *American Journal of Psychiatry, 132,* 1187–1192.

CURRENT STATUS OF THE FIELD

RESEARCH DIRECTIONS

Functional Component

As noted earlier in this chapter, the cognitive and volitional functional capacities delineated in the two major insanity standards cannot reasonably be assessed with the same type of instrumentation and strategies devised for other legal competencies such as competency to stand trial (Chapter 4) or competency to waive rights to silence and counsel (Chapter 5). The insanity standards require an assessment of the defendant's psychopathology, thought processes, and emotional characteristics *at the time of the offense.* Thus, defendants' *current* performance has less legal relevance.

Only two forensic assessments instruments have been designed for use in clinical assessments of insanity. Both of them—the MSE and the R-CRAS—structure the analysis of data in forming a clinical opinion about the defendant's mental state at the time of the offense. Rather than focusing on specific cognitive of volitional capacities, which cannot reasonably be retrospectively assessed, both instruments focus on symptoms of psychopathology.

Further research might determine whether the content categories used in these instruments adequately cover the range of data that experts generally collect or find to be relevant in insanity assessments. Absent this research, the opinions of experienced forensic examiners regarding important types of data needed for insanity assessment reports (Borum & Grisso, 1996) suggest that the MSE and R-CRAS call for an adequate range and type of information.

Causal Component

In clinical assessments of insanity, the presence of a substantial mental disorder (disease or defect) at the time of the offense is a predicate condition. Unless such a condition existed, any inquiry or data concerning cognitive, affective, and volitional capacities is essentially moot. In most legal competency assessments, the examiner first assesses and notes functional deficits in relevant capacities, then determines the most likely cause. The reverse process is more characteristic of criminal responsibility evaluations, where the examiner first considers whether there is reasonable evidence for a mental disorder (e.g., psychosis) and/or symptoms (e.g., delusions) that might have produced (caused) deficits in cognitive or volitional capacity.

Neither of the two FAIs reviewed here provide much specific guidance regarding how the examiner should establish a causal connection or verify the causal element. The MSE focuses primarily on screening for the existence of a predicate mental condition, with very little attention to the causal dimension. The R-CRAS addresses the causal requirements in the rated items and in the decision model, but it does not specify or suggest how to establish whether the requirement was met. For example, the R-CRAS calls for a rating of the examiner's estimate of "patient's self-control" at the time of the offense (Item 24), based on the examiner's "integration of other data and clinical judgment" (Rogers, 1984, p. 31). Item 25 calls for a rating concerning whether loss of control was "a result of a psychosis": for example, whether a "direct relationship" existed between delusions and the alleged offense (Rogers, 1984, p. 31). The data and the decision in these instances are relatively clear, but how the inferences are to be made is not. Nevertheless, there is value in having instruments that guide the collection and organization of assessment data and specify the sequential decisions that must be made.

Whether and how these inferences could be structured and specified is an open question. What kinds of data would inform efforts to develop structured decision guidelines? One approach would be to investigate the decisional processes of expert and/or legal decision makers and to identify and weigh the factors that influence causal inference decisions. This has been done for other psycholegal issues (e.g., Grisso, Tomkins, & Casey, 1984). Alternatively (or in addition), one could directly survey experts and judges about the factors that should be considered in this decision and which should hold a greater or lesser degree of importance.

Research efforts of this type may lead to structured guidelines for the causal inferences underlying these various clinical judgments. This might increase the expert's ability not only to engage in the process more reliably, but also to describe to courts more clearly how the inferential conclusions are reached. The development of similar research efforts focused on clinical reasoning in arriving at opinions about elements of the insanity standards could be of considerable benefit to this most difficult area of assessment and clinical judgment.

Interactive Component

As explained in the first section, the legal concept of insanity does not call for an evaluation of the examinee's capacities relative to the demands of the environmental context in which the alleged offense occurred. Environmental circumstances may be important for understanding how the event occurred, for checking the reality testing of the defendant at that time, for questioning the accuracy of the examinee's report, and for reconstructing the nature of the defendant's pathology. Yet the insanity standard does not ask whether the defendant could conform his or her conduct "under the totality of circumstances," and courts do not seem to perceive this as an underlying question in insanity cases. For example, whether or not a victim had threatened a male insanity defendant (and thereby given him cause to believe that there was a plot against him by the victim) generally will not be an important argument for an insanity defense. What is important is how the defendant's mental disorder might have contributed to this belief. Thus there would seem to be little reason to pursue research on insanity assessment methods employing an interactive perspective.

Judgmental and Dispositional Components

In the first section of this chapter we described the professional and legal debate about whether is it appropriate for mental health professionals to offer opinions on the "ultimate issue" of a defendant's sanity. Although it is possible to use either instrument without making such a conclusion, the existing structure of the MSE and R-CRAS do seem to pull one toward an ultimate opinion. The MSE provides for a conclusion that certain defendants do not have probable grounds for an insanity defense, and the R-CRAS decision model asks the examiner to arrive at a sanity/insanity decision. This could pose a challenge for those who feel obligated to navigate widely around ultimate issue conclusions.

CLINICAL APPLICATION

Description

The strength and promise of both the MSE and the R-CRAS lies in their potential to guide the collection and analysis of data in insanity assessments. Accordingly, in many ways they are more appropriately viewed as "guides" rather than tests. An additional function of FAIs is to provide (normative) data on individuals who have been evaluated or adjudicated for a particular legal competency to serve as a point of comparison for subsequent assessments. The potential to describe examinees in relation to other insanity defendants is somewhat better for the R-CRAS than for the MSE.

Although preliminary evidence suggests that both instruments can facilitate high rates of inter-examiner agreement on the final conclusion (sane vs. insane), the judgments themselves depend greatly on the general clinical skills of the examiner. In addition, the instruments are dependent on other assessment methods for the collection of reliable data. These may include interviews, psychological and neuropsychological tests, and a considerable range of secondary sources of information reviewed in the first section of this chapter.

Explanation

Chief among the potential causal conditions for insanity are inferred relations of the defendant's mental disorder (at the time of the offense) to specific cognitive, affective and volitional capacities noted in insanity standards. For example, one may be required to explain causal links between diagnoses, more specific features of thought disorder, and their relation to capacity to have appreciated the wrongfulness of the act. In addition, one may need to be able to rule out malingering as an explanation for data that otherwise are suggestive of critical thought disorder or incapacity.

The two insanity instruments guide these inferential processes only to the extent of highlighting certain data to be used and the types of inferences to be made. Just as they rely on clinical expertise to determine how data are to be collected, they also depend on the examiner's judgment to determine how the causal inferences and explanations are to be achieved.

Postdiction

One of the unique challenges in insanity assessments is that it requires an appraisal of the defendant's precise mental state at a particular point in time. There can be no objective empirical data to determine that decision. Indeed, there are not even any existing studies demonstrating the ability of mental health professionals to judge—through a postdictive investigation—the nature and degree of a person's particular mental condition or symptom pattern at a given point in the past with any degree of reliability or accuracy. Although this would not address directly the MSO question in insanity cases, it would at least provide some indication of the feasibility of postdictive assessments. The two insanity instruments and their existing research base do not alter this state of affairs.

Conclusions

The first section of this chapter discussed in some detail the argument that threshold decisions (e.g., sane/insane, "lacks *substantial* capacity") actually require moral not scientific judgments. Neither instrument directly addresses this issue, nor do they alter the boundaries of a mental health professional's expertise. As noted above, however, either instrument can be used without reaching or offering conclusions on the ultimate legal issue. For example, the R-CRAS asks the examiner to rate the defendant's degree of awareness of the act's criminality (Item 19). An expert might wish to provide the court with a rating of the defendant on this dimension, and to offer explanations for that opinion without necessarily going further to infer that the defendant did or did not "lack substantial capacity."

Parenting Capacity

RANDY K. OTTO AND JOHN F. EDENS

THE COMPETENCE QUESTION

Mental health professionals typically assess the capacity of parents to care for and meet the needs of their children in two types of legal cases:

- divorce proceedings in which the parents contest custody, and
- abuse, neglect or termination of parental rights proceedings in which the state alleges that the parent is unable or unfit to care for the child (sometimes collectively described as dependency proceedings).

Although courts consider a variety of factors in divorce custody and dependency proceedings, the legal decision maker in both types of case is concerned with the behaviors and capacities of adults as child caretakers. Yet any attempt to define the parental characteristics relevant for these decisions, as well as the relevance of mental health professionals' evaluations, must begin by acknowledging the unruly nature of custody and dependency law. The strands of law referenced above often are not represented by distinct bodies of law in a state's statutes, and different statutes within a state may produce similar custodial consequences. Further, the development of laws for dealing with the array of custody questions noted above often has not been uniform across states. Nevertheless, as is the case with all forensic evaluations, statutes and case opinions provide a starting point for describing the nature of child custody and parenting capacity questions that mental health professionals may be asked to address.

ABUSE, NEGLECT, AND TERMINATION OF PARENTAL RIGHTS

It was not until the early part of the 20th Century that a consensus emerged that child protection was the responsibility of the state (as opposed to private foundations and charities) (Myers, 1998). The state can respond to allegations of abuse and neglect via the criminal justice system (through prosecution of the alleged perpetrating parent or care taker) and the civil system, by way of dependency proceedings designed to protect the child and provide services and conditions necessary to remedy problems that brought the family before the court. It is mental health professionals' involvement in these civil proceedings that we focus on below.

Contemporary child maltreatment laws allow for state supervision of the child and family, temporary removal of the child for protective and rehabilitative purposes, and permanent removal and termination of parental rights (TPR) in the most extreme cases. Dependency cases first require a court's determination that some form of maltreatment (i.e., either abuse or neglect) has occurred. In these hearings the court attempts to identify (Melton et al., 1997; Barnum, 1997):

- the alleged abusive or neglectful behaviors that are said to have occurred
- any harm that resulted to the child
- the parent's capacities to care for and protect the child
- the risk for future harm, and
- prognosis for change and reunification through various interventions, if appropriate and necessary.

In addition, the breadth and vagueness of some child maltreatment laws (see Budd, 2001 and Azar et al., 1995 for further discussion) allow for consideration of indirect evidence concerning the parent's character and general "way of life" (Weisberg & Wald, 1984).

A finding of abuse or neglect is followed by a determination or disposition. Chief among the questions at the disposition phase is whether the child's welfare is adequately protected by allowing continued residence with the parents under supervision of social service agents, or whether temporary or permanent placement outside of the home is required. It is especially at this stage that the parent's qualities for ensuring the future welfare of the child are scrutinized by the court.

All states allow a court to sever completely the legal ties between parent and child under certain circumstances (Sales et al., 1982). Such dispositions, however, represent a minority of all dependency proceedings. Herring (1992), citing data from a Michigan study, estimated that no more than 15% of all dependency cases result in termination of parental rights. Many states include termination of parental rights as an optional disposition within their neglect and abuse laws, while other states address issues of termination of parental rights (TPR) in a separate chapter or code (Weisberg & Wald, 1984). Termination provisions also appear elsewhere in most statutes, however, where they apply to a far wider range of cases than those in which abuse or neglect has actually occurred (as will be described in more detail later in this chapter). Social service or mental health professionals' evaluations of a parent's potential to meet a child's needs are considered in many termination cases.

DIVORCE AND CUSTODY

While custody is contested in a minority of divorce proceedings involving children (Maccoby & Mnookin, 1992; McIntosh & Prinz, 1993), the high rate of divorce in the United States makes clear that courts will be faced with issues of child custody in a fair number of cases. In contrast to dependency proceedings, the legal issue in cases of disputed custody in the context of divorce is not one of parental "unfitness" or "incompetence." Both parents are presumed "fit" or "competent," so the legal decision maker in custody cases seeks to compare the two parents regarding their abilities to meet the "best interests" of their children.

Central to the custody decision-making process is the definition of, and distinction between, different types of custody (Melton et al., 1997; Otto, 2000; Schutz et al., 1989). State law typically makes reference to and distinguishes between decision-making authority for the children (referred to as legal custody or parental responsibility in some jurisdictions) and the issue of physical placement or residence of the children (referred to as residential or physical custody in some jurisdictions). The courts, therefore, must not only make rulings about the living arrangements and visitation schedule for the children post-divorce, but also about who will be involved in making decisions about them (Gunnoe & Braver, 2001). Historically, courts have awarded both physical and legal custody to one parent (typically the mother), but in the past 25 years joint custody has been awarded with increasing frequency. Despite this recent

trend, courts direct that children will live with each parent for equal
amounts of time in only a minority of custody cases (Nord & Zill, 1997;
Maccoby & Mnookin, 1992).

LAW AND CURRENT PRACTICE

Legal Standards

ABUSE, NEGLECT, AND TERMINATION OF PARENTAL RIGHTS PROCEEDINGS.   In
English Common Law, the state's power to intervene between parents
and their children was quite limited, and parents enjoyed essentially
unbridled authority in their interactions with their children. Until this
past century, children were considered property or chattel (typically of
their fathers) and treated as such. Parents in 10th Century England had
the authority to kill an unweaned child or sell a child under the age of
seven into slavery (Foster & Freed, 1964). By the 17th Century, Common
Law prohibited parents from killing their offspring, the state continued to
have limited authority to intervene in matters of the family, and parents
were not required by law to provide their children with basic necessities
(McGough & Shindell, 1978).

    With the development of the state's parents patriae power, however,
the autonomy and control parents had with respect to their children was
diminished, and the state gained the right to protect children from maltreatment at the hands of their parents (McGough & Shindell, 1978;
Custer, 1978). Children are no longer viewed as property and, although
parents enjoy considerable autonomy and protection from the state with
respect to child rearing matters, their power or authority is not absolute,
and states have the right to protect children (see, e.g., Reppucci & Crosby,
1993; *Griswold v. Connecticut*, 1965; *Meyer v. Nebraska*, 1923; *Prince v.
Massachusetts*, 1944; *Quilloin v. Walcott*, 1978; *Santosky v. Kramer*, 1982;
Stanley v. Illinois, 1972). With respect to child maltreatment law, there is
some consistency between states as a result of the federal Child Abuse
Prevention and Treatment Act, which was originally passed in 1974 and
ties federal funding for state child abuse activities to specific legislative
requirements. Nonetheless, there remain significant differences across
states in their laws and legal process.

    Although all states allow for state intervention in cases of child abuse
or neglect, definitions of abuse and neglect vary. Some definitions are
inherently value laden and culturally determined and, consequently,
states vary with respect to the exemptions or exceptions they consider
(e.g., on issues related to corporal punishment, refusal of medical services
on religious grounds, poverty as a cause of failure to provide) (National
Clearinghouse on Child Abuse and Neglect Information, 2001a). Sexual

abuse of a child by a parent or other care taker is also typically identified as a basis for state intervention, although this form of maltreatment, as compared to physical abuse or neglect, is more likely to be processed through the criminal justice system (Daro, 1996; Melton, 1995). Emotional abuse or neglect, sometimes referred to as psychological maltreatment, is considered by some to be the most controversial of grounds for state intervention since there is the least consensus about definitions and criteria, and it is arguably the most value-laden form of maltreatment (Melton et al., 1997).

As noted above, all states authorize family or juvenile courts to terminate parental rights without agreement or consent by the parents (Sales et al., 1982). Until the latter part of the 20th Century, courts often used the mere presence of certain parental behaviors or characteristics as sufficient grounds for a termination decision. Thus, parents who were known to have been adulterous or who had been diagnosed as mentally ill or mentally disabled might, on these bases alone, be declared incompetent or unfit, thereby losing all parental rights (Dyer, 1999; Melton et al., 1997). For the past several decades, however, case law and most statutes changed in this regard, reorienting to the approach that all such conditions are relevant for the termination decision, but that none are sufficient by themselves to conclude unfitness (Feller et al., 1992).

Although the law regarding abuse and neglect of children is vague and varied with the exception of some areas, there appears to be more specificity and consistency across jurisdictions in the law regarding termination of parental rights. This may reflect, in part, the state's recognition of the more serious consequences associated with terminations proceedings (i.e., permanent removal of parental rights and contact). Concerns related to value laden concepts and the lack of a consensus regarding minimal parenting abilities (see above) also apply in TPR proceedings, and may be more of a concern, given the grave implications of such legal decisions (Melton et al., 1997).

Predicate conditions necessary for a termination of parental rights are typically identified by statute, although some states simply use broader and more general language (National Clearinghouse on Child Abuse and Neglect Information, 2001b). Termination of parental rights laws generally require that the petitioner seeking termination of parental rights (the state) prove, by clear and convincing evidence (*Santosky v. Kramer*, 1982), that the parent is unfit in some way and cannot become minimally fit within a specified period of time. Many states also require a showing that the petitioner prove that the state child welfare agency made "reasonable efforts" to reunify the parent and child prior to seeking termination of parental rights (Herring, 1992). Although there is variability between jurisdictions, a number of conditions or circumstances serve as the predicate for termination of parental rights in the majority of states (National Clearinghouse on Child Abuse and Neglect Information, 2001b; Feller et al., 1992; Neal, 1989 cited in Dyer, 1999):

- parental incapacity to care for the child as a result of mental disorder or substance abuse,
- abandonment (e.g., failure to visit or communicate, abandonment of an infant, failure to provide a home),
- occurrence of extreme or chronic abuse or neglect,
- failure of the parent to improve in response to agency interventions, and
- long term incarceration.

By way of the Adoption and Safe Families Act of 1997 and related legislation, congress provided financial incentives for states to restructure their child welfare systems. The Act, which has been described as emphasizing the health and safety of the child while de-emphasizing the rights of biological parents (Venier, 2000), uses funding mechanisms to encourage states to minimize the amount of time children spend in foster care by:

- shortening the length of time before a state seeks to terminate a parent's rights
- identifying exceptions to the general requirement that a state need make a showing that reasonable effort to reunify the family were made (e.g., the parent has committed murder or manslaughter of another child of the parent), and
- increasing rates of adoption (National Clearinghouse on Child Abuse and Neglect Information, 2001b).

Recent appellate cases reflect a movement to ensure that functional abilities of parents (which may or may not be related to conditions such as mental disorder, mental retardation or substance abuse) are the basis for making decisions about termination of parents' rights rather than simply the presence of various conditions (Melton *et al.*, 1997). In *Davis v. Davis* (1977), for example, the court warned that an adulterous parent is not presumptively unfit for custody of a child; the parent's behavior is relevant, but its weight depends on the extent to which it is likely to affect the child's welfare in the particular case in question. Once it is clear that the child's welfare is substantially threatened by the parent's immorality, custody may be terminated; but it is the threat to the child, not the parent's immorality *per se*, that justifies the finding of unfitness and termination of custody. Many courts have ruled similarly concerning parents' past or present mental illness, retardation or other disabilities (e.g., *In re the Custody of a Minor*, 1990; *K.N. v. State*, 1993; *In re Kelly*, 1992), and with regard to sexual orientation (Brownstone, 1980). A corollary of this conceptualization is that the fitness of the parent is to be determined not solely on the basis of the parent's past behavior (although often this will be relevant), but on the basis of judgments concerning the parent's likely future behavior and its influence on the child's growth and development.

Most states consider the *child's best interests* to be paramount in TPR proceedings, with consideration of the child's health, safety, and well being informing this decision (Feller et al., 1992; National Clearinghouse on Child Abuse and Neglect Information, 2001b). The precise wording, however, varies across states, placing somewhat different emphasis on the role of children's best interest in relation to other considerations. In general, these variations create three kinds of standards:

- the *jurisdictional* standard, reflecting a balanced appreciation of both parental rights and the best interests of the child
- the *parental rights* standard, directing that the child's well being is relevant but that the parent's right to parent is paramount absent a showing of unfitness, and
- the *psychological parent* standard, in which termination of parental rights is only allowed when the biological parents of the child have deprived the child in a way that threatens normal development.

Once parental rights have been severed, the parent enjoys no right to contact, visitation or decision making, and adoption of the child can occur without the parent's consent (Feller et al., 1992).

Because of the court's desire to keep families unified and remedy any deficits that lead to abuse or neglect in maltreatment cases, and because of the predicate requirement of a finding of harm and "parental unfitness" in TPR cases (with the exception of some cases, see above for a discussion), evaluations in abuse, neglect and TPR proceedings are focused on minimal parenting competence or adequacy rather than identifying ideal circumstances for the child. Of course, such a process is complicated by the fact that there is no universally accepted standard for "minimal parenting competence" (Azar & Benjet, 1994; Azar, Benjet, Fuhrmann, & Cavallero, 1995; Budd, 2001).

DIVORCE CUSTODY PROCEEDINGS. Courts did not need to concern themselves with questions of custody and parenting fitness until this century since, at Common Law, children were considered property and, in cases of divorce, ownership of all property was enjoyed by the husband-father (Jacob, 1988; Sorenson & Goldman, 1990; Wyer, Gaylord, & Grove, 1987). This right may have been partly embedded in beliefs that fathers were better parents. In its review of child custody law, the court in *Ex Parte Devine* (1981) quoted a Mississippi Chief Justice who offered in an 1842 case:

> The authority of the father is superior to that of the mother. It is the doctrine of all civilized nations. It is according to the revealed law and the law of nature, and it prevails even with the wandering savage, who has received none of the lights of civilization. (p. 688)

But the law began to change in the late 1800s, likely as a result of two factors. First, legal authorities explicitly acknowledged new conceptualizations of the needs of children. An example of the legal system's stated rationale for reconstructing the primary legal consideration in divorce custody cases is provided below:

> Right to custody of the child will depend mainly upon the question of whether such custody will promote the welfare and the interest of such child .... Above all things, [this] is the paramount consideration. (*Chapsky v. Wood*, 1881, p. 321; see also *Finlay v. Finlay*, 1925)

Also identified as an explanation of the shift from father's rights has been the transition of children at the turn of the century from economic assets who could earn income, to economic liabilities who were protected from the workforce via compulsory education laws.

From the mid-19th Century onward women gained increasing rights (Mason, 1994), and by the end of the century we see development and formal acknowledgement of the *"tender years"* doctrine, which held that mothers were uniquely qualified to rear children (*Ex Parte Devine*, 1981; Lyman & Roberts, 1985). Reflecting the common belief about the unique contributions and nature of women as parents at the time, one court wrote: "there is but a twilight zone between a mother's love and the atmosphere of heaven" (*Tuter v. Tuter*, 1938, p. 205). Thus, the legal presumption was that children's best interests were served by granting custody of them to their mother in cases of divorce (Wyer et al., 1987). Although the presumption that a particular mother was best suited to meet a child's needs could be overcome in a particular case by showing that the mother was unfit in some way, this rarely occurred.

The tender years doctrine controlled custody decision-making until the 1960s when significant changes in family law occurred (Hall, Pulver, & Cooley, 1996; Mason, 1994). With shifting conceptualizations of sex roles and movement to '"no fault" divorce, the tender years doctrine was challenged as sexist and lacking in logic (Horne, 1993). One judge offered the following challenge to the tender years doctrine and its associated presumptions: "What a mother's care means to her children has been so much romanticized and poeticized that its reality and its substance have sometimes been lost in the flowers of rhetoric. Not all mothers can lay claim to such eulogy" (*Stanfield V. Stanfield*, 1968, p. 692).

Because women were no longer considered to make better parents as a function of innate abilities, the tender years doctrine was replaced with the *best interests of the child* standard, which has been adopted by all United States jurisdictions (Hall, Pulver, & Cooley, 1996; Rohman, Sales, & Lou, 1987). Despite rejection of the tender years doctrine, mothers continue to be granted custody in 85% to 90% of all divorce custody cases (Victor & Winkler, 1977; US Bureau of the Census, 1989). The reasons for this are unclear. This circumstance may reflect (1) that mothers continue to be the primary parent in the majority families despite changing social conceptions, (2) biases of the courts despite changes in law, (3) a reluctance for fathers to try to gain custody because they perceive the system to be biased to favor mothers as caregivers, or (4) some combination of the above (Horne, 1993; Mnookin, Maccoby, Albiston, & Depner, 1990; Polikoff, 1983).

With the "best interests" standard came greater judicial discretion in deciding custody based on the unique characteristics of each child and a child's potential caretakers. The complexity of factors and circumstances to be considered anew in each case, without formulas or clear decision rules, is cited as contributing to idiosyncratic and inconsistent decision making (Charlow, 1994; Crosby-Currie, 1996; Mnookin, 1975; Pearson & Luchesi-Ring, 1983; Weinstein, 1997), leading judges to look for assistance from mental health professionals in the decision process (Feller et al., 1992; Wald, 1976). Thus, courts have sought and accepted the assistance of mental health professionals in divorce custody cases, especially for their expertise in the evaluation of children's needs, parents' care taking qualities, and description of their implications for the child's welfare. This has continued despite questions offered by mental health and legal commentators alike regarding whether mental health professionals have true expertise to offer in such cases (see, e.g., O'Donahue & Bradley, 1999; Okpaku, 1976; see below for further discussion).

Although it is the "best interests" standard that has prevailed for purposes of custody decision making in cases of divorce, alternative standards have been offered (Melton et al., 1997). The "least detrimental alternative" standard is based on theoretical arguments of Goldstein, Freud, and Solnit (1973) and focuses the custody decision on determining the child's "psychological parent," who then is granted unilateral decision making authority with respect to the child. Melton et al. (1997) also describe the "primary-caretaker" standard, in which custody is granted to that parent who has been primarily responsible for care and nurturance of the child, an arguably more objective and provable matter. Finally, Scott (1992) has proposed the "approximation standard," which dictates that custody arrangements following divorce should approximate, to the extent possible, child rearing arrangements in existence prior to the marital separation and dissolution.

While the "best interests" standard reveals in whose interests custody-related decisions are to be made, it provides little direction regarding the factors or criteria that should be considered when determining a child's interests (Gould, 1998; Otto, 2000; Horne, 1993). Consequently, the large majority of states have operationalized and defined the best interests standard legislatively. Many state's codes are based in part on the custody section of the Uniform Marriage and Divorce Act (1979):

- The wishes of the child's parent or parents as to his custody
- The wishes of the child as to his custodian
- The interaction and interrelationship of the child and his parent or parents, his siblings, and any other person who may significantly affect the child's best interests
- The child's adjustment to his home, school, and community, and
- The mental and physical health of all individuals involved.

Michigan's Child Custody Act (Michigan Compiled Laws Service, 2001) has served as a model for many state legislatures in their attempts to identify factors that the legal decision-maker and custody evaluator are to consider with respect to determining children's best interests. Michigan's law, like that of many states, identifies both psychological factors (e.g., the "love, affection and other emotional ties existing between the parties involved and the child", the "mental and physical health of the parties", "the capacity and disposition of the parties involved to give the child love, affection, and guidance and to continue the education and raising of the child involved in his or her religion or creed, if any", "domestic violence, regardless of whether the violence was directed against or witnesses by the child") and a variety of non-psychological factors (e.g., "moral fitness of the parties involved") that are to be considered by the court, as well as case specific factors that might not have been anticipated by the legislature (i.e., "any other factor considered by the court to be relevant to a particular child custody dispute"). How the child's best interests are operationalized varies from state to state. In their review of state child custody statutes in place in 1993, Hall, Pulver, and Cooley (1996) concluded that "best interests" criteria varied considerably across the 50 states. Schutz et al. (1989), however, were able to identify general consistencies across the various state statutes:

For children—

- Age and sex
- Adjustment to current and prior environments, including the length of time in each
- History of child abuse/victimization
- Educational needs
- Special mental health or medical care
- Wishes or desires regarding placement, if of sufficient age
- Effects of separation of siblings

For parents—

- History of spouse abuse
- Economic status and stability
- Wishes and desires regarding placement and custody
- Mental and physical health
- Substance abuse
- Level of hostility
- Flexibility
- Parenting skills
- Care taking involvement before and after separation

Although the legislatures' attempts to operationalize the best interests standards provide custody evaluators and legal decision-makers with some direction, how decisions are to be made remains unclear. Most apparent is that, when considering issues of custody and placement of children, the relative importance of the various factors identified by statute and the weight they are to be accorded go unstated. This likely reflects acknowledgement by both the judiciary and mental health professionals that, because parents and children in each family are very different, questions of custody and what is in the best interests of children can vary significantly from case to case. Thus, a concretized formula is not appropriate, and courts and legislators have chosen to resist the development of rigid rules for deciding custody (Schutz et al., 1989).

The statutes and the history of their application reflect the highly discretionary use of the factors in divorce custody decisions (Pearson & Luchesi-Ring, 1983). No particular fact (other than a finding of unfitness or incompetence as defined by standards for termination of parental rights) automatically disqualifies a parent as a custodian. No factor is construed *per se* as more important than another; different factors may be given more or less weight by the fact finder in different cases. Further, the court may consider any other factors that are not named in statutes, as long as they can be construed as relevant for the child's welfare. Many states have adopted joint custody as a legal option (i.e., both parents retain equal, shared responsibility and control for a child's upbringing), and about half the states have legislated joint custody as a preferred arrangement (Schutz et al., 1989). The latter states presume that joint custody is the best outcome unless individual circumstances suggest otherwise.

Legal Process

ABUSE, NEGLECT AND TERMINATION OF PARENTAL RIGHTS PROCEEDINGS. Although all states have in place a government system to protect children from abuse and neglect, the child protection process varies considerably. Additionally, within a particular jurisdiction the legal standards can vary across various parts of the dependency process.

A detailed discussion of the child protection process is beyond the scope of this chapter (see Feller et al., 1992; Myers, 1990; or Melton et al., 1997, for a more in-depth coverage). In brief, the first decision point in child protection proceedings occurs in response to an allegation of abuse or neglect. After contact with or screening by a child protective services worker an initial decision is made regarding the child's placement. The child may remain in the home or be removed from the home on an emergency basis, depending on various factors including the likelihood of harm to the child, the parent's or other caretaker's willingness and ability to protect the child, and availability of alternative living arrangements.

Once a child is taken from the parents and placed in emergency protective custody, the protective services agency must immediately initiate proceedings in dependency court. Even in cases where the child remains with his or her parents, proceedings will be initiated to determine whether the child is "dependent" (i.e., has been subjected to abuse or neglect) and falls under its jurisdiction as a result. Upon adjudicating a child dependent, the court may order the parents and child to undergo evaluations and participate in treatment services, with the intention of remedying any deficits and problems that resulted in the dependency adjudication (Caufield & Horowitz, 1987; Feller et al., 1992). In cases where the child has been removed from the home, the ultimate goal is returning the child to the parents' care (reunification). If it is determined that the parent presents an unacceptable risk of harm to the child (as a function of the parents' past behavior, the parent's inability to learn skills necessary for appropriate care taking, or the parent's failure to comply with orders of the court regarding intervention and treatment), the state can seek to terminate the parent's parental rights.

Although there is variability across jurisdictions, different standards of proof are required at different stages in the dependency process (Feller et al., 1992). While probable cause may be all that is required for emergency removal from the home at a subsequent hearing, a slightly higher standard of proof, "preponderance of the evidence," typically will be required at adjudicatory and dispositional hearings. Although Sales et al. (1982) found that many states employed that same standard in termination of parental rights cases, recent years have seen the standard for TPR determinations raised to "clear and convincing evidence" (Dyer, 1999).

In dependency cases, mental health professionals may be called on to evaluate the child and/or parent and engage in one of four assessment activities in the context of these evaluations (Barnum, 1997):

- determine whether abuse occurred (potentially the most problematic and controversial task)
- describe any harm that has resulted to the child as a result of alleged or proven abuse or neglect
- describe the parent's care taking capacities, and
- offer a prognosis with recommendations for treatment and interventions.

Very few states provide procedures for mental health evaluations to determine the mental status of parents alleged to be unfit, or to examine other factors that might be related to parents' child-rearing capacities. Most statutes make some provision for legal counsel for the parent and for the child (Dyer, 1999). The actual frequency with which courts request evaluations and legal representation, however, has not been documented.

DIVORCE CUSTODY PROCEEDINGS.   It is beyond the scope of this discussion to detail the circumstances and legal requirements associated with the appearance of two parents before a juvenile or family court to contend for a child's custody (see, e.g., Goldzband, 1982; Group for the Advancement of Psychiatry, 1980; Schutz et al., 1989). Many cases involve parents who are already in substantial agreement on custody arrangements, whereas others come prepared for battle, either adamantly or with ambivalence. Jurisdictional law or policy may have required that the parties attempt to negotiate a settlement of their differences concerning custody, reserving adversarial resolution for those cases in which negotiation has failed (Elrod & Spector, 1998). Generally, both parents will have legal counsel, and most jurisdictions now provide for separate representation of the child by a guardian *ad litem*.

Mental health professionals may be asked by a parent's attorney to evaluate one or both parents and the children whose custody is in question. Courts sometimes must intervene to order the parent who is the current custodian to cooperate with the other parent's request for access to the children or the parent him or herself. Generally, courts are authorized to appoint mental health professionals to examine any of the parties involved.

Information available to the judge in a divorce custody proceeding might include not only the arguments and evidence offered by legal counsel at the custody hearing, but also the report of the court's mental health examiner (whose findings generally will be presented at the hearing), records and investigations of social service agencies or probation departments, and the results of the judge's own conference with the children to explore their custody preferences or apparent attachments to the parents.

Custody decisions may range from joint custody, in which the parents share the responsibility for all matters of the child's welfare, to a custody arrangement that invests one of the parents with total authority and bars the other parent from contact with the child. Between these two extremes are a variety of possible dispositions involving degrees of parental authority, distinctions between legal and physical custody, enforced arrangements concerning the child's access to both parents, financial support arrangements, and custody arrangements that place some of the children with one parent and some with the other.

The legal process for divorce custody arrangements often does not end with the custody decision. Courts may respond to the petitions of social service agencies or parents concerning failure of a parent to abide by certain court-ordered arrangements (e.g., visitation requirements, support payments). Further, issues related to custody may be revisited as a result of changes in the circumstances of parents or children. For example, parents who are not awarded custody may claim changes in their own circumstances or those of the custodial parent, which may justify reconsideration of the custody issue (e.g., involvement with a significant other that presents a risk to the child, successful treatment of a mental disorder or substance abuse problem). Alternatively or in addition, either parent may be accused of maltreatment or incapacity manifested subsequent to the original custody decision and a change in custody conditions requested. These circumstances might require reevaluation by a mental health professional and a hearing on the need to alter the original divorce custody decision.

Competence Assessment: Current Practice

ABUSE, NEGLECT, AND TERMINATION OF PARENTAL RIGHTS. The mental health professional's evaluation in the context of abuse, neglect, and termination of parental rights will be shaped in part by the law controlling such issues. These evaluations, however, are also shaped by relevant practice guidelines and standards. Although no formal practice standards or guidelines have been developed for conducting evaluations specifically for abuse, neglect and TPR proceedings, a number of organizations have promulgated more general guidelines that go some distance toward identifying a standard for dependency evaluations.

The *Guidelines for Psychological Evaluations in Child Protection Matters* published by the American Psychological Association in 1998 "promote proficiency using psychological expertise in conducting psychological evaluations in child protection matters" (American Psychological Association, Committee in processional Practice and Standards, 1998, p. 2). The guidelines are advisory in nature and are focused on the format or process of the evaluation more than on substance. They advise psychologists conducting such evaluations to:

- seek to provide the legal decision maker with helpful information
- place the interests of the child first
- remain objective, impartial and unbiased
- only conduct assessments that they are qualified to conduct
- avoid multiple roles and relationships with parties
- determine the nature and scope of the evaluation on a case by case basis
- obtain informed consent and assent as appropriate, including notification of limits of confidentiality
- use multiple methods of data gathering
- offer clinical opinions that are appropriately supported by assessment data
- clarify financial arrangements in advance, and
- maintain adequate records.

The American Professional Society on the Abuse of Children (APSAC) published *Practice Guidelines for Psychosocial Evaluation of Suspected Psychological Maltreatment of Children and Adolescents* (APSAC, 1996). Like the APA guidelines, the APSAC guidelines focus heavily on form and include sections devoted to confidentiality and privilege, informed consent, competence of examiners, report writing, and testifying. In addition, however, the guidelines discuss more substantive issues such as prevalence, forms, and impact of abuse and neglect; assessment techniques; impact of child development in assessment; and sources of information typically utilized. APSAC also has published *Practice Guidelines for Psychosocial Evaluation of Suspected Sexual Abuse in Children* (APSAC, 1996). Similar to the more general maltreatment evaluation guidelines, these sexual abuse evaluation guidelines address both format and substantive evaluation issues.

Finally, the American Academy of Child and Adolescent Psychiatry (1997) published the *Practice Parameters for the Forensic Evaluation of Children and Adolescents Who May Have Been Physically or Sexually Abused.* These guidelines discuss both the format and process of the evaluation as well as substantive issues related to evaluation in cases of child abuse, neglect, and maltreatment. The "Forensic Issues" section addresses matters such as role definition, notification and informed consent, confidentiality and privilege, the need for unbiased and objective work, competence and acknowledgement of professional limitations, and knowledge of relevant law. The "Forensic Evaluation" section is devoted to substantive issues including definitions, clinical presentation, and epidemiology of abuse and neglect, and various assessment techniques.

There is little literature available regarding the practice of mental health professionals who evaluate parents in the context of abuse and neglect proceedings. Some authorities (Azar et al., 1995; Budd, 2001; Jacobsen, Miller, & Kirkwood, 1997; Weinstein, 1997) have suggested that mental health professionals should proceed cautiously when offering information about parents to legal decision makers, in light of:

- the lack of universal agreement about minimal parenting competencies
- the absence of structured instruments or assessment formats directly relevant to these cases
- problems inherent to the prediction of low base rate behaviors such as serious violence, and
- cultural differences in parenting styles and values

Articles written for clinicians provide some consensus regarding what areas should be addressed in parenting capacity evaluations. Factors frequently mentioned include the nature of the alleged abuse and neglect, parents' mental status, parenting skills and abilities, the child's needs, compliance with and success of prior interventions, consideration of cultural issues, and current and anticipated living environments (Azar et al., 1995; Budd & Holdsworth, 1996; Dyer, 1999; Kuehnle, Coulter, & Firestone, 2000).

Of course, what authorities offer as appropriate practice and what mental health professionals do in such cases are separate issues. Although select appellate cases reveal highly questionable practice in some TPR cases, there is no reason to believe that these cases reflect practice in general. For example, the primary evidence for mental retardation of a parent in one case involving termination consisted of IQ test results obtained more than five years earlier when the individual was in high school (*State v. McDonald*, 1972). In another case, the examiner equated "mental retardation" with a "personality defect" and therefore as "mental illness" (*In re Rathburn* 1970). Although these cases tell us little about general practice in termination assessments, they warn us that we must not rely on courts to set the standards for the quality or type of assessment methods that we use, because at least some courts will accept data obtained or interpreted in ways that fall well below professional standards of practice.

In the only study to examine the evaluations completed by mental health professionals in maltreatment cases, Budd, Poindexter, Felix, and Naik-Polan (2001) randomly selected 190 evaluations of parents who were involved in abuse and neglect cases in Cook County (Chicago). A total of 84 mental health professionals completed the 190 evaluations; over half (54%) were psychologists, 15% were psychiatrists, and 21% were masters level professionals. Evaluations were categorized as psychological (typically evaluations involving intellectual and personality or psychopathology assessment conducted by psychologists; $n = 103$, 54%), psychiatric (clinical interviews and mental status examinations conducted by psychiatrists; $n = 25$, 13%), bonding-focused (quality of the parent-child relationship and or care giving skills; $n = 21$, 11%), substance abuse (focused on substance abuse history and typically including drug or alcohol testing; $n = 15$, 8%), parenting assessment team (assessment of the parent and child conducted by a team of mental health professionals; $n = 18$, 9%), and other/undefined ($n = 8$, 4%).

With the exception of evaluations completed by a parent assessment team, all types of evaluations were completed, on average, in one session, and typically in a court clinic or professional office. Parent assessment team evaluations averaged nearly five sessions per assessment and typically included both clinic contact and home visits. Various third party sources of information were cited in the evaluations (e.g., collateral informants, child, therapist), and reports completed by parent evaluation teams accessed and made use of third party information more frequently than other types of evaluation. A minority of reports included behavioral observations of parent-child interactions, and descriptions of the parents' child-rearing abilities or parent-child relationships were often lacking. The majority of evaluations completed by psychologists included psychological tests, with measures of personality or psychopathology and cognitive/intellectual functioning being most frequently employed.

Although most evaluations identified one or more general purposes (e.g., to assess the parent's cognitive functioning, to assess the nature and quality of the parent-child relationship), far fewer described a more specific purpose. Only evaluations conducted by mental health professionals working in the court clinic identified a specific forensic-legal issue that the evaluation was designed around. The presenting problem or issue that led to the referral and evaluation was identified in 5% to 41% of the evaluations, depending on the assessment provider group. Identification of the options under consideration occurred in 13% to 67% of the evaluations, depending on the assessment provider group.

Considering the results overall, Budd et al. (2001) concluded that "these shortcomings render many clinical assessment of parents inadequate to serve as a basis for child protection decisions" (p. 105). These somewhat discouraging results are important because so little is known empirically about evaluations of this type. Yet the investigators appropriately note that their findings were based on assessments completed in one judicial circuit, which may or may not reflect forensic practice in other settings.

DIVORCE CUSTODY PROCEEDINGS. Child custody evaluations will be shaped in part by the law controlling child custody decision-making in the jurisdiction in which he or she practices. In addition, three national organizations (and some state organizations) have promulgated custody evaluation guidelines (see Otto, Buffington, & Edens, in press, for further discussion of the strengths and weaknesses of these practice guidelines).

Guidelines for Child Custody Evaluations in Divorce Proceedings, published by the American Psychological Association (1994, APA), focus primarily on format and process (e.g., the goal of the evaluation, the role and orientation of the examiner, the competence and ability of the examiner, and procedural matters related to confidentiality, informed consent, record keeping, financial arrangements, and use and interpretation of data). Like the APA Guidelines, the Model Standards of Practice for Child Custody Evaluations of the Association of Family and Conciliation Courts (undated) (AFCC) offer direction to the evaluator regarding role definition, structuring the evaluation process, and competence. They are more substantive than the APA guidelines in that they also discuss areas of inquiry in the evaluation process (e.g., quality of the relationships between the parents and the child, quality of the relationships between the parents, domestic violence history, psychological adjustment of the parents). Thus, the AFCC guidelines provide more direction to the custody evaluator. The Practice Parameters of Child Custody Evaluation published by the American Academy of Child and Adolescent Psychiatry (1994) (AACAP) include sections devoted to both the process and substance of the evaluation and is the most detailed of the three. It identifies areas of inquiry for the examiner to address, as well as evaluation techniques and some special topics (e.g., parents' sexual orientation, grandparents' rights, child sexual abuse allegations, reproductive technology issues).

A number of investigators have surveyed mental health professionals who conduct child custody evaluations. Keilin and Bloom (1986) described the practices of 82 custody evaluators, the majority of whom were psychologists (78%). Respondents were queried about how they were involved in cases, evaluation techniques they employed, and their impressions of various custody decision making criteria or factors. A large majority (91%) indicated a preference to be retained by the attorneys of both parents or appointed by the court, yet this was the nature of their involvement in only about one-half of the cases in which they were involved. They were retained by the attorney representing one of the parents in almost all of the remaining cases.

There was a fair degree of consensus regarding the mechanics of the evaluation at the most general level. Virtually all respondents reported interviewing each parent and the children. A significant numbers reported using psychological testing with adults (76%) and children (74%), and observing parent-child interactions (69%). Half of the respondents reported that they observed interactions between the two parents, and slightly less than one-third reported engaging in home visits and school visits. Interviews of informed third parties (e.g., friends and relatives) were conducted by approximately one-half of the evaluators.

There was less consensus regarding the use of psychological testing. No single measure was used by a majority of the respondents when assessing children. Intelligence tests were the most frequently used tests, with almost one-half using some measure of intelligence in the majority (85%) of their cases. The next most frequently used instruments were the Thematic Apperception Test or the Children's Apperception Test (39% of the respondents reporting use of these measures in most of their evaluations), then miscellaneous projective drawings, the Rorschach Inkblot Technique, and the Bender-Gestalt Visual Motor Test. For assessing parents, respondents identified the Minnesota Multiphasic Personality Inventory (MMPI) as the most commonly used assessment technique with adults (70% of the examiners in almost all of their cases), followed by the Rorschach Inkblot Technique (42%) and the Thematic Apperception Test (38%).

Updating Keilin and Bloom's survey, Ackerman and Ackerman (1997) obtained usable responses from 201 of the 800 doctoral level psychologists to whom they sent surveys regarding their child custody evaluation practices. Similar to the findings of Keilin and Bloom, almost all of the respondents reported a preference for retention by both parties' attorneys or court appointment. Ackerman and Ackerman noted that their respondents reported spending considerably greater periods of time reviewing adjunctive materials and writing reports than did those surveyed by Keilin and Bloom 10 years earlier. Consistent with Keilin and Bloom's findings, however, intelligence tests and projective measures continued to be the instruments most frequently employed with children, and the MMPI/MMPI-2 remained the most frequently used assessment instrument for parents, followed by the Rorschach.

Many custody evaluators also reported using assessment instruments with children that were developed specifically for use in custody contexts. Over one-third of the respondents reported using the *Bricklin Perceptual Scales* (Bricklin, 1990a), and 16% reported frequent use of the *Perceptions of Relationship Test* (Bricklin, 1989).

Fewer respondents reported using specific custody measures designed for use with families or adults. Only 11% of the psychologists reported using the *Ackerman-Schoendorf Parent Evaluation for Custody Test* (Ackerman & Schoendorf, 1992), but those who used it did so in almost all (89%) cases. The only other custody-specific measures endorsed were the *Parent Awareness of Skills Survey* (Bricklin, 1990b; PASS) and the *Custody Quotient* (Gordon & Peek, 1989), both used by less than 10% of the respondents.

Finally, findings similar to those obtained by Keilin and Bloom (1986) and Ackerman and Ackerman (1997) were reported by Bow and Quinnell (2001), who received usable surveys from 198 of 563 psychologists who were identified as conducting child custody evaluations. Involvement as a custody evaluator came via court appointment in the majority (84%) of cases. The respondents reported spending between 24.5 and 28.5 hours per evaluation, on average. Almost all respondents reported interviewing each parent and the children. Significant numbers of evaluators reported employing psychological testing with adults (91%) and children (61%), and observing parent-child interactions (92%). One third of the respondents reported making home visits, whereas the majority (78%) indicated that they made some contact with the children's teachers. Interviews of informed third parties (e.g., family physician, pediatrician, neighbors, friends, relatives) were employed by approximately one-half of the respondents, whereas virtually all reported relying on adjunctive documents. The authors did not report data regarding specific test selection and use.

In addition to the above, a number of commentators have offered suggestions for comprehensive child custody evaluations (see, e.g., Bricklin,

1995; Gould, 1998; Otto, 2000; Melton et al., 1997; Stahl, 1994). There appears to be a consensus among these authorities that custody evaluations in the context of divorce should describe:

- the child's cognitive, emotional, social and academic needs and abilities,
- the parents' understanding of the child's needs and abilities to meet those needs,
- any factors that may limit a parent's ability to understand or meet a child's needs,
- the nature of the relationship between the child and each parent,
- the relationship between the parents as it affects their interactions with the child, and
- the custodial arrangement proposed by each parent and the possible effects of the child's functioning.

A review of these same commentators, however, does not produce a consensus regarding evaluation techniques that should be employed to provide the information noted above, other than the general agreement that interviews with all relevant parties are necessary.

Many commentators have expressed skepticism regarding the value of forensic examinations in divorce custody cases. Brodzinsky (1993) and Grisso (1984) raised concerns about the specific evaluation techniques employed by mental health professionals in child custody evaluations, while other have asserted that there is little evidence for the validity of professionals' predictions concerning which arrangement will best suit children's needs in custody cases (e.g., Halleck, 1980; Melton et al., 1997; Mnookin, 1975; O'Donahue & Bradley, 1999; Okpaku, 1976). Critics have been concerned especially about examiners' use of theoretical assumptions to speculate about outcomes of various custody arrangements, without empirical support for the speculations and sometimes without clear reference to data specific to the individual case. Goldzband (1982) offered instructive examples of testimony that substitutes untested theory and assumptions (e.g., preference for maternal care in "tender years," the concept of the "psychological parent") for data and careful scrutiny of a case's unique circumstances

Although Melton (1999) has begrudgingly acknowledged that mental health professionals may have something to offer the legal decision maker in cases of contested custody, he and his colleagues (Melton et al., 1997) asserted that mental health professionals "may have little expertise that is directly relevant to custody disputes" and concluded that "there is probably no forensic question on which overreaching by mental health professionals has been so common and so egregious" (pp. 483–484). Perhaps the strongest criticism has been offered by O'Donahue and Bradley (1999), who questioned whether mental health professionals enjoy specialized knowledge about custody relevant issues. They characterized custody evaluations as "no more than educated guesswork, or worse, recommendations based on personal opinions and values," and called for a moratorium on psychologists' participation in custody evaluations (p. 321). This, of course, has not occurred.

FROM LEGAL STANDARD TO FORENSIC ASSESSMENT

Functional Component

It is clear from the preceding review that the legal concepts of parental competency (in abuse, neglect, and TPR cases) and parenting capacity (in divorce custody cases) refer to the functional abilities of caretakers and potential caretakers. Parents' characteristics and abilities are not the only factors considered in courts' deliberations in dependency or custody proceedings (see "Legal Standard"), but they are among the most important factors.

Courts sometimes have used a parent's psychiatric diagnosis as the primary or sole factor for inferring impaired or inadequate parenting ability. This practice ignores current legal precedent requiring consideration of functional consequences of mental disabilities, rather than presuming incapacity on the basis of mental disability alone. Thus, forensic assessments that describe only diagnoses, personality characteristics, or general intellectual capacities of parents and fail to assess the caretaker's child-rearing abilities are of little value (Budd, 2001; Gould & Stahl, 2000). Diagnoses may be relevant, but the competency concept requires a description of what the caretaker understands, believes, knows, does, and is capable of doing by way of parenting (Budd, 2001; Stahl, 1994).

The examiner wishing to fulfill this objective must have a notion of functional ability concepts or behavioral dimensions constituting the relevant domain of parenting abilities. Parenting abilities that are relevant to the court's decisions in cases of dependency and custody have been identified in statutes and case opinions. Generally the abilities mentioned are vague and undifferentiated or cover only a narrow range. Further, different legal sources use different terminology to refer to relevant parenting abilities, making it difficult to determine whether they are referring to the same or different dimensions of parenting.

In contrast to the law's more general construction of parenting, there is a greater appreciation by mental health professionals that parenting tasks are affected by the child's needs and development (e.g., Lerner et al., 1995; Stahl, 1994). For example, Clausen (1968, p. 41) provided a list of parenting tasks derived from a consideration of children's developmental needs:

- provision of nurturance and physical care,
- training and channeling of physiological needs in toilet training, weaning, provision of solid foods,
- teaching and skill-training in language, perceptual skills, physical skills, self care skills in order to facilitate care and insure safety;
- orienting the child to his immediate world of kin, neighborhood, community, and society, and to his own feelings,
- transmitting cultural and subcultural goals and values and motivating the child to accept them for his own,
- promoting interpersonal skills, motives, and modes of feeling and behaving in relation to others, and
- guiding, correcting, and helping the child to formulate his own goals and plan his own activities.

In his discussion of maltreatment evaluations, Barnum (1997) identified two basic responsibilities of parents: advocacy/protection and socialization. Advocacy and protection primarily involves insuring the child's safety in his or her interactions in the outside world. Socialization is broadly conceived by Barnum and includes teaching a child in three fundamental areas: cognitive, behavioral, and emotional. Azar et al. (1998) outlined five broad domains of parenting that may be related to risk for abuse and neglect: parenting skills, social cognitive skills, self control skills, stress management skills, and social skills.

Attempts like these to identify the domain of parenting ability dimensions tend to have begun with a conceptualization of the domain of children's needs. The law clearly establishes children's needs for growth and development as the context in which to consider the functional abilities of parents. This approach draws one to developmental psychology, which may provide conceptual schemata for the domain of children's needs and, thus, essential parenting abilities.

The advantages of conceptualizations of this sort are several. Each parenting task is amenable to translation into one or more parenting ability concepts, and each of these can be related conceptually to psychological evidence (both theoretical and empirical) concerning the developmental needs of children.

Psychologists have developed a number of assessment instruments (reviewed later in this chapter; also see Heinz & Grisso, 1996; Otto, Edens, &

Barcus, 2000) to examine parents' assumptions about children's needs and their past child-rearing behaviors. Unfortunately, few of them have derived from a developmental and legal conceptualization of children's essential needs or parents' essential abilities.

A somewhat different approach to the conceptualization of parenting dimensions is to describe caretakers according to their parenting styles. Researchers have identified two basic dimensions of parenting that appear to play an important role in the socio-emotional development of children. The first of these dimensions—sometimes described as *nurturance*—reflects the degree of affective warmth or coldness in the relationship. The second broad dimension, sometimes referred to as *control or restrictiveness*, describes the type and degree of supervision, monitoring, and/or limit-setting employed by the parent. These two factors (nurturance and control) have been used to classify basic parenting styles (Baumrind, 1967; Campbell, 1997; Reitman & Gross, 1995), such as *authoritative* (high nurturance, high control), *authoritarian* (low nurturance, high control), and *permissive* ([high or low] nurturance, low control).

Classifications of parenting styles do not attempt to define a domain of parenting abilities. Nor do they necessarily use a consideration of children's needs as a conceptual touchstone for their formation. Instead, they seek to describe the range of parenting behavioral styles that are apparent in clinical observations or empirical investigations of parents. Further, the beneficial and deleterious effects of various behavioral styles of parenting are amenable to empirical investigation, using developmental theories and assumptions about children's needs to form hypotheses about these effects. Considerable research on parenting styles (for reviews, see Dishion & Patterson, 1997; Hetherington & Parke, 1975; Loeber & Stouthamer-Loeber, 1986) has provided some empirical grounds for interpretation of their meaning or importance when they are manifested by caretakers. Several methods for assessing these behavioral styles of parenting have been developed, and some of them are reviewed later in this chapter.

Causal Component

Causal inferences will be required in many custody cases, in order to interpret the meaning of parents' manifestations of adequate or deficient parenting abilities. A manifestation of desirable or adequate abilities and attitudes, for example, might reflect either actual strengths or dissimulation. Parties in both dependency and divorce custody cases often wish to appear to be good caretakers. Gardner (1982) commented on the frequency with which examiners encounter "super-parents" who proclaim attitudes and approaches to child rearing that seem (literally) too good to be true. Research examining the response styles of parents participating in child custody evaluations have borne this out, identifying a tendency for parents to minimize shortcomings and foibles that they may perceive as relevant to the custody question (Bathurst, Gottfried, & Gottfried, 1997; Bagby, Nicholson, Buis, Radovonovic, & Fiedler, 1999; Otto & Collins, 1995). Thus, as with all forensic evaluations, examiners must seek to explain the meaning of examinees' adequate performances in custody evaluations, rather than assuming that their admirable behaviors always reflect strengths in everyday parenting behaviors.

When the examinee manifests deficits in parenting abilities, a number of causal explanations are possible, each having important implications for legal deliberations and dispositions of custody cases. Several explanations may be listed, with no claim that these exhaust the possibilities:

- *Life situational stress.* When a parent's recent record of parenting behaviors at home (or abilities as assessed in an examination session) manifests inadequate or detrimental responses to a child, these behaviors might be a reaction to life circumstances (e.g., abandonment by spouse, death of family members, recent economic crisis) of relatively recent onset, rather than being characteristic of the parent's abilities across a longer period of time.
- *Situational or examination-related stress.* Some parents may react more than others to the circumstances of being evaluated or judged in terms of their parenting ability, with the result that their performance may be impaired in direct assessment observations and be non-representative of their usual parenting behaviors.
- *Ambivalence.* Some parents who manifest a poorer ability to meet the needs of the child than might be expected given their parenting history may do so in response to ambivalence about obtaining custody of the child. While the ambivalence might not be expressed openly, it may be manifested indirectly in impairment of the parent's demonstration of adequate parenting abilities.
- *Lack of information.* Some parents might perform poorly on assessments of their knowledge or sensitivity to certain aspects of child rearing merely because they lack the information or awareness required to perform otherwise. Given that they have adequate capacities to learn more appropriate or effective behaviors, their parenting deficits might be negligible if they received appropriate instruction.
- *Mental disorder or disability.* Parenting deficits might be related to underlying deficiencies in intellectual capacity, mental disorder,

or pervasive and persistent problems of personality or behavioral style.

Some of these issues bear on how remediable the parent's deficits are. For example, in a case involving the possible termination of a parent's right due to past neglect, it would certainly be important for a court to know if the parent's past inadequate care-taking behaviors could be easily remedied by instruction concerning some essential aspects of child rearing. It would seem fundamentally unfair to limit or sever a child's relationship with a parent for reasons that are so easily remedied. In contrast, there may be no alternative to terminating or significantly limiting the parent-child relationship when parenting deficits require substantial remediation and change in chronic, underlying characteristics of personality or psychopathology.

One must look beyond the measurement or observation of current parenting abilities, of course, to obtain data with which to address these explanatory possibilities. Some of these optional interpretations may be considered with data obtained from a broad, clinical assessment of the parent's intellectual and personality, characteristics, mental status examination, and interview exploration of the parent's motives and desires. In addition, several of the potential explanations for deficits will require historical information on the parent's life situation and pattern of childrearing practices, outside of the present examination or before the immediate period of time in the examinee's life. This information sometimes can be obtained directly from the examinee in interviews or with structured methods for assessing life stress. Extensive reviews of past records or the reports of third parties might sometimes be helpful. Whatever the specific method, the intent to address causal explanations will require the use of ancillary data with which to assist the court in its interpretation of observed deficits in the parent's specific care taking abilities.

Interactive Component

The logic of standards applied in divorce custody, dependency, and termination cases requires a comparison of *this* parent's abilities to the particular needs of *this* child (Bray, 1991; Bricklin, 1995). Children vary in the degree to which they are in need of various parenting abilities (see generally, Bornstein, 1995). For example, children with special health problems may require especially consistent attention to nutritional or pharmacological schedules and potential medical emergencies, whereas other children may be able to tolerate greater laxity regarding physical care. Some children have developed behavior patterns that require greater structure, discipline, or control, whereas others manage well with considerable autonomy. Some of these differences are related to children's developmental ages or stages, whereas others are more idiosyncratic. These individual differences in children demand somewhat different parenting capacities.

Therefore, deficiencies in certain parenting abilities may have greater or lesser significance in various cases, depending on the needs of the specific child in question. Stated another way, if two parents in two different custody cases manifest relatively equivalent parenting abilities, it is possible that one may be perceived as adequately equipped for custody whereas the other may not, given that the children in the two cases manifest very different needs.

It follows that forensic examiners in dependency and custody cases should obtain information that will help the court to consider congruency or incongruency between the examinee's parenting abilities and the particular needs and characteristics of the specific child whose custody is in question. Assessments in the context of dependency and custody proceedings, therefore, should include assessment of parent and child, individually and in interaction if possible (Bricklin, 1995; Budd & Holdsworth, 1996; Budd, 2001; Gould, 1998; Gould & Stahl, 2000; Stahl, 1994).

Most cases will require a review of the child's medical history, a detailed developmental, social, and family history, and information concerning the child's behavior and performance in various everyday settings, especially schools. Child psychiatrists and developmental and clinical psychologists should be familiar also with the wide range of available instruments and techniques for assessing children's behavioral predispositions, needs, emotional states, and abilities.

The selection of assessment instruments to be employed should also take into consideration the examiner's intention to compare the parent's abilities to the child's emotional needs and abilities. Descriptions of congruency or incongruency between parental ability and a child's needs may be enhanced by selecting instruments for the two assessments that have parallel dimensions: for example, an evaluation of the parent's capacity to provide structure, and the child's capacity for self-control with a minimum of externally imposed structure.

The interactive component also directs one to consider the parent's spouse, other adult and child members of the family, non-family residents, or nonresident social supports within the caretaker's foreseeable future. Individuals of these types in some cases might manifest the potential to compensate for certain functional deficits of the caretaker in meeting a child's needs. In other cases, individuals with whom the caretaker will share child-rearing responsibilities might have characteristics that increase the demand for certain abilities on the part of the caretaker.

These possibilities suggest that some forensic assessments in custody cases will require assessment of ancillary caretakers. Different cases might require more or less intensive assessment of these individuals, but with attention generally to the same set of functional abilities and explanatory considerations as discussed above in relation to the caretaker. Some cases might call for family or conjoint assessments to evaluate the caretaker and ancillary persons as a unit.

In summary, the interactive perspective reminds us that no particular degree of deficit in parenting abilities is suggestive of inadequate care taking. There may be exceptions to this perspective when certain abilities are gravely deficient and important for meeting the needs of any child. Generally, however, the significance of a particular weakness or deficit in parenting ability will lie in its comparison to the needs or demands of the specific child and the resources or deficits of ancillary caretakers. In theory, at least, a parent may be incompetent or inadequate to care for one child in a particular social context, yet adequate to care for another child or to do so within some other social context.

Judgmental and Dispositional Components

A description of the degree of incongruency between a caretaker's parenting abilities and a child's needs is not the sole determining factor in legal custody decisions. Ultimately a judgment must be made concerning whether this degree of congruency or incongruency is sufficient to warrant the decision to terminate or reinstate custody, or to decide which of two potential caretakers, each with patterns of congruencies or incongruencies, warrants the better prospect for custody. It is clear from past appellate decisions (see "Legal Standard" discussion earlier) that no particular degree of ability or person-situation congruency answers the ultimate legal question, "What custody decision should be made?"

Several factors may enter into this judgment. In removal and termination cases, one of these factors is the degree of risk to children that society is willing to take, relative to its interpretation of the rights of parents and society's intervention to limit those rights. The decision that a parent's custody of a child should be terminated because of incompetence (i.e., that the parent is "unfit") is a decision that the risk of harm to the child justifies the state's intrusion to sever a relationship recognized almost universally as having no equal for intimacy and privacy. This balance of interests requires social and moral judgments of the utmost gravity. Empirical evidence and opinions about a child's welfare are critical to this decision, but they do not constitute sufficient grounds for an opinion that it is morally justifiable to remove a child from a parent's custody.

Even setting aside the moral quality of the legal question, mental health professionals apparently have little empirical foundation with which to foresee the long-range effects of termination of parental custody on a child. A child's "best interests" must consider not only the child's immediate care, but also such unpredictable matters as the effects of termination on the child when, as an adult, his or her relationship with the parent has been irreparably altered across time. Therefore, as noted earlier, some commentators have argued that forensic examiners should not offer an opinion concerning whether or not custody should be terminated. Instead, they assert, examiners should go no further than describing parents and children, offering opinions about the immediate, foreseeable consequences of termination or continuation of parental custody, to the extent that data will allow for more than speculation on these matters.

The same conclusion can be reached concerning testimony in divorce custody cases. Often both caretakers present both advantages and disadvantages for the welfare of the child. For example, on what empirical grounds would a mental health professional be able to recommend that one parent, who is somewhat excessively protective but will provide sound religious training, offers a better or poorer prospect for a child than another parent, who encourages autonomy and responsibility but is an atheist? Deciding which of various characteristics is more or less desirable is not an empirical question. It requires moral judgments that subjectively assign different values or different degrees of importance to various aspects of human development. Put simply, decisions about child custody and severance of parental rights are ultimately legal and moral and are best left to the legal decision maker (Azar et al., 1995; Emery, 1999; Melton, 1999; Melton et al., 1997; O'Donahue & Bradley, 1999; Weisz, 1999).

Courts generally allow expert witnesses to offer an opinion concerning whether a parent is minimally competent to parent or concerning who would be the better caretaker of a child (Derdeyn, 1975). Except in extreme circumstances, however, any opinions on these matters stated by a forensic examiner are likely to reflect, at least in part, personal values often devoid of support by medical or behavioral sciences (Mnookin, 1975; O'Donahue & Bradley, 1999). Further, in the extreme cases such as a choice between the risk of life-threatening abuse by one parent and some unfortunate but less detrimental prospect with the other, an expert opinion on the ultimate legal question would offer no more than would already be apparent to others. In any circumstance, then, the forensic examiner rarely can justify stating an opinion about how a custody case should be settled given the competing factors that are to be considered, some of which go beyond the expertise of the mental health professional.

REVIEW OF FORENSIC ASSESSMENT INSTRUMENTS

In the first edition of this book, nine instruments that had been designed to assess various parenting attitudes, behaviors, abilities, or styles were reviewed. Since that time, an extensive number of new parenting measures have appeared in the literature, some of them specifically intended for use in forensic assessments of parents' capacities and custody cases.

The sheer volume of parenting measures that have been developed does not allow their review here. Therefore, parenting instruments that are not reviewed in this chapter are listed in Table 2. Some of them are primarily research scales, while others are commercially marketed and intended for applied use in clinical or forensic settings. What is known about the psychometric properties of these scales varies widely, as some have been heavily researched whereas others have received scant attention. Moreover, there appears to be little relationship between an instrument's empirical support and availability for use. For example, some of the instruments that are available commercially have been subjected to minimal research and, in some cases, are supported by no peer-reviewed publications in scientific journals detailing their characteristics.

Instruments reviewed in this chapter were selected on the basis of two general guidelines. First, some of the instruments that were included in the first edition that have continued to generate a significant amount of research have been retained in order to provide an update regarding their status. Second, we included some measures developed since the first edition because they are used frequently by forensic practitioners. *Exclusion of an instrument from this review should not be considered as an indication that a measure has been judged to be flawed or inappropriate for applied use, and inclusion in this review should not be interpreted as a recommendation that a particular instrument should be used.*

ACKERMAN-SCHOENDORF SCALES FOR PARENT EVALUATION OF CUSTODY (ASPECT)

Authors

Ackerman, M. T., & Shoendorf, K.

Author Affiliation

Wisconsin School of Professional Psychology

TABLE 2. MEASURES OF PARENTING ATTITUDES, SKILLS, AND PARENT-CHILD INTERACTION

Instrument	Author	Described as an assessment of	Published reviews	Publisher
Adult-Adolescent Parenting Inventory-2	Bavolek & Keene (1999)	parenting attitudes and behaviors known to contribute to abuse and neglect	Grisso (1986)	Family Development Resources Inc
Assessment of Interpersonal Relations	Bracken (1993)	the quality of relationships with mothers, fathers, male peers, female peers, and teachers	Keith (1998); Medway (1998)	PRO ED
Assessment of Parenting Skills: Infant and Preschooler	Elliott (1998)	parenting skills	Watson (2001)	Village Publishing
Child-rearing Style Scale and Means-end Problem-solving Test Child-related Stories	Shure & Spivack (1978)	the style of communication with one's child in everyday parent-child interaction	Grisso, 1986	Unpublished
Children's Reports of Parental Behavior	Schaefer (1965)	parenting attitudes and behaviors	Grisso, 1986	Unpublished
Developmental Observation Checklist System	Hresko et al. (1994)	general development, adjustment behavior, and parent stress and support	Bernt (1998); Schwarting (1998)	PRO ED
Dyadic Parent-Child Interaction Coding System II	Eyberg et al. (1994)	the quality of parent-child social interaction	Keyser & Sweetland (1987); McMahon (1985); Strain (1985)	Unpublished
ECOScales	MacDonald et al. (1989)	interactive and communicative skills of preconversational children and adult caregivers	Edwards (1995a); Telzrow (1995)	Riverside Publishing

TABLE 2. CONTINUED

Instrument	Author	Described as an assessment of	Published reviews	Publisher
Family Assessment Form	Children's Bureau of Southern California (1997)	family functioning and service planning needs	Carlson (2001); Kelley (2001)	Child Welfare League of America Inc
Family Assessment Measure Version III	Skinner et al. (1995)	quantitative indices of family strengths and weaknesses	Manges (2001); Spillane (2001)	Multi Health Systems Inc
Family Environment Scale (3rd ed.)	Moos & Moos (1994)	family members' perceptions of their social environment	Mancini (2001); Sporakowski (2001)	Consulting Psychologists Press Inc
Family Risk Scales	Magura et al. (1987)	a child's risk of entering foster care	Dixon (1998); Williams (1998)	Child Welfare League of America Inc
HOME Inventory	Caldwell & Bradley (1984)	the quantity and quality of social, emotional, and cognitive support available to children	Boehm (1985)	University of Arkansas
Iowa Parent Behavior Inventory	Crase et al. (1979)	parental behavior in relation to a Child	Hart (1985); Wikoff (1985)	Iowa State University Research Foundation Inc
Michigan Screening Profile of Parenting	Helfer et al. (1978)	a parent's background	Grisso, 1986; Keyser & Sweetland (1987)	Test Analysis and Development Corporation

Instrument	Author (year)	Description	Citations	Publisher
Parent-Adolescent Communication Scale	Barnes & Olson (1982)	the views of adolescents and parents regarding perceptions and experience of communication	Edwards (1995b); Pfeiffer (1995)	Unpublished
Parent Attitude Survey	Hereford (1963)	parental attitudes and behaviors	Grisso, 1986	Unpublished
Parent Behavior Checklist	Fox (1994)	a family's strengths and needs	Benson (1998); Bernard (1998)	PRO ED
Parent Opinion Questionnaire	Azar et al. (1994)	unrealistic parental expectations regarding appropriate child behavior		Unpublished
Parental Attitude Research Instrument	Schaefer & Bell (1958)	parent attitudes	Grisso, 1986	Unpublished
Parenting Satisfaction Scale	Guidubaldi & Cleminshaw (1994)	parents' attitudes toward parenting	Katz (2001); Smith (2001)	Psychological Corporation
Parenting Scale	Arnold et al. (1993)	dysfunctional parenting in discipline situations		Unpublished
Perceptions of Parental Role Scales	Gilbert & Hanson (1982)	perceived parental role responsibilities	Carlson (1992); Roberts (1992) Grisso, 1986	Marathon Consulting and Press
Single Parenting Questionnaire	Stolberg & Ullman (1983)	aspects of single parenting which impact upon post-divorce child development		Unpublished
Stress Index for Parents of Adolescents	Sheras et al. (1998)	the level of stress in parents of adolescents	Jones (2001); Swearer (2001)	PAR Inc
Uniform Child Custody Evaluation System	Munsinger & Karlson (1994)	data necessary to determine the child's best interests	Zucker (1998)	PAR Inc

Primary Reference

Ackerman, M. T., & Schoendorf, K. (1992). *Ackerman-Schoendorf Scales for Parent Evaluation of Custody manual*. Los Angeles: Western Psychological Services.

Description

The *Ackerman-Schoendorf Scales for Parent Evaluation of Custody* (ASPECT) is "a clinical tool designed to aid mental health professionals in making child custody recommendations" (a, p. 1). The ASPECT is a composite measure that aggregates data from several sources (e.g., interviews and various psychological tests with parent and child, and behavioral observation). In terms of general psychological testing, parents are administered the MMPI-2, Rorschach, and an intelligence test. Children are administered the Rorschach, intelligence and achievement tests, and projective story-telling measures. Parents also complete a Parenting Questionnaire comprised of 57 open-ended questions regarding various issues related to parenting and child custody.

Information from these sources is combined into a "Parental Custody Index" (PCI), which is intended to provide a summary index of parenting effectiveness. The PCI comprises 56 yes/no items and can be broken down into three subscales assessing parents' self-presentation (Observational), the appropriateness of the social environment provided (Social), and the extent of parents' cognitive and emotional capacity to provide for their children (Cognitive-Emotional). Raw scores on these scales are converted to T-scores, which are based on data from the normative sample. The ASPECT also contains 12 "critical items" used to identify areas in which there may be more serious deficits in parenting than are summarized in the PCI or individual subscale scores. (For other reviews of the ASPECT, see references e, f, and h.)

Conceptual Basis

CONCEPT DEFINITION. Chapter 5 of the ASPECT manual describes the derivation of the concepts thought to be germane to effective parenting and custody decision-making, which are described in the introduction as "issues deemed essential by researchers and other mental health professionals in determining appropriate custody recommendations" (a, p. 1). It appears that the authors relied on diverse sources for delineating the domains that they believed were important to assess as part of the PCI, as the literature review includes references to empirical research on parenting, surveys of judges and practitioners, and theoretical reviews of custody standards. Relatively little mention is made of relevant legal standards and definitions, other than that the authors note that these are too vague to offer much specific guidance regarding how to operationalize the key constructs most relevant to custody decision-making.

Item-by-item rationales for each of the 56 PCI items are provided, with occasional citations to others who have argued for the importance of these content areas in relation to parenting ability. For example, support for inclusion of the Observational scale item, "Was the parent appropriately attired?" and the Social scale item, "Does the parent provide appropriate discipline?" is based on reference to other commentators who have asserted that these represent important domains of parenting competence. Similarly, support for the content domain associated conceptually with the Cognitive-Emotional scale item "Were there indicators of difficulty with emotional control on the Rorschach?" is based on reference to psychological theory regarding parenting competence and emotional regulation, as well as on survey findings that the Rorschach is used widely in custody evaluations. Inclusion of some component areas, however, appears to reflect the choices of the authors independent of citations to external support. For example, inclusion of the Social scale item, "Is the child placed next to the parent on the Draw-A-Family Test?" apparently is based on the premise that children's "indirect" parental preferences are relevant to parental competence—and that this component can be assessed via projective methods (see below).

Although the ASPECT appears primarily to be a rationally-derived instrument, the manual notes that an initial collection of items presumed to measure the constructs of interest for the three subscales were examined to determine their internal consistency. Items that did not "maximize the item-to-total correlations" (a, p. 48) apparently were dropped. No other information is provided about these constructs or analyses, however.

OPERATIONAL DEFINITION. The attribute dimensions defined by the ASPECT developers as relevant to parenting capacity are operationalized by using the procedures noted earlier (e.g., standardized tests, unstructured interviews) to reach conclusions about each facet. At the most basic level, each of the 56 items is dichotomized by the examiner as either being present or absent, and these dichotomous decisions are then combined to form a global index of parenting capacity. As can be inferred from the examples above, some of these operationalizations appear to be reasonably consistent with legal constructs regarding custody (e.g., "Does the parent provide appropriate discipline?"), whereas others are further removed from such dimensions (e.g., "Is the parent currently taking any psychiatric medications?" and "Is the Comprehension subtest scale score on the WAIS-R at least 9?").

CRITIQUE.   Other than the authors' literature review, procedures often used to establish the content validity of psychological tests were not employed in the development of the ASPECT. The conceptual bases of the PCI and its subscales primarily were rationally derived, and their connection to relevant functional abilities regarding parenting is unclear in many cases (e, f). Many of the domains presumed by the authors to be important to parenting have weak, indirect, or unknown connections to parenting competence, both in terms of legal standards as well as psychological theory. Equally important, other content areas that may be critical for ascertaining the best placement for the child (e.g., relevant social supports) are not incorporated into the ASPECT. The statistical analyses that were used to eliminate certain domains are not described adequately in the manual.

Operationalization of the content domains that the PCI and its subscales claim to measure is problematic in some cases, relying on procedures or instruments of unknown or questionable reliability and validity (d, i). Moreover, each content area in the ASPECT is equally weighted, even though there is no conceptual reason to assume that all of these factors are equivalent in terms of parenting skill or the custody decision-making process. Similarly, the "averaging" of information across multiple children (if there is more than one whose custody is in dispute) appears to be driven more by convenience than any reliance on legal standards or psychological theory.

Scoring of many items is influenced by observation of unstructured parent-child interactions of relatively limited duration ("Observations can be brief; 15 to 20 minutes should suffice": a, p. 6). The scoring of other items (e.g., "Did the parent provide oral hygiene training?") is described as "self-explanatory" (a, p. 14), although it is unclear what to do if both parents claim to have taught this skill to the child(ren). Conversely, the cognitive-emotional abilities of the parent are operationalized mostly in very concrete terms (e.g., "Was the L scale on the MMPI below 60T (65T for the MMPI-2)?"), yet there is little offered to suggest that these specific factors actually tap the dimensions of parenting relevant to making a custody decision.

In short, a considerable degree of inference would be needed to conclude that the content of the 56 item PCI has captured the requisite dimensions of parenting capacity germane to custody decision-making, or that it has operationalized these content domains in a manner that provides a great deal of confidence that these dimensions actually are being assessed in a reliable and valid manner. Moreover, it is difficult to accept the logic of the instrument's presumption that the multifaceted constructs relevant to determining parental competence can be condensed and reduced to a single quantitative indicator.

Psychometric Development

STANDARDIZATION.   Procedures used to score the PCI itself appear to be relatively straightforward. However, administration and scoring procedures for the ASPECT are dependent upon the measures and procedures that contribute to the PCI. Given recent concerns about the standardization of the Exner Comprehensive System for the Rorschach and its tendency to overpathologize (see h), there is reason for concern about its inclusion from the point of view of standardization. Even more problematic is the use of unstructured projective methods, in light of concerns about their lack of psychometric rigor (d). Finally, both clinical interviews and parent-child observation are designed to be unstructured, although some basic content areas to be covered in the interview are suggested.

RELIABILITY.   The authors report analyses for protocols of 88 examinees that were coded by two raters, but the specific statistic used (e.g., pearson correlation, intra-class correlation) is not indicated. More importantly, the procedure used to ascertain reliability consisted of two raters who "independently reviewed interview notes and tests from examiners using the ASPECT" (a, p. 51). Such a procedure is somewhat limited since it simply indicates that the items comprising the PCI can be coded reliably from summary information collected by individual examiners.

Not addressed by this statistic is how reliably underlying data and observations are collected and coded, which is a reasonable concern in light of the unstructured nature of the interviews and behavioral observations. Thus, the authors do not provide information regarding the reliability of the components themselves (e.g., Form level on the Rorschach; evaluations of the appropriateness of the attire worn by the parent), but merely address whether or not this information can be coded reliably into the PCI. In particular, it is unknown whether the items comprising the Observational scale would be coded similarly if raters had watched videotapes of these interviews, or conducted separate interviews themselves, rather than read someone else's interview notes. For example, two raters could agree that an evaluator indicated in his or her notes that an examinee was "cooperative," but this does not necessarily support the conclusion that they would concur if they actually had observed or participated in these interactions.

Temporal stability of the ASPECT is unknown. No test-retest analyses are reported.

NORMS.   The standardization sample for the ASPECT consisted of 200 families involved in contested custody cases. The demographic composition of the sample is primarily Caucasian (96.9%) and upper middle class. Thus the ASPECT normative sample is not representative of divorcing families in general, although it may not be as discrepant from the population of divorcing families who contest custody and undergo evaluations by mental health professionals. It is also noteworthy that the disposition of the cases in the ASPECT normative sample appears to be unusual, in that fathers obtained custody in a disproportionate number of cases.

CRITIQUE. There are significant problems with the psychometric properties of the ASPECT. Several of the procedures used are unstandardized, reliability information is lacking, and the normative group is not representative of the majority of custody litigants or the typical outcome of these types of cases.

Construct Validation

The internal consistency of the ASPECT is unclear. The manual (a) notes on page 51 that the alphas for the Observational and Cognitive-Emotional subscales were reported as .00, yet in Table 10 (a, p. 52) they are reported as .50. Internal consistency for the Social subscale is reported as .72, whereas the PCI alpha is .76. Given the diversity of content areas tapped by these items, it is not surprising that internal consistency would be somewhat low. Interestingly, item-to-total correlations for several of the individual items are negative, although these items are not reverse-scored.

Evidence of construct validity for the ASPECT is based solely on the content validity issues noted above and the predictive utility research noted in the manual (see below). Despite first becoming commercially available in 1992, as of this date no peer-reviewed research has been published on the ASPECT.

CRITIQUE. Clearly, further research is needed before any strong conclusions can be offered regarding the construct validity of the ASPECT (e, f). Early reviews (c, for example) identified this as an important next step in the development of the scale, and the authors themselves noted the need for such research in the manual (p. 54), but none has been forthcoming.

Many of the components of the PCI may in fact have some indirect connection to parenting capacity (e.g., psychopathology as identified by select MMPI-2 scores, which may limit a parent's ability to parent in some cases). But the burden is on the developers to demonstrate this connection, particularly given the very concrete manner in which several of these indices are employed (e.g., MMPI-2 MacAndrews Alcoholism scale > 65T). Moreover, the bifurcation and summation of these diverse dimensional measures (even if reliable and valid themselves) into a single numerical indicator needs to be justified by data suggesting that such methods are actually measuring some homogeneous construct of "parenting." The relatively low alpha level (.76 for a 56 item scale) reported in the instrument manual indicates that such an approach may not be warranted. Factor analyses of the ASPECT might provide a better conceptualization of the instrument's underlying dimensions than the rationally-derived subscales currently used (b).

Predictive or Classification Utility

The ASPECT manual describes analyses on 57 couples from the standardization sample, the results of which were compared to judges' custody determinations. For those 25 cases in which there was less than one standard deviation (i.e., 10 point) difference between the parents' PCI scores, the overall hit rate was .60. In those 32 cases in which there was more than a 10-point difference, the ASPECT results were consistent with judges' decisions in 91% of the cases.

CRITIQUE.   Although somewhat informative, inferences from these results are limited by several factors. First, the sample is described inadequately, as is the performance of the participants on the PCI. No other information is presented regarding the range of scores these examinees produced other than that there was at least a "10-point difference" between parent couples in some cases. In addition, representation of minority group members in the normative sample is limited or non-existent, and a remarkably high number of fathers were awarded custody, both of which call into question the representativeness of the sample.

Perhaps most importantly, the criterion being predicted—judges' decisions—is an unknown proxy for what constitutes children's best interests. Moreover, although the PCI results apparently were not presented to the judges, it is unclear exactly what (if any) mental health information they were provided about the parents and whether or not this had any impact on their custody determinations.

Aside from these issues, other reviewers have expressed concerns that construction of a score such as the PCI encourages psychologists to overstep their roles in child custody cases. Melton (f) has argued that the numeric identification of the "better" custodial parent places the examiner in the position of attempting to address the ultimate issue before the trier-of-fact, rather than remain in the more appropriate role of the mental health expert who simply provides relevant information to the courts. (See Chapter 1 for a discussion of views for and against addressing the ultimate legal question.)

Potential for Expressing Parent-Child Congruency

In theory, the ASPECT should provide useful information regarding the fit between the parent's abilities and the child's needs, because of the incorporation of information related to their overall functioning and the type and quality of interactions between them. In practice, however, the lack of information about the validity of the instrument leaves unanswered whether the methods used and the ways in which the information has been combined produce PCI scores that actually reflect the true degree of congruence between the parent and the child(ren).

References

(a) Ackerman, M., & Schoendorf, K. (1992). *ASPECT: Ackerman-Schoendorf Scales for Parent Evaluation of Custody-Manual.* Los Angeles, CA: Western Psychological Services.
(b) Arditti, J. A. (1995). Ackerman-Schoendorf Scales for Parent Evaluation of Custody. In J. C. Conoley & J. C. Impara (Eds.), *The twelfth mental measurements yearbook* (pp. 20–22). Lincoln, NE: Buros Institute of Mental Measurements.
(c) Brodzinsky, D. (1993). On the use and misuse of psychological testing in child custody evaluations. *Professional Psychology: Research and Practice, 24,* 213–219.
(d) Garb, H., Wood, J., & Nezworski, M. (2000). Projective techniques and the detection of child sexual abuse. *Child Abuse and Neglect, 24,* 437–438.
(e) Heinze, M., & Grisso, T. (1996). Review of instruments assessing parenting competencies used in child custody evaluations. *Behavioral Sciences and the Law, 14,* 293–313.
(f) Melton, G. B. (1995). Ackerman-Schoendorf Scales for Parent Evaluation of Custody. In J. C. Conoley & J. C. Impara (Eds.), *The twelfth mental measurements yearbook* (pp. 22–23). Lincoln, NE: Buros Institute of Mental Measurements.
(g) Otto, R. K., Edens, J. F., & Barcus, E. (2000). The use of psychological testing in child custody evaluations. *Family and Conciliation Courts Review, 38,* 312–340.
(h) Wellman, M. (1994). Ackerman-Schoendorf Scales for Parent Evaluation of Custody. In D. Keyser & R. Sweetwater (Eds.), *Test critiques, Volume X* (pp. 13–19). Austin, TX: PRO-ED.
(i) Wood, J. M., Nezworski, M. T., Garb, H. N., & Lilienfeld, S. O. (2001). The misperception of psychopathology: Problems with norms of the Comprehensive System for the Rorschach. *Clinical Psychology: Science and Practice, 8,* 350–373.

BRICKLIN PERCEPTUAL SCALES (BPS)

Author

Bricklin, B.

Author Affiliation

Widener University

Primary Reference

Bricklin, B. (1990). *Bricklin Perceptual Scales manual*. Furlong, PA: Village Publishing.

Description

The *Bricklin Perceptual Scales* (BPS) (b) were specifically designed for use in child custody evaluation contexts. The developer describes the BPS as a projective measure of parents' competence, supportiveness, follow-up consistency, and possession of admirable traits (b). Scores for four scales derived from the 64 items (the same 32 for each parent) are obtained by having a child punch holes through a card with a stylus. On the cards are lines with the two extremes marked as "very well" to "not so well." The "parent of choice" is the one who receives the most positive ratings overall across the 32 responses. Thus, conclusions about parental capacity or competence are drawn based on the child's representation of his or her interactions with the parent. Bricklin claims that the information derived from the BPS is a reflection of the child's "unconscious preferences" and that this preference is more important than "objective" measures of parental behavior. Moreover, this preference is said to be of the utmost importance to custody decision-making because "parental behavior can only be evaluated in terms of its meaning and utility to a particular child" (b, p. 14).

Conceptual Basis

CONCEPT DEFINITION.   As noted above, Bricklin (b) indicates that the BPS is designed to measure children's parental preferences across four domains: competence, supportiveness, followup consistency, and possession of admirable traits. Inclusion of these dimensions appears to reflect the author's belief that "conscious processes" are more vulnerable to distortion precipitated by parents motivated to have their child present a particular picture to the examiner. There are, however, no citations to other authorities or specific psychological theories on this point, other than generic references to how "unconscious processes" of the child are more accurate measures of children's best interests than are "conscious" indicators.

OPERATIONAL DEFINITION.   Because the developer believed that more objective measures of parenting capacity (e.g., children's oral reports on the BPS) were of limited value in custody cases, projective methods are used to operationalize the four domains of parenting capacity noted above. The "unconscious preferences" of children are quantified by the extent to which the parents are judged to differ based on the hole punches on the 32 items covered in the BPS. The content of most of these questions is relatively straightforward (e.g., *Card 20*: "If this is Mom doing very well at helping you to calm down, and this is Mom doing not so well at helping you to calm down, where on this line would Mom be?;" *Card 33*: "If this is Dad doing very well at solving a fight over toys, and this is Dad doing not so well at solving a fight over toys, where on this line would Dad be?"). From the comparison of the line punches across the Mother and Father cards, it can then be inferred that the optimal parent is being identified.

CRITIQUE.   The conceptual underpinning of the BPS is not clearly described. As noted above, although there are vague references to the importance of children's "unconscious" preferences, the notion is not linked to psycholegal constructs in ways to support the significance of the content areas purportedly assessed by the BPS (f, j). Moreover, it is unclear why the author considered overt markings on a card with clearly defined parameters (*very well* to *not so well*) to be indicative of unconscious processes and less transparent than verbal responses, and no data are offered to support such a claim (e.g., data examining correlations between children's description of their parents via card marks and verbal reports).

Contrary to Bricklin's claims, the relatively narrow range of the content domains covered by the BPS severely limits the extent to which it could be considered a comprehensive measure of parenting capacity or the fit between the parent's actual abilities and the child's needs, regardless of the adequacy of the projective nature of the data collected regarding the child's "true" perceptions of the parent. Despite these concerns, it should be noted that the overt content of the BPS does tap some issues important to understanding the general nature and strength of the parent-child relationship, providing it with some measure of face validity.

Finally, as noted above and consistent with concerns expressed by Melton (g) regarding the ASPECT, the structuring of BPS results such that they claim to identify the "better" parent may encourage examiners to offer opinions about matters that are ultimately legal determinations, thus overstepping their roles in relation to custody evaluations. This is particularly troubling in relation to the BPS, in that it purports to accomplish this task based solely on input from the child.

Psychometric Development

STANDARDIZATION.   Some general guidelines for administration and scoring are described in the manual, but the manual encourages examiners to deviate from these procedures (see, e.g., p. 22 and p. 58 in reference b). Thus, the BPS is only loosely standardized in its administration format. Scoring is relatively straightforward, in that each card has a grid on the back that provides a numeric indicator identifying where the hole has been placed by the child.

RELIABILITY. Adequate reliability data for the BPS are lacking. Although no information regarding inter-rater reliability is provided, inter-rater reliability may not prove problematic given the objective scoring of the instrument (assuming it is administered in a reliable manner and deviations from recommended procedures do not occur). Test-retest data ($n = 12$) are described in a format that is difficult to comprehend, but they offer some indication of stability over relatively short time frames (i.e., "parents of choice" apparently remained the same over a time frame that was seven months or less). The description of the studies providing this information is insufficient to judge their methodological rigor. Unpublished dissertations that have examined the test-retest reliability of the BPS (d, i, k) have not been so encouraging.

NORMS. There is no clearly delineated normative sample for the BPS. Although the author makes various references to a "data-based system," mostly this appears to consist of anecdotal accounts of other clinicians who have used the instrument. These accounts apparently have not led to accumulation of cases to provide a normative sample.

CRITIQUE. Previous reviewers (e, f, j, l) consistently have noted the problems described above (subjective administration, unknown reliability, absence of norms), which have yet to be addressed in any meaningful fashion. The logic for the instrument as described by its developer suggests that these issues may never be addressed by the instrument's developer; the manual indicates that issues such as test-retest reliability are of limited concern and that there are "no reasons to expect the measures reported here to exhibit any particular degree of stability" (b, p. 42).

Construct Validation

No information has been provided regarding the internal consistency of the BPS.

Construct validation data reported in the BPS manual focuses on the instrument's relationship with another measure designed by the same author, the *Perception of Relationships Test* (PORT; described later in this chapter), and from the instrument's association with other examiners' perceptions of which of the two parents would be the better caretaker.

Regarding the PORT, Bricklin (b) cites two studies in which the BPS and PORT resulted in the same "parent of choice" in a total of 46 of the 55 cases (84%). As further evidence of the validity of the BPS, Bricklin (a) administered the BPS and a set of questionnaires to 23 children and their parents. The questionnaires queried the children and parents regarding the parents' child rearing behaviors and responsibilities. Parents who were identified by the children as taking on more child rearing responsibilities were identified as the "parent of choice." In 21 of 23 cases (91%), the same "parent of choice" was identified by the children's responses to the questionnaires and the BPS.

Interestingly, Bricklin claims that this level of agreement provides even greater support for the validity of the BPS than a higher rate of agreement might have demonstrated. He argues that children's responses to the BPS are non-verbal and represent less conscious feelings about their parents, whereas their responses to questionnaires represent more conscious perceptions. Thus, perfect agreement between the two measures would not be expected and indeed would prove problematic, Bricklin argues. With the same sample, Bricklin also examined the rates of agreement between the "parent of choice" as identified by the children's BPS responses and the parents' perceptions of their involvement with their children. In 13 of 17 (76%) cases there was agreement between parents' perceptions and the "parent of choice" identified by the BPS.

A number of other studies examining the validity of the BPS are described in a photocopied test manual supplement (c), but the descriptions are so limited (one to two lines per study) that it is not possible to adequately critique them. Of particular interest is the claim that in a sample of 1,765 cases, the "parents of choice" identified by the children's BPS responses was consistent with the judgments of psychologists who had access to "clinical and life history data." These findings appear essentially to be psychologists reporting to Bricklin how frequently the BPS results were consistent with their clinical impressions in custody cases they evaluated.

One study (d) examined the association between the BPS and a widely used and extensively researched measure of parent-child functioning, the *Family Environment Scale* (FES; h). Fifty-eight children between the ages of 6 and 12, and their parents, were administered the BPS, *Children's Version of the Family Environment Scales* (CVFES), and FES at two sessions, one week apart. There was very little association between these measures, with poor agreement between the child's "parent of choice" as identified by the BPS and the parents' consensus agreement of who was the "parent of choice."

CRITIQUE. Although the BPS' status as a projective measure for assessing unconscious process creates some methodological obstacles, it would not be difficult to conduct factor analyses on existing BPS data. One might also consider a multi-trait, multi-method research project to investigate its construct validity, but this is made difficult by the lack of a clear description concerning what construct the BPS claims to measure.

There have been no BPS studies published in peer reviewed outlets, and the research data provided in the manual and its supplements are so abbreviated that it is not possible to judge the adequacy of the samples, methodology or the results reported. Studies with large sample sizes are minimally described, and may simply reflect the extent to which examiners who have bought and used the BPS form clinical opinions consistent with its conclusions (and which may have been shaped by the BPS results themselves). Such information does little to support the argument that results of the BPS actually can identify the more appropriate custodial parent.

Predictive or Classification Utility

Bricklin (a) described 29 cases of contested custody in which he conducted evaluations using the BPS. In 27 of these cases (93%) the parent identified as the "parent of choice" by the BPS was awarded custody by the judge. It is not reported whether Bricklin offered an ultimate opinion on custody in these cases that was consistent with BPS scores, which obviously would raise concerns about criterion contamination.

CRITIQUE. The same criticisms noted above regarding the relative absence of construct validation data also apply here. The predictive utility of the BPS is essentially unknown.

Potential for Expressing Parent-Child Congruency

The identification of the "parent of choice" assumes that the BPS provides an index of the degree of fit between the parents' capacities and the child's needs. As such, in principle the BPS should provide a good indication of the degree of congruence between each parent and the child. Unfortunately, the conceptual, psychometric, and validation limitations of the BPS preclude such a conclusion from being drawn. Even assuming that the BPS measures children's perceptions in a reliable and valid manner, the presumption that these perceptions of the parent are de facto indicators of the true level of fit between them is an unsubstantiated claim in need of empirical support before it should be used to influence custody decisions.

References

(a) Bricklin, B. (1990). *Parent Awareness Skills Survey manual*. Furlong, PA: Village Publishing.
(b) Bricklin, B. (1990). *Bricklin Perceptual Scales manual*. Furlong, PA: Village Publishing.

(c) Bricklin, B., & Elliott, G. (1997). *Critical child custody evaluation issues: Questions and answers. Test manuals supplement for BPS, PORT, PASS, PPCP.* Furlong, PA: Village Publishing.

(d) Gilch-Pesantez, J. (2001). *Test-retest reliability and construct validity: The Bricklin Perceptual Scales.* Unpublished doctoral dissertation. Indiana University, Pennsylvania.

(e) Hagin, R. A. (1992). Bricklin Perceptual Scales. In J. L. Conoley & J. C. Impara (Eds.), *The twelfth mental measurements yearbook* (pp. 117–118). Lincoln, NE: Buros Institute of Mental Measurements.

(f) Heinze, M. C., & Grisso, T. (1996). Review of instruments assessing parenting competencies used in child custody evaluations. *Behavioral Sciences and the Law, 14,* 293–313.

(g) Melton, G. B. (1995). Ackerman-Schoendorf Scales for Parent Evaluation of Custody. In J. C. Conoley & J. C. Impara (Eds.). *The twelfth mental measurements yearbook* (pp. 22–23). Lincoln, NE: Buros Institute of Mental Measurements.

(h) Moos, R., & Moos, B. (1994). *Family Environment Scale: Manual* (3rd ed.). Palo Alto, CA: Consulting Psychologists Press.

(i) Muir, K. (1997). *Children's perceptions of their parents and susceptibility to suggestion.* Unpublished doctoral dissertation. California School of Professional Psychology, San Diego.

(j) Otto, R. K., Edens, J. F., & Barcus, E. (2000). The use of psychological testing in child custody evaluations. *Family and Conciliation Courts Review, 38,* 312–340.

(k) Scallon, C. (1997). *Changes in children's perceptions of their 'parent of choice' following participation in a Roman Catholic post-divorce support group.* Unpublished doctoral dissertation. Chicago School of Professional Psychology, Chicago.

(l) Shaffer, M. B. (1992). Bricklin Perceptual Scales. In J. L. Conoley & J. C. Impara (Eds.), *The twelfth mental measurements yearbook* (pp. 118–119). Lincoln, NE: Buros Institute of Mental Measurements.

Perception of Relationships Test (PORT)

Author

Bricklin, B.

Author Affiliation

Widener University

Primary Reference

Bricklin, B. (1989). *Perception of Relationships Test manual.* Furlong, PA: Village Publishing.

Description

The *Perception of Relationships Test* (PORT) (a) was designed specifically for use in child custody evaluation contexts and is described as a projective test that is based on the placement of the child's human figure drawings.

It was designed to assess the "psychological closeness" of the child to each parent, as well as the types of interactions that occur with each parent. The PORT is comprised of seven drawing tasks and is scored based on the configuration of the child, parents, and family within the child's drawings. For example, distances are measured between the child's drawing of the child and the parents in some items. Scores result in the identification of a "primary caretaking parent." Thus, the PORT is not a measure of parenting capacity or ability, but rather is offered as an objective, structured measure of the connection between the parent and child, based on the child's representations. (For a complete review of the PORT, see d).

Conceptual Basis

CONCEPT DEFINITION.   Bricklin (b, p. 1) writes that the PORT measures the "whole organism or gut-level responses a child has toward a parent [which] are much more reflective of what the child's actual interactions or experiences with that parent have been." As with the BPS, apparently no attempts were made to connect the content of the PORT to legal standards, and the theory upon which it is based, as described in the manual, is difficult to discern.

OPERATIONAL DEFINITION.   The relevant content domains operationalized by the PORT appear to be similar to the BPS, in that unconscious preferences for one parent over the other are proposed to be reflected in the obtained drawings. The content of interest to determine this preference is not overtly manifest, and must be assessed via indirect methods. Thus, the PORT presumably assesses the "best interests of the child" by delineating latent constructs that reflect the quality of the relationship between the parent and the child.

CRITIQUE.   The PORT lacks a firm connection between the content of the test, parenting capacity, and relevant legal standards. However, the PORT does claim to assess a general factor (i.e., the child's perception of his or her relationship with each parent) that is nonetheless relevant to issues of custody. The absence of a coherent, empirically supported theory regarding the relationship between human figure drawings and parenting is a particular limitation, however, as are data casting doubt on the reliability and validity of projective drawing techniques more generally (see, e.g., e).

Psychometric Development

STANDARDIZATION.   Administration and scoring guidelines in the PORT manual are inconsistent and difficult to comprehend. The manual (a), which is augmented by various supplements (c), provides little coordinated structure for how to administer the test.

RELIABILITY. Limited reliability data are provided in the manual. Inter-rater reliability is not described, and test-retest estimates are based on very small studies that are not described in sufficient detail to address their methodological adequacy. One unpublished dissertation examining the reliability of the PORT offered little support for the PORT's stability (f).

NORMS. No normative group and no normative data are offered for the PORT.

CRITIQUE. Limitations of the PORT regarding standardization and reliability are similar to those for the BPS (subjective administration, unknown reliability, absence of norms). Despite publication of the PORT over 13 years ago, no published research to remedy these limitations has appeared.

Construct Validation

Information about internal consistency analyses is not available. Research described in the manual (a) compares the identification of the "primary caretaking parent" by the PORT with other instruments and procedures of questionable validity. Bricklin (a) reported that the "primary caretaking parent" identified by the PORT was identical to the "parent of choice" identified by the BPS in 19 of 23 (83%) cases. In another study, clinicians used extensive clinical data to make judgments about 30 children and their parents. These determinations were consistent with the PORT findings in 28 of the 30 cases. The PORT manual also describes a study that compared PORT scores to judgments of clinicians who viewed 30 parent-child interactions. According to Bricklin (a), the PORT-identified "primary caretaking parent" agreed with the clinical opinions regarding parent of choice with better than 90% accuracy.

A number of other studies are referenced in a later published supplement (c), but the descriptions of the studies are too brief (i.e., one to two lines per study) to allow for an adequate critique of their methodology. Of these studies, perhaps most interesting is the description of a sample of 1038 cases, in which an agreement rate of 89% was obtained when PORT "primary caretaking parents" were compared to the judgments of "independent psychologists based on all clinical and life-history data available." These findings, however, appear to be psychologists reporting to Bricklin how frequently the PORT results were consistent with their clinical impressions in custody cases they evaluated.

CRITIQUE. Given the theoretical basis of the PORT and the method it uses to operationalize key variables, it would be difficult to conduct well-controlled studies to examine whether it is measuring the construct of interest, because its author considers overt measures to be invalid indicators of the child's "true" parent. The studies noted above, which appear to lack experimental rigor and/or suffer from various methodological limitations (e.g., criterion contamination), at best provide limited support for the construct validity of the PORT, which is insufficient to justify its use in applied settings.

Predictive or Classification Utility

The PORT manual (a) describes a series of studies that compared PORT scores to judges' decisions regarding custody. In 80 of 87 cases (92%), the judges granted custody to the parent identified as the PCP by the PORT.

Bricklin also claims (a, pp. 43–47) that the PORT may be useful for identifying children who have been physically or sexually abused, because their responses to the projective method can reveal the consequences of such abuse. No data supporting these claims are provided and general concerns regarding the utility of projective drawings more generally raise questions about the validity of such claims (see, e.g., f).

CRITIQUE. One could conduct well-controlled studies using traditional research methodologies that assess whether the "primary caretaking parent" identified by the PORT is "objectively" preferred by the child, and or is actually competent to care for the child. But such studies have not been done. Concerns about the predictive utility of the PORT parallel the concerns noted above for the BPS. There are only limited data to support the conclusion that the PORT identifies the better custodial parent, as defined by a judge's determination, and this information itself may have influenced the outcome being predicted. More generally, concerns have been expressed regarding whether this criterion measure is particularly informative regarding what actually constitutes a child's 'best interests' (g).

Potential for Expressing Parent-Child Congruency

Similar to the BPS, in theory the PORT was developed specifically to provide an index of the congruence between a child and his or her parents. In the absence of better data, however, the case has not been made that this task is accomplished using the results of this measure.

References

(a) Bricklin, B. (1989). *Perception of Relationships Test manual.* Furlong, PA: Village Publishing.
(b) Bricklin, B. (1993). *Test Manuals Supplement #9.* Furlong, PA: Village Publishing.
(c) Bricklin, B., & Elliott, G. (1997). *Critical child custody evaluation issues: Questions and answers.* Test manuals supplement for BPS, PORT, PASS, PPCP. Furlong, PA: Village Publishing.

(d) Conger, J., (1995). Perception-of-Relationships Test. In J. Conoley & J. Impara (Eds.), *The twelfth mental measurements yearbook* (pp. 747–748). Lincoln, NE: Buros Institute of Mental Measurements.
(e) Garb, H., Wood, J., & Nezworski, M. (2000). Projective techniques and the detection of child sexual abuse. *Child Abuse and Neglect, 24,* 437–438.
(f) Muir, K. (1997). *Children's perceptions of their parents and susceptibility to suggestion.* Unpublished doctoral dissertation. California School of Professional Psychology, San Diego.
(g) Otto, R. K., Edens, J. F., & Barcus, E. (2000). The use of psychological testing in child custody evaluations. *Family and Conciliation Courts Review, 38,* 312–340.

Parent Awareness Skills Survey (PASS) and Parent Perception of Child Profile (PPCP)

Author

Bricklin, B.

Author Affiliation

Widener University

Primary References

Bricklin, B. (1990). *Parent Awareness Skills Survey manual.* Furlong, PA: Village Publishing; Bricklin, B., & Elliott, G. (1991). *Parent Perception of Child Profile manual.* Furlong, PA: Village Publishing.

Description

The *Parent Awareness Skills Survey* (PASS) is described as a "clinical tool designed to illuminate the strengths and weaknesses in awareness skills a parent accesses in reaction to typical child care situations" (a, p. 4). The PASS is comprised of 18 childcare scenarios and was designed to sample relevant parenting behaviors that could be employed with children of various ages. After being presented with a particular situation the parent provides his or her reaction, with follow-up questioning by the examiner as needed. Responses are evaluated and scored based on guidelines in the manual.

The *Parent Perception of Child Profile* (b) was designed to assess parental understanding and awareness of a child's development and needs across eight areas: interpersonal relations; daily routine; health history; developmental history; school history; fears; personal hygiene;

and communication style. According to the manual, the PPCP can be self-administered or administered by an examiner in an interview format. The manual indicates that data need not be gathered in all eight categories, and the examiner can decide which issues are most critical for a particular child and parent.

Conceptual Basis

CONCEPT DEFINITION.   The content domains assessed by the PASS and the PPCP are face valid and have some intuitive appeal. The dimensions thought to be relevant to custody decision-making appear to have been delineated by Bricklin and his colleagues using rational means and reviews of the child development and parent-child interaction literature.

OPERATIONAL DEFINITION.   For the PASS, operationalization of the functional parenting abilities appears to be rooted in the common sense belief that strengths and weaknesses in child rearing abilities can be assessed, in part, by querying parents directly about how they would respond to various child care scenarios. The method presumes that verbal responses are useful indicators of the actual abilities thought to be germane to effective parenting.

Similarly, the functional abilities needed for effective parenting are presumed to be represented by the overt responses parents make to inquiries on the PPCP that reflect their level of knowledge about a child's needs and development. Quantification of these responses is presumed to lead to the identification of the parent who is better able to meet these needs.

CRITIQUE.   The content of the PASS and the PPCP generally appears to assess relevant domains of parenting. However, the adequacy and thoroughness of content coverage has not been evaluated systemically, and the choice of dimensions was not linked with any particular psychological model of parenting or legal criteria regarding custody issues. Further content validation procedures would be useful for determining the appropriateness and comprehensiveness of these measures.

Psychometric Development

STANDARDIZATION.   Neither measure can be described as standardized. The PASS manual provides some scoring guidelines, although the author notes, "The evaluator ... can apply his or her own standards in assigning the suggested scores. The PASS allows for wide latitude in scoring since its main purpose is to discover the relative (rather than absolute) strengths and weaknesses any individual or compared set of respondents manifest" (a, p. 11). The PPCP manual provides no scoring guidelines and, as noted above, examiners are free to administer only certain sections of the instrument.

RELIABILITY.   Reliability estimates for these measures have not been reported.

NORMS.   No norms are available for either measure.

CRITIQUE.   Despite the fact that both measures can be scored, there is no evidence that these scores are reliable, nor is there a way to compare them to the performance of anything approaching a reference group. Importantly, although the authors note that the PASS is supposed to provide a relative comparison of the parents (which does not obviate the need for reliability data and a standardization sample), it also is claimed that the PASS can be administered to one parent with scores having interpretive significance (a, p. 16). Given the absence of more supportive information, this would seem to be an overstatement of what the PASS can provide. At best, both measures should be considered semi-structured interviews rather than methods for psychometrically sound quantification of parenting knowledge or ability.

Construct Validation

No data are provided to support the construct validity of either the PASS or the PPCP. No peer-reviewed, published reports have examined their validity.

CRITIQUE.   It is unclear exactly what the scores on these measures mean, although it is likely that they reflect to some extent the clinical judgment and intuition of the examiner, given the non-standardized nature of the tasks and the lack of normative data. Unlike the child-report measures developed by Bricklin that claim to offer projective measures of "unconscious" preferences, the PASS and the PORT easily could be validated using commonly employed methodologies and statistics (e.g., factor analysis, multi-trait and multi-method approaches).

Predictive or Classification Utility

No data are available to examine the predictive utility of either measure.

CRITIQUE.   Clearly, the absence of such data place serious restrictions on what examiners may conclude about the meaning of scores on the PASS or the PPCP in relation to custody decision-making. As such, the reporting of specific scores does not appear warranted at present.

Potential for Expressing Parent-Child Congruency

Similar to Bricklin's child-report measures, in theory the PASS and PPCP could provide useful information regarding the parent's functional abilities and their fit with the needs of the specific child, if there were data available to judge the adequacy of the instruments. Used as semi-structured interviews, these two adult measures might be able to identify potential strengths and weaknesses of parents at a more global (i.e., less quantitative) level, which could then be combined with information from other relevant data sources about the child's needs.

References

(a) Bricklin, B. (1990). *Parent Awareness Skills Survey manual.* Furlong, PA: Village Publishing.
(b) Bricklin, B., & Elliott, G. (1991). *Parent Perception of Child Profile manual.* Furlong, PA: Village Publishing.

CHILD ABUSE POTENTIAL INVENTORY (CAPI)

Author

Milner, J. S.

Author Affiliation

Department of Psychology, Western Carolina University

Primary Reference

Milner, J. S. (1986). *The Child Abuse Potential Inventory manual* (2nd ed.). Webster, NC: Psytec Corporation.

Description

The *Child Abuse Potential Inventory* (CAPI) (i) was developed by Milner and his colleagues to assess parental risk for physical child abuse. It was designed to be a screening tool for use by protective service workers when investigating suspected cases of child abuse. The CAPI Inventory Form IV was released for use in applied settings in 1986. It uses a 160-item forced-choice questionnaire on which examinees indicate that they agree or disagree with the question when applied to themselves or their own circumstances. The items typically refer to some psychological condition or opinion (e.g., "I am often lonely inside," "Children should never be bad"). Items were written at a third-grade reading level and typically can be administered in 10 to 20 minutes. A Spanish version of the instrument also is available (c, i).

Within the 160 items of the CAPI are 77 items constituting a physical abuse scale. Scoring templates, providing weighted scores for each item, are used to obtain a raw score sum across the 77 items. The abuse scale also provides six factor scores (distress, rigidity, unhappiness, problems with the child and oneself, problems with the family, and problems with others). However, the author recommends only the total physical abuse scale score for use in assessing the potential for physical child abuse.

Although the items composing the physical abuse scale have remained unchanged since the inventory's introduction in 1977, three validity scales more recently have been included to assist in detecting response distortion. These validity scales (a lie scale, a random response scale, and an inconsistency scale) are used in various combinations to form three validity indexes: Faking Good, Faking Bad, and Random Response. Most recently, two special scales (ego-strength scale, j; loneliness scale, l) were designed to provide the test user with additional clinical information about the respondent. An applied manual (l) provides information to assist test users in administration and interpretation, and a revised technical manual (i) provides information about the development and validity of the inventory.

Milner cautions the user against applying the CAPI as a diagnostic tool for labeling purposes, recognizing that a score on this instrument alone does not warrant any diagnosis or conclusion about an examinee. Yet many clinical situations could make use of an instrument of this type for purposes of identifying the need for further assessment, cross-checking data from other sources in a more comprehensive evaluation, exploring potential treatment needs, or evaluating treatment programs designed to modify parental dysfunction. Based on an accumulation of many high risk and control samples, the Manual identifies cutoff scores for the upper 5% of normative samples. Milner cautions that these cutoffs are arbitrarily chosen, and notes that cutoff criteria must be determined by individual users based on their own purposes and local samples. The manual contains a detailed discussion of the effects of base rates on predictive accuracy, as well as their importance when interpreting CAPI scores.

Conceptual Basis

CONCEPT DEFINITION.   Milner (i) began with a survey of over 700 articles and books, cataloguing personality traits and background variables that research and theory suggested were characteristic of parents who abuse or neglect their children. The variables were grouped logically into homogeneous categories (e.g., feelings of isolation and loneliness, negative childhood experiences often including abuse). Milner notes that, although "psychiatric and interpersonal perspectives" on child abuse were considered important in defining the relevant content domain, they did not rely on any one particular theory of abuse when developing the item pool.

As can be ascertained by the review of special scales noted above, the CAPI was designed with awareness that respondents might not approach the testing situation in a completely forthright manner. As such, constructs related to response distortion were also identified and attempts were made to operationalize and measure these factors that might affect the validity of the assessment process.

OPERATIONAL DEFINITION.   In terms of delineating the criterion of interest, the CAPI manual indicates that child abusers were operationally defined during the development of the scale as those parents who were defined by social service workers as having committed abuse, based primarily on the North Carolina child abuse reporting law in place at that time. Notably, this did not necessarily mean that the case had been adjudicated, only that it was the case worker's opinion that sufficient evidence was present to warrant such a conclusion.

Regarding the instrument itself, item generation and evaluation was an iterative process. First, the test developers wrote 15 to 20 items for each of the concepts derived from their literature review, creating a 334-item pilot form of the CAPI. This stage involved input from child protective service workers in the field and research staff members. In the first pilot test of this measure, Milner and Wimberley (t) identified the items that best discriminated between 19 abusive and 19 non-abusive parents (matched on nine demographic and background variables). Through a series of analyses, a subsample of items was identified that appeared most promising for differentiating abusers from non-abusers. A revised, 160-item measure was then constructed, which incorporated all of the promising items (some with slight modifications) and several new ones based on input from social service workers. A second study, using a much larger sample ($n = 130$), was conducted to further examine the utility of the 160 items. A total of 77 items significantly discriminated between the abusive and non-abusive parents. These items ultimately were used to create the Abuse scale (the predictive accuracy of which is described below).

The three validity scales included in the CAPI were developed independent of the above process. In order to create the Lie scale, Milner first developed 59 items that focused on denial of common but undesirable attributes (e.g., "I never act silly"). These items were then presented to samples of college students and P.T.A. groups to identify those that were endorsed relatively infrequently (i.e., response rates approximating 15%). A total of 18 items with socially desirable item content and low endorsement rates were identified that ultimately were incorporated into a later edition of the CAPI.

For the Random Response (RR) scale, the manual (i) describes two studies in which 65 filler items from an earlier version of the CAPI were used to develop an 18-item index of infrequent responding. Although also comprised of items with low endorsement rates, unlike the content of the Lie scale these items were not intended to reflect socially desirable behaviors. Also, items initially were selected for inclusion only if they failed to correlate with the Abuse scale score.

Finally, the Inconsistency scale was developed by identifying item pairs that were either similar (10 item pairs) or opposite (10 item pairs) in content. Response patterns that indicate inconsistent responding to similar items or consistent responding to dissimilar items are scored as evidence of inconsistent or random responding.

Because none of these scales was considered by Milner to be a pure measure of a specific response style (e.g., high scores on the Lie scale ostensibly can indicate either socially desirable or random responding), response distortion indices based on the configuration of these scales were developed. For example, the Faking-good index is derived based on consideration of both Lie scale scores and RR scores. Faking good is considered to be present when there is an elevated Lie scale score combined with a normal range RR score.

CRITIQUE. The CAPI was not developed as an index of dimensions of parenting attitudes or abilities generally, but specifically to identify parents who are at high risk for abuse. Thus, the CAPI appropriately began with a survey of research on that parent type, not a review of important parental attitudes in general. Its content, therefore, is relevant for addressing questions of high risk of abuse, but it may not be relevant for addressing other questions of parental ability that may be important for custody decision-making. One would expect, for example, that there are more and less adequate parents, by some other criterion, among non-abusive parents, and the CAPI was not designed to address such questions.

The concept and operational definitions of the CAPI appear to provide adequate content relevance and content coverage for its intended purpose. One question that might be raised is whether the process of item reduction (from 334 to the shorter, final version) employed test development samples of subjects with an adequate range of sociodemographic features to avoid selection of items relevant for only certain subgroups of abusers. This question will be addressed later in the review of validity studies.

Psychometric Development

STANDARDIZATION. The CAPI can be administered to individuals or groups and requires only a pencil and four-page questionnaire for each respondent. Items are rated dichotomously (*agree-disagree*). The inventory can be hand-scored using templates or computer-scored. To decrease scoring errors, computer scoring is recommended by the test author.

RELIABILITY. For the 77 items that contribute to the Abuse scale, internal consistency estimates are reported in the technical manual and can be found in many subsequent studies. For the general population, at-risk, neglectful, and physically abusive groups, split half reliabilities range from .96 to .98, and KR-20 reliabilities range from .92 to .95. Split half reliabilities and KR-20 coefficients by age, gender, ethnic, and education within the above groups range from .93 to .98 and .85 to .96 respectively. Temporal stability estimates are not available for abusers. For nonabusive examinees, however, test-retest reliability for the Abuse scale for 1-day, 1 week, 1 month, and 3 month intervals has been reported as .91, .90, .83, and .75, respectively (i). Internal consistency reliabilities for the six abuse factor scales are lower than the full abuse scale and more variable.

For the Lie scale, KR-20 reliability coefficients have been reported in the .70s for most samples. Relatively similar values have been reported for the Random Response and Inconsistency scales. Test-retest reliability (non-abusive subjects) has been reported as .86 (one day) and .83 (one week) for the Lie scale, although lower values have been obtained for the other two validity scales.

Notably, in addition to general reliability information, the CAPI manual also provides an overview of the Standard Error of Measurement (SEM) for the Abuse scale, subscales, and validity scales, as well as a description of how these values should be used in interpreting individual scores.

NORMS. Descriptive statistics for 836 respondents are presented in the CAPI manual (i, Table 2.7). In addition, similar information is presented for various subgroups, with a cumulative N of over 5,000 respondents drawn from various studies. The manual notes that "while these data are provided for general comparison purposes, they must be viewed with caution because the studies are not always directly comparable" (i, pp. 13–14). In situations in which samples of parents are being assessed who are demographically similar, it is suggested that users consider developing their own local norms.

CRITIQUE. The structure of the CAPI allows for ease of administration and scoring, although Milner reports unpublished data in the manual to suggest that field workers often make errors in the computation of scale scores. Also, substantial evidence supports the internal consistency and temporal stability of measurement with the CAPI scales and subscales. The clear presentation of information related to the SEM in the manual also is an advantage. One somewhat unusual aspect of the CAPI is that it does not use standardized scores, which makes interpretation of the information provided cumbersome at times.

Although the CAPI manual is exhaustive in many respects, the normative group could be described in greater detail and, like the subgroups reported in other tables, this group appears to be primarily a sample of convenience. No discussion is provided to indicate that the sample was census-matched or geographically diverse. Although the various subsamples referenced in the manual appear to be diverse (e.g., location, age, socioeconomic status), the usefulness of the CAPI would be enhanced by a more extensive description of the available normative data.

Construct Validation

Initial factor analyses conducted on a sample of 65 abusing and 65 non-abusing parents revealed seven factors: Distress, Rigidity, Child with Problems, Problems from Family and Others, Unhappiness, Loneliness, and Negative Concept of Child. Factor scores for Distress, Rigidity, and Unhappiness most significantly distinguished abusers from the non-abusers. Subsequent factor analyses of unpublished data ($n = 220$) are reported in the manual and used to support a six-factor structure that generally is similar to the seven factors noted above (see i, Table 3.2). Despite some support for these subscales, the manual indicates that only the total Abuse score should be used to screen for child abuse.

Substantial data in addition to theses factor analytic results support the construct validity of the CAPI abuse scale. The studies are far too extensive to review here in adequate detail, so only a brief summary will be provided. (For more extensive reviews, see i, n, o). The majority of this research has found expected correlational relationships between CAPI abuse scores and a variety of individual, family, and environmental risk factors. Positive relationships generally have been reported between CAPI scores and examinees' childhood history of abuse, social isolation and lack of social support, and negative family interactions and family problems. Studies also have found that individuals with higher CAPI scores report higher levels of negative affective states such as anger, depression, and anxiety. Relationships in the expected direction (i.e., an inverse relationship) have been reported for CAPI scores and personal characteristics such as self-esteem and ego-strength. Individuals with elevated CAPI scores also tend to have an external locus of control. Higher levels of perceived life stress and distress have been related to elevated scores on the CAPI Abuse scale, as well as deficits in knowledge regarding child development issues.

Expected relationships also have been observed between negative evaluations of children's behavior, inappropriate expectations for children's behavior, and CAPI abuse scores. Parenting characteristics such as use of harsh discipline and parenting practices have been studied and findings are in the expected direction, i.e., elevated CAPI scores are associated with use of more harsh discipline techniques, less positive parenting practices, and problems in parent-child interactions. Mixed findings have been found for studies investigating the relationship between CAPI abuse scores and authoritarianism, however, as well as their association with infant attachment problems.

Another line of research supporting the validity of the CAPI has addressed whether it is sensitive to the effects of treatment. Several studies have found that CAPI abuse scores decrease after treatment interventions such as an ecological-based intervention program, a parent training program, in-home treatments, and an intensive multi-modal intervention program. For example, the CAPI was administered pre- and post-treatment to a sample of 42 high-risk parents who participated in a 16-week program of films, speakers, and small group discussions designed to prevent child abuse and improve parenting knowledge and abilities. Prior to receiving this training, these high-risk parents scored significantly higher when compared to the CAPI normative sample, and their post-training scores were significantly lower than their pre-training scores. CAPI scores obtained for 33 of these parents seven weeks after post-training evaluation were also significantly lower than pre-training scores and not significantly different from post-training scores (x). Similar results have been obtained in other treatment outcome studies as well (see reference o for a review).

Support for the validity scales of the CAPI also has been demonstrated. The Lie scale correlates positively with the Marlowe-Crown Social Desirability Scale (.32) and with the MMPI Lie scale (.49) (d). Discriminant validity is evidenced by insignificant correlations between the CAPI Lie scale and scores on Rotter's Locus of Control scale (d), the MMPI Ego Strength scale and parents' grade point average (v), and the CAPI Abuse scale (h). More recent results indicated that parents instructed to fake good, fake bad, or respond randomly were identified with a high rate of accuracy using the CAPI validity measures (p). The validity indexes correctly detected as invalid 94.7% of the protocols generated by general-population parents and 91.1% of those generated by at-risk parents.

CRITIQUE. The available data provide considerable support for the construct validity of the CAPI scales. The factor structure is reasonably stable and generally consistent with the concepts originally derived from the literature on child abuse. CAPI scores relate to several other measures of personality and response distortion in theoretically consistent ways. Further, the CAPI Abuse scale appears to be sensitive to change as a function of remediation directed toward reducing child abuse potential. In the context of forensic evaluations, the accumulated evidence provides important convergent validity for interpreting a parent's CAPI Abuse score as an indicator of potential risk with regard to a child's welfare. Further, the CAPI validity scales may be helpful in detecting cases in which the CAPI Abuse scale results cannot be interpreted in the usual manner, due to the examinee's attempts to create an overly favorable impression or failure to attend to the item content.

In the first edition of this text, two cautions were noted regarding the construct validity of the CAPI. The first was the caveat that the results reviewed in support of the CAPI Abuse scale did not allow one to assume that a high score on the CAPI is indicative of past or future child abuse. The studies reported here do not eliminate that concern, although there is now greater evidence that non-abusing parents who are simply distressed are relatively unlikely to get extremely high scores on the CAPI. The second concern related to the potential impact of sociodemographic characteristics. The early studies employed samples consisting predominantly of white, lower socioeconomic females, with a tendency toward rural residence, and it was unclear whether the same relationships between CAPI scores and variables examined in these studies would be found with ethnic minority samples, with fathers, or with middle- to upper- socioeconomic class samples. Research addressing many of these questions has now been conducted and, although differences have been noted in terms of group mean scores (see Table 2.7; Milner, 1986), the studies generally seem to suggest that the CAPI measures a similar construct in these populations.

Predictive or classificatory utility

Both concurrent and predictive validity studies have been conducted in order to investigate the ability of the CAPI Abuse scale to discriminate between known abusers and non-abusers. In an initial study (u) using discriminant analysis, the CAPI Abuse scale correctly classified 125 out of 130 subjects (96% hit rate, all misclassifications false negatives), using a sample of 65 abusive parents and 65 non-abusive parents matched on nine demographic and familial variables, including ethnic background.

In more diverse populations, subsequent studies using discriminant analysis have resulted in classification rates in the mid-80% to low-90% range (e.g., references r, s). Use of the conservative standard-weighted scoring procedures (as opposed to statistically optimized cut scores) in one study resulted in an overall classification rate of 90.2% for a sample of physical child abusers and comparison parents (k). This study used only valid protocols and the 215-point cut score recommended in the manual. A slightly lower overall rate of correct classification (86.4%) was obtained when invalid protocols were included in the analyses. Use of an optimally-derived 166-point cut-off resulted in a slightly higher overall classification rate compared to the 215 point cut-off. Similarly, another study (a) reported correct classification rates of 87.7%, 73.3% and 100% of physical child abusers, non-abusive comparison parents with childhood history of abuse, and non-abusive comparison parents without childhood history of abuse, respectively, using standard scoring procedures and the 215 point cut-off, and including invalid protocols. Use of the 166-point cut-off resulted in correct classification rates of 96.7%, 60.0%, and 83.3% for the three groups of subjects previously mentioned.

In a truly predictive (rather than concurrent or retrospective) validity study (q), a group of 200 participants were followed in a treatment program for parents at risk for parenting problems. Forty-two parents were reported for confirmed abuse (11), neglect (15) or failure-to-thrive (16) during the follow-up. Pretreatment CAPI scores were above the cutoff score for all of the abusive parents, and CAPI scores correlated with abuse (.34), neglect (.19), but not failure-to-thrive findings (.12). Despite these generally positive findings, the abusive parents accounted for only 10.7% of the 103 at risk parents who had pretreatment CAPI scores above the cutoff; that is, the majority of parents with pretreatment scores above the cutoff criterion apparently did not subsequently abuse their children.

Use of the CAPI Abuse scale to classify other types of abusive groups (as compared to the identified target group of suspected physical child abusers) has resulted in somewhat lower classification rates (e.g., lower 70%s). Such abusive groups include "mildly" abusive parents (g) and physically abusive and neglectful parents (b). One study has reported markedly lower classification rates for the CAPI than have been obtained in most other research (e), finding that only 28% of a combined group of physically and sexually abusive parents referred from a treatment group were correctly classified using the CAPI. Milner (o) has criticized this methodology, however, due to the inclusion of sexual offenders and use of persons already in treatment.

Finally, the classification accuracy of the CAPI has also been studied using non-abusive groups. Specificity rates for low-risk mothers (f), nurturing mothers (i, k), and nurturing foster parents (b) have been 100%. However, there is some evidence that parents of children with a history of medical illnesses and injuries (m) and developmental disabilities (w) may be at greater risk to be misclassified on the Abuse scale. Milner has tentatively noted that the higher scores of parents with children who have suffered injuries may suggest that some of these injuries actually resulted from abusive behavior, although this has not been tested directly.

CRITIQUE. Published studies clearly indicate the ability of the CAPI to discriminate between parents who have or have not abused their children in the past, including samples with diverse sociodemographic characteristics. However, one should remember that these results are not sufficient to conclude that abuse has occurred, or will in the future, based on the CAPI alone.

There are various reasons for this assertion, including ethical issues regarding appropriate test use, impact of varying base rates across samples, and costs of both false positive and false negative errors. Central to these reasons is the fact, recognized by Milner (i), that the cost of identifying 100% of the future abusive parents in his samples has been a very large false positive rate. Almost 90% of the parents with above-cutoff scores did not subsequently abuse their children (although all abusers did meet this criterion). It should be noted, however, that all of the parents were receiving treatment (which also highlights the importance of situational/contextual factors that are not accounted for by instruments such as the CAPI). At least some of the high pretreatment CAPI parents who did not subsequently abuse their children might have done so if treatment had not been provided. Nevertheless, the study results serve as a graphic reminder that an instrument can be highly successful at identifying abusers, yet incapable of being used alone as a practical and accurate diagnostic indicator of future abuse because of its potential for overprediction.

Potential for Expressing Parent-Child Congruency

The CAPI was not intended to assess various parenting abilities or skills. Thus it is not meaningful to consider how parenting dimensions on the measure might be used to compare a parent's abilities to the parallel needs of a specific child.

References

(a) Calisco, J., & Milner, M. (1992). Childhood history of abuse and child abuse screening. *Child Abuse and Neglect, 16,* 647–659.

(b) Couron, B. (1982). Assessing parental potentials for child abuse in contrast to nurturing (Doctoral dissertation), United States International University, 1981. *Dissertation Abstracts International, 42,* 3412B.

(c) De Paul, J., Arruabarrena, I., & Milner, J. S. (1991). Validation de una version Espanola del Child Abuse Potential Inventory para su uso en Espana. *Child Abuse and Neglect, 15,* 495–504.

(d) Ellis, R., & Milner, J. (1981). Child abuse and locus of control. *Psychological Reports, 48,* 507–510.

(e) Holden, E., Willis, D., & Foltz, L. (1989). Child abuse potential and parenting stress: Relationships in maltreating parents. *Psychological Assessment, 1,* 64–67.

(f) Lamphear, V., Stets, J., Whitaker, P., & Ross, A. (1985, August). *Maladjustment in at-risk for physical child abuse and behavior problem children: Differences in family environment and marital discord.* Paper presented at the meeting of the American Psychological Association, Los Angeles.

(g) Matthews, R. (1985). Screening and identification of child abusing parents through self-report inventories (Doctoral dissertation, Florida Institute of Technology, 1984). *Dissertation Abstracts International, 46,* 650B.

(h) Milner, J. (1982). Development of a lie scale for the Child Abuse Potential Inventory. *Psychological Reports, 50,* 871–874.

(i) Milner, J. (1986). *The Child Abuse Potential Inventory: Manual (2nd ed.).* Webster, N.C: Psytec.

(j) Milner, J. (1988). An ego-strength scale for the Child Abuse Potential Inventory. *Journal of Family Violence, 3,* 151–162.

(k) Milner, J. (1989). Additional cross-validation of the Child Abuse Potential Inventory. *Psychological Assessment: A Journal of Consulting and Clinical Psychology, 1,* 219–223.

(l) Milner, J. (1990). *An interpretative manual for the Child Abuse Potential Inventory.* Webster, N.C: Psytec.

(m) Milner, J. (1991). Medical conditions and the Child Abuse Potential Inventory specificity. *Psychological Assessment: A Journal of Consulting and Clinical Psychology, 3,* 208–212.

(n) Milner, J. (1994). Assessing physical child abuse risk: The Child Abuse Potential Inventory. *Clinical Psychology Review, 14,* 547–583.

(o) Milner, J., Murphy, W., Valle, L., & Tolliver, R. (1998). Assessment issues in child abuse evaluations. In J. Lutzker (Ed.), *Handbook of child abuse research and treatment* (pp. 75–115). New York: Plenum.

(p) Milner, J., & Crouch, J. (1997). Impact and detection of response distortions of parenting measures used to assess risk for child physical abuse. *Journal of Personality Assessment, 69,* 633–650.

(q) Milner, J., Gold, R., Ayoub, C., & Jacewitz, M. (1984). Predictive validity of the Child Abuse Potential Inventory. *Journal of Consulting and Clinical Psychology, 52,* 879–884.

(r) Milner, J., Gold, R., & Wimberley, R. (1986). Prediction and explanation of child abuse: Cross-validation of the Child Abuse Potential Inventory. *Journal of Consulting and Clinical Psychology, 54,* 865–866.

(s) Milner, J., & Robertson, K. (1989). Inconsistent response patterns and the prediction of child maltreatment. *Child Abuse and Neglect, 13,* 59–64.

(t) Milner, J., & Wimberley, R. (1979). An inventory for the identification of child abusers. *Journal of Clinical Psychology, 35,* 95–100.

(u) Milner, J., & Wimberley, R. (1980). Prediction and explanation of child abuse. *Journal of Clinical Psychology, 36,* 875–884.

(v) Robertson, K., & Milner, J. (1983). Construct validity of the Child Abuse Potential Inventory. *Journal of Clinical Psychology, 39,* 426–429.

(w) Rodriguez, C., & Murphy, L. (1997). Parenting stress and abuse potential in mothers of children with developmental disabilities. *Child Maltreatment: Journal of the American Professional Society on the Abuse of Children, 2,* 245–251.

(x) Thomasson, E., Berkovitz, T., Minor, S., Cassle, G., McCord, D., & Miner, J. (1981). Evaluation of a family life education program for rural "high risk" families: A research note. *Journal of Community Psychology, 9,* 246–249.

PARENTING STRESS INDEX (PSI)

Author

Abidin, R. R.

Author Affiliation

University of Virginia

Primary Reference

Abidin, R. (1995). *Parenting Stress Index manual* (3rd ed.). Odessa, FL: Psychological Assessment Resources.

Description

The *Parenting Stress Index* (PSI) (a) was developed to assess stress within parent-child systems. Based on Abidin's model of dysfunctional parenting, the PSI in its current form is a 120-item self-report measure that assesses stressors related to both child and parent issues, as well as life event stressors. The PSI, which is intended for parents who have children between the ages of one month and 12 years, is comprised of several scales and subscales. In a portion of the PSI called the "parent domain" (54 items), three subscales are intended to assess the "personality and pathology" (a, p. 30) of the parent: Depression, Competence, and Attachment. Another 4 subscales were developed to assess situational stressors thought to be influential regarding the level of distress experienced by the parent: Spouse, Health, Role Restriction, and Isolation. Subscales within the 47-item "child domain" scale included four thought to be characteristics of temperament: Adaptability, Demandingness, Mood, and Distractibility-Hyperactivity. Finally, two subscales—Acceptability and Reinforces Parent—were considered to reflect interactive aspects of the parent-child relationship. The 19-item Life Stress scale, which assesses the presence of various stressors outside the parent-child relationship, contains no subscales and is considered optional. The PSI also includes a measure of defensiveness called the Defensive Responding scale.

These subscales can be aggregated to form separate Child Domain and Parent Domain scores, as well as a combined Total Stress score. The Life Stress scale is not included in this total. Raw scores on these scales are converted to percentile scores that are based on the normative group (described below).

Conceptual Basis

CONCEPT DEFINITION. Abidin (a) offers a detailed model of parenting stress that is reflected in the subscales developed for the PSI. The PSI is based on the premise that dysfunctional parenting results from stressors related to the three areas noted above (parent and child characteristics, life events) and that the effects of these stressors on parenting ability are additive. Abidin identified these content domains using primarily a rational-theoretical approach, based on reviews of the infant development, parent-child interaction, attachment, child abuse and neglect, child psychopathology, childrearing practices, and stress literatures, as well as his clinical experience.

The PSI is presented as an instrument that may provide information that is relevant to legal decision-making. For example, it is described in the publisher's test catalogue as being useful in assessing for child abuse potential and custody decision-making. However, it does not appear to have been designed with this particular objective in mind. The manual does not discuss legal constructs and issues in the context of the instrument's conceptualization or development in any significant way, although the psychological content domains that the PSI is intended to assess clearly have implications for legal decision-making in these areas.

OPERATIONAL DEFINITION. An iterative process was used to operationalize the content domains of the PSI. This began with the development of a large item pool by the author and his colleagues, followed by pilot testing with mothers of children younger than three years of age, then a review by a panel of six experts in the area of parent-child interaction. The experts appear to have addressed the content and construction of each individual item, although it is not clear that they were involved in refining the broader content domains the items were intended to measure. (An unpublished doctoral dissertation provides a comprehensive overview of the content validational procedures employed for the PSI: see reference d). For the original 150-item PSI, the manual notes that 95% of the items directly focused on content that had been demonstrated to be relevant to parenting stress in at least one research study.

Unlike previous editions, each item on the PSI now contributes only to one subscale. Most of the items are rated by the parent on a 5-point

Likert scale (*Strongly agree* to *Strongly disagree*) although there are a few exceptions to this format (e.g., the Life Stress scale uses a dichotomous format). Some of the items are descriptive in nature (i.e., reflecting specific behaviors the child does or does not engage in), whereas others are framed to reflect how the child's behavior affects the parent or whether the child's behavior deviates from the parent's expectations. Raw scores for the scales and subscales are converted to percentile ranks, which are reported in 5-point intervals.

CRITIQUE. Although somewhat more detail could be provided in the manual, the content validation procedures used in the development of the PSI are a step ahead of many instruments that currently are in use. There is a clearly identified psychological theory on which the PSI is based, and the content of the items themselves has been derived from empirical research. Moreover, unlike other instruments included in this review, the PSI does not purport to measure legal constructs specifically; thus it avoids some of the pitfalls associated with such claims (e.g., that perform-ance on this scale can identify the "better" custodial parent).

Psychometric Development

STANDARDIZATION. The paper-and-pencil format of the PSI is such that administration and scoring are relatively straightforward. Both hand-scoring and computer scoring options are available.

RELIABILITY. Test-retest reliability estimates are reported over rela-tively short durations (e.g., 3 weeks, 3 months) as well as a one-year follow-up. In a relatively small sample ($n = 37$), the one-year stability coefficients for the Child, Parent, and Total Stress scores were .55, .70, and .65, respectively (a).

NORMS. The normative sample reported in the PSI manual (a) con-sisted of 2,633 mothers who were recruited primarily from "well-child-care" pediatric clinics in central Virginia. Others were recruited from day care centers, health maintenance organizations, and general pediatric clinics. A small number of subjects (3.6%) had been referred for diagnostic services related to behavioral or health problems. Almost all were from the East Coast of the United States. No attempt was made to match census data or stratify the sample, and the author acknowledges that the norma-tive group is a sample based on opportunity.

A description of a much smaller normative group of men ($n = 200$) also is included in the manual. Unlike the maternal sample (11% African American, 10% Hispanic), the male group was almost exclusively (95%) Caucasian. They also appear to be more educated than would be expected, in that almost half were college graduates (compared to 27% of the mothers). PSI scores for men were somewhat lower than for women, although it is not clear if this is in any way a function of demographic differences.

The manual also includes statistics for a sample of 223 Hispanic parents from New York City who completed a Spanish-language version of the PSI. Raw scores for this sample appear to be somewhat elevated in comparison to the English-language version, although it is unclear whether the Hispanic sample included data from fathers rather than mothers only. Also, SES level appears to be lower for the Hispanic sample overall.

CRITIQUE. The PSI appears to be reasonably sound psychometrically. Administration and scoring are straightforward. Given that stress is not construed necessarily as a stable construct, the test-retest reliability estimates seem appropriate. Further detail would be helpful regarding some issues, especially inclusion of the Standard Error of Measurement for the scales and subscales. The biggest limitation of the PSI is the normative sample, which is essentially a very large sample of convenience. More detail could be provided regarding various issues, such as some breakdown of PSI scores in relation to the race/ethnicity of the mother.

Construct Validation

Internal consistencies for the normative group in the manual ranged from .70 to .83 for the child subscales and from .70 to .84 for the parent subscales. The Child Domain, Parent Domain, and Total Stress scores all were above .90. Somewhat lower values have been reported for a cross-cultural sample in the manual.

The published literature relating to the construct validity of the PSI is voluminous and cannot be reviewed here in detail. (See references a and b for more detailed reviews.) Results of this research generally are supportive, although there are significant concerns regarding the factor structure of the scale. Analyses reported in the manual indicate that many (and in some cases, the majority) of the items on the subscales do not load substantially on the underlying dimensions of interest, and some items cross-load onto other scales (see Tables 7–9, a).

Concerns regarding its factor structure notwithstanding, the convergent validity of the PSI has been well established, in that the scales and subscales tend to correlate in expected directions with other theoretically relevant constructs (e.g., marital dissatisfaction, childhood illnesses, childhood behavior problems, social isolation). Importantly, criterion measures in many of the studies cited in the manual and in professional journals are structured behavioral observations of parent-child interactions, rather than simply other self-report measures. For example, one study (h) found that, in a sample of 49 pre-schoolers and their mothers, scores from the Child Domain correlated highly with Maternal Involvement, Negative Affectivity, and Sociability scores coded from another instrument (*Parent-Child Early Relational Assessment System*), as well as with attachment status.

It also should be noted that the PSI has been translated into several other languages, and these versions appear to have psychometric properties that are reasonably similar to the English version. Such cross-cultural stability would appear to support the significance of the parenting constructs assessed by the PSI.

CRITIQUE.   The body of research on the PSI is so extensive that simple, evaluative summary statements are difficult to provide. The factor structure reported in the manual is problematic, which raises some concerns about the dimensions that actually underlie the subscales (although these subscales generally do have adequate internal consistencies). Another (potentially related) criticism is that the intercorrelations between some of the subscales are rather high, suggesting that the constructs being assessed are not as distinctive as theorized. Clearly, however, the PSI appears to be embedded in a conceptual and nomological net that supports its use as a global measure of stress, even if some issues have yet to be resolved.

Predictive or Classification Utility

Scores on the PSI have been shown to correlate with several outcome measures of interest to forensic psychologists. For example, parents' PSI scores are sensitive to the effects of intervention. One study (c) reported decreases in PSI scores following completion of an intervention program for parents of children with aggression management problems. PSI scores also are associated with abuse potential. For example, one study (f) found significant differences on all PSI scales and subscales when comparing samples of physically abusive and non-abusive mothers, and also obtained theoretically consistent correlations between PSI scores and behavioral observation of abusive mothers' interactions with their children in a structured activity. Similarly, another study (e) reported that negligent mothers obtained much higher PSI scores than did controls.

Only one published study could be located that examined the predictive validity of the PSI Defensiveness scale (g). That study reported that, in a sample of parents instructed to "fake good," the classification accuracy of this scale was below 50%.

CRITIQUE.   There is clear evidence that parenting stress is associated with adverse outcomes, and that PSI scores seem to be capable of identifying those who, in a relative sense, are at greater risk for engaging in dysfunctional behaviors such as abuse or neglect. Of some concern with the PSI, however, is the suggestion in the manual to use a normatively-based cut score (85th percentile) for determining when to make referrals. The basis for this recommendation is not particularly clear and should be described in greater detail. More generally, given concerns about the normative sample, making absolute (as opposed to relative) predictions about abuse potential based on the percentile scores seems questionable at this time. For example, even if large, positive correlations are obtained between PSI scores and abusive behavior, or group differences are obtained between abusing and non-abusing parents, such information does not address the accuracy of specific cut scores, nor does it take into consideration the importance of base rates when examining predictive accuracy.

Potential for Expressing Parent-Child Congruency

The PSI was not designed specifically to address parent-child congruence, although the scores obtained do purport to provide information regarding the extent to which various characteristics of the child in question appear to be a significant source of distress for the parent. As such, it seems that information from the PSI might be useful in conjunction with other data about the child's functioning, which might allow for a comparison of the parent's attributions to more "objective" measures. For example, a child may be quite accurately perceived by one parent as a significant source of stress because the child very clearly has an externalizing behavior problem (and realistically would strain the resources of anyone), whereas another child is seen as a source of stress by a parent when in fact the child would be considered "low maintenance" by most standards. Also, there would be reason to believe that comparisons might be possible across two parents in a custody dispute regarding the extent to which whatever stress they are experiencing is considered to be attributable to the child.

References

(a) Abidin, R. (1995). *Parenting Stress Index: Professional manual (3rd ed.)*. Odessa, FL: Psychological Assessment Resources.
(b) Abidin, R. (1997). Parenting Stress Index: A measure of the parent-child system. In C. P. Zalaquett & R. J. Wood (Eds), *Evaluating stress*. Lanham, MD: Scarecrow Press.
(c) Acton, R., & During, S. (1992). Preliminary results of aggression management training for aggressive parents. *Journal of Interpersonal Violence, 7*, 410–417.
(d) Burke, W. (1978). *The development of a technique for assessing the stresses experienced by parents of young children*. Unpublished doctoral dissertation. University of Virginia, Charlottesville.

(e) Ethier, L., Lacharite, C., & Couture, G. (1993). *Childhood adversity, parental stress and depression of negligent mothers.* Unpublished manuscript, University of Quebec at Trois-Rivieres, Canada.

(f) Mash, E., Johnston, C., & Kovitz, K. (1983). A comparison of the mother-child interactions of physically abused and non-abused children during play and task situations. *Journal of Clinical Child Psychology, 12,* 337–346.

(g) Milner, J., & Crouch, J. (1997). Impact and detection of response distortions of parenting measures used to assess risk for child physical abuse. *Journal of Personality Assessment, 69,* 633–650.

(h) Teti, D., & Gelfand, D. (1991). Behavioral competence among mothers of infants in the first year: The mediational role of maternal self-efficacy. *Child Development, 62,* 918–929.

PARENT-CHILD RELATIONSHIP INVENTORY (PCRI)

Author

Gerard, A. B.

Author Affiliation

Western Psychological Services

Primary Reference

Gerard, A. B. (1994). *Parent-Child Relationship Inventory manual.* Los Angeles: Western Psychological Services.

Description

The *Parent-Child Relationship Inventory* (PCRI) (b) is a self-report questionnaire that was designed to assess adults' attitudes regarding parenting and their children. The 78 Likert-type items (rated from *strongly agree* to *strongly disagree*) combine into seven content areas: Parental Support; Satisfaction with Parenting; Involvement; Communication; Limit Setting; Autonomy; and Role Orientation. Two validity scales also are included. One is intended to identify socially desirable responding, whereas the other is comprised of highly inter-correlated item pairs and functions as an indicator of response inconsistency.

Conceptual Basis

CONCEPT DEFINITION.   The content domains that the PCRI was designed to measure (noted above) were identified through a fairly rigorous process, involving both qualitative (e.g., expert judges, literature reviews) and quantitative (e.g., factor analytic) methods (b).

OPERATIONAL DEFINITION.   Initial item generation for a 345-item version was driven by a review of existing research on parenting, followed by factor analyses of the prototype measure that identified 14 relevant dimensions.

CRITIQUE.   The content validation procedures used in the development of the PCRI seem to have resulted in the development of scales that represent at least some of the most relevant dimensions of relationship quality. Concerns have been expressed, however, that it is not comprehensive enough in terms of important content domains and that the construct of parenting itself may be too contextual to assess using a self-report measure (d).

Psychometric Development

STANDARDIZATION.   Given the self-report nature of the instrument and the simplicity of the scoring procedures (hand- and computer-scored options are available), it seems unlikely that any significant problems would occur with the PCRI in relation to administration or scoring.

RELIABILITY.   Reliability estimates for the PCRI generally have been acceptable. In the standardization sample, the median alpha reported for the scales was .80 (range = .70 to .88) and the mean test-retest correlation for a subsample of 82 participants over a 5-month follow-up ranged from .44 to .71 (b).

NORMS.   As reported in the manual (b), the normative sample for the PCRI consisted of 1,139 parents who were identified through schools and day-care centers, but with an overall response rate of only 4.4% to the initial solicitation letter. The resulting sample was better educated and less culturally diverse than the U.S. population. Race and education effects were examined by pulling a stratified sample of 240 parents who approximated census data. Although results indicated some significant differences in relation to both demographic factors, separate norms for racial and educational groups were not developed because the obtained differences were presumed to identify substantive differences in parenting across these groups. Separate norms were developed for mothers and fathers, however, given that significant differences were obtained between these groups on five of the seven PCRI scales.

CRITIQUE.   As with most of the parenting measures reviewed, the normative sample for the PCRI has some limitations. The initial 4.4% response rate is reason for concern and, although it may be that the differences between racial groups may in fact represent legitimate differences, at present this assertion remains unsubstantiated.

Construct Validation

Relatively few studies have been conducted on the PCRI, although results have been encouraging. The factor structure of the instrument seems to be reasonably well supported. Aside from these results, the manual notes three studies that have examined the validity of the PCRI. First, in a sample of 35 couples undergoing court-ordered mediation, PCRI scores were generally low and correlated in expected directions with the Personality Inventory for Children (c). Second, a shortened version of the PCRI was used to predict disciplinary styles among a sample of 174 parents. Those who had higher scores on the Communication scale were more likely to reason with their child and less likely to use spanking. The third study reported analyses on 26 adolescent mothers who were considered to be 'at-risk.' As expected, these mothers obtained mean scores that were below the standardization sample on all scales. (See references a and d for reviews of these studies.)

CRITIQUE. More research is needed regarding the construct validity of the PCRI. Although the factor analytic and other item-level analyses are encouraging, more extensive research using better samples and methodologies (e.g., employing adequate control groups) is needed before strong claims can be made regarding exactly what it is that the PCRI measures.

Predictive or Classification Utility

At present, no data are available that address the predictive or classification utility of the PCRI.

CRITIQUE. In the absence of such information, examiners should be very cautious regarding any claims made about the predictive validity of this instrument in forensic contexts. With essentially no data to suggest that PCRI scores identify those whose parenting abilities actually result in children who experience "better" developmental outcomes (e.g., higher academic achievement, lower rates of delinquency or substance abuse), it would be difficult to defend empirically claims that higher scores predict "better" parenting or that low scores predict inadequate parenting (a, d).

Potential for Expressing Parent-Child Congruency

If further empirical support can be provided for the PCRI, it seems that its use in combination with measures of child functioning might provide relevant information regarding congruence. However, at present such results would have to be considered speculative.

References

(a) Boothroyd, R. (1998). Review of the Parent-Child Relationship Inventory. In J. C. Impara & B. S. Plake (Eds.), *The thirteenth mental measurements yearbook* (pp. 717–720). Lincoln, NE: Buros Institute of Mental Measurements of the University of Nebraska-Lincoln.

(b) Gerard, A. (1994). *Parent-Child Relationship Inventory (PCRI): Manual.* Los Angeles, CA: Western Psychological Services.

(c) Lachar, D. (1984). *Personality Inventory for Children manual.* Los Angeles: Western Psychological Services.

(d) Marchant, G., & Paulson, S. (1998). Review of the Parent-Child Relationship Inventory. In J. C. Impara & B. S. Plake (Eds.), *The thirteenth mental measurements yearbook* (pp. 720–721). Lincoln, NE: Buros Institute of Mental Measurements of the University of Nebraska-Lincoln.

CURRENT STATUS OF THE FIELD

There were no specialized forensic instruments for parenting abilities available for review in the Parenting chapter of the first edition of EC. In contrast, most of the instruments reviewed here were designed either specifically to address legal questions of parent competency or capacity (the first five "custody" instruments) or to provide information that would be useful in judicial reviews of cases involving suspected maltreatment of children. The following commentary will reflect on the instruments that have arisen for these purposes, in terms of their guidance for future research and development of FAIs and their use by clinicians.

RESEARCH DIRECTIONS

Functional Component

The adequacy of parenting instruments for maltreatment and divorce child custody assessments will depend on how well they address the functional nature of parenting capacity as a legal construct. Instruments in this context will be helpful if they describe what parents know, believe, and can do in the context of child rearing, in a way that offers guidance to decision makers in legal child custody or abuse and neglect cases.

Development of the new, specialized measures for use in child custody evaluations show some awareness of the importance of parenting functions in assessments for custody cases. The ASPECT, for example, includes items related to parents' caretaking knowledge and skills, as do the PASS and PORT. Future efforts could do better, however, by attending to several things that are dissatisfying about the present instruments.

First, decisions about the specific types of caretaking knowledge, abilities, or skills to include seem to have been based on intuition more than a careful effort to use psychology's knowledge about caregiving as a source of guidance. The *primary* field of study to be consulted in this matter is not clinical psychology (although it has much to offer) but rather developmental psychology. The ability dimensions to be included should be those that constitute some consensus among developmental psychologists regarding essential functions for the proper care and emotional support of children. The instruments thus far developed for child custody evaluations do not appear to have made systematic use of developmental psychology's wealth of information in this regard.

Second, the manner in which parents' skills and abilities has been assessed manifests clinical psychology's traditional over-reliance on interview questioning and on methods of measurement that involve several levels of inference to arrive at one's conclusion about parents' abilities. Asking people things to determine what they know, or what they would do in various situations, is always a good idea. Similarly, asking children to describe their parents' functioning, or how they feel about their caretaking, is advisable in custody evaluations. But both of these methods are always of limited value if what one learns is not supported by direct observation of the parents' skills or abilities in action.

Third, research to examine the construct validity of some of the instruments has been disappointing. For example, it is possible that our concerns about the relationship between reports of parental caretaking behavior and actual caretaking behavior are unfounded, and that asking parents and children about parental functioning is actually a fairly good index of parents' actual functioning. Indeed, the wealth of research with the CAPI and the PSI indicates that much can be done with self-report measures. But the evidence for or against our skepticism regarding the child custody measures has not been produced. Developers of some of the instruments seem to have directed whatever precious resources for research were available toward determining whether their instruments reach conclusions with which judges would agree. If judges agree with the instruments 100% of the time, this will still not tell us the degree to which the instruments produce reliable and valid indexes of parents' functioning as caretakers. At some point the developers of child custody instruments must do (or convince someone else to do) meaningful research that examines parents' actual functioning as caretakers in relation to the scores of the instruments. If they do not, their future is probably limited.

The field should consider whether it is time to take a different direction in developing instruments to assess parenting abilities related to custody questions. These might profitably focus on instruments that do not try to do so much (that is, determine what is in the best interests of the child), and instead focus specifically on functional abilities of parents based on both verbal report and behavior. Suggestions for developing such measures have been provided (e.g., Azar, Lauretti, & Loding, 1998). Moreover, there is a wealth of existing parenting instruments from which to borrow concepts and methods. The 25 parent ability instruments in Table 2 (earlier in this chapter) are only a fraction of available tools. Holden and Edwards (1989) have reviewed 80 measures on parental attitudes toward child rearing, and Holden (1990) reviewed over 150 instruments devoted to parental attitudes, behaviors, and abilities more generally. Although most of these instruments probably would not be appropriate for forensic application, they provide a foundation from which more specialized parenting ability instruments for child custody and termination of parental rights could be developed.

Causal Component

Generally there has been little research on the relations between current parenting scales and various psychological measures of mental disorder, or between parents' scores on these scales and their diagnostic classifications. Knowledge of relations of these types is important for clinical interpretation of the results of parenting instruments in individual cases. For example, an examiner is in a better position to offer the examinee's mental disorder as a plausible explanation for observed deficits in parenting abilities (poor scores on a parenting instrument) if research has demonstrated (and the examiner knows) that many individuals with this disorder produce the pattern of poor parenting scores made by the examinee. Alternatively, research is needed to indicate ways in which psychopathology does not necessarily correspond to (or predict) deficits in parenting abilities. Recent literature has provided some conceptual guidance for conducting research of this type (e.g., Budd & Holdsworth, 1996; Jacobsen, Miller, & Kirkwood, 1997).

Interactive Component

The interactive nature of parental competence requires that we understand not only the parent's capacities, but also the demands of the legally relevant circumstance that the parent faces. This is, in part, the nature of the child. Children in general have certain needs, but specific children will vary with regard to their own special needs. Assuming that adults also vary in their capacities to meet different needs of children, it is reasonable to speak of more or less congruent matches between adults and their children.

It is interesting that some of the child custody measures reviewed in this chapter have the potential to make use of this perspective. Some assess parents' abilities in reference to the specific child in question, and others use children's own reports of parents' behavior, which is one way of capturing the interactive perspective. Unfortunately, so little research has been done with the instruments that their value in this regard remains unknown.

The first edition of EC discussed two implications of the interactive component for the development of tests of parenting capacities. These are worth restating, because the field has not yet responded to the challenge.

INTEGRATING PARENT AND CHILD ASSESSMENT. The interactive perspective just described calls for empirical methods to compare or contrast the capacities of a specific parent to the needs of a specific child. One approach would be to develop an instrument to assess a child's needs in relation to a set of need constructs, and a parallel instrument using the same constructs to assess a parent's functional capacities and dispositions to meet a child's needs. Multidimensional instruments of this type might provide a profile of the child's particular pattern of needs, the parent's particular pattern of functional parenting behaviors, and a description of the congruency between these two profiles. No particular parent profile would be inherently good or bad. That is, the parenting instrument would not attempt to describe more or less competent parenting. Indeed, any particular parenting profile might be considered as more or less desirable in different cases, depending on the profiles on the parallel child instrument in each of these cases. Further, a parent's very low score in some particular area of functioning would not automatically signal a deficiency. The low score might be of little consequence, if the child's need in that particular conceptual area is also low.

The interpretation and utility of parallel parent/child instruments would require considerable research on the validity of the congruency assumption—that is, that better matches between parent-functioning and child-need profiles result in favorable development of children. The assumption could be naive. For example, while parent-child congruency would be estimated at a given point in time, child custody decision makers must examine in part the custody arrangement that offers the best prospects for meeting the child's needs in the future, some of which will not yet be manifested. Would a congruent profile match at a given stage in a child's development (and a given stage in a parent's development) necessarily suggest that the match will remain congruent as the child matures?

ATTENDING TO AGE AND DEVELOPMENTAL DIFFERENCES. Current parenting instruments generally fail to take into account the effect that a child's age or developmental stage might have on the examinee's responses to the parenting instrument. For example, many items in existing parenting instruments refer the respondent merely to children in general, while other items refer to the parent's own child.

A parent's beliefs about when to ignore a child's crying, what rights a parent has in relation to a child, or how much the parent should be responsible for a child's attire may be more or less appropriate, correct, or wise, depending (among other things) on the age of the child in question. Similarly, one wonders whether it is possible to speak of a parent's "attitudes toward children" or "parenting abilities" in general. Do we possess a given attitude toward preschoolers and eighth graders alike? Do we manifest the same functional responses to children of these two age groups? Do they require the same kinds of parenting skills, or might different parenting concepts be needed to assess parenting effectiveness for different ages and stages among children? Do parents themselves go through stages during which they are adapting to new meanings of parenthood? Some of these questions need to be addressed if we are to develop more meaningful clinical and forensic tools for assessing parenting adequacy.

Judgmental and Dispositional Components

Custody decisions frequently require a moral judgment concerning when a parent-child incongruency has been raised above some subjective threshold for a decision to remove a child from a parent's custody or to place the child in the custody of the other parent. Parallel parent-child instruments, or existing parenting instruments, might be helpful in providing information with which courts can conceptualize the extent of a parent's child-rearing abilities or the degree of parent-child incongruency. Neither the instruments nor the forensic examiner, however, should attempt to define how incongruent a parent-child interaction must be in order to justify a particular custody decision.

Some of the instruments reviewed in this chapter, however, contain features that could encourage one to violate this principle. The BPS, for example, results in a comparison of the scores of the two parents, with the recommendation that the parent with the higher score is to be favored for custody. It is highly recommended that future instruments for assessing parenting capacities should not use cut-off scores or parent comparisons in ways that encourage the notion that instruments can provide answers to the ultimate legal question of custody.

CLINICAL APPLICATION

Description

The child custody instruments reviewed in this chapter have little to no research evidence supporting their construct validity or reliability. Even a relatively low standard for empirical support that is required for test use in legal settings would not encourage the use of the child custody instruments for most purposes. Instruments like the BPS might be useful for simply acquiring information concerning how a child sees his or her parent in terms of parenting behaviors and emotional support. But use of the instrument to describe parents themselves in custody cases cannot be recommended.

At least two of the instruments, the CAPI, and PSI, have a great amount of empirical support and, if interpreted carefully, may be of considerable value. Typically they should be used as but one part of a broader assessment. But their current level of sophistication suggests that abuse/neglect evaluations that do not use them may represent substandard practice.

Explanation

Special care must be taken to entertain various possible explanations for a parent's manifest weaknesses or strength on the parenting instruments. Desirable scores on various attitude or ability dimensions might indicate strengths or merely dissimulation of strengths. Only the CAPI provides an empirical indicator of an examinee's social desirability response bias. Less desirable scores may indicate actual weaknesses or merely the effect of situational variables, among other possibilities.

Generally, other assessment methods will be required to obtain data with which to infer the potential meanings of high or low scores on most of the instruments. In addition, past research with some of the instruments suggests their relation to other parent characteristics (e.g., psychopathology, personality characteristics). If a parent's status on these related characteristics is known, then the research results may assist in interpretation of parenting instrument results.

Prediction and Classification

The CAPI and PSI manifest some ability to discriminate between groups of parents who have or have not abused/neglected their children. Nevertheless, one should be especially careful not to diagnose or label parents as "abusive" or "neglectful" on the basis of their scores failing above published cutoff scores or within ranges of scores made by abusive/neglectful research samples. For forensic use, the instruments can be used to identify parents about whom the risk of abuse is greater, while requiring a wider range of data to reach any further.

Conclusions

Nothing concerning the current status of these custody and abuse/neglect instruments would contradict the general recommendation that forensic examiners should avoid conclusory opinions concerning whether a particular parent is or is not competent to care for a particular child, or which of two parents should receive custody of a child. In general, the instruments do not provide a direct empirical indication of present or future functional ability. Further, current instruments will not provide empirical descriptions of the congruency or incongruency between a parent's abilities and a particular child's needs. Finally, they address only one factor—characteristics of parents—among many that must be taken into consideration in clinical or legal decisions about a child's living arrangements.

8

Guardianship and Conservatorship

JENNIFER MOYE

THE COMPETENCE QUESTION

Every state provides by law for the assignment of a guardian or conservator for adults when they are considered unable to care for themselves or to manage their own property. The term *guardianship* traditionally refers to guardianship of the person, whereby a court appoints an individual or agency to be the substitute decision maker and supervisor for decisions regarding day-to-day life, including matters such as living arrangements, health care, finances, and provision of other basic needs. The term *conservatorship* typically refers to guardianship of the estate whereby a court appoints a substitute decision maker and manager only for finances, i.e., managing assets and financial transactions.

Assessments for guardianship of person are among the most challenging because the abilities and skills to be evaluated can be so broad as to include functioning in almost all aspects of life. Likewise, the consequences are of great significance for the individual who, if considered incompetent, may lose autonomy in decisionmaking for almost all aspects of his or her life.

Legal decisions about an adult's need for a guardian most often involve individuals who are significantly mentally impaired due to psychiatric illness (including alcohol or drug dependence), neurological illness (including dementing illnesses), or developmentally disability. The question of need for guardianship often is raised by the individual's relatives who petition the court for guardianship so that they may make decisions for the family member concerning, for example, placement in treatment facilities or protection of financial assets. Not all guardianship arrangements, however, involve relatives; in many states, courts may appoint a person who has developed a reputable practice as a guardian and who acts as guardian and/or conservator for many mentally ill and disabled individuals. Because of the increasing numbers of elderly adults without relatives or friends to serve as guardians of person, and without the funds to pay for guardianship services, most states have established public guardianship commissions or expanded the powers of state Departments of Mental Health or Adult Protective Services to serve in this manner.

All adults are presumed to be legally competent to make decisions regarding self and estate unless determined in a court of law to be otherwise. The appointment of a guardian for person or estate follows a judicial determination that an individual is legally incompetent, after a petition for guardianship has been filed and a hearing held.

Although clinicians may refer to a patient's competence status and may request other clinicians to evaluate a patient's competence, a *clinical* finding of incompetence should not be confused with a *judicial* determination of incompetence. The clinical use of the term competence refers to a clinical opinion regarding the patient's decisional capacities. Such an opinion does not and cannot alter the individual's legal competence status. In addition, such an opinion generally does not grant clinicians or family members the right to make decisions for the patient even though they may feel a patient's decision is imprudent. There are exceptions to this in the area of health care decisions which at times fall under guardianship law and (sometimes conflicting) at other times fall under other statutes such as those providing for advance medical directives (Moye & Zehr, 2000). For example, when a patient has previously been appointed a durable power of attorney for health care, this can and would spring into effect (for medical decisions only) upon a clinical finding of incapacity. The area of health care management (managing one's own health on a day to day basis) generally falls under guardianship law and will be addressed in this chapter. Evaluating capacities for making specific medical decisions is discussed further in chapter 9.

The distinction between legal versus clinical competence is empha-sized because some clinicians may confuse clinical and legal uses of the term competence and thus intervene without the legal authority, often when intervening with paternalistic albeit benevolent motivations (Kane, 2001). One useful approach to avoiding such confusion is to be quite spe-cific in language use: for example, to refer to one's clinical evaluation as a clinical assessment of abilities and capacities for the purposes of evaluat-ing the need for guardianship.

In recent years most states recognized the need to move away from the notion of legal incompetency as a global or all-inclusive characteristic. Instead, states are focusing on the concept of *incapacity* which is meant to avoid the sweeping all-or-nothing implications and social stigma of the term *incompetence* (Sabatino, 1996). Theoretically, this also allows for tai-loring *limited* guardianships to address the specific legal incapacities of an individual, often described in terms of specific behavioral limitations (e.g., unable to manage bank accounts but able to manage a weekly allowance). Such an approach works well for clinicians who address spe-cific functional abilities and capacities in their evaluations.

Later discussions of assessments in this area will focus especially, although not exclusively, on elderly adults whose competence to care for self or property is questioned. This is because the large majority of guardian-ships concern elderly individuals with psychiatric or neurological diagnoses (Barnes, 1992; Krauss & Sales, 1997). This trend will increase as the number of older adults increases; in 1985, 11.9% of the U.S. population was 65 years of age or older, and this will increase to about 13% by 2005 and about 20% by 2025 (Myers, 1990), with greatest growth in the over-80 age range.

A common underlying condition leading to adjudication for guardianship in older adults is dementing illness, including dementia caused by Alzheimer's disease, Parkinson's disease, multiple infarcts, and alcohol-induced persisting disorders which increase in prevalence with advancing age. The majority of older adults, of course, do not have dementia (Regier et al., 1988). The question of an elderly person's need for a guardian may be raised, however, as a consequence of any disorder that significantly and continually limits mental abilities for self-management.

While older adults more often are subject to guardianship than younger adults, it is worth pointing out that advancing age or physical frailty in itself is not grounds for guardianship. For example, the inability to write checks related to severe arthritis in an older adult does not imply the individual is incapable of managing funds, in the same way that a spinal cord injury in a younger adult does not assume any incompetence, but rather that assistance may be needed in completing a task. The need for psychosocial or nursing services to accomplish a task at the elder's direction should not be confused with impairments in judgment and deci-sion making that may underlie the need for a substitute decision maker (Anderer, 1997).

In addition, it is important to note that most older adults, even those with some functional limitations, are independent and can rely upon the support of family. Most older adults live with spouses (64% of those aged 65–74), have weekly contact with children (86% with living children report weekly contact), and live independently (American Psychological Association, 1997). For those older adults who need assistance with tasks of daily living, family and friends continue to be the primary source of assistance for seniors in the United States. Even for adults with significant functional impairments, the family (most often wives and daughters) pro-vide the bulk of the care (Chappell, 1990).

Declarations of incompetency and assignments of guardianship are not required, of course, for many of the elderly with functional limita-tions, because cognitive abilities are intact and substitute decision making is not necessary. In cases when decisional support or substitution is help-ful, many alternatives to guardianship can be exercised, such as health care proxies, durable powers of attorney, shared bank accounts, and trusts (Cross, Fleischner, & Elder, 1996). Even when there is no family or friend to serve as caregiver, alternative mechanisms to guardianship may be available. Adult protective services working in conjunction with home health care agencies can provide many of the services that a guardian would normally offer. Guardianship as a most restrictive alternative should be reserved as a last resort.

Many adults who are made wards of guardians probably experience considerable benefits from the arrangement. At best, the individual receives needed care at home, with the guardian attending to and coordi-nating services for his or her needs. The guardian may assure that the individual's disability allowances, social security receipts, retirement ben-efits, or savings work to ensure continuity of care and are directed and invested according to the individual's plans and preferences. The arrangement may offer the individual protection from persons who would dupe the disabled individual into unscrupulous financial arrange-ments. Furthermore, a guardian can be an important advocate for a men-tally compromised and vulnerable adult who is unable to advocate for him or herself. For example, there is concern about vulnerable older adults in psychiatric or long term care institutions who must rely on the beneficence of their care providers without the benefit of a third party to insure that their needs are met and preferences respected (Altman & Parmelee, 1989), including consent (or non-consent) for psychotropic medication (Parry, 1986a). At worst, however, guardians may arrange for their wards' involuntary and unnecessary hospitalization in public mental hospitals or placement in substandard residential facilities, the guardian having been motivated primarily by the desire to protect as much of the ward's estate as possible for personal use or inheritance.

Whatever the consequences, they occur at a considerable expense to the ward. Appointment of a guardian results in loss of the right to make choices about residency, health care, medication, relationships, marriage, contracts, voting, driving, use of leisure time, and spending (Krauss & Sales, 1997). In addition to these legal consequences, a loss of decisional autonomy may have considerable psychological consequences, impacting mental well being, personal control, ability to cope with changes and stressors, and physical health (Moye, 1996; Rodin, 1986; Stancliffe, Avery, Springborg, & Elkin, 2000).

These potential deprivations of freedom, as well as the risk of petitions that are primarily motivated by potential gains for the guardian, point up the importance of due process in guardianship cases. They underscore as well the special care that should be taken in clinical evaluations for guardianship, upon which the courts rely heavily when determining a person's capacity to care for self or property.

LAW AND CURRENT PRACTICE

During the 1960s and 1970s, reviews of guardianship standards and procedures repeatedly noted significant problems in legal standards (the statutory definitions of incompetency) and in legal procedures (the process by which guardians were appointed and monitored). Legal definitions and processes were built on the presumption that the state or family member was acting in the best interest of the proposed ward and thus few due process protections were needed. While most guardianship petitions are filed by family members wishing to protect the best interests of an elderly adult, the system has been open to potential abuses by those seeking guardianship or conservatorship for financial exploitation of an elderly adult (Parry, 1988). For example, while being a guardian for an incapacitated adult with early onset disability (e.g., an adult with life long developmental disability and minimal employment) would be unlikely to provide personal financial gain, this is not the case when being a guardian for a recently incapacitated adult with late onset disability (e.g., an adult who has amassed considerable assets who now has dementia) (Ritter, 1995).

Problems with legal standards and procedures allowed such poten-tial abuses. Specifically, reviews of earlier standards and procedures (e.g., Anderer, 1990; Hommel, 1996; Moye, 1999; Tor & Sales, 1994; Wang, Burns, & Hommel, 1990) found that:

- statutory definitions for competency were vague
- medical evidence to establish decisional deficits was often sketchy or conclusory
- there were no standards regarding who was qualified to complete clinical evaluations
- those completing clinical evaluations were not required to be pres-ent at hearings for questioning of their expertise and findings
- the proposed ward was rarely advised of the hearing, present at hearing, or represented by counsel, and
- guardians and conservators often were not monitored.

The past twelve years has seen extremely active guardianship law reform throughout the country, although some states lag behind. From 1988–2000 a total of 302 guardianship bills were passed in the United States (Wood, 2000). These bills, some a massive overhaul of guardianship procedures and others addressing minor points in guardianship law, focused on the legal standard for defining and determining incapacity, discussed below, and the legal procedures for appointing a guardian, discussed later.

Legal Standard

States have moved away from standards of legal incapacity that are based on diagnoses to more specific and functional standards (Anderer, 1990, 1997; Tors & Sales, 1994; Wood, 2000). Although the presence of a mental condition is typically still a part of legal standards for incapacity, it is considered the necessary "causal" element, but not a sufficient element to establish the need for guardianship. Revised statutes for legal incapac-ity tend to have three components (Anderer, 1997): mental or physical condition; cognitive or decision making impairment; and behavioral results or consequences. Some states do not specify all three components, although in some of these states they are implied and required in practice. Most statutes link two or more of these elements with the causal phrases "by reason of which" or "as a result of."

The many ways in which these elements have been combined in various states make a description of a typical statutory definition virtually impossible. The first of the above components (the disabling condition component) will be discussed in more detail under the "Causal Component" section of this chapter. The cognitive and behavioral components will be discussed under the "Functional Component" section of this chapter. What follows are some examples of more recently revised statutes to give the reader a sense of evolving legal standards for defining incapacity. Because of discrepancies between states, clinical evaluators should be familiar with statutes in their jurisdiction.

The Uniform Guardianship and Protective Proceedings Act (Revised 1997; also known as Article V of the Uniform Probate Code, abbreviated UPC) provides a basis for statutes regarding guardianship in some states, and defines legal incapacity of the person as: "any person who is impaired by reason of mental illness, mental deficiency, physical illness or disability, chronic use of drugs, chronic intoxification, or other cause (except minority) to the extent of lacking sufficient understanding or capacity to make or communicate responsible decisions." Recently revised codes emphasize the relationship between decisional or cognitive impairments and functional outcomes. In Virginia's 1997 code revision, appointment of a guardian is indicated by "a lack of capacity to meet the essential requirements for health, care, safety or therapeutic needs" or to "manage property or financial affairs" (VA. H.B. 2027). In Iowa's 1997 code revision, appointment of a guardian follows the incompetency of an adult when decision making capacity is so impaired that the individual is "unable to care for the person's personal safety, or to attend to or provide for necessities for the person such as food, shelter, clothing, or medical care, without which physical injury or illness may occur," or the individual is "unable to make, communicate or carry out important decisions concerning the person's financial affairs" (IA. S.F. 241). Similarly, in 1995 Oregon over-hauled its guardianship law, including a new definition of legal incapacity as "a person's ability to receive and evaluate information effectively or to communicate decisions is impaired to such an extent that the person presently lacks the capacity to meet the essential requirements for the person's physical health or safety" (OR. S.B. 61).

In 1996 California passed a ground breaking reform to guide evaluations for guardianship of persons and property, epitomizing the move away from diagnosis as sufficient to establish incapacity (Wood, 2000). California's "Due Process in Competency Determinations Act" (CA. S. B. 730) specifically states that legal incapacity is based on evidence of a deficit in one or more of the person's mental functions, noting that the mere diagnosis of a mental or physical disorder shall not be sufficient in and of itself to support a determination that the proposed ward is of unsound mind or lacks the capacity to do a certain act. Four categories of mental functions are detailed:

- *alertness and attention*, including deficits in level of arousal, consciousness, orientation, attention, or concentration
- *information processing*, including deficits in memory, understanding and communicating with others, recognition of objects and persons, understanding and appreciating quantities, reasoning abstractly and logically, planning, organizing and carrying out actions
- *thought process*, including hallucinations, delusions, and intrusive thoughts
- *modulation of affect*.

The statute specifies that impairments in any of these mental functions may be considered only if the deficit "significantly impairs the person's ability to understand and appreciate the consequences of his or her actions with regard to the type of act or decision in question" in consideration of the "frequency, severity, and duration of impairment." A detailed form describing these deficits must be completed by a licensed psychologist or physician (Hankin, 1995). The form is not meant as a rating tool but provides a common language to clinicians, attorneys, and judges with which to speak about functional incapacities.

Many statutes include a qualifying term in their descriptions, such as *responsible* or *effective* decision making without which there will be some degree of harm that crosses a theoretically unacceptable risk threshold (Anderer, 1997). Such wording clarifies that determination of incompetence involves a value judgment. The removal of the right to self determination is so significant that it is expected to occur only in cases without which there would be substantial risks to the individual.

In summary, the revisions to legal standards of incompetence for guardianship include the presence of a mental disorder and specific functional consequences, be they decisional and/or behavioral, that exceed an unacceptable risk or harm threshold. The intent is to require evidence of specific and significant functional incapacities that will:

- protect individuals from guardianships based on the presence of a mental disorder alone
- install guardians and invoke the potentially sweeping loss of rights only when functional consequences are extreme

- require evaluations that provide the courts specific functional data to create limited rather than plenary guardianships.

Research to evaluate the impact of recent revisions to legal standards would investigate whether clinical evaluations are indeed focusing on specific and significant functional incapacities (e.g., are functionally oriented instruments used in the evaluation) and whether guardianships are limited. While the former question has not been investigated, research on the latter question (Barnes, 1996; Hommel, 1996; Keith & Wacker, 1992; Lisi & Barinaga-Burch, 1995) has found that limited guardianships are not often utilized. Across ten states surveyed between 1989–1992 only 13% of guardianships were limited, except in Minnesota which provides a separate form for plenary versus limited guardianships (and conservatorships), in which case 54% of guardianships were limited (Lisi & Barinaga-Burch, 1995). Another study found little increase in the use of limited guardianship and least restrictive alternatives before and after statutory reform in Iowa and Missouri (Keith & Wacker, 1992).

Legal Process

The legal guardianship process begins with the filing of a petition in the correct court according to the jurisdiction of the proposed ward, which in most states may be done by any interested person (Hafemeister & Sales, 1984). After this, medical evidence (a clinical evaluation) is collected, a hearing is held, and a guardian is appointed and monitored if the person is found incompetent.

MEDICAL EVIDENCE. Pre-1980 reviews found problems with the low quality of clinical evaluations and the sometimes questionable qualifications of the evaluator. Observers noted that examiners' testimony usually was either merely a conclusion about competence ("I have examined the individual and find him to be incompetent") or an identification of a particular disorder followed by the conclusory comment (Alexander, 1977; Allen, Ferster, & Weihofen, 1968; Horstman, 1975; Stone, 1975).

States have addressed the problem of inadequate evaluations by providing more detail and direction to the evaluator. For example, many states now list the required elements of a clinical evaluation (e.g., diagnosis, cognitive limitations, functional consequences) and provide a multipart medical certificate form. For example, Florida's form lists numerous specific incapacities to be considered separately; Rhode Island's "Decision

Making Assessment Tool" form provides separate checklists for biological, psychological, and social assessments.

States have also developed guidelines for examiner qualifications. Physicians have been recognized as qualified to perform competence evaluations and complete medical certificates, although reforms have specified that the physician must be specialized in the area. In additions, reforms have expanded the list of professions considered qualified, especially because laws tend now to focus more on cognitive and behavioral data regarding capacity. Expanded definitions typically include licensed psychologists, social workers, or other psychiatric or geriatric specialists. Some states have recognized the importance of a clinical team. For example, Florida requires a three-person examining team appointed by the court, including psychiatrist or physician, physician or gerontologist, nurse, or social worker, or anyone chosen by the court but not the family's physician (FL. Stat. Ch. 744.331(3), 1989). Maryland requires evaluation by two licensed physicians or by one licensed physician and one licensed psychologist (MD. Est. & Trust, § 13–705, 1999).

HEARING. Pre-1980's reviews of guardianship also registered great concern with procedures governing hearings. For example, Horstman (1975) found that the alleged incompetent individual was not present at the hearing in about 85% of cases. Counsel representing the elderly person was present in less than 3% of the cases. Most hearings lasted only a few minutes, and only about 4% of the petitions were denied. Health professionals who had examined the elderly individuals were present in only one case (out of more than 1000); examination results were conveyed to the court by affidavit in the remainder of the cases.

Subsequently, states tend to have enhanced due process protections in these areas. First, many states have instituted more stringent notice requirements, specifying that the respondent must be served in person and must be provided an explanation of the individual's rights (Wang, Burns, & Hommel, 1990). For example, in 1996, Maryland substantially changed its rules of procedure now requiring the respondent to be served with an "advice of rights" form plainly spelling out the consequences of guardianship and the rights to defend against it. Similarly, in 1995 Oregon replaced most of its existing guardianship law (S.B. 61), in particular requiring notice to the proposed ward that must be served personally, must be in understandable language and large type, and must explain the consequences of the petition as well as the respondents' rights.

A second issue related to hearings is whether the respondent is present at hearings. Many states have modified their statutes so that the respondent is more likely to be present at the hearing by either mandating or encouraging attendance, with a provision that the respondent can be absent if physically or mentally unable to attend the hearing. The spirit of the law is that respondent's may be excused if comatose or otherwise extremely impaired, but not because of the absence of notice, opportunity, or access (Tor & Sales, 1994). However, a more recent study still found that respondent attendance at hearings was low (28%), noting that mandating respondent presence or mandating counsel increased respondent attendance, while only encouraging or allowing respondent presence was less effective (Lisi & Barinaga-Burch, 1995). Of note, guardianship proceedings should comply with the American with Disabilities Act of 1990 which prohibits discrimination on the basis of disability (Stiegel, Mason, Morris, Gottlich, & Rave, 1993). But most states are behind in this area. A few have expanded the options for the hearing location, such as holding hearings at nursing homes or hospitals with little disruption in the judicial process (Stiegel, et al., 1993; Colorado H.B. 00-1375, 2000).

A third issue related to hearings is whether the respondent is represented by counsel. Many states have modified statutes by either mandating or encouraging representation. Representation by counsel would seem to have a significant impact on due process protections by providing the respondent a third party to insure all intended protections (e.g., notice of hearing, presence at hearing, right to object). Again, a key issue appears to be whether counsel is encouraged or mandated. In their 1995 study of guardianship reform across 10 states, Lisi and Barinaga-Burch (1995) found only 17–20% of respondents were represented by court-appointed attorneys and another 9% represented by private counsel, except in states requiring counsel where 80–93% of respondents had legal representation. When counsel is present, it is sometimes unclear if counsel is to act as a guardian ad litem (GAL) or as an advocate. An attorney acting as GAL may represent the individual's best interests and argue for the position that the GAL believes benefits the client, even if it conflicts with the client's expressed wishes. An attorney acting as advocate would represent the client's wishes and require the petitioner to prove his or her case (Stiegel et al., 1993).

The impact of representation deserves further study. For example, Keith and Wacker (1993) found that wards who retained their own counsel were more likely to receive limited guardianship or have the petition denied, while wards with court appointed counsel more often received full guardianship.

APPOINTMENT AND MONITORING OF GUARDIANS. States have been altering guardianship statutes for better inquiry into the fitness of the proposed guardian. For example, in Oregon, in a petition for guardianship the proposed fiduciary must now answer whether he or she has ever been convicted of a crime or had a professional license revoked and whether he or she intends to place the respondent in an institution (O.R.S. 126.003 et .seq., 1995). Similarly, Nevada (NV. S.B. 414, 1995) requires the petition to state that the proposed guardian has not been convicted of a felony. Texas (TX. H.B. 1195, 1995) disallows appointment of persons convicted of an assault on an elderly or disabled individual.

Guardians' accountability and courts' monitoring of guardianship have posed special challenges. Many states have enhanced the reporting requirements by guardians, including the filing of annual reports and inventories with the court, and added provisions to guide the actions of guardians. Some states are modifying law to better guide the actions of guardians. West Virginia and New York now require that guardians receive educational material or complete educational training, unless otherwise directed by the court (WV. Code sec 44A-1–10, 1995; NY. S.B. 4498-D, 1992). Utah now requires that conservators act as "prudent investors," exercise reasonable skill and caution, and evaluate decisions in light of the estate as a whole (UT. H.B. 121, 1995). Florida (S. B. 1734, 1996), Mississippi (H.B. 1420, 1996), and Illinois (S. B. 1527, 1996) recently clarified the power of the guardian to purchase property or borrow money from the ward and to make gifts to him/herself as an heir, now providing for court authorization if it can be established that the action is consistent with the ward's wishes. States are also stipulating when guardians can be removed. For example, in Nevada, a guardian can now be removed if found to be abusing, neglecting, or exploiting the ward (NV. A.B. 585, 1995).

In summary, the revisions to the legal procedures for guardianship have addressed many areas of concern, including the nature of the clinical evaluation and evaluator, the due process protections associated with the hearing, and the selection and monitoring of the guardian. Initial studies suggest that these reforms have enhanced the rights and protections provided to the proposed ward, but that the incremental gain may be modest if the added protections are only encouraged rather then mandated.

Competency Assessment: Current Practice

To catch up with the sweeping legal reforms, the clinical literature on competence assessment for the purposes of guardianship has begun to provide general guidelines for the entire assessment, discussed below, including specific criteria for the functional component of these assessments.

One example of guidelines is that of the Department of Veterans Affairs (1997), which convened a technical advisory group of VA and non-VA psychologists, neuropsychologists, and geropsychologists. The guideline is aimed at psychologists but may be useful to any clinician.

Of interest, the technical advisory group chose the topic because an electronic survey of more than 500 psychologists revealed a dire need for guidance in the burgeoning demand for these assessments.

The guideline recommends that a guardianship assessment include:

- a detailed clinical interview with the patient, family, and involved professionals which includes an assessment of the patient's values, goals, and preferences, and an assessment of mental health conditions (i.e., which would lead to a psychiatric diagnosis)
- a performance based assessment of cognition, and
- a performance based assessment of the specific capacity in question (e.g., writing checks and counting change) (Department of Veterans Affairs, 1997).

The guideline gives equal weight to the steps that precede and follow the actual assessment. Preceding the assessment is: *referral clarification*, including determining what specific issues are in question, whether it is appropriate to be making an evaluation concerning competency (or if alternatives to guardianship should be pursued), and considering one's own qualifications; and, *general assessment planning*, including special issues in obtaining informed consent for the evaluation. Following the evaluation is: *synthesis of data and communication of findings*, which specifies how data might be brought together to develop conclusions, what should be included in the report, and to whom the results of the report should be communicated; and *follow-up evaluation* that tracks the impact of the evaluation and recommended interventions.

Weiner and Wettstein (1993) provided a useful set of general principles for competence evaluations for guardianship: evaluating on more than one occasion, considering the effect of the evaluator and the evaluation setting on the evaluee, evaluating performance under conditions relevant to the competency, and conducting multidisciplinary evaluations. In the assessment phase itself they encourage an assessment of the examinee's personal values and goals, as well as functional assessments using standardized inventories, direct observation, and information from third parties. The evaluator is encouraged to become familiar with the relevant issues of the specific functional capacities to be addressed, become knowledgeable about the legal standards in one's state, and consider the reason and rationale for the patient's decision(s) as well as appreciate the affective and cognitive dimensions of decision making. They stressed that full informed consent must be obtained prior to the assessment and that the ultimate decision of competence is deferred to the courts after the assessment.

Writing from a Canadian legal perspective, Verma and Silberfeld (1997) also provided a useful set of general principles to be used in competency evaluations for guardianship. Their principles include the notation that informal assessments of capacity are made every day, but that if there is ever a doubt, a formal assessment should be pursued but not only when behavior is merely eccentric or unusual. The assessment is justified when a person is at risk of significant harm to self or others or when the individual requests it for him or herself. They also noted that the evaluator is always to serve the interests of the individual being assessed, observe the principle of the least restrictive alternative, and presume the individual competent until proven otherwise. Assessments should be preceded by full informed consent, focus on task specific capacities, state the expected duration of any incapacity, and provide for a re-assessment plan.

From Legal Standard to Forensic Assessment

Functional Component

Statutes, case law, and the commentary of legal scholars make it clear that the central question of law in competence determinations for guardianship is the individual's functional abilities. When used in guardianship law, "functional" refers to descriptions of day to day capacities—what the person is capable of *doing* in the everyday management of person or estate. The strong emphasis on function directs courts and clinicians not to accept a diagnosis alone as a justification for legal incapacity.

Functional assessments for guardianship should evaluate cognition and behavior through testing, observation, and third party informant report. There may be some confusion for clinicians who think of the word "functional" as relating only to activities of daily living (ADL's; i.e., eating, toileting, dressing, grooming, walking) and independent activities of daily living (IADL's; i.e., managing money, home, health, transportation, and meals). The law uses the term functional more broadly to refer to everyday behavior, meaning behavior that is observed, and the cognitive abilities—thinking, memory, judgment, and planning—that support and interact with that behavior. For example, an IADL test might determine if a person can write a check, while a cognitive test might determine whether a person can exercise judgment about when and to whom checks should be written. In this way, cognition and behavior, specifically overlearned daily living skills, are separate but related concepts and together predict everyday functioning (Zimmer, Hayden, Deidan, & Loewenstein, 1994).

Having said this, selecting the appropriate functional abilities relevant for guardianship and conservatorship cases presents several problems. The parameters for the hypothetical domain of abilities defined by these contexts are so broad that they seem to encompass almost all of the functions and skills that we employ in our adaptations to everyday life. When this is considered in light of the diversity of demands placed on us in all walks of life, the problem of defining dimensions of functional abilities related to "caring for self and/or property" is intimidating.

Several authors have suggested hierarchical schemes for organizing functional abilities associated with everyday life (Lawton, 1990; Spector, Katz, Murphy, & Felton, 1987), progressing from the more physically determined to the more socially determined: for example, from physical health to ADL's, IADL's, learning and problem solving, and social roles. Evaluations of functional abilities for guardianship tend to focus on basic, safe functioning in the intermediate areas in these models, assuming enough physical capacity for some minimal functioning (e.g., it is not necessary or possible to evaluate functional abilities in an individual who is in a persistent vegetative state), but not requiring a "high" level of social capacity (e.g., having optimal social and occupational success is not relevant to guardianship).

A general consideration of the domain of abilities often described in this area suggests the following grouping of abilities: Finances, Health, Independent Living, and Transportation (see Table 3). This grouping is handy for clinical evaluation as it combines conceptually similar tasks and is consistent with social services and legal mechanisms (statutes, case law, and regulations) specific to these areas. Each of these categories deserves a brief description.

FINANCES.   The area of finances includes managing assets and spending money, managing debts and obligations and paying bills, and also the more specific issues of contracts, disposition of property, and wills (i.e., including testamentary capacity; Heinik, Werner, & Lin, 1999; Regan & Gordon, 1997). Financial management can be conceptualized to involve three classes of cognitive skills: declarative knowledge, procedural knowledge, and judgment (Loeb, 1996; Marson, 2001; Willis, 1996). *Declarative knowledge* for finances involves the store of facts, concepts and events related to financial activities and accessible to conscious recollection, examples of which are knowledge regarding currency, bank statements, insurance, investments, and other personal financial data. *Procedural knowledge* for finances involves a variety of pragmatic skills, routines, and action sequences that are performance based and may be less accessible to conscious recollection, such as counting coins and currency, making

TABLE 3. CATEGORIES OF FUNCTIONAL TASKS AND CORRESPONDING SOCIAL AND LEGAL
INTERVENTIONS

Category	Tasks	Social Services	Legal Mechanisms

Finances	Managing assets
	Paying bills
	
	Writing will
		Bill paying services
		Money management
		  services
			Conservatorship
			Durable Power
			  of Attorney
			Representative
			  Payee
			Trustee

Health	Medical decision making
	Health care management
	  including medications
		Visiting nurse
		Pill box and pill
		  dispensing systems
		Telephone reminder
		  systems
			Guardianship
			Durable Power
			  of Attorney
			Healthcare
			  Proxy

Independent living	Household cleaning and
	  maintenance
	Laundry
	Meal shopping and
	  preparation
	Communication
	Personal hygiene
		Homemaker services
		
		Meals on wheels
		Emergency call
		  systems
		Home health aide
		Care Management
		Adult protective
		  services
		Assisted living
		Adult foster care
			Guardianship

Transportation	Driving
	
	Use of public transit
		Skill training classes
		
		Rides to appointments
		  and services
		Assisted public
		  transportation
			Driver testing
			  and license
			  revocation

change, writing checks and paying bills, using credit cards, and completing teller transactions. *Financial judgment* involves the capacity for rational, practical, considered and astute decisions in novel, ambiguous, or complex social situations. Examples of good financial judgment include minimizing the risk of financial loss, sensitivity to fraud and con schemes, invulnerability to coercion, and prudent investment.

HEALTH. The area of health includes consent to treatment and may be managed through health care proxies and durable powers of attorney for health care, or through guardianship. Consent to treatment may arise outside of the broader guardianship arena, often in the case of treatment refusal, and is discussed in detail in Chapter 9. However, consent to treatment, including psychiatric treatment for which some states have specific laws, may be a part of guardianship evaluations and of a guardian's obligations. Other areas of health care, such as managing day to day health (e.g., diet, wound care, and medication management) often come under the purview of guardianship.

INDEPENDENT LIVING. This third area is a broad category having to do with individuals' capacities to manage their person and place of residence. Specific functional tasks relevant to this domain include household cleaning and maintenance, laundry, meal shopping and preparation, and communication (e.g., talking by telephone and letter). Senior service agencies have a wealth of services to assist vulnerable adults in living independently including homemaker services that will come to the home to cook, clean, do laundry, prepare meals, and even tackle larger outside tasks such as lawns, leaves, and snow removal. Communication aids include large button telephones, assistive devices, and animals for the deaf and hard of hearing. Medical alert systems can be installed for seniors to activate in the event of a disabling emergency. With all these service options the question is usually whether the adult, with social support if available, can manage the safety and well being of their home and person, noting that some degree of risk is reasonable for all adults.

TRANSPORTATION. A narrower category of functional abilities concerns transportation and the capacity to drive. This question more often arises outside of the guardianship arena after an adult has had a series of motor vehicle accidents. Visual processing (Owsley et al., 1998) and attention (Parasuraman & Nestor, 1993) are important to driving, and direct assessment of driving is best (Hunt et al., 1997; Kapust & Weintraub, 1992).

Clinicians may also be asked to evaluate other specific functional tasks, although again, often these come up outside of guardianship *per se*, including the capacity to vote and the capacity to engage in social relationships such as marriage or sexual intimacy (Berger, 2000; Lichtenberg & Strzepek, 1990). However, any of these specific issues may be addressed in a guardianship evaluation, and when a plenary guardianship is granted decisions regarding these tasks become the responsibility of the guardian.

Causal Component

Almost all state codes require the establishment of a causal relationship between a medical or psychological condition and a deficiency in the abilities necessary to care for self and/or property. The deficit must be the product of some underlying, enduring, and disabling condition that currently is beyond the individual's ability to alter or control. This is of importance because there may be no need for a guardian if the functional deficiency can be modified or remediated easily. Alternatively, incompetence might be declared for only that period of time necessary for remediation; statutes generally provide for review of incompetency status, restoration of competency, and termination of guardianship when the need for it has diminished (see, generally, Sales et al., 1982).

States vary in how they describe the medical or psychological condition. Many states refer to general terms such as mental illness, mental disability, or mental condition. In a recent review, Anderer (1997) noted that 31 states make specific reference to chronic use of alcohol or drugs and 35 states make reference to physical illness or incapacity (added in some states to account for guardianship petitions for individuals with Alzheimer's disease). As states have undertaken guardianship reform, advanced age has been eliminated from statutes in recognition that advanced age itself does not imply deterioration in mental faculties, recognizing such wording as "blatantly discriminatory" (Wood, 2000).

This description of the causal issue might seem to suggest that the presence of an irreversible brain dysfunction or a chronic psychotic condition, in conjunction with functional deficits relevant for self-care, satisfies the causal question. In practice it might, although logically it does not. The apparent functional deficits may be coincidental to the disorder rather than caused by it. Brain dysfunctions, for example, occur in varying degrees and with considerably different consequences for different individuals. Some cerebral conditions may have few important consequences for everyday functioning of some individuals. The mere coexistence of brain dysfunction and functional ability deficits, therefore, does not necessarily establish a relation between them.

There are at least three types of circumstances in which apparent functional deficits, although occurring in conjunction with cerebral dysfunction, might be attributable to other causes. First, examiners selecting methods for assessing the elderly must consider several test-taking characteristics of this population that may produce measurement error. Included among these are limitations in hearing, vision, speed of processing, (Department of Veterans Affairs, 1997), susceptibility to fatigue for some elderly individuals (MacNeill & Lichtenberg, 1999), and the possibility that some elderly persons, and younger persons as well, will be reluctant to take formal tests because of fears of not doing well or because the process reminds them of school (LaRue, 1999). In addition, individual differences related to education, cohort, and ethnic differences may lead to misinterpretation of test scores by unqualified users (LaRue, 1999).

Judicious selection of assessment methods and careful interpretation by qualified evaluators should reduce error related to these characteristics (Moye, 2000). In addition, the error inherent in any instrument for assessing functional abilities will produce a need to evaluate abilities by several methods. These might include not only standardized test methods, but also methods for determining the examinee's functioning outside the examination setting.

The second general circumstance derives from perspectives in gerontology concerning the effect of environmental circumstances on the manifest capacities of the elderly (see, e.g., Lawton, 1990; Lawton, Windley, & Byerts, 1982; Scheidt & Schaie, 1978). An elderly individual's functional abilities at a given point in time might reflect an interaction between the individual and an environmental situation, rather than merely a personal deficit. For example, an elderly person's self-care skills may seem deficient because of a current living arrangement that has allowed the atrophy of personal skills or has discouraged autonomous functioning. The deficiencies might be remediated by planned change in the elderly individual's environmental circumstances. The mere presence of a potential biological cause (e.g., brain dysfunction), therefore, does not rule out an alternative, environmental explanation. Older adults may be particularly sensitive to changes in environment and at higher risk for confusion or delirium in acute medical and psychiatric settings than individuals at other ages (Broshek & Marcopulos, 1999). Older adults may appear to be functionally impaired when instead they are experiencing an acute confusional state related to infection, fever, use of long acting benzodiazepines or narcotics (Broshek & Marcopulos, 1999). This points to the need for multidisciplinary assessment and multiple evaluations, as well as consideration of the role of the environmental circumstances on the individual's test performance.

A third alternative to brain dysfunction as an explanation for current functional deficits is the possibility that the deficiency might have predated the organic condition. The importance of determining premorbid functioning in cerebrally impaired individuals is widely recognized as essential to an effective determination of the relation between current brain dysfunction and functional ability, and underscores the importance of taking a careful history gathered from the individual, family, and medical records (LaRue, 1999). Some adults who have always had some degree of cognitive impairment and some propensity for eccentric decision making will be targeted for guardianships only when they become older, because of ageism or other inappropriate motivations such as financial exploitation.

Examining the potential causal explanations for functional deficits in the elderly, therefore, presents a considerable challenge to the forensic examiner. The evaluator must be sure of the reliability and validity of the assessment; the assessment must reflect true deficits and these deficits must be meaningful for the individual's environmental demands. The evaluator must also be clear about the time line of the onset of the organic condition and functional deficits to insure that they began on or around the same time. Interviews with informants including family members, neighbors, physicians, social workers, or home health care agencies may be required.

Neuropsychological data can also help in the integration of diagnostic and functional data. There is a growing body of literature to establish the ways in which cognitive deficits may predict behavioral deficits. Performance on ADL's has been linked to specific neuropsychological tests and general cognition (Lichtenberg et al., 1994; Moore & Lichtenberg; Lowenstein et al., 1992; Nadler et al., 1993; Searight et al., 1989). Performance on tests measuring visual-spatial problem solving and memory has been linked to performance on tasks assessing medication management (Isaac & Tambly, 1993; Palmer & Dobson, 1994; Richardson, Nadler, & Malloy, 1995) as well as financial management (Richardson et al., 1995). Driving skills have been related to tests of general cognition, visual attention and memory (Odenheimer et al., 1994).

Not all incompetency cases will require the same degree of detail in data collection within the medical, neuropsychological, functional ability, and social environmental spheres of the competency assessment. Yet most cases probably require some attention to each of these spheres. The diverse expertise required by these assessments has led some commentators to recommend (Barnes, 1992; Hafemeister & Sales, 1984), and some states to require (Wang, Burns, & Hommel, 1990), multidisciplinary teams for evaluating disabled adults in guardianship cases.

Interactive Component

The construct of incompetence to care for self and/or property is not merely a question of the absolute level of functional deficit caused by physical or mental disability. The individual's capacities must also be described and considered in relation to several contextual factors, including the situational demands (e.g., living arrangements or financial assets) and social supports or stressors (Krauss & Sales, 1997). One of the legal fact finder's objectives is to determine the degree of incongruence between the person's abilities and these contextual demands. Thus, the outcome of a capacity evaluation for guardianship is the clinical interpretation of assessment data in light of the interaction of everyday functioning and contextual factors.

Observers of guardianship proceedings frequently have referred to this interactive quality of competence determinations. Similarly, Sales et al. (1982) observed that the type and degree of abilities perceived as necessary to care for property depends on the size, type and complexity of the estate. Inability to manage one's estate sometimes occurs not because of changes in the elderly person's functioning, but rather because of changes in property or income, to which the elderly person might not have adjusted. Thus, the evaluator should assess recent changes in the individual's financial or social situation.

Some disabled individuals may be so deficient in relevant functional abilities that they would be unable adequately to care for themselves or property under almost any independent living arrangement or financial circumstances. Some cases, however, will not have such extreme disability. In these instances, the absolute level and type of functional ability is not the sole question. Given two disabled persons with equal degrees and types of incapacity, one may be declared incompetent to manage some portion of self-care whereas the other may not, if the environmental circumstances of the former are more demanding than those of the latter. The law's declaration of the disabled person as incompetent obscures the fact that the legal competence construct focuses on a person-environment interaction as incongruent, therefore representing an ecological condition of incompetency that endangers the disabled person.

The interactive perspective in guardianship law is paralleled by gerontological theory emphasizing the congruence of person-environment fit (Kahana, 1982) or environmental press (Lawton, 1982; 1983). Descriptions of environments for purposes of evaluating the disabled person's capacities to function in those settings must take into account not only the physical environment, but the social characteristics of environments as well. For example, the presence or absence of sources of social support-relatives, friends, or supportive agencies-may enhance or frustrate the person's ability to function, thus creating greater or lesser demands for self-management skills. Social supports, such as neighbors who willingly watch out for and assist an elderly adult, may allow the use of guardianship alternatives. Conversely, other social situations may demand a move towards a more intensive intervention such as conservatorship by adult protective agencies, for example when a relative is accessing an elder's assets not for the well being of the elder but for personal use, such as to support drug abuse. Because such financial considerations may not always be readily apparent, the evaluator should be attentive and inquisitive about the social context and related financial outcomes of guardianship petitions.

Some assessment methods designed for use with the elderly attempt to identify not only the individual's functional abilities, but also the physical demands and social supports of their present environments. These instruments, two of which are reviewed later in this chapter, may provide data necessary for the forensic examiner's attempt to describe congruencies and incongruencies between a disabled individual's abilities and environmental demands.

The impact of the interactive characteristic also relates to the person side of the person-environment interaction. An individual's awareness of deficit or insight may be key in determining how or whether they might be able to use modified environments to enhance decisional impairments (Anderson & Tranel, 1989). For example, many home health care agencies have money management services, which can help the individual in balancing a check book and other minor financial transactions, but only if the individual is insightful about his or her deficit and maintains some judgment about making decisions about self or property in light of those deficits. The individual's preferences, values, and coping strategies contribute to contextual considerations. For example, loneliness or a desire for more contact with family may underlie a vulnerable adult's request for instatement or removal of a guardian.

This interactive characteristic of competence is seen also in the move toward limited guardianship that supports the concept of *least restrictive alternative* in guardianship proceedings (Anderer, 1990; Verma & Silberfeld, 1997), as well as the idea that incapacitated persons still participate as fully as possible in decisions affecting them (e.g., Idaho code § 15-5-503) and the emerging concept of assisted decision making (Gordon, 2000). This concept requires a consideration of alternative "environmental" arrangements that might satisfy the individual's need for protection without a declaration of incompetence or assignment of a guardian. In essence, this perspective requires a search for congruent matches between a person and the situational, social, and individual contexts rather than focusing merely on the individual's functional deficiencies as a determinant of incompetence.

Judgmental and Dispositional Components

The law describes no absolute degree of functional deficiency or person-situation incongruence that defines when an individual should be declared incompetent and in need of a guardian. Statutes frequently employ terms like *sufficient, grave,* or *substantial* to refer broadly to the necessary degree of deficit, yet these are little more than markers signifying that a highly discretionary judgment must be made. That is, the determination of incompetence requires a judgment that the individual's functional deficit and the degree of situational demand are sufficiently incongruent to warrant a finding of incompetence.

This judgment also requires a consideration of the dispositional consequences of incompetence for the disabled person. The fact finder must determine when the potential benefits of guardianship have reached some threshold, defined only by a sense of justice, warranting the consequences of nullification of fundamental rights and freedoms.

Empirical information discussed in relation to the other characteristics of the legal competency construct clearly is relevant for making competence decisions about disabled adults. Yet it cannot answer the ultimate question of an individual's legal competence or incompetence, because that question requires the application of moral and social assumptions to the data.

Therefore, the purpose of a competence assessment for guardianship cases should be to describe what the individual can and cannot do, the apparent neurological (or other) reasons for those observed deficits, their relation to environmental demands, and (if possible) the practical consequences for the individual with or without a guardian in various, relevant residential or financial arrangements. If there is every reason to believe that the disabled person will perish or be in great peril without guardianship, the examiner should say so and explain why. Yet the question of the individual's legal competence or incompetence logically cannot be answered solely by any of these scientific data or opinions.

This is why it is important that clinicians distinguish between the clinical use of the term *incompetence* and its legal use. Clinicians who make evaluations of an adult's decisional and self-management abilities may have different tolerance for risk and a different sense of professional and personal liability. Clinicians involved in discharge planning for adults may have different opinions about whether an elderly adult's difficulties exceed an acceptable risk threshold (Clemens & Hayes, 1997), perhaps related to experience in the field or, for some, ageism. For this reason, it is important that judgmental and dispositional issues should be the responsibility of courts rather than clinicians.

REVIEW OF FORENSIC ASSESSMENT INSTRUMENTS

Clinicians who are asked to evaluate an adult's capacity to care for self or financial resources will likely rely on four sources of standardized assessment data:

- independent activities of daily living (IADL) rating scales
- specific guardianship or conservatorship instruments
- neuropsychological or cognitive testing
- mental health diagnostic interviews and scales.

It is beyond the scope of this chapter to review procedures for neuropsy-chological testing and diagnostic assessment, although a few points on these instruments will be made.

As noted, neuropsychological assessment is likely to be a key compo-nent of assessments of capacities for independent functioning. They help to describe the extent of cognitive and decisional impairments, may assist in differential diagnosis and prognosis, and may help to clarify the link between disabling conditions and functional outcomes and between personal deficits and environmental resources. Furthermore, the bulk of referrals for assessments regarding guardianship will be for elderly adults and the majority of these will be for adults with dementing illnesses. Since deficits in memory and cognition are the hallmark of dementing illness, an assessment of these deficits is key. Neuropsychological assessment is discussed by Lezak (1995) and LaRue (1992) and others.

In most cases a brief screening of cognition (e.g., Mini-Mental Status Exam) would not be sufficient to be informative, but a full neuropsycholog-ical battery will not always be necessary. Evaluators may wish to select spe-cific tests that are likely to be informative about the specific capacity in question (e.g., a test of arithmetic when financial capacities are questioned) and about the disabling condition presented (e.g., tests of memory when the individual presents with dementia). Visual-spatial problem solving and visual memory appear to be especially predictive for some tasks of every-day functioning (Isaac & Tambly, 1993; Palmer & Dobson, 1994; Richardson, Nadler, & Malloy, 1995). The recent revision of the *Wechsler Adult Intelligence Scale-III* (Wechsler, 1997) has adapted many stimuli and procedures to be more suitable for evaluating visual-spatial problem solving in the elderly (e.g., enlarged stimuli). There are many visual memory tests from which to select, including the *Wechsler Memory Scale-III* (Wechsler, 1997), the *Biber Figure Test* (Glosser, Goodglass, & Biber, 1989), the *Continuous Paired Associate Test* (Newton & Brown, 1985), and the *Continuous Visual Memory Test* (Trahan & Larrabee, 1988) (see generally, Moye, 1997). Executive func-tion also is often important to assess in competency evaluations (Marson et al., 1995; Reid-Proctor, Galin, & Cummings, 2001).

A large number of instruments have been developed to assess the mental or psychological capacities of elderly individuals, as well as symp-toms of psychopathology in the elderly (see Lichtenberg, 1999). These are not reviewed here merely because they do not focus on functional abilities of everyday life, but rather on such general constructs as depression, anx-iety, delusions, and behavioral self-control. Nevertheless, many of them may be of considerable benefit in examinations in guardianship cases, in order to obtain information with which to provide psychological explana-tions for functional deficits.

The remainder of this chapter reviews instruments developed to assess everyday functioning, including IADL rating scales and guardianship or conservatorship instruments. The latter are more rightly considered FAI's, but IADL instruments are close and may be especially useful in forensic evaluations.

Regarding IADL rating scales, a number of scales have been designed to assess independent activities of daily living (some including sections on activities of daily living and cognitive abilities) by means of patient or informant report. These scales are useful in organizing assessments of and reports about functioning and are appropriate when there is good evidence that an informant's report is reliable or when the examiner has observed the patient completing tasks in the home or residential setting. Research has suggested that patient report of IADL performance can be reliable for some patients, especially those with minimal cognitive difficulties (Myers, Holliday, Harvey, & Hutchinson, 1993). However, as cognitive deficits worsen, a significant percentage of patients are not reliable informants of their IADL's (Sager et al., 1992). Performance based scales are useful in determining functioning in such cases.

IADL scales selected for inclusion in this chapter met certain specific criteria. They:

- employed a multidimensional approach;
- focused on instrumental or higher-order activities of daily living;
- had multiple studies or citations; and
- were appropriate for use with older adults.

Instruments that assess and describe only the most basic ADL functions probably will be of limited importance in forensic assessments for guardianship cases, for which reason they were not selected for review. Examiners who do have a need for them may choose from several instruments with adequate conceptual and empirical backgrounds, such as the *Katz Index of ADL* (Katz et al., 1963) or the *Barthel Index* (Mahoney & Barthel, 1965).

Several promising scales that were not reviewed (because they did not meet certain inclusion criteria) deserve special mention for completeness:

- *Assessment of Living Skills and Resources* (ALSAR; Williams et al., 1991)
- *Comprehensive Assessment and Referral Evaluation* (CARE; Gurland et al., 1977) (assessing situational and environmental resources)
- *Performance Assessment of Self-Care Skills* (PASS; McCue, Rogers, & Goldstein, 1990)
- *Structured Assessment of Independent Living Skills* (SAILS; Mahurin, DeBettignies, & Pirozzolo, 1991).

In addition, the chapter does not review occupational therapy instruments such as the *Kohlman Evaluation of Living Skills* (KELS; McGourty, 1979) and the *Functional Independence Measure* (FIM; Research Foundation, 1987), because they tend to be developed for and used by occupational therapists only.

In the remainder of the chapter, nine instruments are reviewed under three headings referring to their type:

A. 3 IADL instruments based on interview
B. 2 IADL instruments based on performance, and
C. 4 instruments designed specifically for guardianship and conservatorship evaluations.

A. IADL INSTRUMENTS BASED ON INTERVIEW OR OBSERVATION

ADULT FUNCTIONAL ADAPTIVE BEHAVIOR SCALE (AFABS)

Author

Philip S. Pierce

Author Affiliation

Department of Veterans Affairs, Togus, ME

Primary Reference

Pierce, P. S. (1989). *Adult Functional Adaptive Behavior Scale (AFABS): Manual of Directions (1989 Edition)*. Togus, ME: Author.

Description

The *Adult Functional Adaptive Behavior Scale* (AFABS) was developed to assist in the assessment of ADL and IADL functions in the elderly to evaluate their capacity for personal responsibility and the matching of a client to a placement setting (c).

The AFABS consists of 14 items. Six items rate ADL's: eating, ambulation, toileting, dressing, grooming, and managing (keeping clean) personal area. Two items tap IADL's: managing money and managing health needs. Six items tap cognitive and social functioning: socialization, environmental orientation (ranging from able to locate room up through able to travel independently in the community), reality orientation (aware of person, place, time, and current events), receptive speech communication, expressive communication, and memory. Items are rated on four levels: 0.0 representing a lack of the capacity, 0.5 representing some capacity with assistance, 1.0 representing some capacity without assistance, and 1.5 representing independent functioning in that area. Individual scores are summed to receive a total score in adaptive functioning.

The AFABS assesses adaptive functioning through interviewing an informant well acquainted with the functioning of the individual in question. The informant data is combined with the examiner's observation of and interaction with the client to arrive at final ratings. The AFABS is designed for relatively easy and brief administration (approximately 15 minutes). The author recommends it be administered only by professionals experienced in psychological and functional assessment, specifically a psychologist, occupational therapist, or psychometrician, although research with the AFABS has also utilized psychiatric nurses and social workers trained in its administration.

The AFABS is administered in a semi-structured format, after client observation and medical record review. During the administration the examiner asks the informant about each area of functioning, first asking a general question as written on the rating form (e.g., "does he eat totally by himself or does he require assistance with preparing and eating meals?"). Follow-up questions are then asked on the basis of clinical judgment until the exact level of performance can be rated (c).

Conceptual Basis

CONCEPTUAL DEFINITION. The AFABS was based on Heber's (a) construct of adaptive behavior developed for the developmentally disabled. Heber proposed that adaptive behavior has two components: being independent in personal function/maintenance and meeting societal rules for personal responsibility. The AFABS focuses on the first of these as a prerequisite for being able to have personal responsibility (d).

OPERATIONAL DEFINITION. Specific items were developed through a review of journal articles, texts, and patient records as well as clinical experience in the fields of developmental disabilities, mental retardation, and psychogeriatrics. Items were piloted and revised in consideration of clarity, content coverage, ease of administration, and age-appropriateness (c). Kerby, Wentworth, and Cotten (b) note that the AFABS is well suited for older clients in contrast to other adaptive behavior scales.

CRITIQUE. A strength of the AFABS is its conceptual basis in a theory of adaptive behavior which is modified for use with the elderly. The AFABS may be well suited to answer questions for evaluations concerning level of placement and requisite supervision. Many of the domains are legally relevant for conceptualization of an individual's functional capacities, including communication, but may not adequately sample issues of decision making and judgment for all issues involved in a specific guardianship. Similarly, an item for managing money relative to adaptive behavior is included, but may be inadequate for determining need for conservatorship.

Psychometric Development

STANDARDIZATION. The AFABS manual provides description of each of the 14 content areas and examples for ratings on each of four levels. A rating form provides a place to rate each item and to note problem areas (e.g., hearing impairment) and daily (e.g., "sundowning") or monthly (e.g., delirium) mental status changes.

RELIABILITY. The Cronbach's alpha reliability coefficient was .95 and the Spearman-Brown and Guttman split-half reliability coefficients were both .96 (d) in a mixed sample ($n = 432$). Similar internal consistency reliability was found in a sample of psychiatric inpatients ($n = 91$), yielding an alpha coefficient of .93 and split half coefficient of .97.

NORMS. Mean score and standard deviation are available for 25 community-dwelling elderly adults who served as a control sample in one study (d).

CRITIQUE. Internal consistency reliability is excellent. Additional normative data are needed. The availability of a clear manual and test rating form is a plus. The scale is intended as a semi-structured interview, and as such, does not provide standardized items for asking specific questions or rating clients' performance. This suggests that adequate training and experience may be necessary to obtain accurate estimations of ratings. Studies of inter-rater reliability would help to establish the extent to which it is possible for independent raters to agree given this format.

Construct Validation

In a factor analytic study of 432 adults from various settings, the AFABS yielded one factor with an eigenvalue greater than 1.00 (d).

Kerby, Wentworth, and Cotten (b) examined the relationship between the AFABS and two other adaptive behavior scales. They found significant correlation between the AFABS and other scores ($r = .72$ and .85), providing support for the construct validity of the AFABS.

CRITIQUE. These studies support the author's contention that the AFABS measures a unidimensional construct, adaptive behavior. Additional studies comparing the AFABS with ADL and IADL scales developed for use with elderly populations would further support its construct validity with older adults.

Predictive or Classificatory Utility

In a study of predictive utility, the relationship between the AFABS total score and a 1–6 "level of placement" was determined (1–5 = inpatient wards graded in their level of supervision and 6 = community senior housing) for 25 community dwelling elderly adults and 126 residents of a multi-level state mental health institution (d). The Spearman *rho* coefficient between the AFABS total score and placement level was statistically significant ($r = .86$). An ANOVA comparing the mean score at each of six levels of placement was also statistically significant, and mean score differences on the AFABS between each level of placement were significant in post-hoc tests.

A second study of predictive validity utilized similar methods to compare AFABS total score and a 1–3 "level of placement" for 91 psychiatric inpatients (e). The Spearman *rho* coefficient was statistically significant ($r = .71$) as were ANOVA and post-hoc tests comparing mean AFABS scores at each of three levels of placement.

CRITIQUE. These studies suggest that the AFABS can be useful in predicting the level of supervision required by adults.

Potential for Expressing Person-Situation Congruency

In that the AFABS begins with a review of history and ends with a review of special problem areas, it would allow for interpretation of adaptive behaviors within a personal and situational context. However, there are not specific items built into the AFABS item ratings to assess person-situation congruency.

References

(a) Heber, R. F. (1961). A manual of terminology and classification in mental retardation (2nd ed.). *American Journal of Mental Deficiency*. Monograph Supplement.

(b) Kerby, D. S., Wentworth, R., & Cotten, P. D. (1989). Measuring adaptive behavior in elderly developmentally disabled clients. *The Journal of Applied Gerontology, 8*, 261–267.

(c) Pierce, P. S. (1989). *Adult Functional Adaptive Behavior Scale (AFABS): Manual of Directions (1989 Edition)*. Togus, ME: Author.

(d) Spirrison, C. L. & Pierce, P. S. (1992). Psychometric characteristics of the Adult Functional Adaptive Behavior Scale (AFABS). *Gerontologist, 32*, 234–239.

(e) Spirrison, C. L., & Sewell, S. M. (1996). The adult functional adaptive behavior scale
     (AFABS) and psychiatric inpatients: Indices of reliability and validity. *Assessment, 3,*
     387–391.

MULTIDIMENSIONAL FUNCTIONAL ASSESSMENT QUESTIONNAIRE (MFAQ)

Authors

Older Americans Resources and Services (OARS) Project

Authors' Affiliation

Center for the Study of Aging and Human Development, Duke
University Medical Center, Durham, NC

Primary Reference

Center for the Study of Aging and Human Development (1978). *Multidimensional functional
assessment: The OARS methodology.* Durham, NC: Duke University.

Description

The *Multidimensional Functional Assessment Questionnaire* (MFAQ)
was developed to provide a reliable and valid method for characterizing
elderly individuals and for describing elderly populations, in ways that
would be "useful to clinicians ... to program analysts, to resource alloca-
tors, and to research scientists in a variety of disciplines" (i, p. 4). The
MFAQ supersedes the nearly identical Community Survey Questionnaire
(CSQ, a predecessor which also was developed by the Duke Center). Both
instruments frequently have been called the OARS, in reference to the
program that developed the instrument throughout the 1970s. The MFAQ
or the CSQ was already in use by well over 50 service centers, researchers,
or practitioners nationally when the MFAQ was published (1978).

The MFAQ is a structured interview with 72 items (105 questions)
requiring about one hour to administer. Part A deals with the examinee's
functioning, and Part B elicits information about the services recently
used by the examinee.

Part A provides information in five areas of functioning (m, pp. 68–70):

- *Social resources:* extent, quality, and availability of social interactions (e.g., whom one lives with, in whom one confides, who is
  willing to provide care in case of illness).

- *Economic resources:* financial ability to meet needs and obtain services (e.g., employment status, sources of income, home ownership).
- *Mental health:* mental status and symptomatology (e.g., orientation, memory, symptoms such as anxiety and depression).
- *Physical health:* physical status (e.g., number of doctor visits, medical prescription drugs, physical handicaps and extent of disability).
- *Activities of daily living:* instrumental-activities necessary to maintain household; and physical-capacity to take care of own bodily functions.

The Activities of Daily Living (ADL) dimension assesses 14 functions including both instrumental and physical ADL's. *Instrumental ADL's* include: use telephone, use transportation, shopping, prepare meals, do housework, take medicine, handle money. *Physical ADL's* include: eat, dress oneself, care for own appearance, walk, get in/out of bed, bath, getting to bathroom, continence.

Each of these ADL functions is represented by one item in which examinees are asked whether they can perform the function. For example, (b, p. 169):

> Can you use the telephone ...
> 2–without help, including looking up numbers and dialing
> 1–with some help
> 0–or are you completely unable to use the telephone?

Part B of the MFAQ assesses the individual's utilization of services, that is, whether and to what extent the examinee has received assistance from various community programs, agencies, relatives, or friends, especially within the latest six months. Questioning also includes the examinee's perceived need for the various services. Services items focus on:

- transportation
- social/recreational services
- employment services
- sheltered employment
- educational services
- remedial training
- mental health services
- psychotropic drugs
- personal care services
- nursing care
- physical therapy
- continuous supervision

- checking services (i.e., services that "check on" the elderly individual periodically)
- relocation and placement service
- homemaker-household services
- meal preparation
- administrative, legal, and protective services
- systematic multidimensional evaluation of status
- coordination, information and referral services

Answers to items in both Parts A and B are given numerical (ordinal) values, but they are not summed to produce scores. Part B answers are left at this level of recording, whereas Part A answers are considered by the examiner when arriving at a rating for each of the five domains of functioning. The examinee may be rated 1 to 6 on each of the five dimensions, with the ratings carrying the following labels: 1 = *excellent*, 2 = *good*, 3 = *mildly impaired*, 4 = *moderately impaired*, 5 = *severely impaired*, 6 = *totally impaired*. This is a subjective rating; the examiner is not instructed how to translate answers in a domain of functioning into a rating for the domain.

The MFAQ manual offers five ways to use these ratings to summarize the examinee's current level of functioning (m).

First, the examinee's *SEMPA profile* (from the first letters of the five dimensions of functioning in Part A) is simply a listing of the five ratings given to the examinee in the order specified by the acronym. For example, a 2-5-3-5-5 examinee has good Social Resources (2), is severely impaired in Economic Resources (5), is mildly impaired in the domain of Mental Health (3), and so forth.

Second, the *Cumulative Impairment Score* (CIS) is the sum of the examinee's five ratings. The above examinee would have a CIS of 20. CIS scores may range from 5 to 30, and these scores are sometimes used to form classes of individuals (e.g., 5–17 and 18–30) for research or descriptive purposes.

Third, examinees may be described in terms of their *number of significant impairments*, a significant impairment being a rating of 4 to 6. Thus the above examinee would be said to have three significant impairments.

Fourth, the above definition of significant impairment may be used to designate the examinee as belonging to one of 32 functionally equivalent classes. These classes cover all of the possible combinations of significant impairments on the five functional dimensions. Class 0 individuals have no significant functional impairments, and Class 31 individuals have significant functional impairment on all five dimensions. A chart in the manual (b, p. 67) allows one to identify the above examinee (2-5-3-5-5), who has significant functional impairment on the Economic, Physical, and Activities of Daily Living dimensions, as belonging to Class 21.

Fifth, a major MFAQ study in Cleveland (j) used a combination of the above criteria to classify individuals on eight levels of well-being (k, p. 91).

Examinees may be compared on many of these summary indexes to large validation samples of elderly individuals described in the manual.

Conceptual Basis

CONCEPT DEFINITION.   The Duke University group responsible for the MFAQ included a wide range of disciplines: physicians, social workers, nurses, sociologists, psychologists, economists, and systems analysts. This group chose the five dimensions of the MFAQ, guided by a survey of literature and clinical experience to determine what information was necessary to characterize functioning of the elderly (d).

OPERATIONAL DEFINITION.   Many items were drawn from other instruments and were used without change or were modified. Each item had to meet one of several criteria concerning known or potential reliability and validity, relevance for present theory, or satisfaction of certain professional standards (d, p. 17). The Activities of Daily Living scale, which assesses instrumental and physical functioning in everyday life, was borrowed directly from an instrument with the same name by Lawton and Brody (l).

CRITIQUE.   The choice and definition of concepts for the MFAQ are a product of consensus among professionals of various disciplines who worked with the elderly and were aware of practical needs for describing their functioning, and literature review. This is an acceptable method for selecting concepts, and the widespread use of the instrument suggests that the group's consensus is supported by the perspectives of mental health professionals who were not party to the MFAQ's authorship. The utility of the concepts from a legal perspective is less certain, because judges' or lawyers' opinions apparently were not included in selection of MFAQ dimensions.

At face value, the items of the MFAQ in most of the five domains seem sufficiently comprehensive with regard to functioning of the elderly. On the other hand, one can question whether specific abilities in the Activities of Daily Living dimension are sampled adequately, because each ability (e.g., management of money, use of transportation) is represented by only one item.

The test authors chose merely to ask examinees whether they could perform particular functions, rather than actually testing their ability to do so. This operational choice is not explained, and it raises the question of the relation between examinees' self reports of abilities and their actual abilities. Two studies have investigated the relationship between self reports on the MFAQ and direct assessment and found consistency for healthy older adults but potential inconsistency with increasing dementia. Rogers et al. (n) found good agreement between self reports and direct assessments at the initial time of evaluation for 58 elderly subjects. However, on subsequent assessments six months later, depressed patients' self reports continued to agree with direct assessments while demented patients' self reports showed widening discrepancy with direct assessments. Doble et al. (c) found a similar pattern for 64 elderly subjects with self reports and direct assessments of motor ability; the pattern, however, was found for the non-demented subsample and not the demented subsample.

Psychometric Development

STANDARDIZATION.   The manual (b) provides very careful instructions for the MFAQ interview and helpful suggestions for interviewing the elderly. It encourages users to obtain training in the MFAQ interview through a training program offered at the Center for the Study of Aging and Human Development at Duke University. Instructions for scoring individual items are clear and objective, although criteria for assigning a rating to each of the five domains allow considerable room for subjective judgment and discretion.

RELIABILITY.   Test-retest reliability for the MFAQ has not been reported. Results with the CSQ (an earlier instrument nearly identical to the MFAQ) suggest that correlations between administrations five weeks apart are best for the Economic and Activities of Daily Living domains (.79 and .81), and poorest for the Mental Health domain (.32–.42) (e).

Interrater agreement for the MFAQ (using summary ratings on each domain) produced intraclass correlations of .80 or better for the Social, Mental Health, and Activities domains, and was lowest (.66) for the Physical Health domain (h). Intrarater reliability for the MFAQ has not been examined, but results with the CSQ indicated generally consistent ratings when examiners rerated their own protocols 12 to 15 months after initial ratings (e).

NORMS.   The manual (b) provides means and standard deviations of ratings on each domain for large samples of elderly persons seen by the Duke University Center. Separate norms are provided for elderly persons sampled randomly from the community, elderly who were referred to a clinic for age-related problems, and elderly living in institutions. A report by Fillenbaum (f) provides additional normative data for individual IADL items for three large community samples of elderly adults.

CRITIQUE.   Standardization and basic information on reliability suggest that the MFAQ can be employed with consistency by examiners. The available normative data for summary ratings (CIS data) and items

(IADL) are with large enough samples to lend confidence to their stability. Additional normative data for individual subscales on Part A and Part B would be useful.

Construct Validation

Fillenbaum (f) described a factor analysis of instrumental and physical ADL items of the MFAQ for two samples, finding two factors with instrumental items on one factor and physical items on another, except for the 75+ age group which found three factors with instrumental items on one factor and physical items split between two factors. Using a factor score of .65 as the acceptance criterion, only five items could be considered to load onto the IADL scale (travel, shop, meals, housework, finances) while two items had insufficient scores (telephone, medication).

Whitelaw and Liang (o) used structural equation modeling to confirm a model in which MFAQ instrumental and physical ADL ratings were linked in a causal framework to functional limitations and physical health using two large elderly samples. They suggest that reports of functional limitations may be a meaningful component of self-rated health.

Blazer (a) reported intercorrelations between scales of the latter instrument. The Social and Economic domains correlated with the other three domains in the .30 to .40 range, whereas the Mental Health and Physical Health domains correlated with the Activities of Daily Living domain in the .50 to .70 range for several different research samples.

Fillenbaum and Smyer (h) examined the relations between various external criteria and summary ratings on four of the five MFAQ dimensions. The Economic domain correlated .68 with scores on another scale (e) based on total income and assets. The Mental Health domain ratings correlated .67 with geropsychiatrists' ratings based on their clinical interviews. Physical Health ratings correlated .82 with physicians' ratings based on their personal examinations, and Activities of Daily Living ratings correlated .89 with the ratings of physical therapists who conducted home visits to examine individuals' capacities to perform everyday functions. Research with the CSQ (e) suggests that the Activities of Daily Living scale produces significantly different estimates of everyday functioning compared to ratings based on clinical interviews, with the clinicians' estimates tending to indicate poorer functioning than the Activities scale.

As previously noted, two studies found good agreement, for nondemented subjects, between scores on the IADL of the MFAQ and scores on instruments that directly assess functional status (c, h).

The MFAQ manual (a, e) reports differences in CSQ scores between three samples: a random sample of 997 community residents over 65 years of age, 98 clients 50 years or older who were referred to a clinic for age-related problems, and 102 elderly individuals in institutions. Differences in expected directions are shown for summary ratings on the five domains, for Cumulative Impairment Scores, and for frequencies of subjects within impaired and unimpaired classes. Evidence for statistical significance of differences, however, is not offered.

Fillenbaum (f) reported the extent of ability to perform IADL's for three groups of community dwelling elderly adults from different states; percentage endorsement is provided separately for each group with no statistically significant differences between the three groups.

CRITIQUE. The initial validity research with the MFAQ, together with past research on its predecessor instrument, provides some evidence that the MFAQ scales measure the aspects of functioning that they claim to measure. Many types of research still need to be accomplished, however, in order to provide clear support for interpretations of MFAQ scores (for example, statistical comparison of criterion groups of elderly individuals living in various degrees of autonomy and dependence).

Predictive or Classificatory Utility

There have been no studies of the ability of MFAQ scales to predict future functioning under specific conditions, or to correctly classify elderly individuals according to their levels of adaptation and functioning in everyday life.

Fillenbaum (f) studied the relationship between five items on the MFAQ IADL scale (travel, shop, meals, housework, finances) and survival rate. Initial IADL ratings were inversely related to the one-year death rate, with those unable to perform any IADL's initially having the highest death rate one year later.

CRITIQUE. Numerous additional studies (not cited here) have used the MFAQ as one measure among many in epidemiological surveys or in regards to resource utilization, but there is no research on its utility in predicting future level of care or legal competency status for clinical groups. This is probably related to the MFAQ's history as a tool developed for use more in describing large samples in survey research than for making specific predictions about individual elderly adults in clinical settings. Mental health professionals are in need of this research in order to facilitate predictive interpretation with MFAQ data for these purposes.

Potential for Expressing Person-Situation Congruency

The Social and Economic items in the MFAQ may be useful in describing the nature of the elderly individual's current environmental circumstances, or at least the individual's perceptions of the demands of current living arrangements.

The description of person-situation congruency might be enhanced by developing normative MFAQ data for samples of persons living successfully in settings with varying degrees of autonomy or structured assistance. For example, greater incongruence would be suggested if an individual's MFAQ ratings were significantly greater (more impaired) than the normative ratings for persons living successfully in a particular environment.

References

(a) Blazer, D. (1978). The OARS Durham surveys: Description and application. In Center for the Study of Aging and Human Development, *Multidimensional functional assessment: The OARS methodology* (pp. 75–88). Durham, NC: Duke University.

(b) Center for the Study of Aging and Human Development (1978). *Multidimensional functional assessment: The OARS methodology.* Durham, NC: Duke University.

(c) Doble, S. E., Fisk, J. D., MacPherson, K. M., Fisher, A. G., & Rockwood, K. (1997). Measuring functional competency in older persons with Alzheimer's disease. *International Psychogeriatrics, 9*, 25–38.

(d) Fillenbaum, G. (1978a). Conceptualization and development of the Multidimensional Functional Assessment Questionnaire. In Center for the Study of Aging and Human Development, *Multidimensional functional assessment: The OARS methodology* (pp. 16–24). Durham, NC: Duke University.

(e) Fillenbaum, G. (1978b). Validity and reliability of the Multidimensional Functional Assessment Questionnaire. In Center for the Study of Aging and Human Development, *Multidimensional Functional assessment: The OARS methodology* (pp. 25–35). Durham, NC: Duke University.

(f) Fillenbaum, G. G. (1985). Screening the elderly: A brief instrumental activities of daily living measure. *Journal of the American Geriatrics Society, 33*, 698–706.

(g) Fillenbaum, G., & Maddox, G. (1977). *Assessing the functional status of LRHS participants: Technique, findings, implications* (Technical report No. 2). Durham, NC: Duke University, Center for the Study of Aging and Human Development.

(h) Fillenbaum, G., & Smyer, M. (1981). The development, validity, and reliability of the OARS Multidimensional Functional Assessment Questionnaire. *Journal of Gerontology, 36*, 428–434.

(i) Fillenbaum, C., Dellinger, D., Maddox, G., & Pfeiffer, E. (1978). Assessment of individual functional status in a program evaluation and resource allocation model. In Center for the Study of Aging and Human Development, *Multidimensional functional assessment: The OARS methodology* (pp. 3–12). Durham, NC: Duke University.

(j) Laurie, W. (1978a). Population assessment for program evaluation. In G. Maddox (Ed.), *Assessment and evaluation strategies in aging,* (pp. 100–110). Durham, NC: Duke University.

(k) Laurie, W. (1978b). The Cleveland experience: Functional status and services use. In Center for the Study of Aging and Human Development, *Multidimensional functional assessment: The OARS methodology* (pp. 89–99). Durham, NC: Duke University.

(l) Lawton, M., & Brody, E. (1969). Assessment of older people: Self-maintaining and instrumental activities of daily living. *Gerontologist, 9*, 179–186.

(m) Pfeiffer, E. (1978). Ways of combining functional assessment data. In Center for the Study of Aging and Human Development, *Multidimensional functional assessment: The OARS methodology* (pp. 65–71). Durham, NC: Duke University.

(n) Rogers, J. C., Holm, M. B., Goldstein, G., McCue, M., & Nussbaum, P. D. (1994). Stability and change in functional assessment of patients with geropsychiatric disorders. *American Journal of Occupational Therapy, 48*, 914–918.

(o) Whitelaw, N. A., & Liang, J. (1991). The structure of the OARS physical health measures. *Medical Care, 29*, 332–347.

PHILADELPHIA GERIATRIC CENTER MULTILEVEL ASSESSMENT INVENTORY (MAI)

Authors

Lawton, M. P., & Moss, M.

Author Affiliation

Philadelphia Geriatric Center, Philadelphia, PA

Primary Reference

Lawton, M. P., & Moss, M. (undated). *Philadelphia Geriatric Center Multilevel Assessment Instrument: Manual for full-length* MAI. Philadelphia, PA: Author.

Description

The *Philadelphia Geriatric Center Multilevel Assessment Inventory* (MAI) was designed to assess characteristics of the elderly relevant for determining their needs for services and placement in residential settings. It was developed for both research and applied use. The authors were motivated "to deal with some deficiencies and gaps in existing assessment systems" for the elderly (k), most notably the OARS instruments (see MFAQ review). Nevertheless, the authors acknowledge having borrowed much from earlier instruments that seemed to be of value.

The MAI is a structured interview procedure that obtains descriptive information about an elderly respondent related to seven domains. Each of the domains (except one) is sampled by interview questions in two or more subclasses, which the authors call sub-indexes. The full-length MAI consists of 165 items; the middle length MAI has 38 items, and the short-form has 24 items.

The domains, their sub-indexes, and the number of items in the long form, are (j):

- *Physical Health* (33 items): Self-rated Health Index (3): examinee rates own health. Health Behavior Index (3): reports activities engaged in for health maintenance or care. Health Conditions Index (25): reports on existence of specific health problems.

- *Cognitive* (15 items): Intellectual Functioning Index (11): mental status exam. Cognitive Symptoms Index (4): reports on memory lapses or confusion.
- *Activities of Daily Living* (16 items): Self-Maintenance Index (7): items focus on basic, life sustaining functions, such as feeding, bathing, dressing.
- *Instrumental Activities of Daily Living Index* (9): items include use of telephone, transportation, doing shopping, preparing meals, doing housework, doing handyman work around the house, doing laundry, taking medicine, managing money.
- *Time Use* (19 items): Time Activities Index (19): reports on frequency with which person has engaged in a variety of leisure and social activities.
- *Personal Adjustment* (14 items): Morale Index (9): reports on feelings of loneliness, discouragement, frustration. Psychological Symptoms Index (5): questions regarding insomnia, depression, fears.
- *Social Interaction* (8 items): Interaction with Friends (5): reports on visits and other contacts. Interaction with Family (3): reports on visits and other contacts.
- *Perceived Environment* (24 items): Subjective Housing Index (9): respondent's description of quality of current housing. Subjective Neighborhood Index (12): respondent's description of quality of neighborhood, convenience for everyday activities, neighbors. Personal Security Index (3): respondent's perception of degree of safety in current environment.

Each item includes one or more interview questions, with specifications for assignment of scores to various possible answers. For example, the Managing Money item is typical of the format of most of the items (j, p. 12):

38a. *Do* you manage your money:
— without help (Score 3, skip to Question 39),
— with some help, (e.g., manage day-to-day buying but have help with checkbook and paying bills) (Score 2) or
— don't you handle money at all (no day-to-day buying) (Score 1)?
38b. Why is it that you (have some help/don't handle money at all)? (No score)
38c. *Can* you manage your own money:
— without help (Score 3)
— with some help (Score 2)
— are you completely unable to handle money? (Score 1)

Scores may be summed for items within an index (giving an index score), and for indexes within a domain (providing a domain score).

In addition, the MAI manual (j, pp. D1–D3) provides a method for the examiner to give an examinee a rating of 1 to 5 on each domain, called the "Domain Rating"; the authors recommend these ratings as more convenient than raw index or domain scores for communicating an examinee's results.

Conceptual Basis

CONCEPT DEFINITION.   The guiding conceptual framework for the MAI was Lawton's model for behavioral competence of the elderly (g, h). This model outlines several spheres or domains of functioning, ranging from biological to social, with functions within a domain ranging from simple to complex. It was the product of over a decade of conceptual and empirical work by Lawton in gerontology and in provision of services for the elderly.

Not all of the domains in Lawton's model are represented in the MAI. Further, the MAI combines certain domains that were separate concepts in Lawton's model (e.g., Physical Self Maintenance and Instrumental Self Maintenance became "Activities of Daily Living" in the MAI, with two sub-indexes corresponding to the two earlier concepts). In addition, the MAI includes certain concepts that are not in Lawton's earlier conceptual model, especially the domains of Personal Adjustment and Perceived Environment. Conceptual background for these latter domains was borrowed from other investigators in the field (d, f, and m for Personal Adjustment; b and e for Perceived Environment). Originally the MAI also included an "Objective Environment" domain (e.g., quality of the plumbing, number of steps in the dwelling), but this was abandoned because of difficulties in operationalization or lack of variability across cases (k).

OPERATIONAL DEFINITION.   Neither the manual nor the journal article on the MAI describes the process by which concepts were translated into items for the instrument. The Activities of Daily Living items, however, clearly were derived from Lawton's earlier work (i) on a scale for this domain.

CRITIQUE.   Lawton's earlier work in conceptualizing behavioral competence of the elderly is highly regarded by other workers in gerontology and development of the elderly. This conceptual base is an asset for the MAI.

Many of the domains and sub-indexes of the MAI would seem to provide legally relevant data for characterizing an individual's functional abilities to care for oneself in everyday life. Noteworthy in this regard are the domains of Activities of Daily Living and Physical Health. Other, less functional domains (e.g., Personal Adjustment, Perceived Environment) may provide relevant background for making inferences about the degree to which individuals will be likely to mobilize their resources to make the most of existing physical and instrumental capacities.

Content coverage of the MAI probably is incomplete for assessing an individual's functional abilities to manage property or financial matters. This content area is sampled in only a limited way by one sub-index in the Activities of Daily Living domain.

It is important to note that the MAI does not require an individual to demonstrate the functional abilities associated with the various conceptual domains. The MAI's operational definition of its domains and sub-indexes is an individual's self-report of the things that one can do (or could do, or typically does), the individual's report of personal feelings or perceptions, and so forth. This method for assessing the domains can be adequate for many purposes.

Psychometric Development

STANDARDIZATION. The MAI manual (j, pp. E17–E19) provides considerable structure for the process of the interview, sequence and content of questions, and scoring. It describes criteria for 1 to 5 rating of each of the domains, but these criteria are not tied specifically to item scores. The manual discusses general considerations for interviewing elderly individuals and dealing with special problems of test administration with this population (e.g., with limited hearing or vision).

RELIABILITY. Interrater agreement in assignment of summary ratings was examined by comparing ratings by interviewers to ratings by trained raters who had not interviewed the respondents (484 elderly individuals). Pairs of raters manifested more than a 1-point discrepancy between their summary ratings in only 5% of cases (ranging from $r = .88$ on Activities of Daily Living to $r = .58$ on Social Interaction). Alexopoulous et al. (a) found a high degree of inter-rater reliability using inter-class correlations ($r = .91–.97$) in a sample of depressed older adults.

Test-retest reliability at a 3-week interval was reported as "acceptable, except for the physical self-maintenance sub-index, where variability was very low, the majority receiving perfect scores" (k, p. 95). Internal consistency (alpha) was reported as acceptable for all but the Health Behavior and Personal Security sub-indexes ($r = .39$ and $.57$, respectively). Alexopoulos et al. (a) found an acceptable degree of test-retest reliability using inter-class correlations ($r = .66–.87$) in a sample of depressed older adults.

NORMS. The MAI manual (j, pp. E17-El9) provides raw score means (not summary rating scale data) for four types of elderly respondents on all domains and their sub-indexes (for the MAI long, middle-length, and short forms). The four samples (obtained in Philadelphia) are: independently living community residents, independently living tenants of public housing, high intensity in-home service recipients, and institutional waiting-list clients living in the community.

CRITIQUE. Users of the MAI will find it somewhat like the well-known *Diagnostic Interview Schedule* in terms of its degree of structure and clarity concerning scoring or coding of data. Its summary rating scales require greater degrees of subjective estimation, yet interrater agreement generally is good even on this less structured feature of the MAI. The normative data are based on sufficiently large sample sizes to warrant their general application, although samples from other geographic areas are needed to verify the generalizability of these results.

Construct Validation

Current data on validity of the MAI are from a publication by Lawton and associates (k) using the samples noted previously. First, MAI scores correlated above .55 with summary domain ratings for most domains and sub-indexes (exceptions: Interactions with Friends, and all sub-indexes in the Perceived Environment domain). Second, multiple correlations between domain items and summary ratings generally were above .40 (exceptions similar to above). Third, 14 of the 21 domain and sub-index scores correlated .20 or better with respondents' independent/dependent living status. Finally, many MAI domain and sub-index scores correlated substantially with ratings of the elderly respondents by clinicians or housing administrators who had no knowledge of the respondents' MAI scores.

Most important for the present review, the sub-index that performed best on each of the above examinations of validity was the Instrumental Activities of Daily Living sub-index, that is, the items evaluating an individual's abilities to perform functions required to manage one's everyday affairs. Raw scores on this sub-index correlated .91 with summary ratings of the Activities of Daily Living domain. In comparison to other sub-indexes, it manifested the best internal validity (.86), correlated greatest with current independent or dependent living arrangement of respondents (.56), and correlated the highest of any sub-index with administrators' independent ratings of the elderly respondents (.59).

CRITIQUE. This study shows that several of the MAI domain or sub-index scales may have satisfactory internal validity, may concur with independent experts' ratings of the functional characteristics of elderly person, and are related as expected to elderly individuals' degree of independent living that they apparently manage to maintain. These results are most satisfactory for the scale that assesses functional abilities in everyday life, a sub-index that would be of special interest in assessments of the elderly in guardianship cases.

Especially helpful to further demonstrate construct validity would be studies examining the relation of each of the domain or sub-index scales to other indexes. For example, one might examine the relation of Physical Health to the results of actual physical/medical diagnoses, the relation of IADL to actual demonstrations of individual's abilities to perform the functions at the level reported to examiners on the MAI, or the relation of Personal Adjustment reports to psychological measures of adjustment.

Predictive or Classificatory Utility

MAI scores predicted classification of cognitive impairment (impaired/ not impaired on MMSE cut score of 24) among 2,713 community dwelling elders (c). MAI scores have been significantly associated with severity of depression in 75 elderly adults with major depressive illness (a) and significantly associated with level of hope in 86 older patients with cancer (l).

CRITIQUE.   Examiners are in need of research demonstrating the relation of MAI scores to examinees' success in managing various levels of independence in living when they are placed residentially after MAI assessment. These results are critical for the use of MAI scores when forming predictive opinions.

Potential for Expressing Person-Situation Congruency

The MAI would seem to have considerable potential for comparing an individual's functional abilities to environmental demands of various living arrangements and settings. Administration of the MAI to elderly individuals who are managing successfully in a particular type of setting could produce normative data on each MAI sale for successful adaptation to that setting. Comparison of an examinee's MAI scores to these setting-specific norms might suggest the degree to which the examinee's characteristics and abilities match, exceed, or fall short of the characteristics of individuals who currently meet that environment's demands. This could be described as the congruence or incongruence between the individual's abilities and situational demands, which addresses the interactive question in legal competency determinations.

Comparison of this type would be meaningful, however, only if it is clear that MAI scales (e.g., the activities scale measuring everyday functional abilities) actually measure what they purport to measure. Currently the greatest need is evidence that examinees' reports of their functional abilities on the MAI correspond to their actual abilities.

References

(a) Alexopoulos, G. S., Vrontou, C., Kakuma, T., Meyers, B. S., Young, R. C., Klausner, E., & Clarkin, J. (1996). Disability in geriatric depression. *American Journal of Psychiatry, 153,* 877–885.

(b) Andrews, R., & Withey, S. (1976). *Social indicators of well-being.* New York: Plenum Press.

(c) Barberger-Gateau, P., Commenges, D., Gagnon, M., Letenneur, L., Sauvel, C., Dartigues, J. (1992). Instrumental activities of daily living as a screening tool for cognitive impairment and dementia in elderly community dwellers. *Journal of the American Geriatrics Society, 40,* 1129–1134.

(d) Brandburn, N. (1969). *The structure of psychological well-being.* Chicago: Aldine.

(e) Campbell, A., Converse, P., & Rodgers, W. (1976). *The quality of American life: Perceptions, evaluations, and satisfactions.* New York: Russell Sage.

(f) George, L., & Bearon, L. (1980). *Quality of life in older persons.* New York: Human Sciences Press.

(g) Lawton, M. (1972). Assessing the competence of older people. In D. Kent, R. Kastenbaum, & S. Sherwood (Eds.), *Research, planning and action for the elderly* (pp. 122–143). New York: Behavioral Publications.

(h) Lawton, M. (1982). Competence, environmental press, and adaptation of older people. In M. Lawton, P. Windley, & T. Byerts (Eds.), *Aging and the environment: Theoretical approaches* (pp. 33–59). New York: Springer.

(i) Lawton, M., & Brody, E. (1969). Assessment of older people: Self-maintaining and instrumental activities of daily living. *Gerontologist, 9,* 179–186.

(j) Lawton, M., & Moss, M. (undated). *Philadelphia Geriatric Center Multilevel Assessment. Instrument: Manual for full length MAI.* Philadelphia, PA: author.

(k) Lawton, M., Moss, M., Fulcomer, M., & Kleban, M. (1982). A research and service oriented multilevel assessment instrument. *Journal of Gerontology, 37,* 91–99.

(l) McGill, J. S., & Paul, P. B. (1993). Functional status and hope in elderly people with and without cancer. *Oncology Nursing Forum, 20,* 1207–1213.

(m) Nydegger, C. (Ed.). (1977). *Measuring morale: A guide to effective assessment.* Washington, DC: Gerontological Society.

B. PERFORMANCE BASED INSTRUMENTS TO ASSESS IADL'S

DIRECT ASSESSMENT OF FUNCTIONAL STATUS (DAFS)

Author

David A. Loewenstein

Author Affiliation

Wien Center for Alzheimer's Disease and Memory Disorders, Mount Sinai Medical Center, Miami Beach and University of Miami School of Medicine

Primary Reference

Loewenstein, D. A., Amigo, E., Duara, R., Guterman, A., Hurwitz, D., Berkowitz, N., Wilkie, F., Weinberg, G., Black, B., Gittlenman, B., & Eisdorfer, C. (1989). A new scale for the assessment of functional status in Alzheimer's disease and related disorders. *Journal of Gerontology, Psychological Sciences, 44*, 114–121.

Description

The *Direct Assessment of Functional Status* (DAFS) was designed to assess functional abilities in individuals with dementing illnesses. The scale assesses seven areas:

- time orientation (16 points)
- communication abilities (including telephone and mail; 17 points)
- transportation (requiring reading of road signs; 13 points)
- financial skills (identifying/counting currency, writing a check, balancing a checkbook; 21 points)
- shopping skills (involving grocery shopping; 16 points)
- eating skills (10 points)
- dressing and grooming skills (13 points).

The composite functional score has a maximum of 93 points, exclusive of the Driving subscale which is considered optional.

The DAFS requires that the patient attempt to actually perform each item (e.g., is given a telephone and asked to dial the operator). The entire assessment is estimated to require 30–35 minutes to complete. The scale can be administered by any psychometrically trained administrator. The DAFS has been used for staging functional impairment in dementia, from one to three, in a group of 205 individuals with probable Alzheimer's disease (b).

Conceptual Basis

CONCEPTUAL DEFINITION.   The conceptual intent of the DAFS scale was to provide an assessment of higher order function to better answer questions regarding independent function and legal competency than neuropsychological testing alone (a). A goal of the scale development was to utilize direct assessment to avoid the potential bias of informant report. Another goal was to assess higher order functional abilities (not just physical ADL's) in some depth and with some degree of discrete measurement. The scale is conceptually based in the IADL literature.

OPERATIONAL DEFINITION.   Scale items were developed by identifying seven domains through review of the IADL literature. Once these domains were selected, experienced geriatricians identified the functional deficits

their patients experienced in each domain, the types of behaviors that
could be assessed in vivo in a laboratory setting, and the types of behaviors that were clinically significant in terms of clinical treatment. Specific
functional behaviors were then developed from these suggestions and
refined through piloting with cognitively impaired older adults. When
possible, a hierarchical format was used for items within domains (a).

CRITIQUE. The DAFS is conceptually related to other IADL scales,
although it seems to be more related to clinicians' reports of functional
abilities of practical clinical significance. The scale has limited coverage of
issues of care for and safety in the home and care of and management
regarding one's health and medications. It samples some traditional physical ADL's but not toileting, transferring, or ambulation. More discussion
of the conceptual relevance of these choices would be useful.

Psychometric Development

STANDARDIZATION. The scale, as provided in the appendix of the primary reference, utilizes a detailed rating form. Specific items are listed,
although standardized prompts are not provided.

RELIABILITY. Interrater reliability for each functional subscale and for
the composite measure was computed for 15 memory disordered patients
and 12 control subjects. Inter-rater agreement was 85%. Kappa coefficients
for subscale and composite scores ranged form .911 to 1.000. Test retest
reliability was computed for a 3–7 week retest for 14 memory impaired
patients and 12 controls. Test-retest reliabilities ranged from .71 to .91 for
the patient group and from .91 to 1.0 for the control group (a).

NORMS. Although formal normative data are not presented, a number of elderly control groups are cited. Mean score and standard deviation
for 18 elderly controls are presented in the primary reference (a). A second
control sample of 50 elderly adults is also referenced (b) although data for
this group are not provided.

CRITIQUE. Although standardized instructions are not provided, a
detailed rating form and high interrater reliability suggest good standardization across examiners. Other reliability estimates confirm the scale has
good reliability. It appears there is a good start on normative data with
two potential samples. More specific information on these samples for
clinicians interested in normative comparisons would be useful.

Construct Validation

Performance on the DAFS was significantly correlated with caregiver
report of functional status in the home (as measured by the Blessed

Dementia Rating Scale) for a sample of 30 general memory disordered patients and a sample of 11 Alzheimer's patients (a). In another study of 72 patients with Alzheimer's disease, caregivers tended to overestimate the functional capacities of patients with objective functional impairment on the DAFS (c), especially those with higher MMSE scores.

A test of global cognition was significantly correlated with five DAFS functional tasks: telling time, using the telephone, counting currency, writing a check, and balancing a checkbook, among 33 individuals with a diagnosis of probable Alzheimer's disease. Additional cognitive tests predicted functional performance in addition to global cognition for some tests. Using the telephone was also predicted by DAFS scores; letter preparation was also predicted by figural memory scores, writing a check was also predicted by WAIS Object Assembly, Fuld retrieval, and DAFS scores; balancing a checkbook was also predicted by WMS figural memory and DAFS scores; shopping was also predicted by WAIS Similarities scores (d). The authors suggest the scale shows modest correlation with cognitive measures, suggesting relationship with cognitive status and also supporting the importance of administering functional scales in addition to cognitive tests (since correlations were moderate not high).

The DAFS appears useful for measuring functional decline over time in a report of 52 patients with Alzheimer's disease who were assessed initially and again one year later (e).

CRITIQUE. Relationships between the DAFS and caregiver reports of function in the home suggest the DAFS is useful in measuring everyday functioning. Relationships between the DAFS and cognitive measures suggest the DAFS is useful in tapping functional difficulties related to cognitive impairments and cognitive decline across time. Additional studies of the internal structure of the DAFS and its relationship to other IADL performance measures would provide additional data on construct validity.

Predictive or Classificatory Utility

DAFS subscale scores were compared between patients judged as impaired or not impaired based on chart review in areas of driving, telling time, remembering a list, and both higher and simple financial skills. Mean subscale scores were significantly different within each group ($n = $ 10–15 per group; a). In addition, DAFS total and subscale mean scores were compared for groups of elderly controls ($n = 18$), Alzheimer patients ($n = 12$), and depressed patients ($n = 11$). On most subscales mean scores were significantly different between normals and Alzheimer patients, and between depressed patients and Alzheimer patients, but not between normals and depressed patients (a). In another study, patients with mild Alzheimer's dementia and mild multi infarct dementia were relatively equivalent in functional abilities and less impaired than patients with moderate Alzheimer's disease (f).

CRITIQUE. Initial studies of the predictive validity of the DAFS are promising. Further studies are recommended to compare the DAFS' ability to predict level of supervision or placement needed and real clinical or legal outcomes relevant to legal competence.

Potential for Expressing Person-Situation Congruency

The DAFS appears to be an ecologically valid measure, tapping performance on functional abilities relative to independent living. The scale itself does not provide instructions or scoring to address situational and environmental differences. These would need to be evaluated clinically given the results of the DAFS and other evaluations.

References

(a) Loewenstein, D. A., Amigo, E., Duara, R., Guterman, A., Hurwitz, D., Berkowitz, N., Wilkie, F., Weinberg, G., Black, B., Gittlenman, B., & Eisdorfer, C. (1989). A new scale for the assessment of functional status in Alzheimer's disease and related disorders. *Journal of Gerontology: Psychological Sciences, 44,* 114–121.

(b) Loewenstein, D. A., & Rupert, M. P. (1995). Staging functional impairment in dementia using performance-based measures: A preliminary analyses. *Journal of Mental Health and Aging, 1,* 47–56.

(c) Loewenstein, D. A., Arguelles, S., Bravo, M., Freeman, R. Q., Arguelles, T., Aceredo, A., & Eisdorfer, C. (2001). Caregivers' judgments of functional abilities of the Alzheimer's disease patient: A comparison of proxy reports and objective measures. *Journal of Gerontology, 56,* P78–P84.

(d) Loewenstein, D. A., Rubert, M. P., Berkowitz-Zimmer, N., Guterman, A., Morgan, R., & Hayden, S. (1992). Neuropsychological test performance and prediction of functional capacities in dementia. *Behavior, Health, and Aging, 2,* 149–158.

(e) Loewenstein, D. A., Duara, R., Rubert, M. P., Arguelles, T., Lapinski, K. J., & Eisdorfer, C. (1995). Deterioration of functional capacities in Alzheimer's disease after a 1-year period. *International Psychogeriatrics, 7,* 495–503.

(f) Zimmer, N. A., Hayden, S., Deidan, C., & Loewenstein, D. A. (1994). Comparative performance of mildly impaired patients with Alzheimer's disease and multiple cerebral infarctions on tests of memory and functional capacity. *International Psychogeriatrics, 6,* 143–154.

EVERYDAY PROBLEMS TEST (EPT)

Author

Sherry L. Willis and colleagues

Author Affiliation

Pennsylvania State University

Primary Reference

Willis, S. L. (1996). Everyday cognitive competence in elderly persons: Conceptual issues and empirical findings. *Gerontologist, 36,* 595–601.

Description

The *Everyday Problems Test* (EPT) was developed to focus on the cognitive demands of IADL tasks, while acknowledging that functional capacity involves multiple dimensions, including physical health and social relationships. The tests consists of six stimuli for each of seven IADL areas: managing medications, shopping for necessities, managing finances, using transportation, using telephone, maintaining a household, and meal preparation and nutrition. For each stimulus presented the examinee is asked to solve 2 problems, making 42 stimuli and 84 items in total. Willis and colleagues have also developed the *Everyday Problems for the Cognitively Challenged Elderly* (EPCCE), a similar but shorter test with 16 stimulus materials for low educated normal adults and early stage Alzheimer's patients (d, e). This review focuses on the EPT.

Conceptual Basis

CONCEPTUAL DEFINITION. The EPT derives from life span developmental theories emphasizing the importance of adults' knowledge of the pragmatics of everyday life, also referred to as practical problem solving, everyday problem solving, everyday cognition, and practical intelligence (b). The EPT builds on concepts of IADL's described by Lawton and Brody (1969), emphasizing performance of IADL's and the cognitive aspects of that performance.

OPERATIONAL DEFINITION. In operationalizing everyday problem solving in the EPT the authors were concerned with maximizing the external or ecological validity of the test, to capture real functioning in the home environment better than previously captured in laboratory measures. It is noted that there is no consensus on what tasks best measure everyday problem solving (b). Items were developed from surveys of IADL tasks, involving actual materials which may be encountered in daily life in solving everyday problems (such as a medicine label) (c).

CRITIQUE. The test is nicely grounded in a theoretical framework derived from models of intelligence combined with previous work on IADL's. The operationalization of items to be ecologically valid, yet still relatively easy to administer in a laboratory setting, is a strength. The test is geared towards assessing functional competence from a psychological perspective, some of which may be relevant to questions of legal competency to care for self and property, although additional testing may be required.

Psychometric Development

STANDARDIZATION. The EPT is a standardized, structured performance test, with standard stimuli and instructions. For example, the examinee is given a phone bill and asked to identify all the days on which calls to a certain city were made. The examiner records whether the examinee finds the right page of the bill and identifies each of four correct dates.

RELIABILITY. Internal consistency reliability measured by Cronbach's alpha in a sample of nondemented elderly ($n = 417$) was .94 (c). Two month test-retest reliability in this sample was .94 (c).

NORMS. Normative data are available via the standardization sample, which consisted of 417 non-demented persons (M age = 74.6, M education = 12.0) (c).

CRITIQUE. The availability of standardized stimuli and prompts is a plus. Information on inter-rater reliability would be useful in establishing the extent of reliability of scores between examiners. Internal consistency reliability and test-retest reliability are excellent. The normative sample is large, although restricted to the older population.

Construct Validation

EPT scores were significantly correlated with direct observation of task performance in homes ($r = .67$), with elderly person's self-ratings of IADL limitations ($r = -.23$), spousal ratings of the elderly person's IADL limitations ($r = -.24$), and a measure of "functional literacy" ($r = .87$) (c). Subscales of the EPT and an observational measure of in-home task performance loaded onto the same factors in confirmatory factor analysis of data from 62 older adults.

In lisrel analyses of the fit of a seven-domain subscale structure, a seven factor solution was obtained although the factors were highly interrelated (b). In lisrel analyses comparing the EPT to two other everyday problem solving tests, the best solution was a model involving factors for each separate instrument rather than one including a general common factor upon which two or more instruments loaded (b).

CRITIQUE.   The studies of the factor structure and inter-test relationships of the EPT suggest the test measures seven domains of IADL's consistent with everyday functioning. While comparisons of the EPT and other IADL tests suggest significant method variance; additional studies which compare the EPT to more similar measures of IADL's for older populations (e.g., DAFS, ILS) would be helpful.

Predictive or Classificatory Utility

There were no studies of the EPT's relationship with level of placement or other clinical or legal status.

CRITIQUE.   The EPT is an exceptionally well-designed test, developed for research purposes concerning studies of everyday cognition. Studies that compare the EPT with various clinical or legal outcomes might extend its validity for clinical and legal applications.

Potential for Expressing Person-Situation Congruency

There are no specific items or scoring built into the EPT to consider person-situation congruency.

References

(a) Diehl, M., Willis, S. L., & Schaie, K. W. (1995). Everyday problem solving in older adults: Observational assessment and cognitive correlates. *Psychology and Aging, 10*, 478–491.
(b) Marsiske, M., & Willis, S. L. (1995). Dimensionality of everyday problem solving in older adults. *Psychology and Aging, 10*, 269–283.
(c) Willis, S. L. (1996). Everyday cognitive competence in elderly persons: Conceptual issues and empirical findings. *Gerontologist, 36*, 595–601.
(d) Willis, S. L., Allen-Burge, R., Dolan, M. M., Bertrand, R. M., Yesavage, J., & Taylor, J. L. (1998) Everyday problem solving among individuals with Alzheimer's Disease. *The Gerontologist, 38*, 569–577.
(e) Willis, S. L., Dolan, M. M., & Bertrand, R. M. Problem solving on health-related tasks of daily living. Unpublished manuscript.

C. PERFORMANCE BASED INSTRUMENTS TO ASSESS NEED FOR GUARDIAN OR CONSERVATOR

DECISIONMAKING INSTRUMENT FOR GUARDIANSHIP (DIG)

Author

Stephen Anderer

Author Affiliation

Schnader, Harrison, Segal and Lewis LLP, Attorneys at Law, Philadelphia, PA

Primary Reference

Anderer, S. J. (1997). *Developing an instrument to evaluate the capacity of elderly persons to make personal care and financial decisions.* Unpublished doctoral dissertation, Allegheny University of Health Sciences.

Description

The *Decisionmaking Instrument for Guardianship* (DIG) was developed to evaluate the abilities of individuals to make decisions in everyday situations often raised in guardianship proceedings. The instrument consists of eight vignettes describing situations involving problems in eight areas: hygiene, nutrition, health care, residence, property acquisition, routine money management in property acquisition, major expenses in property acquisition, and property disposition. Examinees are read a brief vignette describing these situations in the second person. For example, the first vignette is "David is an 80 year old man. His wife died two years ago and he lives alone in his home. He has severe arthritis. For two months, David has had difficulty washing himself because of his arthritis. He has not been able to do his cleaning. Food scraps have been left out in the kitchen. The rugs have become dirty." Gender is varied to match the examinee's gender. To facilitate disclosure, individuals are provided a list of major points in each vignette in large print. For example, in the vignette above the list reads: "lives alone, severe arthritis, difficulty washing self, not able to do cleaning, food scraps left out, rugs dirty."

Each disclosure is followed by a series of questions to evaluate problem solving for that situation, such as:

- What is the problem?
- What could David do to solve the problem?
- Which solution to David's problem do you think is the best one?
- How would you describe to David the reasons that he should prefer this solution?

Scoring criteria are used to assign points for aspects of problem solving including defining the problem, generating alternatives, consequential thinking, and complex/comparative thinking.

Conceptual Basis

CONCEPTUAL DEFINITION.   The DIG was based on social problem solving theory, using a social problem solving model developed by D'Zurilla and

Nezu (b). The model has two components: a general motivational component known as "problem orientation," and a set of four problem solving skills. Problem solving skills include the ability to define the problem, generate alternatives, evaluate alternatives, and implement and verify the solution.

OPERATIONAL DEFINITION.   These concepts were operationalized in the context of guardianship through a multi-step process to insure legal relevance (a). First, interviews were conducted with legal and social service professionals experienced with issues of guardianship. Interviewees were asked to identify typical problematic situations confronted by elderly individuals for whom guardianship is sought. These interviews were used to generate a list of problematic situations which was distributed to a second sample of legal and social service professionals. Respondents were asked to rate each situation in terms of frequency of occurrence in their experience and relevance to legal competency. Vignettes were developed to address situations rated as most frequent and most relevant and to cover a range of different decision making situations.

CRITIQUE.   The DIG appears to be nicely and appropriately grounded in problem solving theory. The efforts to operationalize this theory in items that are legally relevant to questions of guardianship through the surveys of legal and social service professionals is a major strength. The DIG appears to be an innovative and promising instrument to assess problem solving for vignettes of everyday situations. Additional performance based testing would supplement the DIG in providing a comprehensive assessment in questions of guardianship. For example, some individuals may have adequate working memory and problem solving, but impaired recent memory. Such individuals could conceivable do well on the DIG yet still be impaired in their everyday function when left at home alone, i.e., memory problems could cause them to mis-pay bills or mistake medications.

Because the DIG has one vignette for eight areas it may inadequately sample all aspects related to functional abilities for legal competencies, such as abilities to care for home via cleaning, maintenance, and personal safety. A strength of the DIG is the inclusion of four vignettes concerning financial management, and in this area the coverage appears to be better.

Psychometric Development

STANDARDIZATION.   The DIG is carefully standardized. Standard instructions, vignettes, questions, and prompts are provided in the manual. In addition, detailed scoring criteria are provided. Sheets with simplified lists of salient points of each vignette are provided (in large type), helping to standardize vignette administration and emphasize the assessment of problem solving and not reading comprehension or memory. Vignettes are kept simple, easy to understand, and brief.

RELIABILITY.   Inter-scorer reliability between three raters ranged from .93 to .97 for the total scale, and .77 to .98 for subscale scores. Internal consistency reliability estimates on the basis of Cronbach's alpha was .92 and Spearman-Brown split half reliability was .93 (a).

NORMS.   Mean and standard deviation scores for 61 individuals ranging in age from 61 to 90 years old are provided (a). Specific information on the neurological and physical health of these individuals is not provided.

CRITIQUE.   This instrument has been extensively standardized in both administration and scoring, and this appears to be reflected in the excellent inter-rater reliability. The standardization sample provides a good start for normative data, but since subjects were drawn from residential facilities, adult day health care programs, and senior centers, the sample is likely to be mixed, reflecting some normal and some potentially neurologically compromised adults. Additional normative data would be useful.

Construct Validation

The DIG total score was significantly correlated with four measures of cognition: the CERAD summary score, WAIS Block Design, WAIS Vocabulary, and a measure of capacity to reason when giving informed consent (*Thinking Rationally About Treatment*, or TRAT: c). Correlations ranged between .54 and .73, with highest correlation between the DIG and the TRAT (a). The DIG total score was significantly correlated with total scores on CERAD tests, ranging from .35 to .59, with highest correlation between the DIG and a test of verbal fluency.

CRITIQUE.   Initial comparisons of the DIG with other cognitive tests find moderate positive correlations. This is a good start to examining construct validity issues. Studies are needed that look further at the internal structure of the DIG and relationship to other functional and guardianship measures.

Predictive or Classificatory Utility

There are no studies of the predictive or classificatory utility of the DIG at this point.

CRITIQUE.   Studies that examine the ability of the DIG to predict level of supervision needed or type of guardianship procured would be useful.

Potential for Expressing Person-Situation Congruency

The DIG is highly standardized and does not contain items within the scale to assess the fit of the functioning on the issue in question with the individual's environmental and situational resources. Such adjustments could be made in interpreting the DIG. Note however that the vignettes on the DIG are very relevant to everyday situations encountered by adults for whom guardianship is in question and in this way appears to be quite ecologically valid.

References

(a) Anderer, S. J. (1997). *Developing an instrument to evaluate the capacity of elderly persons to make personal care and financial decisions.* Unpublished doctoral dissertation, Allegheny University of Health Sciences.
(b) D'Zurilla, T. J., & Nezu, A. M. (1982). Social problem solving in adults. In P. C. Kendall (Ed.), *Advances in cognitive-behavioral research and theory* (Vol. 1). New York: Academic.
(c) Grisso, T., & Appelbaum, P. S. (1993). *Manual for Thinking Rationally about Treatment.* Worcester, MA: University of Massachusetts Medical School.

FINANCIAL CAPACITY INSTRUMENT (FCI)

Author

Daniel Marson and colleagues

Author Affiliation

Department of Neurology, Alzheimer's Disease Center, and Center for Aging at University of Alabama at Birmingham, Birmingham, AL

Primary Reference

Marson, D. C., Sawrie, S. M., Snyder, S., McInturff, B., Stalvey, T., Boothe, A., Aldrige, T., Chatterjee, A., & Harrell, L. E. (2000). Assessing financial capacity in patients with Alzheimer's disease: A conceptual model and prototype instrument. *Archives of Neurology, 57,* 877–884.

Description

The *Financial Capacity Instrument* (FCI) (d) was designed to assess abilities associated with management of everyday financial activities. The instrument assesses six domains of financial activity: basic monetary skills, financial conceptual knowledge, cash transactions, checkbook management, bank statement management, and financial judgment.

The FCI is reported to require between 30–50 minutes to administer, depending on the cognitive level of the examinee. Of note, Marson and his group are also validating a semi-structured interview to assess financial capacity, the Clinical Assessment Interview for Financial Capacity (CAI) (e).

Conceptual Basis

CONCEPTUAL DEFINITION. Financial capacity was identified as an advanced ADL, said to be conceptually and statistically distinct from other ADL's such as those related to household management, and is associated with cognitive functioning. The authors define financial capacity as a multidimensional construct involving declarative knowledge, procedural knowledge, and judgment, and requiring simple and complex processing (b).

OPERATIONAL DEFINITION. An interactive process of test development was used to operationalize financial capacity into domains, with tasks for each domain (c). Inclusion criteria for domains were: theoretical relevance to independent functioning; clinical relevance to health care professionals; and general relevance to Alabama statutes for financial competency. Tasks within each of these domains were identified as being: theoretically relevant to the domain; practical to implement in the laboratory; representative of procedural knowledge, declarative knowledge, or judgment; and of varying difficulty levels sensitive to dementia at different stages.

CRITIQUE. The FCI is nicely grounded in theories of declarative and procedural knowledge. One of its strengths is the consideration of the multiple types of cognitive skills hypothesized to be important for different types of financial capacities. Although many IADL tests have included items for money management, the FCI represents a significant improvement over these through its use of six domains, providing for comprehensive assessment.

Psychometric Development

STANDARDIZATION. The FCI uses an explicit protocol for administration and scoring (a).

RELIABILITY. Test-retest reliability was investigated on a subset of 17 Alzheimer's patients and controls and was found to range from .85 to .98 for the six domains of financial capacity (d). Percent exact inter-rater agreement was examined on another subset of 11 patients and controls using two independent raters and was found to range from 86.4 to 99.7 for the six domains (d). Internal consistency reliability was computed using Cronbach's alpha and was found to range from .85 to .93 over the six domains (d).

NORMS.   Normative data are available for 23 normal older controls, mean age 70.3 years, recruited for initial reliability and validity studies who were assessed to have sufficient pre-existing experience in all of the financial domains (to exclude individuals who may not have been involved in specific financial tasks and whose performance on these would reflect lack of experience rather than capacity impairment) (d).

CRITIQUE.   Initial reliability estimates are excellent and suggest the FCI has acceptable test-retest, interrater, and internal consistency reliability. The normative sample is appropriate for use in early test development, and the sample appears to be appropriately selected with an ingenious consideration of previous financial experience. Additional normative data are needed to enable more broad scale clinical use.

Construct Validation

Performance on the FCI was compared with performance on a neuropsychological battery for 35 Alzheimer's patients (b). In these analyses, Basic Monetary Skills were predicted by performance on Trails A and Tokens; Conceptual Knowledge was predicted by performance on Boston Naming and Dementia Rating Scale Attention; Cash Transactions were predicted by performance on Trails A; Checkbook Management was predicted by performance on Dementia Rating Scale Attention; Bank Statement Management was predicted by performance on Tokens, WAIS Similarities and Dementia Rating Scale Construction; Financial Judgment was predicted by performance on the Boston Naming Test (b). Working memory was found to be key in financial capacity (a).

CRITIQUE.   Early construct validation work is interesting and promising. Additional construct validation that considers performance on the FCI across multiple groups is needed. Factor analyses that explore the six domains of financial capacity developed on the FCI would be most interesting, possibly proving useful in relating performance on the FCI to different legal capacities regarding estate management that are in question in a specific guardianship situation.

Predictive or Classificatory Utility

The performance of 23 normal controls was compared to the performance of 30 individuals with mild Alzheimer's disease and 20 individuals with moderate Alzheimer's disease (d). Mean performance of controls differed from patients with moderate Alzheimer's disease for all six domains, and from patients with mild Alzheimer's disease for five of six domains (the exception being basic monetary skills involving naming, valuing, and counting coins and currency). Patients with mild versus moderate Alzheimer's disease were classified as "capable," "moderately capable," and "incapable" according to FCI scores, based on control-referenced methods. Distributions across categories were statistically different for the two groups (d).

CRITIQUE.   These studies suggest the FCI can be useful in predicting the level of financial incapacity and subsequent financial management needed. The authors nicely include the consideration of a "marginally incapable" group to allow for finer discriminations appropriate to modern limited guardianships.

Potential for Expressing Person-Situation Congruency

There are no specific items within the FCI to address person-situation congruency. However, performance on each of the six domains could be clinically compared to the financial demands and resources in individual cases.

References

(a) Earnst, K. S., Wadley, V. G., Aldridge, T. M., Steenwyk, A. B., Hammond, A. E., Harrell, L. E., & Marson, D. (2000). Loss of financial capacity in Alzheimer's disease: The role of working memory. *Aging, Neuropsychology, and Cognition, xx*, 1–11.
(b) Marson, D. C. (2001). Loss of financial competency in dementia: Conceptual and empirical approaches. *Aging, Neuropsychology, and Cognition, xx*, 1–17.
(c) Marson, D. C., Sawrie, S., Stalvey, T., McInturff, B., & Harrell, L. (1998, February). *Neuropsychological correlates of declining financial capacity in patients with Alzheimer's disease*. Paper presented at the meeting of the International Neuropsychological Society, Honolulu, Hawaii.
(d) Marson, D. C., Sawrie, S. M., Snyder, S., McInturff, B., Stalvey, T., Boothe, A., Aldrige, T., Chatterjee, A., & Harrell, L. E. (2000). Assessing financial capacity in patients with Alzheimer's disease: A conceptual model and prototype instrument. *Archives of Neurology, 57*, 877–884.
(e) Marson, D. (2000, November). *Assessing financial capacity in Alzheimer's disease: A clinical interview approach*. Paper presented at the meeting of the Gerontological Society of America, Washington DC.

HOPEMONT CAPACITY ASSESSMENT INTERVIEW (HCAI)

Author

Barry Edelstein

Author Affiliation

West Virginia University

Primary Reference

Edelstein, B. (1999). *Hopemont Capacity Assessment Interview manual and scoring guide.* West Virginia University: author. (Available from Barry Edelstein, Department of Psychology, P.O. Box 6040, West Virginia University, Morgantown, WV 26506.)

Description

The *Hopemont Capacity Assessment Interview* (HCAI) (b) is a semi-structured interview in two sections. The first section is for assessing capacity to make medical decisions. The second section, discussed here, assesses capacity to make financial decisions.

In the interview the examinee is first presented with concepts of choice, cost, and benefits and these concepts are reviewed with the examinee through questions and answers. The examinee is then presented three financial scenarios. In the first, the examinee has a limited amount of money (40 cents) and only he or his friend can use it to make a purchase. In the second scenario, the examinee wants to make a purchase and is offered that item or is offered twice the money. In the third scenario, a friend has a limited amount of money (5,000 dollars) and is trying to choose between using the money for a child's college tuition versus saving the money for his nursing home care needs. For each scenario the individual is asked basic questions about what he or she has heard, and then asked to explain costs and benefits, to make a choice, and to explain the reasoning behind that choice. There are 30 items in all. Detailed scoring procedures are not described, but the examiner is referred to score the results with respect to legal standards articulated by Appelbaum and Grisso (1988).

Conceptual Basis

CONCEPTUAL DEFINITION. The HCAI was developed in reference to four legal standards described by Appelbaum and Grisso (1988) relevant for assessing civil competencies. Questions in response to disclosed information are intended to assess the capacities to *understand* relevant information, demonstrate *appreciation* of the significance of the information for the circumstance, *rationally consider* the risks and benefits of different choices, and *express a choice*.

OPERATIONAL DEFINITION. The interview was structured and made simple to be suitable for cognitively impaired elderly adults, including those residing in nursing homes. Two scenarios were chosen with different levels of risk to increase generalizability. Items were developed based on a standard sixth grade reading level.

CRITIQUE. The HCAI is appropriate for older cognitively impaired adults, but may be too easy to provide fine discriminations for adults with mild or more subtle impairments. The conceptual relation of the HCAI to legal standards identified in the literature is a strength.

Psychometric Development

STANDARDIZATION. The HCAI uses a semi-structured format. General instructions are provided. Specific standardized introductions, scenarios, and follow-up questions are on the rating form. A three point rating system was developed for research purposes (2 = *adequate*, 1 = *partially adequate*, 0 = *inadequate*) (a,b).

RELIABILITY. Inter-rater reliability was calculated by comparing the scoring of two raters for 17 protocols (c). Inter-rater reliability, assessed through the exact agreement formula, was .93. Two week test-retest stability was .50 (d).

NORMS. Normative data are not available.

CRITIQUE. Standardization of administration is excellent. Inter-scorer reliability is good. Test-retest reliability is moderate. However, few instruments even provide such estimates, so the investigators are commended for their efforts in this area. As the authors note, reasons for lower test-retest reliability need to be determined (d). Normative data are needed.

Construct Validation

The correlation between the HCAI-financial section and the MMSE for 93 residents of a long term care facility was .60 (a). Correlations between the HCAI-financial section and nine cognitive measures for 50 residents of several long term care facilities were calculated in a second study (b). All correlations were positive and statistically significant. The highest correlation was with WAIS Vocabulary, and this test also emerged as the best predictor of HCAI-financial scores in multiple regression analyses.

CRITIQUE. These initial studies of relationships between the HCAI-financial and other cognitive measures are useful and may suggest what abilities are important for good performance on the HCAI instrument. Additional studies comparing the HCAI-financial to other measures of financial decision making would help to extend the construct validity of the test.

Predictive or Classificatory Utility

Mean MMSE score for 74 individuals judged to have poor financial capacity on the basis of the HCAI was 12.8, while mean MMSE score for 19 individuals judged to have adequate financial capacity was 24.4 (c). Similar mean differences were found in a second study (d).

CRITIQUE.   Additional studies are needed to determine whether the HCAI accurately predicts capacity to manage finances as determined by other methods (e.g., other financial measures or consensus opinion).

Potential for Expressing Person-Situation Congruency

The HCAI is highly standardized and does not include items to assess the fit of financial capacities as assessed on the instrument with environmental or situational circumstances (e.g., the extent of the individual's estate needing management).

References

(a) Edelstein, B. (2000). Challenges in the assessment of decision making capacity. *Journal of Aging Studies, 14*, 423–437.
(b) Edelstein, B. (1999). *Hopemont Capacity Assessment Interview manual and scoring guide.* West Virginia University: author. (Available from Barry Edelstein, Department of Psychology, P.O Box 6040, West Virginia University, Morgantown, WV 26506.)
(c) Edelstein, B., Nygren, M., Northrop, L., Staats, N., & Pool, D. (1993, August). *Assessment of capacity to make financial and medical decisions.* Poster presentation at the APA Annual Convention, Toronto, Canada.
(d) Staats, N. (1995). *Psychometric evaluation of the Hopemont Capacity Assessment Interview.* Unpublished Master's Thesis, West Virginia University.

INDEPENDENT LIVING SCALES (ILS)

Author

Loeb, P. (Anderten)

Author Affiliation

Private Practice

Primary Reference

Loeb, P. A. (1996). *Independent Living Scales.* San Antonio: Psychological Corporation.

Description

The *Independent Living Scales* (ILS) is an individually administered instrument developed to assess abilities of the elderly associated with

caring for oneself and/or for one's property. The ILS is a significantly modified version of the earlier *Community Competence Scale* (CCS) (reviewed in
the first edition of this book). The CCS was constructed specifically to be
consistent with legal definitions, objectives, and uses, in order to enhance
its value for expert testimony about capacities of the elderly in legal
guardianship cases.

The ILS consists of 70 items in five subscales:

- Memory/Orientation (awareness of surroundings and short-term
  memory)
- Managing Money (ability to count money, do monetary calculations, pay bills, and take precautions with money)
- Managing Home and Transportation (ability to use telephone, public
  transportation, and maintain a safe home)
- Health and Safety (awareness of personal health, ability to evaluate
  health problems, handle medical emergencies, take safety precautions), and
- Social Adjustment (mood and attitude towards social relations)

The five subscales may be summed to obtain an overall score which is
meant to reflect the individual's capacity to function independently overall. Two factors may be derived from items across the five subscales:
Problem Solving and Performance/Information.

ILS items use a direct performance format (e.g., examinee is asked to
demonstrate how to dial the operator) and Wechsler subscale type format
(e.g., examinee is asked to explain a situation or solve a problem). Direct
performance items require examinees to engage in some activity that will
show the degree to which they know or can do a specific thing. Some of
these items require special testing materials: for example, blank checks,
schematic maps, money, an envelope (for the examinee to address), a
checking account balance record, a key. The ILS kit includes many of these
items, although examiners supplement these with common items in their
possession (e.g., telephone, coins).

Scoring requires the assignment of 2 to 1 to 0 or 2 and 0 point credits
based on scoring criteria provided in the manual for each item. Scoring
criteria formats are similar to Wechsler Information, Comprehension, or
Vocabulary subscale formats. For example, Item 6 regarding use of a bus
schedule in "Managing Home and Transportation" is scored as follows:

- *2 points:* Mentions two or more facts (route bus follows, when bus
  arrives, where the stops at a destination, how much it costs to ride)
- *1 point:* Mentions one fact
- *0 point:* Does not know

Testing begins with seven screening items to assess ability to see, read, hear, speak, write and walk to assess the examinee's test taking ability in light of these functions. All items may be presented in a written format for individuals with poor hearing but intact vision and reading. The manual encourages examiners to use nonleading questions to allow examinees to clarify their responses ("explain what you mean," "tell me more about that") or to give more than one answer (where relevant), in light of the instrument's intent to assess maximum functional ability of the examinee. Administration typically requires 45 minutes.

Conceptual Basis

CONCEPT DEFINITION.   Loeb used an empirical method to select and define the component concepts for the ILS (a, Loeb and Anderten are the same author). "Caring for self and/or property" was identified as the primary legal construct, and "caring for self" and "caring for property" were considered to be two subconcepts. Loeb reviewed relevant statutes of all states, major relevant case law, and legal scholarly writings to collect an initial list of components, that is, broad categories of human abilities referred to in these sources. In addition, Loeb used an exploratory interview procedure to elicit additional components, as well as more specific abilities (referred to as "attributes" contributing conceptually to a component). Interviews were conducted with probate judges, attorneys, physicians, psychiatrists, psychologists, nurses, and social workers who worked with or made decisions about the elderly, as well as with many elderly individuals themselves. Major interview questions focused on the respondent's perceptions of the things that elderly individuals need to be able to do in order to care for themselves or their property. A composite set of tentative components and their specific ability attributes was constructed from the literature review and interview results.

Loeb (a) then employed a two-stage survey process in which respondents rated the components and their attributes for their importance in relation to the care-for-self subconcept and separately for importance regarding the care-for-property subconcepts. The 288 respondents in the final survey included Missouri probate judges, a random national selection of members of the Gerontological Society and of Division 20 (Adult Development and Aging) of the American Psychological Association, mental health professionals who regularly performed guardianship assessments in St. Louis, and elderly individuals who advised a local agency for the aging. (Significant differences between respondent groups in importance ratings were found on only five of the components.)

Nineteen components receiving the highest importance ratings for either the self or property concepts became the subscales: judgment, emergencies, acquire money, compensate incapacities, manage money, communication, care medical, adequate memory, satisfactory living arrangement, proper diet, mobility, sensation, motivation, personal hygiene, maintain household, utilize transportation, verbal/math, social adjustment, and dangerousness. Attributes (specific abilities) with the highest importance ratings within a component provided the conceptual definition for the given component.

The above procedures were employed for developing the CCS from which the ILS was developed (by the author in collaboration with the Psychological Corporation: g). This revision resulted in 118 prototype items, including 94 from the CCS and 24 new items added with the intention of improving reliability (g). These were administered to a nonclinical sample of 590 adults and a clinical sample of 248 adults. This process resulted in a final selection of 70 items for the ILS; 48 items were dropped because of lack of discrimination between adults at different levels of dependence, low inter-item correlation, and/or sex bias.

OPERATIONAL DEFINITION.   Items were constructed to reflect the specific abilities (attributes) that were determined in the above procedure as defining a given component. Whenever possible, Loeb (f) constructed items that required the examinee to demonstrate the specific ability in question, to demonstrate knowledge or relevant factual information, or to demonstrate the use of information in solving hypothetical, everyday problems in living. The number of items for a component was dictated primarily by the number of constituent attributes arising from the earlier empirical analysis, as well as the need to have adequate samples of behavior related to each attribute. Wechsler's item and scoring formats offered a general model for the ILS.

CRITIQUE.   Loeb's empirical approach to conceptual definition provides the ILS with a firm base in terms of content validity. The components and specific abilities represent the combined perspectives of legal professionals who address the legal construct of competency in guardianship cases, the psychological and behavioral perspectives of mental health and social service personnel who assess and serve the elderly, and the practical perspectives of the elderly themselves. (Interestingly, the perspectives of these various groups did not differ markedly (a).) Thus, the process allows one to postulate that the components have conceptual ties to both the legal notion of competency to care for self/property and clinical notions of capacities relevant for independent functioning. The extent to which the final scale is a comprehensive reflection of these efforts is less clear, since so many items were eliminated.

Loeb also seems to have been successful in constructing items that require an examinee's demonstration of the abilities (attributes) associated with the various components. The MAI and the MFAQ (reviewed earlier) ask examinees to report whether or not they can perform a certain function; in contrast, the ILS asks them to perform it. This approach has considerable benefits for the examiner who wishes to use assessment data to make inferences about everyday functioning, because ILS responses may be much closer conceptually to everyday functioning than are self-reports. On the other hand, one must remember that performance in test situations—even performing everyday functions–may not always reflect an examinee's behavior in everyday life.

A variety of short forms of the original scale (CCS) have been suggested involving 42 items or 50 items (h, i), but currently only the 70 item standardized ILS is available (g).

Psychometric Development

STANDARDIZATION. Wording and sequence of items were carefully developed (f) and refined (b) in the initial scale, and further specified in the standardization efforts. Examiner comments about the clarity of rules for administration and scoring were compiled. Ambiguities were resolved and in some cases items that were difficult to score or administer were eliminated from the final scale (g). The final test kit contains a detailed administration form with each item appearing as read to the subject in its entirety and a scoring manual with examples of 2, 1, and 0 point responses.

RELIABILITY. Internal consistency in the standardization sample consisting of 590 nonclinical cases was .88 for the full scale. Subscale alphas were: .77 for Memory/Orientation, .87 for Managing Money, .85 for Managing Home and Transportation, .86 for Health and Safety, .72 for Social Adjustment. The developers note that the Memory/Orientation scales and the Social Adjustment scales have the fewest items, likely attenuating alpha. Factor score alphas were .86 for Problem Solving and .92 for Performance/Information.

Test-retest reliability estimates in 80 adults from the standardization sample who were administered the test approximately 2 weeks post initial test (range 7–24 days) were .91 for the full scale, .84 for Memory/Orientation, .92 for Managing Money, .83 for Managing Home and Transportation, .88 for Health and Safety, .81 for Social Adjustment, .90 for the Problem Solving factor, and .94 for the Performance/Information factor. Test-retest decision consistency was compared by looking at the distributions of individuals classified as high, moderate, or low functioning (determined on the basis of ILS cut-off scores) developed by examining current living situation and self-reports of areas of need for assistance, initially and at retest. In general test-retest decision consistency was good except for the Social Adjustment scale. Individuals tended to improve over time, which may reflect clinical improvement and/or experience with the test. Test security is emphasized (g).

Interrater reliability for the ILS is excellent at .99 for the total scale and .95–.99 over subscales and factor scores (g).

NORMS.   Normative data are available for 590 adults age 65+, approximately evenly split by gender and ranging across educational levels (g).

CRITIQUE.   The ILS has evidence for excellent reliability in all domains. The normative sample is adequate for assessing older adults, although additional normative data would be required if the test were to be used with younger, for example psychiatrically ill, adults. ILS development included extensive attention to standardization of procedures and scoring, resulting in an instrument that is relatively easy to administer and score. Overall, the test has exceptional psychometric properties.

Construct Validation

The ILS aims to have good validity for the legal construct of capacity to care for self and property through the identification of content domain through extensive survey methods described earlier. The final subscale development was guided by item q-sorts by four experts in the field. As noted earlier, factor analysis of the ILS revealed two factors: Problem solving, comprised of questions that demand complex reasoning and problem solving, and Performance/Information, comprised of questions that require knowledge of factual information.

Early studies of the ILS in its original form, the CCS, examined correlations between the CCS and other measures. The CCS correlated poorly (.21) with scores on the *Geriatric Profile* (a measure of symptomatic behavior in the elderly, d, f) and only moderately (.40) with scores on Zigler and Phillips' (k) *Social Competence Scale* (h). In both of these studies, however, the CCS was more closely related to the degree of independence that subjects maintained in living arrangements than were the measures to which the CCS was being compared (see Predictive and Classificatory Utility below). Dunn (c) found that the seven core measures in the *Halstead-Reitan Battery* for neuropsychological assessment were capable of accounting for 41% of the variance (multiple regression) in total CCS scores, in an elderly sample being assessed for suspected dementia related to brain pathology. The highest Pearson correlations between Halstead measures and total CCS scores were for the Halstead's *Speech Sounds*

Perception Test (−.56), *Rhythm Test* (−.47), and *Tactual Performance (Memory) Test* (.38).

Subsequent work with the ILS itself also examined correlations with cognitive measures (including WAIS-R subscale and IQ scores) among 90 adults in a nonclinical sample, and Microcog index scores among 47 adults in a nonclinical sample. In general, correlations were moderate except for Social Adjustment, suggesting the constructs are related but not identical.

In another study of the CCS (the predecessor to the ILS) Dunn (c) compared CCS scores with relatives' ratings of the examinee's functioning in each area. Correlations between CCS subscale scores and their corresponding SCIL ratings by relatives were above .40 for Communications and Money Management; between .30 to .39 for Care for Medical Needs, Emergencies, Personal Hygiene, and Utilize Transportation; and below .30 for Acquire Money, Compensate for Incapacities, Diet, and Manage Household. Total CCS and total SCIL scores correlated .41. Subsequent work with the ILS itself found that among 90 adults in a nonclinical sample, ILS subscales correlated between .53 to .67 with MAI total scores, and ILS total scores correlated .71 with MAI total scores (g).

A series of studies examined the use of the ILS with clinical populations including adults with mental retardation, traumatic brain injury, dementia, chronic psychiatric disturbance, schizophrenia, and major depression. In general, patients performed worse on ILS scales than did controls although this varied across groups and was not statistically significant for every subscale for every group, especially not for Memory/Orientation and Social Adjustment (g).

CRITIQUE. It is interesting that the ILS factor analysis suggests two factors that are consistent with two of the three item types that were identified on the CCS. It is unclear whether this represents two important elements in the construct of capacity to care for self and property or merely "method variance" associated with the items. It would have been interesting if factor analyses found more support for the ILS subscales and particularly the notion of financial management as being somewhat different from Health and Safety or Home and Transportation skills. Patterns of correlation with the WAIS-R suggest these subscales may rely on slightly different abilities.

There is some evidence that the ILS and its predecessor, the CCS, are related to the degree of independent living that one can maintain in everyday life, and that they relate more closely to this criterion than do indexes of general cognition or social competence. It would be interesting to compare scores on the ILS with scores on other performance-based IADL instruments like the DAFS or EPT.

The ILS exceeds other IADL scales in the quantity of data available comparing it with other tests and between patient groups. Yet the ILS is in need of research showing that the scores on various component subscales correspond to external indicators of the same specific functional abilities that the subscales claim to measure. For example, do Managing Money scores correlate highly with the degree of responsibility for personal financial dealings actually assumed by individuals in everyday life? Furthermore, do Managing Money scores correlate with judicial assessments of need for a conservator? The ILS was carefully developed to correspond with the legal construct of capacity to care for self and property, although some of the content coverage and specificity may have been diminished in the standardization efforts which reduced the number of items to less than half developed in the original clinical and legal surveys. Studies comparing the current version of the ILS to expert assessments of relevant legal constructs would be interesting.

Predictive or Classificatory Utility

In early studies, total CCS scores were related significantly to the degree of independence in examinees' current living arrangements. Loeb (f) found highly significant differences (for total CCS scores and for 14 of the 19 CCS subscales) between elderly individuals in three living arrangements: living independently, living in a home for the aged with little daily assistance, and living in a home for the aged with much daily assistance and structure. Post hoc analyses identified significant differences primarily on Communication, Emergencies, Personal Hygiene, Manage Money, Utilize Transportation, and Verbal/Math Skills. In a different population, Searight (i) found significant total CCS score differences (using a 16 subscale version of the CCS) between boarding home and independent apartment dwellers (not geriatric), all of whom were recently discharged from a psychiatric hospital. Searight (h) found the same result in another deinstitutionalized psychiatric sample involving both urban and rural settings.

Caul (b) examined the ability of the CCS to predict the future community adjustment of psychiatric patients examined with the CCS during hospital treatment. Community adjustment was assessed with the *Brockton Social Adjustment Scale* (j, a rating of living and employment independence) and the *Katz Adjustment Scale* (e, professionals' ratings of behavioral symptomatology) approximately three months after CCS examination in the hospital. The CCS correlated .49 with later Brockton adjustment, but only .10 with Katz adjustment.

Subsequent work with the standardized ILS established cut scores on the ILS to correspond with level of independent functioning in the community (g). The cut scores are useful in interpretation of the scale for clinical purposes.

CRITIQUE. When added to the results described above under Construct Validation, these findings lend further support to the inference that the ILS measures functional abilities of some importance in managing one's everyday life and financial resources. With the development of cut-scores during the standardization of the ILS, the classificatory utility of the instrument is increased, although still must be provided in light of other data. The score may suggest a level of supervision needed and would need to be combined with other data to make recommendations regarding legal adjudication for guardianship.

Potential for Expressing Person-Situation Congruency

It is possible to interpret the ILS on several levels. The examiner can consider the full scale score as an indicator of level of functioning, high for independent functioning, moderate for semi-independent functioning, and low for dependent functioning. However, there is the possibility for more refined interpretation, considering person-situation congruency at other levels of interpretation. Subscale scores and individual item information may be interpreted in light of information about the individual's situation and resources. The extent to which family or professional assistance is available and the extent to which the individual will use and can benefit from that assistance all need to be considered.

The most direct approach to expressing person-situation congruency with the ILS in individual cases would be to establish normative data for ILS subscales in a variety of environmental living arrangements. This approach would determine the mean subscale scores for individuals who are manifesting adequate functional adaptation to completely independent residential and financial situations, to settings that provide varying degrees of assistance, and finally for individuals who have adapted only under situations of extreme assistance and dependency. An examinee's ILS subscale scores then could be compared to the norms for these various settings. For example, a setting in which residents have ILS scores notably greater than those of the examinee might be seen as making demands that are incongruent with the abilities of the examinee. Examinees with scores more congruent with individuals in highly protective settings may be perceived as more likely to be in need of some form of guardianship, conservatorship, or other assistance in the relevant areas of functioning suggested by their poorer scores on certain ILS subscales.

Another method for expressing person-situation congruency with the ILS would be to develop methods for assessing and describing environments using dimensions that are parallel to various components of the ILS. Thus an elderly individual's particular circumstances might be described as demanding greater or less ability to manage money, to respond to emergencies, and so forth. The environment's demands could then be compared to the degrees of ability that the elderly person would bring to that situation. The development of this type of assessment system is discussed further in the third section of this chapter.

References

(a) Anderten, P. (1979). *The elderly, incompetency, and guardianship.* Unpublished master's thesis, St. Louis University.
(b) Caul, J. (1984). *The predictive utility of the Community Competence Scale.* Unpublished doctoral dissertation, St. Louis University.
(c) Dunn, T. (1984). *Halstead-Reitan Neuropsychological Battery and its prediction of functional daily living skills among geriatric patients with suspected dementia.* Unpublished doctoral dissertation, St. Louis University.
(d) Evenson, R. (1976). *Geriatric Profile: Manual.* Unpublished, Missouri Institute of Psychiatry, St. Louis, MO.
(e) Katz, M., & Lyerly, S. (1963). Methods for measuring adjustment and social behavior in the community: 1. Rationale, description, discriminative validity, and scale development. *Psychological Reports, 13,* 503–535.
(f) Loeb, P. A. (1983). *Validity of the Community Competence Scale with the elderly.* Unpublished doctoral dissertation, St. Louis University.
(g) Loeb, P. A. (1996). *Independent Living Scales.* San Antonio: Psychological Corp.
(h) Searight, H. R. (1983). *The utility of the Community Competence Scale for determining placement site among the deinstitutionalized mentally ill.* Unpublished doctoral dissertation, St. Louis University.
(i) Searight, H. R., Oliver, J., & Grisso, T. (1983). The Community Competence Scale: Preliminary reliability and validity. *American Journal of Community Psychology, 11,* 609–613.
(j) Walker, R. (1972). The Brockton Social Adjustment Scale. *Diseases of the Nervous System, 33,* 542–545.
(k) Zigler, E., & Phillips, L. (1961). Social competence and outcome in psychiatric disorders.*Journal of Abnormal and Social Psychology, 63,* 264–271.

CURRENT STATUS OF THE FIELD

RESEARCH DIRECTIONS

Functional Component

The following discussion relies on the instruments reviewed in the second section of this chapter to examine several issues in the development of methods for assessing the abilities of disabled persons in guardianship cases.

TABLE 4. CONTENT AREAS ON IADL AND FAI INSTRUMENTS

	AFABS	MAI	MFAQ	DAFS	EPT	DIG	FCI	HCAI	ILS
Money									
Cash/Check		X	X	X		X	X	X	X
Knowledge/ judgment	X				X	X	X	X	X
Home									
Cleaning	X	X	X		X	X			X
Maintenance		X				X			X
Safety									X
Laundry		X			X				
Health									
Medication	X	X	X		X				
Health Maintenance	X				X	X			X
Transportation									
Using bus/taxi		X	X		X				X
Driving		X		X					
Meals									
Shopping		X	X	X	X				
Food preparation		X	X		X	X			
Communication									
Telephone		X	X	X	X				X
Mail			X						X

SELECTING FUNCTIONAL ABILITY CONSTRUCTS. Numerous instruments have been developed to assess functional capacities related to questions of guardianship and conservatorship. A comparison of the constructs in tests reviewed in this chapter appears in Table 4.

The various instruments reviewed in this chapter exemplify three different ways to identify the ability constructs relevant for describing everyday functioning of disabled adults. The MAI was based substantially on a conceptual model that defined domains of functioning—ranging from physical to social—and organized abilities within each domain in order of complexity. The AFABS, EPT, DAFS, and MFAQ derived their domains from a logical synthesis of gerontological literature on intellectual abilities (especially the EPT) and functional abilities, and the clinical experience of selected experts, as were the FCI and HCAI, with particular attention to issues of legal capacities. Selection of DIG and ILS dimensions was based on an empirical consensus of a wide range of groups, including the elderly and clinicians working in clinical and legal contexts.

How should future test development proceed? Developers of similar instruments in the future should not automatically select any one of these methods over the others, because none is inherently best. Each has its own values and limitations. Instruments based on a conceptual approach have a clear advantage over the other two approaches in that their results can then be interpreted in light of the conceptual model itself. On the other hand, concepts and theories sometimes confine thinking, so that the product might not be as responsive to real-world concerns and phenomena as an instrument based on a logical synthesis of practical, clinical experience. Clinical notions about what to measure, however, may be open to bias or narrowness of perspective. This can be mitigated by an empirical approach to gaining consensus among a broader range of individuals for whom the instrument will be relevant.

A fourth empirical approach, however, would offer advantages not afforded by any of the three approaches demonstrated in the current instruments. Each of these approaches assumes that a single set of domain concepts will serve the need to describe elderly individuals equally well across all environmental settings in which elderly persons function. In contrast, a behavioral-ecological approach would seek several domains of functioning that may be salient for various, specific environmental settings, rather than assuming that one set of domains could serve to describe essential functions across all settings and circumstances of the elderly.

Two methods would seem to be suitable for pursuing this objective. The more costly and difficult of the two would require researchers to observe, record, and categorize the specific functions performed by individuals in various settings (e.g., residential options for disabled elderly or nonelderly adults) requiring different degrees of independent functioning. These results would define the conceptual dimensions for subsequent instruments, each instrument having been designed to assess abilities relevant for functioning only in a particular type of setting.

The second method, exemplified by the initial investigations of Scheidt and Schaie (1978), would use survey procedures to determine the frequency with which residents in various living arrangements encounter various possible environmental demands (e.g., dealing with broken appliances, cleaning one's residence, responding to emergencies). The more frequent demands of various settings could then be translated into "critical behaviors necessary to meet these demands" (Scheidt & Schaie, 1978, p. 85). Both the behavioral observation and survey-of-demand approach would provide a more direct, empirical base for the selection of functional-ability domains of measurement than the three approaches in the current instruments.

Whatever approach is used, the relevance of the instrument's concepts and scales for legal decisions about the need for a guardian will depend on the degree to which the use of the instrument in legal cases was considered at the outset. For example, a set of ability dimensions derived for the study of institutionalized elderly individuals, for whom basic functions of feeding and bathing are paramount considerations, is not likely to provide adequate coverage for the range of elderly and nonelderly disabled individuals (and their environments) encountered in guardianship cases.

Merely surveying judicial concerns may not be sufficient to determine which functional abilities are most relevant for legal guardianship cases. For example, although the ILS began with such a survey, this did not result in money-management content that might be relevant for assessing a person's capacity to manage larger estates. Test developers need to consider the range of case circumstances that actually confront legal decision makers. Unfortunately, there has been no empirical research that describes specific types of guardianship cases typically seen in probate courts. Without this information, researchers are at a disadvantage in constructing assessment instruments of relevance for that decision-making process.

In general, more study is needed to delineate the conceptual coherence of specific functional tasks and the relationship of performance on these with various criteria for "competent" functioning. In considering "capacity to care for self," it is unclear what items should be incorporated, and whether these should focus on direct behavior, reasoning about everyday activities, or higher level abilities (e.g., memory) important for safely carrying out everyday activities. It would be helpful to know how performance on different tasks relates to each other. Does an individual's abilities to prepare a meal relate to abilities to clean a house? Do different everyday activities rely on different cognitive abilities? Does the capacity to independently and prudently manage finances rely on different cognitive abilities then the capacity to independently and safely drive a car? There has been decades of research exploring the "structure of intellect," such as Guilford's work on model's of intelligence (1967), Cattell's work differentiating fluid from crystallized abilities (1963), and Schaie's (1994) and Baltes (1987) work on the course of intellectual development across the lifespan. Efforts to relate these structures to areas of brain function (c.f. Lezak, 1995) provide a conceptual and biologically based framework to guide cognitive assessments. Similar empirical work on the "structure of function" is needed and can build upon work by Kane and Kane (1981), Lawton (1982), Spector et al. (1987), and Marsiske and Willis (1995). With a conceptual framework that links everyday functioning to measures of cognition and behavior, and everyday behaviors to each other, clinicians will have an empirically and conceptually coherent structure to guide their assessments. As it is now, each individual assessment is primarily a clinical, personal, and subjective task, evaluating specific tasks in a mostly face valid fashion. While specificity and ecological validity is important, empirical and conceptual grounding should ultimately enhance the reliability and meaningfulness of guardianship decisions.

METHODS FOR ASSESSING ABILITIES. The various instruments manifest several different response modes for indexing functional abilities. Each of these offers different sources of potential error in relation to external criteria.

The MFAQ asks examinees to report whether or not they "can do" particular things. Some individuals, however, might not have had to perform the function in question for some time (e.g., housecleaning, if they have hired a maid for several years) and may not be aware that their abilities have diminished over the years. In addition, some elderly individuals might have a need to report being able to do things that in fact they cannot do. The MAI potentially mitigates these problems by asking not only what examinees "can do," but also whether or not they now perform the function. Nevertheless, this method is still open to error in self-report of one's performance.

Asking examinees to demonstrate the ability in question, as do many of the DAFS, EPT, and ILS items, avoids self-report error. Nevertheless, this method requires attention to another question of generalizability— whether individuals might sometimes perform the function better or more poorly in the artificial test situation than in the real world.

Another approach, used on the AFABS, is to ask individuals who are familiar with the examinee's everyday functioning to describe or rate it. This method, though, is highly dependent on the integrity and motivation of the informant. In guardianship cases, relatives who are close to the examinee may be the petitioners; they might be motivated to accentuate the individual's specific inabilities, consistent with their general opinion about the need for guardianship. The examiner's direct observation of examinees in their natural setting, also encouraged with the AFABS, may be possible in institutional or nursing home environments; but this may be more difficult when the examinee is living in a private setting.

CRITERION VALIDITY. The most common strategies for validation of the instruments reviewed here have been the comparison of their results to clinicians' ratings and comparison between groups of elderly individuals living in settings requiring various degrees of independence. These are important criteria, but they do not directly address the question of generalizability of test results to the real world. Mental health professionals and legal decision makers who will use the instruments and their results need to know whether performance on the test corresponds to functioning in everyday life. For example, one needs to know whether the behavior sampled in the ILS Money Management items provides results that correspond to the same levels of performance in the actual management of money in everyday life. Research efforts to validate these instruments eventually must turn to the use of behavioral criteria in examinees' natural environments, rather than relying solely on clinical judgments and group classification as external criteria.

Another important validation strategy is to compare multiple instruments designed to measure the same abilities with one another in multiple homogenous subgroups. Given the expansion of the number of tests to measure everyday functioning, a critical next step of inquiry is to test the same sample with multiple measures intending to measure capacities in multiple areas (home, health, finances, etc). Multi-trait multi method analyses would serve to validate the instruments and the concepts.

PSYCHOMETRIC PROPERTIES. Many of the instruments presented have good reliability. Additional information on inter-rater reliability is needed for the AFABS and EPT, and on test-retest stability is needed for the AFABS, MFAQ, and DIG. Normative data are critically important to provide information on the performance of healthy samples against which to compare the performance of impaired individuals to get a sense of the relative deficit of any individual. Normative data are needed for the AFABS, DAFS, DIG, and HCAI. Furthermore, information on the performance of healthy individuals is important in establishing the meaningfulness (validity) of the test and concepts. If healthy people do poorly or change over time, concepts or their measurement need to be re-evaluated.

Many of the instruments demonstrate considerable ingenuity in the development of systems for combining item scores to obtain summary indexes of functioning. Many of the summary score systems will be quite useful in research for validating the instrument. On the other hand, researchers and test developers should be aware that summary scores will be of limited use in applications of instrument results to legal guardianship cases. An overall impairment score, for example, does not communicate a person's strengths and weaknesses on specific areas of functioning within the test. The latter differentiation will become increasingly important in crafting limited guardianships. Therefore, validation research should not focus entirely on summary impairment scores at the expense of validating individual items or subsets of items.

Causal Component

Current research with the three instruments does not adequately prepare examiners to interpret the reasons or potential explanations for deficient performance on the instruments. For example, interpretations about causal relations between performance on these instruments and brain pathology or psychological symptoms would be aided by more research on the performance of individuals with known types of pathology. Research on the relation between results on these instruments and results on neuropsychological assessment instruments would also be helpful (e.g., see Dunn, 1984, in the ILS review). The inclusion of neuropsychological testing, as well as other data (such as medical record information), is necessary to establish causal links.

Some elderly individuals might manifest relatively poor performance in certain areas of functioning not because of an inability to perform the function, but because of inexperience or a reversible atrophy of skills. Kane and Kane (1981), for example, point out that some residential settings for the elderly do not encourage the maintenance or development of "IADL skills," producing a risk that they will lose these skills permanently. On the other hand, some individuals may have become deficient in certain skills yet be capable of relearning them relatively quickly under proper conditions (Willis, 1990). Poor performances on the functional ability instruments, therefore, should not automatically be interpreted as fixed incapacities. This observation has legal relevance, in that placing legal control of an individual's life in the hands of a guardian might seem unjust when the individual may be capable, with minimal assistance, of assuming self-control.

Examiners, however, have little research to guide them in determining whether a current performance deficit suggests an irretrievable loss of function or a reversible deficit. Further, existing instruments do not provide methods for examining these alternative interpretations. One approach to developing such methods would be to devise supplementary test procedures designed to teach the skill in question to the examinee, then to reassess performance. For example, if an examinee performed poorly when locating a name in the telephone book (an item in the ILS), a supplementary procedure could instruct the examinee how to perform this task, then retest at a later time with a different name to locate. Thus, the development of a "learning capacity" supplement to an instrument like the ILS might be of assistance to examiners in interpreting the nature and implications of performance deficits on the instrument.

Overall, forensic examiners should bear in mind that while new statutes focus on "functional" definitions of incapacity, accurate diagnosis of the "disabling condition" is still an essential part of the forensic evaluation, especially in guardianship. Diagnosis will often be the best indicator of prognosis and will guide guardianship decisions, which focus on more than the competency of the individual for a single task at a single point in time (i.e., competency to stand trial), but on many tasks over an indefinite period of time. A diagnosis of dementia of the Alzheimer type would suggest the incapacities will progress; a diagnosis of alcohol dependence could mean the incapacities might remit if the drinking stopped.

Interactive Component

A disabled individual's functional deficit may be of greater or lesser consequence depending on the person's current living arrangements, family supports, financial estate, and other environmental or situational circumstances. This has several implications for the development of instruments like those reviewed earlier.

First, test developers should not encourage the use of cutoff scores for determining a person's impaired or unimpaired status. Absolute performance criteria of this type may be useful for various research purposes. Yet impairment is a relative rather than fixed condition, depending in part on the demands of the examinee's own environmental circumstance. This is recognized not only in legal reasoning (see Interactive Component, in the first section of this chapter), but also in the ecological perspectives of gerontologists themselves (see the same discussion noted above). Kane and Kane (1981), for example, discuss the fact that "not all persons are required to manage skills at the same level of complexity … Some have more of the advantages of modern devices and human help than do others" (p. 57). They note also that certain geriatric rehabilitation settings in England evaluate competence "by performance relative to the actual home environment rather than by an absolute set of skills" (p. 57).

Second, this view suggests the need for ways to describe the demands of disabled individuals' specific environments relative to their own level of functional abilities. The MAI and MFAQ provide certain types of information that may be used to characterize the physical demands and social supports in an elderly examinee's current environment. Part B of the MFAQ may be especially helpful in determining the supportive services currently at work in the examinee's life. Nevertheless, the ideal assessment system would provide a method for assessing and describing the examinee's environment on dimensions that directly parallel each of the functioning domains on which the examinee has been assessed. The ALSAR and CARE instruments attempt to measure resources for each capacity in question. They were not reviewed here since they have been the subject of limited study and validation. Clearly more research on these instruments is warranted.

Another key area for research is the individual-family dynamic in the interactive component. Although capacity assessments focus of the abilities of the identified individual, competency concerns often arise in a family system. Some family members support their parents' and grandparents' autonomous decision making and only step-in via guardianship when it is really necessary to protect the individual and estate from real danger to the individual (i.e., financial exploitation by a scam-artist that would result in the loss of a home for the elder). Unfortunately some guardianship petitions are from families with decades of conflict and the petition may really represent a desire of an adult child or other relative to gain financial control for their own (the "fiduciary's" own) current and future financial needs. Drug addiction and excessive credit spending are among the habits that may lead adult children to look at compromised parents as a source of income; cohort differences whereby currently older cohorts see themselves in a role of sacrificing for their children may also shape the spending decisions and expectations of elderly parents and their adult children. Determining when to respect the beliefs and norms of individual families versus when to intercede in situations of financial exploitation of the elders can be difficult. Clearly, the role of family dynamics needs to be evaluated in considering the disabled adult's capacities in the context of evaluations for guardianship, especially where the guardian may benefit from their position.

Judgmental and Dispositional Components

Even with the eventual development of instruments for expressing person-situation incongruence, test developers should not be concerned with determining the degrees of incongruence that might define legal incompetence to care for one's property or oneself. Incompetence decisions require the application of judgments and moral values in order to conclude whether the weight of evidence tips the scales in favor of protection of the individual at the expense of loss of freedom and self-determination. This is not an empirical question and therefore is not properly addressed with predetermined, absolute criteria of a scientific nature.

It is important to recognize that decisions regarding self-determination are moral and legal and must therefore be judicial. It is also important to acknowledge that such decisions are only as good as the data upon which they rely. Judges and juries generally do not have clinical training and rely upon the expertise of clinicians to complete evaluations of functioning that are comprehensive, valid, and age appropriate.

In addition, we should recognize that judicial determinations may be subject to the same ethical dilemmas clinicians face in balancing beneficence which promotes autonomy versus paternalism, especially for elderly adults about whom paternalistic instincts may run high. One area for future research consists of ethics studies of the judgmental and dispositional outcomes of guardianship proceedings. Potential racial (Vasvada, Masand, & Nasra, 1997) and age-based discrimination (Altman & Parmelee, 1989) in guardianship decisions could be further explored.

CLINICAL APPLICATION

Description

Not all guardianship cases involving disabled individuals will require a description on the full range of functional abilities represented in the instruments reviewed in this chapter. For example, some individuals may be so severely disabled physically (e.g., bed-ridden) that this condition alone will rule out the need to assess many behavioral tasks so that the evaluation may focus on cognitive capacities to direct others in self and estate care.

When a full assessment of capacities related to ability to care for self and/or property is needed, the instruments reviewed here offer several benefits, including standardization of procedure, generally acceptable reliability, and an assurance that the examinee will be described on a range of functions. Further, their use mitigates one's over-reliance on speculation about practical, functional abilities based on symptoms of physical or psychopathological disorder alone.

Examiners should not emphasize the use of summary scores at the expense of individual item responses when describing examinees' performance on the instruments. The concept of limited guardianship is best served by providing information about discrete abilities; summary impairment scores may inappropriately encourage all-or-none notions of incompetency.

Explanation

Indications of poor ability on the instruments may be obtained for a variety of reasons. Among these are temporary conditions of fatigue, certain motivational states, misunderstanding of the examiner's inquiries (e.g., due to visual or hearing difficulties), atrophy of skills that conceivably could be relearned, or actual deficit as a direct consequence of brain pathology or other disorder. Further, instruments that ask the examinee "Do you ... " or "Can you ... " (the MAI and MFAQ) may produce responses that are motivated by the examinee's self-perceptions and feelings of adequacy or inadequacy, such as exaggerated feelings of helplessness or a need to appear competent. Therefore, all indexes of functional strengths or deficits must be interpreted concerning their probable cause or their relation to other conditions of the examinee.

As previously noted, interpretation of performance on functional ability instruments will require a variety of other types of data concerning the examinee. Generally this might require assessment with neuropsychological instruments, psychological tests of affect and personality, medical and neurological examination, including labs and scans, or other methods. In addition, several discussions in this chapter have pointed to the importance of information about examinees' current social and physical environments when explaining their functional abilities and deficits. Thus a direct examination (observation) of their home environment and associates may be necessary. The range of information that will be needed in many of these assessments again supports an interdisciplinary approach.

Special consideration should be given to the possibility that some disabled individuals may be capable of learning skills that they do not possess currently, rather than merely assuming that current inabilities are fixed and unchangeable (Willis, 1990). Thus assessments should include an evaluation of learning potential.

Prediction

Generalization of the instruments' results to functioning in everyday life presents several difficulties. Currently there is evidence that performance on such instruments reflects systematic differences between elderly or nonelderly disabled groups who function in living arrangements requiring more or less self-sufficiency. Yet the instruments vary regarding empirical evidence that their indexes of specific abilities correspond to actual performance of those abilities outside the testing situation. Construct validity studies suggest that they do, but direct evidence is minimal.

Any use of the instruments' results to infer functioning or to predict future functioning in everyday settings must consider the fact that environmental settings themselves contribute greatly to an individual's manifestation of the ability in question outside the test situation. Thus generalization of the results to external situations will require data on the current or future physical and social environment in which the examinee will be functioning. Any speculations on the basis of examination of the individual alone, without a corresponding environmental assessment, are improper and highly suspect. Certain features of the instruments themselves provide some information about the examinee's environment. Nevertheless, the self report does not offer a substitute for obtaining and considering environmental data from other sources.

Conclusions

The instruments obviously cannot define legal competence or incompetence, because these determinations require moral and social judgments about justice that are not empirical in nature (see Judgmental and Dispositional Components, in the first section of this chapter). However, these instruments can be extremely helpful in providing a way to assess behavioral and cognitive skills important for everyday functioning and for organizing the courts' thinking about these matters for the purpose of deciding questions of legal competence. Like all assessment instruments, those reviewed here must be used by qualified examiners familiar with the population and disorders presented, as well as the psychometric properties that support or limit interpretation of tests (Moye, 2000).

Examiners may be especially helpful for the legal decision maker if they can characterize the congruency or discrepancy between the disabled individual's functional abilities and the demands or supports that are characteristic of specific environments. Expert testimony about the significance or severity of functional disability should be based on the previously mentioned person-situation comparisons, not on an absolute level of functioning alone. This is because very poor functioning in a certain area of ability may be of little consequence or of great consequence, depending on the nature of the examinee's everyday environment. Thus describing an individual as impaired should be qualified, that is, impaired in relation to some particular demand of the relevant environment.

Degrees of discrepancy between an individual's manifest abilities and environmental demands might allow the examiner to testify about the risks associated with a decision not to provide the individual with guardianship assistance in various spheres of self-care or management of property. This testimony would not violate the general principle to avoid stating a conclusion on the ultimate legal question. That is, the assessment results might allow the examiner to conclude that the individual would be exposed to a particular degree of peril without a guardian's assistance; this could be stated without concluding that a legal threshold for a determination of incompetency has or has not been reached.

However, as previously noted, forensic evaluations for the purposes of guardianship of person and estate rarely involve in-person testimony and cross-examination of the evaluator. This means there is not an opportunity for the proposed ward and their counsel (if they are even present) to challenge the adequacy and appropriateness of the evaluation. There should be continued efforts to advocate for legislation that can increase the quality of competency evaluations in this area (e.g., bills which require the evaluator to provide detailed reports or to appear in person).

In conclusion, numerous instruments are available for use in guardianship evaluations. The examiner can choose the most appropriate instrument based on the best method and task appropriateness for the specific capacity area in question. Future research should extend the validity and normative data for these instruments. In the interim, clinicians involved in these evaluations can carefully evaluate the disabling condition, cognitive abilities, and behavioral outcomes specific to any individual and guardianship issue presented and support the courts in arriving at fair and, if appropriate, limited guardianships.

9

Competence to
Consent to Treatment

THE COMPETENCE QUESTION

Western traditions of respect for individual choice, as exemplified for several centuries in Anglo-American law, have protected the right of persons to decide for themselves whether to undergo medical treatment (Faden & Beauchamp, 1986). Medical professionals have long been prohibited from treating people against their will, both by ethical tradition and by laws that defined physicians' treatment without consent as the basis for a suit for battery. Often, however, the patients' consent to treatment was less than explicit and might be implied, for example, if the patient did not object to a course of treatment as it was being implemented.

By the mid-twentieth century, however, traditional approaches to consent to treatment came under greater scrutiny. In a series of cases from 1955 to 1972, the courts formulated a radically different approach that came to be called *informed consent* (Berg, Appelbaum, Lidz, & Parker, 2001). As it evolved, informed consent came to require three elements: (a) the *disclosure* of treatment-relevant information to patients by clinicians, (b) that the patients' decision must be *voluntary*, and (c) that the patient

391

must be *competent* to make the treatment decision (Grisso & Appelbaum, 1998a; *Kaimowitz v. Department of Mental Health*, 1973). The necessity for informed consent could be set aside only in certain emergency situations (for some treatments). For patients who were incompetent to provide consent, typically the decision about treatment would be made by a proper substitute decision maker or by court order.

The competence element of informed consent is the primary focus of this chapter, although it will become clear that questions of competence are not separable from the disclosure and voluntariness requirements. The term *competence to consent* refers to an individual's legal capacity to accept a proposed treatment, to refuse treatment, or to select among treatment options.

Questions of competence to consent may be raised for many types of patients. They may be persons with physical traumas or illnesses requiring medical treatment, or they may be persons who require treatment for mental illness. Although mental illness, mental retardation, and degenerative neurological conditions often precipitate the need for an evaluation of a person's competence to consent, the question may be raised in cases involving no mental illness but rather the presence of significant cognitive deficits related to a trauma or the effects of prolonged illness.

The mere fact of mental illness, disability, or involuntary hospitalization does not create a presumption of incompetence to consent to or refuse most treatments (*Rennie v. Klein, 1982; Rogers v. Okin*, 1982). In contrast, the law related to the treatment of minors generally presumes that they are incompetent to consent; yet special statutory provisions and case law recognize several exceptions (e.g., "mature minor," and consent for certain types of treatment: Melton, Petrila, Poythress, & Slobogin, 1997), sometimes requiring a determination of a minor's competence to consent.

The importance of defining competence to consent among these types of patients is underscored by the risks associated with various treatments about which they are asked to decide. In addition to surgical procedures, treatments that often receive special attention in discussions of informed consent include electroconvulsive therapy, psychotropic medication, psychotherapy and behavior modification techniques, and elective medical interventions such as sterilization and termination of pregnancy.

Questions of competence to consent to treatment arouse conflicting social values concerning patient autonomy and beneficent protection of patients (Lidz et al., 1984; Faden & Beauchamp, 1986). We value individual freedom to exercise self-determination in matters intimately affecting one's own life, even if one's choices may be perceived by others as odd or unreasonable. This view often includes arguments against presumptions of incompetence based merely on an individual's status as mentally ill.

Sometimes in conflict with this value, however, is the humanitarian concern that disabled or immature individuals should be protected from suffering that they might endure because of their unreasonable or imprudent choices. Debate concerning competence to participate in treatment decisions has been fueled by conflict between these competing values.

Furthermore, the law's definitions of patients' right to refuse treatment, and of the parameters of competence to consent, establish the contours of professional responsibility in clinical decisions. These contours in turn define the basis for claims of professional liability for damage. The types of claims for potential litigation in this area are numerous: for example, a patient's claim to having been competent when he was treated without his consent by doctors who perceived the patient as incompetent to consent; a consenting patient's claim that she was not adequately informed of the treatment risks; or the claim that doctors did not seek appropriate surrogate consent to treat a patient who had incompetently refused a treatment that was needed (Berg et al., 2001). The careful assessment of competence to consent, therefore, is of special importance in order to fulfill professional obligations (Grisso & Appelbaum, 1998a).

Finally, the limits and side effects of many medical and psychological treatments (e.g., tardive dyskinesia with prolonged antipsychotic medication) intensify the argument that, whenever possible, patients should be allowed to choose whether they will endure these treatments. In turn, patients' competence to consider the information that professionals give them about the risks of such treatments takes on greater urgency in light of our increased knowledge of the risks.

LAW AND CURRENT PRACTICE

Legal Standard

As noted earlier, the doctrine of informed consent requires three elements: (a) *disclosure* of relevant treatment information, (b) *voluntariness*, and (c) *competence* of the person giving consent. Thus the major focus of this chapter—the competence element—is only one element that may legally invalidate consent or refusal.

The *disclosure* element requires that patients must be informed of five things (*Natanson v. Kline*, 1960; *Canterbury v. Spence*, 1972):

- the nature of the disorder for which treatment is being proposed,
- the nature of the proposed treatment,
- the benefits associated with the treatment as well as the likelihood of their occurrence,

- the risks and discomforts associated with the treatment, and their likelihood, and
- the alternative treatments available (including no treatment), as well as their risks and benefits.

The specific information and disclosure procedures that constitute adequate disclosure in a given case have been judged by three somewhat different legal standards: whether the disclosure represents what the average, reasonable practitioner would provide under similar circumstances (*Natanson v. Kline*, 1960); whether the disclosure would be adequate to inform the average, reasonable patient (*Cobbs v. Grant*, 1972); and/or whether the clinician disclosed any information that this specific patient might find relevant when making the treatment decision (see generally, Berg et al., 2001). It is also clear that courts have expected disclosure to occur in a manner that is designed to facilitate patients' understanding (Grisso & Appelbaum, 1998a).

The *voluntariness* element requires that a patient's consent must not be the product of coercion, unfair persuasions, and inducements (*Relf v. Weinberger*, 1974). The law has not outlined the specific contours of these conditions. But voluntariness is not in question merely because one is hospitalized and therefore dependent on hospital personnel (Perlin, 1989) or because family members may have convinced the patient to make a particular decision (Grisso & Appelbaum, 1998a).

Until the 1970s, relatively little attention was given to identifying legal standards to be employed in determining *competence* to consent to treatment. One of the initial attempts by Roth, Meisel, and Lidz (1977) concluded that trying to identify a single operative standard for legally defining competence to consent to treatment was "a search for the holy grail." Nevertheless, their seminal work has led to an evolving consensus about the standards that are generally applied by the courts when determining competence to consent to treatment. This consensus was recently summarized by Grisso and Appelbaum (1998a) as a set of "maxims" for legal competence to consent to treatment.

First, courts have consistently made it clear that the mere fact of serious mental illness, mental retardation, or cognitive impairment does not create a presumption of incompetence. One may, in fact, be seriously mentally ill yet competent to consent to treatment.

Second, the law's fundamental concern is with the effects of patients' mental states on their actual cognitive functioning. In this regard, reviews of the law (Annas & Densberger, 1984; Appelbaum & Grisso, 1988; Appelbaum & Grisso, 1995; Drane, 1984; Grisso, 1986; Grisso & Appelbaum, 1998a; McKinnon, Cournos, & Stanley, 1989; Tepper &

Elwork, 1984) have identified four functional abilities that are relevant. These include the ability to:

- communicate a choice,
- understand relevant information,
- appreciate the relevance of the information for one's own circumstances, and
- manipulate information rationally.

These legal concepts will be examined further in a later section in which they are translated for purposes of forensic assessment. Courts typically do not apply any one of these abilities uniformly or in all cases; they generally choose from among them depending on the facts of the case and precedent within a particular legal jurisdiction.

Third, whether courts will consider a person competent or incompetent to consent to treatment will depend in part on the demands of the particular treatment decision that they face. Not all treatment situations require the same degree of decisionmaking abilities. Drane (1984) referred to this maxim as the "sliding scale" of competence, meaning that more or less ability may be required by courts depending on the nature and complexity of the treatment decision that needs to be made.

Fourth, courts' decisions about competence are influenced by the consequences of the treatment decision (Grisso & Appelbaum, 1998a). For example, greater ability may be required when a patient's decision is very likely to lead to death than when the consequences are less certain or severe. This does not mean that patients automatically should be considered incompetent simply because they are opting for a choice that the court believes is unwise. But a patient whose decision creates a higher level of risk regarding the patient's health is likely to receive greater scrutiny.

Finally, the law presumes that one's competence or incompetence can change. Incompetence is not construed as a static condition, but instead requires periodic reassessment and reinstatement of legal competence status when the patient's capacities have improved.

The law deals with the issue of minors' competence to consent to treatment in a different way. As noted earlier, statutes generally deny minors the right to an independent consent or refusal regarding their treatment, because of presumed incompetence to consent. This has been based not only on legal and social assumptions about the effects of immaturity on minors' decisions, but also on social values concerning the rights of parents to control the activities of dependent children for whom they are legally responsible. Nevertheless, the law recognizes a number of exceptions (Melton et al., 1997):

- Most statutes recognize the right of consent for a "mature minor," often defined as a child in the later years of minority status who is living independently of parents or other caretakers.
- Most states recognize a child's consent to treatment (independent of parental involvement) for certain problems, such as venereal disease or drug abuse.
- Courts have recognized minors' rights to make certain decisions concerning birth control and termination or continuation of pregnancy (Melton et al., 1983; *Planned Parenthood v. Danforth, 1976*).

In these exceptional instances, a child's competence to consent to treatment presumably is controlled by the same law of informed consent and competence that prevails in adult cases.

Legal Process

The question of a patient's competence to consent generally will be raised when a treating professional believes that the patient is deficient in the ability to make a competent decision about a treatment that the professional has proposed or is planning to propose. In many jurisdictions, however, this will not result in a judicial review. Several other resolutions are more common.

First, the professional often will proceed with the proposed treatment if the patient consents, even though the professional may have some doubt about the patient's actual competence to make the decision. In other words, the question of competence simply might not be raised if the patient does not refuse the proposed treatment (Berg et al., 2001).

Second, the treating professional might acknowledge the patient's incompetence or relative incapacity and seek the substitute decision of a member of the patient's family. This is routine, of course, in obtaining parents' consent for treatment of children, who for most purposes are considered by statute incompetent to consent. With adults, this approach is most likely to be taken when the patient appears confused or when mental illness is evident and the patient is refusing the proposed treatment (President's Commission for Ethical Problems, 1982), especially when the treatment itself does not present unusually high risks compared to its potential benefits.

Third, treating professionals sometimes attempt to deal with a potentially incompetent patient's refusal of treatment by using logical persuasion, patience, or a prolonged decision process. Lidz et al. (1984), for example, noted that patients' decision-making processes and their actual decisions frequently change during hospitalization. They described cases in which hospital staff, being aware of this variability in patients' decisions, raised the proposed treatment option with the patients repeatedly until such time as they were disposed to agree with the proposal.

Finally, the professional might request a review by an institutional ethics committee or other nonjudicial review mechanism (Levine, 1977; Grisso & Appelbaum, 1998a; Veatch, 1977). Alternatively, the patient may ask the nonjudicial review board to rule on a professional's proposal to proceed to treatment against the allegedly incompetent patient's wishes. Nonjudicial review is required routinely in some institutions for cases in which the proposed treatment (which the patient has refused) is highly intrusive, represents a relatively high risk, or involves an irreversible surgical procedure.

If these various nonjudicial approaches to the question are not available, or do not succeed in allowing treatment over the allegedly incompetent patient's refusal, and if the treating professional is intent on providing the proposed treatment, then the professional may seek judicial review of competence. Most states provide for this review either specifically or under their guardianship laws (see Chapter 8). If the court finds the patient incompetent, the court typically will appoint someone—often a family member—to make treatment decisions for the patient. Various states, however, provide that the court itself may act as the substitute treatment decision maker on behalf of the patient.

Competency Assessment: Current Practice

In preceding chapters dealing with other legal competencies, assessments for competence have been discussed as relatively formal activities designed to obtain information with which to advise legal decision makers. In contrast, most cases in which patients' treatment decision-making capacities are questionable do not reach judicial scrutiny. As noted earlier, more often they result in clinical decisions to forego or delay proposed treatments, or to seek consent from relatives or authorized nonjudicial review boards. Assessments for competence to consent ultimately may reach a legal forum, and in some states they must for certain purposes (e.g., medication of patients involuntarily admitted to psychiatric hospitals). Yet generally they have been "forensic assessments" (in the sense described earlier for other legal competencies) only in those special circumstances or jurisdictions in which judicial review of evidence and declaration of incompetence has been required.

Thus it is not surprising that most evaluations for competence to consent are not formal procedures. Instead, they generally occur in the context of doctor-patient discussions in which a treatment is about to be proposed or when informed consent procedures are implemented (Grisso & Appelbaum, 1998a; Lidz et al., 1984). Thus the treating professional forms an impression of the patient's capacities prior to seeking informed consent (based on overall medical and psychological information about the patient), or the professional evaluates the quality of the patient's actual responses to disclosure of information about the proposed treatment plan. Then, if the case seems ambiguous, the clinician may request a competence evaluation from a specialized forensic mental health professional.

Prior to the past 15 years it was not uncommon to find clinicians basing their competence judgments on global evaluations of mental status, rather than on an evaluation of abilities specific to understanding and weighing treatment options (Grisso, 1986; Lidz et al., 1984). More recent legal and clinical analyses, however, have offered recommendations concerning the specific cognitive or behavioral characteristics of patients that ought to be evaluated when examining competence to consent to treatment, and have provided methods for those evaluations (e.g., see Appelbaum & Grisso, 1988). Many of these recommendations are described in the next section, which examines the translation of the legal construct into psychological concepts. There have been no studies, however, that provide empirical data on "average" or typical practice concerning how competence to consent evaluations are performed.

FROM LEGAL STANDARD TO FORENSIC ASSESSMENT

Functional Component

We noted earlier that as a result of two decades of legal reviews of informed consent and competence (Annas & Densberger, 1984; Appelbaum & Grisso, 1988; Appelbaum & Grisso, 1995; Drane, 1984; Grisso, 1986; Grisso & Appelbaum, 1998a; McKinnon, Cournos, & Stanley, 1989; President's Commission for Ethical Problems, 1982; Roth, Meisel, & Lidz, 1977; Tepper & Elwork, 1984), a consensus has arisen concerning the specific types of abilities that are legally relevant for patients' participation in treatment decisions. These analyses have identified four types of abilities as constituting the domain of functional abilities that might be related to legal definitions of competence to make treatment decisions. (For more detailed descriptions, see especially: Appelbaum & Grisso, 1988; Appelbaum & Grisso, 1995; Grisso & Appelbaum, 1998a).

ABILITY TO COMMUNICATE A CHOICE. This standard focuses simply on patients' abilities to state a preference, indicating to their caregivers what course of treatment they desire (e.g., see *Matter of Conroy*, 1985; *Matter of*

O'Brien, 1986; President's Commission on Ethical Issues, 1982). Some patients are unable to state a choice, while others express decisions that are extremely unstable, vacillating from moment to moment to such an extent that treatment cannot proceed in any specific direction.

As a legal matter, the ability to communicate a choice is a "threshold" issue; if patients are unable to express a choice, usually there is no need to consider their status regarding other abilities. On the other hand, if patients have serious deficits in other abilities described below, rarely will they be considered competent merely because they can state a preference.

ABILITY TO UNDERSTAND RELEVANT INFORMATION. The functional ability most commonly applied by courts in weighing matters of competence to consent to treatment is patients' ability to understand the information that is disclosed to them about the treatment decision. This requirement is often overtly derived from contract law (White & Denise, 1991), where it serves as the basis for determinations of competence to contract. Among the conceptual analyses listed at the beginning of this discussion, all have included the ability to comprehend what one is being told about the disorder, its treatment, and its benefits and risks as a fundamental ability associated with competence to consent to treatment.

ABILITY TO APPRECIATE THE RELEVANCE OF INFORMATION. Many courts have found that patients were incompetent to consent to treatment because, although they appeared to understand what they were being told about their condition, they did not appreciate the significance of the information for their own situation. Thus, patients may be said to lack appreciation when they understand that their doctors believe they are ill, but they deny that they are ill despite solid objective evidence to the contrary. In other cases, they may understand that an effective treatment exists, but cannot believe that it is likely to help them. Typically such cases involve persons with delusions associated with psychotic mental disorders. While they might show evidence of understanding what they are being told, their delusional beliefs (e.g., about the doctor as an agent of the devil) interfere with their realistic application of the information to their own situation.

ABILITY TO MANIPULATE INFORMATION RATIONALLY. Some courts have found that patients were incompetent because they were unable to reason with and process the information disclosed to them about their disorder or treatment, even if they understood it and appreciated its significance for themselves. The focus of this reasoning standard is on the individual's difficulties in weighing multiple treatments, each with different types of benefits and risks, and is most likely to be of concern in more complex treatment decisions or when patients manifest confusion as they proceed to "work with" the information that apparently they can grasp "piece by piece." This circumstance might be found for some persons with developmental disabilities, patients who are suffering from specific brain dysfunctions, or patients who are highly anxious or confused as a result of recent physical or psychological trauma immediately prior to the situation.

Not all jurisdictions will employ all four of these abilities in weighing matters of competence to consent to treatment. Nevertheless, all of them are important to consider when determining what functional abilities are relevant for forensic evaluations of competence, because one or more of them will be used by virtually all courts.

Causal Characteristic

Legal standards for competence to consent to or refuse treatment do not specifically require that deficits in relevant functional abilities must be a "product" of mental illness. In fact, it is not clear that the law requires any particular explanation for a patient's apparent deficits in understanding, appreciation, or reasoning about treatments. Logically, however, explanations for deficits in relevant functional abilities would seem to be a necessary part of assessments for competence to consent to treatment.

For example, imagine that one has assessed a patient's capacity to understand or process treatment-related information prior to undertaking an informed consent procedure. Deficits observed in these capacities might be related to enduring conditions of the patient (e.g., irreversible cerebral damage). On the other hand, they might be related to temporary conditions, such as mental states induced by drugs (self-administered prior to hospitalization), pain related to physical trauma that can be reduced with an analgesic, or bereavement at the recent death of a loved one. A knowledge of these causal conditions might be important in deciding whether the patient is in need of a substitute decision maker or whether one might merely delay the consent process (if treatment is not needed for an emergency condition) until the patient's manifest abilities have improved. These possibilities suggest the need for assessment data to illuminate the medical, psychological, and social circumstances of the patient that might account for observed deficits in the patient's understanding and reasoning with treatment-related information.

Therefore, if patients manifest deficits during assessments of their functional abilities relevant to decision making when confronted with treatment-related information, further assessment may be necessary in order to explore more specific explanations for these deficits. Typically this will involve mental status examination and clinical diagnosis of mental conditions. Typically neuropsychological testing or other more complex assessment methods are not feasible at the time a patient is required to make a treatment decision. On occasion, though, they may be helpful when the decision is of substantial consequence, documentation of competence is critical, and the circumstances allow it—for example, a person with a history of cognitive deficits who wishes to consent to kidney donation to assist another family member.

There has been some research on the relation between mental illness and the functional abilities associated with treatment decision making. Concerning understanding as a functional ability in consent, a large number of studies have found that persons with mental illness understand alarmingly little about their treatment, such as the medications they are taking or how often they are administered (Appelbaum et al., 1981; Hoffman & Srinivasan, 1992; Jaffe, 1986; Linden & Chaskel, 1981; Norko, Billick, McCarrick, & Schwartz, 1990; Olin & Olin, 1975; Soskis, 1978; Soskis & Jaffe, 1979). These studies, however, do not tell us much about the relation of mental illness to poor treatment understanding, because they assumed rather than demonstrated that patients had been given the information in the first place.

Other studies have controlled for this, for example, by providing standardized treatment information to patients as part of their research design (e.g., Benson, Roth, Appelbaum, Lidz, & Winslade, 1988; Beck, 1988; Irwin et al., 1985; Janofsky, McCarthy, & Folstein, 1992). However, often they did not examine the possibility that their disclosures were overly complex, or that factors other than mental illness might be reducing level of understanding. Although patients' poor understanding of treatment-related information is often due to their incapacities, one must consider that a patient's deficiencies in actual understanding might be a consequence of the manner in which the treating professional disclosed the information to the patient. Thus the causal question might require investigation of the method of disclosure itself. Disclosure variables requiring consideration are the clarity and difficulty level of verbal explanations, the length of consent forms, the amount of time the patient was allowed for assimilating information, and the method of disclosure.

A patient might also perform poorly in an assessment of understanding of disclosed treatment information merely as an artifact of the method of assessment. For example, several studies of patients' abilities related to informed consent have examined their understanding of disclosed information at a point in time ranging from days to weeks after the information was disclosed to them (e.g., Barbour & Blumenkrantz, 1978; Bergler, Pennington, Metcalfe, & Freis, 1980; Freeman, Pichard, & Smith, 1981; Kaufer, Steinberg, & Toney, 1983; Morrow, Gootnick, & Schmale, 1978; Robinson & Meray, 1976). Measures of this type assess memory for the treatment information, but not necessarily comprehension of the information at the time that consent or refusal was given by the patient in response to original disclosure.

While reasoning as a functional ability among persons with mental illnesses has not received much research attention, failure to appreciate the nature of one's own mental illness has been studied extensively as "lack of insight" (for a review of these studies, see Appelbaum and Grisso, 1995). Although results have been varied, overall they suggest that denial of illness is a significant feature among many persons with schizophrenia.

It is important to realize, however, that the appearance of a failure to acknowledge that one has a mental disorder (when it is diagnosed by clinicians) may arise for reasons other than mental illness, such as differing cultural perspectives. Saks and Behnke (1999) have suggested that beliefs should have the quality of "patently false beliefs" in order to be considered a failure of appreciation sufficient to constitute a basis for incompetence. Their concern, which is generally recognized in the literature, is that persons with beliefs that are simply different from those of the treating professional (not associated with mental disorder) should not be considered a sign of incapacity to decide about treatment. Distinguishing "patently false (delusional) beliefs" from merely idiosyncratic beliefs is sometimes important in satisfying the causal questions that will arise when patients appear to "lack appreciation" or "lack insight" with regard to their disorder or treatment options.

Interactive Characteristic

There are three ways in which the demands of treatment situations are relevant for weighing the significance of individuals' functional deficits for treatment decision making.

COMPLEXITY OF THE CIRCUMSTANCES.   Medical and mental health diagnoses, treatment proposals, and risk/benefit situations differ in their complexity. Some treatments can be understood by a wide range of patients because of the general population's familiarity with the treatments. Other treatments are more esoteric, experimental, or complex in their procedures and implications. In addition, while some treatment situations may be made over a course of time, others require an immediate decision because the illness is rapidly progressing toward a potentially fatal outcome. Thus some treatment situations demand a greater capacity for understanding or reasoning in order for a patient's decision to meet criteria for the competence element of informed consent.

SERIOUSNESS OF POTENTIAL CONSEQUENCES.   Some illnesses and treatment situations are more consequential than others. The degree of ability that is required to decide about a treatment that can be characterized as "high benefit, low risk" may be less than the degree of ability required for deciding about a high risk treatment that is of uncertain benefit. From time to time the law has recognized that mental patients may be competent to deal with some treatment decisions (e.g., medication: *Rennie v. Klein*, 1982) but not others (e.g., psychosurgery: *Kaimowitz v. Department of Mental Health*, 1973).

ASSISTANCE AS COMPENSATION. External assistance for a patient during the treatment decisionmaking process may sometimes compensate for deficits in relevant functional abilities, thus reducing the argument for a finding of incompetence. Some patients are fortunate to have relatives or friends who can assist them, cognitively and emotionally, in thinking through the treatment decision. Sometimes it is possible to give a patient time to recover from the initial anxiety associated with the diagnosis of the disorder, or to talk to other patients who have had to make a similar decision. When ways might be found to compensate for the patient's functional deficits, this places less demand on the patient's own abilities, thus increasing the possibility that the patient's abilities will better match the demands of the situation (Grisso & Appelbaum, 1998a).

Therefore, it is helpful if assessments for competence to consent to treatment can describe the nature of the treatment situation, in ways described above, and to consider these demands in relation to the degree of the patient's decision making abilities. The congruency or incongruency between these two factors offers an interactive perspective that would assist courts or hospitals in their judgments about patients' competency in relation to specific external demands. Possible ways to achieve these descriptions will be raised in the last section of this chapter.

Judgmental and Dispositional Characteristics

In the five chapters preceding this one, each of the areas of competence required a legal judgment that individuals' circumstances and abilities met the law's standards for incompetence. Only in this way could certain individuals' fundamental rights and privileges be set aside in order to execute a disposition that would protect them (e.g., guardianship) or would recognize the important needs of others (e.g., of children, in cases of termination of parental rights because of incompetence).

In this respect, most determinations of patients' competence to consent are different from determinations of other competencies. Most patients who are treated as incompetent to consent do not seek (and are not provided) judicial review of the decision (Grisso & Appelbaum, 1998a; Lidz et al., 1984; President's Commission for Ethical Problems, 1982). Hospital personnel often make the decision, either on their own or on the advice of a nonjudicial review committee. Determination of psychiatric patients' incompetence to consent to or refuse various treatments is more likely to come under judicial scrutiny as a result of laws that specifically require it (see this chapter's introduction and "Legal Standard"). In the past, however, courts tend to have viewed patients' competence to consent primarily as a medical question controlled by professional rather than legal standards (President's Commission for Ethical Problems, 1982).

This perspective often has encouraged medical and mental health professionals to make judgments about patients' competence to consent to treatment. The judgments that must be made are similar to those made by legal decision makers in other areas of competence, in that the decisions require a sense of fairness and a recognition of the importance of basic rights of self-determination, balanced against the patient's best interests in terms of medical and mental health treatment needs. Often a patient's need for a particular treatment is not absolutely compelling, but instead can be expressed as preferable to some degree by medical or mental health standards. Similarly, many patients are not grossly deficient in consent-related abilities, but instead manifest degrees of understanding and reasoning capacity. Determining the degree of treatment urgency that will outweigh the refusal of a patient with a particular degree of capacity requires a moral judgment. State legislatures and courts, of course, have made these judgments a matter of law in certain jurisdictions, or for certain types of treatments when an allegedly incompetent patient has refused them. Yet in many cases it is the responsibility of health and mental health professionals to make this judgment.

Assessment data related to the question of a patient's competence to consent should not be expected to make these judgments for us. Assessment tools may provide standardized information that can clarify the extent of a patient's relevant capacities, and they can promote a consistent quality of information across competency cases. Yet no particular assessment result will relieve the professional of the responsibility for discretion in dealing with the moral quality of the judgment.

REVIEW OF FORENSIC ASSESSMENT INSTRUMENTS

This section reviews 8 instruments that have been developed for assessing individuals' functional abilities to participate in decisions about their treatment. All of these instruments have been developed within the past 15 years, so none of them were reviewed in the first edition of this book. In contrast, the 3 instruments reviewed in the first edition are not reviewed here, because there has been no new research on those instruments in the interim.

The first 4 instruments in this section were developed for use as clinical tools to assess patients' capacities for competent consent: the *Capacity to Consent to Treatment Instrument*, the *Hopemont Capacity Assessment Interview*, the *Hopkins Competency Assessment Test*, and the *MacArthur Competence Assessment Tool for Treatment*. These are followed by the *MacArthur Competence Assessment Tool for Clinical Research*, intended for use in evaluating competence of patients to consent to participate in clinical research associated with their need for treatment. Finally, reviews are provided for three instruments (*Understanding Treatment Disclosures; Perceptions of Disorder; Thinking Rationally About Treatment*) that were developed as research tools to examine hypotheses regarding the capacities of persons with mental illness to make treatment decisions.

An additional instrument, the *Standardized Consent Capacity Interview* (SCCI), deserves mention but is not reviewed here because there was not yet information on its psychometric properties at the time of this review. The SCCI was derived from Marson's *Capacity to Consent to Treatment Instrument* (CCTI), which is reviewed in this section. It was designed specifically for routine clinical use and therefore attempts some of the same objectives as the CCTI but in more economical fashion. Descriptions of the SCCI have been published in studies in which it formed the structure for interviews of patients to serve as stimuli in competence to consent research (Marson, McInturff, et al., 1997; Marson, Hawkins et al., 1997) that examined clinician's competency judgments. But the clinicians were not asked to score the SCCI itself, so the existing reports do not speak to the instrument's reliability or validity. We anticipate that reports of the psychometric properties and clinical utility of the instrument are forthcoming.

CAPACITY TO CONSENT TO TREATMENT INSTRUMENT (CCTI)

Author

Marson, D.

Author Affiliation

Department of Neurology, University of Alabama at Birmingham

Primary Reference

Marson, D., Ingram, K., Cody, H., & Harrell, L. (1995). Assessing the competency of patients with Alzheimer's Disease under different legal standards. *Archives of Neurology, 52,* 949–954

Description

The *Capacity to Consent to Treatment Instrument* (CCTI) was originally developed in the early 1990s to assess patients' capacities related to competence to consent to treatment, especially for persons with dementias. The manual is available from the CCTI's primary author. The instrument was introduced as a "prototype" in the primary 1995 reference noted above, although it did not have a name at that time. It was identified as the CCTI in later publications, and the instrument was not altered from its "prototype" form. Some later publications, however, employ only parts of the CCTI and therefore do not present a few of the original items. The present description is based on the Marson, Ingram, Cody and Harrell (1995) article, as well as materials (including scoring criteria) provided by the instrument's author in a January 1999 CCTI revision.

The CCTI consists of two clinical vignettes, each of which presents a hypothetical medical problem and symptoms, as well as two treatment alternatives with associated risks and benefits. The two vignettes are labeled "neoplasm" (a brain tumor and its possible treatments) and "cardiac" (heart blockage problem). The wording of the vignettes is highly standardized, and they were written at a fifth- to sixth-grade reading level. After listening to a vignette (aided by a printed copy in hand during the oral presentation), the patient is asked 14 questions that elicit information with which to evaluate the patient's capacities relevant for competence to consent to treatment. Administering both vignettes and their questions requires about 20 to 25 minutes (f).

The patient's answers contribute to two types of scores, called the "Quantitative Scoring System" and the "Qualitative Scoring System."

The *Quantitative Scoring System* provides scores on the following subscales, which are referred to as "legal standards" (or "LS") (referring to standards for legal competence):

- LS1: The capacity to *evidence a treatment choice*. This is assessed with a single item asking patients what treatment in the vignette they would choose.
- LS2: The capacity to *make a "reasonable" choice*. This is also assessed with the item that asks for the patient's treatment choice, and is defined as the choice that most reasonable people would make.
- LS3: The capacity to *appreciate the emotional and cognitive consequences of a treatment choice*. This is assessed with 3 questions in the original CCTI, and with 2 questions in the January 1999 revision, that asks patients what plans they need to make for the future and

what they believe their life will be like (with or without the proposed treatment).

- LS4: The capacity to provide *rational reasons for a treatment choice*, or to use logical processes to compare benefits and risks of various treatments. This is assessed with a request for patients to provide all of the reasons why they chose or rejected the proposed treatment.
- LS5: The capacity to *understand the treatment situation and choices*. This is assessed with 9 questions that require patients recall and comprehension of the various pieces of information provided in the vignette regarding symptoms, treatment, risks, benefits, and likelihood of various outcomes.

Responses are recorded by the examiner and scored according to detailed criteria for each item, providing for scores of 2, 1, and 0 points per answer. Some items allow the patient to get credit for several answers (e.g., when asked about symptoms, a score of 2 for each of 4 symptoms in the vignette). The highest possible score for each legal standard is 2 for LS1, 1 for LS2, 4 for LS3, 26 or 6 for LS4 (depending on whether the patient chose the treatment—which leads to more opportunities to obtain points—or rejected the treatment), and 64 for LS5. Cut-off scores are not provided for adequate or inadequate (competent or incompetent) performance, although the CCTI author has used two standard deviations below the group mean as a convenient way to define a relatively "low" score on an LS. There is no "total CCTI score;" each LS score stands on its own.

The *Qualitative Scoring System*, also called the "Error Code Scoring System," provides for the identification of 16 types of errors conceptually organized into 4 domains: language dysfunction, executive dysfunction, affective dysfunction, and compensatory responses. This part of the CCTI does not provide actual scores; it is intended instead to allow the examiner to identify the simple presence or absence of various types of errors.

Conceptual Basis

CONCEPT DEFINITION. The five "legal standards" that guided the CCTI's development were derived from previous legal analyses of competence to consent to treatment (g). Conceptualization of the Rational Reasons and Understanding standards were derived from Appelbaum and Grisso (see reviews later in this chapter for *Understanding Treatment Disclosures* and *Thinking Rationally about Treatment*).

The 16 error codes were developed in part on the basis of the authors' experience with verbal responses observed in persons with Alzheimer's Disease, and in part on the Exner special scoring system for the Rorschach.

OPERATIONAL DEFINITION.   In determining how to operationally represent these constructs, the authors endeavored to develop a format that
"approximates 'real life' medical treatment decision making by requiring a
subject to elect and explain a treatment decision in a verbal dialogue format" (a). The choice of the two medical conditions (neoplasm and cardiac) is
not explained, but the content of the vignettes was reviewed by independent physicians for accurate representation of the conditions and treatments.

    CRITIQUE.   One of the CCTI's strengths is its use of constructs that are
based on legal analysis of competence. The method was devised for use in
the study of competence among patients with Alzheimer's Disease, but
the format and interview items are such that there is no reason why they
could not be used with other persons whose competence is questioned.

    The vignettes are standardized (using hypothetical neoplasm and
heart disorder cases), which has its advantages and disadvantages. This
maximizes the opportunity to develop meaningful norms for use in clinical cases and to make group comparisons in research. But in clinical
cases the method would leave open the possibility that the patient might
do better (or worse) in comprehending their own disorder, in that the
method does not assess patients' capacities in the context of a disorder or
treatment that they are currently experiencing.

    Two cautions should be noted regarding the legal constructs used in
the CCTI. First, not all of the legal constructs that structure the CCTI will
be relevant in all states for legal determinations of competence to consent.
Virtually all states' laws recognize the importance of the patient's understanding of the disclosed information, but only some states specifically
refer to appreciation and reasoning.

    Second, the standard called LS2, the patient's capacity to make a
"reasonable choice," was originally one entry in a well-known list of legal
standards for competence to consent to treatment compiled by Roth, Lidz,
and Meisel (g). However, within the past two decades, this concept has
disappeared from virtually all legal and conceptual analyses of competence to consent. This standard, found in some states in the first half of
the 20th century, allowed courts to find people incompetent if they chose
a treatment that others (or the court itself) would consider odd or ill
advised. In contrast, it is fundamental to the modern doctrine of informed
consent that patients are allowed the autonomy to make any choice they
wish, unpopular as it might be, as long as they are doing so with abilities
(to understand, appreciate, and reason) that are sufficiently intact. Based
on this analysis, clinicians should be aware that using LS2 in the CCTI
when reasoning about a patient's competence, or when offering information to a court in a competence proceeding, is inconsistent with current
legal standards for competence in almost all states.

The conceptualization of the error codes is novel. One can imagine their use particularly in research that relates specific types of clinical dysfunctions to deficits in performance on the formal quantitative scales of the CCTI. In clinical cases, the error codes could offer the potential for providing causal explanations for a patient's deficits in understanding, appreciating consequences, and rational reasons in the CCTI vignette.

Psychometric Development

STANDARDIZATION. Administration procedures, interview questions, and scoring criteria for the quantitative (LS) scales are quite specific. Every patient receives the same disclosure about the same disorders, allowing for the development of norms for comparative purposes. The criteria for assigning error codes are a good deal more complex than for the quantitative scales, but they are succinctly defined and are accompanied by examples of responses that suggest each type of error code.

RELIABILITY. Three trained raters (number of protocols scored was not specified) achieved interrater reliability of $r = .83$ on the scales that use interval scoring (LS3, LS4 and LS5) and 96% agreement on the categorical scales (LS1 and LS2) (f). Three raters trained in the error codes achieved 81% agreement for 644 text observations within 23 protocols, with all three raters agreeing on code assignments in 65% of the observations.

NORMS. No formal set of norms has been provided for the CCTI. However, normative performance for groups of persons with Alzheimer's Disease and for normal comparison groups can be found in various publications of research with the CCTI. Some of these norms are stated as means and standard deviations for the various LS scales (f, with 29 persons with Alzheimer's Disease and 15 normal comparison subjects; also b, for 72 persons with Alzheimer's Disease and 21 normal comparison subjects), while others are provided as percent of subjects who were defined as "Incompetent" based on their performance below the -2 standard deviation of normal comparison samples (for example, c, with 29 persons with Alzheimer's disease and 15 normal comparison subjects).

CRITIQUE. Interrater reliability for the LS scales appears to be acceptable, and the rate of agreement for the error coding is relatively good in light of the complexity of the judgments that this aspect of the CCTI scoring requires. Users should note that considerably less reliability may be expected for the error coding method, especially by clinicians who may not be highly trained in the method.

The CCTI would benefit by the publication of a set of norms that clinicians can use for comparing the level of performance of their own patient to the performance of various patient groups or normal comparison subjects. Current norms are based on relatively small samples, and they are expressed in means rather than the percent of subjects making various scores on the LS scales. Caution is required in using the "Incompetence" criterion employed in the CCTI research studies. This method of expressing a group's performance is helpful for research purposes, but should not be extended to decisions about individual patients' competence or incompetence to consent treatment.

Construct Validation

The authors performed several factor analyses of the 14 items that make up the LS3–5 scales (appreciating consequences, rational reasons, and understanding, respectively) (a). Two factors best accounted for the variance, with all items from LS3 and 4 (rational reasons and appreciating consequences) and about half of the items from LS5 (understanding, primarily items about risks and benefits of treatment) loading highest on Factor 1, and the other half of the LS5 items (primarily about symptoms and details involving memory of numerical probabilities) loading highest on Factor 2. An additional factor analysis included a number of neuropsychological measures that had been given to this group of Alzheimer's Disease patients ($n = 82$) along with factor scores created with the previous factor analysis. The content of the two emerging factors, interpreted based on the nature of the neuropsychological measures that loaded on them, suggested that Factor 1 pertained to verbal conceptualization and reasoning, while Factor 2 was related primarily to verbal memory.

Three reports using the same two groups of subjects (29 patients with mild or moderate symptoms of Alzheimer's Disease and 15 normal older comparison subjects) found significantly lower mean scores for the Alzheimer's Disease patients on LS3 (rational reasons), LS4 (appreciating consequences), and LS5 (understanding), but not for LS1 and 2 (c, d, f). The study's method for classifying patients as "incompetent" (below -2 SD for the normal comparison sample) classified the patients with moderate symptoms of Alzheimer's disease as incompetent in 50% of the cases on LS3 (appreciating consequences), 71% of the cases on LS4 (rational reasons), and 100% of the cases in LS5 (understanding) (c, f).

The CCTI authors have examined the relation of the instrument's LS scores to a number of neuropsychological measures of cognitive functioning. Virtually all such measures were correlated significantly with performance on LS1 and 3–5 (LS2, "reasonable choice," was not examined in these analyses). Using stepwise multiple regression analyses, LS1 scores (evidencing a choice) were best identified by an auditory comprehension test, LS3 scores (appreciating consequences) by executive function measures such as Controlled Oral Word Fluency and Trail Making A, and LS5 scores (understanding) by Dementia Rating Scale Conceptualization and the Boston Naming Test (c). LS4 scores (rational reasons) were best identified by Dementia Rating Scale Initiation/Perseveration scores (d).

Error code incidence rates were significantly greater for Alzheimer's Disease patients (n = 72) than for normal older comparison subjects (n = 21) on 9 of the 19 error types (b). Types of error codes correlated with the LS scores were different for the various LSs, with correlations in the range of .14 to .36.

CRITIQUE.   There is substantial support here for the CCTI's construct validity and its conceptualization of abilities related to competence to consent to treatment. The studies provide good evidence for expected differences between Alzheimer's Disease patients and normal older comparison subjects. It is reasonable to believe that the CCTI would identify similar differences between normal comparison subjects and persons with serious mental disorders other than Alzheimer's Disease (e.g., schizophrenia, depression). Research to examine the application of the CCTI to other patient populations could be quite helpful in expanding the range of the CCTI's use in clinical evaluations related to competence to consent to treatment.

The authors explanations for the correlations that they found between neuropsychological test findings and various LS scores are too complex to summarize here, but they provided sound logic for explaining deficits in the various LS areas. The only caution to raise on this point is that the explanations for the relationships that were found were *post hoc* and that many of the neuropsychological measures were substantially related to many of the LS scores. Future research that examines *a priori* hypotheses about these relationships would be helpful. Research should also include *a priori* hypotheses about neuropsychological indices with which specific LS constructs would *not* be expected to relate.

Predictive or Classificatory Utility

No studies have examined the relation of CCTI scores to clinical or judicial judgments about competence or incompetence to consent to treatment, nor to patients' performance in actual consent circumstances.

CRITIQUE.   Although not directly related to classificatory utility of the CCTI, it is worth noting that the CCTI authors examined the ability of clinicians to use the LS format as a structure for organizing their judgments about patients' competence to consent to treatment (e). Five competency-experienced clinicians observed competence interviews of Alzheimer's disease patients and normal older controls. The interviews used the CCTI vignettes and interview questions. Clinicians were asked to make competence/incompetence judgments for each of the LSs (without benefit of the CCTI scoring system) and an overall competence judgment. The relation of the overall competence judgments to actual LS scores for these patients on the CCTI was not reported. The report focuses on agreement between clinicians, which was highest for LS1 (evidencing a choice) and lowest for LS3 (appreciating consequences).

Potential for Expressing Person-Situation Congruency

The treatment situations used in the CCTI vignettes were purposely standardized, not tailored to the conditions of the individual patient. Thus they provide no opportunity to examine patients' performance in relation to varying demands in terms of complexity of the treatment options.

References

(a) Dymek, M., Marson, D., & Harrel, L. (1999). Factor structure of capacity to consent to medical treatment in patients with Alzheimer's Disease: An exploratory study. *Journal of Forensic Neuropsychology, 1*, 27–48.
(b) Marson, D., Annis, S., McInturff, H., Bartolucci, A., & Harrell, L. (1999). Error behaviors associated with loss of competency in Alzheimer's Disease. *Neurology, 53*, 1983–1992.
(c) Marson, D., Chatterjee, A., Ingram, K, & Harrell, L. (1996). Toward a neurologic model of competency: Cognitive predictors of capacity to consent in Alzheimer's Disease using three different legal standards. *Neurology, 46*, 666–672.
(d) Marson, D., Cody, H., Ingram, K., & Harrell, L. (1995). Neuropsychologic predictors of competency in Alzheimer's Disease using a rational reasons legal standard. *Archives of Neurology, 52*, 955–959.
(e) Marson, D., Earnst, K., Jamil, F., Bartolucci, A., & Harrell, L. (in press). Consistency of physicians' legal standard and personal judgments of competency in patients with Alzheimer's Disease. *Journal of the American Geriatrics Society.*
(f) Marson, D., Ingram, K., Cody, H., & Harrell L. (1995). Assessing the competency of patients with Alzheimer's Disease under different legal standards. *Archives of Neurology, 52*, 949–954.
(g) Roth, L., Meisel, A., & Lidz, C. (1977). Tests of competency to consent to treatment. *American Journal of Psychiatry, 134*, 279–284.

HOPEMONT CAPACITY ASSESSMENT INTERVIEW (HCAI)

Author

Barry Edelstein

Author Affiliation

West Virginia University

Primary Reference

Edelstein, B. (1999). *Hopemont Capacity Assessment Interview manual and scoring guide.* West Virginia University: Author. (Available from Barry Edelstein, Department of Psychology, P.O. Box 6040, West Virginia University, Morgantown, WV 26506.)

Description

The *Hopemont Capacity Assessment Interview* (HCAI) (c) is a semi-structured interview in two sections. The first section, discussed here, is for assessing capacity to make medical decisions. The second section, discussed in Chapter 8, assesses capacity to make financial decisions.

The interview begins with a brief explanation that when doctors want to propose a course of treatment, they explain the benefits and risks to the individual who is given a choice of that treatment or other courses of action. The first 3 items ask the examinee to offer definitions of "benefit," "risk," and "choice."

Then a brief (six-sentence) "scenario" of a disorder (eye infection) and treatment choices is provided (described as the examinee's "friend" whom the examinee will be asked to advise). This is followed by nine items (questions) designed to identify whether the examinee can describe the medical problem, the proposed treatment, the reason for it, the possible benefits and risks, and the choices, then can offer a choice and explain the reasons for choosing it. This process is repeated with another scenario (advance directive to allow or refuse CPR) and a similar set of nine questions. The manual provides an answer sheet to record examinees' responses.

Answers to the 21 items are scored according to 2, 1, and 0 or 1 and 0 scoring criteria provided in the manual. No instructions for combining the scores are provided, but one reported study has added the scores on all items to produce a total HCAI score (with a possible range of 0–33) (d).

Conceptual Basis

CONCEPTUAL DEFINITION.   The HCAI was developed in reference to four legal standards described by Appelbaum and Grisso (a) relevant for assessing civil competencies (b). Questions in response to disclosed information are intended to assess the capacities to understand relevant information, demonstrate appreciation of the significance of the information for the circumstance, rationally consider the risks and benefits of different choices, and express a choice.

OPERATIONAL DEFINITION.   The interview was structured and made simple to be suitable for cognitively impaired elderly adults, including those residing in nursing homes. Two scenarios were chosen with different levels of risk to increase generalizability. Items were developed based on a standard nursing reference at a sixth grade reading level.

CRITIQUE.   The structure of the HCAI is based on modern notions of the abilities associated with competence to consent to treatment. No effort was made, however, to create scales associated with those abilities (e.g., Understanding, Appreciation or Reasoning scales). The author's intentions were to provide a structured interview with questions that could be evaluated with ratings, but that was not intended to provide norms to which individual examinees could be compared (b). This offers the benefit of flexibility and avoidance of a rigid focus on additive scores. The disadvantage of this approach is that reporting of performance must proceed item by item, given that no scale or summary scores are offered. In addition, it requires that researchers determine for themselves how they will combine the item ratings, and there is no assurance that all researchers will do it the same way. Thus across time, results of studies using the HCAI may become hard to compare.

Psychometric Development

STANDARDIZATION.   The HCAI uses a structured interview format in that specific questions are asked, but it is semi-structured in that it allows flexibility for probing. The criteria provided for assigning 2, 1, and 0 ratings to each item are explicit and clear.

RELIABILITY.   Inter-rater reliability has been reported as .93 (90% agreement) (e). However, repeat testing after about 2 weeks indicated a .29 correlation between first and second administrations (e). These data came from a study of 50 psychogeriatric nursing home residents.

NORMS.   Normative data are not available.

CRITIQUE.   Standardization of the procedure and scoring appear to be good, as well as initial indication of inter-rater reliability. The reports test-retest correlation is troubling, but may be related to the specific sample that was used. It is hoped that use in research with elderly persons, as well as other populations, will result in a better indication of the instrument's psychometric properties, as well as normative samples to which individual cases can be compared. At present, one study has examined the utility of the HCAI in assessing treatment decision making capacities among elderly persons in a long term care facility (d). But the study did not describe the samples' scores sufficiently to offer comparative potential for clinicians.

Construct Validation

Internal consistency as measured by coefficient alpha was .94 in a study of elderly persons in a long term care facility (d). In the same study, the summed score of the HCAI ratings for treatment decision making capacity correlated .66 with the *Mini Mental Status Exam* (MMSE) and .50 with the Element Disclosure version of *Understanding Treatment Disclosures* (see review later in this chapter).

CRITIQUE.   Results of construct validity are encouraging but await further support before one can judge the value of the instrument.

Predictive or Classificatory Utility

In the study noted above, HCAI summed ratings for treatment decision making capacity correlated .61 with competence or incompetence judgments provided by two "clinical interns" who "together [had] integrated information from [a] battery" including a number of psychometric tests of general cognitive, intellectual, and psychological characteristics (d, p. 626).

CRITIQUE.   The results tell us little about the utility of the HCAI, because there is no reason to believe that two "clinical interns," even supplied with very large amounts of data regarding individuals' cognitive capacities, represents a reliable criterion for competence. The authors of the study (d) suggested that this "gold standard" was appropriate because "clinicians traditionally have been called upon" to make these decisions. By this logic, it is up to the researcher to demonstrate that the two interns made decisions with which most clinicians would have agreed. The mere fact that they were "clinicians" does not necessarily mean that they represent standard clinical practice.

Potential for Expressing Person-Situation Congruency

The HCAI is highly standardized and does not include items to assess the fit of financial capacities as assessed on the instrument with environmental or situational circumstances (e.g., the extent of the individual's estate needing management).

References

(a) Appelbaum, P., & Grisso, T. (1988). Assessing patients' capacities to consent to treatment. *New England Journal of Medicine, 319,* 1635–1638.
(b) Edelstein, B. (2000). Challenges in the assessment of decision making capacity. *Journal of Aging Studies, 14,* 423–437.
(c) Edelstein, B. (1999). *Hopemont Capacity Assessment Interview manual and scoring guide.* West Virginia University: Author. (Available from Barry Edelstein, Department of Psychology, P.O Box 6040, West Virginia University, Morgantown, WV 26506.)

(d) Pruchno, R., Smyer, M., Rose, M., Hartman-Stein, P., & Henderson-Laribee, D. (1995). Competence of long-term care residents to participate in decisions about their medical care: A brief, objective assessment. *The Gerontologist, 35,* 622–629.
(e) Staats, N., & Edelstein, B. (1995). *Cognitive predictors of medical decision-making capacity.* Paper presented at the meeting of the Gerontological Society of American, Los Angeles.

HOPKINS COMPETENCY ASSESSMENT TEST (HCAT)

Author

Janofsky, J.

Primary Author Affiliation

Johns Hopkins School of Medicine, Baltimore MD

Primary Reference

Janofsky, J., McCarthy, R., & Folstein, M. (1992). The Hopkins Competency Assessment Test: A brief method for evaluating patients' capacity to give informed consent. *Hospital and Community Psychiatry, 43,* 132–136

Description

The *Hopkins Competency Assessment Test* (HCAT) (c) was developed "to screen patients for competency to make treatment decisions and to write advance directives" (c, p. 132). It was intended as a screening tool that could be used by nonclinicians to determine whether the issue of patients' capacities should be raised for further evaluation. It is further described as an "instrument for quantitative assessment of clinical competency" and that it "does not determine legal competency but rather is an aid to the clinician in forming an opinion about clinical competency" (c, p. 132).

The HCAT consists of a four-paragraph "essay" that was written at three reading comprehension levels (6th grade, 8th grade, and 13th grade). The content of the essay informs patients about:

1. the nature of informed consent (e.g., that the patient must be informed and understand in order to provide consent to treatment),
2. that "chronic disease" can decrease a patient's ability to make decisions,
3. that patients can state their wishes in advance of disease in instructions that are called durable power of attorney, and

4. the effect this will have on future treatment.

Thus the focus of the content is partly on understanding what is required in order to consent to treatment and partly on understanding the nature and value of advance directives.

Presentation of the essay is followed by six questions, four of them open-ended, one true-false, and one a sentence completion. Two questions focus on assessing #1 above, two on #2 above, one on #3 and one on #4. Clinicians are provided an example of an adequate answer for each of these questions and are asked to assign a score of 1 for each correct answer. Scoring range is 0–10, because four points (four correct answers) are possible for one of the questions. The authors suggest a score of 3 or below as indicative of incompetence (based on research results explained later).

In research procedures (c), patients were given the 13th grade disclosure version first and, after scoring, were given the 8th grade version if they achieved a score of 7 or lower, and then received the 6th grade version if a similarly low score was made on the 8th grade version.

Conceptual Basis

CONCEPT DEFINITION. Primary publications for the HCAT do not define the concepts that the instrument is intended to measure. In their preface, however, the authors indicate the intention to assess "competency to consent to treatment" (c, p. 132), and they define this as the ability to "understand the discussion of the proposed treatment and its risk, benefits, and alternatives" and to "understand … the right to informed consent" (c, p. 132).

OPERATIONAL DEFINITION. The authors did not describe their process for interpreting and operationalizing the above concepts. The four paragraphs of the essay and the six questions appear to focus on the latter of the two concepts above—that is, "understand the right to informed consent"—in that the content focuses on the patient's understanding of what informed consent is, what can impair it, and how one can provide informed consent in advance of its need.

CRITIQUE. The authors say that the instrument is designed to "aid clinicians in forming an opinion about clinical competency." The HCAT's content and conceptual definition, however, provide no reason to believe that the HCAT measures the range of abilities associated conceptually with competence to consent to treatment. As others have observed (e, f, g), clinicians who administer the HCAT will have acquired no information about the essentials for competence to consent to treatment—for example, how well the patient understands a disorder, a potential treatment, its risks and benefits, and alternative treatments; the patient's capacity to reason about the information; and the patient's appreciation of the significance of the information for his or her own situation.

The importance of this cannot be overstated. For example, later researchers (a) selected the HCAT, "based on these previous findings [referring to reference c] as a measure of subjects decision-making capacities" (a, p. 957). Yet the conceptualization, content, and format of the HCAT require no decisions and no decision-like processes on the part of patients to whom it is administered. The instrument only scores patients' understanding of what they are told, and what they are told does not include some of the information that patients are expected to understand (e.g., the nature of their disorder) for purposes of informed consent to treatment.

In sum, it is best to consider the HCAT as a possible means to assess patients' abilities to understand what informed consent is and what advanced directives are, but not an assessment of their "capacity to give informed consent" (as claimed in Janofsky, c, p. 132).

Psychometric Development

STANDARDIZATION. Administration procedures and questions are highly standardized and clearly described (a). Scoring instructions are relatively specific and simple to use.

RELIABILITY. Interscorer reliability has been examined twice. Two of the HCAT authors administered and scored 16 HCAT protocols (sample characteristics not described) (c). They reported a Pearson correlation coefficient of .95 for total HCAT scores. In another study (a), three researchers administered and scored 15 subjects (sample characteristics not described). Spearman's rank-order correlation coefficients for all possible pairs of scorers were .96, .97, and .99.

NORMS. HCAT results for various groups of patients are provided in some of the articles reporting research with the HCAT (b, c, d). In some cases these are means, while in others they are percent of subjects below the HCAT's competence cut-off score (that is, 3 or below = incompetent).

CRITIQUE. The tests of interscorer reliability are difficult to interpret. The types of individuals (e.g., patients, non-patients, etc.) who produced the protocols are poorly identified in those reports. Similarly, the manner in which the patient samples are described in the reports makes it difficult to use them to make meaningful comparisons of patients' HCAT scores to past research results.

Construct Validation

In the original HCAT study (c) involving 41 medical and psychiatric patients, the mean HCAT score for psychiatric patients was lower than for medical patients, but not significantly. Jones et al. (1998) found that HCAT scores in a psychiatric sample (n = 43) were related to age ($-.46$) and education (.50). Another study (b) reported that HCAT scores were significantly lower for 16 patients (medical and neuropsychiatric) whom hospital staff judged as "incompetent" compared to 15 patients judged "competent" for purposes of providing informed consent.

The HCAT and the Mini-Mental Status Exam (MMSE) were employed together in the original study (c). The report offered no direct comparison between them, but it demonstrated that the HCAT compared more favorably with clinicians' competence judgments than did the MMSE (see review of this result in the following subsection). Another study (b), however, found that the HCAT correlated .75 with MMSE results in a psychiatric sample (and .68 with a daily living skills test).

CRITIQUE. It is not possible to draw any inferences about construct validity of the HCAT from these results. Part of the problem is that the construct on which the HCAT is based is ambiguous, as noted earlier. Their intention to measure "clinical competence," "competence to consent," and "decision making about treatment" is never conceptually defined, so that it is not clear what construct to employ in making inferences about the above results.

In general, one might think that the fact that a psychiatric sample scored no differently than a medical sample (c) would challenge the construct validity of the HCAT, but this cannot be inferred since the nature of the psychiatric sample was never described. One would expect a measure of capacity to consent to be related to MMSE scores; one study reports that HCAT and MMSE scores are highly correlated, while Janofsky et al. (c) remark primarily on their differences.

Jones et al. (d) found that only 7 of 43 patients scored below the cut-off on the HCAT. Their observations of those seven patients is worth noting: "[They were] cooperative and appeared generally competent to discuss health problems, and if consent had been needed ... there would have been no obvious reason to suspect their ability to consent" (d, p. 53–54).

Predictive or Classificatory Utility

Several studies have examined the ability of the cut-off score on the HCAT (incompetent = 3 or lower) to identify patients found incompetent by clinicians performing their own independent evaluations of competence.

Janofsky et al. (c) found that this cut-off score identified all of the patients
found incompetent, and misclassified none of the patients found competent, by a forensic psychiatrist who performed "clinical competency evaluations" and made competence/incompetence decisions on each patient.
Another study (a), using clinical judgments of nursing home professionals regarding their patients' competence, found that staff considered 65%
of the HCAT-incompetent patients to be incompetent, and 90% of the
HCAT-competent patients to be competent.

Holzer et al. (b) compared HCAT results to consulting or admitting
clinicians' formal evaluations of patients' capacities to give informed consent. The HCAT identified as competent 73% of the patients whom clinicians considered competent, and identified as incompetent 81% of the
patients whom clinicians considered incompetent. In this study (b), four
other measures of mental capacity and neuropsychological functioning
were employed as well. All of these measures did better than the HCAT
at identifying the patients judged competent by the clinicians, while the
HCAT performed as well as two of the other measures in identifying
patients judged incompetent by clinicians.

CRITIQUE.   These results do not provide information of value regarding
the HCAT's clinical utility. In general the proportions of "correct" classifications are neither very good nor very bad, and an instrument called a screening test should not be held to a very high classificatory standard. But in this
case one cannot judge the value of the results because the standard itself is
unknown. In the original study (c), for example, there was no description of
what the forensic clinician was evaluating. The term used to describe the
focus of their evaluations was "clinical competency," but it is not clear
which clinical competency they were intending (or asked) to evaluate
(e.g., competence to consent to treatment, competence to understand the
meaning of informed consent, competence to execute advance directives).
The other two studies also provided no way of knowing what was meant by
"competency" as judged by consulting psychiatrists or nursing home staff.

Potential for Expressing Person-Situation Congruency

The HCAT "essays" are highly standardized and are not intended
to assess patients' own circumstances. Thus they provide no opportunity
to examine patients' performance in relation to varying demands in terms
of complexity of various treatment options.

References

(a) Barton, D., Mallik, H., Orr, W., & Janofsky, J. (1996). Clinicians' judgment of capacity or
    nursing home patients to give informed consent. *Psychiatric Services, 47,* 956–960.

(b) Holzer, J., Gansler, D., Moczynski, N., & Folstein, J. (1997). Cognitive functions in the informed consent evaluation process: A pilot study. *Journal of the American Academy of Psychiatry and the Law, 25*, 531–540.
(c) Janofsky, J., McCarthy, R., & Folstein, M. (1992). The Hopkins Competency Assessment Test: A brief method for evaluating patients' capacity to give informed consent. *Hospital and Community Psychiatry, 43*, 132–136.
(d) Jones, B., Jayaram, G., Samuels, J., & Robinson, H. (1998). Relating competency status to functional status at discharge in patients with chronic mental illness. *Journal of the American Academy of Psychiatry and the Law, 26*, 49–55.
(e) Kaye, N. (1992). Assessing competency: Comment. *Hospital and Community Psychiatry, 43*, 648.
(f) Lavin, M. (1992). Assessing competency: Comment. *Hospital and Community Psychiatry, 43*, 646–647.
(g) Sales, G. (1992). Assessing competency: Comment. *Hospital and Community Psychiatry, 43*, 646.

MACARTHUR COMPETENCE ASSESSMENT TOOL FOR TREATMENT (MACCAT-T)

Authors

Grisso, T., & Appelbaum, P. S.

Primary Author Affiliation

Department of Psychiatry, University of Massachusetts Medical School, Worcester MA

Primary Reference

Grisso, T., & Appelbaum, P. S. (1998). *MacArthur Competence Assessment Tool for Treatment (MacCAT-T)*. Sarasota, FL: Professional Resource Press

Description

The *MacArthur Competence Assessment Tool for Treatment* (MacCAT-T) was designed to offer practical guidance to health professionals in their assessments of patients' decisionmaking capacities in the context of informed consent to treatment (c). As an interview guide, it was intended to assist clinicians in obtaining from patients information that is especially relevant for judgments about patients' competence to consent to treatment. It also provides a procedure for rating the quality of patients' responses to the interview questions. The MacCAT-T was published as an appendix to a book by the authors (b) and in commercial test form with a manual and materials (c).

The MacCAT-T is related to three research instruments reviewed later in this chapter: the UTD, POD, and TRAT. All four instruments were developed by a research initiative of the MacArthur Research Network for Mental Health and Law between 1989 and 1998. The three research instruments were developed first, followed by the MacCAT-T. Its purpose was to assess the same decisionmaking abilities measured by these more lengthy research instruments, but in a format that was easier to use in the course of clinical work. Whereas the research instruments used standardized disclosures and hypothetical vignettes that do not refer to patients' own specific conditions, the content of the MacCAT-T focuses specifically on the patient's own disorder, symptoms, and treatment options. Whereas the research instruments employed highly detailed and specific scoring criteria, the MacCAT-T offers more general criteria to assist clinicians in rating patients' responses. This method runs the risk of reduced precision in return for greater feasibility for clinical use in a wide range of settings and diagnostic conditions.

The MacCAT-T interview combines the process of preparing patients to make informed treatment decisions with the assessment of their capacities to decide. The parts of the interview and the sequence in which they occur are as follows:

- *Understanding—Disorder*: A structured format is provided for disclosing to the patient the nature of his or her own disorder. To prepare for this, the clinician lists several symptoms observed in clinical evaluation of the patient as a guide for the disclosure. This is followed by structured inquiry (open-ended) and probing questions to assess the degree to which the patient recalls and understands the various elements of the disorder that were disclosed.
- *Appreciation—Disorder*: The patient is then asked if he or she has any reason to doubt that he or she has the disorder that was disclosed, including an exploration of the patient's belief.
- *Understanding—Treatment*: A structured format is provided for disclosing to the patient the nature of the clinician's proposed treatment (prepared and presented similarly to the procedure in "Understanding-Disorder"), followed by structured inquiry to assess the degree to which the patient has understood the various elements of the treatment that were disclosed.
- *Understanding Benefits and Risks*: A structured format is provided for disclosing to the patient two or more main benefits and two or more main risks or discomforts of the proposed treatment (prepared and presented in a manner similar to that described in "Understanding-Disorder"), followed by structured inquiry to

assess the degree to which the patient has understood the various elements of the treatment that were disclosed.

- *Appreciation—Treatment*: The patient is asked whether it seems possible that this treatment might be of some benefit to himself or herself, including an exploration of the reasons for the patient's belief.
- *Alternative Treatments*: Any other possible treatments are disclosed. (Assessment of understanding of the alternative treatments is optional.)
- *First Choice and Reasoning*: The patient is asked which of the treatments seems best (or that the patient is most likely to want), followed by a structured process for exploring the patient's reasoning for that choice.
- *Generating Consequences*: The patient is asked to describe some ways that the benefits and risks discussed earlier "might influence your everyday activities at home or at work."
- *Final Choice*: The patient is asked to make a final choice.

Administration requires about 20–25 minutes. A record form is provided for the clinician to use for organizing the disorder and treatment information to be presented to the patient and for recording the patient's responses to the assessment inquiries. The manual describes a method that clinicians can use to rate each of the patient's responses (2, 1, 0), using definitions and examples in the manual as a guide, and to use the individual response ratings to calculate ratings for each component of the process. The final page of the MacCAT-T record form provides spaces for adding up the ratings to produce four Summary Ratings: Understanding, Appreciation, Reasoning, and Expressing a Choice.

The Understanding Summary Rating (range = 0–6) is based on ratings for the patient's responses to the three Understanding sections of the interview (for Disorder, Treatment, and Benefits-Risks). The Appreciation Summary Rating (range = 0–4) is based on ratings for the patient's responses on the two Appreciation sections (Disorder, Treatment). The Reasoning Summary Score (range = 0–8) is based on evidence of four types of functions in the patient's explanation for his or her choice: Consequential Thinking, Comparative Thinking, Generating Consequences, and Logical Consistency. These Reasoning functions were derived from a research instrument reviewed later in this chapter, *Thinking Rationally About Treatment* (TRAT). Finally, the patient's ability to express a choice is signified by an Expressing a Choice Summary Rating of 2 if they are able and 0 if they are not.

The MacCAT-T manual does not provide "cut-off" scores on these Summary Rating scales for adequate or inadequate performance. The authors explain that in theory there is no absolute level of ability that indicates competence or incompetence, because this will vary with the demands of a patient's particular situation (a). Moreover, there is no "total MacCAT-T" score. The Summary Ratings simply allow clinicians to document their impressions of the degree of adequacy of patients' Understanding, Appreciation, and Reasoning, provide a means of expressing that opinion when offering explanations to others (that is, other clinicians or courts), and offer the possibility of comparison of the clinician's ratings to those of other clinicians involved in the same case.

Conceptual Basis

CONCEPT DEFINITION.   The concepts of Understanding, Appreciation, and Reasoning used in the MacCAT-T are identical to the concepts underlying the three research instruments reviewed later in this chapter (see descriptions in reviews of the UTD, POD, and TRAT, respectively). (Expressing a Choice is also measured with a single item in the TRAT during the process of assessing the patient's reasoning about a choice.) The authors' decision to use these concepts to represent abilities related to competence to consent to treatment was based on legal research that had identified the legal relevance of these categories of abilities for conceptualizing competence (see later reviews of the three research instruments).

OPERATIONAL DEFINITION.   The decision to use an interview format involving the patient's own symptoms and disorder, rather than a psychological testing format with standardized stimuli, was based on the desire to develop an instrument that could be used primarily in clinical work. Most medical circumstances in which competence to consent to treatment is evaluated do not lend themselves to protracted testing sessions. Moreover, it is often patients' ability to understand and appreciate specifically their own disorder and treatment options, not those of hypothetical cases, that is at issue in making legal, ethical and medical decisions about patients' consent.

The structure of the interview itself was drawn from legal and ethical guidelines regarding the essentials for disclosure of information in an informed consent process, including disclosure of the disorder, disclosure of the treatment, description of the benefits and risks of the treatment, and any alternative treatments and their risks and benefits. To this was added a process of decisionmaking such as would normally occur in a doctor-patient relationship (but with exploration of the patient's' choice that reveals the patient's reasons for making the decision).

The construction of Understanding ratings followed closely the format used in the parallel research instrument to measure *Understanding Treatment*

Disclosure (UTD), but differs in that the MacCAT-T provides one general definition for rating each Understanding response as 2, 1, or 0, not separate criteria for each Understanding item as in the UTD. The Appreciation ratings are very different from the format and criteria used in the Appreciation instrument called *Perception of Disorder*, involving no scoring of patients' responses to hypotheticals that negate their faulty beliefs. Instead it employs much simpler criteria that focus on the presence or absence of delusional content in cases in which the patient fails to believe that he or she is ill. The Reasoning section employs several of the same operations and scoring criteria found in the parallel research measure, the TRAT (e.g., "Consequential Thinking"), but uses an abbreviated number of them.

CRITIQUE.   A strength of the MacCAT-T is its use of constructs that are based on legal analysis of competence and that have proved useful in studies with the parallel research instruments that influenced the development of the MacCAT-T. Its format is especially suitable for clinical practice, in that it guides clinicians through the process of informing patients about their disorders and treatments while simultaneously assessing their capacities to make treatment decisions. Moreover, its format allows it to be tailored to the individual disorders and treatment situations of patients.

The absence of a total MacCAT-T score may seem unfortunate to some users, but it makes sense conceptually because "competence" is not unidimensional. For example, if there were a MacCAT-T total score, some people might obtain a high score yet still be considered incompetent. This could happen if they performed well on two subtests (for example, perfect Understanding and Reasoning) but poorly on one other subtest (e.g., poor Appreciation due to total denial that the disorder applies to oneself). In addition, a total MacCAT-T score would not be meaningful from a legal perspective. Most states do not recognize all four of the constructs for purposes of legal definition of competence. Understanding is used in most states, but Appreciation and Reasoning are used more variably. Thus a total MacCAT-T score would misrepresent the applicable standards in some states.

Psychometric Development

STANDARDIZATION.   Administration procedures, interview questions, probing, and rating criteria are clearly described in the manual. While the procedure is standardized in its sequence and the types of information provided and questions asked, it is not standardized with regard to content. For example, each patient will receive somewhat different information about symptoms of disorder (because the symptoms described are those of the individual patient). For this reason, the rating criteria are general rather than specific. For example, the rating criteria for Understanding cannot spell out exactly the response that is "adequate" for every possible symptom, but relies instead on the clinician's impression that the patient's symptom description was generally accurate or inaccurate (in the clinician's opinion).

RELIABILITY.   Interrater reliability (a, c) was determined for 3 trained raters who independently rated 40 protocols (20 patients, 20 community comparison subjects). Intraclass correlations were .99 for understanding, .87 for Appreciation, and .91 for Reasoning. Pearson correlations between pairs of raters were in the high .90s for Understanding but ranged from .59 to .83 for Appreciation and Reasoning. Test-retest reliability with the MacCAT-T has not been examined.

NORMS.   The manual provides comparative data based on two samples: 40 patients hospitalized with schizophrenia or schizoaffective disorder, and 40 individuals without mental illnesses and matched with the patient group on age, gender, race and socioeconomic status.

CRITIQUE.   Interrater reliability was surprisingly good, given that the nature of the instrument required less standardization and broader rating criteria than for the research instruments that preceded it. It should be noted, however, that the raters used in the test of interrater reliability were highly trained in the method. Clinicians who attempt to use the instrument only occasionally and only after casual reading of the manual might not do as well. Nevertheless, the results indicate that the MacCAT-T rating procedure has enough structure to offer potential not only for clinical work but also as an instrument in applied clinical research, given that the clinician participants receive adequate training.

The norms provided in the manual may be of some use in judging whether the scores of a particular patient are generally lower in relation to a psychiatric patient sample and a non-patient sample. The sample sizes for these norms, however, were relatively small and must be used cautiously when interpreting individual cases.

Construct Validation

MacCAT-T scores were examined in a sample of 40 patients hospitalized with schizophrenia or schizoaffective disorder and compared to those of a matched sample (age, gender, race, SES) of patients in the community without mental disorder (a). Understanding and Reasoning means for patients were significantly lower than for the community comparison group. Scores were 4 or below on Understanding (range 0–6) for 32.5% of patients and only 5% of community subjects, and were 3 or below on Reasoning (range = 0–8) for 20% of patients and 5% of community subjects.

The Appreciation components could not be administered to community subjects because this requires references to one's belief about one's own disorder. Clear deficiencies in Appreciation (0 credit) were found for 12% of patients on Appreciation of Disorder and 7.5% of patients on Appreciation of Treatment. In the same study, distributions of scores for patients and community comparison subjects were very similar to those found for the more comprehensive and standardized research measures of Understanding, Appreciation, and Reasoning from which the MacCAT-T was derived.

Total BPRS scores were not significantly related to any of the MacCAT-T summary ratings, but strong negative correlations were found between Understanding and BPRS Conceptual Disorganization and BPRS Hallucinations (a). These findings replicated the findings of earlier results with the parallel research measure of Understanding (UTD) (d). The correlation between MacCAT-T Understanding and Factor III of the BPRS (Thought Disorganization: items 4, 8, 12, 15), was −.21 (not statistically significant), considerably lower than the −.44 in an earlier study using the parallel research measure of Understanding (UTD) (d).

None of the MacCAT-T scales were correlated at a statistically significant level with patients' age, gender, race, number of prior hospitalizations, age at first hospitalization, highest occupation, or education.

CRITIQUE.   The results are consistent with the general notion that persons with schizophrenia, expected to have problems in processing information due to conceptual disorganization, would have greater difficulty in abilities related to treatment decision making. Other than good face validity, however, evidence to date is not available to assure that the MacCAT-T is measuring the specific abilities that it claims to measure. It has produced distributions of ratings on the various summary scales that were similar to those produced by the more sophisticated research measures of the same constructs. But no direct comparison has been made to determine the correlation between scores on the research measures and the summary rating scores of the MacCAT-T. Moreover, apart from poorer scores for persons with schizophrenia, no studies have examined whether the summary rating scores are related to behaviors (within or outside the consent context) to which one would expect understanding, appreciation, or reasoning to be related.

Predictive or Classificatory Utility

No studies have examined the relation of MacCAT-T ratings to clinician or judicial judgments about competence or incompetence to consent to treatment, nor to patients' performance in actual consent circumstances.

CRITIQUE.   Even if the MacCAT-T were known to measure accurately the concepts that it claims to measure, it is not clear that MacCAT-T ratings would necessarily be related substantially to competence decisions by judges or even by clinicians. This is because incompetence does not necessarily relate to poor capacities overall, but may also be related to deficits in a specific capacity when other capacities are intact. For example, theoretically one might have excellent Understanding and Reasoning yet poor Appreciation, with incompetence decided on the latter basis. Across cases, such circumstances probably would create only marginal correlations between competence judgments and any one type of ability assessed by the MacCAT-T.

Potential for Expressing Person-Situation Congruency

The MacCAT-T uses the patient's own disorder and treatment options as the stimuli for the inquiry about the patient's functioning on decisionmaking abilities. The ratings that it provides, therefore, are influenced not only by the patient's capacities, but also by the complexity of the patient's disorder and the particulars of the patient's treatment options. In this sense, the MacCAT-T is an index of person-situation congruency in the context of consent to treatment. Indeed, some patients who receive low ratings when being seen for a particular disorder might receive relatively higher ratings if they are seen again for a much different ("simpler") disorder and treatment circumstance.

References

(a) Grisso, T., Appelbaum, P., & Hill-Fatouhi, C. (1997). The MacCAT-T: A clinical tool to assess patients' capacities to make treatment decisions. *Psychiatric Services, 48,* 1415–1419.
(b) Grisso, T., & Appelbaum, P. (1998a). *Assessing competence to consent to treatment: A guide for physicians and other health professionals.* New York: Oxford University Press.
(c) Grisso, T., & Appelbaum, P. (1998b). *MacArthur Competence Assessment Tool for Treatment (MacCAT-T).* Sarasota, FL: Professional Resource Press.
(d) Grisso, T., & Appelbaum, P.S. (1995). The MacArthur Treatment Competence Study, III: Abilities of patients to consent to psychiatric and medical treatment. *Law and Human Behavior, 19,* 149–174.

MacArthur Competence Assessment Tool for Clinical Research (MacCAT-CR)

Authors

Appelbaum, P. S., Grisso, T.

Primary Author Affiliation

Department of Psychiatry, University of Massachusetts Medical School, Worcester MA

Primary Reference

Appelbaum, P. S., & Grisso, T. (2001). *MacArthur Competence Assessment Tool for Clinical Research (MacCAT-CR)*. Sarasota, FL: Professional Resource Press

Description

The *MacArthur Competence Assessment Tool for Clinical Research* (MacCAT-CR) was designed as a "structured interview schedule for assessing decision-making abilities relevant for judgments about subjects' competence to consent to participation in research" (c, p.1). It was derived from the *MacArthur Competence Assessment Tool for Treatment* (see previous review). It provides an interview procedure and a method for rating the quality of subjects' responses to the interview questions. Its objective is to provide ratings and summary scores for four constructs, called "Understanding," "Appreciation," "Reasoning," and "Expressing a Choice."

The MacCAT-CR content is drawn from the specific research study for which a person is being asked to provide consent. The researcher selects information about the study taken from the study's basic informed consent disclosure, which is then used to formulate various parts of the MacCAT-CR interview process. Those contents also become the basis for the ratings of subjects' responses concerning their adequacy.

The interview begins with a section called "Understanding," involving 5 brief disclosures regarding the nature of the study, with each disclosure paragraph being followed by 1 or more questions (13 questions in all). These are outlined as follows:

- Disclosure of Nature of the Project, followed by 4 questions, 1 assessing understanding of the nature of the project and 3 assessing understanding of any 3 primary procedural elements of the project (e.g., duration, daily doses of medication).

- Disclosure that the primary purpose of the project is research, followed by 1 question assessing understanding.
- Disclosure concerning how this differs from individualized health care, and 3 questions assessing understanding of that element.
- Disclosure of the study's potential benefits and risks/discomforts, and 4 questions assessing understanding of them.
- Disclosure of subject's right to refuse or withdraw after consent, and 1 question assessing its understanding.

Subjects' 13 answers contribute to an Understanding score, based on ratings of their answers to each question on a 0–2 basis (total Understanding scores ranging from 0–26).

The second major section of the procedure ("Appreciation") focuses on subjects' abilities to acknowledge how they themselves will be affected by a decision to participate. The 3 questions focus on recognition that the study is not being done for their personal benefit, that there is a possibility of reduced benefit compared to other clinical options, and recognition that they can withdraw from the study. Their 3 answers contribute to an Appreciation score based on ratings of 0–2 for each answer (total Appreciation scores ranging from 0–6).

Next the subject is asked to make a choice about participation, contributing to a 0–2 rating indicating their ability to "Express a Choice."

Finally, subjects are asked to explain the reasons for their choice ("Reasoning"). In this context, they are also asked to describe some of the ways that participating in the project will "affect your everyday activities," then asked to provide a final decision about participation. Answers are scored for 4 matters (patterned after elements in *Thinking Rationally about Treatment*, reviewed later in this chapter, as well as the MacCAT-T):

- *Consequential Thinking*: A person's consideration of the consequences of a treatment alternative when deciding whether to reject or accept that alternative (or others).
- *Comparative Thinking*: A person's "simultaneous" processing of information about two treatment alternatives, such that they receive consideration in relation to each other, not merely as separate facts.
- *Generating Consequences*: A person's capacity to generate potential real-life consequences of the liabilities described in an informed consent disclosure of a treatment alternative.
- *Logical Consistency*: Degree to which one's choice follows logically from one's explanation for the choice.

Ratings of 0–2 for each of these concepts contribute to a Reasoning score that ranges from 0–8.

Administration requires about 20–25 minutes. The manual (c) provides an example of the use of the MacCAT-CR in a study of a new medication for schizophrenia, demonstrating for researchers how to transport research protocol information into the MacCAT-CR interview. A record form is provided for the clinician to use for organizing the project information to be presented to the subject and for recording the subject's responses to the assessment inquiries. A procedure and criteria for rating subjects' responses is also provided, as well as a summary rating form.

The MacCAT-CR manual does not provide cut-off scores on these Summary Rating scales for adequate or inadequate performance. The authors explain that in theory there is no absolute level of ability that indicates competence or incompetence, because this will vary with the demands of a subject's particular situation (c). Moreover, there is no "total MacCAT-CR" score; each of the four elements is communicated as individual scales.

Conceptual Basis

CONCEPT DEFINITION. The concepts of Understanding, Appreciation, Reasoning, and Expressing a Choice used in the MacCAT-CR are identical to the concepts underlying the MacCAT-T (reviewed earlier) and the three research instruments reviewed later in this chapter (see descriptions of the UTD, POD, and TRAT, respectively). The authors' decision to use these concepts to represent abilities related to competence to consent to research participation was primarily in deference to theoretical consistency with the area of competence to consent to treatment, which has received much more attention with regard to legal conceptualization of relevant functional abilities.

OPERATIONAL DEFINITION. The structure of the interview was drawn from legal and ethical guidelines regarding the essentials for disclosure of information in an informed consent process. To this was added a process of decisionmaking such as would normally occur in a subject's response to disclosure and invitation to participate in research. As noted in the description above, the logic and construction of the items and ratings for the MacCAT-CR followed closely the format used by its predecessor, the MacCAT-T.

CRITIQUE. The MacCAT-CR uses constructs that are based on legal analysis of competence and that have proved useful in other research on civil competencies (a, b). Like the MacCAT-T, its format is especially adaptable to individual circumstances associated with the range of disorders and treatments that may be the subject of clinical research. This same format, however, makes the MacCAT-CR a somewhat different "test" from one study to another. Thus its design sacrifices some degree of cross-study comparison (e.g., generalized psychometric reliability, the ability to develop generalized norms) for the sake of versatility in covering the range of content and circumstances represented in clinical research studies.

The absence of a total MacCAT-CR score may seem unfortunate to some users, but it makes sense conceptually because "competence" is not unidimensional. For example, if there were a MacCAT-CR total score, some people might obtain a high score yet still be considered incompetent. This could happen if they performed well on two subtests (for example, perfect Understanding and Reasoning) but poorly on one other subtest (e.g., poor Appreciation due to total denial that the disorder applies to oneself).

Psychometric Development

STANDARDIZATION. Administration procedures, interview questions, probing, and rating criteria are described in the manual. While the procedure is standardized in its sequence and the types of information provided and questions asked, it is not standardized with regard to content. For example, patients in different studies will receive somewhat different information about symptoms of disorder (because the symptoms described are those relevant for a specific study). For this reason, the rating criteria are general rather than specific. For example, the rating criteria for Understanding cannot spell out exactly the response that is "adequate" for every possible research condition, but relies instead on the clinician's impression that the subject's description was generally accurate or inaccurate (in the clinician's opinion).

RELIABILITY. For two studies reporting interrater reliability (e, f), intraclass correlations were .98 and .94 for Understanding, .84 and .90 for Appreciation, and .84 and .80 for Reasoning. In one of these studies (f), interexaminer reliability (two separate interviews of the same subject by different interviewers) was .77 for Understanding, .68 for Appreciation, and .82 for Reasoning.

An examination of test-retest performance with a sample of persons with major depression found no significant increase in mean scores on any of the MacCAT-CR scales (d). However, correlations between scores on first and second administration were relatively low for Understanding (.26) and Appreciation (.36), and there was no significant relation between first and second Reasoning scores (−.15). The latter result may have been produced by the tendency of some subjects to truncate their Reasoning explanations on the second administration.

NORMS. No norms are provided. Three studies provide data for samples of prospective research participants with schizophrenia (e), major depression (d), and Alzheimer's Disease (f).

CRITIQUE. Interrater reliability as reported was quite good. One is cautioned, however, that such findings might not generalize to other studies using the MacCAT-CR, because each study employs somewhat different content based on the specific projects for which subjects are being recruited. Nevertheless, the results suggest that MacCAT-CR rating procedures have enough structure to offer potential not only for reliable scoring. It is unlikely that meaningful norms can be produced for an instrument like the MacCAT-CR, because the mean and distribution of scores for any given project are likely to be dependent on the specific content of the study in question.

Construct Validation

Three studies have examined MacCAT-CR scores in psychiatric samples (major depression, d; schizophrenia, e; Alzheimer's Disease, f). The latter two studies employed comparison groups with only minor medical or psychiatric problems; their mean performance on the main MacCAT-CR scales was very high. The study with a sample of patients with major depression (d) reported similarly high scores. Their *Hamilton Depression Rating* scores, however, suggested only "moderate" depression.

In contrast, significantly lower mean scores on Understanding, Appreciation and Reasoning were obtained by persons with schizophrenia compared to individuals recruited from a medical clinic (without mental disorder) (e). Similarly, significantly lower mean scores on these scales were found for Alzheimer's Disease patients compared to non-Alzheimer individuals of similar age and education (f).

Correlations between MacCAT-CR scores and *Brief Psychiatric Rating Scale* scores for patients with schizophrenia were moderate ($r = -.34$ for Understanding, $-.27$ for Appreciation, and $-.47$ for Reasoning) (e). Substantial r-squares were found in this sample for the relation of MacCAT-CR scores to scores on the Repeatable Battery for the Assessment of Neuropsychological Status ($R^2 = .67$ with Understanding, .66 with Appreciation, and .58 with Reasoning). In this study, using an educational intervention following first administration of the MacCAT-CR significantly increased schizophrenic patients' Understanding scores to a level that was not statistically significant from the non-schizophrenic comparison group.

CRITIQUE. The results are generally consistent with expectations based on the nature of symptoms associated with the psychiatric groups in these studies. MacCAT-CR tasks are substantially cognitive in nature, and the patient groups for whom symptoms that impair cognitive functioning are most typical performed poorest. Moreover, MacCAT-CR scores were related to severity of symptoms and indexes of the serious of cognitive impairment in the expected direction. The resulting improvement in MacCAT-CR scores with educational intervention is intriguing, suggesting not only the instrument's responsiveness to expected changes but also the potential to improve patients' abilities to provide competent consent despite initial appearance of incapacity.

Predictive or Classificatory Utility

The study noted above involving Alzheimer's Disease patients (f) used a consensus of clinicians (without access to the MacCAT-CR scores) to categorize the patients as "capable" or "incapable" of providing competent consent to research participation. In Receiver Operating Characteristics analyses, "areas under the curve" were .90 for Understanding, .86 for Appreciation, and .88 for Reasoning. Using optimal cut-offs created by these analyses, about 62% of the subjects were "incapable" on at least one of the three ability measures.

CRITIQUE. These are promising results, despite the fact that one cannot be certain about the reliability of the clinician judgments as the criterion for evaluating the MacCAT-CR.

Potential for Expressing Person-Situation Congruency

The MacCAT-CR uses the research project's own protocol and circumstances as the stimuli for the inquiry about the patient's functioning on decisionmaking abilities. The ratings that it provides, therefore, are influenced not only by the patient's capacities, but also by the complexity of the design of the research project in which they are being asked to participate. Thus the method automatically evaluates the person's abilities in relation to the demands of the specific project for which they are deciding about participation.

References

(a) Appelbaum, P., & Grisso, T. (1988). Assessing patients' capacities to consent to treatment. *New England Journal of Medicine, 319,* 1635–1638.
(b) Appelbaum, P., & Grisso, T. (1995). The MacArthur Treatment Competence Study: I, Mental illness and competence to consent to treatment. *Law and Human Behavior, 19,* 105–126.
(c) Appelbaum, P. S., & Grisso, T. (2001). *MacArthur Competence Assessment Tool for Clinical Research (MacCAT-CR).* Sarasota, FL: Professional Resource Press.
(d) Appelbaum, P. S., Grisso, T., Frank, E., O'Donnell, S., & Kupfer, D. (1999). Competence of depressed patients for consent to research. *American Journal of Psychiatry, 156,* 1380–1384.
(e) Carpenter, W., Gold, J., Lahti, A., Queern, C., Conley, R., Bartko, J., Kovnick, J., & Appelbaum, P. S. (2000). Decisional capacity for informed consent in schizophrenia research. *Archives of General Psychiatry, 57,* 533–538.
(f) Kim, S., Caine, E., Currier, G., Leibovici, A., & Ryan, J. (2001). Assessing the competence of persons with Alzheimer's Disease in providing informed consent for participation in research. *American Journal of Psychiatry, 158,* 712–717.

Understanding Treatment Disclosures (UTD)

Authors

Grisso, T., & Appelbaum, P. S.

Primary Author Affiliation

Department of Psychiatry, University of Massachusetts Medical School, Worcester MA

Primary Reference

Grisso, T., & Appelbaum, P. S. (1992). *Manual for Understanding Treatment Disclosures.* Worcester MA: University of Massachusetts Medical School. (Available from the authors.)

Description

Understanding Treatment Disclosures (UTD) (d) was developed as a research instrument to measure patients' understanding of information similar to disclosures in informed consent for treatment. The UTD was developed for use in a project, the MacArthur Treatment Competence Study (b), focused on identifying patients' capacities to make decisions about consent to or refusal of treatment when they are hospitalized for mental disorders.

The instrument consists of three subtests that involve disclosing a standardized treatment situation to the respondent, followed by questions to assess the respondent's understanding of the information. This may be done with any of three forms that pertain to three different disorders: Schizophrenia, Major Depression, and a non-psychiatric disorder, Ischemic Heart Disease. All three forms have the same format and length. In the research study for which the instrument was developed, patients received the form that corresponded to their own disorder, although the instrument provides standardized disclosures to all patients with that disorder, not disclosures that are "tailored" precisely to their own symptoms.

The respondent is first given (in oral and written form) five brief paragraphs (two to three short sentences each) of information about the disorder and its treatment:

- General description of the disorder and its symptoms.
- Brief description of a medication that is frequently prescribed for the disorder.
- Symptoms that the medication is expected to relieve, and the likelihood of relief.

- Possible side-effects and their likelihood.
- Alternative treatment (psychotherapy for the psychiatric disorders, surgery for the medical disorder) and a comment about a benefit and risk for this alternative.

The information is provided to the examinee in a procedure that is called "uninterrupted disclosure," meaning that the information is provided from beginning to end before any questioning occurs. Then 10 standardized questions are asked to assess understanding of the information, with respondents answering by offering their own paraphrase of the information presented. This is called "paraphrased recall."

The respondent then receives a procedure called "element disclosure," in which each of the same five paragraphs is presented again, but one paragraph at a time, with questioning occurring immediately after each paragraph disclosure. The questioning at this point is of two kinds: "paraphrased recall," and then "recognition." The latter questioning involves the presentation of four standardized statements about information of a type in the disclosure. Two of these statements say the same thing as the information in the disclosed paragraph but in different words, while the other two say something different. The respondent must indicate whether each statement is "the same" or "different" from the disclosed information. Together these procedures create the instrument's three subtests:

- Uninterrupted Disclosure, Paraphrased Recall
- Element Disclosure, Paraphrased Recall
- Element Disclosure, Recognition

The UTD manual provides objective criteria for scoring responses. Answers to each of the five questions per subtest may receive from 0 to 2 points. There is no single "UTD Score;" that is, the scores on the three subscales are not summed to provide a summary score. The instrument yields three subscales scores—UD-PR, ED-PR, and ED-RC—ranging from 0 to 10 points each.

Conceptual Basis

CONCEPT DEFINITION. The decision to measure understanding of information that is typically provided in the informed consent process was based on the authors' review of relevant law that identified four constructs that are used in legal definitions of competence to consent to treatment: Understanding, Appreciation, Reasoning, and Ability to Express a Choice (a, b). (See the next two reviews for instruments related to the other legal constructs.) Understanding was defined as the ability to "comprehend the meaning and intent of that which they have been told in the informed consent process" (d, p. 2).

OPERATIONAL DEFINITION. The authors developed disclosures for three different disorders in preparation for including these three patient groups in a major study of patients' treatment decision-making abilities. The five types of information provided in the disclosures were selected specifically because legal cases have established these as the necessary elements of of adequate disclosure for informed consent.

Information included in each element of the disclosure was not intended to be comprehensive, but rather to be representative of the type of information the element represents. Moreover, the information disclosed to examinees was standardized, not adjusted to the individual circumstances of each patient, because the UTD was developed specifically for use in a research study in which the design required similar stimulus conditions across participants. The disclosure elements were written rather simply, creating a level of "reading ease" that was calculated at about the average for 7th to 9th grade. Pilot studies indicated that the various forms of the UTD did not differ in their level of difficulty in understandability or readability.

The various stimulus and response subtests were selected in order to be able to control for various sources of error in the assessment of individuals' understanding. Examinees' responses to Uninterrupted Disclosure, for example, might be impaired because of poor comprehension or because of difficulty in recalling pieces of the disclosure embedded in a large amount of information. The Element Disclosure procedure, in contrast, provides an index of comprehension in a process that minimizes demands on memory. The use of a Recognition response mode in addition to Paraphrased Recall response mode recognizes that some examinees' might understand information they are provided but might not have the capacity to express it.

CRITIQUE. The logic for the selection of content and the various response formats seems sound. The standardization of the content is a significant advantage in research situations, although it necessarily reduces the value of the instrument in individual forensic cases. Used for clinical purposes, the instrument could provide an index of the person's capacities for understanding the type of information associated with a particular disorder, but not necessarily the information that is specific to his or her case.

Psychometric Development

STANDARDIZATION. Administration procedures, interview questions, probing, and scoring criteria are very specific. The level of scoring judgment required by the criteria is no greater than is employed in standardized intelligence tests like the Wechsler.

RELIABILITY.   Interscorer reliability (f) was determined for 10 recently-trained research assistants, based on independent scoring of 20 protocols. Kappa correlations for individual UTD items were .60 or above for 90% of the comparisons, and .70 or above for 74% of the comparisons. Intraclass correlations for subtests scores (for Uninterrupted-Paraphrase and Element-Paraphrase) were all above .84. (Reliability was not checked for Element-Recognition scores, which are entirely objective.) Test-retest reliability with a two-week interval ranged from .50–.80, depending on the subtest and the diagnostic identification of the participant samples.

NORMS.   The UTD manual does not provide norms, but normative data are available in the report of the study for which the instrument was developed (e). Mean scores and distributions for the three subscales are provided for hospitalized patients, 75 with schizophrenia, 92 with major depression, and 82 with angina, as well as three comparison groups of similar size comprising persons in the community without mental disorders.

CRITIQUE.   The UTD's psychometric properties are generally acceptable.

Construct Validation

Internal consistency based on alpha coefficients and corrected item-total correlations were best on all three subscales for patients with schizophrenia (alpha = .75–.85; average item-total r's = .52–.66), and lowest for persons in the community with no mental disorder (alpha = .55–.70; average item-total r's = .31–.46) (f). In a factor analysis that included the three disclosure procedures of the UTD together with 10 other subtests from two measures of Appreciation and Reasoning abilities (two other abilities related to legal competence: see later reviews of POD and TRAT), the highest loading subtests on the first factor were the three disclosure procedures (e). This is consistent with the assumption that the instrument measures a construct that is distinct from other legal constructs employed in competence determinations.

For long-term care residents, Pruchno et al. (g) reported a higher relation between the UTD Recognition task and MMSE scores (.68) than between UTD recall (paraphrase) tasks and MMSE scores (.50). UTD Recognition tasks were also more highly correlated to clinicians' independent judgments about competence (.60) than were UTD recall (paraphrase) tasks (.45).

Grisso and Appelbaum (e) reported significantly lower UTD scores on all subscales for persons hospitalized for schizophrenia than for their community (non-mentally ill) comparison group, and lower UTD scores on Element-Paraphrase and Element-Recognition for persons hospitalized for major depression than for their community comparison group. Chronicity of disorder (age at first hospitalization, number of prior admissions) was not related to UTD scores. Among persons with major depression, significant correlations were reported for IQ and performance on all three subtests, but not for persons with schizophrenia. In contrast, among persons with schizophrenia, significant negative correlations ($-.33$ to $-.41$) were reported between symptom severity (Brief Psychiatric Rating Scale) and performance on all three subtests (especially for symptoms of thought disorganization), but not for persons with major depression. Similarly, in a separate study, symptom severity among depressed patients was not significantly related to UTD performance (c).

CRITIQUE. Some caution is warranted in regard to internal consistency for persons without mental disorders. It is possible that higher internal consistency was obtained for patients as an artifact of general negative effects of psychopathology on performance (affecting item responses relatively consistently), whereas understanding is less consistent (that is, more dependent on inherent differences in difficulty of the various elements in the disclosure) for persons without mental disorders.

UTD scores were lower for diagnostic groups and measures of psychopathology that would be expected to increase the risk of poor understanding of information presented in the context of informed consent procedures. The correlation between symptoms severity and performance within the schizophrenia group, however, indicates that "poor understanding" as measured by the UTD is not synonymous with serious mental disorder. Variability among persons with schizophrenia was considerable, whereas performance was uniformly high among persons in the non-ill comparison.

Predictive or Classificatory Utility

Studies thus far have not examined the degree to which UTD scores correspond to external criteria for understanding of other information or for competence to consent to treatment.

CRITIQUE. Tests of the relation of UTD scores to courts' determinations of competence to consent to treatment would need to take into account that courts may find patients incompetent for many reasons other than deficiencies in their ability to understand treatment information.

Potential for Expressing Person-Situation Congruency

Various disorders and treatment situations differ in the complexity of their options, risks, benefits, and the difficulty level of the concepts or treatments that must be understood. The disclosed treatment situations used in the UTD were purposely standardized to meet the needs of a research study. Thus they provided no opportunity to examine patients' performance in relation to varying demands in terms of complexity of the treatment options.

References

(a) Appelbaum, P., & Grisso, T. (1988). Assessing patients' capacities to consent to treatment. *New England Journal of Medicine, 319,* 1635–1638.
(b) Appelbaum, P., & Grisso, T. (1995). The MacArthur Treatment Competence Study, I: Mental illness and competence to consent to treatment. *Law and Human Behavior, 19,* 105–126.
(c) Frank, L., Smyer, M., Grisso, T., & Appelbaum, P. S. (1999). Measurement of advance directive and medical treatment decision-making capacity of older adults. *Journal of Mental Health and Aging, 5,* 257–274.
(d) Grisso, T., & Appelbaum, P. S. (1992). *Manual for Understanding Treatment Disclosures.* Worcester MA: University of Massachusetts Medical School.
(e) Grisso, T., & Appelbaum, P. S. (1995). The MacArthur Treatment Competence Study, III: Abilities of patients to consent to psychiatric and medical treatment. *Law and Human Behavior, 19,* 149–174.
(f) Grisso, T., Appelbaum, P. S., Mulvey, E., & Fletcher, K. (1995). The MacArthur Treatment Competence Study, II: Measures of abilities related to competence to consent to treatment. *Law and Human Behavior, 19,* 127–148.
(g) Pruchno, R., Smyer, M., Rose, M., Hartman-Stein, P., & Henderson-Laribee, D. (1995). Competence of long-term care residents to participate in decisions about their medical care: A brief, objective assessment. *The Gerontologist, 35,* 622–629.

PERCEPTIONS OF DISORDER (POD)

Authors

Appelbaum, P. S., & Grisso, T.

Primary Author Affiliation

Department of Psychiatry, University of Massachusetts Medical School, Worcester MA

Primary Reference

Appelbaum, P. S., & Grisso, T. (1992). *Manual for Perceptions of Disorder.* Worcester MA: University of Massachusetts Medical School. (Available from the authors.)

Description

Perceptions of Disorder (POD) (b) was developed as a research instrument to measure patients' acknowledgement of their disorders and acknowledgement of the potential value of treatment for their illnesses. The POD was developed for use in a project, the MacArthur Treatment Competence Study (c), focused on identifying patients' capacities to make decisions about consent to or refusal of treatment when they are hospitalized for mental disorders. The authors clearly describe the POD as a tool for research investigation of non-acknowledgement of one's disorder or the potential for treatment to be beneficial, not as a clinical instrument to be used in forensic assessments intended for use in determining a patient's competence to consent to treatment (b).

The instrument is designed for use with patients who have a mental disorder or medical illness. The instrument has three parts, two of which are called "Non-Acknowledgement of Disorder" (NOD) and "Non-Acknowledgement of Treatment Potential" (NOT). (The third part is not discussed here, because it consisted of exploratory items for which no scoring or research results were reported.) Both of these procedures have three interview questions.

For "Non-Acknowledgement of Disorder" (NOD), the first item is introduced by the examiner using standardized wording to describe symptoms, but allows the patient's own symptoms (from their hospital chart) to be inserted in the narrative. Patients' are then asked whether they believe that they have those symptoms, and are asked to indicate the degree of affirmative or negative opinion they have about this on a card showing a 6-point range of options. The second NOD item asks patients how serious they believe their symptoms are and obtains their answer on the same rating card. The third item uses a standardized format to indicate the name of their disorder (e.g., "schizophrenia"), to characterize its symptoms, and to tell the patient that the patient's doctor has made this diagnosis in their case. Then the patient is asked (using the same 6-point rating card) the degree to which the patient agrees or disagrees with the diagnosis.

Scoring for each of the NOD items is based on the patient's rating for Items 1 and 3, and on Item 2, a formula that indicates the correspondence or discrepancy between the patient's rating of perceived severity of symptoms and the actual severity of the patient's symptoms (which requires a measure of severity such as the Brief Psychiatric Rating Scale or the Beck Depression Inventory). Scores of 0, 1, or 2 are possible on each item, leading to NOD scores ranging from 0–6, with lower scores indicating greater non-acknowledgement of disorder.

For "Non-Acknowledgement of Treatment Potential" (NOT), the first item uses a standardized script to inform the patient of several types of treatment for the patient's disorder, then asks the patient to rate the degree to which he or she believes that "you have the kind of condition for which some types of treatment might be helpful." The second NOT item describes medication as an option, indicates that it is often helpful (for "75–90% of patients"), and obtains the patient's rating of the degree to which the patient believes that medication "might be helpful for you." Finally, the third item uses a standardized format to inform the patient that patients with mental disorders who decide not to take medications often do not improve or get worse. Then the rating card is used to obtain their level of belief that "you might get better without medication."

Whenever patients indicate any degree of disagreement with NOT items 1 or 2, or in any degree show belief that they might get better without medication on item 3, they are asked to explain their answer ("What makes you believe that ..."). Their answer is then used to select from the manual any of several "hypotheticals" that have been written to "negate" the underlying presumption, or "premise," in the patient's explanation. For example, if the patient's explanation indicates the basic premise, "I'm too far gone for anything to help," the examiner selects the "Too Sick" hypothetical, and it is administered to the patient: "Imagine that a doctor tells you that there is a medication that has been shown in research to help 90% of people with problems just as serious as yours. Do you think this medication, if it existed, might be of more benefit to you than getting no treatment at all?" The patient answers on the 6-point rating form. Patients then receive a score based on their answer to the hypothetical, not on the answer they provided when rating the original question. Scores of 0, 1, and 2 are possible on each item, leading to NOT scores ranging from 0–6, with lower scores indicating greater non-acknowledgement of treatment potential.

Conceptual Basis

CONCEPT DEFINITION. The decision to measure a construct of Appreciation was based on the authors' review of relevant law that identified four constructs that are used in legal definitions of competence to consent to treatment: Understanding, Appreciation, Reasoning, and Ability to Express a Choice (a, c; also see h). (See the previous and following reviews for instruments related to the other legal constructs.) The authors identified the construct to be measured as "appreciation of the significance of the information (in a treatment disclosure) for one's own circumstances" (b). The authors further defined Appreciation as "non-acknowledgement of disorder" and "non-acknowledgement of treatment potential." They identified several reasons that a person might disavow that they have a disorder or that treatment might be of value. These include reality-based reasons, value-based reasons, coping and defense-based reasons, and organically-based reasons. Only "defense-based" disavowals are relevant for weighing competence to consent to treatment, they claimed, in that this is closest to the "lack of insight" into one's illness that is of concern in many cases of incompetence to consent to treatment, especially in clinical cases involving psychotic symptoms. Thus it is not mere disavowal of symptoms or potential values of treatment that must be measured, but rather disavowal that is the product of mechanisms of denial or psychological distortion of reality, such as is found in some cases of psychosis involving delusional thinking.

OPERATIONAL DEFINITION.   The decision to create two types of questions, focused on possible disavowal of one's illness and disavowal of the value of treatment, was based on the authors' review of the types of concerns about "appreciation" most often raised in cases involving questionable competence to consent to treatment. Similar guidance was used to arrive at the specific items within the two parts of the measure. The decision to base NOT scores on patients' responses to hypothetical questions that negate their disavowal of the value of treatment was based on the notion that only beliefs that are held rigidly in the face of contradictory information (albeit hypothetical information) should represent lack of appreciation, as that concept is used in literature on competence to consent to treatment.

CRITIQUE.   There has been spirited commentary regarding the POD's operationalization of the concept of appreciation (i, j, k). The debate focused primarily on three things:

- whether the nature of the measure might discriminate against persons with ethnic/cultural or religious views that are contrary to medical or psychological notions of "disorder" and "treatment"
- whether the POD authors adequately defined the concept of appreciation, and
- whether their operational definition of the concept adequately represents the concept.

The authors addressed the first question (raised by Stefan, k), at least regarding ethnic/cultural issues, by determining that there were no significant differences between African-Americans and other subjects in their study on relevant POD measures (f). Saks and Behnke (i), however, contend that "lack of appreciation" for purposes of competence to consent should be restricted to those cases in which a person's denial of illness or treatment potential is clearly associated with "patently false beliefs" (see also Slobogin, j). They would not interpret a person's beliefs that are contrary to psychiatric diagnoses or empirical notions of treatment benefit as being a "lack of appreciation" if they are based on religious beliefs or on mere "defensiveness."

The POD authors claim that the nature of the POD's questioning typically will not result in a low score for persons with religious beliefs against treatment (examinees are not required to "accept" the treatment or approve of it, only to acknowledge that it might be of some benefit). On the other hand, the authors have acknowledged that after considerable efforts they were unable to devise an operational definition of a "patently false belief" (f). To this extent the POD falls short of representing the narrow definition of appreciation that some theorists would prefer.

Psychometric Development

STANDARDIZATION.   Administration procedures, interview questions, probing, and scoring criteria are very specific. The process for discovering the patient's symptoms in order to insert them in the standardized script is described, although there is no protection against individual differences between examiners in their selection of symptoms among the materials that they encounter on a patient. Some judgment is needed to discover the examinee's premise for having rejected the potential value of treatment and in selecting a hypothetical based on that premise.

RELIABILITY.   Interscorer reliability was not examined in the primary study for which the POD was developed because its scoring is based solely on examinees' own ratings (g). Test-retest reliability with a two-week interval was .90 on the NOD for patients with schizophrenia and .59 for patients with major depression, and on the NOT they were .66 for patients with schizophrenia and .48 for patients with major depression (g).

NORMS.   The POD manual does not provide POD norms, but normative data are available in the report of the study for which the instrument was developed (e). Mean scores and distributions for the three subscales are provided for 75 patients hospitalized with schizophrenia, 92 patients hospitalized with major depression, and 82 hospitalized with angina.

CRITIQUE.   The POD's psychometric properties suggest somewhat less stability than one would hope for. Some possible reasons for this are discussed below, with reference to internal consistency.

Construct Validation

Internal consistency based on alpha coefficients was .80 for NOD and .67 for NOT. Corrected item-subtest correlations were better for items in NOD (.59 to.70) than for items in NOT (.43 to .60) (g). A factor analysis (e) that included the two POD subtests together with three disclosure procedures of the UTD (previous review) and 8 subtests of the TRAT suggested that the POD measured a construct that was quite distinct from these other two measures (neither POD subtest loaded on the two factors that emerged. In addition, the two POD subtests themselves did not share enough similarity to represent a separate factor. Consistent with this finding, the NOD and NOT were correlated only .23.

Grisso and Appelbaum (e) reported significantly more non-acknowledgement of one's disorder (lower NOD scores) for persons hospitalized for schizophrenia (about one-third of these patients showed significant signs of non-acknowledgement of disorder) than for persons hospitalized for major depression. No significant difference was found between these two groups regarding non-acknowledgement of the potential value of treatment (NOT scores), and only about 15% of both groups showed significant signs of non-acknowledgement of treatment potential. Among schizophrenia patients, those who had high BPRS scores on "Conceptual Disorganization" were more likely to disavow their symptoms (50%) than were those with low Conceptual Disorganization scores (12%). No significant relations were found between NOD or NOT scores and measures of symptom severity, IQ, or indexes of chronicity of disorder.

CRITIQUE. Concerning the evidence regarding questionable internal consistency, the authors of the POD comment that these results suggest that the POD and its two subtests might not have the properties of scales. They suggest that the "POD is best seen as a set of interview screening questions, with non-acknowledgement on any one of them raising a concern about a respondent's unrealistic rejection of the relevance of diagnostic or treatment information for his or her own circumstances" (g, p. 146). This dictates against interpreting POD scores as though they represented a "trait" such as generalized denial.

The results of the factor analyses suggest that the POD measures abilities or response tendencies that are quite distinct from its two companion measures (UTD and TRAT). Moreover, the two subtests of the POD do not seem to measure the same construct, or the construct that they measure can manifest itself quite differently in references to patients' beliefs about their disorder versus their beliefs about treatment.

The relations between the POD and clinical variables are generally as one would expect regarding the presumed relation between failure to acknowledge one's illness and the extent of one's psychopathology. For example, the evidence suggests that POD scores were not impaired generally across persons with significant psychopathology, but that they were impaired for persons with delusional (that is, conceptually disorganized) thinking.

Predictive or Classificatory Utility

Studies thus far have not examined the degree to which POD scores correspond to external criteria for appreciation, other measures of "insight," or other judgments about competence to consent to treatment.

CRITIQUE. Tests of the relation of POD scores to courts' determinations of competence to consent to treatment would need to take into account that courts may find patients incompetent for many reasons other than deficiencies in their ability to appreciate the relevance of treatment information for their own circumstances.

Potential for Expressing Person-Situation Congruency

The questions associated with the POD were purposely standardized to meet the needs of a research study. Thus they provided no opportunity to examine patients' performance in relation to varying demands in terms of complexity of the treatment options.

References

(a) Appelbaum, P., & Grisso, T. (1988). Assessing patients' capacities to consent to treatment. *New England Journal of Medicine, 319,* 1635–1638.
(b) Appelbaum, P., & Grisso, T. (1992). *Manual for Perceptions of Disorder.* Worcester MA: University of Massachusetts Medical School.
(c) Appelbaum, P., & Grisso, T. (1995). The MacArthur Treatment Competence Study, I: Mental illness and competence to consent to treatment. *Law and Human Behavior, 19,* 105–126.
(d) Appelbaum, P., & Roth, L. (1982). Competency to consent to research: A psychiatric overview. *Archives of General Psychiatry, 39,* 951–958.
(e) Grisso, T., & Appelbaum, P. S. (1995). The MacArthur Treatment Competence Study, III: Abilities of patients to consent to psychiatric and medical treatment. *Law and Human Behavior, 19,* 149–174.
(f) Grisso, T., & Appelbaum, P. (1996). Values and limits of the MacArthur Treatment Competence Study. *Psychology, Public Policy, and Law, 2,* 167–181.
(g) Grisso, T., Appelbaum, P. S., Mulvey, E., & Fletcher, K. (1995). The MacArthur Treatment Competence Study, II: Measures of abilities related to competence to consent to treatment. *Law and Human Behavior, 19,* 127–148.
(h) Roth, L., Meisel, A., & Lidz, C. (1977). Tests of competency to consent to treatment. *American Journal of Psychiatry, 134,* 279–284.
(i) Saks, E., & Behnke, S. (1999). Competency to decide treatment and research: MacArthur and beyond. *Journal of Contemporary Legal Issues, 10,* 103–129.
(j) Slobogin, C. (1996). "Appreciation" as a measure of competency: Some thoughts about the MacArthur group's approach. *Psychology, Public Policy, and Law, 2,* 18–30.
(k) Stefan, S. (1996). Race, competence testing, and disability law: A review of the MacArthur competence research. *Psychology, Public Policy, and Law, 2,* 31–44.

Thinking Rationally about Treatment (TRAT)

Authors

Grisso, T., & Appelbaum, P. S.

Primary Author Affiliation

Department of Psychiatry, University of Massachusetts Medical School, Worcester MA

Primary Reference

Grisso, T., & Appelbaum, P. S. (1993). *Manual for Thinking Rationally about Treatment*. Worcester MA: University of Massachusetts Medical School. (Available from the authors.)

Description

Thinking Rationally about Treatment (TRAT) (d) was developed as a research instrument to measure patients' cognitive functions that are employed in the process of deciding among alternative treatments. The TRAT was developed for use in a project, the MacArthur Treatment Competence Study (a), focused on identifying patients' capacities to make decisions about consent to or refusal of treatment when they are hospitalized for mental disorders. The instrument consists of two parts, the "TRAT Vignette" and the "TRAT Tasks."

The *TRAT Vignette* is provided in three forms: Schizophrenia, Depression, and Ischemic Heart Disease. (In the study for which the instrument was developed, patients received the form that corresponded to their own disorder.) The individual is asked to "assist" the hypothetical patient by recommending one of three treatment alternatives, which are provided in the vignette along with a number of their benefits and liabilities. In a standardized interview procedure, a series of questions are asked in order to elicit the subject's explanation for his or her choice, providing data for scores on five of the eight cognitive functions measured in the TRAT. These five functions are conceptually and operationally defined as follows:

- *Seeking Information*: A person's tendency to seek information beyond that which is provided in the disclosure of a decisionmaking problem. Credit is received if the examinee requests further specific information when offered a chance to do so.
- *Consequential Thinking*: A person's consideration of the consequences of a treatment alternative when deciding whether to reject

or accept that alternative (or others). Credit for this function is received if the examinee's explanation for choice of an alternative manifests the use of consequences in the reasoning for the choice.

- *Comparative Thinking*: A person's "simultaneous" processing of information about two treatment alternatives, such that they receive consideration in relation to each other, not merely as separate facts. Credit is received if the examinee's explanation for choosing a particular alternative refers to the consequences of two alternatives in reasonably close juxtaposition.
- *Complex Thinking*: A person's attention to the range of treatment alternatives available within a decision problem, even if only to reject them, rather than avoiding or neglecting consideration of some alternatives. Credit for this function is given if the examinee's explanation for an alternative manifests reference to the full range of treatment alternatives (three) offered in the vignette.
- *Generating Consequences*: A person's capacity to generate potential real-life consequences of the liabilities described in an informed consent disclosure of a treatment alternative. Credit is received if examinees are able to describe ways that medical consequences (e.g., medication side-effects) might influence their own everyday activities.

The examinee's responses to the TRAT Vignette interview questions are recorded verbatim on a structured response sheet by the examiner. They are then scored (2, 1, 0) for each of the five functions according to guidelines that are provided in the manual in two forms: as scoring criteria, and as a set of decision rules outlined in the form of flow diagrams.

The three *TRAT Tasks* are unrelated to the vignette. They are individual tasks that assess three additional cognitive functions associated with decision making or problem solving:

- *Weighing Consequences*: A person's tendency for consistent application of his/her own preferences when evaluating the desirability of consequences of the various alternatives. This function is assessed in two stages separated by other tasks. In Part I, examinees are presented with ten cards, each offering a pair of everyday activities (e.g., "Buy something at a bargain"), thus presenting all possible pairs of five activities, and in each case they are asked to choose which of the two activities they prefer. These are recorded on a response sheet. In Part II, examinees are asked to place in order of preference each of the five activities now listed singly on cards. The scoring procedure allows the examiner to score (2, 1, 0) the consistency of the examinee's stated preferences on Part I and Part II.

- *Transitive Thinking*: A person's functioning on a task requiring logical inferences about the relative quantitative relationships between several alternatives based on paired comparisons. Credit for this function is given for the examinee's performance on several transitive problems (e.g., A is larger than B, B is larger than C: Chose the largest).
- *Probabilistic Thinking*: A person's demonstration of the ability to distinguish correctly the relative values of numerical (percentage) probabilities. This is assessed with several problem questions requiring an understanding of simple percentage probability statements.

Scores are obtained for each of the eight functions, then summed to produce a total TRAT score. For reasons explained below, the authors eventually developed a TRAT-2 score, based on the sum of scores on six of the TRAT subtests (deleting Weighting Consequences and Seeking Information).

Conceptual Basis

CONCEPT DEFINITION.   The authors explain that their intention in developing the TRAT was to measure the capacity to process information rationally in order to arrive at a treatment decision. The decision to measure this capacity was based on the authors' review of relevant law that identified four constructs that are used in legal definitions of competence to consent to treatment: Understanding, Appreciation, Reasoning, and Ability to Express a Choice (a). (See the previous two reviews for instruments related to the other legal constructs.) They provide evidence that this capacity is relevant (among other capacities) for legal determinations of competence to consent to treatment.

To select and define the various abilities to be assessed, the authors reviewed psychological theories of decision making and problem solving in order to identify abilities that seemed conceptually related to the capacity with which the law was concerned. The specific ability constructs were borrowed from several models of decision making and problem solving with special attention to abilities that the various theories had in common (e.g., c, g, h, i, j).

OPERATIONAL DEFINITION.   The decision to create TRAT vignettes for three different disorders was based on the authors' intentions to use these three diagnostic patient groups in a major study of patients' treatment decision-making abilities. The various treatment alternatives provided in each vignette were based on actual treatment options that were typical for the disorders in question. Separate "TRAT tasks" were developed for three of the eight functions because they would have been difficult to include in the vignette procedure without greatly complicating the process. The tasks themselves were developed wholly as the authors' inventions, not borrowed from other tests.

CRITIQUE.   To the extent that the law is interested in patients' capacity to process information in reaching a treatment decision, the TRAT presents a reasonable effort to represent that capacity operationally. The specific abilities were selected, however, solely on the basis of their relation to psychological theories of decision making. Thus the relevance of the specific functions measured in the TRAT (e.g., *Generating Consequences*) for legal concerns is theoretical, not specifically referenced in past legal decisions.

PSYCHOMETRIC DEVELOPMENT

STANDARDIZATION.   Administration procedures, interview questions, probing, and scoring criteria are clearly described in the manual. The degree of scorer judgment required by the criteria for scoring the vignette subscales is somewhat greater than for the instrument's companion measures (the UTD and POD, reviewed earlier).

RELIABILITY.   Interscorer reliability (f) was determined for 10 recently-trained research assistants, based on independent scoring of 20 protocols. Kappa correlations for individual TRAT items were .60 or above for 76% of the comparisons, although about 7% of the comparisons were below the accepted level of statistical significance. Intraclass correlations for total TRAT scores all were above .88, and kappa correlations for individual TRAT subtests were .60 or above for 77% of the comparisons.

Test-retest reliability (f) with a two-week interval ranged from .66–.68, depending on the subtest and the diagnostic identification of the participant samples, with no significant difference between means at first and second administration.

NORMS.   The TRAT manual does not provide norms, but normative data are available in the report of the study for which the instrument was developed (e). Mean scores and distributions for the three subscales are provided for hospitalized patients, 75 with schizophrenia, 92 with major depression, and 82 with angina, as well as three comparison groups of similar size comprising persons in the community without mental disorders.

CRITIQUE.   The TRAT psychometric properties are generally acceptable, but not as good as for the UTD (reviewed earlier). Interrater reliability is somewhat weak; some of the criteria for scoring responses to the vignette procedure, although carefully described, are in some cases complex.

Construct Validation

Internal consistency based on alpha coefficients and corrected item-total correlations were best for patients with schizophrenia (alpha = .74; average item-total $r = .42$), and lowest for persons with ischemic heart disease (alpha = .39; average item-total $r = .25$) (f). A series of factor analyses of the subscales indicated that *Weighing Consequences* and *Seeking Information* were outliers in relation to the other six subscales. Thus for research purposes the authors employed only the six inter-related subscales to form a TRAT score called TRAT-2.

In a factor analysis that included the 8 TRAT subtests together with the 3 disclosure procedures of the UTD and the two subtests of the POD, the highest loading measures for the second factor were four of the TRAT subtests that employ the TRAT vignette (f). This is consistent with the assumption that the instrument measures a construct that is distinct from the other legal constructs employed in competence determinations.

Grisso and Appelbaum (e) reported significantly lower TRAT-2 scores for persons hospitalized for mental disorders (schizophrenia, or major depression) than for their community (non-mentally ill) comparison groups. Similarly, Frank et al. (b) found a significant negative relation between depressive symptom severity and TRAT scores.

Differences between patients with schizophrenia and their community comparison group (e) were apparent across most of the eight TRAT subscales, but apparent on only 4 of the subscales for patients with major depression and their community comparison group. TRAT-2 scores were significantly related to verbal cognitive functioning (measured with selected subtests from the Wechsler Adult Intelligence Scale-Revised), but were not significantly related to chronicity of disorder (age at first hospitalization, number of prior admissions).

CRITIQUE. Two of the subscales apparently do not tap the same construct as the remainder of the TRAT subscales. One of these, *Seeking Information*, may simply measure inquisitiveness or degree of involvement, rather than rational processing of information. The other, *Weighing Consequences*, measures the stability of one's everyday preferences—a characteristic that may influence decision making but which is quite different in nature from the other cognitive functions measured by the TRAT. These two subtests may be worth administering for the additional information that they provide, but the authors' data suggest that they impair the internal consistency of the TRAT when they are allowed to contribute to a TRAT total score.

TRAT-2 scores were lower for diagnostic groups with disorders that would be expected to manifest poorer processing of information presented in the context of a treatment decision. But the fact that TRAT-2 scores were unrelated to symptom severity is not consistent with expectation, presuming that greater severity of symptoms would interfere with information processing. The study's measure of symptom severity (Brief Psychiatric Rating Scale), however, is based on many types of symptoms that are not cognitive in nature, and this could account for the insignificant correlation between symptom severity and TRAT-2 scores.

Predictive or Classificatory Utility

Studies thus far have not examined the degree to which TRAT scores correspond to external criteria for processing of information to make a decision or for clinical or judicial judgments about competence to consent to treatment.

CRITIQUE.   Tests of the relation of TRAT scores to courts' determinations of competence to consent to treatment would need to take into account that courts may find patients incompetent for many reasons other than deficiencies in their ability to process information rationally.

Potential for Expressing Person-Situation Congruency

Various disorders and treatment situations differ in the complexity of their options, risks, benefits, and the difficulty level of the concepts or treatments that must be understood. The treatment situations used in the TRAT vignettes were purposely standardized to meet the needs of a research study. Thus they provided no opportunity to examine patients' performance in relation to varying demands in terms of complexity of the treatment options.

References

(a) Appelbaum, P.S., & Grisso, T. (1995). The MacArthur Treatment Competence Study, I: Mental illness and competence to consent to treatment. *Law and Human Behavior, 19*, 105–126.
(b) Frank, L., Smyer, M., Grisso, T., & Appelbaum, P. S. (1999). Measurement of advance directive and medical treatment decision-making capacity of older adults. *Journal of Mental Health and Aging, 5*, 257–274.
(c) Goldfried, M., & D'Zurilla, T. (1969). A behavioral-analytic model for assessing competence. In C. D. Spielberger (Ed.), *Current topics in clinical and community psychology* (pp. 151–196). New York: Academic Press.
(d) Grisso, T., & Appelbaum, P. S. (1992). *Manual for Thinking Rationally About Treatment.* Worcester MA: University of Massachusetts Medical School.
(e) Grisso, T., & Appelbaum, P. S. (1995). The MacArthur Treatment Competence Study, III: Abilities of patients to consent to psychiatric and medical treatment. *Law and Human Behavior, 19*, 149–174.

(f) Grisso, T., Appelbaum, P. S., Mulvey, E., & Fletcher, K. (1995). The MacArthur Treatment Competence Study, II: Measures of abilities related to competence to consent to treatment. *Law and Human Behavior, 19*, 127–148.
(g) Hogarth, R. (1987). *Judgement and choice: The psychology of decision.* New York: John Wiley.
(h) Janis, I., & Mann, L. (1977). Decision making: A psychological analysis of conflict, choice, and communication. New York: Free Press.
(i) Spivack, G., Platt, J., & Shure, M. (1976). *The problem solving approach to adjustment.* San Francisco, CA: Jossey-Bass.
(j) Spivack, G., & Shure, M. (1974). *Social adjustment of young children: A cognitive approach to solving real-life problems.* San Francisco, CA: Jossey-Bass.

CURRENT STATUS OF THE FIELD

RESEARCH DIRECTIONS

The first edition of *Evaluating Competencies* reviewed three instruments in this area, all of them characterized as "prototypes" because their authors considered them "experimental" and not yet ready for clinical or forensic use. Those instruments received no further research attention during the past 15 years. But their efforts to explore ways to operationalize the relevant abilities for the legal concept of competence to consent to treatment had an impact on the instruments that we have reviewed here. One can see in some of these instruments an adoption of strategies explored by Weithorn (1980; Weithorn & Campbell, 1982) in her prototype instrument, *Measure of Competency to Render Informed Treatment Decisions* (see pp. 330–335 in the first edition).

Functional Component

Weithorn had turned to the analyses of Roth, Meisel, and Lidz (1977) for the ability constructs that that she used in her competence to consent to treatment instrument. These were also the starting point for Appelbaum and Grisso (1988) as they began their work on the UTD, POD, TRAT, and eventually the MacCAT-T, and they were employed also in Marson's CCTI. This may indicate that researchers and legal analysts in this area have reached a consensus about the fundamental abilities that need to be assessed in competency to consent instruments: the abilities to *express a choice*, to *understand* information that is disclosed, to *appreciate the significance* of its consequences for oneself, and to *reason* with (or *logically process*) the information when arriving at a decision. Moreover, the various instruments suggest a consensus, with adequate legal foundation, about what a person must be able to understand and cognitively process for informed consent (the disorder, treatment, its risks and benefits, and alternative treatments and their risks and benefits).

A note of caution is in order, however, for persons who pursue further research with these instruments or who seek to develop new ones. First, Roth et al.'s (1977) original scheme included a fifth ability: that the patient can make a "rational choice" (that is, can arrive at the "best" decision, the one that most "reasonable" people would make). Marson's CCTI includes this concept. In contrast, it was specifically set aside by Appelbaum and Grisso (1988) because legal and ethical views subsequent to the Roth et al. seminal analysis have recognized that as a legal standard this concept is antithetical to the fundamental notion of autonomy. It suggests that individuals are competent if they choose what others would choose, whereas modern notions of informed consent allow individuals to make whatever choice they wish as long as they have the capacities to understand, appreciate, reason, and express a choice.

Second, as demonstrated by the previous reviews, the definition of "appreciation" is not the same across the measures that claim to identify it. The POD and MacCAT-T focus on what has been called "lack of insight" into one's disorder and need for treatment (Appelbaum & Grisso, 1995). This definition focuses on cases in which people do not believe that the information they are being given about their disorder applies to their own situation. In contrast, the CCTI focuses on lack of awareness of potential consequences of one's treatment. Moreover, the actual stimuli and scoring or rating criteria used in the POD and MacCAT-T suggest somewhat different definitions of appreciation. The POD scores appreciation as poor if individuals fail to acknowledge their illness (or the value of treatment) even when given hypotheticals that challenge the premises behind their beliefs, suggesting a rigid discounting of reality. The MacCAT-T, however, scores failure to acknowledge one's illness based on a specific reason for non-acknowledgement: when the patient has a delusional premise that distorts reality and does not have a basis in the patient's cultural or religious background. As noted in the review of the POD, the meaning of "appreciation" as a legal standard for competence to consent to treatment is currently a matter of intellectual debate with contributions from several different perspectives.

The differences in definitions of appreciation have several implications. Future researchers who seek to measure the concept must be clear about their definitions, and comparisons between instruments will have to take into account the fact that different measures, though similarly titled, might not be conceptualized or operationalized to measure the same thing. Unfortunately, the law does not currently provide a sufficiently fine-grained definition to allow us to judge which of the instruments' definitions of appreciation is more legally relevant. The debate to watch in this regard may be that of ethicists more than legal analysts.

Second, the differences will influence research that examines the relation of appreciation to the other psycholegal constructs (understanding and reasoning). Both the CCTI and the MacArthur research measures have been used in this type of research. Studies that compare patients' performance on measures of the various psycholegal constructs address questions about the necessity or redundancy of using all three constructs in clinical practice. They seek to address whether states that employ different legal standards are likely to find different types or proportions of patients incompetent to consent (Dymek et al., 1999; Grisso & Appelbaum, 1995b; Berg et al., 1996). But the results are likely to be different for studies that employ different conceptual and operational definitions of appreciation.

Finally, the first edition discussed confusion at that time concerning whether the law defined "understanding" as *actual understanding* (the condition of a patient's knowledge of his or her own treatment situation) or the *capacity to understand* (one's ability to understand hypothetical, treatment-like information). Subsequently the issue has caused neither legal controversy nor ethical debate. This suggests that there is room for instruments that use either of these approaches to defining "understanding," as long as we are clear about their different implications when used in research and in forensic cases.

The difference is important for the test developer, because assessment of *actual* understanding requires an instrument that uses the patient's own symptoms and treatment options as the test stimulus (like the MacCAT-T, as well as the SSCI now being developed by Marson: see introduction to the instrument review section of this chapter). In contrast, assessment of *capacity* to understand allows for a measure that uses one or two standardized symptom and treatment vignette disclosures (like the CCTI and the three research measures).

Of course, there are substantial differences in what the researcher can confidently do with these two types of instruments from the point of view of standardized control that allows for inferences and comparisons involving groups of patients. Both methods allow for standardization of format, so that the same general *types* of information are provided to all patients and the same inquiries are made. But the use of hypotheticals allows the same *content* to be included in that format across patients. In contrast, instruments like the MacCAT-T and the SSCI (see the paragraph introducing the instrument review section) allow for the patient's own symptoms and treatment to be inserted in the format, thus producing nonstandardized content across patients. Examining patients' actual understanding of their own circumstances, therefore, requires a methodological concession that weakens one's ability to make meaningful group comparisons. While this is a limitation, it need not deter researchers from using "actual understanding" instruments in research if they create conditions that will minimize those limitations. For example, the matter would be less critical in a study in which all of the patients at least had the same disorder (e.g., schizophrenia) but with the disclosure including the patient's own pattern of symptoms, compared to a study involving patients with a wide variety of psychiatric diagnoses.

Causal Component

The first edition urged future researchers to examine the relation between performance on competence to consent to treatment instruments and various psychological conditions that might impair abilities associated with competence. This has been an integral part of the projects that spawned the instruments reviewed here. Performance on the various elements of these competence to consent instruments have been examined for persons with various psychiatric and medical disorders (e.g., schizophrenia, major depression, Alzheimer's Disease, and several non-psychiatric medical conditions), as well as persons with no disorders. Further studies with other patient populations (for example, persons with mental retardation) would be especially helpful.

Most impressive has been the interest in examining the relation of scores on these instruments to performance on various neuropsychological measures that may account for deficits in the psycholegal abilities in question. Such studies are especially helpful in addressing the construct validity of the instruments, as well as providing information for clinicians who may use the same neuropsychological measures to explain the decision making deficits of persons whom they are asked to evaluate in competence cases.

Research should also use these instruments to examine the decision-making capacities of children and adolescents. Early in the 1980s there was a brief surge of interest in the capacities of children and adolescents to make treatment decisions (e.g., Melton et al., 1983) among researchers who addressed psychological questions related to law and policy. This was stimulated in part by considerable interest among child advocates in promoting children's participation in decisions about their medical care. Policy issues that research in this area addressed ranged from youths' role in their own commitment to inpatient psychiatric facilities, to adolescent girls' capacities to make decisions about abortions. This line of research, however, was less often pursued in the 1990s. The reasons for this are probably complex, including the relative lack of options for measuring the abilities in question. There would seem to be no reason why the new instruments reviewed here could not be used to examine children's and adolescents' capacities for treatment decision making.

Interactive Component

As noted in the introduction to this chapter, patients' competence to consent is judged not by their absolute abilities alone, but by the degree to which those abilities are challenged by the demands of their own treatment situation and the decisions they must make. Actual understanding instruments like the MacCAT-T and the anticipated SCCI (using patients' own symptoms and treatment options as the stimuli) will give more relevant data for judging patients' capacities in the context of the specific demands of their own situation. In the language of the interactive component of competence, patients' performance on instruments that use their own specific treatment situation is an index of person-situation congruency.

This does not mean that instruments using hypothetical situations in vignettes have no role in research on the interactive nature of competence to consent to treatment. The interactive, person-situation construction of legal competencies reminds us that people whose capacities are marginal may nevertheless be considered competent if we can manipulate the circumstances of their consent process, such that the level of demand is decreased and/or their understanding and processing of information is increased. This strategy is called "assisted competence" (Grisso & Appelbaum, 1998). For example, people with marginal abilities to understand or reason about treatment information may be assisted by visual aids, simplifying the wording of the disclosure, having family members or companions assist them in thinking through the alternatives, and other strategies for manipulating the environment in ways that might incrementally compensate for their limited capacities. To date there have been few studies of the degree to which such strategies can be used to improve patients' understanding and processing of treatment information in informed consent situations. The instruments reviewed here that use hypothetical vignettes would be entirely suitable as pre-and-post measures to examine the effects of compensatory strategies on the improvement of patients' abilities to make treatment decisions.

Judgmental and Dispositional Components

The MacCAT-T and the CCTI have set a fortunate precedent by not summing patients' scores across the various psycholegal scales. To do otherwise, producing a total "competence" or "capacity" score, would not be logical. It would suggest, for example, that a high score in understanding can compensate for a low score in reasoning, despite the fact that understanding of information is useless if one cannot process the information rationally to arrive at a decision.

Research with the HCAT used a cut-off score to signify probable incompetence, setting the score on the basis of empirical comparisons of HCAT scores to independent clinical judgments of competence. The developers of the MacArthur instruments and the CCTI chose not to develop cut-off scores, but rather to signify a higher level of risk of incompetence by using various points of comparison. In their studies with the UTD, POD and TRAT, the researchers used the range of scores below the minus-2 standard deviation point for the total distribution of scores (combining patients and non-patients) as an index of impairment. The CCTI authors did the same but used their non-patient samples alone to establish the minus-2 standard deviation point. Such indexes are helpful in expressing degrees of serious impairment, as long as they are not translated automatically into statements that individuals below those scores are "incompetent."

The use of "normal" comparison groups is especially helpful and consistent with the law's way of thinking about legal competencies. The "average adult" is considered competent to decide most things. We know, however, that even "average adults" manifest limitations in their understanding and reasoning abilities. Using their imperfect abilities as a standard guards against penalizing patient samples simply because they, too, manifest some deficits in those abilities. Their deficits should be substantially greater than the "average" person's abilities in order to raise the question of their competence.

CLINICAL APPLICATION

Description

The assessment of patients' competence to consent to treatment is a routine obligation for every health and mental health professional. Typically it is assessed by default; nothing occurs in the normal course of the doctor-patient interaction to even raise the question. In this sense, the clinician is obligated simply to be vigilant for cues that might reasonably raise the question of competence (Grisso & Appelbaum, 1998a).

Once a cue does raise the question, typically a full "forensic" evaluation of the patient's competence to consent still will not be required. A more informal process will evolve in which the clinician will explore the possibility that the initial cues need to be taken more seriously. If they do, it is at this point that some cases may call for the use of a standardized process represented by the instruments in this chapter. The instruments may be used by the attending clinician or by a specialist with whom the clinician may consult (e.g., a forensic psychologist, or a psychiatrist providing consultation-liaison to various medical departments in a hospital).

The value of these instruments is especially great when it may be important to document the data and reasons for one's judgments about a patient's competence and to clearly describe those matters to others, be they colleagues or courts. This may be necessary if the clinician intends to proceed with a treatment, perhaps on the family's agreement, after deciding that the patient is incompetent. In many states, doing this requires the decision of a court, and the instruments can be especially useful for describing one's data and logic in those cases because of the instruments' relationship to the legal and ethical standards for competence to consent to treatment.

Concerning the selection of instruments, it is difficult to imagine many clinicians employing the UTD, POD, and TRAT together in their assessments of patients' treatment decision making capacities. They require considerable time, and the TRAT's use of card-sorts is not particularly amenable to bedside use. The HCAT cannot be recommended for descriptive objectives of these evaluations, because the data that it obtains simply are not relevant in most cases. The HCAT allows one to describe what a person can understand about the concept of informed consent, but it does not provide evidence for patients' abilities to understand their disorder or the nature of the treatment that is being proposed.

In contrast, the CCTI and the MacCAT-T require no materials other than the examiner's clipboard and recording forms, and they require only about 20 minutes on average. They provide information relevant for the full range of abilities with which legal and ethical analyses of competence to consent to treatment are likely to be concerned. The CCTI does this for the patient's capacities to respond to hypotheticals rather than the patient's own disorder, but it offers normative points of comparison for expressing the patient's abilities in relation to others. The MacCAT-T allows one to describe patients' actual understanding and processing of their own disorder and treatment situation, which is an advantage for presentation to courts. However, opportunities for comparing the patient's performance to that of others is not as good as with the CCTI, because the use of the patient's own disorder limits standardization and the opportunity for true norms to have been developed.

As noted earlier in this chapter, not all states use all four of the psycholegal constructs represented in these two instruments. This need not deter their use by clinicians who must often make their own decisions, without legal intervention, about patients' competence to consent. But examiners who are performing competence evaluations for courts' determinations of patients' competence to consent should be aware of the standards that apply in their own state. While they may administer all of the instrument in question, only some of the information might be considered legally relevant in their jurisdiction.

Explanation

Clinicians will need to explain the reasons for patients' deficits on the instruments. These may occur for a wide variety of reasons, such as symptoms of psychotic disorders that can affect cognitive and emotional functioning, neuropsychological disorders, mental retardation, dementias, and temporary but extreme symptomatic conditions sometimes associated with medical conditions (e.g., trauma-related anxiety and compensatory defense mechanisms to cope with stress). Often these conditions are obvious and within the boundaries of discovery in ordinary clinical observation. At other times they may require confirmation with additional psychological and diagnostic tests.

Prediction

The measures described in this chapter do not have a predictive objective. They seek to describe what people can do now, at the time they need to make a treatment decision. However, sometimes courts will want to address whether a person may be able to make future treatment situations. In such cases, the instruments themselves provide no basis for making that prediction. The clinician's attempts to do so would be based primarily on an assessment of the cause of the patient's deficits in performance on the instruments, some of those causes logically being more enduring or remedial than others.

Conclusions and Opinions

The instruments reviewed here obviously cannot define legal competence or incompetence. This is true whether the clinician uses the data from the instruments in the course of making a clinical decision or offers the data in a court where a legal decision about competence or incompetence will be made. The data from some of these instruments certainly provide relevant information for making the competence decision. But additional clinical data as well as the application of moral and legal considerations will be required to make the final judgment concerning whether the patient's incapacities, and the consequent risks, are sufficient to curtail his or her right to make the treatment decision.

———10———

Developing and Using Forensic Assessment Instruments

Chapters 4 through 9, each devoted to assessment for a specific legal competence, ended with discussions of the current status of the field. These discussions examined research directions for the development of FAIs, as well as clinical applications to guide the use of FAIs, related to the specific legal competence featured in each chapter.

Looking across all of these areas of legal competency, what general messages arise that would guide the future development of specialized instruments for competence assessments? And what general recommendations are suggested for their use? The present chapter addresses these questions in a section on "Developing Forensic Assessment Instruments" and another on "Using Forensic Assessment Instruments." The final section on "Continuing the Improvement of Forensic Assessments" comments on the continuing value of the book's five-concept model for legal competencies and discusses issues that may promote or inhibit the development and use of FAIs in the future.

DEVELOPING FORENSIC ASSESSMENT INSTRUMENTS

In each of the preceding six chapters, the Research Directions subsection has identified conceptual and methodological issues in the construction and validation of FAIs, as well as strategies for dealing with these issues. Some of these issues and strategies have been unique to a particular legal competence, whereas others have recurred across competencies. The following discussion identifies some of the major, recurrent issues and strategies in FAI development in those reviews.

FUNCTIONAL COMPONENT

Chapter 3 identified the use of functional ability concepts (C in Figure 1) to provide a conceptual link between legal constructs of competence (A) and psychological principles concerning human behavior in general (B). FAIs (C') are operational definitions of the functional ability concepts. The reviews of researchers' experiences in developing FAIs have revealed certain recurrent issues and strategies in forming conceptual and operational definitions of legally relevant functional abilities.

Concept Formulation: Finding the Relevant Functional Abilities

The formation of functional-ability concepts for a legal competence seems to require strategies for dealing with: (a) the law's definition of the competence, (b) psychology's and psychiatry's ways of conceptualizing human behavior in general, and (c) the empirical domain of abilities associated with the relevant environmental and social context.

DISCOVERING THE LAW'S DEFINITION. Chapter 3 pointed out that researching the law, as well as researching judges', lawyers', and legal scholars' interpretations of the law, are important steps in developing ability concepts that will stand the test of perceived relevance for the legal competence construct. Past efforts by FAI developers to achieve this have involved three strategies, all with some merit:

- Comprehensive reviews of law
- Observation of the law in action
- Surveys of expert opinions about the law's intent

Reviews of law typically involve comprehensive analyses of relevant statutes, case law, proposed legal standards, and legal commentary (e.g., law review journals). This produces material that can guide the researcher in efforts to interpret the law's intent regarding competence abilities. This strategy has been employed for at least some instruments in all of the areas of legal competence. The process often will require that the instrument developer—typically a psychologist or psychiatrist—obtain interpretive assistance from law scholars and practitioners with greater experience in interpreting the law.

Observation of the law in action involves studies of the decision-making strategies of judges themselves in cases requiring competence determinations. Research to identify the information to which legal decision makers attend, and how they weigh and combine this information to make competence decisions, may raise suggestions for legally relevant ability constructs that often are not apparent in black letter law or written case opinions. This strategy rarely has been employed in the form of systematic and controlled research by FAI developers. Less systematic but direct observations of judicial behavior, however, have preceded development of some competence to stand trial instruments (Chapter 4) as well as the ILS for competence of disabled adults in guardianship cases (Chapter 8).

Consensus research with samples of judges and lawyers asks them to nominate or rate functional abilities that they perceive to be relevant to the legal competence construct. This strategy has been used not only to generate functional ability concepts, but also to obtain consensual validation of the legal relevance of ability concepts generated by other means. Here the research team's social scientist may take the lead, constructing the proper interview or survey tools that will produce information to be considered by the interdisciplinary team. Several past FAI projects have used this strategy in one form or another (e.g., the CMR in Chapter 3, and the ILS in Chapter 8).

USING PSYCHOLOGICAL CONSTRUCTS.   Researchers who have developed FAIs have frequently used psychological constructs and theories to help clarify and structure the law's relatively ambiguous references to functional abilities in an area of competence. For example, cognitive and social problem-solving theories have shaped the conceptualization of functional abilities related to waiver of rights (Chapter 5) and consent to treatment (Chapter 9). Constructs derived from psychiatry and clinical psychology have played an important role in conceptualizing capacities related to assessments in criminal responsibility cases (Chapter 6), and neuropsychological theories have contributed to conceptualization of abilities related to everyday living skills for questions of the need for guardianship (Chapter 8).

EMPIRICAL STRATEGIES.   A third strategy is to obtain empirical information about the types of abilities actually required in order to perform a role in the environmental context related to a particular legal competence: for example, in the role of defendant in trials, or in the role of parent for young children. Quite a number of approaches to obtaining empirical information of this type are demonstrated in the preceding chapters.

First, empirical research in psychology might already have identified essential or important abilities associated with role performance in some contexts. For example, developmental psychologists have identified at least some of the important abilities associated with caring for children and meeting their needs (Chapter 7); gerontologists have identified abilities associated with adaptive functioning of the elderly in everyday life (Chapter 8). Generally, however, basic research will not have examined the abilities associated with the environmental contexts and roles related to legal competencies. For example, there have been no systematic studies of the actual knowledge and skills that individuals must employ in their role as a defendant in criminal trials.

A second strategy, therefore, would involve performing a functional analysis of the role in question prior to FAI development. This would require direct observation of individuals performing in that role, in order to catalogue the nature and frequency of those things that individuals in that role seem to be required to understand or do. Such "job analyses" could be especially useful in suggesting a range of abilities that might not have been considered in legal or scientific theoretical conceptualizations. Interestingly, none of the FAI projects reviewed earlier has employed this strategy systematically.

Finally, one can interview individuals who have performed in the role in question (or are especially familiar with it), asking them to describe the full range of abilities required by the role. This strategy is subject to error in the observations or reports of those individuals who are queried. Nevertheless, role participants (and those who have directly observed them in the legal process) often are in a unique position to describe ability requirements that would not be apparent to casual observers. This strategy was employed with elderly individuals and caretakers or professionals who work with the elderly as one step in the procedure for developing the ILS (Chapter 8), and it is demonstrated in some studies of competence to stand trial involving interviews of defendants and/or their attorneys (e.g., Tobey et al., 2000; Hoge et al., 1992).

ARRIVING AT FINAL CONCEPTS.   One will find that analyses based on the various methods above do not always lead to the same sets of concepts with which to structure FAIs. This arises in at least two ways.

First, legal standards regarding any one type of legal competence are not entirely uniform across U.S. jurisdictions (or those of other countries). For example, analyses of law leading to development of the MacCAT-T (Chapter 9) indicated that the legal standards for competence to consent to treatment include "understanding" of relevant information in almost all states, but only some states' laws specify a consideration of patients' "reasoning" abilities (Appelbaum & Grisso, 1995). At a more specific level

of content, what a suspect must understand to provide a valid waiver of
Miranda rights (Chapter 5), and the level of understanding required, will
vary somewhat from one jurisdiction to another as manifested in inter-
jurisdictional differences in the words and phrases of standard "*Miranda*
warnings." These differences across jurisdictions present special challenges to the FAI developer, because the selection of specific concepts or
a single standardized content for the FAI will render the final product less
relevant and applicable for some jurisdictions than for others.

Second, scholarly legal analyses, expert surveys, and theoretical and
empirical methods for identifying concepts to guide FAI development
may sometimes reveal abilities that are important to functioning and decision making in an area of legal competence, but that are not specifically
identified in analyses of statutes and case law. Should these abilities be
excluded as guides for FAI development because they are not specifically
acknowledged in legal standards?

One view would suggest that a FAI that includes ability constructs
not currently defined in law will offer information that is legally irrelevant and therefore open to challenge as providing inadmissible (or at least
irrelevant) evidence. A second view would argue that ability constructs
outside the law can be included, as long as they have a sound logic associated with the role context for the legal competence in question. Several
reasons can be offered in defense of this approach:

- Legal competence standards often are general in their definition of
  competence, in order to allow for the evolution of law in dealing
  with evidence when applying the standards to diverse cases. They
  allow room for expansion of meaning and improvement in application of the law, in the normal course of legal challenges and judicial
  acceptance of new concepts that will "fit into" existing legal theories and definitions.
- Psychology and psychiatry have a role to play in assisting the law
  to clarify the domain of abilities associated with individuals' functioning in the contexts to which legal competencies refer.
- Courts are always free to reject the relevance of specific types of
  information provided by a FAI (e.g., information about an ability
  concept that the court deems irrelevant) without necessarily
  rejecting all of the information that the instrument provides.

Operationalization: Creating the Stimulus and Response Formats

The six competence chapters have identified a number of critical
questions concerning the translation of functional ability concepts into

instruments for measurement or rating of the abilities. Three of these questions deserve special mention because of their importance across all competence areas.

CHOOSING THE STIMULUS.   Rarely will the FAI developer be able to select stimuli (e.g., questions and the context in which they are asked) that simulate the circumstances of the legal competence construct (e.g., the trial experience for defendants). The proper objective may be to develop a stimulus format that merely approximates the legally relevant environmental context as closely as important practical and ethical constraints will allow.

Strategies for approximating relevant external contexts within the assessment setting are well known among test developers. Placing examinees in highly realistic simulations of the real world context—for example, observing a parent and child interacting in their own home or in the clinic—offers the closest approximation, although these strategies frequently are not feasible for assessments of legal competence. Picture stimuli to accompany hypothetical dilemmas offer closer approximations than presenting examinees with dilemmas in verbal form alone. Stimuli that ask about the examinee's own circumstances come closer than stimuli that ask the examinee to respond to hypothetical (third-person) circumstances.

FAIs developed in the areas of competence to waive rights (Chapter 5) and to consent to treatment (Chapter 9) offer closer approximations of their respective contexts than do FAIs in other areas where clinical interview formats have predominated as the model for obtaining information about abilities (e.g., competence to stand trial, Chapter 5). The first-person format of the MacCAT-T (Chapter 9) seems to approximate more closely the relevant context for capacity to consent to treatment than would a hypothetical or paper and pencil instrument. FAI developers working in a given competence area may wish to examine stimulus strategies used in other competence areas as alternatives to abstract interview or questionnaire items.

CHOOSING THE RESPONSE.   The six competence reviews reveal two important considerations when determining the response format of a FAI. These include decisions about modes of verbal expression to employ, as well as options for verbal or performance demonstrations of ability.

Concerning modes of verbal expression, the preceding chapters offer numerous examples of FAIs that ask examinees to demonstrate their abilities by verbalizing their thoughts to open-ended questions, choosing between multiple alternatives, or making dichotomous choices. The previous reviews have pointed out several reasons to choose carefully the verbal expressive requirements of a FAI. For example, some expressive modes are more similar than others to the mode required by the environmental context to which a legal competence refers. Further, error is introduced when an instrument requires a mode of verbal expression in which the examinee is deficient, so that some examinees might understand and be able to process the information in question but not be able to verbalize what they have understood or inferred. It is for this reason that the reviews frequently have recommended the development of FAIs to assess a given set of functional abilities using more than one expressive mode (e.g., the CAST-MR in Chapter 4 and the *Miranda* comprehension measures in Chapter 5).

Second, some FAIs rely on examinees' verbal descriptions of their own abilities, whereas others require a functional demonstration of the relevant ability. The latter, performance-based approach can be in verbal form (e.g., asking people to use information in solving a problem) or motor form (e.g., asking people to do something—e.g., to count out change for a dollar—rather than asking them if they can do it). Comments throughout these chapters have suggested that whenever it is feasible, FAI developers should consider the greater merits of the "demonstration" or performance-based approach when deciding on a response format. There is often some discrepancy between what people do, or are capable of doing, and what they say they can or would do.

CHOOSING SCORING CRITERIA.   Many of the FAIs require that responses be designated "correct or incorrect," "adequate or inadequate," "good, marginal/questionable, or poor," or some more extensive rating. Examiners often are provided with descriptive definitions to guide them in assigning the scores or ratings. These criterion definitions, therefore, constitute standardized, evaluative judgments about correctness or adequacy.

FAI developers have used several strategies to choose standardized criteria for correctness or adequacy on individual FAI items. In general, instruments in the criminal competencies (Chapters 4, 5 and 6) have sought the opinions of legal professionals concerning the degrees of adequacy of pilot responses to draft items for a FAI. In contrast, instruments in the civil competencies (Chapters 7, 8 and 9) tend to have sought the opinions of medical and mental health professionals. Some FAI developers have involved both of the above professional groups, either in working panels or through more extensive survey procedures.

The importance of this stage in FAI development cannot be stressed enough. FAI developers have no reason to expect that their own intuitive judgments about the correctness or adequacy of particular test responses will carry much weight with colleagues in either the legal or mental health professions. Standardized scoring criteria should represent consensual judgments of representative FAI users and appropriate authorities, rather than the potentially idiosyncratic views of the FAI developer.

Validation: Demonstrating the Value of the Instrument

The earliest data-collection efforts with a FAI generally involve establishing relevant types of reliability (e.g., interscorer and test-retest reliability). This is followed by initial investigations of the FAI's construct or predictive validity.

As with any psychological instrument, a FAI's validity is not defined by any single type of validity study, nor can any one research project provide definitive evidence of validity. Validity is always cumulative and relative, rather than conclusive and absolute. Consequently, FAI developers should introduce their instrument to colleagues in their field when its basic reliability and the first steps in examining validity are sufficient to suggest its potential. This allows other researchers to begin the process of accumulating information bearing on validity, through exposure of the instrument to a greater range of methodologies, theoretical perspectives, and populations than usually will be available to any single FAI developer or research team.

The six competence reviews provide examples of a great many strategies for establishing construct validity. Especially evident have been statistical methods for determining:

- internal consistency of an instrument's scales, including alpha coefficients and factor analyses
- comparisons of criterion groups selected on the basis of empirical or theoretical rationale (e.g., for the ILS in Chapter 8, elderly persons living independently compared to those living with moderate assistance or substantial assistance), and
- concurrence with clinical diagnoses or the results of psychological tests manifesting characteristics with theoretical relevance for a FAI's functional ability concepts.

The scope of these strategies would be difficult to summarize here. Studies that have examined FAIs' predictive utility, however, deserve special comment.

In general, few of the FAIs reviewed here have been studied for their predictive or postdictive utility. The previous reviews suggest a number of reasons for this. Predictive studies often are time consuming and expensive. Examining the outcome of child custody as a function of parental capacity, for example, might require monitoring of a large number of families across a period of many years. In some areas of legal competence it might be very difficult to determine a criterion with which to assess an instrument's predictive accuracy. For example, what outcome should be considered in follow-up studies of child custody arrangements?

What types of outcomes represent adequate competence to stand trial? Further, some legal competencies focus on a person's abilities in the past rather than the future (e.g., competent waiver of rights in interrogation), so that one would be concerned with a related FAI's postdictive rather than predictive utility. Yet researchers may have no way to obtain data on individuals' performance in the past.

The most common criterion used to examine predictive or classificatory utility has been judicial decisions or clinical experts' judgments about competence that were made without knowledge of the FAI scores for examinees about whom competence was judged. As discussed in detail in Chapter 3, however, there are significant problems with judicial or clinical judgments as a "gold standard" for FAIs:

- the unknown reliability of those judgments
- lack of evidence regarding the degree to which those judgments are related to the actual abilities of competence examinees, and
- the fact that legally relevant functional abilities (which FAIs claim to measure) are presumed to be only one important type of legally-relevant information contributing to legal or clinical judgments about competence.

To the extent that FAIs are validated against judicial or clinical judgments, those studies should aspire to (but need not always manifest) several features displayed in some of the FAI reviews in earlier chapters:

- comparison groups of substantial size
- samples obtained from multiple jurisdictions
- FAI data obtained as close to the point of criterion judgment as is feasible, and
- analyses that fully describe the degree to which results of the FAI are related to the criterion judgments in question (e.g., ROC analyses).

CAUSAL COMPONENT

Chapter 2 and each of the review chapters have explained the importance of providing possible explanations for an individual's deficits in functional abilities relevant for a legal competence. Therefore, it is important to obtain empirical information with which to interpret deficits manifested on FAIs. Strategies associated with this objective in the six competence chapters have focused on: (a) reliability, (b) concurrent psychological characteristics, and (c) the detection of malingering or dissimulation.

Reliability

Studies of interscorer and test-retest reliability are helpful in addressing proposals that an individual's deficits on a FAI may be due to error inherent in the instrument itself (e.g., scoring error, test-related fatigue, or variations in administration allowable by the instrument's procedure). Most FAI developers have included examinations of instrument reliability within their research agendas, and FAIs seem to have required no special strategies in this regard.

Concurrent Psychological Characteristics

In the FAI reviews, studies that have examined FAI deficits in relation to concurrent biological or psychological pathology often provide information that will be helpful when proposing explanations for functional deficits related to a legal competence (see especially the Construct Validation sections of instrument reviews in Chapters 4, 6 and 7). Developmental characteristics often have been investigated concerning their relation to FAI performance, offering empirical bases for explaining some FAI deficits with reference to an individual's age or cognitive developmental status.

A major problem in some areas of FAI development (e.g., measures for parenting in child custody, Chapter 7) has been the relatively narrow range of the demographic, racial, and socioeconomic characteristics of sample norms for any given FAI. Legally relevant functional abilities, like any other performance variables, may vary for different reasons within different demographic or socioeconomic groups. For example, pathology may be a reasonable explanation for FAI deficits in one demographic group but not in another.

Malingering and Dissimulation

The fact that deficient FAI performance might sometimes be due to malingering (faking bad) and that meritorious performance might sometimes amount to dissimulation (faking good) has been noted for each legal competence in which these response styles might produce certain benefits for the examinee (especially Chapters 4 through 7). Any assessment of this explanation for an examinee's performance typically must use data from a range of sources other than a FAI itself. Nevertheless, some FAIs have demonstrated strategies for contributing to this assessment.

One approach is to develop several FAIs that evaluate the same knowledge or skills in different ways. Results across FAIs can then be examined for consistencies or inconsistencies in the types of errors made by the examinee. Consistency would suggest that the individual is not malingering. Inconsistencies would raise the question of malingering, although other possible reasons for the inconsistencies (e.g., psychotic confusion) would need to be examined before drawing conclusions. The measures of *Miranda* comprehension provide one example of FAIs that offer this potential (Chapter 5).

A second approach is to include test items specifically for the purpose of detecting malingering or dissimulation response tendencies. For example, the ECST-R (forthcoming: see Chapter 4) includes items specifically for purposes of detecting malingering in competence to stand trial evaluations. It includes items (the Atypical Presentation Scale) contributing to an index of potential for feigning psychotic and non-psychotic symptoms. Generally, however, existing FAIs have not used this internal index approach as much as would seem to be warranted by the types of assessments in which FAIs are used.

Finally, FAIs may be examined for their correlation with other indexes of malingering or dissimulation. Some instruments in Chapters 4 and 7, for example, have been examined for their relation to tests of social desirability response set.

INTERACTIVE COMPONENT

Chapter 2, as well as the first section in each of the competence review chapters, discussed the need to compare an individual's degree of functional abilities to the demands of the specific, competence-related situation that the individual faces. For competence to stand trial, this means the demands of the defendant's own future trial; for divorce custody cases, it refers to the demands and needs of a specific child who might be given into the examinee's care. To do this, one must have meaningful concepts with which to categorize and describe environmental situations relevant for a legal competence, as well as methods for obtaining these descriptive data for a specific situation.

Discussions at the end of each FAI review, and at the end of each review chapter, have explored the potential for developing dimensions of situational demand with which to describe the situations relevant for a particular legal competence. Chapter 8, for example, described work in the assessment and taxonomy of environments for the elderly and Chapter 4 discussed strategies for developing methods to describe trial situations (Chapter 4). Special emphasis was placed on finding dimensions of environmental demand that parallel the ability dimensions relevant for legal competencies. These discussions, then, were directed toward the development of what might be called "environmental FAIs" methods to describe an environmental situation in a way that will promote comparison of its demands to an individual's degree of legally relevant abilities.

None of the FAIs reviewed in the first edition of this book (in 1986) had undergone systematic development of such methods, and this is still the case for the instruments reviewed in this second edition (most of which were developed after the first edition). Certain FAIs were found to be more amenable than others for comparison of an individual's FAI results to relevant situations (especially the civil competence measures in Chapters 7, 8 and 9). Yet these comparisons currently would require a good deal of clinical speculation, largely without systematic conceptual guidelines or empirically based validity.

It is not clear why more recent FAIs have not adopted empirical strategies for comparing examinees' abilities to the degree of demand posed by their own circumstances. The logic to justify this effort continues to be sound. Moreover, the interactive component has been acknowledged in other scholarly discussions of legal competencies and in studies of the quality of competence evaluations (e.g., for competence to stand trial, see Skeem, Golding, Cohn, & Berge, 1998). To be sure, the necessary research to provide empirical indexes of relevant environmental demands would be difficult and potentially expensive. Perhaps the additional effort is simply more than most projects can undertake, simultaneous with the development of FAIs to assess examinees' legally relevant abilities. Nevertheless, the need and the challenge remain, and it would be exciting to see more attention to the Interactive component in the development of our next generation of FAIs for legal competencies.

JUDGMENTAL AND DISPOSITIONAL COMPONENTS

Chapter 2 explained that legal competence decisions are judgments that confer a dispositional status on individuals. Moral and societal values must be considered when deciding whether or not the circumstances of a particular case warrant a finding of incompetence and its dispositional consequences. Therefore, neither forensic assessments nor FAIs can define legal competence or incompetence. Assessments are the product of scientific expertise, which does not include special authority in the application of moral values to legal decisions.

It is appropriate, therefore, that researchers who have developed FAIs specifically for use in forensic assessments (especially Chapters 4, 5 and 6) often have been careful to state that their instruments were not intended to operationalize legal competence itself. Nevertheless, the reviews pointed out several ways in which certain features of some of the instruments could mislead others to perceive FAIs as defining competence. Among these are:

- the use of titles that may be translated too literally (e.g., "Competence Assessment Instrument")
- rating systems or FAI summary statements that state conclusions about competence/incompetence, and
- publication of cutoff scores below which one is expected to make an interpretation of incompetence.

It is possible that in actual practice these features of FAIs do little harm. Developing a FAI without them, however, does nothing to weaken the value of the instrument. Therefore, discussions in the review chapters urged FAI developers to avoid them. This will help to maintain conceptual clarity regarding the objectives of FAIs, and it may mitigate misunderstanding of the instruments' purposes when their results are reported in legal hearings.

Few FAIs have been developed to assist in judgments about the remediation of examinees' deficits in functional abilities relevant for legal competence. Often this must be inferred from other clinical data regarding the most likely causes of those deficits. Future development of FAIs, however, might consider the inclusion of methods to determine the tractability of examinees' functional capacities. The MacCAT-CA (Chapter 4), for example, includes several items that use a two-step assessment of understanding of criminal trials. Beginning with questions that assess the examinee's current knowledge, these items then instruct the examiner to teach and re-test when the examinee's first response is deficient. Such mechanisms provide an indication of the degree to which examinees' poor understanding is easily remediable or less tractable.

USING FORENSIC ASSESSMENT INSTRUMENTS

The five-component model in Chapter 2 outlined the objectives of an integrated assessment process that can increase the legal relevance of assessments related to legal competencies. Chapter 3 described the potential role of FAIs in this process. The contributions and limitations of specific FAIs within this process were described in the final discussions (Clinical Application) in each of the six review chapters.

This section offers comments on using this structure in the process and reporting of forensic assessments for legal competencies. The discussion does *not* describe all of the steps or requirements for performing such assessments. It comments only on the relevance of the components in the model as a structuring devise, as well as the role of FAIs in the assessment process. Descriptions of the full requirements for forensic clinical evaluations in legal competence cases can be found in other sources (e.g., Grisso, 1988; Heilbrun, 2001; Melton et al., 1997).

FORMING THE QUESTION

The five-component model can be used to organize one's view of the purposes of an assessment related to a question of legal competence:

- to describe relevant functional abilities (Functional component)
- to provide explanations for any deficits in abilities manifested in the assessment data (Causal component)
- where possible, to relate these results to the specific future or past situational circumstances in the case, including their relevance for prediction or postdiction of the examinee's behavior when possible (Interactive component), and
- to provide summary or concluding opinions regarding the referral question (the clinical equivalent of the Judgmental component, although as noted later, a conclusion that the examinee is or is not competent is not necessarily offered)
- to describe the prospects for remediation of the examinee's deficits in relevant functional abilities (Dispositional component)

The referral question actually posed to the examiner will almost never be structured in this format. The examiner, however, can use these categories to structure the more global request for a "competency evaluation," and to orient attorneys and judges to the information they will be receiving. If possible, the examiner's translation of the referral question should be discussed with the referring attorney or communicated to the court and should be stated clearly at the outset of the final report.

SELECTING ASSESSMENT METHODS

Assessment methods should be selected on the basis of their prospect for meeting the assessment's five objectives (as outlined above, parallel to the five components of legal competencies).

Evaluations for legal competencies typically should employ a variety of sources of data. Depending on the type of legal competence, these might include archival information (e.g., hospital reports, court records), interviews with the examinee, and interviews with relevant third parties who may be able to provide additional information about the examinee, and standardized tests or structured interview procedures. When they are included in evaluations, FAIs typically represent only one source of data within a broader data-gathering process (Heilbrun, 2001).

FAIs are recommended in order to provide a standardized index of functional abilities relevant for the legal competence in question. Those functional abilities often are assessed also through interviews with the examinee, which sometimes provide information about functional abilities unique to the individual that are not possible to obtain with available FAIs. On the other hand, FAIs provide the benefits of standardization, including minimization of examiner bias and the ability to directly compare the performance of the examinee to norms based on the same instrument. Together, interviews and FAIs provide a crosscheck on inferences about functional abilities, as well as a safeguard against the different limitations of both methods.

Typically, examiners who use psychological tests also will employ tests of general intellectual abilities, personality characteristics, or psychopathology of the examinee. These are often important to fulfill the Causal objective of competence evaluations. They can supplement interview and archival data for purposes of explaining legally-relevant deficits in functional abilities identified by FAIs.

Finally, efforts to meet the objective related to the Interactive component of a legal competence will require that the examiner employ some means for assessing the degree of functional demands placed on the examinee in his or her own specific situation. As noted in the reviews of FAIs, currently there are very few systematic methods for assessing such demands and comparing them to the examinee's level of ability. Typically examiners must obtain such information through unstandardized observations and interviews with the examinee and relevant third parties who know the examinee's circumstances.

DESCRIBING FUNCTIONAL ABILITIES

FAIs are especially useful when examiners provide written reports or oral testimony in legal competence cases. They allow the examiner to convey to the court, abstractly (in constructs and dimensions) and in concrete terms (item responses and scores), specifically what the examinee can and cannot do, does or does not know, and believes or does not believe with relevance to the definition of the specific legal competence in question. In addition, for FAIs that are fully developed, scores on these instruments often allow the examiner to provide the court:

- a description of the degree of confidence that can be placed on the reliability of the score
- comparative statements that express the examinee's performance in relation to reference groups (e.g., "His score on the MacCAT-CA indicated that his understanding of the trial process was in the bottom 10% of persons his age, and was in the middle of the range of scores made by persons who have been found incompetent to stand trial")
- evidence regarding the validity of the method from which the scores were derived

Note that clinicians who rely only on unstructured interviews may be able to describe the same abilities, but they have no means to offer courts information about the reliability, validity, or comparative meaning of the information.

EXPLAINING FUNCTIONAL DEFICITS

The six review chapters have described a number of possible explanations for functional deficits as manifested on FAIs and in other contexts. One purpose of an assessment related to a legal competence is to provide information that will assist the legal fact finder in weighing the plausibility of these explanations.

This will require that the examiner form a number of causal hypotheses. The hypotheses might include any mental conditions to which the statutory definition of the legal competence refers (e.g., conditions that the law has accepted as relevant for addressing "mental disease or defect" as a statutory requirement). In addition, however, the examiner may form hypotheses based on psychiatric and psychological explanations that are not specifically noted in statutory definitions of the law, but that are not excluded in case precedent regarding the legal competence. Other potential hypotheses are offered by situational factors related to the examination session itself (e.g., distractions), as well as possible malingering or dissimulation.

The examiner must collect and synthesize information that will test these hypotheses. Rarely can this be done with the precision of a controlled research study. The quality of the process will depend primarily on the standardization, reliability, and validity of the data collection methods used, as well as the logical and theoretical rationale employed in the interpretation. Sometimes FAIs have a nonquantitative role to play in this process, as when the content of an examinee's specific response to a question on a FAI reveals a delusional idea that impairs the examinee's response to the question.

MAKING PREDICTIONS OR POSTDICTIONS

The six review chapters have pointed out that it is rarely possible to support specific predictions or postdictions about the performance of an examinee in a time and place removed from the examination, and FAIs themselves do not provide these types of results. Nevertheless, FAIs may be helpful in contrasting an individual's functional abilities with the demands of situations or contexts external to the examination session (in other words, addressing the Interactive component). For example, a defendant's difficulty in communication on the MacCAT-CA can be compared to the demands of the defendant's trial, which are believed to include the need for the defendant to testify. Poor scores on "judgment" in *Independent Living Scale* items focused on personal safety may be contrasted with the individual's isolated living arrangement and a tendency to wander outside in dangerous circumstances in the middle of the night (or with the person's residence in an assisted living center where others provide considerable protection for the person).

When this comparison manifests substantial logical incongruency between the individual's abilities and situational demands, the examiner may find it possible to express an opinion about the individual's functioning in the future or past situation that forms the environmental context for the legal competence question. This will assist the legal fact finder to consider legal competence from an interactive perspective, as described in Chapter 2.

STATING CONCLUSIONS

Nothing about FAIs contradicts the general position taken in previous chapters concerning conclusory testimony by mental health professionals in legal competence cases. An expert opinion that answers the ultimate legal question is not an "expert" opinion, but a personal value judgment. No amount or type of empirical and scientific information alone can answer the question of legal competence, because the degree of ability required for legal competence is not definitive, absolute, or consistent across cases.

On the other hand, an examiner's data might often be sufficient to state other conclusions falling short of the ultimate legal question. Examples include statements about the degree of an examinee's deficits in relation to validation samples of persons who have been found incompetent, and an expert's opinion that the examinee would or would not be able to perform particular functions that are relevant for the legal competence in question. FAIs will also improve clinicians' abilities to describe conditions under which the examinee might be able to develop (or regain) the abilities required for legal competence, or ways in which assistance may compensate for the individual's deficits in a manner that would mitigate the need for a finding of incompetence.

A Note on Potential Misuse of FAIs

Risks of misuse arise in the development of any new technology, and the use of FAIs in clinical forensic practice is no exception. Misuse of FAIs can occur in their interpretation not only by clinicians, but also by attorneys who translate and "package" evidence for presentation to the court. Sometimes this will happen because of lack of understanding of the nature of FAIs. At other times misuse or misinterpretation of FAIs is the product of advocacy, an essential feature of the legal process that inevitably influences even the "impartial" clinician's participation in it (Otto, 1989).

Some forms of misuse of FAIs are the same as those sometimes found in the use of other psychological tests. For example, examiners may administer the instrument in ways that are inconsistent with the instrument's standardized procedure. Or they may use test norms for making interpretations about examinees belonging to classes (e.g., race, gender) that were not included in the development of the instrument's norms.

Other misuses of FAIs, however, are more specific to their intended use in legal settings. For example:

- *It is misuse for competence evaluations to rely on FAIs as the sole source of data.* No FAI measures the full range of abilities that might be relevant for a question of competence.
- *Scores on FAIs (especially an instrument's so-called "cut-off scores")* *should not be interpreted as defining legal competence or incompetence.* FAIs measure certain functional abilities relevant for that decision. But a person's functional abilities are only part of the data that must be considered in reaching conclusions about legal competence (e.g., along with data related to the Causal component). Moreover, no level of disability is automatically associated with incompetence, because its relevance for competence must always be considered in light the demands of the person's situation (the Interactive component).

- *The significance of scores on FAIs is misinterpreted when they are said to "predict" functioning in future situations relevant for the question of legal competence.* Many FAIs have established validity based on the relation of their scores to past functioning of examinees, concurrent functioning in other contexts, or the relation of scores to various criteria of theoretical relevance (e.g., demographic characteristics, diagnoses, or independent competence judgments). Thus far, however, no FAI has been examined for its ability to truly predict behavior subsequent to the examinee's evaluation.

Most of these misuses of FAIs may be classified as misrepresentation. They offer the results of FAIs to the consumer (the legal decision maker in the form of judge or jury) as more than they are intended to be. The consequences of misuse of FAIs are both case-specific and general. In a specific case, misinterpretation risks misunderstanding by the fact finder and the potential for a miscarriage of justice for the individual whose rights and welfare are at stake. The cumulative effect of such misuses across time creates misunderstanding and erodes the confidence of legal decision makers in FAIs as a type of evidence on which expert opinions may be based.

CONTINUING THE IMPROVEMENT OF FORENSIC ASSESSMENTS

Chapter 1 described apparent improvements in the quality of forensic assessments for legal competencies during the 15 years between first and second editions of this book. It also described ways in which average practice in forensic assessment still falls short of objectives offered in various professional guidelines. What has been the role of the present model of legal competencies, and the development and use of FAIs, in helping us to improve the quality of our forensic evaluations of competencies? Does the future prospect of FAIs appear to be promising, or have FAIs had their day?

THE CONCEPTUAL MODEL

Let us first summarize some of the advantages of the five-component model as they were described in the conclusion of the first edition:

- The analysis described in this book demonstrates the feasibility of a single model to structure our conceptualization of the nature of diverse legal competencies. This is heuristically desirable for reasons of parsimony and efficiency.

- The concepts that formed the model were not novel, but were borrowed and synthesized from legal and psychological perspectives throughout competence law, judicial opinion, and scholarly analysis. Thus the model requires no radical restructuring of the law itself, but rather conforms to it, amplifies it, and encourages its growth.
- The model forces us to take seriously certain assumptions in the law of competencies that have not been carried through to their logical conclusions, especially the interactive quality of legal competencies.
- The model provides a systematic structure for translation from law to clinical practice. It makes the law's definition of legal competence accessible from the psychological and psychiatric perspective of the clinician who provides information for decision making by the courts.

The five-part model of legal competencies has obtained general acceptance in the literature of forensic assessment. In past years it has been widely cited, has encouraged the development of forensic assessment instruments, has influenced the development of professional guidelines for forensic assessments, and has offered structure for research to study the quality of forensic assessment practices. Review chapters in this book indicate that the model continues to be useful in guiding the development of FAIs, describing their features, and evaluating their quality. The values of the model, therefore, have been manifested in the field's development, and nothing has arisen to contradict the "fit" of the model in legal and forensic clinical analyses of competencies. No better structure for conceptualizing legal competencies and related forensic assessments has been proposed. Therefore, it is likely that the model will continue to provide good service to legal scholars, law-and-psychology theorists, assessment researchers, and clinical forensic practitioners for some time to come.

THE FUTURE OF FAIs

More questionable is the future of forensic assessment instruments. The first edition of EC described the promise:

> The development of forensic assessment instruments (FAIs) was proposed as a strategy for increasing the empirical integrity of assessments that use the conceptual model. The review chapters have demonstrated FAIs' potentials for

> providing standardized, quantitative data to meet the needs of courts for
> reliable and valid information ... In summary, we have a clear option to commit
> ourselves to this empirical technology as one important means for improving
> forensic assessments. (Grisso, 1986, p. 362)

During the past 15 years since this challenge was issued, clearly we have witnessed substantial advances in the development of FAIs to assess functional abilities related to legal competencies. The first edition provided only a few examples of instruments that were developed specifically as FAIs, supplemented by many that could serve that purpose although they had not been developed with that intention. In contrast, the great majority of the instruments reviewed in this second edition were developed specifically as FAIs, their number having grown exponentially and with no sign of abatement in recent years. Moreover, in most areas of legal competence, their quality has steadily improved, providing the opportunity for the promise of empirically-aided assessments for legal competencies to become reality.

In contrast, evidence provided in Chapter 1 and in the "Current Practice" sections of the review chapters suggests that the use of these instruments has not yet become standard practice for forensic clinical experts. They are used by many forensic clinicians but not the majority, and those that use them do not do so routinely. This can no longer be explained by the novelty of FAIs or lack of clinicians' knowledge of their existence. They have been in the mainstream of our journals for some time. Within the past few years, test publishers' catalogues have featured special sections to describe and advertise their collection of "forensic tests."

Why have forensic clinicians not wholly embraced FAIs as standard practice? The most likely reason is the costs associated with their use. There are three types of costs that warrant consideration.

First, *it is easier and financially less expensive to perform legal competence evaluations without administering FAIs* (or any other empirical measures of the examinee's characteristics). The addition of FAIs to one's current evaluation procedures does not produce a case-by-case financial benefit, and it requires time that must be subtracted from one's already busy assessment schedule in public forensic evaluation services. The additional costs can be absorbed when clinicians' evaluation services are paid by the hour. But the addition of a FAI is difficult for clinicians who receive state or county funds to provide assessments for a fixed per-case cost (the amount often already being inadequate to compensate for the time required).

Second, *cases differ with regard to the need for finer-tuned assessments.* Some percentage of competence cases involve individuals who are "clearly competent," while others involve persons with mental illnesses that grossly effect their cognitive abilities, rendering opinions about "incompetence" fairly easy to justify with minimal data on functional abilities. Clinicians typically are urged to use psychological testing selectively, employing it in cases that fall between these two extremes. Thus one must anticipate that clinicians will use FAIs only in those minority of cases that warrant the additional effort and cost of a standardized, empirical tool for assessing legally-relevant functional abilities.

Finally, *clinicians who base their opinions for courts on data derived from new FAIs open themselves to greater scrutiny and challenge by attorneys during their expert testimony.* Traditional requirements for admissibility of expert evidence (*Frye v. U.S.*, 1923) have been supplemented by important, more recent standards (*Daubert v. Merrell Dow Pharmaceuticals*, 1993; *Kumho Tire Company, Ltd. v. Carmichael*, 1999) that have increased attorneys' challenges of the instruments used by clinicians to provide data for their opinions. Criteria for admissibility associated with these cases include scrutiny of the demonstrated reliability and validity of the instruments, their error rates, their logic, and demonstration of professional peer acceptance of new methods. Such scrutiny can have a beneficial effect on the quality of information provided to the courts. But most FAIs, regardless of their ability to meet these challenges, are relatively new and therefore have not built a history of acceptance in the courts. Therefore, clinicians who adopt new FAIs open themselves to the potential for more intense challenges by attorneys. Ironically, forensic clinicians' opinions are accepted by most courts as a routine matter (on the basis of their adequate training and expertise) if their opinions rely on nonstandardized interviews and clinical inferences for which no evidence of reliability or validity can be offered. These conditions are not conducive to adoption of new FAIs, despite their potential for a more reliable and valid basis for opinions, except by some minority of clinicians who are willing to endure the rigors associated with being the "test case" for establishing an instrument's acceptance by the courts.

Thus, after 15 years, the closing paragraph of the first edition of this book continues to be a fitting conclusion to the second edition:

> We must decide [the] cost-benefit issues on the basis of our own professional standards. This book has argued that the integrity and credibility of our forensic assessments require an investment in a more standardized, empirical approach than we have employed in the past. Whether we will make the investment depends on our perceptions of the weight of that argument, [placing] our professional standards in the balance against the effort that the commitment would require. The law eventually may answer that question for us, although it would be better for forensic examiners themselves to address it now. This is an ultimate question that mental health professionals are indeed qualified to answer. (Grisso, 1986, p. 363).

References

Abidin, R. (1995). *Parenting Stress Index: Professional manual* (3rd ed.). Odessa, FL: Psychological Assessment Resources.

Abidin, R. (1997). Parenting Stress Index: A measure of the parent-child system. In C. P. Zalaquett & R. J. Wood (Eds.), *Evaluating stress*. Lanham, MD: Scarecrow Press.

Ackerman, M., & Ackerman, M. (1997). Custody evaluation practices: A survey of experienced professionals (revisited). *Professional Psychology: Research and Practice, 28*, 137–145.

Ackerman, M., & Schoendorf, K. (1992). *ASPECT: Ackerman-Schoendorf Scales for Parent Evaluation of Custody-Manual*. Los Angeles, CA: Western Psychological Services.

Acton, R., & During, S. (1992). Preliminary results of aggression management training for aggressive parents. *Journal of Interpersonal Violence, 7*, 410–417.

Albers, A., & Pasewark, R. (1976). Involuntary hospitalization: The social construction of dangerousness. *American Journal of Community Psychology, 4*, 129–131.

Alexander, G. (1977). On being imposed upon by artful or designing persons: The California experience with involuntary placement of the aged. *San Diego Law Review, 14*, 129–131.

Alexopoulos, G. S., Vrontou, C., Kakuma, T., Meyers, B. S., Young, R. C., Klausner, E., & Clarkin, J. (1996). Disability in geriatric depression. *American Journal of Psychiatry, 153*, 877–885.

Allen, R., Ferster, E., & Weihofen, H. (1968). *Mental impairment and legal incompetency*. Englewood Cliffs, NJ: Prentice-Hall.

Altman, W. M. & Parmelee, P. A. (1989). Discrimination based on age: The special case of the institutionalized age. In D. Kagehiro & W. Laufer (Eds.), *Handbook of psychology and the law* (pp. 408–431). New York: Springer.

American Academy of Child and Adolescent Psychiatry (1994). Practice parameters for child custody evaluation. *Journal of the American Academy of Child and Adolescent Psychiatry, 36,* 57S–68S.

American Bar Association (1989). *ABA criminal justice mental health standards.* Washington DC: American Bar Association.

American Law Institute. (1962). *Model Penal Code.* Washington, DC: ALI.

American Professional Society on Abuse of Children (1996). *Psychosocial evaluation of suspected sexual abuse in children: Practice guidelines* (2nd ed.). Chicago, IL: American Professional Society on Abuse of Children.

American Psychiatric Association (1980). *Diagnostic and Statistical Manual of Mental Disorders (3rd ed.).* Washington, DC: American Psychiatric Association.

American Psychiatric Association. (1982). *Statement on the insanity defense.* (Released January, 1983). Washington, DC: American Psychiatric Association.

American Psychiatric Association (1994). *Diagnostic and statistical manual of mental disorders (4th ed.).* Washington, DC: American Psychiatric Association.

American Psychological Association (1994). Guidelines for child custody evaluations in divorce proceedings. *American Psychologist, 49,* 677–682.

American Psychological Association (1997). *What practitioners should know about working with older adults.* Washington, DC: American Psychological Association.

American Psychological Association (1998). *Guidelines for psychological evaluations in child protection matters.* Washington, DC: American Psychological Association.

Anderer, S. J. (1990). A model for determining competency in guardianship proceedings. *Mental and physical disability law reporter, 14,* 107–114.

Anderer, S. J. (1997). *Developing an instrument to evaluate the capacity of elderly persons to make personal care and financial decisions.* Unpublished doctoral dissertation, Allegheny University of Health Sciences.

Anderson, S. W., & Tranel, D. (1989). Awareness of disease states following cerebral infarction, dementia, and head trauma: Standardized assessment. *Clinical Neuropsychologist, 3,* 327–339.

Anderten, P. (1979). *The elderly, incompetency, and guardianship.* Unpublished master's thesis, Psychology Department, St. Louis University.

Andrews, R., & Withey, S. (1976). *Social indicators of well-being.* New York: Plenum Press.

Annas, G., & Densberger, J. (1984). Competence to refuse medical treatment: Autonomy vs. paternalism. *University of Toledo Law Review, 15,* 561–596.

Appelbaum, P.S. (1999). Missing the boat: Competence and consent in psychiatric research. *American Journal of Psychiatry, 155,* 1486–1488.

Appelbaum, B., Appelbaum, P., & Grisso, T. (1998). Competence to consent to voluntary hospitalization: A test of the APA's proposal. *Psychiatric Services, 49,* 1193–1196.

Appelbaum, P., & Grisso, T. (1988). Assessing patients' capacities to consent to treatment. *New England Journal of Medicine, 319,* 1635–1638.

Appelbaum, P., & Grisso, T. (1992). *Manual for perceptions of disorder.* Worcester MA: University of Massachusetts Medical School.

Appelbaum, P., & Grisso, T. (1995). The MacArthur Treatment Competence Study: I, Mental illness and competence to consent to treatment. *Law and Human Behavior, 19,* 105–126.

Appelbaum, P. S., & Grisso, T. (2001). *MacArthur Competence Assessment Tool for Clinical Research (MacCAT-CR).* Sarasota, FL: Professional Resource Press.

Appelbaum, P.S., Grisso, T., Frank, E., O'Donnell, S., & Kupfer, D. (1999). Competence of depressed patients for consent to research. *American Journal of Psychiatry, 156,* 1380–1384.

Appelbaum, P., & Gutheil, T. (1992) *Clinical handbook of psychiatry and the law.* Baltimore, MD: William and Wilkins.

Appelbaum, P., Mirkin, S., & Bateman, A. (1981). Empirical assessment of competency to consent to psychiatric hospitalization. *American Journal of Psychiatry, 138,* 1170–1176.

Appelbaum, P., & Roth, L. (1982). Competency to consent to research: A psychiatric overview. *Archives of General Psychiatry, 39,* 951–958.

Arditti, J. A. (1995). Ackerman-Schoendorf Scales for Parent Evaluation of Custody. In J. C. Conoley & J. C. Impara (Eds.), *The twelfth mental measurements yearbook* (pp. 20–22). Lincoln, NE: Buros Institute of Mental Measurements.

Arnold, D., O'Leary, S. G., Wolff, L. S., & Acker, M. M. (1993). The Parenting Scale: A measure of dysfunctional parenting in discipline situations. *Psychological Assessment, 5,* 137–144.

Association of Family and Conciliation Courts (undated). *Model standards of practice for child custody evaluation.* Milwaukee, WI: Author.

Ausness, C. (1978). The identification of incompetent defendants: Separating those unfit for adversary combat from those who are fit. *Kentucky Law Journal, 66,* 666–706.

Azar, S. T., & Benjet, C. L. (1994). A cognitive perspective on ethnicity, race, and termination of parental rights. *Law & Human Behavior, 18,* 249–268.

Azar, S. T., Benjet, C. L., Fuhrmann, G. S., & Cavallerao, L. (1995). Child maltreatment and termination of parental rights: Can behavioral research help Solomon? *Behavior Therapy, 26,* 599–623.

Azar, S. T., Lauretti, A. F., & Loding, B. V. (1998). The evaluation of parental fitness in termination of parental rights cases: A functional-contextual perspective. *Clinical Child and Family Psychology Review, 1,* 77–100.

Azar, S., Robinson, D., Hekiman, E., & Twentyman, C. (1984). Unrealistic expectations and problem-solving ability in maltreating and comparison mothers. *Journal of Consulting and Clinical Psychology, 52,* 687–691.

Bagby, M., Nicholson, R., Buis, T., Radanovic, H., & Fidler, B. (1999). Defensive responding on the MMPI-2 in family custody and access evaluations, *Psychological Assessment, 11,* 24–28.

Bagby, R., Nicholson, R., Rogers, R., & Nussbaum, D. (1992). Domains of competence to stand trial: A factor analytic study. *Law and Human Behavior, 16,* 491–506.

Baltes, P. B. (1987). Theoretical propositions of life-span developmental psychology: On the dynamics between growth and decline. *Developmental Psychology, 23,* 611–626.

Barberger-Gateau, P., Commenges, D., Gagnon, M., Letenneur, L., Sauvel, C., & Dartigues, J. (1992). Instrumental activities of daily living as a screening tool for cognitive impairment and dementia in elderly community dwellers. *Journal of the American Geriatrics Society, 40,* 1129–1134.

Barbour, G., & Blumenkrantz, N. (1978). Videotape aids informed consent decision. *Journal of the American Medical Association, 240,* 2741–2742.

Barnes, A. P. (1992). Beyond guardianship reform: A reevaluation of autonomy and beneficence for a system of principled decision-making in long term care. *Emory Law Journal, 41,* 633–760.

Barnes, H., & Olson, D. (1982). *Parent–Adolescent Communication Scale manual.* Unpublished manuscript, University of Minnesota.

Barnum, R. (1997). A suggested framework for forensic consultation in cases of child abuse and neglect. *Journal of the American Academy of Psychiatry and Law, 25,* 581–593.

Barnum, R. (2000). Clinical and forensic evaluation of competence to stand trial in juvenile defendants. In Grisso, T., & Schwartz, R. (eds.), *Youth on trial: A developmental perspective on juvenile justice* (pp. 193–223). Chicago, IL: University of Chicago Press.

Barthel, J. (1977). *A death in Canaan.* New York: Dell.

Barton, D., Mallik, H., Orr, W., & Janofsky, J. (1996). Clinicians' judgment of capacity or nursing home patients to give informed consent. *Psychiatric Services, 47,* 956–960.

Bathurst, K., Gottfried, A., & Gottfried, A. (1997). Normative data for the MMPI-2 in child custody litigation. *Psychological Assessment, 9,* 205–211.

Baumrind, D. (1967). Child care practices anteceding three patterns of preschool behavior. *Genetic Psychology Monographs, 75,* 43–88.

Bavolek, S., & Keene, R. (1999). *Adult-Adolescent Parenting Inventory-2 manual*. Park City, Utah: Family Development Resources Inc.

Bazelon, D. (1974). Psychiatrists and the adversary. *Scientific American, 230,* 18–23.

Bazelon, D. (1975). A jurist's view of psychiatry. *Journal of Psychiatry and Law, 3,* 175–190.

Bazelon, D. (1982). Veils, values, and social responsibility. *American Psychologist, 37,* 115–121.

Bem, D., & Allen, A. (1974). On predicting some of the people some of the time: The search for cross-situational consistencies in behavior. *Psychological Bulletin, 81,* 506–520.

Benson, M. (1998). Parent Behavior Checklist. In J. C. Impara & B. S. Plake (Eds.), *The thirteenth mental measurements yearbook.* Lincoln, NE: Buros Institute of Mental Measurements.

Benson, P., Roth, L., Appelbaum, P., Lidz, C., Winslade, W., (1988). Information disclosure, subject understanding, and informed consent in psychiatric research. *Law and Human Behavior, 12,* 455–476.

Berg, J., Appelbaum, P., & Grisso, T. (1996). Constructing competence: Formulating standards of legal competence to make medical decisions. *Rutgers Law Review, 48,* 345–396.

Berg, J., Appelbaum, P. S., Lidz, C., Parker, B. (2001). *Informed consent: Legal theory and clinical practice (2nd ed.).* New York: Oxford University Press.

Berger, J. T. (2000). Sexuality and intimacy in the nursing home: A romantic couple of mixed cognitive capacities. *The Journal of Clinical Ethics, 11,* 309–313.

Bergler, J., Pennington, A., Metcalf, M., & Freis, E. (1980). Informed consent: How much does the patient understand? *Clinical Pharmacology Therapeutics, 27,* 435–440.

Bernard, H. (1998). Parent Behavior Checklist. In J. C. Impara & B. S. Plake (Eds.), *The thirteenth mental measurements yearbook.* Lincoln, NE: Buros Institute of Mental Measurements.

Bernt, F. (1998). Developmental Observation Checklist System. In J. C. Impara & B. S. Plake (Eds.), *The thirteenth mental measurements yearbook.* Lincoln, NE: Buros Institute of Mental Measurements.

Bersoff, D., Goodman-Delahunty, J., Grisso, T., Hans, V., Poythress, N., & Roesch, R. (1977). Training in law and psychology: Models from the Villanova Conference. *American Psychologist, 52,* 1301–1310.

Bittman, B., & Convit, A. (1993). Competency, civil commitment, and the dangerousness of the mentally ill. *Journal of Forensic Sciences, 38,* 1460–1466.

Blazer, D. (1978). The OARS Durham surveys: Description and application. In Center for the Study of Aging and Human Development, *Multidimensional functional assessment: The OARS methodology* (pp. 75–88). Durham, NC: Duke University.

Boehm, A. (1985). Home Observation for the Measurement of the Environment. In J. V. Mitchell (Ed.), *The ninth mental measurements yearbook.* Lincoln, NE: Buros Institute of Mental Measurements.

Bonnie, R. (1992). The competence of criminal defendants: A theoretical reformulation. *Behavioral Sciences and the Law, 10,* 291–316.

Bonnie, R. (1993). The competence of criminal defendants: Beyond Dusky and Drope. *University of Miami Law Review, 47,* 539–601.

Bonnie, R., & Grisso, T. (2000). Adjudicative competence and youthful offenders. In T. Grisso & R. Schwartz (Eds.), *Youth on Trial: A developmental perspective on juvenile justice* (pp. 73–104). Chicago: University of Chicago Press.

Bonnie, R., & Slobogin, C. (1980). The role of mental health professionals in the criminal process: The case for informed speculation. *Virginia Law Review, 66,* 427–522.

Bonovitz, J., & Bonovitz, J. (1981). Diversion of the mentally ill into the criminal justice system: The police intervention perspective. *American Journal of Psychiatry, 138,* 973–976.

Boothroyd, R. (1998). Review of the Parent–Child Relationship Inventory. In J. C. Impara & B. S. Plake (Eds.), *The thirteenth mental measurements yearbook* (pp. 717–720). Lincoln, NE: Buros Institute of Mental Measurements of the University of Nebraska-Lincoln.

Bornstein, M. (Ed.). (1995). *Handbook of parenting Volumes 1–4.* Mahwah, NJ: Erlbaum.

Borum, R., & Fulero, S. (1999). Empirical research on the insanity defense and attempted reforms: Evidence toward informed policy. *Law and Human Behavior, 23,* 117–135.

Borum, R., & Grisso, T. (1995). Psychological test use in criminal forensic evaluations. *Professional Psychology: Research and Practice, 26,* 465–473.

Borum, R., & Grisso, T. (1996). Establishing standards for criminal forensic reports: An empirical analysis. *Bulletin of the American Academy of Psychiatry and the Law, 24,* 297–317.

Bow, J., & Quinnell, F. (2001). Psychologists, current practices and procedures in child custody evaluations; Five years after American Psychological Association Guidelines. *Professional Psychology: Research and Practice, 32,* 261–268.

Bracken, B. (1993). *Assessment of Interpersonal Relations manual.* Austin, TX: PRO-ED.

Brakel, S. (1974). Presumption, bias, and incompetence in the criminal process. *Wisconsin Law Review,* pp. 1105–1130.

Brakel, S., & Rock, R. (1971). The *mentally disabled and the law.* Chicago, IL: University of Chicago Press.

Brandburn, N. (1969). *The structure of psychological well-being.* Chicago: Aldine.

Campbell, A., Converse, P., & Rodgers, W. (1976). *The quality of American life: Perceptions, evaluations, and satisfactions.* New York: Russell Sage.

Bricklin, B. (1989). *Perception of Relationships Test manual.* Furlong, PA: Village Publishing.

Bricklin, B. (1990a). *Parent Awareness Skills Survey manual.* Furlong, PA: Village Publishing.

Bricklin, B. (1990b). *Bricklin Perceptual Scales manual.* Furlong, PA: Village Publishing.

Bricklin, B. (1993). *Test Manuals Supplement #9.* Furlong, PA: Village Publishing.

Bricklin, B. (1995). *The custody evaluation handbook: Research-based solutions and applications.* New York: Brunner/Mazel.

Bricklin, B. (1999). The contributions of psychological tests to child custody evaluations. In. R. M. Galatzer-Levy & L. Kraus (Eds.), *The scientific basis of child custody decisions* (pp. 120–156). New York: Wiley.

Bricklin, B., & Elliott, G. (1991). *Parent Perception of Child Profile manual.* Furlong, PA: Village Publishing.

Bricklin, B., & Elliott, G. (1997). *Critical child custody evaluation issues: Questions and answers. Test manuals supplement for BPS, PORT, PASS, PPCP.* Furlong, PA: Village Publishing.

Brodzinsky, D. (1993). On the use and misuse of psychological testing in child custody evaluations. *Professional Psychology: Research and Practice, 24,* 213–219.

Broshek, D., & Marcopulos, B. (1999). Delirium assessment in older adults. In P. Lichtenberg (Ed.) *Handbook of assessment in clinical gerontology,* (pp. 167–204). New York: Wiley.

Brownstone, H. (1980). The homosexual parent in custody disputes. *Queen's Law Journal, 5,* 119–240.

Budd, K. S. (2001). Assessing parenting competence in child protection cases: A clinical practice model. *Clinical Child and Family Psychology Review, 4,* 1–18.

Budd, K. S., & Holdsworth, M. J. (1996). Issues in clinical assessment of minimal parenting competence. *Journal of Clinical Child Psychology, 25,* 2–14.

Budd, K. S., Poindexter, L. M., Felix, E. D., & Naik-Polan, A. T. (2001). Clinical assessment of parents in child protection cases: An empirical analysis. *Law and Human Behavior, 25,* 93–108.

Bukatman, B., Foy, J., & DeGrazia, E. (1971). What is competency to stand trial? *American Journal of Psychiatry, 127,* 1225–1229.

Bulcroft, K., Kielkopf, M., & Tripp, K. (1991). Elderly wards and their legal guardians: Analysis of county probate records in Ohio and Washington. *The Gerontologist, 31,* 156–164.

Burke, W. (1978). *The development of a technique for assessing the stresses experienced by parents of young children.* Unpublished doctoral dissertation. University of Virginia, Charlottesville.

Caldwell, B. M., & Bradley, R. H. (1984). (Rev. ed.). Unpublished manuscript, University of Arkansas.

Calisco, J., & Milner, M. (1992). Childhood history of abuse and child abuse screening. *Child Abuse and Neglect, 16,* 647–659.

Campbell, S. B. (1997). Behavior problems in preschool children: Developmental and family issues. In T. H. Ollendick & R. J. Prinz (Eds.), *Advances in clinical child psychology, Vol. 19* (pp. 1–26). New York: Plenum.

Carlson, C. I. (1992). Perceptions of Parental Role Scales. In J. J. Kramer & J. C. Conoley (Eds.), *The eleventh mental measurements yearbook.* Lincoln, NE: Buros Institute of Mental Measurements.

Carlson, C. I. (2001). Family Assessment Form. In B. S. Plake & J. C. Impara (Eds.), *The fourteenth mental measurements yearbook.* Lincoln, NE: Buros Institute of Mental Measurements.

Carpenter, W., Gold, J., Lahti, A., Queen, C., Conley, R., Bartko, J., Kovnick, J., & Appelbaum, P. S. (2000). Decisional capacity for informed consent in schizophrenia research. *Archives of General Psychiatry, 57,* 533–538.

Cattell, R. B. (1963). Theory of fluid and crystallized intelligence: A critical experiment. *Journal of Educational Psychology, 54,* 1–22.

Caul, J. (1984). *The predictive utility of the Community Competence Scale.* Unpublished doctoral dissertation, St. Louis University.

Caulfield, B., & Horowitz, R. (1987). *Child abuse and the law: A primer for social workers.* Chicago: National Committee for Prevention of Child Abuse.

Center for the Study of Aging and Human Development (1978). *Multidimensional functional assessment: The OARS methodology.* Durham, NC: Duke University.

Chappell, N. (1990). Aging and social care. In R. H. Binstock & L. K. George (Eds.), *Handbook of aging and the social sciences.* New York: Academic.

Charlow, A. (1994). Awarding custody: The best interests of the child and other fictions. In S. R. Humm et al. (Eds.), *Child, parent, and state: Law and policy reader* (pp. 3–37). Philadelphia: Temple University Press.

Children's Bureau of Southern California (1997). *Family Assessment Form manual.* Washington, DC: Child Welfare League of America, Inc.

Cirincione, C., Steadman, H., & McGreevy, M. (1995). Rates of insanity acquittals and the factors associated with successful insanity pleas. *Bulletin of the American Academy of Psychiatry and Law, 23,* 399–409.

Clausen, J. (1968). Perspectives in childhood socialization. In J. Clausen (Ed.), *Socialization and society* (pp. 130–181). Boston, MA: Little, Brown.

Clemens, E., & Hayes, H. (1997). Assessing and balancing elder risk, safety, and autonomy: Decision making practices of elder care workers. *Home Health Care Services Quarterly, 16,* 3–20.

Cole, D. E. (1995). Parent Awareness Skills Survey. In J. L. Conoley & J. C. Impara (Eds.), *The twelfth mental measurements yearbook* (p. 735). Lincoln, NE: Buros Institute of Mental Measurements.

Committee on Ethical Guidelines for Forensic Psychologists (American Psychology-Law Society) (1991). Specialty guidelines for forensic psychologists. *Law and Human Behavior, 15,* 655–665.

Conger, J. (1995). Perception-of-Relationships Test. In J. C. Conoley & J. C. Impara (Eds.), *The twelfth mental measurements yearbook* (pp. 747–748). Lincoln, NE: Buros Institute of Mental Measurements.

Cooper, D. (1997). Juveniles' understanding of trial-related information: Are they competent defendants? *Behavioral Sciences and the Law, 15,* 167–180.

Cooper, D., & Grisso, T. (1997). Five year research update (1991–1995): Evaluations for competence to stand trial. *Behavioral Sciences and the Law, 15,* 347–364.

Couron, B. (1982). *Assessing parental potentials for child abuse in contrast to nurturing.* Dissertation Abstracts International, 42, 3412B.

Crase, S., Clark, S., & Pease, D. (1979). Iowa Parent Behavior Inventory manual. Ames, IA: Iowa State University Research Foundation.

Crosby-Currie, C. A. (1996). Children's involvement in contested custody cases: Practices and experiences of legal and mental health professionals. *Law & Human Behavior, 20,* 289–311.

Cross, J., Fleischner, R., & Elder, J. (1996). *Guardianship and conservatorship in Massachusetts.* Charlottesville: The Mitchie Company.

Curran, W., McGarry, A., & Shah, S. (Eds.), *Forensic psychiatry and psychology* (pp. 65–82). Philadelphia, PA: F. A. Davis.

Daro, D. (1996). Current trends in child abuse reporting and fatalities: NCPCA's 1995 Annual State survey. *APSAC Advisor,* Summer.

Department of Veterans Affairs (1997). *Clinical assessment for competency determination: A practice guideline for psychologists.* Milwaukee: National Center for Cost Containment.

DePaul, J., Arruabarrena, I., & Milner, J. S. (1991). Validation de una version Espanola del Child Abuse Potential Inventory para su uso en Espana. *Child Abuse and Neglect, 15,* 495–504.

Derdeyn, A. (1975). Child custody consultation. *American Journal of Orthopsychiatry, 45,* 791–801.

Diehl, M., Willis, S. L., & Schaie, K. W. (1995). Everyday problem solving in older adults: Observational assessment and cognitive correlates. *Psychology and Aging, 10,* 478–491.

Dishion, T. J., & Patterson, G. R. (1997). The timing and severity of antisocial behavior: Three hypotheses within an ecological framework. In D. M. Stoff, J. Breiling, & J. Maser (Eds.), *Handbook of antisocial behavior* (pp. 205–217). New York: Wiley.

Dixon, D. (1998). Family Risk Scales. In J. C. Impara & B. S. Plake (Eds.), *The thirteenth mental measurements yearbook.* Lincoln, NE: Buros Institute of Mental Measurements.

Doble, S. E., Fisk, J. D., MacPherson, K. M., Fisher, A. G., & Rockwood, K. (1997). Measuring functional competency in older persons with Alzheimer's disease. *International Psychogeriatrics, 9,* 25–38.

Drane, J. (1984). Competency to give an informed consent: A model for making clinical assessments. *Journal of the American Medical Association, 252,* 925–927.

Dunn, T. (1984). *Halstead-Reitan Neuropsychological Battery and its prediction of functional daily living skills among geriatric patients with suspected dementia.* Unpublished doctoral dissertation, St. Louis University.

Dyer, F. (1999). *Psychological consultation in parental rights cases.* New York: Guilford.

Dymek, M., Marson, D., & Harrel, L. (1999). Factor structure of capacity to consent to medical treatment in patients with Alzheimer's Disease: An exploratory study. *Journal of Forensic Neuropsychology, 1,* 27–48.

D'Zurilla, T. J., & Nezu, A. M. (1982). Social problem solving in adults. In P. C. Kendall (Ed.), *Advances in cognitive-behavioral research and theory (Vol. 1).* New York: Academic.

Earnst, K. S., Wadley, V. G., Aldridge, T. M., Steenwyk, A. B., Hammond, A. E., Harrell, L. E., & Marson, D. (2000). Loss of financial capacity in Alzheimer's disease: The role of working memory. *Aging, Neuropsychology, and Cognition, 8,* 1–11.

Edelstein, H. (1999). *Hopemont Capacity Assessment Interview manual and scoring guide.* West Virginia University, Morgantown, WV: Author.

Edelstein, H. (2000). Challenges in the assessment of decision making capacity. *Journal of Aging Studies, 14,* 423–437.

Edelstein, B., Bygren, M., Northrop, L., Staats, N., & Pool, D. (1993, August). *Assessment of capacity to make financial and medical decisions.* Presented at the annual convention of the American Psychological Association, Toronto, Canada.

Edens, J. F., Poythress, N. G., Nicholson, R. A., & Otto, R. K. (1999). Effects of state organizational structure and forensic examiner training on pretrial competence assessments. *Journal of Behavioral Health Services and Research, 26,* 140–150.

Edwards, A. J. (1995a). ECOScales. In J. C. Conoley & J. C. Impara (Eds.), *The twelfth mental measurements yearbook.* Lincoln, NE: Buros Institute of Mental Measurements.

Edwards, A. J. (1995b). Parent–Adolescent Communication Scale. In J. C. Conoley & J. C. Impara (Eds.), *The twelfth mental measurements yearbook.* Lincoln, NE: Buros Institute of Mental Measurements.

Elliot, G. (1998). *Assessment of Parenting Skills: Infant and Preschooler manual.* Furlong, PA: Village Publishing.

Ellis, J., & Luckasson, R. (1985). Discrimination against people with mental retardation. *Mental Retardation, 23,* 249–252.

Ellis, R., & Milner, J. (1981). Child abuse and locus of control. *Psychological Reports, 48,* 507–510.

Elrod, L. D., & Spector, R. G. (1998). A review of the year in family law: A search for definitions and policy. *Family Law Quarterly, 31,* 613–666.

Emery, R. E. (1999). Changing the rules for determining child custody in divorce cases. *Clinical Psychology: Science and Practice, 6,* 323–327.

Ennis, B., & Litwack, T. (1974). Psychiatry and the presumption of expertise: Flipping coins in the courtroom. *California Law Review, 62,* 693–752.

Ethier, L., Lacharite, C., & Couture, G. (1993). *Childhood adversity, parental stress and depression of negligent mothers.* Unpublished manuscript, University of Quebec at Trois-Rivieres, Canada.

Evenson, R. (1976). *Geriatric Profile: Manual.* Unpublished manuscript, Missouri Institute of Psychiatry, St. Louis, MO.

Everington, C. (1990). The Competence Assessment for Standing Trial for Defendants with Mental Retardation (CAST-MR): A validation study. *Criminal Justice and Behavior, 17,* 147–168.

Everington, C., & Dunn, C. (1995). A second validation study of the Competence Assessment for Standing Trial for Defendants with Mental Retardation (CAST-MR). *Criminal Justice and Behavior, 22,* 44–59.

Everington, C., & Fulero, S. (1999). Competence to confess: Measuring understanding and suggestibility of defendants with mental retardation. *Mental Retardation, 37,* 212–220.

Everington, C., & Luckasson, R. (1992). *Competence Assessment for Standing Trial for Defendants with Mental Retardation (CAST*MR): Test manual.* Worthington, OH: IDS Publishing Corporation.

Eyberg, S., Bessmer, J., Newcombe, K., Edward, D., & Robinson, E. (1994). *Dyadic Parent–Child Interaction Coding System II manual.* Unpublished manuscript, University of Florida.

Faden, R., & Beauchamp, T. (1986). *A history and theory of informed consent.* New York: Oxford University Press.

Fein, R., Appelbaum, K., Barnum, R., Baxter, P., Grisso, T., & Leavitt, N. (1991). The "Designated Forensic Professional" Program: A state government–university partnership to improve forensic mental health services. *Journal of Mental Health Administration, 18,* 223–230.

Feld, B. (2000). Juveniles' waiver of legal rights: Confessions, Miranda, and the right to counsel. In T. Grisso & R. Schwartz (Eds.), *Youth on trial: A developmental perspective on juvenile justice* (pp. 105–138). Chicago: University of Chicago Press.

Feller, J. N., Davidson, H. A., Hardin, M., & Horowitz, R. M. (1992). *Working with the courts in child protection.* Washington, DC: US Department of Health and Human Services.

Ferguson, A., & Douglas, A. (1970). A study of juvenile waiver. *San Diego Law Review, 7,* 39–54.

Fillenbaum, G. (1978a). Conceptualization and development of the Multidimensional Functional Assessment Questionnaire. In Center for the Study of Aging and Human Development, *Multidimensional functional assessment: The OARS methodology* (pp. 16–24). Durham, NC: Duke University.

Fillenbaum, G. (1978b). Validity and reliability of the Multidimensional Functional Assessment Questionnaire. In Center for the Study of Aging and Human Development, *Multidimensional functional assessment: The OARS methodology* (pp. 25–35). Durham, NC: Duke University.

Fillenbaum, G. (1985). Screening the elderly: A brief instrumental activities of daily living measure. *Journal of the American Geriatrics Society, 33,* 698–706.

Fillenbaum, C., Dellinger, D., Maddox, G., & Pfeiffer, E. (1978). Assessment of individual functional status in a program evaluation and resource allocation model. In Center for the Study Of Aging and Human Development, *Multidimensional functional assessment: The OARS methodology* (pp. 3–12). Durham, NC: Duke University.

Fillenbaum, G., & Maddox, G. (1977). *Assessing the functional status of LRHS participants: Technique, findings, implications* (Technical report No. 2). Durham, NC: Duke University, Center for the Study of Aging and Human Development.

Fillenbaum, G., & Smyer, M. (1981). The development, validity, and reliability of the OARS Multidimensional Functional Assessment Questionnaire. *Journal of Gerontology, 36,* 428–434.

Fitten, L. J., & Waite, M. S. (1990). Impact of medical hospitalization on treatment decision-making capacity in the elderly. *Archives of Internal Medicine, 150,* 1717–1721.

Fitzgerald, J., Peszke, M., & Goodwin, R. (1978). Competency evaluations in Connecticut. *Hospital and Community Psychiatry, 29,* 450–453.

Folstein, M., Folstein, S., & McHugh, P. (1975). Mini-mental state: A practical method of grading cognitive state of patients for the clinician. *Journal of Psychiatric Research, 12,* 189–198.

Foster, H., & Freed, D. (1964). Child custody. *New York University Law Review, 39,* 423–443.

Frank, L., Smyer, M., Grisso, T., & Appelbaum, P. S. (1999). Measurement of advance directive and medical treatment decision-making capacity of older adults. *Journal of Mental Health and Aging, 5,* 257–274.

Freeman, W., Pichard, A., & Smith, H. (1981). Effect of informed consent and educational background on patient knowledge, anxiety, and subjective responses to cardiac catheterization. *Catheterization and Cardiovascular Diagnosis, 7,* 119–134.

Frumkin, B. (2000). Competency to waive Miranda rights: Clinical and legal issues. *Mental and Physical Disabilities Law Reporter, 24,* 326–331.

Fukunaga, K., Pasewark, R., Hawkins, M., & Gudeman, H. (1981). Insanity plea: Inter-examiner agreement and concordance of psychiatric opinion and court verdict. *Law and Human Behavior, 5,* 325–328.

Fulero, S., & Everington, C. (1995). Assessing competency to waive Miranda rights in defendants with mental retardation. *Law and Human Behavior, 19,* 533–543.

Fulero, S., & Finkel, N. (1991). Barring ultimate issue testimony: An "insane" rule? *Law and Human Behavior, 15*, 495–507.

Gannon, J. (1990). Validation of the Competence Assessment Instrument and elements of competence to stand trial. *Dissertation Abstracts International, 50-B*, 3875.

Garb, H., Wood, J., & Nezworski, M. (2000). Projective techniques and the detection of child sexual abuse. *Child Abuse and Neglect, 24*, 437–438.

Gardner, R. (1982). *Family evaluation in child custody litigation.* Cresskill, NJ: Creative Therapeutics.

George, L., & Bearon, L. (1980). *Quality of life in older persons.* New York: Human Sciences Press.

Gerard, A. (1994). *Parent–Child Relationship Inventory (PCRI): Manual.* Los Angeles, CA: Western Psychological Services.

Gilbert, L., &, Hanson, G. (1982). *Perceptions of Parental Role Scales manual.* Columbus, OH: Marathon Consulting and Press.

Gilch-Pesantez, J. (2001). *Test-retest reliability and construct validity: The Bricklin Perceptual Scales.* Unpublished doctoral dissertation. Indiana University, Pennsylvania.

Glosser, G., Goodglass, H., & Biber, C. (1989). Assessing visual memory disorders. *Psychological Assessment, 1*, 82–91.

Goldfried, M., & D'Zurilla, T. (1969). A behavioral-analytic model for assessing competence. In C. D. Spielberger (Ed.), *Current topics in clinical and community psychology* (Vol. 1, pp. 151–196). New York: Academic Press.

Golding, S. L., Roesch, R., & Schreiber, J. (1984). Assessment and conceptualization of competence to stand trial: Preliminary data on the Interdisciplinary Fitness Interview. *Law and Human Behavior, 8*, 321–334.

Goldstein, A. (1967). *The insanity defense.* New Haven, CT: Yale University Press.

Goldstein, J., Freud, A., & Solnit, A. (1973). *Beyond the best interest of the child.* New York: Free Press.

Goldzband, M. (1982). *Consulting in child custody.* Lexington, MA: Lexington Books.

Gordley, J. (1984). Legal reasoning: An introduction. *California Law Review, 72*, 138–177.

Gordon, R. (2000). The emergence of assisted (supported) decision-making in the Canadian law of adult guardianship and substitute decision-making. *International Journal of Law and Psychiatry, 25*, 61–77.

Gordon, R., & Peek, L. A. (1989). *The Custody Quotient: Research manual.* Dallas, TX: Wilmington Institute.

Gothard, S., Rogers, R., & Sewell, K. (1995). Feigning incompetency to stand trial: An investigation of the GCCT. *Law and Human Behavior, 19*, 363–373.

Gould, J. (1998). *Conducting scientifically crafted child custody evaluations.* Thousand Oaks, CA: Sage.

Gould, J., & Stahl, P. (2000). The art and science of child custody evaluations: Integrating clinical and forensic mental health models. *Family and Conciliation Courts Review, 38*, 392–414.

Grisso, T. (1980). Juveniles' capacities to waive *Miranda* rights. An empirical analysis. *California Law Review, 68*, 1134–1166.

Grisso, T. (1981). *Juveniles waiver of rights: Legal and psychological competence.* New York: Plenum Press.

Grisso, T. (1984, June). *Forensic assessment in juvenile and family cases: The state of the art.* Keynote address at the Summer Institute on Mental Health Law, University of Nebraska, Lincoln.

Grisso, T. (1986). *Evaluating competencies: Forensic assessments and instruments.* New York: Plenum.

Grisso, T. (1988). *Competence to stand trial evaluations: A manual for practice.* Sarasota, FL: Professional Resource Press.

Grisso T. (1992) Five-year research update (1986–1990): Evaluations for competence to stand trial. *Behavioral Sciences and the Law, 10,* 353–369.

Grisso, T. (1997). The competence of adolescents as trial defendants. *Psychology, Public Policy, and Law, 3,* 3–32.

Grisso, T. (1998a). *Forensic evaluation of juveniles.* Sarasota, FL: Professional Resource Press.

Grisso, T. (1998b). *Instruments for assessing understanding and appreciation of Miranda rights.* Sarasota, FL: Resource Press.

Grisso, T. (2000). What we know about youths' capacities as trial defendants. In T. Grisso & R. Schwartz (Eds.), *Youth on trial: A developmental perspective on juvenile justice* (pp. 139–172). Chicago: University of Chicago Press.

Grisso, T., & Appelbaum, P. S. (1992). *Manual for thinking rationally about treatment.* Worcester MA: University of Massachusetts Medical School.

Grisso, T., & Appelbaum, P. S. (1992). *Manual for understanding treatment disclosures.* Worcester MA: University of Massachusetts Medical School.

Grisso, T., & Appelbaum, P. S. (1995). The MacArthur Treatment Competence Study, III: Abilities of patients to consent to psychiatric and medical treatment. *Law and Human Behavior, 19,* 149–174.

Grisso, T., & Appelbaum, P. S. (1996). Values and limits of the MacArthur Treatment Competence Study. *Psychology, Public Policy, and Law, 2,* 167–181.

Grisso, T., & Appelbaum, P. S. (1998a). *Assessing competence to consent to treatment: A guide for physicians and other health care professionals.* New York: Oxford University Press.

Grisso, T., & Appelbaum, P. S. (1998b). *MacArthur Competence Assessment Tool for Treatment (MacCAT-T).* Sarasota, FL: Professional Resource Press.

Grisso, T., Appelbaum, P. S., Mulvey, E., & Fletcher, K. (1995). The MacArthur Treatment Competence Study, II: Measures of abilities related to competence to consent to treatment. *Law and Human Behavior, 19,* 127–148.

Grisso, T., Cocozza, J., Steadman, H., Fisher, W., & Greer, A. (1994). The organization of pretrial forensic evaluation services: A national profile. *Law and Human Behavior, 18,* 377–393.

Grisso, T., Miller, M., & Sales, B. (1987). Competency to stand trial in juvenile court. *International Journal of Law and Psychiatry, 10,* 1–20.

Grisso, T., & Pomicter, C. (1977). Interrogation of juveniles: An empirical study of procedures, safeguards, and rights waiver. *Law and Human Behavior, 1,* 321–342.

Grisso, T., & Ring, M. (1979). Parents' attitudes toward juveniles' rights in interrogation. *Criminal Justice and Behavior, 6,* 221–226.

Grisso, T., & Schwartz, R. (Eds.) (2000). *Youth on trial: A developmental perspective on juvenile justice.* Chicago, IL: University of Chicago Press.

Group for the Advancement of Psychiatry. (1974). *Misuse of psychiatry in the criminal courts: Competency to stand trial.* New York: Committee on Psychiatry and Law.

Group for the Advancement of Psychiatry, Committee on the Family. (1980). *Divorce, child custody and the family.* New York: Mental Health Materials Center.

Grunder, T. (1978). Two formulas for determining the readability of subject consent forms. *American Psychologist, 33,* 773–775.

Gudeman, H. (1981). Legal sanctions and the clinician. *The Clinical Psychologist, 34,* 15–17.

Gudjonsson, G. (1992). *The psychology of interrogations, confessions, and testimony.* London: Wiley.

Gudjonsson, G., Rutter, S., & Clare, C. (1995). The relationship between suggestibility and anxiety among suspects detained at police stations. *Psychological Medicine, 25*, 875–878.

Gudjonsson, G., & Sigurdsson, J. (1995). The relationship of confabulation to the memory, intelligence, suggestibility, and personality of juvenile offenders. *Applied Cognitive Psychology, 10*, 85–92.

Gudjonsson, G., & Sigurdsson, J. (1996). The relationship of confabulation to the memory, intelligence, suggestibility and personality of prison inmates. *Nordic Journal of Psychiatry, 49*, 373–378.

Guidubaldi, J., & Cleminshaw, H. (1994). *Parenting Satisfaction Scale manual*. San Antonio, TX: Psychological Corporation.

Guilford, J. P. (1967). *The nature of human intelligence*. New York: McGraw Hill.

Guion, R. (1983). Standards for psychological measurement. In B. D. Sales (Ed.), *The professional psychologist's handbook* (pp. 111–140). New York: Plenum Press.

Gunnoe, M. L., & Braver, S. L. (2001). The effects of joint legal custody on mothers, fathers and children controlling for factors that predispose a sole maternal versus joint legal award. *Law & Human Behavior, 25*, 25–43.

Gurland, B. J., Juriansky, J., Sharpe, L., Simon, R., Stiller, P., & Birkelt, P. (1977–78). The Comprehensive Assessment and Referral Evaluation (CARE): Rationale, development and reliability. *International Journal of Aging and Human Development, 39*, 129–137.

Gutheil, T., & Appelbaum, P. S. (1982). *Clinical handbook of psychiatry and the law*. New York: McGraw-Hill.

Hafemeister, T., & Sales, B. (1984). The use of interdisciplinary teams of health related professionals in guardianship and conservatorship proceedings. *Law and human behavior, 8*, 335–354.

Hagin, R. A. (1992). Bricklin Perceptual Scales. In J. L. Conoley & J. C. Impara (Eds.), *The twelfth mental measurements yearbook* (pp. 117–118). Lincoln, NE: Buros Institute of Mental Measurements.

Hall, A. S., Pulver, C. A., & Cooley, M. J. (1996). Psychology of the best interests standard: Fifty state statutes and their theoretical antecedents. *American Journal of Family Therapy, 24*, 171–180.

Halleck, S. (1980). *Law in the practice of psychiatry: A handbook for clinicians*. New York: Plenum Press.

Halpern, A. (1975). *Use and misuse of psychiatry in competency examination of criminal defendants*. New York: Insight Communications.

Haney, C. (1982). Employment tests and employment discrimination: A dissenting psychological opinion. *Industrial Relations Law Journal, 5*, 1–86.

Hankin, M. B. (1995). A brief introduction to the due process in competency determinations act: A statement of legislative intent. *California Trusts and Estates Quarterly, 1(4)*, 36–49.

Hart, V. (1985). Iowa Parent Behavior Inventory. In J. V. Mitchell (Ed.), *The ninth mental measurements yearbook*. Lincoln, NE: Buros Institute of Mental Measurements.

Heber, R. F. (1961). A manual of terminology and classification in mental retardation (2nd ed.). *American Journal of Mental Deficiency*. Monograph Supplement.

Heilbrun, K. (2001). *Principles of forensic mental health assessment*. New York: Kluwer Academic/Plenum Publishers.

Heilbrun, K., Bennett, W., White, A., & Kelly, J. (1990). An MMPI-based model of malingering and deception. *Behavioral Sciences and the Law, 8*, 43–53.

Heinik, J., Werner, P., & Lin, R. (1999). How do cognitively impaired elderly patients define "testament": Reliability and validity of the Testament Definition Scale. *International Journal of Psychiatry and Related Sciences, 36*, 23–28.

Heinze, M., & Grisso, T. (1996). Review of instruments assessing parenting competencies used in child custody evaluations. *Behavioral Sciences and the Law, 14*, 293–313.

Helfer, R., Hoffmeister, J., & Schneider, C. (1978). *A manual for the use of the Michigan Screening Profile of Parenting*. Boulder, CO: Test Analysis and Development Corporation.

Hereford, C. (1963). *Changing parental attitudes through group discussion*. Austin, TX: University of Texas Press.

Herring, D. J. (1992). Symposium: Inclusion of the reasonable efforts requirement in termination of parental rights statutes: Punishing the child for the failures of the state child welfare system. *University of Pittsburgh Law Review, 54*, 139–209.

Hetherington, E. M., & Parke, R. (1975). *Child psychology: A contemporary viewpoint*. New York: McGraw-Hill.

Hoffman, B., & Srinivasan, J. (1992). A study of competence to consent to treatment in a psychiatric hospital. *Canadian Journal of Psychiatry, 37*, 179–182.

Hogarth, R. (1987). *Judgement and choice: The psychology of decision*. New York: Wiley.

Hoge, S., Bonnie, R., Poythress, N., & Monahan, J. (1992). Attorney-client decisionmaking in criminal cases: Client competence and participation as perceived by their attorneys. *Behavioral Sciences and the Law, 10*, 385–394.

Hoge, S., Bonnie, R., Poythress, N., Monahan, J., Feucht-Haviar, T., & Eisenberg, M. (1997). The MacArthur adjudicative competence study: Development and validation of a research instrument. *Law and Human Behavior, 21*, 141–179.

Holden, E., Willis, D., & Foltz, L. (1989). Child abuse potential and parenting stress: Relationships in maltreating parents. *Psychological Assessment, 1*, 64–67.

Holden, G. (1990). Parenthood. In J. Touliatos, B. Perlmutter, & M. Strauss (Eds.), *Handbook of family measurement techniques*. Newbury Park: Sage.

Holden, G., & Edwards, L. (1989). Parental attitudes toward child rearing: Instruments, issues, and implications. *Psychological Bulletin, 106*, 29–58.

Holmstrup, M., Fitch, W., & Keilitz, I. (1981). *Screening and evaluation in centralized forensic mental health facilities*. Williamsburg, VA: National Center for State Courts.

Holzer, J., Gansler, D., Moczynski, N., & Folstein, J. (1997). Cognitive functions in the informed consent evaluation process: A pilot study. *Journal of the American Academy of Psychiatry and the Law, 25*, 531–540.

Hommel, P. A. (1996). Guardianship reform in the 1980's: A decade of substantive and procedural change. In M. Smyer, K. W. Schaie, & M. P. Kapp (Eds.), *Older adults decision making and the law* (pp. 225–253). New York: Springer.

Horne, J. E. (1993). The Brady Bunch and other fictions: How courts decide child custody disputes involving remarried parents. *Stanford Law Review, 45*, 2074–2142.

Horstman, P. (1975). Protective services for the elderly: The limits of parens patriae. *Missouri Law Review, 40*, 215–278.

Hresko, W., Miguel, S., Sherbenou, R., & Burton, S. (1994). *Developmental Observation Checklist System manual*. Austin, TX: PRO-ED.

Hunt, L. A., Murphy, C. F., Carr, D., Duchek, J. M., Buckles, V., & Morris, J. C. (1997). Reliability of the Washington University Road Test: A performance-based measure assessment for drivers with dementia of the Alzheimer's type. *Archives of Neurology, 54*, 707–712.

Inbau, F., Reid, J., & Buckley, J. (1986). *Criminal interrogation and confessions (3rd ed.)*. Baltimore, MD: Williams and Wilkins.

Irwin, J., Lowitz, A., Marder, S., Mintz, J., Winslade, W., Van Putten, T., & Mills, M. (1985). Psychotic patients' understanding of informed consent. *American Journal of Psychiatry, 142*, 1351–1354.

Isaac, L. M., & Tamblyn, R. M. (1993). Compliance and cognitive function: A methodological approach to measuring unintentional errors in medication compliance in the elderly. *Gerontologist, 33*, 772–781.

Jacob, H. (1988). *Silent revolution: The transformation of divorce law in the United States.* Chicago: University of Chicago Press.

Jacobsen, T., Miller, L. J., & Kirkwood, K. P. (1997). Assessing parenting competency in individuals with severe mental illness: A comprehensive service. *Journal of Mental Health Administration, 24*, 189–199.

Jaffe, R. (1986). Problems of long-term informed consent. *Bulletin of the American Academy of Psychiatry and the Law, 14*, 163–169.

Janis, I., & Mann, L. (1977). *Decision making: A psychological analysis of conflict, choice, and communication.* New York: Free Press.

Janofsky, J., McCarthy, R., & Folstein, M. (1992). The Hopkins Competency Assessment Test: A brief method for evaluating patients' capacity to give informed consent. *Hospital and Community Psychiatry, 43*, 132–136.

Jones, B., Jayaram, G., Samuels, J., & Robinson, H. (1998). Relating competency status to functional status at discharge in patients with chronic mental illness. *Journal of the American Academy of Psychiatry and the Law, 26*, 49–55.

Jones, E. (2001). Stress Index for Parents of Adolescents. In B. S. Plake & J. C. Impara (Eds.), *The fourteenth mental measurements yearbook.* Lincoln, NE: Buros Institute of Mental Measurements.

Kahana, E. (1982). A congruence model of person–environment interaction. In M. Lawton, P. Windley, & T. Byerts (Eds.), *Aging and the environment* (pp. 97–121). New York: Springer.

Kane, M. (2001). Legal guardianship and other alternatives in the care of elders with Alzheimer's disease. *American Journal of Alzheimer's Disease and Other Dementias, 16*, 89–96.

Kane, R., & Kane, R. (1981). *Assessing the elderly: A practical guide to measurement.* Lexington, MA: Lexington.

Kapp, M. B. (1994). Ethical aspects of guardianship. *Clinics in Geriatric Medicine, 10*, 501–512.

Kapust, L. R., & Weintraub, S. (1992). To drive or not to drive: Preliminary results from road testing of patients with dementia. *Journal of Geriatric Psychiatry and Neurology, 5*, 210–216.

Karel, M. J. (2000). The assessment of values in medical decision making. *Journal of Aging Studies, 14*, 403–422.

Kassin, S. (1997). The psychology of confession evidence. *American Psychologist, 52*, 221–233.

Kassin, S., & McNall, K. (1991). Police interrogations and confessions: Communicating promises and threats by pragmatic implication. *Law and Human Behavior, 15*, 233–251.

Katz, I. (2001). Parenting Satisfaction Scale. In B. S. Plake & J. C. Impara (Eds.), *The fourteenth mental measurements yearbook.* Lincoln, NE: Buros Institute of Mental Measurements.

Katz, M., Ford, A., Moskowitz, R., Jackson, B. & Jaffee, M. (1963). Studies of illness in the aged: The Index of ADL, a standardized measure of biological and psychosocial function. *Journal of the American Medical Association, 185*, 94–99.

Katz, M., & Lyerly, S. (1963). Methods for measuring adjustment and social behavior in the community: 1. Rationale, description, discriminative validity, and scale development. *Psychological Reports, 13*, 503–535.

Kaufer, D., Steinberg, E., & Toney, S. (1983). Revising medical consent forms: An empirical model and test. *Law, Medicine and Health Care, 11*, 155–184.

Kaye, N. (1992). Assessing competency: Comment. *Hospital and Community Psychiatry, 43*, 648.

Keilin, W., & Bloom, L. (1986). Child custody evaluation practices: A survey of experienced professionals. *Professional Psychology: Research and Practice, 17,* 338–346.

Keilitz, I. (1982). *Mental health examinations in criminal justice settings: Organization, administration, and program evaluation.* Williamsburg, VA: National Center for State Courts.

Keilitz, I., Farthing-Capowich, D., McGraw, B., & Adams, L. (1984). *The guilty but mentally ill verdict: An empirical test.* Williamsburg, VA: National Center for State Courts.

Keith, P. (1998). Assessment of interpersonal relations. In J. Impara & B. Plake (Eds.), *The thirteenth mental measurements yearbook.* Lincoln, NE: Buros Institute of Mental Measurements.

Keith, P., & Wacker, R. (1992). Guardianship reform: Does revised legislation make a difference in outcomes for proposed wards? *Journal of Aging & Social Policy, 4,* 139–155.

Keith, P., & Wacker, R. (1993). Implementation of recommended guardianship practices and outcome of hearings for older persons. *The Gerontologist, 33,* 81–87.

Kelley, M. (2001). Family Assessment Form. In B. S. Plake & J. C. Impara (Eds.), *The fourteenth mental measurements yearbook.* Lincoln, NE: Buros Institute of Mental Measurements.

Kerby, D. S., Wentworth, R., & Cotten, P. D. (1989). Measuring adaptive behavior in elderly developmentally disabled clients. *The Journal of Applied Gerontology, 8,* 261–267.

Keyser, D. & Sweetland, R. (1985). *Michigan Screening Profile of Parenting.* Test Critiques, Volume IV. Austin, TX: PRO-ED.

Keyser, D. & Sweetland, R. (1987). *Dyadic Parent–Child Interaction Coding System.* Test Critiques, Volume VI. Austin, TX: PRO-ED.

Kim, S., Caine, E., Currier, G., Leibovici, A., & Ryan, J. (2001). Assessing the competence of persons with Alzheimer's Disease in providing informed consent for participation in research. *American Journal of Psychiatry, 158,* 712–717.

Kovar, M. G., & Lawton, M. P. (1994). Functional disability: Activities and instrumental activities of daily living. In M. Lawton & J. Teresi (Eds.), *Annual review of gerontology and geriatrics: focus on assessment techniques, (Vol. 14.* pp. 57–75). New York: Springer.

Krauss, D. A., & Sales, B. D. (1997). Guardianship and the elderly. In P. Nussbaum (Ed.), *Handbook of neuropsychology and aging* (pp. 528–540). New York: Plenum.

Kuehnle, K., Coulter, M., & Firestone, G. (2000). Child protection evaluations: The forensic stepchild. *Family and Conciliation Courts Review, 38,* 368–391.

Laboratory of Community Psychiatry, Harvard Medical School (1973). *Competency to stand trial and mental illness* (DHEW Publication No. ADM77-103). Rockville, MD: Department of Health, Education and Welfare.

Lachar, D. (1984). *Personality Inventory for Children manual.* Los Angeles: Western Psychological Services.

LaFortune, K. A., & Carpenter, B. N. (1998). Custody evaluations: A survey of mental health professionals. *Behavioral Sciences and the Law, 16,* 207–224.

LaFortune, K., & Nicholson, R. (1995). How adequate are Oklahoma's mental health evaluations for determining competency in criminal proceedings? The bench and the bar respond. *Journal of Psychiatry and Law, 23,* 231–262.

Lamphear, V., Stets, J., Whitaker, P., & Ross, A. (1985, August). *Maladjustment in at-risk for physical child abuse and behavior problem children: Differences in family environment and marital discord.* Paper presented at the meeting of the American Psychological Association, Los Angeles.

LaRue, A., (1992). *Aging and neuropsychological assessment.* New York: Plenum.

Laurie, W. (1978a). Population assessment for program evaluation. In G. Maddox (Ed.), *Assessment and evaluation strategies in aging* (pp. 100–110). Durham, NC: Duke University.

Laurie, W. (1978b). The Cleveland experience: Functional status and services use. In Center for the Study of Aging and Human Development, *Multidimensional functional assessment: The OARS methodology* (pp. 89–99). Durham, NC: Duke University.

Lavin, M. (1992). Assessing competency: Comment. *Hospital and Community Psychiatry, 43,* 646–647.

Lawrence, S. (1981). *Manual for the Lawrence Psychological-Forensic Examination.* San Bernardino, CA: Author.

Lawton, M. (1982). Competence, environmental press, and adaptation of older people. In M. Lawton, P. Windley, & T. Byerts (Eds.), *Aging and the environment: Theoretical approaches* (pp. 33–59). New York: Springer.

Lawton, M. P. (1983). Environment and other determinants of well-being in older people. *The Gerontologist, 23,* 349–357.

Lawton, M. P. (1990). Residential environment and self-directedness among older people. *American Psychologist, 45,* 638–640.

Lawton, M. P., & Brody, E. (1969). Assessment of older people: Self-maintaining and instrumental activities of daily living. *Gerontologist, 9,* 179–186.

Lawton, M. P., & Moss, M. (undated). *Philadelphia Geriatric Center Multilevel Assessment Instrument: Manual for full-length MAI.* Philadelphia, PA: Author.

Lawton, M. P., Moss, M., Fulcomer, M., & Kleban, M. (1982). A research and service oriented multilevel assessment instrument. *Journal of Gerontology, 37,* 91–99.

Lawton, M.P. Windley, P., & Byerts, I. (Eds.). (1982). *Aging and the environment.* New York: Springer.

Lehman, V. (1963). *Guardianship and protective services for older people.* Albany: National Council on Aging Press.

Lerner, R. M., Castellino, D. R., Terry, P. A., Villarruel, F. A., & McKinney, M. H. (1995). A developmental contextual perspective on parenting. In M. H. Bornstein (Ed.), *Handbook of parenting: Biology and ecology of parenting* (pp. 285–309). Mahwah, NJ: Erlbaum.

Lezak, M. (1995). *Neuropsychological assessment* (3rd ed.). New York: Oxford.

Lichtenberg, P. A. (Ed.) (1999). *Handbook of assessment in clinical gerontology.* New York: Wiley.

Lichtenberg, P. A., Christensen, B., Metler, L., Jones, G., Reyes, J., & Blumenthal, F. (1994). A preliminary investigation of the role of cognition and depression in predicting functional recovery among geriatric rehabilitation patients: A program of neuropsychological research. *Advances in Medical Psychotherapy, 8,* 121–136.

Lichtenberg, P. A., & Strzepek, D. (1990). Assessments of institutionalized dementia patients' competencies to participate in intimate relationships. *The Gerontologist, 30,* 117–120.

Lidz, C., Meisel, A., Zerubavel, E., Carter, M., Sestak, R., & Roth, L. (1984). *Informed consent: A study of decisionmaking in psychiatry.* New York: Guilford.

Linden, M., & Chaskel, R. (1981). Information and consent in schizophrenic patients in long-term treatment. *Schizophrenia Bulletin, 3,* 372–378.

Lipsitt, P., Lelos, D., & McGarry, A. L. (1971). Competency for trial: A screening instrument. *American Journal of Psychiatry, 128,* 105–109.

Lisi, L. B., & Barinaga-Burch, S. (1995). National study of guardianship systems: Summary of findings and recommendations. *Clearinghouse Review, October,* 643–653.

Loeb, P. A. (1983). *Validity of the Community Competence Scale with the elderly.* Unpublished doctoral dissertation, St. Louis University.

Loeb, P. A. (1996). *Independent Living Scales.* San Antonio: Psychological Corporation.

Loeber, R., & Stouthamer-Loeber, M. (1986). Family factors as correlates and predictors of juvenile conduct problems and delinquency. In M. Tonry & N. Morris (Eds.), *Crime and justice* (Vol. 17, pp. 29–149). Chicago: University of Chicago Press.

Loftus, E., & Monahan, J. (1980). Trial by data: Psychological research as legal evidence. *American Psychologist, 35,* 270–283.

Loewenstein, D. A., Amigo, E., Duara, R., Guterman, A., Hurwitz, D., Berkowitz, N., Wilkie, F., Weinberg, G., Black, B., Gittlenman, B., & Eisdorfer, C. (1989). A new scale for the assessment of functional status in Alzheimer's disease and related disorders. *Journal of Gerontology: Psychological Sciences, 44,* 114–121.

Loewenstein, D. A., Arguelles, S., Bravo, M., Freeman, R. Q., Arguelles, T., Aceredo, A., & Eisdorfer, C. (2001). Caregivers' judgments of functional abilities of the Alzheimer's disease patient: A comparison of proxy reports and objective measures. *Journal of Gerontology, 56,* P78–P84.

Loewenstein, D. A., Duara, R., Rubert, M. P., Arguelles, T., Lapinski, K. J., & Eisdorfer, C. (1995). Deterioration of functional capacities in Alzheimer's disease after a 1-year period. *International Psychogeriatrics, 7,* 495–503.

Loewenstein, D. A., & Rupert, M. P. (1995). Staging functional impairment in dementia using performance-based measures: A preliminary analyses. *Journal of Mental Health and Aging, 1,* 47–56.

Loewenstein, D. A., Rubert, M. P., Berkowitz-Zimmer, N., Guterman, A., Morgan, R., & Hayden, S. (1992). Neuropsychological test performance and prediction of functional capacities in dementia. *Behavior, Health and Aging, 2,* 149–158.

Lyman, R., & Roberts, M. C. (1985). Mental health testimony in child custody evaluations. *Law and Psychology Review, 9,* 15–34.

Maccoby, E. E., & Mnookin, R. H. (1992). *Dividing the child: Social and legal dilemmas of custody.* Cambridge, MA: Harvard University Press.

MacDonald, J., Gillette, Y., & Hutchinson, T. (1989). *ECO Scales manual.* Chicago: Riverside Publishing.

MacNeill, S. E., & Lichtenberg, P. A. (1999). Screening instruments and brief batteries for assessment of dementia. In P. A. Lichtenberg (Ed.), *Handbook of assessment in clinical gerontology* (pp. 417–441). New York: Wiley.

Magnusson, D., & Endler, N. (Eds.). (1977). *Personality at the crossroads: Current issues in interactional psychology.* Hillsdale, NJ: Erlbaum.

Magura, S., Moses, B., Jones, M. (1987). *Family Risk Scales manual.* Washington, DC: Child Welfare League of America, Inc.

Mahoney, F., & Barthel, D. (1965). Functional evaluation: The Barthel Index. *Maryland State Medical Journal, 14,* 61–65.

Mahurin, R. K., DeBettignies, B. H., & Pirozzolo, F. J. (1991). Structured assessment of independent living skills: Preliminary report of a performance measure of functional abilities in dementia. *Journal of Gerontology: Psychological Sciences, 46,* P58–P66.

Mancini, J. A. (2001). Family Environment Scale: Third Edition. In B. S. Plake & J. C. Impara (Eds.), *The fourteenth mental measurements yearbook.* Lincoln, NE: Buros Institute of Mental Measurements.

Manges, K. (2001). Family Assessment Measure Version III. In B. S. Plake & J. C. Impara (Eds.), *The fourteenth mental measurements yearbook.* Lincoln, NE: Buros Institute of Mental Measurements.

Marchant, G., & Paulson, S. (1998). Review of the Parent-Child Relationship Inventory. In J. C. Impara & B. S. Plake (Eds.), *The thirteenth mental measurements yearbook* (pp. 720–721). Lincoln, NE: Buros Institute of Mental Measurements of the University of Nebraska-Lincoln.

Marsiske, M., & Willis, S. L. (1995). Dimensionality of everyday problem solving in older adults. *Psychology and Aging, 10,* 269–283.

Marson, D. (2000, November). *Assessing financial capacity in Alzheimer's disease: A clinical interview approach.* Paper presented at the meeting of the Gerontological Society of America, Washington, DC.

Marson, D. C. (2001). Loss of financial competency in dementia: Conceptual and empirical approaches. *Aging, Neuropsychology, and Cognition, 8,* 1–17.

Marson, D., Annis, S., McInturff, H., Bartolucci, A., & Harrell, L. (1999). Error behaviors associated with loss of competency in Alzheimer's Disease. *Neurology, 53,* 1983–1992.

Marson, D., Chatterjee, A., Ingram, K., & Harrell, L. (1996). Toward a neurologic model of competency: Cognitive predictors of capacity to consent in Alzheimer's Disease using three different legal standards. *Neurology, 46,* 666–672.

Marson, D.C., Cody, H. A., Ingram, K. K., & Harrell, L. E. (1995). Neuropsychologic predictors of competency in Alzheimer's disease using a rational reasons legal standard. *Archives of Neurology, 52,* 955–959.

Marson, D., Earnst, K., Jamil, F., Bartolucci, A., & Harrell, L. (in press). Consistency of physicians' legal standard and personal judgments of competency in patients with Alzheimer's Disease. *Journal of the American Geriatrics Society.*

Marson, D. C., Sawrie, S. M., Snyder, S., McInturff, B., Stalvey, T., Boothe, A., Aldrige, T., Chatterjee, A., & Harrell, L. E. (2000). Assessing financial capacity in patients with Alzheimer's disease: A conceptual model and prototype instrument. *Archives of Neurology, 57,* 877–884.

Marson, D. C., Sawrie, S., Stalvey, T., McInturff, B., & Harrell, L. (1998, February). *Neuropsychological correlates of declining financial capacity in patients with Alzheimer's disease.* Paper presented at the meeting of the International Neuropsychological Society, Honolulu, Hawaii.

Mash, E., Johnston, C., & Kovitz, K. (1983). A comparison of the mother–child interactions of physically abused and non-abused children during play and task situations. *Journal of Clinical Child Psychology, 12,* 337–346.

Mason, M. A. (1994). *From father's property to children's rights: The history of child custody in the United States.* New York: Columbia University Press.

Matthews, R. (1985). *Screening and identification of child abusing parents through self-report inventories* (Doctoral dissertation, Florida Institute of Technology, 1984). Dissertation Abstracts International, 46, 650B.

McClelland, D. (1973). Testing for competence rather than for "intelligence." *American Psychologist, 28,* 1–14.

McCue, M., Rogers, J., & Goldstein, G. (1990). Relationships between neuropsychological and functional assessment in elderly neuropsychiatric patients. *Rehabilitation Psychology, 35,* 91–99.

McDonald, D., Nussbaum, D., & Bagby, R. (1991). Reliability, validity and utility of the Fitness Interview Test. *Canadian Journal of Psychiatry, 36,* 480–484.

McGarry, A., Curran, W., & Kenefick, D. (1968). Problems of public consultation in medico-legal matters: A symposium. *American Journal of Psychiatry, 125,* 42–45.

McGill, J. S., & Paul, P. B. (1993). Functional status and hope in elderly people with and without cancer. *Oncology Nursing Forum, 20,* 1207–1213.

McGough, L. S., & Shindell, L. M. (1978). Coming of age: The best interests of the child standard in parent-third party custody disputes. *Emory Law Journal, 27,* 209–252.

McGourty, L. K. (1979). *Kohlman Evaluation of Living Skills* (2nd ed.). Seattle: Linda Kohlman McGourty.

McIntosh, J. A, & Prinz, R. J. (1993). The incidence of alleged sexual abuse in 603 family court cases. *Law and Human Behavior, 17,* 95–101.

McKinnon, K., Cournos, F., & Stanley, B. (1989). *Rivers* in practice: Clinicians' assessments of patients' decision-making capacity. *Hospital and Community Psychiatry, 40,* 1159–1162.

McMahon, R. J. (1985). Dyadic Parent–Child Interaction Coding System. In J. V. Mitchell (Ed.), *The ninth mental measurements yearbook.* Lincoln, NE: Buros Institute of Mental Measurements.

Medway, F. J. (1998). Assessment of Interpersonal Relations. In J. C. Impara & B. S. Plake (Eds.), *The thirteenth mental measurements yearbook.* Lincoln, NE: Buros Institute of Mental Measurements.

Meehl, P. (1970). Some methodological reflections on the difficulties of psychoanalytic research. In M. Radner & S. Winokur (Eds.), *Minnesota studies in the philosophy of science: Vol. 4. Analyses of theories and methods of physics and psychology* (pp. 403–416). Minneapolis, MN: University of Minnesota Press.

Meehl, P. (1971). Law and the fireside inductions: Some reflections of a clinical psychologist. *Journal of Social Issues, 27,* 65–100.

Meisel, A., Roth, L., & Lidz, C. (1977). Toward a model of the legal doctrine of informed consent. *American Journal of Psychiatry, 134,* 285–289.

Melton, G. B. (1995). Ackerman-Schoendorf Scales for Parent Evaluation of Custody. In J. C. Conoley & J. C. Impara (Eds.), *The twelfth mental measurements yearbook* (pp. 22–23). Lincoln, NE: Buros Institute of Mental Measurements.

Melton, G. B. (1999). Due care, not prohibition of expert opinions. *Clinical Psychology: Science and Practice, 6,* 335–338.

Melton, G., Koocher, G., & Saks, M. (Eds.) (1983). *Children's competence to consent.* New York: Plenum Press.

Melton, G., Petrila, J., Poythress, N., & Slobogin, C. (1987). *Psychological evaluations for the courts: A handbook for mental health professionals and lawyers.* New York: Guilford.

Melton, G., Petrila, J., Poythress, N., & Slobogin, C. (1997). *Psychological evaluations for the courts: A handbook for mental health professionals and lawyers* (2nd ed.). New York: Guilford.

Melton, G., Weithorn, L., & Slobogin, C. (1987). *Community mental health centers and the courts: An evaluation of community-based forensic services.* Lincoln, NE: University of Nebraska Press.

Mental Disability Law Reporter (1978). Incompetency to stand trial on criminal charges. *Mental Disability Law Reporter, 2,* 615–663.

Messick, S. (1980). Test validity and the ethics of assessment. *American Psychologist, 35,* 1012–1027.

Milner, J. (1982). Development of a lie scale for the Child Abuse Potential Inventory. *Psychological Reports, 50,* 871–874.

Milner, J. (1986). *The Child Abuse Potential Inventory: Manual* (2nd ed.). Webster, NC: Psytec.

Milner, J. (1988). An ego-strength scale for the Child Abuse Potential Inventory. *Journal of Family Violence, 3,* 151–162.

Milner, J. (1989). Additional cross-validation of the Child Abuse Potential Inventory. *Psychological Assessment, 1,* 219–223.

Milner, J. (1990). *An interpretative manual for the Child Abuse Potential Inventory.* Webster, NC: Psytec.

Milner, J. (1991). Medical conditions and the Child Abuse Potential Inventory specificity. *Psychological Assessment, 3,* 208–212.

Milner, J. (1994). Assessing physical child abuse risk: The Child Abuse Potential Inventory. *Clinical Psychology Review, 14,* 547–583.

Milner, J. & Crouch, J. (1997). Impact and detection of response distortions of parenting measures used to assess risk for child physical abuse. *Journal of Personality Assessment, 69,* 633–650.

Milner, J., Gold, R., Ayoub, C., & Jacewitz, M. (1984). Predictive validity of the Child Abuse Potential Inventory. *Journal of Consulting and Clinical Psychology, 52,* 879–884.

Milner, J., Gold, R., & Wimberley, R. (1986). Prediction and explanation of child abuse: Cross-validation of the Child Abuse Potential Inventory. *Journal of Consulting and Clinical Psychology, 54,* 865–866.

Milner, J., & Robertson, K. (1989). Inconsistent response patterns and the prediction of child maltreatment. *Child Abuse and Neglect, 13,* 59–64.

Milner, J., & Wimberley, R. (1979). An inventory for the identification of child abusers. *Journal of Clinical Psychology, 35,* 95–100.

Milner, J., & Wimberley, R. (1980). Prediction and explanation of child abuse. *Journal of Clinical Psychology, 36,* 875–884.

Mischel, W. (1983). Alternatives to the pursuit of the predictability and consistency of persons: Stable data that yield unstable interpretations. *Journal of Personality, 51,* 578–604.

Mischel, W. (1984). Convergences and challenges in the search for consistency. *American Psychologist, 39,* 351–364.

Mnookin, R. (1975). Child custody adjudication: Judicial functions in the face of indeterminacy. *Law and Contemporary Problems, 39,* 226–293.

Mnookin, R., Maccoby, E. E., Albiston, C. R., & Depner, C. E. (1990). Private ordering revisited: What custodial arrangements are parents negotiating? In. S. D. Sugarman & H. H. Kay (Eds.), *Divorce reforms at the crossroads.* New Haven, CT: Yale University Press.

Monahan, J. (1981). *The clinical prediction of violent behavior.* Rockville, MD: National Institute of Mental Health.

Moore, C. A., & Lichtenberg, P. L. (1995). Neuropsychological prediction of independent functioning in a geriatric sample: A double cross validation study. *Rehabilitation Psychology, 41,* 115–130.

Moos, R., & Moos, B. (1994). *Family Environment Scale manual* (3rd ed.). Palo Alto, CA: Consulting Psychologists Press.

Morris, G. (1975). The *insanity defense: A blueprint for legislative reform.* Lexington, MA: Lexington.

Morrow, G., Gootnick, J., & Schmale, A. (1978). A simple technique for increasing cancer patients' knowledge of informed consent to treatment. *Cancer, 42,* 793–799.

Morse, S. (1978a). Crazy behavior, morals, and science: An analysis of mental health law. *Southern California Law Review, 51,* 527–654.

Morse, S. (1978b). Law and mental health professionals: The limits of expertise. *Professional Psychology, 9,* 389–399.

Morse, S. (1982). Failed explanations and criminal responsibility: Experts and the unconscious. *Virginia Law Review, 68,* 971–1084.

Morse, S. (1983). Mental health law: Governmental regulation of disordered persons and the role of the professional psychologist. In B. D. Sales (Ed.), *The professional psychologist's handbook* (pp. 339–422). New York: Plenum Press.

Moye, J. (1996). Theoretical frameworks for competency assessments in cognitively impaired elderly. *Journal of Aging Studies, 10,* 27–42.

Moye, J. (1997). Nonverbal memory assessment with designs: Construct validity and clinical utility. *Neuropsychology Review, 7,* 157–170.

Moye, J. (1999). Assessment of competency and decision making capacity. In P. Lichtenberg (Ed.), *Handbook of Assessment in Clinical Gerontology* (pp. 488–528). New York: Wiley.

Moye, J. (2000). Mr. Franks refuses surgery: Cognition and values in competency determination in complex cases. *Journal of Aging Studies, 14,* 385–401.

Moye, J., & Zehr, M. (2000). Resolving ethical challenges in psychological practice for long term care. *Clinical Psychology: Science and Practice, 7*, 337–344.

Muir, K. (1997). *Children's perceptions of their parents and susceptibility to suggestion.* Unpublished doctoral dissertation. California School of Professional Psychology, San Diego.

Mumley, D., Tillbrook, C., & Grisso, T. (in press). Five year research update (1996–2000): Evaluations for competence to stand trial (adjudicative competence). *Behavioral Sciences and the Law.*

Munsinger, H., & Karlson, K. (1994). *Uniform Child Custody Evaluation System manual.* Odessa, FL: PAR.

Murray, H. (1938). *Explorations in personality.* New York: Oxford University Press.

Myers, G. (1990). Demography of Aging. In R. H. Binstock & L. K. George (Eds.), *Handbook of aging and the social sciences.* New York: Academic.

Myers, A., Holliday, P., Harvey, K., & Hutchinson, K. (1993). Functional performance measures: Are they superior to self-assessments? *Journal of Gerontology: Medical Sciences, 48,* M196–M206.

Nadler, J., Richardson, E., Malloy, P. (1993). The ability of the Dementia Rating Scale to predict everyday functioning. *Archives of Clinical Neuropsychology, 8,* 449–460.

National Clearinghouse on Child Abuse and Neglect Information (2001a). *Statutes at a glance: Definitions of child abuse and neglect.* Washington, DC: Author.

National Clearinghouse on Child Abuse and Neglect Information (2001b). *Statutes at a glance: Grounds for termination of parental rights.* Washington, DC: Author.

Newton, N. A., & Brown, G. G. (1985). Construction of matched verbal and design continuous paired associate tests. *Journal of Clinical and Experimental Neuropsychology, 7,* 97–110.

Nicholson, R., Briggs, S., & Robertson, H. (1988). Instruments for assessing competence to stand trial: How do they work? *Professional Psychology: Research and Practice, 19,* 383–394.

Nicholson, R., & Kugler, K. (1991). Competent and incompetent criminal defendants: A quantitative review of comparative research. *Psychological Bulletin, 109,* 355–370.

Nicholson, R., LaFortune, K., Norwood, S., & Roach, R. (1995, August). *Quality of pretrial competency evaluations in Oklahoma: Report content and consumer satisfaction.* Paper presented at the annual convention of the American Psychological Association, New York City.

Nicholson, R., & Norwood, S. (2000). The quality of forensic psychological assessments, reports, and testimony: Acknowledging the gap between promise and practice. *Law and Human Behavior, 24,* 9–44.

Nicholson, R., Robertson, H., Johnson, & Jensen, G. (1988). A comparison of instruments for assessing competence to stand trial. *Law and Human Behavior, 12,* 313–321.

Nord, C., & Zill, N. (1997). Noncustodial parents' participation in their children's lives. *Child Support Report, 19,* 1–2.

Norko, M., Billick, S., McCarrick, R., & Schwartz, M. (1990). A clinical study of competency to consent to voluntary psychiatric hospitalization. *American Journal of Forensic Psychiatry, 11,* 3–15.

Nottingham, E., & Mattson, R. (1981). A validation study of the Competency Screening Test. *Law and Human Behavior, 5,* 329–335.

Nussbaum, D., Mamak, M., Tremblay, H., Wright, P., & Callaghan, J. (1998). The METFORS Fitness Questionnaire (MFQ): A self-report measure for screening competency to stand trial. *American Journal of Forensic Psychology, 16,* 41–65.

Nydegger, C. (Ed.) (1977). *Measuring morale: A guide to effective assessment.* Washington, DC: Gerontological Society.

Oberlander, L., & Goldstein, N. (2001). A review and update on the practice of evaluating *Miranda* comprehension. *Behavioral Sciences and the Law, 19*, 453–471.

Odenheimer, G., Beaudet, M., Jette, A., Albert, M., Grande, L., & Minaker, K. (1994). Performance-based driving evaluation of the elderly driver: Safety, reliability, and validity. *Journal of Gerontology: Medical Sciences, 49*, M153–M159.

O'Donohue, W., & Bradley, A. R. (1999). Conceptual and empirical issues in child custody evaluations. *Clinical Psychology: Science and Practice, 6*, 310–322.

Okpaku, S. (1976). Psychology: Impediment or aid in child custody cases? *Rutgers Law Review, 29*, 1117–1153.

Olin, G., & Olin, G. (1975). Informed consent in voluntary mental hospital admissions. *American Journal of Psychiatry, 132*, 938–941.

Otto, R. (1989). Bias and expert testimony of mental health professionals in adversarial proceedings: A preliminary investigation. *Behavioral Sciences and the Law, 7*, 267–273.

Otto, R. K. (2000). *Child custody evaluation: Law, ethics, and practice.* Tampa, Florida: Louis de la Parte Florida Mental Health Institute.

Otto, R., Buffington, J., & Edens, J. (in press). Child custody evaluations: research and practice. In A. Goldstein (ed.), *Volume 11: Forensic psychology, Handbook of psychology.* New York: Wiley.

Otto, R., & Collins, R. (1995). *Use of the MMPI/MMPI-2 in child custody evaluation. In Y. Ben-Porath, J. Graham, G. C. N. Hall, and M. Zaragoza (Eds.), Forensic applications of the MMPI-2. Newbury Park, CA: Sage.

Otto, R., Edens, J., & Barcus, E. (2000). The use of psychological testing in child custody evaluations. *Family and Conciliation Courts Review, 38*, 312–340.

Otto, R., Heilbrun, K., & Grisso, T. (1990). Training and credentialing in forensic psychology. *Behavioral Sciences and the Law, 8*, 217–231.

Otto, R., Poythress, N., Edens, N., Nicholson, R., Monahan, J., Bonnie, R., Hoge, S., & Eisenberg, M. (1998). Psychometric properties of the MacArthur Competence Assessment Tool-Criminal Adjudication. *Psychological Assessment, 10*, 435–443.

Owsley, C., Ball, K., McGwin, G., Sloane, M. E., Roenker, D. L., & White, M. F. (1998). Visual processing impairment and risk of motor vehicle crash among older adults. *Journal of the American Medical Association, 279*, 1083–1088.

Palmer, H. M. & Dobson, K. S. (1994). Self-medication and memory in an elderly Canadian sample. *The Gerontologist, 34*, 658–664.

Parasuraman, R., & Nestor, P. (1993). Attention and driving: Assessments in elderly individuals with dementia. *Clinics in Geriatric Medicine, 9*, 377–387.

Parry, J. (1986a). Decision-making rights over persons and property. In S. J. Brakel, J. Parry, & B. A. Weiner (Eds.), *The mentally disabled and the law* (pp. 435–470). Chicago: American Bar Foundation.

Parry, J. (1986b). Incompetency, guardianship, and restoration. In S. J. Brakel, J. Parry, & B. A. Weiner (Eds.), *The mentally disabled and the law* (pp. 369–394). Chicago: American Bar Foundation.

Parry, J. (1988). Selected recommendations from the national guardianship symposium at Wingspread. *Mental and physical disability and law reporter, 12*, 398–406.

Pasewark, R. (1981). Insanity plea: A review of the research literature. *Journal of Psychiatry and Law, 9*, 357–401.

Pasewark, R., & McGinley, H. (1986). Insanity plea: National survey of frequency and success. *Journal of Psychiatry and Law, 13*, 101–108.

Pasewark, R., Pantle, M., & Steadman, H. (1979a). Characteristics and dispositions of persons found not guilty by reason of insanity in New York State, 1971–1976. *American Journal of Psychiatry, 136,* 655–660.

Pasewark, R., Pantle, M., & Steadman, H. (1979b). The insanity plea in New York State, 1965–1976. *New York State Bar Journal, 52,* 186–189.

Pasewark, R., Pantle, M. & Steadman, H. (1982). Detention and rearrest rates of persons found not guilty by reason of insanity and convicted felons. *American Journal of Psychiatry, 139,* 892–897.

Pearson, J., & Luchesi-Ring, M. A. (1983). Judicial decision-making in contested custody cases. *Journal of Family Law, 21,* 703–724.

Perlin, M. (1989). *Mental disability law: Civil and criminal.* Charlottesville, VA: Mitchie.

Perlin, M. (1994). *Law and Mental Disability.* Charlottesville, VA: Mitchie.

Petrella, R., & Poythress, N. (1983). The quality of forensic evaluations: An interdisciplinary study. *Journal of Consulting and Clinical Psychology, 51,* 76–85.

Pfeiffer, E. (1978). Ways of combining functional assessment data. In Center for the Study of Aging and Human Development, *Multidimensional functional assessment: The OARS methodology* (pp. 65–71). Durham, NC: Duke University.

Pfeiffer, S. (1995). Parent–Adolescent Communication Scale. In J. C. Conoley & J. C. Impara (Eds.), *The twelfth mental measurements yearbook.* Lincoln, NE: Buros Institute of Mental Measurements.

Phillips, B., & Pasewark, R. (1980). Insanity plea in Connecticut. *Bulletin of the American Academy of Psychiatry and the Law, 8,* 335–344.

Pierce, P. S. (1989). *Adult Functional Adaptive Behavior Scale (AFABS): Manual of Directions (1989 Edition).* Togus, ME: Author.

Polikoff, N. D. (1982). Why are mother losing custody?: A brief analysis of criteria used in child custody determinations. *Women's Rights Law Reporter, 7,* 235–243.

Pope, B., & Scott, W. (1967). *Psychological diagnosis in clinical practice.* New York: Oxford University Press.

Poythress, N., Bonnie, R., Hoge, S., Monahan, J., & Oberlander, L. (1994). Client abilities to assisst counsel and make decisions in criminal cases: Findings from three studies. *Law and Human Behavior, 18,* 437–452.

Poythress, N., Nicholson, R., Otto, R., Edens, J., Bonnie, R., Monahan, J., & Hoge, S. (1999). *The MacArthur Competence Assessment Tool – Criminal Adjudication: Professional manual.* Odessa, FL: Psychological Assessment Resources.

Poythress, N., Otto, R., & Heilbrun, K. (1991). Pretrial evaluations for criminal courts: Contemporary models of service delivery. *Journal of Mental Health Administration, 18,* 198–208.

President's Commission for the Study of Ethical Problems in Medicine and Biomedical and Behavioral Research. (1982). *Making health care decisions.* Washington, DC: U.S. Government Printing Office.

Pruchno, R., Smyer, M., Rose, M., Hartman-Stein, P., & Henderson-Laribee, D. (1995). Competence of long-term care residents to participate in decisions about their medical care: A brief, objective assessment. *The Gerontologist, 35,* 622–629.

Randolph, J., Hicks, T., & Mason, D. (1981). The Competence Screening Test: A replication and extension. *Criminal Justice and Behavior, 8,* 471–481.

Randolph, J., Hicks, T., Mason, D., & Cuneo, D. (1982). The Competence Screening Test: A validation in Cook County, Illinois. *Criminal Justice and Behavior, 9,* 495–500.

Regan, W. M., & Gordon, S. M. (1997). Assessing testamentary capacity in elderly people. *Southern Medical Journal, 90,* 13–15.

Regier, D. A., Myers, J. K., Kramer, M., Robins, W. W., George, L. K., Karno, M., & Locke, B. Z. (1988). One-month prevalence of mental disorders in the United States. *Archives of General Psychiatry, 45,* 977–986.

Reid-Proctor, G. M., Galin, K., Cummings, M. A. (2001). Evaluation of legal competency in patients with frontal lobe injury. *Brain Injury, 15,* 377–386.

Reitman, D., & Gross, A. (1995). Familial determinants. In M. Hersen & R. T. Ammerman (Eds.), *Advanced abnormal child psychology* (pp. 87–104). Hillsdale, NJ: Erlbaum.

Reppucci, N. (1984). The wisdom of Solomon: Issues in child custody determination. In N. Reppucci, L. Weithorn, E. Mulvey & J. Monahan (Eds.), *Children, mental health, and the law* (pp. 59–78). Beverly Hills, CA: Sage.

Reppucci, N. D., & Crosby, C. A. (1993). Law, psychology, and children: Overarching issues. *Law and Human Behavior, 17,* 1–10.

Research Foundation (1987). *Functional Independence Measure.* State University of New York: Research Foundation.

Richardson, E. D., Nadler, J. D., & Malloy, P. F. (1995). Neuropsychological prediction of performance measures of daily living skills in geriatric patients. *Neuropsychology, 9,* 565–572.

Ritter, J. P. (1995). Preparation for guardianship cases poses a constant challenge. *The Journal of Long Term Care Administration, Fall,* 14–17.

Robbins, E., Waters, J., & Herbert, P. (1997). Competency to stand trial evaluations: A study of actual practice in two states. *Journal of the American Academy of Psychiatry and the Law, 25,* 469–483.

Roberts, M. (1992). Perceptions of Parental Role Scales. In J. J. Kramer & J. C. Conoley (Eds.), *The eleventh mental measurements yearbook.* Lincoln, NE: Buros Institute of Mental Measurements.

Robertson, K., & Milner, J. (1983). Construct validity of the Child Abuse Potential Inventory. *Journal of Clinical Psychology, 39,* 426–429.

Robey, A. (1965). Criteria for competency to stand trial: A checklist for psychiatrists. *American Journal of Psychiatry, 122,* 616–623.

Robey, A. (1978). Guilty but mentally ill. *Bulletin of the American Academy of Psychiatry and Law, 6,* 374–381.

Rodin, J. (1986). Aging and health: Effects on the sense of control. *Science, 233,* 1271–1276.

Rodriguez, J., LeWinn, L., & Perlin, M. (1983). The Insanity Defense under Siege: Legislative Assaults and Legal Rejoinders. *Rutgers Law Journal, 14,* 397–430.

Rodriguez, C. & Murphy, L. (1997). Parenting stress and abuse potential in mothers of children with developmental disabilities. *Child Maltreatment: Journal of the American Professional Society on the Abuse of Children, 2,* 245–251.

Roesch, R., & Golding, S. L. (1980). *Competency to stand trial.* Urbana-Champaign, IL: University of Illinois Press.

Roesch, R., Jackson, M., Sollner, R., Eaves, D., Glackman, W., & Webster, C. D. (1984). The Fitness to Stand Trial Interview Test: How four professions rate videotaped fitness interviews. *International Journal of Law and Psychiatry, 7,* 115–131.

Roesch, R., Webster, C. D., & Eaves, D. (1984). *The Fitness Interview Test: A method for examining fitness to stand trial.* Toronto, Ontario, Canada: Research Report of the Centre of Criminology, University of Toronto.

Roesch, R., Zapf, P. A., Eaves, D., & Webster, C. D. (1998). *Fitness Interview Test (Revised Edition).* Burnaby, British Columbia, Canada: Mental Health, Law and Policy Institute, Simon Fraser University.

Rogers, J., Holm, M., Goldstein, G., McCue, M., & Nussbaum, P. (1994). Stability and change in functional assessment of patients with geropsychiatric disorders. *American Journal of Occupational Therapy, 48,* 914–918.

Rogers, R. (1984). *Rogers Criminal Responsibility Assessment Scales*. Odessa, FL: Psychological Assessment Resources.

Rogers, R. (2001). Focused forensic interviews. In R. Rogers (Ed.), *Handbook of diagnostic and structured interviewing* (pp. 296–357). New York: Guilford.

Rogers, R., Bagby, R., Crouch, M., & Cutler, B. (1990). Effects of ultimate opinions on juror perceptions of insanity. *International Journal of Law and Psychiatry, 13*, 225–232.

Rogers, R., & Cavanaugh, J. (1981). The Rogers Criminal Responsibility Assessment Scales. *Illinois Medical Journal, 160*, 164–169.

Rogers, R., Dometsch, R., & Cavanaugh, J. (1981). An empirical approach to insanity evaluations. *Journal of Clinical Psychology, 37*, 683–687.

Rogers, R., & Ewing, C. (1989). Ultimate opinion proscriptions: A cosmetic fix and a plea for empiricism. *Law and Human Behavior, 13*, 357–374.

Rogers, R., Grandjean, N., Tillbrook, C., Vitacco, M., & Sewell, K. (2001). Recent interview-based measures of competence to stand trial: A critical review augmented with research data. *Behavioral Sciences and the Law, 19*, 503–518.

Rogers, R., Seman, W., & Wasyliw, O. (1983). The RCRAS and insanity: A cross-validation study. *Journal of Clinical Psychology, 39*, 554–559.

Rogers, R., & Sewell, K. (1999). The R-CRAS and insanity evaluations: A reexamination of construct validity. *Behavioral Sciences and the Law, 17*, 181–194.

Rogers, R., Sewell, K., Grandjean, N., & Vitacco, M. (in press). The detection of feigned mental disorders on specific competency measures. *Psychological Assessment*.

Rogers, R., & Shuman, D. (2000). *Conducting insanity evaluations* (2nd ed.). New York: Guilford.

Rogers, R., Tillbrook, & Sewell, K. (undated). *Evaluation of Competency to Stand Trial-Revised (ECST-R): Professional manual.* (In preparation.)

Rogers, R., Ustad, K., Sewell, K., & Reinhardt, V. (1996). Dimensions of incompetence: A factor analytic study of the Georgia Court Competence Test. *Behavioral Sciences and the Law, 14*, 323–330.

Rogers, R., Wasyliw, O., & Cavanaugh, J. (1984). Evaluating insanity: A study of construct validity. *Law and Human Behavior, 8*, 293–304.

Rohman, L., Sales, B., & Lou, M. (1987). The best interests of the child in custody disputes. In L. Weithorn (Ed.), *Psychology and child custody determinations* (pp. 59–105). Lincoln, NE: University of Nebraska Press.

Roth, L., Lidz, C., Meisel, A., Soloff, P., Kaufman, F., Spiker, D., & Foster, R. (1982). Competency to decide about treatment or research: An overview of some empirical data. *International Journal of Law and Psychiatry, 5*, 29–50.

Roth, L., Meisel, A., & Lidz, C. (1977). Tests of competence to consent to treatment. *American Journal of Psychiatry, 134*, 279–284.

Sabatino, C. (1996). Competency: Refining our legal fictions. In M. Smyer, K. W. Schaie, & M. B. Kapp (Eds.), *Older adults decision making and the law*. New York: Springer.

Sager, M. A., Dunham, N. C., Schwantes, A., Mecum, L. Halverson, K., & Harlowe, D. (1992). Measurement of activities of daily living in hospitalized elderly: A comparison of self-report and performance-based methods. *Journal of the American Geriatrics Society, 40*, 457–462.

Saks, E., & Behnke, S. (1999). Competency to decide treatment and research: MacArthur and beyond. *Journal of Contemporary Legal Issues, 10*, 103–129.

Sales, B. D., Powell, D., Van Duizend, R., & Associates (1982). *Disabled persons and the law*. New York: Plenum.

Sales, G. (1992). Assessing competency: Comment. *Hospital and Community Psychiatry, 43*, 646.

Scallon, C. (1997). Changes in children's perceptions of their 'parent of choice' following participation in a Roman Catholic post-divorce support group. Unpublished doctoral dissertation. Chicago School of Professional Psychology, Chicago.

Schaefer, E. (1965). Children's reports of parental behavior: An inventory. *Child Development, 36*, 417–423.

Schaefer, E., & Bell, R. (1958). Development of a parental attitude research instrument. *Child Development, 29*, 339–361.

Schaie, K. W. (1994). The course of adult intellectual development. *American Psychologist, 49*, 304–313.

Scheidt, R., & Schaie, K. (1978). A taxonomy of situations for an elderly population: Generating situational criteria. *Journal of Gerontology, 33*, 848–857.

Schreiber, J. (1978). Assessing competency to stand trial: A case study of technology diffusion in four states. *Bulletin of the American Academy of Psychiatry and the Law, 6*, 439–457.

Schreiber, J. (1983). *Evaluation of procedures for assessing competency to stand trial* (Final Report on NIMH Research Grant No. R01-MH33669). Rockville, MD: Center for Studies of Antisocial and Violent Behavior, National Institute of Mental Health.

Schreiber, J., Roesch, R., & Golding, S. L. (1987). An evaluation of procedures for assessing competence to stand trial. *Bulletin of the American Academy of Psychiatry and the Law, 15*, 143–150.

Schutte, H., Malouff, J., Lucore, P., & Shern, B. (1988). Incompetency and insanity: Feasibility of community evaluation and treatment. *Community Mental Health Journal, 24*, 143–150.

Schutz, B., Dixon, E., Lindenberger, J., & Ruther, N. (1989). *Solomon's sword: A practical guide to conducting child custody evaluations.* San Francisco, CA: Jossey-Bass.

Schwarting (1998). Developmental Observation Checklist System. In J. C. Impara & B. S. Plake (Eds.), *The thirteenth mental measurements yearbook.* Lincoln, NE: Buros Institute of Mental Measurements.

Scott, E. (1992). Pluralism, paternal preference, and child custody. *California Law Review, 80*, 615–672.

Scott, E., Reppucci, N. D., & Woolard, J. (1995). Evaluating adolescent decisionmaking in legal contexts. *Law and Human Behavior, 19*, 221–244.

Searight, H. R. (1983). *The utility of the Community Competence Scale for determining placement site among the deinstitutionalized mentally ill.* Unpublished doctoral dissertation, St. Louis University.

Searight, H. R., Dunn, E. J., Grisso, J. T., Margolis, R. B., & Gibbons, J. L. (1989). The relation of the Halstead-Reitan neuropsychological battery to ratings of everyday functioning in a geriatric sample. *Neuropsychology, 3*, 135–145.

Searight, H. R., Oliver, J., & Grisso, T. (1983). The Community Competence Scale: Preliminary reliability and validity. *American Journal of Community Psychology, 11*, 609–613.

Seeburger, R., & Wettick, R. (1967). *Miranda* in Pittsburgh: A statistical study. *University of Pittsburgh Law Review, 29*, 1–26.

Shaffer, M. B. (1992). Bricklin Perceptual Scales. In J. L. Conoley & J. C. Impara (Eds.), *The twelfth mental measurements yearbook* (pp. 118–119). Lincoln, NE: Buros Institute of Mental Measurements.

Shah, S. (1981). Legal and mental health system interventions: Major developments and research needs. *International Journal of Law and Psychiatry, 4*, 219–270.

Shapiro, D. (1999). *Criminal responsibility evaluations: A manual for practice.* Sarasota, FL: Professional Resource Press.

Sheras, P., Abidin, R., & Konold, T. (1998). *Stress Index for Parents of Adolescents manual.* Odessa, FL: PAR.

Shure, M., & Spivack, G. (1978). *Problem-solving techniques in child-rearing.* San Francisco: Jossey-Bass.

Silver, E., Cirincione, C., & Steadman, H. (1994). Demythologizing inaccurate perceptions of the insanity defense. *Law and Human Behavior, 18*, 63–70.

Skeem, J., & Golding, S. (1998). Community examiners' evaluations of competence to stand trial: Common problems and suggestions for improvements. *Professional Psychology: Research and Practice, 29*, 357–367.

Skeem, J., Golding, S. L., Cohn, N., & Berge, G. (1998). Logic and reliability of evaluations of competence to stand trial. *Law and Human Behavior, 22*, 519–547.

Skinner, H., Steinhauer, P., & Santa Barbara, J. (1995). *Family Assessment Measure Version III manual*. North Tonawanda, NY: Multi-Health Systems Inc.

Slobogin, C. (1989). The "ultimate issue". *Behavioral Sciences and the Law, 7*, 259–266.

Slobogin, C. (1996). "Appreciation" as a measure of competency: Some thoughts about the MacArthur group's approach. *Psychology, Public Policy, and Law, 2*, 18–30.

Slobogin, C., Melton, G., & Showalter, C. R. (1984). The feasibility of a brief evaluation of mental state at the time of the offense. *Law and Human Behavior, 8*, 305–320.

Smith, J. (2001). Parenting Satisfaction Scale. In B. S. Plake & J. C. Impara (Eds.), *The fourteenth mental measurements yearbook*. Lincoln, NE: Buros Institute of Mental Measurements.

Sorenson, E.D., & Goldman, J. (1990). Custody determinations and child development: A review. *Journal of the American Academy of Child and Adolescent Psychiatry, 30*, 439–460.

Soskis, D. (1978). Schizophrenic and medical inpatients as informed drug consumers. *Archives of General Psychiatry, 35*, 645–647.

Soskis, D., & Jaffe, R. (1979). Communicating with patients about antipsychotic drugs. *Comprehensive Psychiatry, 20*, 126–131.

Spector, W. D., Katz, S., Murphy, J. B., & Fulton, J. P. (1987). The hierarchical relationship between activities of daily living and instrumental activities of daily living. *Journal of Chronic Disease, 40*, 481–489.

Spillane, S. (2001). Family Assessment Measure Version III. In B. S. Plake & J. C. Impara (Eds.), *The fourteenth mental measurements yearbook*. Lincoln, NE: Buros Institute of Mental Measurements.

Spirrison, C. L. & Pierce, P. S. (1992). Psychometric characteristics of the Adult Functional Adaptive Behavior Scale (AFABS). *Gerontologist, 32*, 234–239.

Spirrison, C. L., & Sewell, S. M. (1996). The adult functional adaptive behavior scale (AFABS) and psychiatric inpatients: Indices of reliability and validity. *Assessment, 3*, 387–391.

Spitzer, R., & Endicott, J. (1978). *Schedule of affective disorders and schizophrenia*. New York: Biometrics Research.

Spitzer, R., Endicott, J., & Rollins, E. (1975). Clinical criteria and DSM-III. *American Journal of Psychiatry, 132*, 1187–1192.

Spivack, G., Platt, J., & Shure, M. (1976). *The problem solving approach to adjustment*. San Francisco, CA: Jossey-Bass.

Spivack, G., & Shure, M. (1974). *Social adjustment of young children: A cognitive approach to solving real-life problems*. San Francisco, CA: Jossey-Bass.

Sporakowski, M. (2001). Family Environment Scale: Third Edition. In B. S. Plake & J. C. Impara (Eds.), *The fourteenth mental measurements yearbook*. Lincoln, NE: Buros Institute of Mental Measurements.

Staats, N. (1995). *Psychometric evaluation of the Hopemont Capacity Assessment Interview*. Unpublished Master's thesis, West Virginia University.

Staats, N., & Edelstein, B. (1995). *Cognitive predictors of medical decision-making capacity*. Paper presented at meeting of the Gerontological Society of America, Los Angeles.

Stahl, P. (1994). *Conducting child custody evaluations: A comprehensive guide*. Thousand Oaks, CA: Sage.

Stancliffe, R. J., Abery B. H., Springborg, H., & Elkin, S. (2000). Substitute decision-making and personal control: Implications for self-determination. *Mental Retardation, 38,* 407–421.

Steadman, H. (1980). Insanity acquittals in New York State, 1965–1978. *American Journal of Psychiatry, 137,* 321–326.

Steadman, H., & Braff, J. (1983). Defendants not guilty by reason of insanity. In J. Monahan & H. Steadman (Eds.), *Mentally disordered offenders: Perspectives from law and social science* (pp. 109–129). New York: Plenum.

Steadman, H., Keitner, L., Braff, J., & Aravanites, T. (1983). Factors associated with a successful insanity plea. *American Journal of Psychiatry, 140,* 401–405.

Steadman, H., McGreevy, M., Morrissey, J., Callahan, L., Robbins, P., & Cirincione, C. (1993). *Before and After Hinckley: Evaluating Insanity Defense Reform.* New York: Guilford.

Steadman, H., Monahan, J., Hartstone, E., Davis, S., & Robbins, P. (1982). Mentally disordered offenders: A national survey of patients and facilities. *Law and Human Behavior, 6,* 31–38.

Stefan, S. (1996). Race, competence testing, and disability law: A review of the MacArthur competence research. *Psychology, Public Policy, and Law, 2,* 31–44.

Steinberg, L., & Cauffman, E. (1996). Maturity of judgment in adolescence: Psychosocial factors in adolescent decision-making. *Law and Human Behavior, 20,* 249–272.

Stiegel, L. A., Mason, D. R., Morris, D., Gottlich, V., & Rave, M. (1993). Three issues still remaining in guardianship reform. *Clearinghouse Review, October,* 577–584.

Stolberg, A., & Ullman, A. (1983). *Single Parenting Questionnaire: Development, validation and applications manual.* Unpublished manuscript, Virginia Commonwealth University.

Stone, A. (1975). *Mental health and law: A system in transition* (DHEW Public, No. ADM-75-176). Rockville, MD: National Institute of Mental Health.

Stone, A. (1984). *Law, psychiatry, and morality: Essays and analysis.* Washington, DC: American Psychiatric Press.

Strain, P. S. (1985). Dyadic Parent–Child Interaction Coding System. In J. V. Mitchell (Ed.), *The ninth mental measurements yearbook.* Lincoln, NE: Buros Institute of Mental Measurements.

Swearer, S. (2001). Stress Index for Parents of Adolescents. In B. S. Plake & J. C. Impara (Eds.), *The fourteenth mental measurements yearbook.* Lincoln, NE: Buros Institute of Mental Measurements.

Telzrow, C. (1995). ECO Scales. In J. C. Conoley & J. C. Impara (Eds.), *The twelfth mental measurements yearbook.* Lincoln, NE: Buros Institute of Mental Measurements.

Tepper, A., & Elwork, A. (1984). Competence to consent to treatment as a psycholegal construct. *Law and Human Behavior, 8,* 205–223.

Teti, D. & Gelfand, D. (1991). Behavioral competence among mothers of infants in the first year: The mediational role of maternal self-efficacy. *Child Development, 62,* 918–929.

Thomasson, E., Berkovitz, T., Minor, S., Cassle, G., McCord, D., & Miner, J. (1981). Evaluation of a family life education program for rural "high risk" families: A research note. *Journal of Community Psychology, 9,* 246–249.

Tillbrook, C. (2001). Competence to proceed: A comparative appraisal of approaches to assessment. *Dissertation Abstracts International, 61,* 5009.

Tor, P. B., & Sales, B. D. (1994). Guardianship for incapacitated persons. In B. D. Sales and D. W. Shuman (Eds.), *Law, mental health, and mental disorder* (pp. 202–218). New York: Brooks/Cole Publishing.

Trahan, D., & Larrabee, G. (1988). *Continuous Visual Memory Test.* Odessa, FL: Psychological Assessment Resources.

Uniform Guardianship and Protective Proceedings Act, Uniform Probate Code, Article V (1997).

Uniform Marriage and Divorce Act (1979). *Uniform Laws Annotated, 9A*.

United States Bureau of the Census (1989). *Statistical abstract of the United States*. Washington, DC: Author.

Ustad, K., Rogers, R., Sewell, K., & Guarnaccia, C. (1996). Restoration of competence to stand trial: Assessment with the Georgia Court Competence Test and the Competence Screening Test. *Law and Human Behavior, 20*, 131–146.

Vasavada, T., Masand, P. S., & Nasra, G. (1997). Evaluations of competency of patients with organic mental disorders. *Psychological Reports, 80*, 107–113.

Veatch, R. (1977). Hospital ethics committees: Is there a role? *Hastings Center Report, 7*, 22–24.

Venier, R. (2000). Parental rights and the best interests of the child: Implications for the Adoption and Safe Families Act of 1997 on domestic violence victims' rights. *American University Journal on Gender, Social Policy, and Law, 8*, 517–552.

Verma, S., & Silberfeld, M. (1997). Approaches to capacity and competency. *International Journal of Law and Psychiatry, 20*, 35–46.

Victor, I., & Winkler, W. (1977). *Fathers and custody*. New York: Hawthorn.

Viljoen, J., Roesch, R., & Zapf, P. (in preparation). *Interrater reliability of the Fitness Interview Test across four professional groups*. Burnaby, British Columbia, Canada: Simon Fraser University.

Wald, M. (1976). State intervention on behalf of "neglected" children: A search for realistic standards. In M. K. Rosenheim (Ed.), *Pursuing justice for the child* (pp. 246–278). Chicago: University of Chicago Press.

Walker, R. (1972). The Brockton Social Adjustment Scale. *Diseases of the Nervous System, 33*, 542–545.

Wang, L., Burns, A. M., & Hommel, P. A. (1990). Trends in guardianship reform: Roles and responsibilities of legal advocates. *Clearinghouse Review*, October, 561–569.

Warren, J., Fitch, L., Dietz, P., & Rosenfeld, B. (1991). Criminal offense, psychiatric diagnosis, and psycholegal opinion: An analysis of 894 pretrial referrals. *Bulletin of the American Academy of Psychiatry and the Law, 19*, 63–69.

Warren, J. I., Rosenfeld, B., Fitch, W. L., & Hawk, G. (1997). Forensic mental health clinical evaluation: An analysis of interstate and intersystemic differences. *Law and Human Behavior, 21*, 377–390.

Watson, T. S. (2001). Assessment of Parenting Skills: Infant and Preschooler. In B. S. Plake & J. C. Impara (Eds.), *The fourteenth mental measurements yearbook*. Lincoln, NE: Buros Institute of Mental Measurements.

Wechsler, D. A. (1997a). *The Wechsler Adult Intelligence Scale – III*. New York: Psychological Association.

Wechsler, D. A. (1997b). *The Wechsler Memory Scale – III*. New York: Psychological Association.

Weiner, B. (1985). Mental disability and criminal law. In S. J. Brakel, J. Parry, & B. Weiner (Eds.), *The mentally disabled and the law* (3rd ed.). Chicago: American Bar Association.

Weiner, B. A., & Wettstein, R. M. (1993). *Legal issues in mental health care*. New York: Plenum.

Weiner, I., & Hess, A. (Eds.). (1987). *Handbook of forensic psychology*. New York: Wiley.

Weinstein, J. (1997). And never the twin shall meet: The best interests of children and the adversary system. *University of Miami Law Review, 52*, 79–175.

Weisberg, R., & Wald, M. (1984). Confidentiality laws and state efforts to protect abused or neglected children: The need for statutory reform. *Family Law Quarterly, 18*, 143–212.

Weisz, V. G. (1999). Commentary on "Conceptual and empirical issues in child custody evaluations." *Clinical Psychology: Science and Practice, 6*, 328–331.

Weithorn, L. (1980). *Competency to render informed treatment decision: A comparison of certain minors and adults.* Unpublished doctoral dissertation, University of Pittsburgh.

Weithorn, L., & Campbell, S. (1982). The competency of children and adolescents to make informed treatment decisions. *Child Development, 53,* 1589–1599.

Wellman, M. M. (1994). Ackerman-Schoendorf Scales for Parent Evaluation of Custody. In D. Keyser & R. Sweetwater (Eds.), *Test Critiques, Volume X* (pp. 13–19). Austin, TX: PRO-ED.

White, P., & Denise, S. (1991). Medical treatment decisions and competency in the eyes of the law: A brief survey. In M. Cutter & E. Shelp (Eds.), *Competency: A study of informal competency determinations in primary care.* Dordrecht: Kluwer Academic Publishers.

Whittemore, K., Ogloff, J., & Roesch, R. (1997). An investigation of competence to participate in legal proceedings in Canada. *Canadian Journal of Psychiatry, 42,* 869–875.

Wikoff, R. (1985). Iowa Parent Behavior Inventory. In J. V. Mitchell (Ed.), *The ninth mental measurements yearbook.* Lincoln, NE: Buros Institute of Mental Measurements.

Wildman, R., Batchelor, E., Thompson, L., Nelson, F., Moore, J., Patterson, M., & deLaosa, M. (1980). *The Georgia Court Competence Test: An attempt to develop a rapid, quantitative measure for fitness for trial.* Unpublished manuscript, Forensic Services Division, Central State Hospital, Milledgeville, GA.

Williams, J. (1998). Family Risk Scales. In J. C. Impara & B. S. Plake (Eds.), *The thirteenth mental measurements yearbook.* Lincoln, NE: Buros Institute of Mental Measurements.

Williams, J., Drinka, T., Greenberg, J., Farrell-Holton, J., Euhardy, R., & Schram, M. (1991). Development and testing of the Assessment of Living Skills and Resources (ALSAR) in elderly community dwelling veterans. *The Gerontologist, 31,* 84–91.

Willis, S. (1990). Current issues in cognitive training research. In E. A. Lovelance (Ed.), *Aging and cognition: Mental processes, self-awareness and interventions* (pp. 263–280). Amsterdam: Elsevier.

Willis, S. (1996). Everyday problem solving. In J. E. Birren & K. W. Schaie (Eds.), *Handbook of the psychology of aging* (4th ed., pp. 287–307). New York: Academic Press.

Willis, S. (1996). Everyday cognitive competence in elderly persons: Conceptual issues and empirical findings. *Gerontologist, 36,* 595–601.

Willis, S., Allen-Burge, R., Dolan, M. M., Bertrand, R. M., Yesavage, J., & Taylor, J. L. (1998) Everyday problem solving among individuals with Alzheimer's Disease. *The Gerontologist, 38,* 569–577.

Willis, S., Dolan, M. M., & Bertrand, R. M. Problem solving on health-related tasks of daily living. Unpublished manuscript.

Wood, E. (2000). *State guardianship legislation: Directions of Reform, Annual Legislative Summaries, 1988–2000.* Washington, DC: Commission on Legal Problems of the Elderly, American Bar Association.

Wood, J., Nezworski, M., Garb, H., & Lilienfeld, S. (2001). The misperception of psychopathology: Problems with norms of the Comprehensive System for the Rorschach. *Clinical Psychology: Science and Practice, 8,* 350–373.

Wyer, M., Gaylord, S., & Grove, E. (1987). The legal context of child custody evaluations. In L. Weithorn (Ed.), *Psychology and child custody determinations* (pp. 4–22). Lincoln, NE: University of Nebraska Press.

Zapf, P. A., & Roesch, R. (1997). Assessing fitness to stand trial: A comparison of institution-based evaluations and a brief screening interview. *Canadian Journal of Community Mental Health, 16,* 53–66.

Zapf, P. A., & Roesch, R. (2001). A comparison of the MacCAT-CA and the FIT for making determinations of competence to stand trial. *International Journal of Law and Psychiatry, 24,* 81–92.

Zapf, P. A., Roesch, R., & Viljoen, J. (2001). Assessing fitness to stand trial: The utility of the Fitness Interview Test (Revised). *Canadian Journal of Psychiatry, 46,* 426–432.

Zigler, E., & Phillips, L. (1961). Social competence and outcome in psychiatric disorders. *Journal of Abnormal and Social Psychology, 63,* 264–271.

Zimmer, N. A., Hayden, S., Deidan, C., & Loewenstein, D. A. (1994). Comparative performance of mildly impaired patients with Alzheimer's disease and multiple cerebral infarctions on tests of memory and functional capacity. *International Psychogeriatrics, 6,* 143–154.

Zucker, S. (1998). Uniform Child Custody Evaluation System. In J. C. Impara & B. S. Plake (Eds.), *The thirteenth mental measurements yearbook.* Lincoln, NE: Buros Institute of Mental Measurements.

Legal Citations

Canterbury v. Spence, 462 F.2d 772 (1972).
Chapsky v. Wood, 26 Kansas 650 (1881).
Cobbs v. Grant, 8 Cal. 3d 229 (1972).
Colorado v. Connelly, 479 U.S. 157 (1986).
Cooper v. Oklahoma, 116 S.Ct. 1373 (1996).
Coyote v. United States, 380 F.2d 305 (1967).
Daubert v. Merrell Dow Pharmaceuticals, 509 U.S. 579 (1993).
Davis v. Davis, 372 A.2d 231 (1977).
Dickerson v. U.S., 166 F.3d 667 (2000).
Drope v. Missouri, 420 U.S. 162 (1975).
Durham v. United States, 214 F.2d 862 (1954).
Dusky v. United States, 362 U.S. 402 (1960).
Ex parte Devine, 398 So. 2d 686 (Ala. 1981).
Fare v. Michael C., 442 U.S. 707 (1979).
Feguer v. United States, 302 F.2d 214 (1962).
Finlay v. Finlay, 148 N.E. 624 (1925).
Frye v. United States, 392 F. 1013 (D.C.Cir. 1923).
Gallegos v. Colorado, 370 U.S. 49 (1962).
Godinez v. Moran, 113 S.Ct. 2680 (1993).
Griswold v. Connecticut, 381, U.S. 479 (1965).
Haley v. Ohio, 332 U.S. 596 (1948).
Hansford v. United States, 124 U.S. App. D.C. 387, 365 F.2d 920 (1966).
Harris v. State, 499 N.E.2d 723 (Ind. 1986).
In re custody of a minor (1990).

In re Gault, 387 U.S. 1 (1967).
In re Kelly (Conn. App. Ct 1992).
In re Patrick W., 148 Cal. Rptr. 735 (1978).
In re Rathburn, 266 A.2d 423 (1970).
In the Interest of S.H., a Child, 469 S.E.2d 810 (Ga. Ct. App. 1996).
Jackson v. Indiana, 406 U.S. 715 (1972).
Johnson v. Zerbst, 304 U.S. 458 (1938).
K.N. v. State, 856 P.2d 468 (Alaska, 1993).
Kaimowitz v. Department of Mental Health, Civ. No. 73-19434-AW (Cir. Ct. Wayne County, July 10, 1973).
Kumho Tire Company, Ltd. v. Carmichael, 526 U.S. 137 (1999)
Lyles v. United States, 254 F.2d 725 (1957).
Matter of Conroy, 486 A.2d 1209 (N.J. 1985).
Matter of O'Brian, 517 N.Y.S.2d 364 (Sup. Ct. 1986).
Miranda v. Arizona, 384 U.S. 436 (1966).
McNaughten's Case, 8 Eng. Rep. 718 (1843).
Meyer v. Nebraska, 262 U.S. 390 (1923).
Michigan v. Daoud, 614 N.W.2d 152 (2000).
Natanson v. Kline, 350 P.2d 1093 (1960).
People v. Bernasco, 562 N.E.2d 958 (Ill. 1990).
Pate v. Robinson, 383 U.S. 375 (1966).
People v. Crews, 122 Ill.2d 266 (1988).
People v. Lara, 432 P.2d 202 (1967).
People v. Pennington, 426 P.2d 942 (1967).
Planned Parenthood of Central Missouri v. Danforth, 428 U.S. 52 (1976).
Prince v. Massachusetts, 321 U.S. 158 (1944).
Quilloin v. Walcott, 434 U.S. 246 (1978).
Relf v. Weinberger, 372 F. Supp. 1196 (1974).
Rennie v. Klein, 462 F. Supp. 1131 (1978); modified, 476 F. Supp. 1294 (1979); stay denied, 481 F. Supp. 552 (1979); modified and remanded, 653 F.2d 836 (1981); vacated and remanded, 50 USLW 3998.27 (1982).
Riggins v. Nevada, 504 U.S. 127 (1992).
Rogers v. Commissioner of Mental Health, 390 Mass. 489 (1983).
Rogers v. Okin, 478 F. Supp. 1342 (1979); affirmed in part, reversed in part, vacated in part, and remanded 643 F.2d 650 (1980); vacated and remanded sub. nom.
Mills v. Rogers, 457 U.S. 291 (1982); certified questions answered sub. nom. Rogers v. Commissioner of Mental Health, 390, Mass. 489 (1983).
Santosky v. Kramer, 455 U.S. 745 (1982).
Sieling v. Eyman, 478 F.2d (9th Cir., 1973).
Stanfield v. Stanfield, 435 S.W.2d 690 (1968).
Stanley v. Illinois, 405 U.S. 645 (1972).
State v. Jackson, 304 S.E.2d 134 (1983).
State v. McDonald, 201 N.W.2d 447 (1972).
State v. Prater, 463 P.2d 640 (1970).
Swisher v. United States, 237 F. Supp. 291 (1965).
Tuter v. Tuter, 120 S.W.2d 203 (1938).
United States v. Adams, 297 F. Supp. 596 (1969).
United States v. Sermon, 228 F. Supp. 972 (W. D. Mo., 1964).
United States *ex rel.* Simon v. Maroney, 228 F. Supp. 800 (1964).

United States v. Wilson, 391 F.2d 460 (1966).
West v. United States, 399 F.2d 467 (1968).
Westbrook v. Arizona, 384 U.S. 150 (1965).
Wieter v. Settle, 193 F. Supp. 318 (W.D. Mo., 1961).
Zinermon v. Burch, 494 U.S. 113 (1990).

Author Index

519

Subject Index

529

Printed in the United States
74203LV00001B/64-69